Lecture Notes in Computer Science   11887

More information about this series at http://www.springer.com/series/7407

Michèle Weiland · Guido Juckeland ·
Sadaf Alam · Heike Jagode (Eds.)

High Performance Computing

ISC High Performance 2019 International Workshops
Frankfurt, Germany, June 16–20, 2019
Revised Selected Papers

 Springer

Editors
Michèle Weiland (ID)
University of Edinburgh
Edinburgh, UK

Guido Juckeland (ID)
Helmholtz-Zentrum Dresden-Rossendorf
Dresden, Sachsen, Germany

Sadaf Alam (ID)
Swiss National Supercomputing Centre
Lugano, Ticino, Switzerland

Heike Jagode (ID)
University of Tennessee at Knoxville
Knoxville, TN, USA

ISSN 0302-9743   ISSN 1611-3349   (electronic)
Lecture Notes in Computer Science
ISBN 978-3-030-34355-2   ISBN 978-3-030-34356-9   (eBook)
https://doi.org/10.1007/978-3-030-34356-9

LNCS Sublibrary: SL1 – Theoretical Computer Science and General Issues

Preface

A separate workshop day attached to the International Supercomputing Conference (ISC) High Performance, formerly known as the International Supercomputing Conference, was first added to the technical program in 2015 under the leadership of Bernd Mohr (Forschungszentrum Jülich GmbH). Supported by the success of the past four years, ISC High Performance renewed and further extended the workshop program in 2018, under the leadership of Sadaf Alam (Swiss National Supercomputing Center) and Heike Jagode (University of Tennessee Knowville). Michele Weiland (The University of Edinburgh) and Guido Juckeland (Helmholtz-Zentrum Dresden-Rossendorf) joined the team as proceedings chair and deputy chair, respectively, and managed the organization of the proceedings for the workshops.

The 21 workshops at ISC High Performance 2019 provided a focused, in-depth platform with presentations, discussion, and interaction on topics related to all aspects of research, development, and application of large-scale, high-performance experimental and commercial systems. Workshop topics included HPC computer architecture and hardware; programming models, system software, and applications; solutions for heterogeneity, reliability, and power efficiency of systems; virtualization and containerized environments; big data and cloud computing; artificial intelligence; as well as international collaborations. Workshops were selected with a peer-review process by an international committee of 16 experts in the field from Europe, the United States, and Asia.

Since 2016, ISC High Performance has provided a platform for workshops with their own call for papers and individual peer-review process through an early deadline in December 2017. In all, 17 workshop proposals were submitted before this deadline from organizers all over the world; 9 full-day and 8 half-day workshops were accepted after a rigorous review process in which each proposal received 3 reviews. Additionally, each reviewer was given the possibility to discuss all the submissions. Workshops without a call for papers were invited to submit their proposals in February 2019. For this second deadline, a further four workshop proposals were accepted by the committee following the same rigorous peer-review process as for workshops with proceedings.

The 21 workshops were held on Thursday, June 20, 2019, at the Frankfurt Marriott Hotel. The workshop proceedings volume collects all the accepted papers of the workshops from the call for papers. Each chapter of the book contains the accepted and revised papers for one of the workshops. For some workshops, an additional preface describes the review process for that workshop and provides a summary of the outcome.

June 2019   Michèle Weiland
                                                                      Guido Juckeland
                                                                          Sadaf Alam
                                                                       Heike Jagode

---

The original version of the book was revised: For detailed information see correction chapter. The correction to the book is available at https://doi.org/10.1007/978-3-030-34356-9_50

Organization

Program Committee

Christoph Angerer	NVIDIA, USA
Hartwig Anzt	University of Tennessee, USA
Abdulrahman Azab	University of Oslo, Norway
Shane Canon	Lawrence Berkeley National Lab, USA
Sunita Chandrasekaran	University of Delaware, USA
Valeriu Codreanu	SURFsara, The Netherlands
Jens Domke	RIKEN Center for Computational Science (R-CCS), Japan
Steffen Frey	Visualisierunsginstitut der Universität Stuttgart, Germany
Siddhartha Jana	Intel, USA
Guido Juckeland	Helmholtz-Zentrum Dresden-Rossendorf (HZDR), Germany
Mozhgan Kabiri Chimeh	The University of Sheffield, UK
Julian Martin Kunkel	University of Reading, UK
Scott Lathrop	Shodor, USA
Jay Lofstead	Sandia National Laboratories, USA
Piotr Luszczek	University of Tennessee Knoxville, USA
David Martin	Argonne National Laboratory, USA
Michael Mascagni	Florida State University, USA
Anastassios Nanos	National Technical University of Athens, Greece
Jan F. Nygård	The Cancer Registry of Norway, Norway
Dirk Pleiter	Jülich Supercomputing Centre, University of Regensburg, Germany
Swaroop Pophale	Oak Ridge National Laboratory, USA
Michael Ringenburg	Cray Inc., USA
Martin Schulz	Technical University of Munich, Germany
Hari Subramoni	The Ohio State University, USA
Nitin Sukhija	Slippery Rock University of Pennsylvania, USA
Thomas Theussl	King Abdullah University of Science and Technology, Saudi Arabia
Mohamed Wahib	AIST, TokyoTech OIL, Japan
Michele Weiland	The University of Edinburgh, UK
Andrew Younge	Sandia National Laboratories, USA

Short Papers

Preface to the First International Workshop on Legacy Software Refactoring for Performance

Artur Podobas[1], Jens Domke[1], and Wahib Attia Mohamed[2]

[1] RIKEN Center for Computational Science, Kobe, Japan
[2] National Institute of Advanced Industrial Science and Technology,
Tokyo, Japan

1 Workshop Background and Description

The First International Workshop on Legacy Software **REFAC**toring for Performance (REFAC'19) is dedicated to the much needed shift in focus from hardware to software to achieve performance gains. Modernizing hardware has too long been the primary method of accelerating legacy software, and close to half of the expected performance improvement in legacy codes can be attributed to improve processor technology. More than half of this improvement was based on Moore's law and its observation that transistors will continue to become smaller every few (originally two) years. The remaining hardware improvements came from architectural innovations, such as deeper cache hierarchies, the migration to more exotic architectures (e.g. GPUs), or the utilization of larger and wider vector-units (SIMD), as well as scaling the HPC systems up by giving them more processors and cores. Unfortunately, we are no longer seeing the consistent technology scaling that Gordon Moore observed. Instead, the technology scaling has significantly slowed down, and is expected to continue only for a few more years. Consequently, in the so-called Post-Moore era, the "performance road" forks three-ways, yielding the following alternatives: (i) architectural innovations will attempt to close the performance gap, and an explosion of diverging architectures tailored for specific science domains will emerge, (ii) alternative materials and technologies (e.g. non-CMOS technologies) allow the spirit of Moore's law to continue for a foreseeable future, or (iii) we abandon the von-Neumann paradigm together and move to a neuromorphic or quantum-like computer (which, in time, might or might not become practical). Independent of which direction we will end up taking in the future, the following will hold: **Software and algorithmic optimization will be transferable to the first two out of the three identified directions. It is these architecture-oblivious software optimizations that are the primary scope of the proposed workshop.**

The workshop offered a forum for technical contributions, invited presentations, and discussions in the following areas:

– All types of general-purpose processor legacy-software optimizations for HPC

- Changes to (collective) communication algorithms or implementations to enable the use of different numerical methods (e.g.: Lagrangian vs. Eulerian)
- Accelerating of pre-/post-processing in scientific workflows or axillary tools
- Improved maintainability/performance through existing production libraries
- Revisiting and applying modern compiler (flag) techniques, performance analysis tools, moderate usage of OpenMP, etc., for performance gains
- Manual code refactoring, such as loop transformations or changing data structures, to acknowledge the shifting ratio in memory vs. compute capabilities of modern architectures, and
- Using mixed or adaptive precision wherever possible.

2   Technical Paper Reviewing Process

The workshop adopted a single-blind reviewing process and was reviewed by the technical program committee (TPC). The TPC consisted of ten (excluding organizers) international experts from workshop-relevant domains: Andreas Knüpfer (TU Dresden), Anshu Dubey (ANL), Barna Bihari, (LLNL), Bernd Mohr (Jülich Supercomputing Centre), Dali Wang (ORNL), Daniel Molka (German Aerospace Center), Didem Unat (Koç University), Hisashi Yashiro (RIKEN R-CCS), Saurabh Chawdhary (ANL), and Seyong Lee (ORNL).

The workshop organizers partook in the reviewing process. Each technical paper contribution was reviewed by at least four TPC members, by sampling from our reviewer pool the most knowledgeable experts for the research area of the paper. The review process resulted in two accepted technical papers:

1. "Asynchronous AMR on Multi-GPUs", *M.N. Farooqi, T. Nguyen, W. Zhang, A. Almgren, J. Shalf and D. Unat*
2. "Modernizing Titan2D, a parallel AMR Geophysical Flow Code to Support Multiple Rheologies and Extendability", *N.A. Simakov, R.L. Jones-Ivey, A. Akhavan-Safaei, H. Aghakhani, M.D. Jones and A.K. Patra*

which were allowed to make minor changes to address the reviewers' feedback.

3   Workshop Summary

The well-attended workshop took place in the Frankfurt Marriott Alabaster 2 conference room on Thursday, June 20th, and featured (apart from the two accepted papers) a keynote by Benoit Marchand (NYU) and two invited speakers, reporting their experiences and approaches for refactoring legacy software.

The presentations were performed in an interactive style, where the audience could (and did) ask questions at any time. This forum-like format encouraged discussions and information exchange throughout the workshop and helped contributing to the success of the workshop. Participants continued to discuss even during the breaks, signifying the importance and timeliness of the workshop. The end of the workshop featured a 30-min free-form debate, where workshop participants actively discussed emerging issues ranging from algorithms to middleware and runtime systems. This free-form discussion successfully brought different researcher and practitioners together, some whom continued the conversation even after the workshop ended. We and the participants are looking forward to the next REFAC'20, and hope this year's workshop kickstarts a broader effort across our HPC community to modernize and speed-up our dated production codes.

P^3MA Workshop 2019

1 Workshop Summary

The 4th International Workshop on Performance Portable Programming models for Manycore or Accelerators (P^3MA) co-located with ISC 2019 was held at Frankfurt, Germany on June 20. The workshop solicited papers on topics covering feature sets of programming models (including, but not limited to, C++, OpenCL, OpenMP, OpenACC, and various DSLs), their implementations, and experiences with their deployment in HPC applications on multiple architectures, performance modeling and evaluation tools, asynchronous task and event-driven execution/scheduling. We received 3 submissions in total. All submitted manuscripts were peer reviewed by at least 3 reviewers. The review process was single blind, i.e., authors were known to reviewers. Submissions were evaluated on correctness, originality, technical strength, significance, quality of presentation, and interest and relevance to the conference. We chose 3 papers to be published in the workshop proceedings, Springer-Verlag Lecture Notes in Computer Science (LNCS) volumes. The workshop was held for a full day on June 20 at ISC and brought together researchers, vendors, users and developers to brainstorm aspects of heterogeneous computing and its various tools and techniques. Around 45 attendees were present. All of the accepted papers were presented at the workshop with topics ranging from using high-level programming models for heterogeneous systems to experiences porting legacy code to accelerators. The workshop organizers also conducted a timely panel moderated by Sunita Chandrasekaran that brought together expert developers from Alpaka (Sergei Bastrakov, HZDR) Kokkos (Christian Trott, Sandia National Lab), SYCL (Morris Hafner, Codeplay), OpenMP (Johannes Doerfert, Argonne National Lab) and OpenACC (Michael Wolfe, PGI/NVIDIA). The panel focused on how an application developer could make an informed choice about using a programming model when there is more than a few available. The first paragraphs that follows a table, figure, equation etc. does not have an indent, either.

2 Organizing Committee

Steering Committee

Matthias Muller	RWTH Aachen University, Germany
Barbara Chapman	Stony Brook University, USA
Oscar Hernandez	ORNL, USA
Duncan Poole	OpenACC

4th International Workshop on In Situ Visualization (WOIV'19)

Steffen Frey[1], Peter Messmer[2] and Thomas Theußl[3]

[1] University of Stuttgart
[2] NVIDIA
[3] KAUST

1 Introduction

Large-scale HPC simulations with their inherent I/O bottleneck have made *in situ* an essential approach for data analysis. In situ coupling of analysis and visualization to a live simulation circumvents writing raw data to disk. Instead, data abstracts are generated that capture much more information than otherwise possible.

The "Workshop on In Situ Visualization" series provides a venue for speakers to share practical expertise and experience with in situ visualization approaches. This 4th edition of the workshop, WOIV'19, took place as a full-day workshop on 20 June 2019 in Frankfurt, Germany, after two half-day workshops in 2016 and 2017 and a full-day workshop in 2018. The goal of the workshop in general is to appeal to a wide-ranging audience of visualization scientists, computational scientists, and simulation developers, who have to collaborate in order to develop, deploy, and maintain in situ visualization approaches on HPC infrastructures.

For WOIV'19 we again also encouraged submissions on approaches that did not live up to their expectations. With this, we expected to get first-hand reports on lessons learned. Speakers should detail if and how the application drove abstractions or other kinds of data reductions and how these interacted with the expressiveness and flexibility of the visualization for exploratory analysis or why the approach failed.

2 Organization of the Workshop

The workshop content was built on two tracks:

Invited talks experts in the field were invited to share their thoughts and insights
Research paper presentations authors were required to submit a full paper before the workshop, which was then reviewed for inclusion in the conference proceedings

After the submission deadline in mid-May 2019, five manuscripts were submitted. Having the time of a full-day workshop at their disposal, the organizing committee was able to select four of these five submissions for presentation at the workshop. After a full review cycle by an international program committee after the workshop presentations, all four papers were selected for inclusion in these conference proceedings. Additionally, five internationally recognized researchers agreed to each give an invited talk at the workshop. Slides for all presentations can be downloaded from the workshop web page at http://woiv.org.

2.1 Organizing Committee

Steffen Frey	University of Stuttgart
Peter Messmer	NVIDIA
Thomas Theußl	KAUST

2.2 Programm Committee

Hadrien Calmet	BSC-CNS
Jose Camata	Federal University of Juiz de Fora
Hank Childs	University of Oregon
Jens Henrik Goebbert	Jülich Supercomputing Centre
Samuel Li	National Center for Atmospheric Research
Kenneth Moreland	Sandia National Laboratories
Benson Muite	University of Tartu
Guido Reina	University of Stuttgart
Joachim Pouderoux	Kitware
Tom Vierjahn	Westphalian University of Applied Sciences
Max Zeyen	Kitware

3 Workshop Summary

3.1 Invited Talks

Burlen Loring and Silvio Rizzi presented the in situ visualization framework SENSEI, which addresses the challenge of toolchain dependent application instrumentation: In order to use in situ visualization the HPC applications needs to be instrumented to expose the simulation data to the visualization application. So far, no single standard interface has emerged, requiring the developers to instrument their applications with different interfaces depending on the targeted in situ visualization toolchain. SENSEI tries to consolidate these different APIs, offering a single mechanism for application instrumentation independent of the selected visualization toolchain. This should help to lower the adoption threshold for in situ visualization and enable a broader range of applications to benefit from it.

In a next presentation, Peter Messmer gave an update on visualization efforts at NVIDIA. Specifically, the arrival of Turing GPUs with hardware accelerated ray tracing put a new emphasis on ray tracing for scientific visualization. Not only does this technology help to produce powerful images for outreach and education, but it also provides better visual cues for e.g. depth and therefore helps a scientist in the day to day work to better understand the spatial relationship of objects in a scene. With the integration of these technologies into popular scientific visualization tools like Para-View, these technologies become available to a broad range of scientific visualization users. In addition to these latest developments on hardware accelerated ray tracing, Peter raised the question whether there is a need for a standardization efforts for ray tracing in scientific visualization in order to free ISV's from developing their own implementations while offering optimal performance on each platform.

In a subsequent presentation, Mike Ringenburg from Cray talked about the con-currently ongoing workshop series on interactive HPC. This conference series has been established to bring together domain scientist, HPC center managers and middleware developers to address the challenges of using HPC systems in an interactive manner. With visualization benefitting significantly from a high degree of interactivity, it was interesting to see the parallels and differences in the two areas. While the focus of the in situ vis workshop series is on the visualization aspect, both interactive or in a batch fashion, the interactive HPC workshops are more interested in the middleware and center policy aspects of interactivity, specifically in light of the convergence of HPC and data sciences. However, despite the differences in the two target audiences, the talk and the subsequent discussion showed that there clearly are common aspects of interest.

Next, Joao Barbosa from TACC presented a summary of the IXPUG In Situ Hackathon 2019. The Hackathon intends to provide a forum to bring simulation developers together with visualization experts for hands-on implementation of in situ analysis. It took first place in 2017 in Austin, Texas hosted at TACC, then in 2018 in Chicago, Illinois hosted at Argonne National Lab, and finally in 2019 Santa Fe, New Mexico hosted by TACC and LAN. Joao presented some statistics of these events with 30–40 participants each, noting that they were successful because they provided a distraction-free environment and a good mix of new and returning participants. He concluded by presenting selected results of the last Hackathon.

Finally, Silvio Rizzi, on behalf of Jim Ahrens, talked about the development and use of in situ visualization and analysis approaches for the U.S. Exascale Computing Project (ECP), an accelerated research and development project funded by the US Department of Energy (DOE). It is a seven-year, $1.7 B R&D effort that launched in 2016 with the participation of six core DOE National Laboratories (Argonne, Lawrence Berkeley, Lawrence Livermore, Los Alamos, Oak Ridge, Sandia), with staff from most of the 17 DOE national laboratories taking part in the project. While ECP applications target national problems, Silvio focussed on the in-situ aspects. He presented an overiew of ECP Software Technology Data and Visualization projects and an outline of several algorithms and subsystems planned within these projects.

3.2   Research Papers

In the first research presentation, Zhang and Entezari discussed their paper "In-Situ Data Reduction via Incoherent Sensing". In this context, they presented study for data reduction in an in-situ situation based on compressed sensing. The volumetric data is first sparsified using wavelet, curvelet, and surfacelet transforms, then compressed sensing techniques are used for compression and reconstruction. The authors demonstrate the effectiveness of their method with examples from chemistry and astrophysics and examine how different methods for compressing the data influence the quality of the reconstruction.

Next, Sarton et al., in their paper "Distributed out-of-core approach for in-situ volume rendering of massive dataset", present a GPU-based volume rendering approach suitable for out-of-core/in-situ visualization of large volumetric data sets. The volume is divided into bricks and managed with a page table layout. An exemplary 2-CPU and 4-GPU server is used for storing, handling, and rendering the volume, the result is then streamed to a thin client for visualization. By providing each GPU with a local brick cache, and by using multi-resolution volume data the system is capable of providing interactive frame rates, which is demonstrated on two volumetric datasets.

In their paper "In-Situ Processing in Climate Science", Röber and Engels, describe the current efforts of leveraging in situ visualization at the German Climate Computing Centre (DKRZ). The paper describes the Catalyst in situ library being integrated into the ICON model and used to generate images and extract geometric features. It also describes some work to write hierarchical data and to compress data with wavelet decomposition. The authors describe a workflow where a special adaptor is developed to fit ICON model to Catalyst, and then the model output is directly visualized through ParaView. The authors also describe a progressive visualization approach where lower resolution data is used for exploration, whereas the original resolution data is used for detailed examination.

Finally, Hummels and van Kooten, in their paper "Leveraging NVIDIA Omniverse for In Situ Visualization", propose a method that allows interactive, high-quality visualization of distilled simulation geometry. Omniverse is NVIDIA's collaboration platform for 3D production pipelines. It is integrated with a number of commercially available 3D software packages and game engines and enables content creators to work on different aspects of models or entire scenes simultaneously. By integrating Para-View and Catalyst with the Omniverse, the visualization geometry becomes immediately accessible to a number of 3D content authoring and rendering tools without the requirement of invasive software changes or tedious postprocessing and conversion workflows.

The workshop was concluded by a panel dicsussion on the "Future of In-situ at ISC", covering a variety of different topics. Among others, we talked about the different directions the workshop could take in future iterations, considering the landscape of related workshops and events in the field of in situ visualization. Here, especially the strong inclusion of simulation and domain scientists, as well as the focus on sharing experiences gained in the development process were identified as important aspects. In addition, the role of interactivity in in-situ visualization was discussed, to identify collaboration potential with the interactivity workshop in future iterations.

Contents

On the Use of Kernel Bypass Mechanisms for High-Performance
Inter-container Communications 1
   Gabriele Ara, Luca Abeni, Tommaso Cucinotta, and Carlo Vitucci

Continuous-Action Reinforcement Learning for Memory Allocation
in Virtualized Servers 13
   Luis A. Garrido, Rajiv Nishtala, and Paul Carpenter

Container Orchestration on HPC Clusters 25
   Marco Enrico Piras, Luca Pireddu, Marco Moro, and Gianluigi Zanetti

Data Pallets: Containerizing Storage for Reproducibility and Traceability 36
   Jay Lofstead, Joshua Baker, and Andrew Younge

Sarus: Highly Scalable Docker Containers for HPC Systems 46
   Lucas Benedicic, Felipe A. Cruz, Alberto Madonna, and Kean Mariotti

Singularity GPU Containers Execution on HPC Cluster 61
   Giuseppa Muscianisi, Giuseppe Fiameni, and Abdulrahman Azab

A Multitenant Container Platform with OKD, Harbor Registry and ELK 69
   Jarle Bjørgeengen

Enabling GPU-Enhanced Computer Vision and Machine Learning
Research Using Containers. 80
   Martial Michel and Nicholas Burnett

Software and Hardware Co-design for Low-Power HPC Platforms 88
   Manolis Ploumidis, Nikolaos D. Kallimanis, Marios Asiminakis,
   Nikos Chrysos, Pantelis Xirouchakis, Michalis Gianoudis,
   Leandros Tzanakis, Nikolaos Dimou, Antonis Psistakis,
   Panagiotis Peristerakis, Giorgos Kalokairinos, Vassilis Papaefstathiou,
   and Manolis Katevenis

Modernizing Titan2D, a Parallel AMR Geophysical Flow Code to Support
Multiple Rheologies and Extendability. 101
   Nikolay A. Simakov, Renette L. Jones-Ivey, Ali Akhavan-Safaei,
   Hossein Aghakhani, Matthew D. Jones, and Abani K. Patra

Asynchronous AMR on Multi-GPUs 113
   Muhammad Nufail Farooqi, Tan Nguyen, Weiqun Zhang,
   Ann S. Almgren, John Shalf, and Didem Unat

Batch Solution of Small PDEs with the OPS DSL.................... 124
Istvan Z. Reguly, Branden Moore, Tim Schmielau, Jacques du Toit,
and Gihan R. Mudalige

Scalable Parallelization of Stencils Using MODA 142
Nabeeh Jumah and Julian Kunkel

Comparing High Performance Computing Accelerator
Programming Models 155
Swaroop Pophale, Swen Boehm, and Verónica G. Vergara Larrea

Tracking User-Perceived I/O Slowdown via Probing 169
Julian Kunkel and Eugen Betke

A Quantitative Approach to Architecting All-Flash Lustre File Systems..... 183
Glenn K. Lockwood, Kirill Lozinskiy, Lisa Gerhardt, Ravi Cheema,
Damian Hazen, and Nicholas J. Wright

MBWU: Benefit Quantification for Data Access Function Offloading 198
Jianshen Liu, Philip Kufeldt, and Carlos Maltzahn

Footprinting Parallel I/O – Machine Learning to Classify
Application's I/O Behavior..................................... 214
Eugen Betke and Julian Kunkel

Adventures in NoSQL for Metadata Management 227
Jay Lofstead, Ashleigh Ryan, and Margaret Lawson

Towards High Performance Data Analytics for Climate Change 240
Sandro Fiore, Donatello Elia, Cosimo Palazzo, Fabrizio Antonio,
Alessandro D'Anca, Ian Foster, and Giovanni Aloisio

An Architecture for High Performance Computing and Data Systems
Using Byte-Addressable Persistent Memory 258
Adrian Jackson, Michèle Weiland, Mark Parsons,
and Bernhard Homölle

Mediating Data Center Storage Diversity in HPC Applications
with FAODEL 275
Patrick Widener, Craig Ulmer, Scott Levy, Todd Kordenbrock,
and Gary Templet

Predicting File Lifetimes with Machine Learning 288
Florent Monjalet and Thomas Leibovici

An I/O Analysis of HPC Workloads on CephFS and Lustre............. 300
Alberto Chiusole, Stefano Cozzini, Daniel van der Ster,
Massimo Lamanna, and Graziano Giuliani

Enabling Fast and Highly Effective FPGA Design Process Using the CAPI
SNAP Framework.. 317
   Alexandre Castellane and Bruno Mesnet

Scaling the Summit: Deploying the World's Fastest Supercomputer........ 330
   Verónica G. Vergara Larrea, Wayne Joubert, Michael J. Brim,
   Reuben D. Budiardja, Don Maxwell, Matt Ezell, Christopher Zimmer,
   Swen Boehm, Wael Elwasif, Sarp Oral, Chris Fuson, Daniel Pelfrey,
   Oscar Hernandez, Dustin Leverman, Jesse Hanley, Mark Berrill,
   and Arnold Tharrington

Parallelware Tools: An Experimental Evaluation on POWER Systems...... 352
   Manuel Arenaz and Xavier Martorell

Performance Evaluation of MPI Libraries on GPU-Enabled OpenPOWER
Architectures: Early Experiences.................................. 361
   Kawthar Shafie Khorassani, Ching-Hsiang Chu, Hari Subramoni,
   and Dhabaleswar K. Panda

Exploring the Behavior of Coherent Accelerator Processor Interface (CAPI)
on IBM Power8+ Architecture and FlashSystem 900.................. 379
   Kaushik Velusamy, Smriti Prathapan, and Milton Halem

Porting Adaptive Ensemble Molecular Dynamics Workflows
to the Summit Supercomputer..................................... 397
   John Ossyra, Ada Sedova, Arnold Tharrington, Frank Noé,
   Cecilia Clementi, and Jeremy C. Smith

Performance Comparison for Neuroscience Application Benchmarks....... 418
   Andreas Herten, Thorsten Hater, Wouter Klijn, and Dirk Pleiter

Evaluating POWER Architecture for Distributed Training of Generative
Adversarial Networks 432
   Ahmad Hesam, Sofia Vallecorsa, Gulrukh Khattak,
   and Federico Carminati

A Study on the Performance of Reproducible Computations............. 441
   Nico Bombace and Michèle Weiland

Three Numerical Reproducibility Issues That Can Be Explained
as Round-Off Error... 452
   Michael Mascagni

Training Multiscale-CNN for Large Microscopy Image Classification
in One Hour... 463
   Kushal Datta, Imtiaz Hossain, Sun Choi, Vikram Saletore, Kyle Ambert,
   William J. Godinez, and Xian Zhang

Benchmarking Deep Learning Infrastructures by Means of TensorFlow
and Containers 478
   Adrian Grupp, Valentin Kozlov, Isabel Campos, Mario David,
   Jorge Gomes, and Álvaro López García

MagmaDNN: Towards High-Performance Data Analytics and Machine
Learning for Data-Driven Scientific Computing 490
   Daniel Nichols, Nathalie-Sofia Tomov, Frank Betancourt,
   Stanimire Tomov, Kwai Wong, and Jack Dongarra

Open OnDemand: HPC for Everyone 504
   Robert Settlage, Alan Chalker, Eric Franz, Doug Johnson, Steve Gallo,
   Edgar Moore, and David Hudak

Highly Interactive, Steered Scientific Workflows on HPC Systems:
Optimizing Design Solutions 514
   John R. Ossyra, Ada Sedova, Matthew B. Baker, and Jeremy C. Smith

The Role of Interactive Super-Computing in Using HPC for Urgent
Decision Making. 528
   Nick Brown, Rupert Nash, Gordon Gibb, Bianca Prodan, Max Kontak,
   Vyacheslav Olshevsky, and Wei Der Chien

Deep Learning at Scale for Subgrid Modeling in Turbulent Flows:
Regression and Reconstruction 541
   Mathis Bode, Michael Gauding, Konstantin Kleinheinz,
   and Heinz Pitsch

Using FPGAs to Accelerate HPC and Data Analytics
on Intel-Based Systems 561
   Thomas Steinke, Estela Suarez, Taisuke Boku, Nalini Kumar,
   and David E. Martin

Exploring the Acceleration of the Met Office NERC Cloud Model
Using FPGAs. 567
   Nick Brown

Acceleration of Scientific Deep Learning Models on Heterogeneous
Computing Platform with Intel® FPGAs. 587
   Chao Jiang, Dave Ojika, Thorsten Kurth, Prabhat, Sofia Vallecorsa,
   Bhavesh Patel, and Herman Lam

In-Situ Data Reduction via Incoherent Sensing 601
   Kai Zhang and Alireza Entezari

In-Situ Processing in Climate Science 612
   Niklas Röber and Jan Frederik Engels

Distributed Out-of-Core Approach for In-Situ Volume Rendering
of Massive Dataset   623
  Jonathan Sarton, Yannick Remion, and Laurent Lucas

Leveraging NVIDIA Omniverse for In Situ Visualization.   634
  Mathias Hummel and Kees van Kooten

Hands-On Research and Training in High Performance Data Sciences,
Data Analytics, and Machine Learning for Emerging Environments.   643
  Kwai Wong, Stanimire Tomov, and Jack Dongarra

Correction to: High Performance Computing C1
  Michèle Weiland, Guido Juckeland, Sadaf Alam, and Heike Jagode

Author Index   657

On the Use of Kernel Bypass Mechanisms for High-Performance Inter-container Communications

Gabriele Ara[1]⑩, Luca Abeni[1]⑩, Tommaso Cucinotta[1](✉)⑩,
and Carlo Vitucci[2]

[1] Scuola Superiore Sant'Anna, Pisa, Italy
{gabriele.ara,luca.abeni,tommaso.cucinotta}@santannapisa.it
[2] Ericsson, Stockholm, Sweden
carlo.vitucci@ericsson.com

Abstract. In this paper, we perform a comparison among a number of different virtual bridging and switching technologies, each widely available and commonly used on Linux, to provide network connectivity to co-located LXC containers for high-performance application scenarios.

1 Introduction

Information and Communication Technologies (ICT) have gone quite a long way, with continuous advances in processing and networking technologies, among others, that resulted into a great push towards distributed computing models. This is witnessed by the widespread diffusion of public cloud computing services, along with private cloud models being employed in nearly every sector/industry. These allow for a greater degree of flexibility in resource management paving the way for on-demand, cost-effective distributed computing solutions progressively replacing traditional dedicated infrastructure management.

In the domain of network operators, recent technological trends led to replacing traditional physical networking infrastructures sized for the peak hour with software-based virtualized network functions (VNFs). These are instantiated on-demand and "elastically", so as to provide the required level of service performance. The new paradigm of Network Function Virtualization (NFV) [11] relies on a flexible general-purpose computing infrastructure managed according to a private cloud paradigm, to provide networking functions at reduced operational costs. As an example, in the Radio Access Network (RAN), a number of different options have been proposed [1] for splitting the functionality among the distributed unit (DU) that needs to stay close to the antenna, vs. the centralized unit (CU) that can be off-loaded to a closeby private cloud data center.

In this context, a number of network functions need high-performance and low end-to-end latency, where a key role is played by the communication overheads experienced by the individual software components participating in each deployed VNF. Such requirements are so tight that NFV has already focused on

© Springer Nature Switzerland AG 2019
M. Weiland et al. (Eds.): ISC 2019 Workshops, LNCS 11887, pp. 1–12, 2019.
https://doi.org/10.1007/978-3-030-34356-9_1

lightweight virtualization solutions based on operating system (OS) containers, rather than traditional virtual machines (VMs). Moreover, in order to reduce even further the per-packet processing overheads, and at the same time allow for the maximum flexibility in packet processing by the VNF, plenty of experimentation is being done on the use of user-space networking, as opposed to traditional TCP/IP based management of network packets within an OS kernel or hypervisor. While using these kernel bypass[1] techniques, among which a prominent position in industry is played by the Data Plane Development Kit (DPDK) [7], one of the key functionality that needs to be preserved is the virtual switching among multiple containers within the same host. This need can occasionally be dropped in presence of hardware support for virtual switching, such as with Single-Root of I/O Virtualization (SR-IOV) [4], letting different containers/VMs use dedicated virtual functions of the same NIC.

Paper Contributions and Structure. In this paper, experimental results are presented comparing different virtual switching and user-space packet processing solutions. The focus is on the maximum achievable throughput for small packets exchanged among containers deployed onto the same host. This highlights the difference in per-packet processing overheads of the compared solutions.

The remainder of this paper is structured as follows. Section 2 introduces basic terminology used throughout the paper, and describes the basic elements of the compared networking/switching technologies. Section 3 describes the testbed we used for the comparative evaluation of the considered technologies, and presents experimental results gathered on a multi-core platform running Linux. Section 4 reviews related literature on the topic, discussing our contribution in relation to prior art. Finally, Sect. 5 contains a few concluding remarks, pointing out future research lines on the topic.

2   Overview of Compared Solutions

This section presents various background concepts about containers on Linux and the various virtual switching solutions that are compared later in Sect. 3.

Containers

Differently from traditional machine virtualization, allowing multiple operating systems to coexist on the same host, virtualizing the available hardware via full emulation or para-virtualization, containers are a lightweight virtualization abstraction realized directly within a single operating system, by recurring to proper kernel-level encapsulation and isolation techniques.

The Linux kernel supports containers by proper configuration of control groups (affecting resource scheduling and control) and namespaces via userspace tools such as Docker or LXC. Namespaces allow to isolate (and virtualize) system resources: a process running in a namespace has the illusion to use a dedicated copy of the namespace resources, and cannot access resources outside

---

[1] See for example: https://lwn.net/Articles/629155/.

of it. The Linux kernel provides different kinds of namespaces, one for each different hardware or software resource that needs to be isolated/virtualized. For example, the network namespace encapsulates all the resources used by the kernel network stack, including network interfaces, routing tables, iptables rules, etc.

Network connections among processes running inside and outside a namespace are generally implemented by using a virtual Ethernet pair, i.e., two software network interfaces (there is no physical NIC attached to them) connected point-to-point, so that packets sent to one of the two interfaces are received by the other, and vice-versa. Hence, if one of the two endpoints is inside the namespace and the other one is outside, it is possible for the applications running in the namespace to communicate with the external world. This is shown in Fig. 1a.

Socket API
Traditionally, the external endpoint of a virtual Ethernet pair is attached to a Linux software bridge or some other kind of virtual switch, while the internal endpoint is accessed via simple blocking system calls exchanging a packet per call, such as when using send() or recv(). As a result, to exchange a UDP packet, at least two system calls are needed, along with various user-space to kernel space switches, data copies, and scheduling decisions. Therefore, when exchanging small packets, the overheads associated to each system call needed by the sender and the receiver grow to prohibitive values. On the other hand, when exchanging large packets, these overheads are amortized over the large amounts of data exchanged per call, but this time performance bottlenecks are due mostly to how many times data is copied to go from the sender to the receiver.

The typical way to mitigate the first issue is by recurring to batch APIs, with which a single system call sends or receives multiple packets, as possible with sendmmsg() and recvmmsg(). The second issue, instead, is mitigated by having the application and the underlying hardware reduce any need for copying data, exploiting memory-mapped I/O, scatter-gather primitives or using zero-copy APIs, such as the MSG_ZEROCOPY flag with standard send().

Use of virtio
To improve the networking performance between containers, system calls, context switches and data copies should be avoided as much as possible. For example, if two containers are co-located on the same physical node, they can exchange data by using shared memory buffers. This requires to bypass the in-kernel networking stack or to use a user-space TCP/IP stack. The latter allows user programs to be developed by using standard networking APIs, where the system is able to use the appropriate optimizations when possible.

This can be achieved by replacing virtual Ethernet pairs with para-virtualized network interfaces based on the virtio standard [18,19]. These use "virtual queues" of received and transmitted packets, that can be shared among different guests and the host, allowing for the implementation of efficient host/guest communications. While virtio virtual NICs are generally implemented by hypervisors such as qemu/kvm, thanks to the recent "vhost-user" introduction

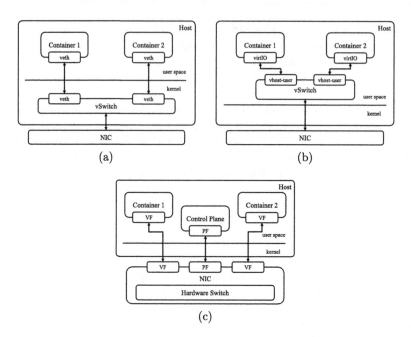

Fig. 1. Different approaches to inter-container networking: (a) kernel-based solution; (b) using DPDK with vhost in user mode; (c) using SR-IOV support.

they can also be used in containerized environments. This way, vhost services [23] can be used to move packets across virtual NICs. These can be implemented either in kernel space (using a kernel thread created by the vhost-net module) or in user-space, using a daemon [12] to implement the vhost functionalities. See also Fig. 1b.

DPDK

The simplest way to use virtio NICs in containers to enable the memory sharing optimizations is through a commonly used kernel bypassing framework: the Data Plane Development Kit (DPDK). While DPDK has been originally designed only for kernel bypassing (implementing the NIC drivers in user space), it now provides some interesting features such as the virtio and vhost drivers. The virtio driver is able to connect to virtio-net virtual interfaces, while the vhost driver can be used to implement vhost functionalities in user space (the so called "vhost-user"). For example, virtual switches can use the DPDK vhost driver to implement virtio-net endpoints connecting different VMs.

When using containers instead of full VMs, the vhost driver can be used to implement virtual NICs for the virtio-user driver; as a consequence, a DPDK-based virtual switch running in the host can create virtio-net interfaces which DPDK-based applications running in the containers can connect to. Different software components (described below) can be used as the vhost-user user-space daemon. Clearly, the inter-container networking performance also depends on the software component used as a vhost-user daemon, as shown in Sect. 3.

Virtual Switches Based on virtio

The following is a list of the most commonly adopted solutions in industry for inter-container communications using virtual switches. For each of these scenarios, two vhost-user ports are connected with each other via a virtual switch application running in user space.

Open vSwitch (OVS) [10] is an open-source software-only virtual switch that can be used with Linux-based hypervisors (e.g., KVM) or container platforms [13]. Since it is a full fledged open-source switching solution, OVS is our reference to evaluate performance of generic virtual switching solutions between vhost-user ports.

DPDK Testpmd can be used to test the functionality of the DPDK PMD driver and can be configured to act as a simple bridge between pairs of virtual or physical ports. Albeit configurable, the default pairing between ports is performed on their ordering (ports 0 and 1, ports 2 and 3, and so on), which means that this software does not contain any actual switching functionality nor packet inspection programmed in it. This is why we will use it as a reference for the maximum performance achievable using PMD driver and vhost-user ports.

Snabb [22] is a simple and fast packet networking toolkit that can be used to program user-space packet processing flows [12]. This is done by connecting functional blocks in a directed acyclic graph, each block performing a specific action or representing a custom driver for an interface. In our tests, we configured it statically as a simple bridge between the two vhost-user ports, and thus it represents the maximum achievable performance by an actual configurable virtual switch solution that performs minimal packet processing on forwarding.

FD.io Vector Packet Processing (VPP) [9] is an extensible framework that provides switching and routing functionalities released in the context of the Fast Data IO (FD.io) Linux Foundation project and that is an open-source implementation of Cisco's VPP technology. The core idea behind VPP is to process more than one packet at a time, taking advantage of instruction and data cache localities to achieve lower latencies and higher throughput [3]. This switch will be used to compare its performance with the one achieved by OVS, which does not have this optimization.

Single Root I/O Virtualization (SR-IOV)

SR-IOV [4] is a specification that allows a single PCIe device to appear as multiple physical PCIe devices. This is achieved by introducing the distinction between Physical Functions (PFs) and Virtual Functions (VFs): the former allow for using the full list of features of the PCIe device, while the latter are "lightweight" functions that have only the ability to move data between an application and the device. VFs can be individually exposed in passthrough to VMs or containers, which can access directly the hardware device, without any need for virtual switching. Most SR-IOV devices contain a hardware layer-2 switch able to forward traffic among PFs and VFs. This is depicted in Fig. 1c. SR-IOV devices can either be accessed trough OS drivers, or via DPDK ones, which allow an application to gain complete control over a VF to access it from user space. In this case, a Testpmd application must run on the host to handle configuration requests from applications, to assign or release VFs and configure the control plane associated with the hardware switch, which will then perform all forwarding operations in hardware.

3   Experimental Results

In this section we introduce the experimental testbed used for evaluating the considered technologies, along with our testing application and environment.

Platform Description and Set-Up

Experiments were performed on a Dell PowerEdge R630 V4 server equipped with two Intel® Xeon® E5-2640 v4 CPUs at 2.40 GHz, 64 GB of RAM and an Intel® X710 DA2 Ethernet Controller for 10 GbE SFP+ (used in SR-IOV experiments). The machine is configured with Linux kernel version 4.15.0, DPDK version 18.11, OVS version 2.11.0, Snabb version 2018.09 and VPP version 19.04. To maximize reproducibility of results, our tests have been run without using hyperthreads and disabling CPU frequency scaling (governor set to `performance` and Turbo Boost disabled).

Testing Application

To evaluate the various local networking alternatives described in Sect. 2, a testing application has been developed, composed of a sender and a receiver exchanging packets at a configurable rate. Each of these programs is deployed on a separate container pinned down on a different CPU of the same CPU package (same NUMA node). The sender program sends packets of a given size in bursts of a given size, matching a desired sending rate. The three parameters can be controlled via command-line options. The receiver program continuously tries to receive packets, measuring the received packet rate.

   In a realistic scenario, when deciding what networking paradigm to adopt, different trade-offs would be possible: for example, traditional `send()` and `recv()` system calls can be used on raw sockets to bypass the networking stack, but not the kernel completely. Or a user-space TCP/IP stack implementation can be used to allow using higher-level networking protocols without giving up on the advantages coming from direct access to the NIC.

   Therefore, the benchmark application comes in various incarnations that use UDP sockets, bypass the networking stack by using raw sockets, or bypass the kernel completely so that:

1. virtio-net is used instead of virtual Ethernet pairs to enable optimizations (based on shared memory buffers) in inter-container communications;
2. DPDK is used to bypass the kernel completely (both in-kernel device drivers and networking stack);
3. polling techniques are used for sending/receiving network packets.

Table 1. Maximum throughput achieved for various socket-based solutions, using packets of 64 bytes and bursts of 64 packets.

Technique	Max throughput (kpps)
UDP sockets using `send/recv`	227
UDP sockets using `sendmmsg/recvmmsg`	276
Raw sockets using `send/recv`	471
Raw sockets using `sendmmsg/recvmmsg`	594

The first version of the benchmark application uses kernel sockets to exchange data; it can be configured to send packets one at a time (using `send/recv`) or in bursts of various sizes (using `sendmmsg/recvmmsg` to perform a single system call per burst) and it can be set to use raw sockets instead of UDP sockets, to bypass part of the network stack during kernel processing. In any case, the two containers communicate through a simple Linux bridge (further benchmarking with alternative bridging techniques is planned in future work).

The other application variant uses DPDK and the PMD driver to bypass the kernel when exchanging data. This allows it to be used both with vhost-user ports or with SR-IOV virtual functions, depending on the test.

Results

Using the described setups, we measured the receiving rate at various UDP packet sizes (from 64 to 1500 bytes) and packet sending rates (from 1 to 20 Mpps) in steady state conditions. Moreover, packets are sent in bursts (of 16, 32, and 64 packets per burst).

The first result that we want to point out is that performance achieved without using kernel-bypass techniques are much lower than the ones achieved using DPDK, either via virtio or offloading to SR-IOV. For example, using packets of 64 bytes all DPDK solutions were able to achieve over 5 Mpps, while traditional sockets were not even able to reach 1 Mpps. Table 1 reports the maximum throughput achieved using the traditional socket APIs and show that bypassing the networking stack can improve the performance from 276 kpps to 594 kpps; however, even with optimizations like sending packets in batches with `sendmmsg` and a burst size of 64 packets, the achieved performance is significantly impaired when a virtual Ethernet port is used to connect the two containers, and it is even lower with smaller burst sizes.

Switching to the higher-performance alternatives relying on kernel bypass, Fig. 2 summarizes the major results from our experimentation, reporting the achieved throughput (on the Y axis) with respect to the desired packet sending rate (on the X axis), using bursts of 16 packets and packet sizes of 64 and 512 bytes. Note that our tests using a burst size of 32 and 64 packets achieved no measurable difference in the results, compared to the showed results, referring to a burst size of 16 packets.

In the plots, each data point is obtained from a 1-min run, by averaging the obtained per-second receive rate for 20 s, discarding as many initial samples for each run, to ensure we skip the initial warm-up phase. Note that the standard deviation among the 20 averaged values was below 2.5% (and around 0.5% on average) for all the runs.

In all our tests, each networking solution is able to achieve the desired throughput up to a certain maximum value, after which any additional packet sent is dropped before reaching its destination. The maximum throughput achieved with each packet size and networking technology is summarized in Fig. 3.

Among the solutions that use kernel-bypass techniques, maximum performance is achieved offloading traffic to the SR-IOV enabled Ethernet controller, taking advantage of its hardware switch. The second best performance is achieved by DPDK Testpmd application used as virtual bridge; while this result was expected among virtio-based solutions, it cannot be used in a realistic scenario because the application itself is not a virtual switch, it just forwards all the packets received from a given port to another statically assigned port. Snabb resulted as the best among software switches during our tests; however, it was configured to act as a simple bridge between the two virtual ports, limiting to the very minimum the amount of processing performed on packet forwarding.

Between the two considered complete virtual switches, VPP and OVS, the former is able to achieve a higher throughput with respect to the latter when the packets are smaller than 512 bytes. This is probably thanks to the batch packet processing features included with VPP, which make it more cache-friendly and lead to higher network performance on larger amounts of packets.

Final Remarks

Results indicate clearly that if the focus of the NFV application being developed is to achieve maximum performance, SR-IOV is the way to go, as it can clearly outperform even Testpmd, which is just a mock bridge application. This however requires custom configuration of containers to access the device in passthrough and introduces some limits to the portability of applications, even if DPDK framework provides a sufficiently generic API to access either virtual or physical devices with little effort on a great variety of platforms. If it is not possible to use a SR-IOV enabled interface, the two most promising alternatives based on vhost-user are Snabb and VPP. It is worth noting that Snabb configuration must be programmed manually in the Lua language, while VPP accepts a simple configuration file on startup.

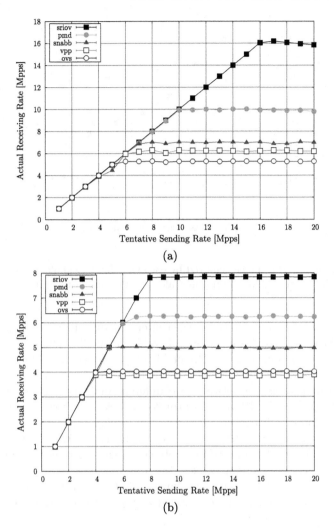

Fig. 2. Receive rate obtained at varying sending rate, with a packet size of 64 bytes (a) and 512 bytes (b).

4   Related Work

Several works appeared in prior research literature addressing how to optimize the networking performance for virtual machines and containers. For example, some authors investigated [2] packet forwarding performance achievable in virtual machines using different technologies to implement the virtual NICs and to connect them to the host network stack or physical NIC.

Many solutions exist to greatly reduce the overheads due to interrupt handlers, like interrupt coalescing and other optimizations available on Linux through New API (NAPI) [21], including hybrid interrupt-handling tech-

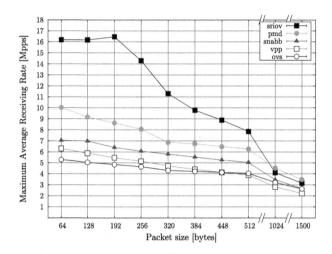

Fig. 3. Maximum performance achieved by each switching technology. Notice that the last two entries on the x axis are not in scale with the rest of the axis.

niques that switch dynamically between interrupt disabling-enabling (DE) and polling (NAPI) depending on the actual traffic on the line [20].

Comparisons among Remote Direct Memory Access (RDMA) [15], DPDK and traditional sockets already exist [5], mainly focusing on the achievable minimum round-trip latencies between two different machines. These works show how both RDMA and DPDK can outperform sockets, achieving much smaller latencies for small UDP packets, at the cost of forcing applications to operate in poll mode, leading unavoidably to high CPU utilizations. Also, authors point out that DPDK can actually be used in combination with interrupts, saving energy, but before sending or receiving packets the program must switch back to polling mode. This reduces CPU utilization during idle times, at the cost of a greater latency when interrupts must be disabled to revert to polling mode, when the first packet of a burst is received.

Another survey among common networking set-ups for high-performance NFV exists [8], accompanied by a quantitative comparison addressing throughput and CPU utilization of SR-IOV, Snabb, OVS with DPDK and Netmap [16]. Authors highlight how the different solutions have remarkable differences in security and usability, and they show that, for local VM to VM communications, Netmap is capable of reaching up to 27 Mpps (when running on a 4GHz CPU), overcoming SR-IOV due to its limited internal switch bandwidth that becomes a bottleneck. While in this paper we provide a thorough performance analysis for many of the networking solutions described in that work, some of them have not been included; in particular, we did not evaluate NetVM [6] and Netmap (along with its associated virtual switch, VALE [17]), because our focus has been here on solutions commonly adopted in current NFV industrial practice. However, their inclusion in the comparison is among our planned future work.

In another interesting work [14], VPP, OVS and SR-IOV are compared with respect to scalability in the number of VMs on a single host. Other works exist in the area, but a complete state of the art review is out of the scope of this paper.

Differently from the above mentioned works that mostly deal with networking performance for virtual machines, in this paper we focused on industrially viable solutions for high-performance networking for Linux containers. Also, this paper extends our preliminary work [24], where a very basic comparison among communication techniques for co-located Linux containers was done, with a strong focus on motivational arguments for the research in the context of NFV.

5   Conclusions and Future Work

In this paper, we compared various switching technologies for inter-container communications, with a focus on high-performance and poll-based APIs employing batch-based packet processing in user-space. In our experimentation, the best performance has been achieved by SR-IOV, followed by Snabb, among DPDK based virtual switching solutions. These all outperform what is achievable with traditional socket-based APIs and a Linux virtual bridge.

In the future, we plan to extend the evaluation by: considering also the latency dimension, along with the throughput one considered in this work; comparing the various solutions when transmitting through a real network, in addition to the local communications considered here; considering additional works in the comparison, such as Netmap, VALE and NetVM; and finally evaluating how the various solutions impact the performance of a realistic NFV use-case, in addition to the low-level benchmark considered so far.

References

1. 3rd Generation Partnership Project; Transport requirement for CU-DU functional splits options; R3-161813. In: 3GPP TSG RAN WG3 Meeting 93, August 2016
2. Abeni, L., Kiraly, C., Li, N., Bianco, A.: On the performance of KVM-based virtual routers. Comput. Commun. **70**, 40–53 (2015). https://doi.org/10.1016/j.comcom.2015.05.005
3. Barach, D., Linguaglossa, L., Marion, D., Pfister, P., Pontarelli, S., Rossi, D.: High-speed software data plane via vectorized packet processing. IEEE Commun. Mag. **56**(12), 97–103 (2018)
4. Dong, Y., Yang, X., Li, J., Liao, G., Tian, K., Guan, H.: High performance network virtualization with SR-IOV. J. Parallel Distrib. Comput. **72**(11), 1471–1480 (2012)
5. Géhberger, D., Balla, D., Maliosz, M., Simon, C.: Performance evaluation of low latency communication alternatives in a containerized cloud environment. In: IEEE 11th International Conference on Cloud Computing (CLOUD), pp. 9–16 (2018)
6. Hwang, J., Ramakrishnan, K.K., Wood, T.: NetVM: high performance and flexible networking using virtualization on commodity platforms. IEEE Trans. Netw. Serv. Manage. **12**(1), 34–47 (2015)

7. Intel Corporation: Data Plane Development Kit (DPDK), February 2019. http://www.dpdk.org

8. Lettieri, G., Maffione, V., Rizzo, L.: A survey of fast packet I/O technologies for network function virtualization. In: Kunkel, J.M., Yokota, R., Taufer, M., Shalf, J. (eds.) ISC High Performance 2017. LNCS, vol. 10524, pp. 579–590. Springer, Cham (2017). https://doi.org/10.1007/978-3-319-67630-2_40

9. LF Projects, LLC: Vector Packet Processing (VPP), February 2019. http://fd.io/technology

10. Linux Foundation Collaborative Project: Open vSwitch (OVS), February 2019. https://www.openvswitch.org

11. NFV Industry Specif. Group: Network Functions Virtualisation. Introductory White Paper (2012)

12. Paolino, M., Nikolaev, N., Fanguede, J., Raho, D.: SnabbSwitch user space virtual switch benchmark and performance optimization for NFV. In: Proceedings of the IEEE Conference on Network Function Virtualization and Software Defined Network (NFV-SDN 2015), pp. 86–92, November 2015

13. Pfaff, B., et al.: The design and implementation of open vSwitch. In: 12th USENIX Symposium on Networked Systems Design and Implementation (NSDI 15), Oakland, CA, pp. 117–130 (2015)

14. Pitaev, N., Falkner, M., Leivadeas, A., Lambadaris, I.: Characterizing the performance of concurrent virtualized network functions with OVS-DPDK, FD.io VPP and SR-IOV. In: Proceedings of the 2018 ACM/SPEC International Conference on Performance Engineering, pp. 285–292. ACM (2018)

15. RDMA Consortium: Architectural Specifications for RDMA over TCP/IP, February 2019. http://www.rdmaconsortium.org

16. Rizzo, L.: netmap: a novel framework for fast packet I/O. In: 21st USENIX Security Symposium (USENIX Security 12), pp. 101–112 (2012)

17. Rizzo, L., Lettieri, G.: VALE, a switched ethernet for virtual machines. In: CoNEXT 2012 - Proceedings of the 2012 ACM Conference on Emerging Networking Experiments and Technologies, December 2012

18. Russell, R., Tsirkin, M., Huck, C., Moll, P.: Virtual I/O Device (VIRTIO) Version 1.0. Standard, OASIS Specification Committee (2015)

19. Russell, R.: VIRTIO: towards a de-facto standard for virtual I/O devices. ACM SIGOPS Oper. Syst. Rev. **42**(5), 95–103 (2008)

20. Salah, K., Qahtan, A.: Implementation and experimental performance evaluation of a hybrid interrupt-handling scheme. Comput. Commun. **32**(1), 179–188 (2009)

21. Salim, J.H., Olsson, R., Kuznetsov, A.: Beyond softnet. In: USENIX (ed.) Proceedings of the 5th Annual Linux Showcase & Conference, vol. 5, pp. 165–172, November 2001

22. SnabbCo: Snabb, February 2019. https://github.com/snabbco/snabb

23. Tsirkin, M.S.: Vhost-net and Virtio-net: need for speed. In: Proceedings of the KVM Forum, May 2010

24. Vitucci, C., Abeni, L., Cucinotta, T., Marinoni, M.: The strategic role of inter-container communications in RAN deployment scenarios. In: ICN 2019: The Eighteenth International Conference on Networks, March 2019

Continuous-Action Reinforcement Learning for Memory Allocation in Virtualized Servers

Luis A. Garrido[1](✉), Rajiv Nishtala[2], and Paul Carpenter[1]

[1] Barcelona Supercomputing Center, Barcelona, Spain
{luis.garrido,paul.carpenter}@bsc.es
[2] Norwegian University of Science and Technology, Trondheim, Norway
rajiv.nishtala@ntnu.no

Abstract. In a virtualized computing server (node) with multiple Virtual Machines (VMs), it is necessary to dynamically allocate memory among the VMs. In many cases, this is done only considering the memory demand of each VM without having a node-wide view. There are many solutions for the dynamic memory allocation problem, some of which use machine learning in some form.

This paper introduces CAVMem (Continuous-Action Algorithm for Virtualized Memory Management), a proof-of-concept mechanism for a decentralized dynamic memory allocation solution in virtualized nodes that applies a *continuous-action* reinforcement learning (RL) algorithm called Deep Deterministic Policy Gradient (DDPG). CAVMem with DDPG is compared with other RL algorithms such as Q-Learning (QL) and Deep Q-Learning (DQL) in an environment that models a virtualized node.

In order to obtain linear scaling and be able to dynamically add and remove VMs, CAVMem has one agent per VM connected via a lightweight coordination mechanism. The agents learn how much memory to bid for or return, in a given state, so that each VM obtains a fair level of performance subject to the available memory resources. Our results show that CAVMem with DDPG performs better than QL and a static allocation case, but it is competitive with DQL. However, CAVMem incurs significant less training overheads than DQL, making the continuous-action approach a more cost-effective solution.

Keywords: Reinforcement learning · Memory · Virtualization

1 Introduction

Cloud infrastructures are built using virtualization technology, which provides isolation for concurrently running applications [5] and allows sharing of the available computing resources [3–6]. When multiple VMs are active in a node, its physical memory is allocated among the VMs in order to optimize throughput

© Springer Nature Switzerland AG 2019
M. Weiland et al. (Eds.): ISC 2019 Workshops, LNCS 11887, pp. 13–24, 2019.
https://doi.org/10.1007/978-3-030-34356-9_2

and prevent memory starvation. This memory allocation problem is difficult to solve because the memory demand of a VM changes continuously. Many solutions for this problem are limited by the complex relationship between the memory allocated to a VM, the applications' behavior and their performance, for which RL provides a good alternative.

Different approaches of RL have been applied to the resource management problem in virtualized nodes [2] which rely on the discretization of states and actions. Discretization introduces some limitations, mainly combinatorial explosion: as the number of states/action grows, the problem becomes unsolvable [17]. In the context of memory allocation, discretization restricts the granularity at which memory can be allocated, limiting the opportunities for better optimization. Another limitation of current RL approaches for resource management is that they deploy a single agent responsible for re-allocating memory. Such a centralized approach has scalability and flexibility restrictions, since it introduces a traffic bottleneck and single points of failure.

This paper presents CAVMem (Continuous-Action Algorithm for Virtualized Memory Management), which serves as a proof-of-concept for a solution to the dynamic memory allocation problem using a distributed continuous-action RL formulation, avoiding the limitations of discretization and centralization. To the best of our knowledge, this is the first such formulation of the memory allocation problem. CAVMem is initially designed with DDPG, but other RL algorithms were also implemented, namely Q-Learning [12] (QL) and Deep Q-Learning [7] (DQL). These are compared in a model environment that simulates certain aspects of a virtualized computing node.

In summary, the contributions of this paper are:

(1) Formulation of the memory management problem as a distributed continuous-action Markov Decision Process (MDP). This formulation supports an unlimited and variable number of VMs.

(2) Development of a continuous-action off-policy model-free RL algorithm for dynamic memory allocation.

(3) Comparison between three RL approaches: (a) CAVMem with DDPG (continuous action space), (b) CAVMem with QL (tabular, non-continuous action) and (c) CAVMem with DQL (non-continuous action). We also compare against the static policy that divides memory equally among VMs.

The rest of this paper is organized as follows. Section 2 provides background information on memory allocation and RL. Section 3 explains the design of CAVMem and its contributions. Section 4 explains our experimental methodology. Section 5 presents the results and discussion. Section 6 presents related work and Sect. 7 presents our conclusions and future work.

2   Background

2.1   Memory Management in Virtualized Nodes

Cloud services are built on top of virtualization technology, which make use of a hypervisor to multiplex certain physical resources such as CPUs and I/O interfaces and allocate others, such as memory. When a VM is created, it is allocated a portion of the node's memory. If the VM increases its memory demand, it may exceed its initial allocation. In this case, the VM may swap data to its (virtual) disk device(s), suffering a significant performance loss. In this case, the VM is *underprovisioned* of memory. A VM with idle memory is *over-provisioned*. When one or more VMs are in this state while others are under-provisioned, it is necessary to re-allocate memory to re-balance the allocation and optimize overall system performance.

Analytical solutions for this problem require the analysis of many VM–application sets and combinations. The number of possibilities is huge, and attempting to obtain solutions in this way is intractable. Instead, heuristics are designed to exploit optimal allocations for known sets. Heuristics are also limited since sometimes they do not generalize well for all possible combinations. Reinforcement learning is a good alternative to overcome these limitations.

2.2   Reinforcement Learning: Markov Decision Process

Reinforcement learning problems involve an agent interacting with an environment, usually stochastic, with the goal of maximising its total (cumulative) discounted reward. These problems are typically modeled as Markov Decision Processes (MDP), which have the following elements:

- State space S, which contains all states in which the environment can be in.
- Action space A, which contains the possible actions the agent can take.
- Transition probability function, denoted by $P : S \times A \times S \rightarrow \mathbb{R}$. This function gives the probability that if the agent is in state s_i in timestep i and it takes action a_i, then it will transition to state s_{i+1} in the following timestep $(i+1)$.
- Reward function $R : S \times A \times S \rightarrow \mathbb{R}$, which gives the immediate reward obtained from the transition from state s_i via action a_i to new state s_{i+1}.

The objective of the agent is to learn the optimal policy $\pi : S \rightarrow A$ (state-to-action mappings) for which the discounted reward $r_t^\gamma = \Sigma_{k=t}^\infty \gamma^{k-t} r(s_k, a_k, s_{k+1})$ is maximized, where $\gamma \in [0, 1]$ is the discount factor. The agent learns the optimal policy by maximizing the (expected) state-action value function $Q^\pi(s, a)$, expressed by the Bellman equation [8]:

$$Q^\pi(s_t, a_t) = \mathbb{E}[r(s_t, a_t) + \gamma Q^\pi(s_{t+1}, \pi(s_{t+1}))] \qquad (1)$$

The Q-function can be represented as 2D matrix of states and actions, where each entry $Q(s, a)$ represents the reward for an action at a given state. This approach is known as Q-Learning [12] *(QL)*. This requires quantizing both the state and action space into discrete values within the minimum and maximum range. The need to build the extensive 2D matrix of state-action space leads to a combinatorial explosion of the state–action space, which could quickly increase the learning time and memory complexity. To solve this, Mnih *et al.* [7] estimate the Q-function through a parametrized neural network (NN) function approximator, an approach called Deep Q-Learning *(DQL)*. However, both DQL and QL estimate the action as a discrete value.

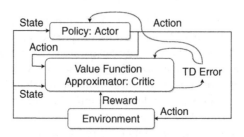

Fig. 1. Diagram of the actor–critic architecture for DDPG.

In this context, Lillicrap *et al.* introduce a method to estimate the actions continuously called Deep Deterministic Policy Gradient [17] *(DDPG)*. DDPG is an off-policy learning algorithm [13], meaning that it learns the optimal policy interacting with the environment.

Figure 1 shows a high-level view of the DDPG learning agent. It includes two neural networks: *actor network* and *critic network*. The input to the actor network is the current state of the environment, while the input to the critic network is both the current state and the continuous actions generated by the actor. Using continuous actions for memory allocation is potentially beneficial since it allows to allocate memory at a finer granularity, and prevents the limitations imposed by discretization.

3   CAVMem: Algorithm for Virtualized Memory Management

In this section, we introduce CAVMem, a mechanism using continuous action RL for memory management in virtualized nodes. We formulate the problem as a Markov Decision Process. The MDP is formulated such that it does not impose limits on the number of VMs. It creates a RL agent per VM which has both a local view and a node-wide view, indirectly passing to a VM information on the behavior of other VMs. The reward is set to optimize aggregate performance while ensuring fairness among the VMs. In the following subsections, we detail how the MDP is formulated, its advantages and the learning mechanism.

3.1   Decentralized Strategy for Memory Management

Determining a priori the memory demands of VMs in virtualized servers is complicated because the nodes seldom have prior knowledge of applications on each VM or the number of concurrently active VMs. Instead, another approach is to let the VMs ask for the memory they need. In this case, each VM monitors its own resource utilization and bids for memory independently, resulting in a decentralized solution.

Decentralization has two advantages. First, CAVMem is designed to adjust itself to any amount of active VMs, a feature allowed by our MDP formulation.

Table 1. State inputs to the actor and critic networks of the DDPG learning agents.

State information from computing node and VMs			
	Name	Range	Description
perVM	$msr_t^{VM_j}$	$[-1, 1]$	RAM miss rate of VM_j, rescaled to range $[-1, 1]$; i.e. a value of -1 means zero miss rate
perVM	$M_t^{VM_j}$	$[0, 1]$	Fraction of total RAM allocated to VM_j
Node	$avgMsr_t^{node}$	$[-1, 1]$	Average RAM miss rate across all VMs, equal to $\frac{1}{N}\sum_j msr_t^{VM_j}$
Node	$msrTgt_t^{node}$	$[-1, 1]$	Target RAM miss rate for all VMs given by Eq. 3
Node	$totalMemUse_t^{node}$	$[0, 1]$	Fraction of the node's physical RAM that is allocated to VMs, equal to $\sum_j M_t^{VM_j}$

Second, CAVMem removes a single point of control, which allows to scale even beyond a single computing node.

3.2 Formulating the Problem as an MDP

[**State space,** S]: Table 1 lists the five state variables for each agent, two of which belong to the VM and the other three are common to all VMs in the node. This state space definition allows the agent to have *some* information about the other active VMs through the information related to the node.

[**Action space,** A]: The action $a_t^{VM_j}$ chosen for VM_j in timestep t is referred to as the VM's **memory bid**, which ranges from -1.0 to 1.0. A positive bid is a request for more memory and a negative bid is an action to release memory. Concretely, the VM agent requests a total memory allocation equal to $(1 + a_t^{VM_j}) \times M_t^{VM_j}$. As discussed later, it may not be possible to fully satisfy the request, for instance when there is insufficient memory for to accommodate every request or when the memory allocation for the VM would become too small.

[**Reward function,** R]: The reward function encourages a fair level of performance across the VMs by making all VMs suffer the same miss rate over each time step. This is done through a penalty (negative reward) proportional to the absolute difference between the RAM miss rate of the VM, given by $msr_{t+1}^{VM_j}$ and the miss rate target, $msrTgt_{t+1}^{node}$:

$$r_t^{VM_j} = -|msr_t^{VM_j} - msrTgt_t^{node}| \times k \tag{2}$$

The parameter k, which we set to 1, affects the learning rate. The miss rate target for the next timestep is given by:

$$msrTgt_{t+1}^{node} = avgMsr_t^{node} \times \sqrt{totalMemUse_t^{node}} \tag{3}$$

Here, $avgMsr_{node}$ is the average RAM miss rate across all active VMs, defined in Table 1. When it is non-zero and there is free memory, the factor $totalMemUse_{node}$ encourages the VMs to use more memory, via a well-known square-root rule of thumb.

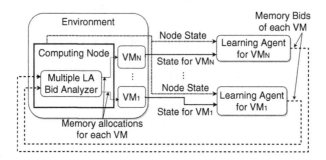

Fig. 2. Diagram of the CAVMem architecture, with one learning agent per VM.

Environment Constraints for Decentralized Control. Figure 2 shows a high-level view of our system, including a module called the Bid Analyzer (BA), the VMs and the learning agents of each VM. The BA checks the bids of the learning agents before issuing them to the node. It prevents VM memory allocation from being less than a given threshold (set manually at 384 MB) and it prevents memory allocation from exceeding the node's capacity. Additionally, it also enforces bid prioritization for VMs that issue negative bids.

Action Space Exploration. A classic problem in RL is the *exploration–exploitation dilemma* [13], which captures the need to exploit the "optimal" solution obtained so far but also explore potential better actions. To explore in continuous action domains, the common approach is to use an Ornstein–Uhlenbeck process [14,15]. This process is a noise signal that creates a Brownian motion around the deterministic action generated by the DDPG agent. At every timestep, a noise signal is added to the action with a probability of ϵ. In our implementation, initially there's a phase of aggressive exploration in which $\epsilon = 1$. This probability reduces over time until it reaches $\epsilon = 0.001$. This process is called epsilon annealing, and it is used to transition from explorative policy to an exploitative one [13].

4 Experimental Framework

CAVMem was implemented in Python 3.6 with Tensorflow 1.12 [11] on a system with a 2.3 GHz Intel Core i7 processor and 16 GB of RAM. CAVMem is designed with an underlying DDPG implementation, but we also tested it with DQL and QL implementations for comparison, and a static allocation policy that divides

Table 2. List of scenarios used for evaluation

Label	Benchmark name	Description
Scenario 1	VM1, VM2: *perlbench*	Both VMs run *perlbench* repeatedly
Scenario 2	VM1: *perlbench*; VM2: *gcc*	VM1 runs *perlbench* repeatedly, VM2 runs *gcc*
Scenario 3	VM1: *gcc*; VM2: *bzip2*	VM1 runs *gcc* repeatedly, VM2 runs *bzip2*

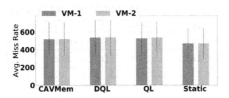

Fig. 3. Average Miss Rate for Scenario 1. Less is better

memory equally among VMs. Whenever CAVMem is mentioned, it is assumed that the agents are DDPG implementations (continuous action).

The neural networks for DDPG are fully-connected with two hidden layers of 64 units with ReLU activation functions, while the output layers use Tanh. The learning rates for the actor and critic networks are 0.0001 and 0.001, respectively, using the Adam optimizer. The annealing phase lasts for 200 episodes, where each episode has 100 steps. All experiments run for 1000 episodes.

DQL has similar parameters, but it only has one learning rate of 0.001 for the Q-function approximator for 3 discrete actions. The QL implementation also consists of 3 actions, and it has each state space variable quantized in 10 discrete values. This results in a state-action matrix of 300,000 entries.

The learning agents are deployed in a simulation environment of a virtualized node, which include models of VMs and some aspects of system memory (capacity, RAM misses, utilization). This evaluation methodology allows to see the effectiveness of the MDP formulation, without intervention of specific hardware.

We evaluate CAVMem in scenarios consisting of different combinations of VMs executing SPEC CPU 2006 benchmarks [16], summarized in Table 2. Every scenario runs two VMs with 6 GB of RAM, with 1 GB allocated initially.

In every scenario, three metrics are evaluated: (1) the average miss rate (pages/second), (2) the average miss rate deviation, and (3) the overhead (time spent in seconds) associated to the training of each agent. Every metric is measured over the last 100 episodes of each experiment. It is desirable that the average miss rate is minimized by the agent, since this would avoid disk accesses on a real system. The miss rate deviation is to compare how well the agent learns the desired behavior according to the reward function. And the overhead allows us to estimate the cost to the deployment of each agent.

5   Results for Evaluation

5.1   Results for Scenario 1

Figure 3 shows the average miss rates for Scenario 1. CAVMem has a miss rate 10% larger than *static*, while *DQL* and *QL* are higher by 14.7% and 13.9% respectively. Since the VMs are executing the same benchmark, an equal memory allocation is optimal resulting in *static* being the best in this case. Nevertheless, we see that CAVMem performs the best among the learning agents.

Figure 4 shows the average miss rate deviations for Scenario 1. CAVMem tracks the target better than all other approaches. CAVMem has a miss rate deviation 82.2% smaller than *static*, and 66.1% and 75.4% smaller than *DQL* and *QL*, respectively.

Figure 5 shows the overheads for Scenario 1. *DQL* presents an overhead 10.64 and 15.0 times larger than CAVMem and *QL* respectively, a major consideration when deploying *DQL*. *QL* presents the smallest overhead, while CAVMem's is 37% larger than *QL*'s.

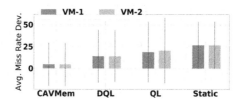

Fig. 4. Average Miss Rate Deviation for Scenario 1. Less is better

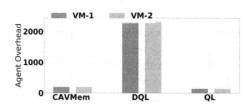

Fig. 5. Overhead (in seconds) for each agent in Scenario 1. Less is better

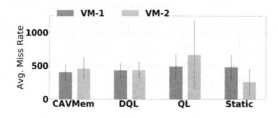

Fig. 6. Average Miss Rate for Scenario 2. Less and equal is better

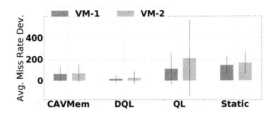

Fig. 7. Average Miss Rate Deviation for Scenario 2. Less is better

5.2 Results for Scenario 2

Figure 6 shows the average miss rates for Scenario 2. *QL* and *static* fail to balance the miss rates, which is an undesirable result, since they both benefit one VM while harming the other. CAVMem and *DQL* maintain the miss rate balance to a better degree by increasing the miss rate of both VMs. CAVMem minimizes the miss rate 6.41% below *DQL* for VM1 and 5.81% above *DQL* for VM2. Seemingly, CAVMem and *DQL* are competitive in performance.

Figure 7 shows the miss rate deviations for Scenario 2. Here, *static* is further away from the target, while CAVMem deviates by 67.6% more than *DQL*, even though they both minimize the miss rate to similar values.

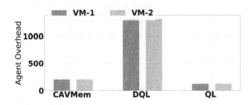

Fig. 8. Overhead (in seconds) for each agent in Scenario 2. Less is better

Figure 8 shows the overhead of the agents for Scenario 2. *DQL* maintains an overhead 5.44 and 9.96 times larger than CAVMem and *QL*, respectively.

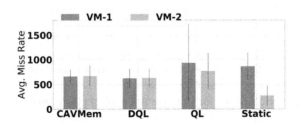

Fig. 9. Average Miss Rate for Scenario 3. Less and equal is better

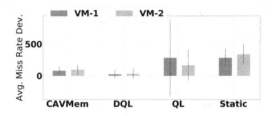

Fig. 10. Average Miss Rate Deviation for Scenario 3. Less is better

CAVMem's overhead is 70% larger than QL's but performs similar to DQL. Thus far, CAVMem provides the best performance-overhead trade-off.

5.3   Results for Scenario 3

Figure 9 shows the average miss rates for Scenario 3. DQL and *static DQL* present imbalanced miss rates for the VMs, while CAVMem and DQL yield similar values, with CAVMem being 5.96% larger than DQL.

Figure 10 shows the miss rate deviations for Scenario 3. DQL tracks the miss rate targets better being 65.92% more accurate than CAVMem, while QL and *static* fail to do so. We omit the overhead charts for this case due to lack of space, but the experiments show that DQL's overhead is 10.9 and 14.2 times larger than CAVMem's and QL's, respectively. CAVMem's overhead is larger than QL's by 28%, still maintaining the cost-effectiveness of CAVMem.

5.4   Discussion

We can summarize the findings as follows: (1) CAVMem with $DDPG$ and DQL are able to minimize and balance the miss rates in a comparable way, better than *static* in most cases, while QL consistently fails to do so, (2) DQL tracks the performance target better than CAVMem with $DDPG$, while *static* and QL fail in most instances, (3) DQL has extremely high learning overheads when compared to CAVMem with $DDPG$ and QL, highlighting a performance-cost trade-off.

6   Related Work

Many solutions have been proposed to solve the resource allocation problem in cloud infrastructures [1–4,10,15] but so far, there have not been too many efforts that use RL to exclusively solve the memory management problem in a single node, and much less continuous-action RL solutions. There are some notable RL-based solutions for the resource allocation problem that targets CPU and memory (and other resources) within a virtualized node. In [2], the authors implemented a model-based DQL algorithm for VM resource configuration, which included CPU time, virtual CPU and memory. CAVMem differs from these RL-based solutions in three ways: (1) CAVMem uses continuous-action RL exclusively for memory management, (2) CAVMem avoids discretization, and (3) it is decentralized.

7 Conclusions and Future Work

This paper proposes CAVMem as a proof-of-concept of a distributed MDP formulation for the memory allocation problem in virtualized nodes. Moreover, CAVMem also offers a continuous-action RL agent to solve the allocation problem, avoiding discretization and exploiting de-centralization. Our results show that CAVMem performs similar to the well-known DQL but with much less learning overhead, making it a very cost effective solution.

For future work, CAVMem should be deployed in a real computing node, and an exhaustive search of the parameter space of the learning agents is also necessary. Likewise, it is necessary to test CAVMem with more combinations of benchmarks and scenarios.

Acknowledgements. This research is part of a project that has received funding from the European Union's Horizon 2020 research and innovation programme under grant agreement No 754337 (EuroEXA) and the European Union's 7th Framework Programme under grant agreement number 610456 (Euroserver). It also received funding from the Spanish Ministry of Science and Technology (project TIN2015-65316-P), Generalitat de Catalunya (contract 2014-SGR-1272), and the Severo Ochoa Programme (SEV-2015-0493) of the Spanish Government.

References

1. Zhang, W., Xie, H., Hsu, C.: Automatic memory control of multiple virtual machines on a consolidated server. IEEE Trans. Cloud Comput. **5**(1), 2–14 (2017)
2. Rao, J., Bu, X., Xu, C.-Z., Wang, L., Yin, G.: VCONF: a reinforcement learning approach to virtual machine auto configuration. In: Proceedings of the 6th International Conference on Autonomic Computing (ICAC 2009), pp. 137–146 (2009)
3. Garrido, L.A., Carpenter, P.: vMCA: memory capacity aggregation and management in cloud environments. In: IEEE 23rd International Conference on Parallel and Distributed Systems (ICPADS) (2017)
4. Garrido, L.A., Carpenter, P.: Aggregating and managing memory across computing nodes in cloud environments. In: Kunkel, J.M., Yokota, R., Taufer, M., Shalf, J. (eds.) ISC High Performance 2017. LNCS, vol. 10524, pp. 642–652. Springer, Cham (2017). https://doi.org/10.1007/978-3-319-67630-2_45
5. Armbrust, M., et al.: A view of cloud computing. Commun. ACM **53**(4), 50–58 (2010)
6. Zhang, Q., Cheng, L., Boutaba, R.: Cloud computing: state-of-the-artand research challenges. J. Internet Serv. Appl. **1**(1), 7–18 (2010)
7. Mnih, V., et al.: Human-level control through deep reinforcement learning. Nature **518**, 529–533 (2015). https://doi.org/10.1038/nature14236

8. Van Hasselt, H.: Reinforcement learning in continuous state and action spaces. In: Wiering, M., van Otterlo, M. (eds.) Reinforcement Learning. Adaptation, Learning, and Optimization, vol. 12. Springer, Heidelberg (2012). https://doi.org/10.1007/978-3-642-27645-3_7

9. Dulac-Arnold, G., Evans, R., Sunehag, P., Coppin, B.: Reinforcement learning in large discrete action spaces. CoRR abs/1512.07679 (2015)

10. Bu, X., Rao, J., Xu, C.Z.: Coordinated self-configuration of virtual machines and appliances using a model-free learning approach. IEEE Trans. Parallel Distrib. Syst. **24**, 681–690 (2013)

11. Abadi, M., et al.: TensorFlow: a system for large-scale machine learning. In: Proceedings of the 12th USENIX conference on Operating Systems Design and Implementation: USENIX Association, CA, USA, Berkeley, pp. 265–283 (2016)

12. Watkins, C.J.C.H.: Learning from delayed rewards. Ph.D. thesis, Cambridge University, Cambridge, England (1989)

13. Sutton, R.S., Barto, A.G.: Introduction to Reinforcement Learning, 1st edn. MIT Press, Cambridge (1998)

14. Bibbona, E., Panfilo, G., Tavella, P.: The Ornstein–Uhlenbeck process as a model of a low pass filtered white noise. Metrologia (2008)

15. Li, T., Xu, Z., Tang, J., Wang, Y.: Model-free control for distributed stream data processing using deep reinforcement learning. In: Proceedings of Very Large Database Endowment, February 2018

16. Henning, J.L.: SPEC CPU2006 benchmark descriptions. SIGARCH Computer Architecture News, pp. 1–17 (2006)

17. Lillicrap, T.P., et al.: Continuous control with deep reinforcement learning. CoRR (2015)

Container Orchestration on HPC Clusters

Marco Enrico Piras, Luca Pireddu$^{(\boxtimes)}$, Marco Moro, and Gianluigi Zanetti

CRS4, Loc. Piscina Manna, 09050 Pula, Italy
{marcoenrico.piras,luca.pireddu,marco.moro,gianluigi.zanetti}@crs4.it

Abstract. Use of software containers and services in science is a rising trend that is not satisfied by the HPC computing resources often available in research contexts. We propose a method to grow Kubernetes clusters onto transient nodes allocated through the Grid Engine batch workload manager. The method is being used to run a mix of data-intensive service applications and bursty HPC-style workflows on an OpenStack-based Kubernetes deployment, while keeping a homogeneous job management, logging, monitoring, and storage infrastructure. Moreover, it is relatively straightforward to convert the implementation to be compatible with other workload managers.

Keywords: Cloud computing · HPC

1 Introduction

There appears to be a trend in several fields of science – and perhaps particularly in the biosciences – to adopt software containers in their workflows [19,20,24], but this user requirement is not met well by the conventional HPC batch-oriented infrastructure available in many scientific institutions. The motivations for using containers span from reproducibility [1,5,27] to ease of installation. Often these containers are used to deploy service-oriented software, which is where batch-oriented systems are particularly lacking. As an example, consider the use of workflow engines or data repositories. Indeed, even the adoption of software containers can drive the need to run internal services such as container image repositories, image building and testing services. Running complex, multi-container applications and services drives the need for container orchestration frameworks, such as Kubernetes [12]. Kubernetes (k8s for short) provides a platform to weave together containers to implement complex applications and automate or simplify much of the work of running and scaling services based on those containers. It is the flagship project of the Cloud Native Computing Foundation and backed by leading industry players.

The adoption of Kubernetes for scientific workloads offers great deployment flexibility and reproducibility, as it provides a platform that decouples users from many of the details of the underlying computing infrastructure. Indeed, this feature is very desirable for an important class of scientific users that regularly assemble scientific workflows from ready-made building blocks or need to easily

© Springer Nature Switzerland AG 2019
M. Weiland et al. (Eds.): ISC 2019 Workshops, LNCS 11887, pp. 25–35, 2019.
https://doi.org/10.1007/978-3-030-34356-9_3

install complex applications – and the k8s community has assembled a selection of prepackaged software. For instance, packages are available and to quickly set up working environments for bioinformaticians [6], metabolomics researchers [22] or data scientists (Kubeflow [11], Kubebench [7]). Unfortunately, Kubernetes is a poor match to the HPC computing resources often found in research contexts. At the same time, Kubernetes on its own does not address all the requirements of the HPC community and it is not feasible for centres to replace their existing HPC infrastructure. Moreover, Kubernetes may also be of interest to HPC centres as a means to open up the infrastructure to a wider array of tools or to integrate service-derived data (e.g., IoT sensors) into the modelling and simulation work often run on HPC platforms [9].

In this work, we propose a hybrid Kubernetes on HPC approach that consists in deploying Kubernetes worker nodes as Grid Engine (GE) [4] batch jobs to dynamically increase the size of a running Kubernetes cluster. This approach provides a solution to accommodate service- and container-oriented workloads while being minimally disruptive to an existing HPC infrastructure. It also provides a means to handle bursty k8s workloads with excess HPC computing capacity – without permanently converting the infrastructure from batch-oriented provisioning. Moreover, should users desire, there is some simple support for batch jobs on Kubernetes which can be a way to maintain a homogeneous platform for all workload types. The manuscript is organized as follows. Section 2 summarizes the related work in the field. Section 3 provides additional background useful to understand the implementation. Section 4 describes the implementation, providing previously configuration details, underlying requirements and code to ensure the reusability of the recipe in a different context. Section 5 describes experiments performed to test scalability of the cluster expansion procedure as the number of nodes increases, while Section 6 discusses various aspects of the work. Section 7 concludes the paper.

2   Related Work

To the best of the authors' knowledge, no previous solution that deploys Kubernetes workloads on a batch system exists in the literature – scientific or otherwise. Nevertheless, work has been done on the general problem of bridging the gap between conventional HPC and service-oriented infrastructure. Recently, work has been published showing how to dynamically migrate computing resources between HPC and OpenStack clusters based on demand [16]. At a higher level, IBM has demonstrated the ability to run Kubernetes pods on Spectrum LSF. Many other batch HPC systems have evolved to support running software containers images rather than plain executables. One of the most common software container formats is the Docker container [18]. However, the Docker daemon, which coordinates the execution of the container on the host system assumes a security model where trusted users are running trusted containers and natively runs containers as uid 0 (root). This configuration is ill-matched to a multi-tenant HPC infrastructure. Solutions have been presented to ameliorate this issue while preserving compatibility with Docker. For instance, Shifter [8] is a system to securely run Docker images at scale on HPC systems. On the other hand, Singularity [15] is an alternative container format that supports a more general "untrusted users running untrusted containers" security model and is thus more readily applicable to an HPC environment. The Slurm workload manager [28,29] has integrated support for both these container engines, while only limited support for Docker is provided (only trusted users which belong to a special group can execute Docker containers). Other common batch workload managers have also adopted support for some combination of these three container solutions – e.g., Spectrum Load Sharing Facility (LSF), Moab, Portable Batch System (PBS), Univa Grid Engine.

3 Background

3.1 Kubernetes

Kubernetes is a container and microservice platform that orchestrates computing, networking and storage infrastructure to support user workloads. It supports the automation of much of the work required to maintain and operate long-running services. Moreover, it enables portability across infrastructure providers. A k8s cluster is composed of one or more master nodes and a set of worker nodes (see Fig. 1). Multiple master nodes can be used to provide high availability and to scale to larger numbers of worker nodes. The Kubernetes master nodes run essential cluster services and form the cluster's *control plane.* On the other hand, worker nodes run the user-scheduled containerized workloads in units called *pods.* A pod encapsulates one or more tightly coupled containers that share resources, including a single IP address, and is the smallest deployable object in k8s. Kubernetes' main services communicate directly through the cluster network, while all pods are directly connected to a *virtual overlay network* which exists only within the cluster. This design allows all pods within the k8s cluster to directly address each other without NAT, even as the number of pods grows.

To implement the overlay network Kubernetes can use any of a number of plugins compatible with the Container Network Interface (CNI) [2]. For the purposes of this work, the authors are using Flannel [3]. Flannel allocates a subnet to each host participating in the overlay network from which pod IP addresses can be allocated [17]. Flannel agents run on each host in the Kubernetes cluster and provide a TUN virtual network device for each pod in the Kubernetes cluster. In typical Flannel-based configuration, IP traffic between the pods on the same node is routed directly through a bridge network device managed by the container engine (e.g., Docker). On the other hand, traffic between pods on different hosts is encapsulated by the flannel agent on the pod's host and transmitted to the destination host through a standard Linux VXLAN – which encapsulates traffic in UDP datagrams; at the destination the corresponding Flannel agent interprets the packet and delivers it to the addressed overlay network device connected to the pod through the container engine's bridge. Flannel can also

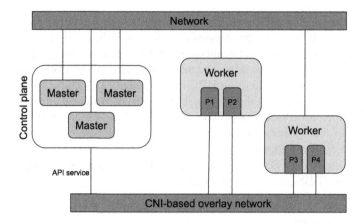

Fig. 1. High-level Kubernetes cluster architecture. Boxes denoted "Pn" are running on worker nodes.

be configured to use backend transmission mechanisms other than VXLAN – for instance, cloud-specific plugins provided by IaaS providers – but those are beyond the scope of this work.

3.2 Kubernetes Deployment

Kubernetes is a system composed of many parts, making its deployment is relatively complex. The complexity has motivated the development of a number of packages that automate the process. For the purposes of this work, only two are relevant: kubeadm and KubeSpray [13]. Kubeadm is a "k8s node management" tool, packaged with Kubernetes, that provides the basic functionality to configure and maintain the k8s machinery installed on a single node. It generally forms the basis for higher-level tools that implement cluster-wide deployment functionality, such as KubeSpray. KubeSpray is a tool that automates the deployment of Kubernetes on a set of pre-deployed nodes – or, optionally, it can also leverage Terraform [26] to automate the deployment of nodes on IaaS.

4 Implementation

4.1 General Approach

The level of integration between Kubernetes and Grid Engine that we seek to achieve is to be able to run k8s worker nodes as Grid Engine jobs. Worker node allocation is to be done by launching a GE job and deallocation by deleting the same job – while manual, this simple approach allows for future automation by implementing a custom Kubernetes controller. However, our k8s worker job imposes some particular requirements:

- k8s worker bootstrap and tear down needs to run with root privileges;
- reliable tear down procedure that always runs;
- gang scheduling required to support allocating blocks of nodes as a group.

Given these requirements, we opt to leverage the Grid Engine `Parallel Environment (PE)` [21] which helps fulfill all of them. Parallel Environments are a construct through which GE prepares the environment for a job to run. From a practical point of view, it allows cluster administrators to configure setup and a tear down scripts that are respectively run before and after the job – both executed with administrative privileges. Thus, we wrap the k8s worker setup and join into the PE setup, while the tear down and node clean-up is wrapped in the PE tear down script. With this strategy the actual job to be run becomes a trivial "`sleep infinity`" only intended to keep the job alive. Kubernetes workers can be allocated in groups by launching a job that requests multiple nodes (and the workers will only be launched when all the nodes are available). On the other hand, the k8s worker(s) is deallocated by deleting the job with the appropriate GE command (`qdel`) using the job id provided by the job allocation command.

In summary, n k8s workers can be launched with the following Bash shell command:

```
qsub -pe k8s $(( $n * $slots_per_node )) -b y sleep infinity
```

The `qsub` invocation returns a job id number that can then be used to delete the k8s workers with `qdel`. In this example, the user does not provide parameters identifying the k8s cluster to which to join the new nodes as we assume a single, always-on k8s deployment; however, a user could pass these parameters as variables to the `qsub` job submission.

4.2   Kubernetes Cluster Deployment

We deployed a Kubernetes cluster on a private OpenStack installation – control plane and a number of worker nodes – with our *manage-cluster* [23] tool. This tool is a front-end to Terraform and KubeSpray. After configuring the deployment parameters, (e.g., number and types of nodes, network configuration, etc.) the tool instantiate the computing resources and deploy Kubernetes.[1]

4.3   HPC Worker Node Software Prerequisites

The HPC nodes to be added to the running k8s cluster must run Linux. Further, the following software components need to be available on the HPC nodes:

1. kubeadm
2. kubelet
3. Docker container runtime

---

[1] **Workaround DNS bug**. In our tests fresh deployments created with the most recent version of KubeSpray were created with an erroneous cluster DNS setting. One must correct it by editing the config map `kubelet-config-X.Y` (where `X.Y` is the k8s version) in the `kube-system` namespace or new nodes will not work correctly.

Components 1 and 2 are core components of the k8s distribution and their version must exactly match the version of Kubernetes deployed on the control plane. The third requirement is the Docker runtime (k8s also supports other container runtimes such as containerd and cri-o, but Docker is still the most widely used). The container runtime must be configured as a system service (e.g., managed through `systemctl`). As a final recommendation, the following kernel modules must be available: `ip_vs`, `ip_vs_rr`, `ip_vs_sh`, `ip_vs_wrr`, `nf_conntrack_ipv4`, `overlay`,

4.4   Networking

Kubernetes nodes and masters all need to be reachable from each other via network. All the traffic specified in Table 1 must be allowed for basic k8s operation. Inter-cluster network communication is not an issue on typical installations of Kubernetes on top of OpenStack or other IaaS. In those cases, nodes typically communicate with each other over a virtual private cluster network, created and managed through the OpenStack networking subsystem Neutron, where traffic is not restricted. However, in this conventional deployment traffic from the outside the OpenStack cluster is only allowed through a few floating IPs mapped to a subset of k8s nodes (typically the master nodes). In our hybrid deployment the original nodes are deployed in OpenStack, while the transient nodes live on an HPC cluster and are on a different network. Therefore, to configure nodes so that they are all interconnected, our k8s deployment on OpenStack foregoes the virtual private network and connects all the k8s nodes to an OpenStack *external network* – i.e., reachable from outside OpenStack. To clarify, this external network merely needs to be accessible from the HPC cluster; it does not need to be accessible from other institutional subnets nor from outside the institutional network. This configuration of Kubernetes on OpenStack can be replicated with the Terraform templates available on our fork of the KubeSpray project [14] (and included in manage-cluster).

Table 1. Inbound Kubernetes traffic between master and worker nodes (including the Flannel overlay network).

Protocol	Port range	Node type	Purpose
TCP	6443	All	Kubernetes API server
TCP	2379–2380	Master Node	etcd server client API
TCP	10250	All	Kubelet API
TCP	10251–10252	Master Node	scheduler and controller manager
TCP	30000–32767	All	NodePort Services
UDP	8472	All	Flannel

4.5   GE Worker Setup and Tear down

The worker node setup is performed in the GE Parallel Environment's *start* phase, which runs on each new node being allocated. After initializing the environment (e.g., loading software modules and kernel modules) the procedure performs a `kubeadm join`, which implements the bootstrapping of the Kubernetes components and the connection to the control plane. This action requires two parameters:

- the endpoint of the k8s API server;
- a secret token to establish mutual trust between the master and a joining node.

The authentication token can be generated on any master node with

```
kubeadm token create --print-join-command
```

Every generated token can be used multiple times until it expires. Its duration can be set depending on the usage scenario: for instance, very brief for a cluster auto-scaler that generates a new token for each allocation, or longer in our manual allocation scenario.

Our implementation uses the default *Token-based discovery with CA pinning* worker-master authentication method. Thus, when the join process is started the worker downloads some initial information from the control plane, including the root certificate authority. The token is used to validate the CA and thus ensure the worker is connecting to the intended masters; likewise the token is used by the masters to authenticate the new worker, thus establishing mutual trust. Finally, the complete configuration is sent to the new worker, the `kubelet` agent is started and the overlay network is configured. Kubelet needs to be restarted until it is able to setup all its components and connect to the control plane. The startup process waits a configurable number of seconds for the correct state before killing `kubelet` and trying again.

Conversely, the worker node tear down is performed in the GE Parallel Environment's *stop* phase, the procedure must stop the k8s daemons and delete the local state with `kubeadm reset`. Further clean-up is performed removing any temporary data and cached container images – both to protect user data and to avoid gradually filling temporary space.

4.6   Kubernetes Cluster Configuration

While the overall configuration of a Kubernetes cluster is beyond the scope of this work, we offer some comments regarding configuration aspects that are specific to the type of deployment described here.

Node Selection. Not all applications would tolerate well having the node on which they are running suddenly terminated by the batch scheduler – for instance, because the batch job running kubelet reached its runtime limit. Thus, it seems reasonable for applications to "opt-in" to the usage of dynamic nodes. This scheduling behaviour can be achieved by *tainting* the transient nodes with effect `NoSchedule` and then having the applications mark their pods as *tolerant* to that tainting condition.

Storage. Kubernetes deployments backed by a cloud infrastructure normally have at their disposal cloud-provisioned storage that is well integrated with k8s, providing functionality such as auto-provisioning and mounting of volumes – features that are likely absent on HPC cluster nodes. As an alternative, users can access regular cluster-shared storage through the `hostPath` volume specification. In addition, if local storage is available the `local-static-provisioner` service (found in https://github.com/kubernetes-sigs) might also be of help.

5   Evaluation

We ran a series of experiments to measure the time required to complete a cluster expansion operation as a function of the number of nodes to be added. Therefore, for each run, a `qsub` job was launched requiring the set number of nodes. We tested adding 1, 5, 10, 15 and 20 nodes. The time between when the GE job entered the "running" state and the last node had successfully joined the k8s cluster (reached the "Ready" state) was measured. Each run was repeated 5 times. Figures 2 and 3 show the results.

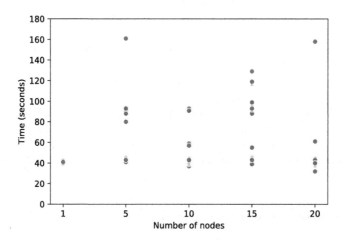

Fig. 2. Scatterplot of cluster expansion time as a function of the number of new nodes.

The measurements show that new nodes are generally ready to work about 40 s after being scheduled by GE. The size of the block of new nodes requested does not seem to impact join time – at least up to the tested size of 20 nodes. The fact that `kubelet` sometimes needs to be restarted more than once for it to

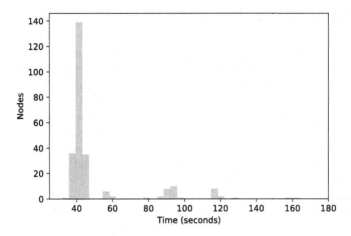

Fig. 3. Histogram of cluster join times for new nodes. The multi-modal distribution is due to the constant timeout before restarting `kubelet` while waiting for it to reach its "Ready" state.

reach its "ready" state raises the variance of the expansion completion time and creates some stragglers. Moreover, the constant wait timeout before the restart results in the multi-modal distribution seen in Fig. 3.

6   Discussion

This work can be the basis for the deployment of managed Kubernetes services at facilities with an infrastructure that is mainly HPC-oriented. The authors are using the functionality presented in this manuscript to run a mix of data-intensive service applications and bursty HPC-style workflows on an OpenStack-based Kubernetes deployment. The computing resources available on the Open-Stack cluster being used are insufficient to fulfill peak requirements. Expanding the Kubernetes cluster with transient nodes from the HPC cluster at the same institute provides sufficient resources to run a Weather Research and Forecasting (WRF) [25] workflow on hundreds of MPI-connected cores on top of Kubernetes, while keeping a homogeneous job management, logging, monitoring, and storage infrastructure. The gang-scheduling requirement imposed by MPI applications is handled by installing the kube-batch scheduler [10] alongside the default Kubernetes scheduler.

While the parallel environment construct is not available in all batch workload managers, our PE-based solution is relatively simple to convert to simpler job-based solution with a setuid-root launcher program. Measures specific to the workload manager would have to be taken to support gang scheduling and to ensure proper clean-up of the node when the k8s worker is deallocated.

7   Conclusion and Future Work

This manuscript presents a new method to expand Kubernetes clusters onto HPC resources managed through Grid Engine. The approach is being used to run services and WRF batch workflows on an always-on Kubernetes cluster deployed on OpenStack that is expanded on-demand onto HPC nodes. The recipe and code provided can be used to replicate this hybrid setup on different batch computing systems. Future work will extend this functionality with a custom Kubernetes controller to support auto-scaling the Kubernetes cluster based on workload. The open source code for this work is available in the following GitHub repository: https://github.com/crs4/ge-k8s.

Acknowledgements. This work was partially supported by the TDM project funded by Sardinian Regional Authorities under grant agreement POR FESR 2014-2020 Azione 1.2 (D. 66/14 13.12.2016 S3-ICT).

References

1. Clyburne-Sherin, A., Fei, X., Green, S.A.: Computational reproducibility via containers in social psychology, April 2019. http://osf.io/s8mz4
2. Container Network Interface - networking for Linux containers, April 2019. https://github.com/containernetworking/cni. Accessed 26 Apr 2019
3. Flannel is a simple and easy way to configure a layer 3 network fabric designed for Kubernetes, April 2019. https://github.com/coreos/flannel. Accessed 26 Apr 2019
4. Gentzsch, W.: Sun grid engine: towards creating a compute power grid. In: Proceedings of the 1st International Symposium on Cluster Computing and the Grid, CCGRID 2001, p. 35. IEEE Computer Society, Washington, DC, USA (2001)
5. Grüning, B., et al.: Practical computational reproducibility in the life sciences. Cell Syst. **6**(6), 631–635 (2018). https://doi.org/10.1016/j.cels.2018.03.014
6. Guerler, A., et al.: The Galaxy platform for accessible, reproducible and collaborative biomedical analyses: 2018 update. Nucleic Acids Res. **46**(W1), W537–W544 (2018). https://doi.org/10.1093/nar/gky379
7. Huang, X., Saha, A.K., Dutta, D., Gao, C.: Kubebench: a benchmarking platform for ML workloads. In: 2018 First International Conference on Artificial Intelligence for Industries (AI4I), pp. 73–76 (2018). https://doi.org/10.1109/AI4I.2018.8665688
8. Jacobsen, D.M., Canon, R.S.: Contain this, unleashing Docker for HPC. In: Proceedings of the Cray User Group (2015)
9. Khalid, A.: HPC-wire: Bridging HPC and Cloud Native development with Kubernetes, April 2019. https://www.hpcwire.com/solution_content/ibm/cross-industry/bridging-hpc-and-cloud-native-development-with-kubernetes/. Accessed 26 Apr 2019
10. kube-batch, April 2019. https://github.com/kubernetes-sigs/kube-batch. Accessed 26 Apr 2019
11. Kubeflow: The machine learning toolkit for kubernetes, April 2019. https://www.kubeflow.org. Accessed 26 Apr 2019
12. Kubernetes: production-grade container orchestration, April 2019. https://www.kubernetes.io. Accessed 26 Apr 2019

13. Deploy a production ready kubernetes cluster, April 2019. https://kubespray.io. Accessed 26 Apr 2019

14. Kubespray, April 2019. https://github.com/tdm-project/kubespray/. Accessed 26 Apr 2019

15. Kurtzer, G.M., Sochat, V., Bauer, M.W.: Singularity: scientific containers for mobility of compute. PLoS ONE **12**(5), e0177459 (2017)

16. Liu, F., Keahey, K., Riteau, P., Weissman, J.: Dynamically negotiating capacity between on-demand and batch clusters. In: SC18: International Conference for High Performance Computing, Networking, Storage and Analysis, pp. 493–503. IEEE, November 2018. https://doi.org/10.1109/SC.2018.00041

17. Marmol, V., Jnagal, R., Hockin, T.: Networking in containers and container clusters. In: Proceedings of NetDev 0.1 (2015)

18. Merkel, D.: Docker: lightweight Linux containers for consistent development and deployment. Linux J. **2014**(239) (2014)

19. Nagler, R., Bruhwiler, D.L., Moeller, P., Webb, S.: Sustainability and reproducibility via containerized computing. CoRR abs/1509.08789 (2015)

20. Nekrutenko, A., Team, G., Goecks, J., Taylor, J., Blankenberg, D.: Biology needs evolutionary software tools: let's build them right. Mol. Biol. Evol. **35**(6), 1372–1375 (2018). https://doi.org/10.1093/molbev/msy084

21. Oracle Inc.: Sun N1 Grid Engine 6.1 Administration Guide, April 2019. Accessed 26 Apr 2019

22. Peters, K., et al.: PhenoMeNal: processing and analysis of metabolomics data in the cloud. GigaScience, **8**(2), giy149 (2018)

23. Piras, M.E., del Rio, M., Pireddu, L., Gaggero, M., Zanetti, G.: Manage-cluster: simple utility to help deploy Kubernetes clusters with Terraform and Kube-Spray, April 2019. https://github.com/tdm-project/tdm-manage-cluster. Accessed 26 Apr 2019

24. Silver, A.: Software simplified. Nat. News **546**(7656), 173 (2017)

25. Skamarock, W.C., et al.: A description of the advanced research WRF model, version 4. Technical report, National Center for Atmospheric Research, Boulder, CO, USA (2008)

26. Terraform, April 2019. https://www.terraform.io. Accessed 26 Apr 2019

27. da Veiga Leprevost, F., et al.: BioContainers: an open-source and community-driven framework for software standardization. Bioinformatics **33**(16), 2580–2582 (2017). https://doi.org/10.1093/bioinformatics/btx192

28. Yoo, A.B., Jette, M.A., Grondona, M.: SLURM: simple linux utility for resource management. In: Feitelson, D., Rudolph, L., Schwiegelshohn, U. (eds.) JSSPP 2003. LNCS, vol. 2862, pp. 44–60. Springer, Heidelberg (2003). https://doi.org/10.1007/10968987_3

29. Zhang, J., Lu, X., Chakraborty, S., Panda, D.K.D.K.: Slurm-V: extending slurm for building efficient HPC cloud with SR-IOV and IVShmem. In: Dutot, P.-F., Trystram, D. (eds.) Euro-Par 2016. LNCS, vol. 9833, pp. 349–362. Springer, Cham (2016). https://doi.org/10.1007/978-3-319-43659-3_26

Data Pallets: Containerizing Storage for Reproducibility and Traceability

Jay Lofstead[1]([envelope]) [ORCID], Joshua Baker[1,2], and Andrew Younge[1]

[1] Sandia National Laboratories, Albuquerque, NM, USA
gflofst@sandia.gov
[2] Georgia Institute of Technology, Atlanta, GA, USA

Abstract. Trusting simulation output is crucial for Sandia's mission objectives. We rely on these simulations to perform our high-consequence mission tasks given national treaty obligations. Other science and modeling applications, while they may have high-consequence results, still require the strongest levels of trust to enable using the result as the foundation for both practical applications and future research. To this end, the computing community has developed workflow and provenance systems to aid in both automating simulation and modeling execution as well as determining exactly how was some output was created so that conclusions can be drawn from the data.

Current approaches for workflows and provenance systems are all at the user level and have little to no system level support making them fragile, difficult to use, and incomplete solutions. The introduction of container technology is a first step towards encapsulating and tracking artifacts used in creating data and resulting insights, but their current implementation is focused solely on making it easy to deploy an application in an isolated "sandbox" and maintaining a strictly read-only mode to avoid any potential changes to the application. All storage activities are still using the system-level shared storage.

This project explores extending the container concept to include storage as a new container type we call *data pallets*. Data Pallets are potentially writeable, auto generated by the system based on IO activities, and usable as a way to link the contained data back to the application and input deck used to create it.

1 Introduction

Making computational experiments capable of being considered a science requires that any data be traceable back to how it was produced. The best practice existing approach relies on external workflow management tools, such as the Sandia Analysis Workbench (SAW), to track artifacts. Unfortunately, these approaches have been problematic because the workflow engines do not manage the artifacts themselves as much as try to keep track of them. If a user or the system migrates data, then SAW has to figure out what happened. When running Modeling and Simulation (ModSim) workloads, "hope of correctness" is the wrong confidence level.

© Springer Nature Switzerland AG 2019
M. Weiland et al. (Eds.): ISC 2019 Workshops, LNCS 11887, pp. 36–45, 2019.
https://doi.org/10.1007/978-3-030-34356-9_4

Existing systems are not built to support provenance by default. Through hacking things like extended POSIX attributes in the file system, some information could be added, but it would have to be explicitly handled by every client and then it may not be portable to other systems that may or not properly support these extended attributes. File format approaches all require manual application changes to write the additional information. The hardest problem to address today is how to uniquely identify an object (e.g., application, input deck, or data set) in a portable way.

Container technology characteristically offers the following features:

1. portability including dependent library support with a web of dependent container instances
2. isolation from other applications
3. encapsulation of a set of files into a single object (most container systems)
4. a unique hash code

Of these attributes, the scale out community has focused on the first two. These features are ideal for offering an immutable application that can be deployed quickly without worrying about which machine it is deployed on and what the dependent libraries are. It also offers invisible scalability by trivializing adding replicas that can all offer the same service without any end-user knowledge or specific action. These features work well to address service-oriented and serverless computing. For ModSim workloads, these same characteristics are useful, but not sufficient. This aspect of using containers for ModSim is being explored in a commercial environment by companies like Rescale that offer SaaS ModSim.

Considering the generated data and the needed confidence of exactly how it was generated, the latter two attributes are the most interesting and must be explored. Encapsulating the application and input deck each into their own container is a necessary first step. By wrapping any generated data into a new container as well ensures that the data set is treated as a whole as well. With some container systems offering the ability to add annotations, it becomes possible to annotate the data, in a fully portable way, to guarantee precise knowledge of the context used to created the data. Using a system that offers these annotations enables this functionality with generally no application code changes.

This project is providing a low-level, first step for a viable fix for this problem. By encapsulating the data (and other generated artifacts) into their own system-generated container wrappers, what we call a *Data Pallet*, we can use the unique ID for each container mounted (e.g., the application and input deck) as annotations directly linking the generated data to what created it. Key to this working is that it is not a dependency that would require the dependent containers be loaded in order to use this container. Then, by inspecting the Data Pallet, it is simple to find the matching container for the application and input deck using the annotation stored container IDs. There is no question of whether or not these are the matching components or not. Further, since the annotations and unique container ID are in the wrapper (i.e., not in the data itself), it is not possible to move the application, input deck, or Data Pallet without moving the IDs and annotations without explicit, difficult work. This makes identifying both the ancestry and dependency webs straightforward.

The potential impact of this work is enormous. For high consequence workloads, having an established provenance record of what source and configuration created a data set offers a guarantee we cannot ensure today. The problematic approaches being pursued both historically and today to address this issue are divorced from the underlying system that users and system processes will manipulate outside the management system causing links to get stale and broken. Only with an approach like this can we have full confidence that our ModSim analysis can be trusted and be traceable back to the original source code and people that created it. For the broader science community, reproducibility is important. To demonstrate reproducibility, a couple metrics must be met. First, data must be sufficiently traceable back to where they came from and how they were created. Second, the higher standard of replicable requires that everything is sufficiently documented to enable someone else to recreate the experiments and generate comparable result. This is what is required for something to be a science. This system enables automatic tracking and use of support information without requiring a separate tool–the information is all inherent in the artifacts themselves–making it science by default.

There are a tremendous number of aspects of this idea to explore before it can be fully exploited in systems. This first step proves the idea is worthwhile and that further exploration is warranted.

The rest of this document is divided into the following sections. First is a short look at related work in Sect. 2. Next, is a description of the design in Sect. 3. Some information about the measured overheads in this approach are included in Sect. 4. Finally, Conclusions and Future Work are described in Sect. 6

2   Related Work

Existing work that attempts to do similar things does not exist. This idea and approach are wholly new. However, there are some systems and work that are doing some more distantly related things that appear similar at first glance.

Workflow systems, such as the Sandia Analysis Workbench (SAW) [7], Pegasus [3]/DAGMan [11], Kepler [10], Swift [14], and many others all focus on providing a way to orchestrate a series of tasks to accomplish a goal. However, they offer little to no support for managing the artifacts, configurations for each component, and component versioning. The lack of system level support for these kinds of activities makes offering tools that provide them difficult to impossible. At best, these tools offer suggestions and hope rather than iron-clad guarantees about provenance. Existing provenance systems such as those in Kepler [1] try to track artifacts, but have no ability to fully associate these relationships with the data such that data manipulations, such as moving a file or renaming, are not broken by these activities.

The Data Pallets idea, at a surface level, is similar to various storage containers ideas. However, these approaches all focus on exposing a shared storage layer into the container context. None of them offer any sort of wrapper approach that could hold attributes linking data back to the antecedents no matter how the data is moved or renamed.

Other approaches, if used correctly, have a potential to achieve similar goals, but with application modification and intrusive data modification. For example, ADIOS [9], NetCDF [12], and HDF5 [4] all offer arbitrary attributes inside the file. If a user were to explicitly add the container IDs, they could achieve a similar goal. However, that would require that the container IDs be apparent in the application's running context and that the application code be modified to include writing such annotations into the file. The Data Pallets approach eliminates all of those requirements by adding the wrapper automatically just by virtue of running the application in a container and the annotations are generated the same way. No changes to the application or how it runs will be required.

Singularity [6] offers a writeable container, but it has some strict limitations. First, the container has to be created prior to running Singularity and mounted as part of the startup process with an option to indicate that it should be writeable. Rather than limit to a single container, manually created by the user prior to starting the application, we are proposing to auto-generate and mount new writeable containers at runtime. Further, we will annotate these generated containers with the IDs from the context in which it was created. This is the key traceability component.

Kubernetes Persistent Volumes [5], like other storage container ideas, allocate storage to persist state. What this and all similar ideas fail to do is to address the need for long-term data archiving and the ability to move these states not just to tape, but to wholly new clusters or desktop machines while maintaining the connection to the generators and environmental information.

A preprint of this work was submitted to arXiv [8].

3 Design

The design for this idea is very simple. Intercept any attempt to create a file on storage and create and mount a new container, with the appropriate annotations applied, to capture that output. While this simple idea is currently not fully attainable for a variety of reasons, there are ways to work around these limitations to demonstrate the idea potential. Further, for this to be a workable approach, it needs to work within a production workflow system, such as the Sandia Analysis Workbench.

To visualize how the Data Pallets work, consider the progression of these figures. Figure 1a is an illustration of what a typical workflow component looks like. It is a node in a graph with an application using input data from somewhere, typically storage, and an input deck that describes how to operate.

Figure 1b shows how this evolves if containers are introduced. Note that the application is wrapped in a container and the input deck is somehow mounted into that container. It may be via mounting a host directory into the container, or as illustrated, as a separate container that is mounted into the same namespace. Most importantly, the input data comes from storage, or other sources, still.

The final version shown in Fig. 1c expands the containerized version to shift input data from being read from some external source to being brought in via either a container or a native mount. We also illustrate the dynamically created Data Pallet containers that are also mounted into the namespace. However, note that the first Data Pallet is potentially a Data Pallet created by a previous component. In this case, the Pallet would likely be read only. Making it writeable may lead to confusion about the data provenance. At a minimum, the annotations would need to be expanded to include the new container context.

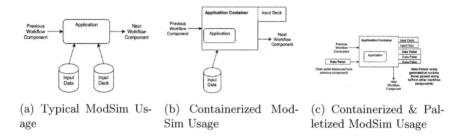

(a) Typical ModSim Usage   (b) Containerized ModSim Usage   (c) Containerized & Palletized ModSim Usage

Fig. 1. Different data organizations

With this new architecture, containers proliferate along with the provenance annotations. This is not a problem-free approach, but it solves the data provenance issue. The implications of this approach are many. Some of them are explored in this paper while others are being better formulated and explored still before being shared.

3.1   Design and Implementation Challenges

The way that containers work makes enabling this approach more difficult than it may appear. Containers are a way to work with the Linux Namespaces [2] easing setup and use. In particular, what happens is that the container system creates a namespace and maps in a series of resources. All other resources on the machine are not accessible. This enables having multiple instances running in isolation from each other with no changes necessary in the application.

The implication of this namespace implementation is that there are no intermediaries between a containerized application and the resources, such as a translation layer. This enables essentially native performance. The difficulty is that it does not enable experimenting with new system-level functionality, such as that proposed with Data Pallets. Instead, it is still necessary to use standard OS implementation techniques to introduce new features. To achieve the Data Pallets idea, a classic file systems research approach was employed.

The initial implementation idea was to intercept a call to the system command `mkdir`, the command to create a directory in storage, and use that as the entry point for creating a new container on the fly and mounting it. Since the container system did not offer an intercept point and instead exposed the kernel directly, FUSE [13] was a natural way to intercept the system call invoking the functionality.

Long term, a system level approach for intercepting POSIX **open** and other file or storage object creation calls would offer a truly native way to accomplish the same goal.

3.2   Design and Implementation Details

To accelerate the idea exploration, we chose to leverage the Singularity system. It already offered a way to mount an existing container as "writeable", but did not offer a way to generate that on-demand nor to annotate it with any sort of context information.

To make this work, we used Singularity 3.0 for two main reasons. First, Singularity's security model offers the best solution for working in the sensitive DOE environment. Docker's passing root access from inside a container to the underlying system is not viable for highly secured systems. Singularity's approach isolates root access in a container to just the container, preserving the security envelope. Second, Singularity introduced enhanced a new container image format that supports multiple streams (partitions) making adding annotations easier. In our case, we add a JSON file with the annotations.

3.3   Integration with Sandia Analysis Workbench (SAW)

Integrating with SAW demonstrates that the Data Pallets idea is compatible with production workflow systems typically used to run ModSim workloads. Making Data Pallets work within SAW required no special changes for the most basic level. Instead, a new object type to handle a container was the only requirement. This capability is a standard end-user enabled feature part of SAW. A richer integration, such as offering an interface to the container hub making selecting an application or inspecting annotations easier, are beyond the scope of this work.

4   Measurements

To evaluate the implementation, tests are performed on a single desktop workstation. While this is not an "at scale" implementation, it is sufficient to show how this can work for file per process workloads. Alternative workloads that use an N-1 pattern will require further exploration.

The testing environment is a Dell Precision 3420 SFF tower. It has an Intel Core i7-6700 CPU @ 3.40 GHz, 32 GB RAM, and a 256 GB ATA SAMSUNG SSD SM87 for storage. It is running Ubuntu 16.04 LTS - 64-bit. The Singularity version is the initial release of 3.0. FUSE 3.3.0 is used.

4.1 Time Overheads

The time overheads for this approach are small, particularly in the context of the application runtimes. To evaluate the time, we use a simple application, gnuplot, and make 1000 tests using the mean of the results for each test.

To determine the overheads, we evaluate the following characteristics. First, we measure the time it takes for the application to run generating output completely outside of the container environment. Second, we measure the time it takes to run the application from within a container, but writing directly to storage. Third, we measure the time with the application in a container writing into a dynamically created container. Using these three metrics, we are able to extract these detailed overheads.

In Table 1, we show the metrics related to running an application, gnuplot, using the structure described in Fig. 1c. By far, the time is spent in the container load overhead. Considering the time to deploy applications in a cluster, around 0.5 s is negligible. For cloud application deployments, this overhead is typical and considered sufficiently fast to be useful for a production environment.

Table 2 shows the time to create the various components. As is shown, the overheads are tiny and acceptably small considering the variability in any parallel storage system. This would be completely lost in the noise.

Table 1. Workflow node overheads

Average time to mount the custom FUSE filesystem	0.037 s
Average time to spin up/tear down Application Container	0.498 s
Average time to run application and create Data Pallets	0.037 s
Average total time to run the Application Container	0.535 s
Average time to unmount the custom FUSE filesystem	0.029 s
Total time taken by the Gnuplot Workflow Node	0.601 s

Table 2. Application containers overheads

Average time to run Gnuplot on input data	0.0284 s
Average time for total Data Pallet creation/storage	0.00133 s
Average time to pull PNG output file from Data Pallet	0.00725 s

4.2 Space Overheads

Since we are incorporating additional data into each output and requiring similar overheads on applications and input decks, it is important to understand the space overheads imposed by this approach. To determine these overheads, we test the following configurations:

- Empty Container - This is the baseline overhead for all applications and input decks. Since we will store all of these artifacts long term, understanding this base overhead will reveal how much additional storage will be required for archiving.
- Basic Writeable Container - This is the size overhead for the generated data sets.
- Attributes Stream - Since each container image can contain multiple data streams, one will be the normal data contents and a second will be the JSON file containing the list of associated container IDs.

The space overheads are shown in Table 3.

Table 3. Space overheads

Empty container	32.2 KB
Writeable container	704.5 KB
Attributes stream	1.1 MB

4.3   Discussion

From this data, it is apparent that the primary source of overhead in running the workflow node is the application container, itself. The time by the Data Pallets creation and management is minimal as compared to the application runtime. The total time taken by the internals of the container are also minimal as compared to the spin up and tear down time of the container itself. Fortunately, the overhead involved in container creation is a prevalent issue in current research, and strides are being made to minimize it. Out of the overhead introduced by the new approach, the majority of increase comes from the mounting of the FUSE filesystem. Actual use of it to create the SIF images is negligible.

The empty container size is small enough to be used as a wrapper around any application. For an input deck, this size is likely larger than the input deck itself (excepting a mesh description), but still small enough to justify using it to wrap around the input deck.

The writeable container size is much larger because the only writeable format is ext3 rather than the more compact squashfs, what is used for read-only containers. The reason ext3 is required is that the container system requires the underlying operating system to handle the writing operations into storage backed container file. The squashfs file system format inherently does not support writing into it except at creation.

The attributes stream overhead is surprisingly large. This would be the minimum size for each additional attribute stream added to a container image. For output data sets on the order of 10% of node memory, this is still a small enough overhead to be acceptable. Our nodes are moving to 128 GB as the base memory making this less than 1% of the total volume written during the output.

5   Integration with Sandia Analysis Workbench

The long-term goal for this work is to be able to deploy fully container wrapped applications and input decks into the SAW system and eliminate the need for SAW to attempt to track generated artifacts and instead rely on the inherent annotations as the source of truth. The previously mentioned limitations with the current system that attempts to track artifacts without owning them is fragile with many exposed areas where the system can be broken either accidentally, on purpose, or by automated system processes.

To test this integration, a simple input deck was wrapped in a container, another container contained an application, and it generated a separate output. We chose to use the gnuplot application as there is a simple example using this provided as part of SAW.

By wrapping everything in a container, we changed the workflow to run the component by using the container runtime command rather than directly running the application. This simple change revealed the simplicity with which this change could be deployed with minimal to no impact on existing users. Further integration is left to future work.

6   Conclusions and Future Work

This work demonstrates that it is possible to shift downward the provenance information necessary to trace from a given data set back to the application and input deck that created it. Unlike other approaches, Data Pallets offers a guarantee of this traceability without having to use a special tool for all data access. Instead, by incorporating the data annotations linking the data back to the application and input deck, the provenance is manifest rather than linked. The potential benefit for both reproducibility and confidence in ModSim results is enormous.

For the future work, many steps will be investigated.

First, considering current limitations in how Singularity mounts containers, we can create a container at runtime, but it only works properly when we add the files to the newly created container after the files are created. Sylabs and Sandia are currently working together to change how things work to allow files to be written to the dynamically created container.

Second, issues surrounding when and how to unmount a writeable container need to be investigated. Currently, we are assuming that the system can flush cold data to storage without having to rely on the container context exiting. If this is not the case, then memory pressures are going to force changes such that we can discover how to unmount the created container to free needed memory.

Third, the SAW integration demonstrated the possibility of running containers. The next step for this to be usable and viable is to offer introspection into things like the JSON attributes stream, seeing a list of dependent containers, and getting a list of available containers to run from a local container "hub". These hubs offer a way to dynamically load a container as needed based on the container ID rather than having to manually pre-deploy all needed containers when running the application. Scalability issues with this are likely at the high end, but well understood and demonstrated techniques to manage this, such as distribution trees, can address the performance issues. Further, the current Singularity container hub uses Docker's system, something not viable within our environment.

Acknowledgements. Sandia National Laboratories is a multimission laboratory managed and operated by National Technology and Engineering Solutions of Sandia, LLC, a wholly owned subsidiary of Honeywell International, Inc., for the U.S. Department of Energy's National Nuclear Security Administration under contract DE-NA0003525. This work is funded through the LDRD program and ASC CSSE.

References

1. Altintas, I., Barney, O., Jaeger-Frank, E.: Provenance collection support in the kepler scientific workflow system. In: Moreau, L., Foster, I. (eds.) IPAW 2006. LNCS, vol. 4145, pp. 118–132. Springer, Heidelberg (2006). https://doi.org/10.1007/11890850_14
2. Biederman, E.W., Networx, L.: Multiple instances of the global linux namespaces. In: Proceedings of the Linux Symposium, vol. 1, pp. 101–112. Citeseer (2006)
3. Deelman, E., et al.: Pegasus: a workflow management system for science automation. Future Gener. Comput. Syst. **46**, 17–35 (2015). Funding Acknowledgements: NSF ACI SDCI 0722019, NSF ACI SI2-SSI 1148515 and NSF OCI-1053575
4. Koziol, Q., Matzke, R.: HDF5-a new generation of HDF: reference manual and user guide. National Center for Supercomputing Applications, Champaign, Illinois, USA 1998. http://hdf.ncsa.uiuc.edu/nra/HDF5
5. Kubernetes. Persistent Volumes (2019). https://kubernetes.io/docs/concepts/storage/persistent-volumes/
6. Kurtzer, G.M., Sochat, V., Bauer, M.W.: Singularity: scientific containers for mobility of compute. PLoS ONE **12**(5), e0177459 (2017)
7. Sandia National Labs: Sandia Analysis Workbench Next Generation Workflows (2018). https://gitlab.com/iwf/ngw
8. Lofstead, J.F., Baker, J., Younge, A.: Data pallets: containerizing storage for reproducibility and traceability. CoRR, abs/1811.04740 (2018)
9. Lofstead, J.F., Klasky, S., Schwan, K., Podhorszki, N., Jin, C.: Flexible IO and integration for scientific codes through the adaptable IO system (ADIOS), In: Proceedings of the 6th International Workshop on Challenges of Large Applications in Distributed Environments CLADE 2008, pp. 15–24. ACM, New York (2008)
10. Ludäscher, B., et al.: Scientific workflow management and the Kepler system: research articles. Concurr. Comput.: Pract. Exper. **18**(10), 1039–1065 (2006)
11. Malewicz, G., Foster, I., Rosenberg, A.L., Wilde, M.: A tool for prioritizing DAG-Man jobs and its evaluation. In: 2006 15th IEEE International Symposium on High Performance Distributed Computing, pp. 156–168 (2006)
12. Rew, R., Davis, G.: NetCDF: an interface for scientific data access. IEEE Comput. Graph. Appl. **10**(4), 76–82 (1990)
13. Szeredi, M.: Fuse: filesystem in userspace 2005 (2005). http://fuse.sourceforge.net
14. Wilde, M., Hategan, M., Wozniak, J.M., Clifford, B., Katz, D.S., Foster, I.: Swift: a language for distributed parallel scripting. Parallel Comput. **37**(9), 633–652 (2011)

Sarus: Highly Scalable Docker Containers for HPC Systems

Lucas Benedicic$^{(\boxtimes)}$, Felipe A. Cruz, Alberto Madonna, and Kean Mariotti

Swiss National Supercomputing Centre, Lugano, Switzerland
`benedicic@cscs.ch`

Abstract. The convergence of HPC and cloud computing is pushing HPC service providers to enrich their service portfolio with workflows based on complex software stacks. Such transformation presents an opportunity for the science community to improve its computing practices with solutions developed in enterprise environments. Software containers increase productivity by packaging applications into portable units that are easy to deploy, but generally come at the expense of performance and scalability. This work presents Sarus, a container engine for HPC environments that offers security oriented to multi-tenant systems, container filesystems tailored for parallel storage, compatibility with Docker images, user-scoped image management, and integration with workload managers. Docker containers of HPC applications deployed with Sarus on up to 2888 GPU nodes show two significant results: OCI hooks allow users and system administrators to transparently benefit from plugins that enable system-specific hardware; and the same level of performance and scalability than native execution is achieved.

1 Introduction

Building and deploying software on high-end computing systems is a challenging task. Recent service models developed for cloud environments are putting additional pressure on the traditional support and maintenance methods of HPC centers. Even regular upgrades of HPC software environments have become more demanding in the presence of applications with shorter release cycles (e.g. TensorFlow [1], Spark [42]). Increasingly complex software stacks are required by certain workflows like Jupyter notebooks, visualization and data analysis. Consequently, finding a mechanism that helps lowering the support burden coming from end users as well as from regular maintenance tasks, while still delivering a rich palette of applications and services running at high performance, is becoming a matter of greater importance for HPC service providers. The progressive integration of cloud computing usage models into HPC should not be viewed as a challenge, but rather as an opportunity to improve existing and future HPC capabilities.

The original version of this chapter was revised: It has been changed to open access under a CC BY 4.0 license and the copyright holder is now "The Author(s)". The correction to this chapter is available at https://doi.org/10.1007/978-3-030-34356-9_50

© The Author(s) 2019, corrected publication 2020
M. Weiland et al. (Eds.): ISC 2019 Workshops, LNCS 11887, pp. 46–60, 2019.
https://doi.org/10.1007/978-3-030-34356-9_5

One such example, which received significant development momentum from cloud services, is represented by software containers, a virtualization technology that can be employed to cope with the requirements of flexible yet increasingly sophisticated application deployments. By packaging applications and their environments into standard units of software, containers feature several benefits: they are portable, easy to build and deploy, they have a small footprint, and also show a low runtime overhead. The portability of containers is achieved through a runtime program that performs the instantiation of images which are agnostic of the host infrastructure [29].

Ensuring their performance and scalability matches native deployments as close as possible is critical to the success of containers in an HPC context. This has a direct impact on particular elements of a container image, such as support for dedicated hardware, drivers and vendor-specific libraries which are usually not part of the image itself due to their emphasis on portability.

Another key aspect to take into consideration is to leverage on existing developments. The technology provided by Docker established itself as the most popular container implementation. For this reason, a container software for HPC providing the capability to deploy Docker-compatible containers at scale will greatly benefit from a rich set of mature tools and practices.

Based on our experience operating containers in an HPC production environment, we identify the following key features for the effective use of containers in HPC:

(F1) Transparently achieve native performance and scalability from specialized hardware at runtime.
(F2) Suitability for parallel filesystems.
(F3) Security measures fitting multi-tenant systems.
(F4) Compatibility with workload managers.
(F5) Easy integration of vendor support.
(F6) Compatibility with Docker's image format and workflow.

The rest of this paper is organized as follows: in Sect. 2 we introduce related work of container runtimes targeted at HPC environments. Section 3 introduces Sarus, describing design and implementation details. In Sect. 4 we illustrate five OCI hooks to satisfy multiple HPC use cases and show how Sarus supports them. In Sect. 5 we proceed to test the capabilities of Sarus by comparing the performance of containerized and native versions from a selection of real-world HPC applications. These tests also demonstrate the use of OCI hooks to provide access to high-performance MPI and GPU acceleration, making full use of the hardware available on a supercomputing system.

2   Related Work

In the scientific computing community there has been a growing interest in running Docker containers on HPC infrastructure [8]. However, Docker was developed to answer the particular needs of web service applications, which feature substantially different workloads from the ones typically found in HPC. For this reason, deploying Docker in a production HPC environment encounters significant technical challenges, like missing integration with workload managers, missing support for diskless nodes, no support for kernel-bypassing devices (e.g. accelerators and NICs), no adequate parallel storage driver, and a security model unfit for multi-tenant systems.

A number of container platforms have thus been created to fill this gap and provide Linux containers according to the demands of HPC practitioners, retaining a varying degree of compatibility with Docker.

Singularity [19] is a container platform designed around an image format consisting of a single file. While it is able to convert Docker images through an import mechanism, it is centered on its own non-standard format and can also build its own images starting from a custom language. Support for specific features, e.g. OpenMPI and NVIDIA GPUs, is integrated into the Singularity codebase.

Charliecloud [33] is an extremely lightweight container solution focusing on unprivileged containers. It is able to import Docker images, requires no configuration effort from system administrator, and it is a user-space application, achieving high levels of security. Charliecloud's minimal feature set allows fine-grained control over the customization of the container. On the other hand, it requires a substantial level of proficiency from the user to set up containers for non-trivial use cases.

Shifter [16] is a software developed to run containers based on Docker images on HPC infrastructures. It is designed to integrate with the Docker workflow and features an image gateway service to pull images from Docker registries. Shifter has recently introduced the use of configurable software modules for improved flexibility. However, the modules and the executables have to be developed and configured specifically for Shifter.

3   Sarus

Sarus is a tool for HPC systems that instantiates feature-rich containers from Docker images. It fully manages the container life-cycle by: pulling images from registries, managing image storage, creating the container root filesystem, and configuring hooks and namespaces. For instantiating the containers, Sarus leverages on `runc` [30]: an OCI-compliant kernel-level tool that was originally developed by Docker [22].

In order to address the unique requirements of HPC installations, Sarus extends the capabilities of `runc` to enable features such as native performance from dedicated hardware, improved security on multi-tenant systems, support for network parallel filesystems, diskless computing nodes, and compatibility with workload managers. Keeping flexibility, extensibility, and community efforts in high regard, Sarus relies on industry standards and open source software.

Similarly, Sarus depends on a widely-used set of libraries, tools, and technologies to reap several benefits: reduce maintenance effort and lower the entry barrier for service providers wishing to install the software, and for developers

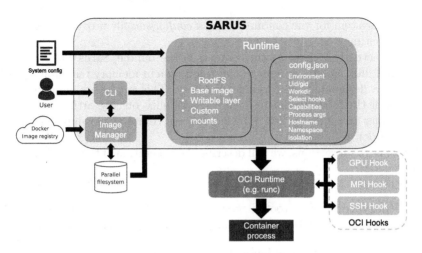

Fig. 1. Sarus architecture diagram.

seeking to contribute code. Sarus builds upon the popularity of Docker, providing the capability of deploying Docker images, the internal structure of which is based on OCI standards.

3.1   Sarus Architecture

The workflows supported by Sarus are implemented through the interaction of several software components (Fig. 1). The **CLI** component processes the command line arguments and calls other components to perform the actions requested by the user. The **Image Manager** component is responsible for importing container images onto the system, converting the images to Sarus' own format, storing them on local system repositories, and querying the contents of such repositories. The **Runtime** component instantiates and executes containers by setting up a bundle according to the OCI Runtime Specification: such bundle is made of a root filesystem directory for the container and a JSON configuration file. After preparing the bundle, the **Runtime** component will call an external **OCI runtime** (runc in this case), which will effectively spawn the container process. Sarus can instruct the **OCI runtime** to use one or more **OCI hooks**. These hooks are often used to customize the container by performing actions at selected points during the container lifetime.

3.2   Container Creation

The Runtime component of Sarus is responsible for setting up and coordinating the launch of container instances. When the user requests the execution of a container process through the **sarus run** command, an OCI bundle is first created in a dedicated directory. The bundle is formed by a *rootfs* directory, containing the root filesystem for the container, and a *config.json* file providing settings to the OCI runtime.

Before actually generating the contents of the bundle, Sarus will create and join a new Linux mount namespace, then mount an in-memory temporary filesystem on the designated OCI bundle directory. This procedure prevents other processes of the host system from having visibility on any artifact related to the container instance [25,26] (F3) and ensures complete cleanup of container resources upon termination.

In the next subsections, we will describe the generation of the bundle contents in more detail.

Root Filesystem. The root filesystem for the container is assembled in a dedicated directory inside the OCI bundle location through several steps:

a. The squashfs file corresponding to the image requested by the user is mounted as a *loop device* on the configured rootfs mount point. The loop mount allows access to the image filesystem as if it resided on a real block device (i.e. a storage drive). This strategy prevents metadata thrashing and improves caching behavior (F2), as all container instances access a single squashfs file on the parallel filesystem. The effectiveness of this approach has already been demonstrated by Shifter [16].

b. Sarus proceeds to create an overlay filesystem [5], using the loop-mounted image as the *read-only* lower layer, while part of the OCI bundle in-memory filesystem forms the *writable* upper layer. An overlay filesystem allows the contents of containers to be transparently modifiable by the users, while preserving the integrity of container images (F6). Additionally, the in-memory filesystem improves the performance of the container writable layer and suits diskless computing nodes (e.g. as those found in Cray XC systems), where the host filesystem also resides in RAM.

c. Selected system configuration files (e.g. `/etc/hosts`, `/etc/passwd`, `/etc/group`) required to setup file permissions in shared directories, or networking with other computing nodes, are copied from the host into the rootfs of the container (F3).

d. *Custom mounts* are performed. These are bind mounts requested by the system administrator or by the user to customize the container according to the needs and resources of an HPC system site or a specific use case, such as providing access to parallel filesystems.

e. The container's rootfs is remounted [43] to remove potential suid bits from all its files and directories (F3).

config.json. The JSON configuration file of the OCI bundle is generated by combining data from the runtime execution context, command-line parameters, and properties coming from the image. We hereby highlight the most important details:

- The uid/gid of the user from the host system are assigned to the container process, regardless of the user settings in the original image. This is done to keep a consistent experience with the host system, especially regarding file ownership and access permissions (F3).
- The container environment variables are created by uniting the variables from the host environment and the variables from the image. If a variable exists in both the host and the image, the value from the image is taken. This ensures a consistent behaviour as expected by image creators (e.g. in the case of PATH). Selected variables are also adapted by Sarus to suit system-specific extensions, like NVIDIA GPU support, native MPI support or container SSH connections (F1, F4, F5, F6).
- Support for image-defined properties like default arguments, entrypoint, and working directory is configured to show consistent behavior with a Docker container (F6).
- The container process is configured to run with all Linux capabilities disabled[1] and it is prevented from acquiring new privileges by any means[2] (F3).
- Settings for OCI hooks are copied from the Sarus configuration file.

4   Extending Sarus with OCI Hooks

OCI hooks are an effective way of extending the functionality provided by a container runtime. The standard interface defined by the OCI Runtime Specification allows the extensions to be developed without understanding the details about how the runtime instantiates a container. This way, vendors can independently develop dedicated hooks to provide support for their products (F5). Likewise, researchers and engineers at computing sites can create additional hooks for enabling innovative capabilities or further integrate containers with their HPC infrastructure. Even hooks developed by the open source community or meant for other areas of IT can be seamlessly and readily adopted by an OCI-compliant runtime.

The nature of hooks as autonomous extensions implies that each one of them can be activated independently from each other. Sarus gives system administrators full flexibility to configure hooks, so installations can be tailored to the characteristic of each individual system.

In the context of HPC, hooks have shown the potential to augment containers based on open standards, including native support for dedicated hardware like accelerators and interconnect technologies (see Sect. 5) (F1).

In the next subsections we highlight several OCI hooks use cases of particular interest for HPC.

---

[1] Linux divides the privileges traditionally associated with superuser into distinct units, known as capabilities [24].

[2] This is achieved by setting the *no_new_privs* process attribute to 1 [22].

4.1 Native MPICH-Based MPI Support (H1)

The MPI [11] is a portable standard for developing distributed memory applications. HPC centers around the globe extensively deploy MPI implementations that can take advantage of the fast network infrastructure while providing message-passing communications that are efficient and scalable.

In 2013 multiple vendors of MPI implementations based on the MPICH library announced an effort to achieve ABI compatibility between their implementations [27]. In practice, applications that have been built with any library complying with the MPICH ABI Compatibility Initiative can later run correctly using other ABI initiative libraries without needing recompilation.

Sarus features a hook able to swap MPICH-based MPI implementations inside a container with an ABI-compatible native implementation from the host. The detection of host MPI libraries is performed through the `ldconfig` system tool [23]. The advantage is that the native library has been optimized for the infrastructure of the HPC system, which is able to leverage hardware acceleration, therefore allowing the container to achieve native performance (F1). ABI compatibility between host and container MPI libraries is fundamental to ensure the replacement works seamlessly at runtime without requiring a recompilation of the application.

4.2 NVIDIA GPU Support (H2)

The use of NVIDIA GPUs as computational accelerators for HPC has become increasingly relevant in recent times. The November 2018 edition of the TOP500 list of supercomputer sites features 123 systems equipped with NVIDIA GPUs, including the top 2 systems [39]. Additionally, several GPU-accelerated codes were recognized as finalists or winners of the ACM Gordon Bell Prize over the years [17,18,37,40].

NVIDIA provides access to GPU devices and their drivers inside OCI containers through the hook component of the NVIDIA Container Runtime [28]. The hook imports the native device files and driver stack into the container, using `ldconfig` to find host shared libraries.

Sarus is able to integrate the use of the NVIDIA Container Runtime hook by modifying the container environment in a way that is completely transparent to both users and system administrators (F1, F5). These modifications ensure that device allocations performed by the workload manager are respected, while guaranteeing the correct operation of CUDA applications inside the container, even in the case of partial or shuffled devices selection on multi-GPU systems (F4). For example, when operating under a workload manager which sets the `CUDA_VISIBLE_DEVICES` environment variable, no user action is required to correctly enable access to GPUs from inside the container.

This is also the first example of a vendor-supplied OCI hook that Sarus is able to seamlessly integrate and apply to high-performance containers.

4.3 SSH Connection Within Containers (H3)

The SSH protocol [41] is used to securely connect machines and services over a network. Such capability is required by distributed applications like Apache Spark [42].

Sarus provides a hook that gives containers the ability to establish SSH connections between them, using a customized OpenSSH software [12], a set of dedicated keys (avoiding reuse of the user's native keys for security reasons), and a non-standard port.

4.4 Slurm Scheduler Synchronization (H4)

The Slurm Workload Manager [35] is an open-source job scheduler adopted by many high performance systems worldwide to allocate system resources in order to carry out different computing jobs. In some cases, the allocated resources are not all made available at the exact same time.

Sarus comes with a hook that implements a synchronization barrier before the user application is started inside the container. This prevents actions (such as attempting SSH connections) towards containers which are not yet available from causing the whole Slurm job step to fail. The synchronization mechanism is based on the environment set up by Slurm with regards to total number of tasks and process identifiers.

5 Performance Evaluation

In this section we discuss the performance aspects of Sarus by comparing data for a variety of workloads, executed by corresponding native and containerized applications. It should be noted that the creation of the container images represents a best reproducibility effort in terms of software releases, compiler versions, compilation tool chains, compilation options and libraries, between native and containerized versions of the applications. Despite this effort, the exact reproducibility of the application binaries cannot be guaranteed. However, this highlights how the Docker workflow of packaging applications using mainstream Linux distributions (e.g. Ubuntu) and basic system tools (e.g. package managers) can seamlessly integrate with HPC environments, since container images targeted at personal workstations can still be used to achieve consistently comparable performance with native installations.

For each data point, we present the average and standard deviation of 50 runs, to produce statistically relevant results, unless otherwise noted. For a given application, all repetitions at each node count for both native and container execution were performed on the same allocated set of nodes.

We conduct our tests on Piz Daint, a hybrid Cray XC50/XC40 system in production at the Swiss National Supercomputing Centre (CSCS) in Lugano, Switzerland. The compute nodes are connected by the Cray Aries interconnect under a Dragonfly topology, providing users access to hybrid CPU-GPU nodes.

Hybrid nodes are equipped with an Intel® Xeon® E5-2690v3 processor, 64 GB of RAM, and a single NVIDIA® Tesla® P100 with 16 GB of memory. The software environment on Piz Daint is the Cray Linux Environment 6.0.UP07 (CLE 6.0) [7] using *Environment Modules* [9] to provide access to compilers, tools, and applications. The default versions for the NVIDIA CUDA and MPI software stacks are, respectively, CUDA version 9.1, and Cray MPT version 7.7.2.

We install and configure Sarus on Piz Daint to use `runc`, the native MPI (H1) and NVIDIA Container Runtime (H2) hooks introduced in Sect. 4, and to mount container images from a Lustre parallel filesystem [31].

5.1 Scientific Applications

In this section, we test three popular scientific application frameworks, widely used in both research and industry. The objective is to demonstrate the capability of Sarus and its HPC extensions (see Sect. 4) to run real-world production workloads using containers, while performing on par with highly-tuned native deployments. All container runs in the following subsections use both the MPI and NVIDIA GPU hooks.

GROMACS. GROMACS [2] is a molecular dynamics package with an extensive array of modeling, simulation and analysis capabilities. While primarily developed for the simulation of biochemical molecules, its broad adoption includes research fields such as non-biological chemistry, metadynamics and mesoscale physics.

For the experiment we select the GROMACS Test Case B from PRACE's Unified European Applications Benchmark Suite [32]. The test case consists of a model of cellulose and lignocellulosic biomass in an aqueous solution. This inhomogeneous system of 3.3 million atoms uses reaction-field electrostatics instead of smooth particle-mesh Ewald (SPME) [10], and therefore should scale well. The simulation was carried out using single precision, 1 MPI process per node and 12 OpenMP threads per MPI process. We perform runs from a minimum of 4 nodes up to 256 nodes, increasing the node count in powers of two, carrying out 40 repetitions for each data point.

As the native application we use GROMACS release 2018.3, built by CSCS staff and available on Piz Daint through an environment module. For the container application, we build GROMACS 2018.3 with GPU acceleration inside a Ubuntu-based container.

The results are illustrated in Fig. 2. We measure performance in ns/day as reported by the application logs. The speedup values are computed using the performance average of each data point, taking the native value at 4 nodes as baseline.

We observe the container application consistently matching the scalability profile of native version. Absolute performance is identical up to 32 nodes. From 64 nodes upwards, the differences (up to 2.7% at 256 nodes) are consistent with empirical experience about sharing the system with other users during

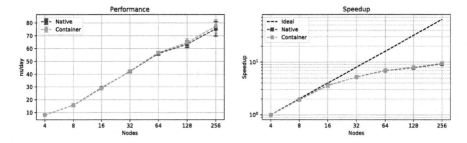

Fig. 2. Comparison of performance and speedup between native and container versions of GROMACS on Piz Daint.

the experiment. Standard deviation values remain comparable across all node counts.

TensorFlow with Horovod. TensorFlow [1] is a popular open source software framework for the development of machine-learning (ML) models, with a focus on deep neural networks.

Horovod [36] is a framework to perform distributed training of deep neural networks on top of another ML framework, like TensorFlow, Keras, or PyTorch. Notably, it allows to replace TensorFlow's own parameter server architecture for distributed training with communications based on an MPI model, providing improved usability and performance.

As test case, we select the `tf_cnn_benchmark` scripts from the Tensorflow project [38] for benchmarking convolutional neural networks. We use a ResNet-50 model [14] with a batch size of 64 and the synthetic image data which the benchmark scripts are able to generate autonomously. We perform runs from a minimum of 2 nodes up to 512, increasing the node count in powers of two.

For the native application, we install Horovod 0.15.1 on Piz Daint on top of a CSCS-provided build of TensorFlow 1.7.0, which is available on Piz Daint through an environment module. For the container application, we customize the Dockerfile provided by Horovod for version 0.15.1, which is based on Ubuntu, to use TensorFlow 1.7.0 and MPICH 3.1.4. Neither application uses NVIDIA's NCCL library for any MPI operation.

The results are shown in Fig. 3. We measure performance in images per second as reported by the application logs and compute speedup values using the performance averages for each data point, taking the native performance at 2 nodes as baseline.

The container application shows a performance trend identical to the native one, with both versions maintaining close standard deviation values. Absolute performance differences up to 8 nodes are less than 0.5%. From 16 nodes upwards we observe differences up to 6.2% at 256 nodes, which are compatible with empirical observations of running experiments on a non-dedicated system.

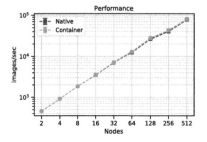 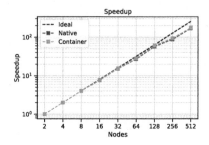

Fig. 3. Performance and speedup comparison between native and container versions of TensorFlow with Horovod.

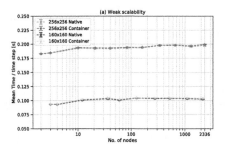 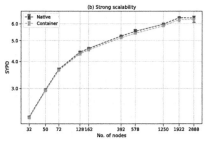

Fig. 4. Weak (a) and strong (b) scalability comparison between native and container versions of the COSMO code.

COSMO Atmospheric Model Code. The Consortium for Small Scale Modeling (COSMO) [6] develops and maintains a non-hydrostatic, limited-area atmospheric model which is used by several institutions for climate simulations [4,21] and production-level numerical weather prediction (NWP) [3,20,34] on a daily basis.

As test cases, we replicate the strong and weak scaling experiments performed in [13]. These experiments use a refactored version 5.0 of the GPU-accelerated COSMO code to simulate an idealized baroclinic wave [15]. The setup expands the computational domain of COSMO to cover 98.4% of the Earth surface and discretizes the vertical dimension using 60 stretched mode levels, going from the surface up to 40 km. For the complete details of the experimental setup, please refer to [13].

For the native application, we build the COSMO code and its dependencies on the Cray Programming Environment 18.08 available on Piz Daint. For the container application, in order to meet the specific requirements of the COSMO code, we package the Cray Linux Environment 6.0UP07 and the Cray Developer Toolkit 18.08 in a Docker image. This image is subsequently used as the base environment in which the containerized COSMO stack is built.

Weak scaling. The experiments for weak scaling employ two domain sizes with 160×160 and 256×256 horizontal grid points per node, respectively. We perform runs from a minimum of 2 nodes up to 2336, carrying out 5 repetitions at each node count. For each run, the mean wall-clock time of a simulation step is calculated by taking the total duration of the time loop as reported by the application log and dividing it for the number of time steps. Figure 4(a) displays the average, minimum and maximum values of mean step duration for each data point. The performance trend of native and container applications is identical across all node counts and domain sizes. The absolute performance differences range from 0.3% to 1% on the 256×256 per-node domain and from 1% to 1.6% on the 160×160 per-node domain, which are within the observed variability for running on a shared system.

Strong scaling. The experiments for strong scaling employ a fixed domain with a 19 km horizontal grid spacing. We perform runs from a minimum of 32 nodes up to 2888, carrying out 5 repetitions at each node count. We measure performance in simulated years per day (SYPD), calculated from the simulation time step and the wall-clock duration of the time loop as reported by the application log. Figure 4 (b) displays the average, minimum and maximum values of SYPD for each data point. Again, native and container performances follow very similar trends throughout all deployment scales and show very small variations. Differences range from 0.8% to 2.1%. In the same fashion of the other experiments, such differences are consistent with previous experience about not having the system dedicated to these experiments.

6   Conclusions

Sarus is a container engine for HPC enabling the deployment of Docker containers which achieve native performance and scalability on supercomputing platforms.

Being designed around the specifications of the OCI, Sarus uses external hooks with a standard interface in order to extend its capabilities and support unique features of HPC environments, like system-tuned libraries and vendor-optimized drivers for dedicated hardware (e.g. accelerators and high-performance interconnects). Sarus integrates an OCI-compliant runtime, such as `runc`, to leverage low-level kernel features while reducing development efforts and architectural complexity. Sarus complements the advantages of the OCI specifications by tailoring containers for multi-tenant cluster systems, with regard to security, access permissions, and superior I/O performance for container images mounted on network parallel filesystems. The capability of importing Docker images and a Docker-compatible CLI increase the convenience of packaging software on personal computing devices, and then using Sarus to deploy containers at scale on HPC systems.

We showed that containerized applications deployed with Sarus on the Piz Daint supercomputing system can perform on par with native implementations by testing three real-world applications with complex dependency stacks: the GROMACS package for molecular dynamics, the combination of TensorFlow and

Horovod frameworks for Machine Learning, and the COSMO atmospheric model simulation code. The presented results show no performance degradation when comparing the natively compiled versions with their containerized counterparts, even when deploying containers on 2888 GPU nodes.

References

1. Abadi, M., et al.: TensorFlow: a system for large-scale machine learning. In: Proceedings of the 12th USENIX Symposium on Operating Systems Design and Implementation (OSDI), Savannah, Georgia, USA (2016)
2. Abraham, M.J., et al.: GROMACS: high performance molecular simulations through multi-level parallelism from laptops to supercomputers. SoftwareX **1**, 19–25 (2015)
3. Baldauf, M., Seifert, A., Förstner, J., Majewski, D., Raschendorfer, M., Reinhardt, T.: Operational convective-scale numerical weather prediction with the cosmo model: description and sensitivities. Mon. Weather Rev. **139**(12), 3887–3905 (2011)
4. Ban, N., Schmidli, J., Schär, C.: Heavy precipitation in a changing climate: does short-term summer precipitation increase faster? Geophys. Res. Lett. **42**(4), 1165–1172 (2015)
5. Brown, N.: Overlay Filesystem (2014). https://www.kernel.org/doc/Documentation/filesystems/overlayfs.txt
6. Consortium for Small-Scale Modeling: Cosmo model (2019). http://www.cosmo-model.org/
7. CRAY: XC Series System Administration Guide (S-2393) Rev B, February 2019. https://pubs.cray.com/content/S-2393/CLE%206.0.UP06/xctm-series-system-administration-guide/about-xctm-series-system-administration-guide-s-2393
8. Deal, S.J.: HPC made easy: using docker to distribute and test trilinos (2016)
9. Delaruelle, X.: Environment Modules open source project. http://modules.sourceforge.net/
10. Essmann, U., Perera, L., Berkowitz, M.L., Darden, T., Lee, H., Pedersen, L.G.: A smooth particle mesh ewald method. J. Chem. Phys. **103**(19), 8577–8593 (1995)
11. MPI Forum: MPI: a message-passing interface standard. version 3.0, September 2012. http://www.mpi-forum.org
12. OpenSSH Foundation: OpenSSH (1999). https://www.openssh.com/
13. Fuhrer, O., et al.: Near-global climate simulation at 1 km resolution: establishing a performance baseline on 4888 GPUs with COSMO 5.0. Geosci. Model Dev. 11(4), 1665–1681 (2018)
14. He, K., Zhang, X., Ren, S., Sun, J.: Deep residual learning for image recognition. In: Proceedings of the IEEE Conference on Computer Vision and Pattern Recognition, pp. 770–778 (2016)
15. Jablonowski, C., Williamson, D.L.: A baroclinic instability test case for atmospheric model dynamical cores. Q. J. R. Meteorol. Soc. **132**(621C), 2943–2975 (2006)
16. Jacobsen, D.M., Canon, R.S.: Contain this, unleashing Docker for HPC. In: Proceedings of the Cray User Group (2015)
17. Joubert, W., et al.: Attacking the opioid epidemic: determining the epistatic and pleiotropic genetic architectures for chronic pain and opioid addiction. In: Proceedings of the International Conference for High Performance Computing, Networking, Storage, and Analysis, SC 2018, Piscataway, NJ, USA, pp. 57:1–57:14. IEEE Press (2018). http://dl.acm.org/citation.cfm?id=3291656.3291732

18. Kurth, T., et al.: Exascale deep learning for climate analytics. In: Proceedings of the International Conference for High Performance Computing, Networking, Storage, and Analysis, SC 2018, Piscataway, NJ, USA, pp. 51:1–51:12. IEEE Press (2018). http://dl.acm.org/citation.cfm?id=3291656.3291724
19. Kurtzer, G.M.: Singularity 2.1.2 - Linux application and environment containers for science, August 2016. https://doi.org/10.5281/zenodo.60736
20. Lapillonne, X., et al.: Operational numerical weather prediction on a GPU-accelerated cluster supercomputer. In: EGU General Assembly Conference Abstracts, vol. 18 (2016)
21. Leutwyler, D., Lüthi, D., Ban, N., Fuhrer, O., Schär, C.: Evaluation of the convection-resolving climate modeling approach on continental scales. J. Geophys. Res.: Atmos. **122**(10), 5237–5258 (2017)
22. Hykes, S.: Spinning Out Docker's Plumbing: Part 1: Introducing runC (2015). https://blog.docker.com/2015/06/runc/. Accessed 22 November 2018
23. Linux man-pages project: ldconfig(8), September 2017. http://man7.org/linux/man-pages/man8/ldconfig.8.html
24. Linux man-pages project: capabilities(7), February 2018. http://man7.org/linux/man-pages/man7/capabilities.7.html
25. Linux man-pages project: mount_namespaces(7), April 2018. http://man7.org/linux/man-pages/man7/mount_namespaces.7.html
26. Linux man-pages project: unshare(2), February 2018. http://man7.org/linux/man-pages/man2/unshare.2.html
27. MPICH: MPICH ABI Compatibility Initiative, November 2013. https://www.mpich.org/abi/
28. NVIDIA: NVIDIA Container Runtime (2018). https://developer.nvidia.com/nvidia-container-runtime
29. Open Container Initiative: The 5 principles of Standard Containers (2015). https://github.com/opencontainers/runtime-spec/blob/master/principles.md
30. Open Containers Initiative: runC: CLI tool for spawning and running containers according to the OCI specification (2014), https://github.com/opencontainers/runc
31. OpenSFS and EOFS: Lustre filesystem. http://lustre.org
32. PRACE: Unified European Applications Benchmark Suite, October 2016. http://www.prace-ri.eu/ueabs/
33. Priedhorsky, R., Randles, T.: Charliecloud: unprivileged containers for user-defined software stacks in HPC. In: Proceedings of the International Conference for High Performance Computing, Networking, Storage and Analysis, p. 36. ACM (2017)
34. Richard, E., Buzzi, A., Zängl, G.: Quantitative precipitation forecasting in the Alps: the advances achieved by the mesoscale alpine programme. Q. J. R. Meteorol. Soc. **133**(625), 831–846 (2007)
35. SchedMD: Slurm Workload Manager, November 2018. https://slurm.schedmd.com
36. Sergeev, A., Del Balso, M.: Horovod: fast and easy distributed deep learning in TensorFlow. arXiv preprint arXiv:1802.05799 (2018)
37. Shimokawabe, T., et al.: Peta-scale phase-field simulation for dendritic solidification on the TSUBAME 2.0 supercomputer. In: Proceedings of 2011 International Conference for High Performance Computing, Networking, Storage and Analysis, p. 3. ACM (2011)
38. TensorFlow Project: Tensorflow Benchmarks (2015). https://github.com/tensorflow/benchmarks
39. TOP500.org: November 2018—TOP500 Supercomputer sites (2018). https://www.top500.org/lists/2018/11/

40. Vincent, P., Witherden, F., Vermeire, B., Park, J.S., Iyer, A.: Towards green aviation with Python at petascale. In: Proceedings of the International Conference for High Performance Computing, Networking, Storage and Analysis, p. 1. IEEE Press (2016)
41. Ylonen, T., Lonvick, C.: The Secure Shell (SSH) protocol architecture (2005)
42. Zaharia, M., et al.: Apache spark: a unified engine for big data processing. Commun. ACM **59**(11), 56–65, October 2016. https://doi.org/10.1145/2934664
43. Zak, K.: mount(8), August 2015. http://man7.org/linux/man-pages/man8/mount.8.html

Singularity GPU Containers Execution on HPC Cluster

Giuseppa Muscianisi[1(✉)], Giuseppe Fiameni[1], and Abdulrahman Azab[2]

[1] CINECA - Interuniversity Consortium, Bologna, Italy
{g.muscianisi,g.fiameni}@cineca.it
[2] University of Oslo, Oslo, Norway
abdulrahman.azab@usit.uio.no

Abstract. This paper describes how to use the Singularity containerization tool in a HPC cluster equipped with GPU accelerators. The application chosen for benchmarking is Tensorflow, the open-source software library for machine learning. The singularity containers built have run into GALILEO HPC cluster at CINECA. A performance comparison between bare metal and container executions is also provided, showing a negligible difference in the number of images computed per second.

Keywords: Singularity · GPU · Tensorflow

1 Introduction

The use of container technology has been increasing in the last years thanks to the diffusion of Docker [1] among researchers both for sharing their applications and to simplify the installation processes on the hosts.

Within containers, it is possible to run the same software on different architectures without installing it and its dependencies every time on different platforms. Since the containers allow a light-weight virtualization of the available resources in the host, it is possible to install a software only one time in the container and then bring and run such container on multiple platforms.

So, thanks to Docker, an extensive diffusion of containers creation and sharing among researchers has motivated their utilization also in the HPC context. Unfortunately, Docker is not suitable for HPC environment because to run a Docker container privileged access rights are needed possibly leading to malicious actions within the container execution.

In the years, many containerization tools have been developed to avoid such security limitations. Among them, since the first official release in 2017, Singularity [2,3] has established itself among the best tools available for the execution of containerized applications in the HPC environment.

Supported by Prace - Partnership for Advanced Computing in Europe - 5IP, http://www.prace-ri.eu/.

M. Weiland et al. (Eds.): ISC 2019 Workshops, LNCS 11887, pp. 61–68, 2019.
https://doi.org/10.1007/978-3-030-34356-9_6

Singularity is able to bring containers and thus improve scientific workflow reproducibility. It is "secure" in the sense that the container execution takes place in the user space, without having demons running in the host as happens for Docker.

Through Singularity it is possible to run parallel applications on HPC cluster, both MPI, OpenMP and hybrid codes. It is possible to leverage accelerators, also, as GPU, FPGA or Intel MIC, that are often available in a supercomputing system. Singularity integrates within common workload managers, as Torque [4], PBS Pro [5] or SLURM [6], always available in HPC environments to orchestrate job execution: from a user perspective, run a bare metal or a containerized application is exactly the same.

In this article, a Singularity GPU containers execution on a HPC cluster is presented. The application chosen for benchmarking is Tensorflow [7], the widely used open-source software library for machine learning. Due to its many dependencies at the installation time, it results to be a good tool to be containerized. The singularity containers built have run into GALILEO supercomputing cluster, located at CINECA, the Italian Interuniversity Consortium [8].

In Sect. 2 both the container building process and run on GALILEO cluster are described. In Sect. 3 the benchmarking results are presented. Finally, in Sect. 4 some consideration are reported.

2   Singularity GPU Containers Building and Running

By design, a container is platform-agnostic and also software-agnostic. But nowadays HPC systems are equipped with accelerators, as GPU, FPGA or Intel MIC, and a relevant number of softwares and libraries have been written and designed to use such specialized hardware.

So to be really useful, a containerized application has to be able to use such kind of hardware. Of course, a solution is to install the accelerator specific drivers and libraries into the container. But for nVidia GPUs, Singularity provide an other solution. In fact, Singularity supports "natively" the GPUs in the sense that all the relevant nVidia/Cuda libraries on the host are found via the ld.so.cache that is bound into a library location within the container automatically. To enable the usage of GPUs in a Singularity container, simply add the flag "–nv" in the singularity execution command line [3]. The Cuda Toolkit has to be available in the container, with a version compatible with the driver version installed on the GPUs in the host.

Different Singularity GPU containers have been built, bootstrapping both from other Docker or Singularity containers already available in the official Docker Hub [9] and Singularity Hub [10], or bootstrapping from Ubuntu or CentOS official distributions. In the first case, few modifications have been done as add a directory for test purposes or install additional packages. In all cases, the simplicity of usage has been noted, both in building and running containers from scratch or using a pre-built ones.

In the tests presented here, two Singularity containers with the widely used machine learning framework "Tensorflow" have been built, both with GPU libraries available, version 1.10.1 and 1.12.1.

Accordingly to the philosophy of reproducibility and sharing that featured the containerization techniques, it has been decided to use the pre-built, official released containers. The containers built have been bootstrapped from the Docker ones available in the official Docker Hub repository of Tensorflow community [12].

To build the containers, the skeleton recipe reported in Table 1 has been used:

Table 1. Singularity recipe skeleton used to build the GPU container.

```
Bootstrap:docker
From:tensorflow/tensorflow:VERSION NUMBER FOR GPUs

%post
mkdir -p /test
chmod 777 -R /test
```

where the directory "test" is local to the container and has been used to bind the input files previously downloaded in the host.

3   Benchmark

3.1   Systems Description

GALILEO. GALILEO [8] is the CINECA Tier-1 "National" level supercomputer. Introduced first in 2015, it has been configured at the beginning of 2018 with Intel Xeon E5-2697 v4 (Broadwell) nodes. Also available in GALILEO is a pool of 15 nodes, each equipped with 2 x 8-cores Intel Haswell 2.40 GHz plus 2 nVidia K80 GPUs, 128 GB/node RAM, and an Infiniband with 4x QDR switches as Internal Network.

3.2   Test Case 1: Containerized Tensorflow Execution on GALILEO Versus Official Tensorflow Performance Data

A Singularity container has been built directly from those available in the official Tensorflow Docker hub. The version of Tensorflow used is the 1.10.0 for GPU. The container has been built using Singularity 2.3.1 version, while on GALILEO the 2.5.2 version. For container test the ResNt-50 [16] neural network has been considered, with a batch size of 32 over the ImageNet [18] data

set. The obtained results have been compared with those provided in the official
Tensorflow nVidia Teska K80 [11] and are reported in Table 2. As it is possible
to note by the reported number, the usage of the containerized application does
not introduce any significant overhead in the computations, since the number of
images computed per second remains of the same order of magnitude.

Table 2. The number of images computed per second is reported both in the simulation
of containerized Tensorflow on 1 GALILEO node with 2 nVidia Tesla K80 and in those
reported in the official Tensorflow performance documentation.

	GALILEO nVidia Tesla K80	Official Tensorflow nVidia Tesla K80
1 gpu	54,968	52
2 gpus	107,916	99
3 gpus	194,15	195

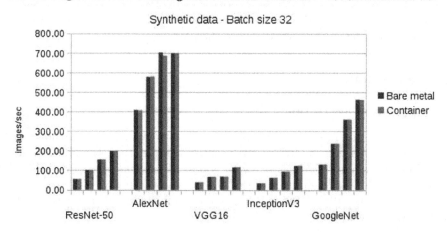

Fig. 1. Number of images per second computed in ResNet-50, AlexNet, VGG16, Inception V3 and GoogleNet model for 1, 2, 3 and 4 K80 NVIDIA GPUs on a single GALILEO node. The batch size used is 32, the dataset is ImageNet - synthetic.

3.3   Test Case 2: Containerized Versus Bare Metal Execution on GALILEO

A Singularity container has been built directly from those available in the official Tensorflow Docker hub. The version of Tensorflow used is the 1.12.0 for

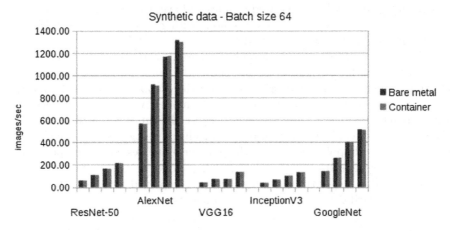

Fig. 2. Number of images per second computed in ResNet-50, AlexNet, VGG16, InceptionV3 and GoogleNet model for 1, 2, 3 and 4 K80 NVIDIA GPUs on a single GALILEO node. The batch size used is 64, the dataset is ImageNet - synthetic.

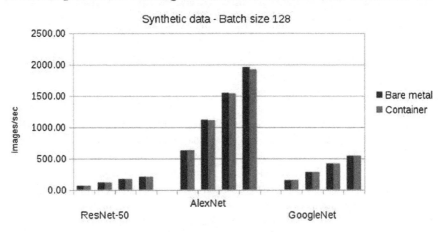

Fig. 3. Number of images per second computed in ResNet-50, AlexNet, and GoogleNet model for 1, 2, 3 and 4 K80 NVIDIA GPUs on a single GALILEO node. The batch size used is 128, the dataset is ImageNet - synthetic.

GPU. The container has been built using Singularity 3.0.2 version, the same also available as a module on GALILEO.

Both for bare metal and container tests, five different neural networks have been considered: AlexNet [13], googLeNet [14], InceptionV3 [15], ResNet-50 [16] and VGG16 [17]. The dataset was ImageNet [18] (synthetic) and three different batch sizes were analyzed: 32, 64 and 128 per device, where the device is the GPU. The tests have been repeated 6 times and averaged on the set of data. All the runs have been executed in a single node with 2*8-cores Intel Xeon E5-2630 v3 at 2.40 GHz and 2 nVidia K80 GPUs.

The number of images per second is reported in the Figs. 1, 2 and 3. The batch size being fixed, each histogram shows the number of images per second computed in each neural network model described above and for 1, 2, 3, and 4 GPUs a single GALILEO node. Note that the models VGG16 and Inception V3 with a batch size of 128 are not shown because the run was out of memory. As shown, no overhead in the execution is introduced using the container instead of the bare metal application, since the number of images computed per second is more or less the same.

In Tables 3, 4 and 5, the number of images is reported for each test, together with the standard deviation of the measurements.

Table 3. Number of images per second computed in ResNet-50, AlexNet, VGG16, InceptionV3 and GoogleNet model for 1, 2, 3 and 4 K80 NVIDIA GPUs on a single GALILEO node. The batch size used is 32, the dataset is ImageNet - synthetic. The standard deviation of the measurements is also reported.

Model	GPUs number	Bare metal	Container
ResNet-50	1 gpu	$54,9 \pm 0,83$	$54,87 \pm 0,98$
	2 gpus	$102,2 \pm 1,3$	$101,4 \pm 1,5$
	3 gpus	$155,4 \pm 2,8$	$155,4 \pm 2,3$
	4 gpus	$197,8 \pm 1,9$	$198,3 \pm 1,4$
AlexNet	1 gpu	$408,6 \pm 5,2$	$406,3 \pm 3,8$
	2 gpus	$578,1 \pm 5,4$	$580,0 \pm 4,2$
	3 gpus	704 ± 24	686 ± 25
	4 gpus	699 ± 20	699 ± 14
VGG16	1 gpu	$38,54 \pm 0,38$	$38,32 \pm 0,43$
	2 gpus	$66,12 \pm 0,82$	$66,06 \pm 0,47$
	3 gpus	$67,36 \pm 0,60$	$66,61 \pm 0,51$
	4 gpus	$115,4 \pm 1,7$	$115,9 \pm 1,5$
InceptionV3	1 gpu	$33,92 \pm 0,34$	$33,85 \pm 0,41$
	2 gpus	$62,17 \pm 0,58$	$62,43 \pm 0,86$
	3 gpus	$94,4 \pm 1,3$	$94,1 \pm 1,4$
	4 gpus	$123,4 \pm 1,4$	$124,2 \pm 1,4$
GoogleNet	1 gpu	$129,9 \pm 1,8$	$129,9 \pm 2,5$
	2 gpus	$237,2 \pm 4,7$	$237,0 \pm 5,1$
	3 gpus	$360,3 \pm 4,9$	$359,8 \pm 4,3$
	4 gpus	$462,9 \pm 3,7$	$461,4 \pm 7,4$

Table 4. Number of images per second computed in ResNet-50, AlexNet, VGG16, InceptionV3 and GoogleNet model for 1, 2, 3 and 4 K80 NVIDIA GPUs on a single GALILEO node. The batch size used is 64, the dataset is ImageNet - synthetic. The standard deviation of the measurements is also reported.

Model	GPUs number	Bare metal	Container
ResNet-50	1 gpu	$59{,}19 \pm 0{,}62$	$58{,}43 \pm 0{,}60$
	2 gpus	$108{,}97 \pm 0{,}94$	$107{,}7 \pm 1{,}8$
	3 gpus	$164{,}3 \pm 2{,}6$	$163{,}0 \pm 1{,}1$
	4 gpus	$213{,}6 \pm 3{,}0$	$211{,}9 \pm 3{,}4$
AlexNet	1 gpu	$568{,}1 \pm 3{,}1$	$565{,}3 \pm 7{,}1$
	2 gpus	$917{,}5 \pm 3{,}8$	$908{,}1 \pm 11{,}7$
	3 gpus	1167 ± 55	1174 ± 22
	4 gpus	1316 ± 38	1299 ± 28
VGG16	1 gpu	$40{,}98 \pm 0{,}35$	$40{,}95 \pm 0{,}42$
	2 gpus	$72{,}64 \pm 0{,}48$	$72{,}36 \pm 0{,}99$
	3 gpus	$71{,}77 \pm 0{,}72$	$71{,}38 \pm 0{,}84$
	4 gpus	$134{,}9 \pm 2{,}1$	$134{,}8 \pm 1{,}8$
InceptionV3	1 gpu	$36{,}01 \pm 0{,}52$	$35{,}99 \pm 0{,}30$
	2 gpus	$66{,}10 \pm 0{,}78$	$65{,}90 \pm 0{,}51$
	3 gpus	$99{,}1 \pm 1{,}2$	$100{,}2 \pm 1{,}2$
	4 gpus	$131{,}6 \pm 1{,}4$	$130{,}8 \pm 1{,}4$
GoogleNet	1 gpu	$139{,}9 \pm 1{,}9$	$142{,}0 \pm 2{,}0$
	2 gpus	$259{,}4 \pm 2{,}1$	$260{,}1 \pm 5{,}2$
	3 gpus	$400{,}1 \pm 3{,}8$	$397{,}4 \pm 4{,}5$
	4 gpus	$513{,}6 \pm 3{,}9$	$509{,}3 \pm 5{,}2$

Table 5. Number of images per second computed in ResNet-50, AlexNet and GoogleNet model for 1, 2, 3 and 4 K80 NVIDIA GPUs on a single GALILEO node. The batch size used is 128, the dataset is ImageNet - synthetic. The standard deviation of the measurements is also reported.

Model	GPUs number	Bare metal	Container
ResNet-50	1 gpu	$61{,}94 \pm 0{,}72$	$61{,}18 \pm 0{,}65$
	2 gpus	$113{,}2 \pm 1{,}3$	$111{,}8 \pm 1{,}7$
	3 gpus	$171 \pm 2{,}4$	$170{,}3 \pm 1{,}1$
	4 gpus	203 ± 3	$202{,}1 \pm 2{,}8$
AlexNet	1 gpu	$626{,}7 \pm 9{,}5$	629 ± 15
	2 gpus	1115 ± 12	1108 ± 16
	3 gpus	1544 ± 25	$1534{,}3 \pm 5{,}3$
	4 gpus	1957 ± 20	1920 ± 72
GoogleNet	1 gpu	$147{,}4 \pm 2{,}2$	$149{,}2 \pm 2{,}4$
	2 gpus	$277{,}9 \pm 2{,}4$	$276{,}6 \pm 2{,}4$
	3 gpus	$414{,}2 \pm 7{,}2$	$412{,}7 \pm 3{,}3$
	4 gpus	$539{,}4 \pm 8{,}5$	$538{,}9 \pm 4{,}9$

4   Conclusion

A possible way to run Singularity GPU containers has been considered. The containers have been built starting from those available in the Tensorflow Docker Hub repository. Two performance tests have been described: in the first, the data obtained run a containerized version of Tensorflow on GALILEO cluster have been compared with those available in the official Tensorflow performance webpage. In the second, a comparison among a bare metal and a containerized executions, both on GALILEO, has been done. Both such tests show that running a GPU containerized version of Tensorflow does not introduce relevant overhead or performance issues.

References

1. Docker. https://www.docker.com/
2. Kurtzer, G.M., Sochat, V., Bauer, M.W.: Singularity: scientific containers for mobility of compute. PLoS ONE **12**(5), e0177459 (2017). https://doi.org/10.1371/journal.pone.0177459
3. Singularity. https://www.sylabs.io/
4. Torque. http://www.adaptivecomputing.com/products/torque/
5. PBS Pro. https://www.pbspro.org/
6. Slurm. https://slurm.schedmd.com/
7. Tensorflow. https://www.tensorflow.org/
8. GALILEO cluster user documentation. https://wiki.u-gov.it/confluence/display/SCAIUS/UG3.3%3A+GALILEO+UserGuide
9. Docker Hub. https://hub.docker.com/
10. Singularity Hub. http://singularity-hub.org/
11. Tensorflow Performance benchmarks. https://www.tensorflow.org/guide/performance/benchmarks
12. Tensorflow Docker Hub. https://hub.docker.com/r/tensorflow/tensorflow/
13. Krizhevsky, A., Sutskever, I., Hinton, G. E.: Imagenet classification with deep convolutional neural networks. In: Advances in Neural Information Processing Systems, pp. 1097–1105 (2012)
14. Szegedy, C., et al.: Going deeper with convolutions. In: Computer Vision and Pattern Recognition (CVPR) (2015)
15. Szegedy, C., Vanhoucke, V., Ioffe, S., Shlens, J., Wojna, Z.: Rethinking the inception architecture for computer vision (2015). https://arxiv.org/abs/1512.00567
16. He, K., Zhang, X., Ren, S., Sun, J.: Deep residual learning for image recognition (2015). https://arxiv.org/abs/1512.03385
17. Simonyan, K., Zisserman, A.: Very deep convolutional networks for large-scale image recognition (2014). https://arxiv.org/abs/1409.1556
18. ImageNet dataset. http://www.image-net.org/

A Multitenant Container Platform
with OKD, Harbor Registry and ELK

Jarle Bjørgeengen$^{(\boxtimes)}$ (iD)

University of Oslo, USIT, Gaustadalléen 23a, 0373 Oslo, Norway
`postmottak@usit.uio.no`
`https://www.usit.uio.no/english/`

Abstract. This paper summarizes the open container [2] journey of
the University of Oslo's Center of Information technology, (Division
for Infrastructure). It describes the background for adopting containers in the first place, the pitfalls of early attempts, the learning that
was obtained from stepping into those pitfalls, how they were mended
and some thoughts about future direction for container usage. Challenges regarding organizational aspects and increased demand for rapid
delivery, combined with the established expectations of security and stability, is also described in relation to container technology. It distills the
findings and explains the rationale behind the chosen direction of adapt-
ing Openshift community Distribution of Kubernetes (OKD) [1] as our
main container platform for long running core services, and how it was
adapted to best integrate it with existing automation, monitoring and
logging: Elasticsearch, Logstash and Kibana (ELK).

Keywords: Open containers · Kubernetes · Docker · Continuous
delivery · Multi tenancy · Self service

1 Introduction

There is an increasing demand for and utilization of open containers [2] by IT-
professionals today. The majority of cloud native technologies utilize container
technology in some form. Containers make promises of advantages like: faster
software delivery, immutable services, portability and dynamic on-demand scaling. Software developers and users of containers and container platforms are
compelled by containers' ease of creating and continuously improving powerful functions that provide businesses value in highly competitive markets that
change ever more rapidly. But containers also introduce new challenges, especially regarding increased complexity and/or security. As the number of software abstraction layers and interfaces from users down to physical infrastructure
increase, the complexity increases too. The exposure for attacks and cascading

---

Supported by University of Oslo, Center for Information Technology (USIT).

© The Author(s) 2019, corrected publication 2020
M. Weiland et al. (Eds.): ISC 2019 Workshops, LNCS 11887, pp. 69–79, 2019.
https://doi.org/10.1007/978-3-030-34356-9_7

failures is increasing accordingly. How to balance the benefits and challenges of containers ? With this context the paper describes the use cases, history, considerations, current state and future vision for container usage in delivery of core services at USIT.

2   Past

2.1   Background

We started using Docker [3] containers for some small web based applications in 2015. Applications like Graphite [4], Grafana [5] and Kibana [6] with our home made role based access control (RBAC) system which is used for filtering Elasticsearch [7] documents based on ownership. We found that containers provided value when making multiple instances of the same application, but with slightly different parameters. Orchestration of containers was mainly done with Ansible [8] and templating was done with Jinja2 templates within Ansible. Containers made it possible to run many applications instances on a few hosts that would otherwise require one host per application.

However we also found that the immutable nature of containers introduced some headache when it came to keeping application stacks up to date with security fixes. Long running service containers tended to stay up for long periods of time and their software stack (being immutable) were unchanged. This is of course wanted behaviour when it comes to predictability of application dependencies, and it is much of the value proposition of containers. But keeping those software stacks unchanged over time led to exposure against vulnerabilities that otherwise would have been automatically updated if they just run as ordinary processes in our standardized Linux server environment. This pattern introduced a business risk that needed to be mitigated, so we made a container policy in order to regulate how containers were to be used and managed for production services running on core server networks. The policy mainly described requirements for:

- Image sources: A local registry with a vetted list of replicated images from external sources.
- Detection and mitigation of vulnerabilities: Automated scanning and actions to take.
- Run time requirements: Don't run as root, allowed version of container run times etc.
- Transparency: All artifact inclusion in version control system (VCS). Tagging images with VCS version. Always use image from local registry (build and push before use)

The main purpose of having an on premise registry is to be able to decouple the dependency from external registries both for confidentiality and availability. For instance Dockerhub has been regarded as safe location for software distribution, but recent security breach [9] shows that attacks can happen and that exposure and tampering are real threats.

At USIT we have standardized on RedHat Enterprise Linux (RHEL) for Linux servers running core datacenter services. Servers are automatically boot-strapped with configuration management agents (Cfengine3 [10]) that converge and maintain the state of server operating systems into a safe baseline. One of the aspects covered by config management is to enforce that SELinux is turned on in version 7 of RHEL. Many people wrongly assume that containers provide stronger isolation than they in fact do [11]. In RHEL7 the Docker engine is inte-grated with SELinux so that containers automatically runs in unique SELinux contexts, and with reduced privilige to access host resources. It means that for RHEL7 with SELinux on containers provide a higher level of isolation between them and against the hosting node, than a vanilla Docker Community Edition installation. This is why our policy require production containers to run on RHEL7 (CentOS7 in IaaS-cloud environments) with SELinux on. SELinux is by no means the only runtime security measure to take regarding securing contain-ers and it definitely does not exclude other best practices to secure containers at runtime, for example seccomp [12] for systemcall filtering, EBPF [14] and user namespace remapping [13], however SELinux comes as an additional security layer on RHEL7 and does not require any extra effort to set up.

For on premise registry we required one with open source license, RBAC and support for external authentication/identity-providers in order to re-use existing business logic and organizational structure. Harbor registry [15] were as close as we got to those requirements at the time. Initially Harbor supported LDAP-authentication but not authorization based on group memberships so we made scripts for synchronizing local Harbor groups with ldap-groups. Also Harbor had no built in vulnerability-scanner, so we used a separate instance of CLAIR [16].

2.2   Challenges

The main problem with vulnerability scanning of container images is getting relevant data. One could scan all contents of the registry, but only a subset of the images in the registry is actually in use. Thus, scanning the whole registry would generate alerts for a lot of irrelevant images. Since we have both configuration management (Cfengine3 [10], and centralized logging (Rsyslog, Logstash and Elasticsearch)) we can collect information about which container images actually is in use on server hosts in our networks. This was done by using Cfengine to inject hourly updates of meta-data to Rsyslog about images used by running containers on hosts that had Docker installed and running. The metadata sent to Rsyslog was parsed and sent to Elasticsearch centrally and thus instantly made available for querying via the Elasticsearch API. Hence, the baseline for what container layers will be scanned and alerted upon is the set of image-ids found in the container meta-data store in Elasticsearch.

Meta-data about ownership of images is also collected and it provides email-addresses for alerting container owners about vulnerabilities in their running containers. If images lacks contact information the owner of the host is alerted via the owner's contact email address, which is collected and provided by another tool created at USIT: Nivlheim [17]. If containers run from images that is not found in the Harbor registry the container owner is notified about this breach of container policy as well.

Even with this pre-seeding of data before vulnerability alerting, the owners got too many alert to handle in an efficient manner. The reasons for this were twofold: there was no option for image owners to flag vulnerabilities for some subset of containers as "acknowledged" and filter them out upon subsequent scanning.

Also the hypothesis were made that many of the alerts may or may not be relevant because of how images are built. Images are frequently built using ordinary package install commands (yum, apt, port, pkg and so on) in the Docker file to add image layers. These tools tend to pull in orders of magnitude more dependencies than the container process needs, and many of the dependencies may or may not be posing a threat to the running process albeit present in the image, and thus can trigger hits by the vulnerability scanner. How to differentiate relevant from irrelevant? Nontrivial. One way of improving this is to put more labour into slimming down the images during builds (this is also mentioned as a desired property of image builds in the container policy). The advantage is that the images produced actually have a smaller attack surface and it will naturally have less likelihood of vulnerability alerts too, and the alerts is assumed to be more relevant. Unfortunately the ability and willingness to make image slimming happen are not very prominent, due to time constraints, labour requirements due to lack of tools for automating the process.

The limitations of Ansible and Jinja2 as a container management and orchestration tool became apparent. There is no rescheduling upon container failure, no service discovery and/or scale out features. The lack of observability is prominent and self service features need to be built using tools like Rundeck [18] and/or Ansible (Tower) and this leads to more infrastructure/platform code to develop, maintain and operate.

Images are replicated from external container registries (dockerhub etc) and into the /library project of our on premise instance of Harbor. Replication is done by script on an hourly basis. The script reads a list of registry/image:tag instances, pulls them to local container storage, re-tag them with the URL of the Harbor registry and pushes them there.

The procedure for adding new image references to be synchronized involves filling out a form with some standard questions about justification and considerations regarding trust. Submission of the form triggers en informational email to it-security and a new ticket to request tracker. If the request looks reasonable I (or someone like me) add the new image reference to the replication list, and it will be included in the hourly synchronization.

3   Present

Armed with experiences with past usage of containers, and conscious of an increasing demand for application containerization we set out to improve the state of containers at USIT. Some parts were working well; the image replication process and the on premise registry storage, so they were kept albeit upgraded, but there were ample room for improvement regarding orchestration, observabilty, self service, support for continuous delivery and deployment automation.

3.1 Evaluation of Container Orchestration Frameworks

During 2018 we ramped up the effort for finding improved alternatives for container orchestration. By this time the whole industry seemed to converge against Kubernetes [19] based solutions in one form or another. Kubernetes being backed by large open source founded companies like Google and RedHat, being the core project of which the Cloud Native Computing Foundation (CNCF) [20] was ignited from [21] and major cloud service providers like Google, Amazon and Azure were offering Kubernetes as a service targeted to increase developer efficiency. Hence we focused on use case experiments with frameworks that were utilizing Kubernetes.

Kubernetes is well defined when it comes to API-functionality for the different versions and this is also the value proposition for developers and/or Kubernetes users. It says: "give me a state declaration for scaling, connectivity and resources of your micro services and I will make it so". However, assembling, improving and maintaining a Kubernetes service that will keep that promise reliably and securely over time is a nontrivial task.

From a platform perspective Kubernetes look more like a set of software components that can be assembled into a service in many different ways. Core Kubernetes developers have been comparing it with the GNU/Linux stack and how that can be assembled into more or less opinionated Linux distributions [22]. Taking upstream Kubernetes and assembling it into a stable production service is hard [23].

For this reason we set out looking for "distributions" of Kubernetes that when installed were assembled automatically in a way that aligned as much as possible with our existing operational practices, policies and strategies: secure, standardized, multitenant with RBAC and integration with identity providers, high degree of developer self service, high degree of deployment and build automation and with an open source licens.

We tried a few Kubernetes installation frameworks: Kubespray [24] and NAISible [25] with some local modifications, but found that some core requirements regarding RBAC, multitenancy and developer self service were lacking. Then we tried OKD. OKD claimed to fulfill all the requirements, however it is also a rather large and complex installation process (although automated) and it would inevitably take time to understand all its moving parts.

Experiments with earlier versions (Openshift Origin) a couple of years back exhibited lack of modularity and poor error messages in the installation process combined with inaccurate and incomplete documentation, thus setting the expectations towards a daunting task. However, after installing v3.10 of OKD it became apparent that much of those earlier problems with installation and documentation were improved. Also there generally were a lot fewer bugs in the installation framework than earlier, particularly for the core functionality (Kubernetes).

OKD is multitenant via the concept of projects. Projects are much the same as Kubernetes name spaces, but with isolation features between them. Kubernetes namespaces is just that: separation of names (unless additional steps are taken). OKD projects have by default isolation on network (OVS multitenant) and process (SELinux) level between projects. There are also default enforcing policies to prevent breakout from containers/pods towards the hosting node (SELinux, SecComp, Security Context constraints (SCC)).

In addition to the core Kubernetes API compability, OKD has self service features for automating deployments and builds via image streams and build configs. Build configs can incorporate Jenkinsfiles and run them on demand by spinning up Jenkins instances on the fly or by having Jenkins running in projects (for shortening pipeline traverse times). Another nice feature of image streams is that running applications can be configured to automatically redeploy with updated base images via event triggers in image streams.

Efforts were increased to verify if OKD was a suitable to become our new container runtime platform. The next step was to adapt the installation to our existing environment and hypothesis testing against application development use cases. This effort was mainly organized as weekly "sprints" with members from departments from opposite sides (dev and ops) of the line organization and initiated only by peers communicating and silent approval by relevant managers. Unsurprisingly this method turned out to be efficient for progress and organizational learning, and we have increased the frequency of sprint weeks in order to reach production ready state by the summer of 2019.

3.2   Observability: Logging and OKD

OKD comes with an optional Elasticsearch, Fluentd and Kibana (EFK) [26] stack which is tightly aligned with the multitenancy in OKD. Project owners automatically get access to logs of their own pods, but not to other projects. However, Elasticsearch is by nature a difficult application to containerize and maintain in a stable manner. Also it has high demand on CPU, memory and storage IOPS resources on each deployed cluster.

Since we already have a rather large ELK installation with Elasticsearch running on 21 bare metal servers, it seemed like a more attractive option to scratch the built in EFK stack of OKD and integrate with USITs ELK instance. Another benefit with this is of course the ability to correlate and aggregate logs between OKD cluster and other log-sources. But how to automate this as a part of the installation, and how to create self service for tenants? Our ELK instance is already multitenant but how to make the connection between OKD tenants and ELK tenants?

The standard configuration management baseline for all our servers include a filebeat agent shipping system logs off to Logstash centrally. It turns out that filebeat in recent versions introduced integration with Kubernetes [27], making it possible to discover pods/containers-ids from the Kubernetes/OKD API and automatically ship log events based on matching conditions like namespace name, labels, annotations etc.

We decided to have logs from cluster components tagged and sent to a separate index prefix in ELK (kube-ops). This is done by matching pod events against list of projects/namespaces known to host system pods.

So now we have cluster system logs sent to ELK and accessible by cluster operators (admins with high level of privilege), but what about application logs? Ideally we would like to have tenants decide by themselves which deployments to enable logging for, to mark them as their own and sub-classify using an application field. It turns out that this is possible by using the same filebeat autodiscovery feature for Kubernetes by matching on labels. We introduced a label `log2elk: true` for tenants to signal that they want to ship logs to ELK.

In ELK it is good practice to log events as JSON-data in order to get maximum value of aggregation and grouping features later. So we decided that applications that apply the "log2elk: true" must log output as JSON. Furthermore the JSON must have a "logowner" field matching a known logowner in ELK (logownertenant), and an "application" field that makes grouping of applications within a logowner possible. So filebeat will send log events from pods with the label `log2elk: true` to Logstash centrally, Logstash input processors will check required fields and if they comply restructure events such that they get ingested and become available through Elasticsearch filter aliases for logowners to access from their dedicated Kibana instance. In USIT-ELK each logowner has their own Kibana instance which is tied to a user group in LDAP and is restricted to that logowners data set.

OKD has an advanced audit logging system [28] that can be configured by a separate audit policy file on the master node(s). It can potentially generate a lot of log-data and needs some iterations of policy modifications to balance value with spuriousness. It can be configured to log JSON, so it is straight forward to drop a filebeat config fragment into the directory `/etc/filebeat/filebeat.d/` on master nodes. Filebeat will then tag and ship the audit log to ELK.

Just like in Kubernetes cluster events are temporarily stored in etcd, and we need a way of exporting them as JSON events. Kubernetes has an events endpoint that can be watched/followed and where events will be published as they happen. We will write a small script or program that captures events from the OKD/Kubernetes API and spool them to file, and drop another filebeat configuration fragment into `/etc/filebeat/filbeat.d/` for tailing and shipping events.

3.3   Observability: Monitoring and OKD

We use Zabbix [29] as the central monitoring framework. Configuration of monitoring templates and access to modify configuration (self service) is completely automated through scripts that ask Nivlheim and LDAP to automatically decide what to monitor and whom to give access at which level. A subset of the monitoring automation is to automatically configure health monitoring for java based web-application. This is also done by asking Nivlheim about what to monitor and how. Nivlheim knows this by means of collected files from hosts running java-applications.

These java-applications are the first candidates for moving into OKD, but when containerized the applications can no longer rely on file access to the host and thus Nivlheim has no knowledge about them (being a file based collection tool for hosts) and installing a Nivlheim agent (or any management agent) inside each container is considered an anti-pattern. Finding an alternative method for monitoring applications running in OKD was the topic of the first sprint week, and a minimum viable product (MVP) was created during that week by application developers and operations cooperating. Two main changes were made: Applications made health information available through a http endpoint in its own service and the route/ingress of the application in OKD were marked with annotations (`uio.no/monitor.with.Zabbix:"true"`) which were picked up by a Zabbix auto discovery script that regularly asks OKD clusters about their routes/ingresses and pick out url-endpoints (stored in another annotation) to be configured for monitoring.

4   Future

4.1   Monitoring

Cluster events in ELK can form the basis for alerting rules by querying ELK for events of a certain severity and with other properties that we find we need to know about. Also v3.11 of OKD comes with an integrated Prometheus operator [30] that can monitor cluster health and resource consumption (both cluster wide and applications). The built in Grafana instance provide tenants the ability to monitor metrics of their own liking and resource consumption of their own applications. Also we already have an LDAP-integrated instance of Grafana running centrally with access to all other infrastructure and application metrics. Adding prometheus instances of OKD-clusters as Grafana datasources is trivial and make it possible to cross correlate and combine OKD metrics with other infrastructure metrics. Since v 4.2 of Zabbix there is a built in integration with Prometheus [31] that makes it easier to monitor cluster health directly with Zabbix.

4.2   Container Policy and OKD

Our container policy requires that all container images are being pulled from a local Harbor registry. The installation playbooks of OKD fetches most of the cluster components from images located in dockerhub by default. Fortunately this can be changed by a parameter named "oreg_url" that specify an alternative registry url-prefix to fetch cluster components from.

In order to have a baseline for all running containers that is not too much out of alignment with our general Linux server update policy it was recently decided to require all container images to be rebuilt and redeployed at least every 30 days. Automating container rebuild and push to registry is quite trivial, but automatically redeploying with rebuilt image and verifying that the service works as expected afterwards is not that trivial. Our hypothesis is that OKD can help with this utilizing image streams combined with deployment configs that trigger automatic rolling redeployment upon new images being pushed into the image stream. Also if the deployment is properly configured with Kubernetes liveness and readiness probes it will decrease or eliminate downtime for updates and make sure that new pods are healthy before service pointers are switched to updated pods.

4.3   Gitops [32] and OKD

We keep all our infrastructure and application code in VCS (git), and we strive for as little human intervention as possible when installing, running, modifying and maintaining infrastructure and platforms. At the moment we have no automatic triggering of configuration changes in OKD clusters after installation. Ideally it would be possible to make a change in the inventory of a running cluster, and it would automatically converge to new desired state when a pull request is merged.

Although Ansible itself have some level of convergence and idempotence, there is too much dependence on order of events in OKD installation playbooks and roles to make such behavior reliable. However, the new major release of OKD (v4) seems promising. It is much more based on self management by means of cluster operators, and will rely less on Ansible. The introduction of operators for managing all cluster life cycle aspects could make OKD more gitops friendly. We plan to try OKD v4 in the future, but meanwhile we will make project configuration (ownerhip, resource quotas, privileges and metadata injection) in OKD completely automated via git, pull requests and application of new state via the `oc apply` command.

4.4   Continuous Delivery in OKD

OKD has features that makes it possible to host complete continuous delivery pipelines inside projects. Today most of our developer groups uses build automation and automatic testing with Jenkins or other tools. There is some operational overhead of running standalone Jenkins instances. Based on our knowledge of OKD features we have a hypothesis that developer efficiency can be boosted and operational overhead reduced by moving the pipelines into OKD.

4.5   OKD in the Cloud

Portability is major benefit of running applications in containers. There pressure for utilizing public cloud services is increasing. The main reasons are bursting resource availability, quick cost scaling and reduction of operational expenses and investments. Just like many other organizations we foresee that public cloud consumption will increase, but it will take time to migrate to a "cloud only" situation, and based on regulation and/or policy some data, and hence the services processing those data, may never be allowed to run in public cloud. For applications with extreme resource consumption over long time it is probably not cost efficient (yet?) to run everything in public cloud. The bottom line is that we will need both on premise and public cloud in the foreseeable future. The ability to quickly move applications between on premise and public cloud in an automated or even autonomous way is often termed "Hybrid cloud", and we think that container platforms like OKD will play an important role in achieving hybrid cloud functionality.

At the moment we are working on automated provision and install of OKD in our community Openstack (RDO) [33] cloud UHIaaS [34] with terraform [35] and OKDs Ansible installer (plus som adaptations). Furthermore the plan is to extend this to work on major public cloud platforms from Google, Microsoft and Amazon, thus enabling maximum applications portability by offering the same run time platform (OKD) both on premise and in different public cloud contexts.

5   Conclusion

So far we have enough evidence that OKD and our approach to integrate with our existing operational systems, and spin up new clusters in different contexts, that we will continue the work along the lines suggested in Sect. 4. The aim has been and continue to be to help application developers and/or container users become more agile and efficient in delivering business value with balanced security, scalability and availability in mind. More automation, probably in the form of GitOps, will help us to improve further.

References

1. Openshift Community Distribution of Kubernetes. https://www.okd.io/
2. Open Container Initiative. https://www.opencontainers.org/
3. Docker Wikipedia Page. https://en.wikipedia.org/wiki/Docker_(software)
4. Graphite Home Page. https://graphite.readthedocs.io/en/latest/
5. Grafana Home Page. https://grafana.com/grafana
6. Kibana Homepage. https://www.elastic.co/products/kibana/
7. Elasticsearch Homepage. https://www.elastic.co/products/elasticsearch
8. Ansible Github Page. https://github.com/ansible
9. Hacker New, Dockerhub Security Breach April 2019. https://thehackernews.com/2019/04/docker-hub-data-breach.html
10. Cfengine Github Page. https://github.com/cfengine/core
11. Walsh, D.: Docker security features in RHEL7. https://opensource.com/business/14/7/docker-security-selinux
12. Seccomp Documentation Page. https://www.kernel.org/doc/Documentation/prctl/seccomp_filter.txt
13. Docker User Namespace Remap Configuration Documentation. https://docs.docker.com/engine/security/userns-remap/
14. Using eBPF to Bring Kubernetes-Aware Security to the Linux Kernel by Dan Wendlandt, Isovalent. https://docker.guru/2019/07/10/using-ebpf-to-bring-kubernetes-aware-security-to-the-linux-kernel-dan-wendlandt-isovalent/
15. Harbor Homepage. https://goharbor.io/

16. CLAIR Github Page. https://github.com/coreos/clair
17. Nivlheim Github Page. https://github.com/usit-gd/nivlheim
18. Rundeck Homepage. https://www.rundeck.com/open-source
19. Kubernetes Homepage. https://kubernetes.io/
20. Cloud Native Computing Foundation Home Page. https://www.cncf.io/
21. Kubernetes Wikipedia Page (Histroy). https://en.wikipedia.org/wiki/ Kubernetes#History
22. Kubernetes Distributions and 'Kernels' - Tim Hockin & Michael Rubin, Google. https://www.youtube.com/watch?v=fXBjA2hH-CQ
23. Isenberg, K.: Hard Problems Regarding Kubernetes in Production. https://twitter. com/KarlKFI/status/1020518198817406976
24. Kubespray Github Page. https://github.com/kubespray
25. NAISible Github Page. https://github.com/nais/naisible
26. Documentation of OKDs EFK Stack. https://docs.okd.io/latest/install_config/ aggregate_logging.html
27. Documentation of Filebeat Advanced Autodiscovery. https://www.elastic.co/ guide/en/beats/filebeat/6.7/configuration-autodiscover-advanced.html
28. Documentation of OKDs Advanced Audit Logging. https://docs.okd.io/latest/ install_config/master_node_configuration.html#master-node-config-advanced-audit
29. Zabbix Home Page. https://www.Zabbix.com/
30. OKD Prometheus Operator and Cluster Monitoring. https://docs.okd.io/3.11/ install_config/prometheus_cluster_monitoring.html
31. Zabbix' Prometheus Integration. https://Zabbix.com/documentation/current/ manual/config/items/itemtypes/prometheus
32. GitOps, Coined by WeaveWorks. https://www.weave.works/blog/gitops-operations-by-pull-request
33. Openstack RDO Project Homepage. https://www.rdoproject.org/
34. Norwegian Cloud Infrastructure for Research and Education (UHIaaS) Homepage. http://www.uh-iaas.no/
35. Terraform Homepage. https://www.terraform.io/

Enabling GPU-Enhanced Computer Vision and Machine Learning Research Using Containers

Martial Michel$^{(\boxtimes)}$ and Nicholas Burnett

Data Machines Corp., Ashburn, VA, USA
{martialmichel,nicholasburnett}@datamachines.io
https://datamachines.io

Abstract. Video analytics frameworks often rely on Neural Networks to perform their tasks. For example, a "You Only Look Once" object detection algorithm applies a single neural network to each image, divides the image into regions, and predicts bounding boxes (weighted by the predicted probabilities) with probabilities for each region. Those algorithms often run more efficiently on hardware accelerators. Libraries which use CUDA enabled GPUs can achieve tremendous advances in speed for those functionalities. Frequently, video analytic researchers develop large solutions to allow them to solve problems with complex setup procedures for other researchers to be able to duplicate their efforts. Here we present a software solution that can be run on multiple computer environments without having to customize systems and software, and support the measurement of the performance of machine learning algorithms on disparate datasets. In this publication, we introduce a common base container that provides GPU-optimized access to common Computer Vision (CV) and Machine Learning (ML) libraries, and can be used as the building container (think Docker `FROM`) for complex analytics to be interactively designed and tested, and as the base for Docker container images that can be shared between analytics researchers.

Keywords: Computer Vision · Machine Learning · GPU · Docker container

1 Introduction

Video analytics and its applications have been a core technical challenge for many years.

The National Institute of Standards and Technology (NIST) Text REtrieval Conference (TREC) Video Retrieval Evaluation (TRECVID) [1] is an evaluation challenge series that has been run annually since 2003 to promote progress in content-based retrieval from digital video via open, metrics-based evaluation. Numerous challenges have been created within this evaluation series, including

© Springer Nature Switzerland AG 2019
M. Weiland et al. (Eds.): ISC 2019 Workshops, LNCS 11887, pp. 80–87, 2019.
https://doi.org/10.1007/978-3-030-34356-9_8

Video Search, Surveillance event detection, Instance search, Multimedia event detection, Localization, Video Hyperlinking and many others.

Similarly, the DARPA Media Forensics [2] program looks to develop technologies for the automated assessment of the integrity of an image or video, and integrate these in an end-to-end media forensics platform.

The Current video analytics solutions and systems that have been evaluated are largely opaque and technology development in this area is generally limited to strategic partnerships and consortia. The resulting proprietary interfaces and stovepipes make it impractical and uneconomical for the research community and burgeoning video analytics businesses to penetrate these established ecosystems.

In order to further development of video technology solutions, the tools, analytics, and best practices for the development, use, and assessment of video analytics data and technologies require an open extensible environment to facilitate state-of-the-art solutions.

One of the many commonalities of a video analytics Research & Development framework is that researchers are using more CUDA GPU, more Computer Vision, and more Machine Learning to solve those challenges. As container orchestration mechanisms (such as Kubernetes) become more available, the design of specialized and optimized containers to solve one problem is commonplace. However, these are large, often contain artifacts of their training, and are not reusable in a repeatable High Performance Computing (HPC) infrastructure.

There is a need to create open and user-friendly development frameworks for Research & Development that enable collaboration where analytics, tools, and systems are available in the context of a scalable, maintainable, secure, and interoperable ecosystem. In the following, we present our first step toward this reference framework by providing a container for video analytics researchers.

In this publication, we define a reference framework base container to enable computer vision researchers be able to integrate often used core technologies, and provide them with a reusable container to build their own research using the provided container as the FROM in their Dockerfile. After discussing this solution, we will introduce researchers to its use through an interactive shell, and demonstrate its utility when running an object detection and object classification on a video.

2   Defining the Base Container

2.1   System Setup: Ubuntu, CUDA, Docker, Nvidia-Docker

For the purpose of this publication, we have set up a system (AMD64 & Intel EM64T based, with at least 2 GHz dual core processor, 8 GB of system memory, and 50 GB of free hard drive space with internet access and a Nvidia CUDA-enabled GPU card (see https://developer.nvidia.com/cuda-gpus for additional information) on an Ubuntu Linux 18.04 LTS [64-bit PC (AMD64) desktop image from http://releases.ubuntu.com/18.04/], and installed the Nvidia CUDA drivers (CUDA 10.1 installation instructions can be found at https://docs.nvidia.com/cuda/cuda-installation-guide-linux/index.html), as well as the stable Community Edition (CE) of Docker[1], and finally, the Nvidia Docker[2] runtime for the Docker daemon that abstracts the Nvidia GPU(s) available to the host OS using the Nvidia driver.

A blog post detailing the complete setup process is available in addition to this paper, to assist users with the installation process, and can be found at http://www.datamachines.io/devrandom/2019/6/20/toward-a-containerized-nvidia-cuda-tensorflow-and-opencv.

2.2   Docker and Container Runtime

Docker (https://www.docker.com/) is an open source platform used to deploy applications or services using containers on different operating systems. Containers are technological solutions to package an application and all its resources and components within a self-contained, isolated environment.

Researchers benefit from a simple-to-install, easy-to-use environment; therefore, we selected the docker container runtime for its ability to build, package, share and run containers. The focus of this use case is to enable the research community to benefit from high-performance computing (HPC) enabling containers to support their needs. For HPC users, the `Dockerfile` and container images for this project are both publicly available, therefore the use of an HPC optimized container ecosystems is possible. For example, the SARUS [3] *OCI-compliant container runtime* can import the Docker container image from its public repository and run at scale on provided HPC systems.

2.3   TensorFlow

TensorFlow (https://www.tensorflow.org/) is an open source library designed to assist researchers in developing and training ML models using a comprehensive, flexible ecosystem of tools and libraries. TensorFlow is available as a GPU-optimized Docker container image, running CUDA 9.0 on an Ubuntu 16.04 to create virtual environments that isolate a TensorFlow installation from the rest of the system while sharing the resources of the host machine.

2.4   OpenCV

The Open Source Computer Vision Library (OpenCV, https://opencv.org/) is an open source computer vision and machine learning software library, with more than 2500 optimized algorithms to support classic and state-of-the-art computer vision and machine learning algorithms. OpenCV can be compiled with CUDA GPU support and OpenMP (https://www.openmp.org/) for shared-memory and high-level parallelism on multi-core CPUs.

---

[1] Docker CE installation instructions can be found at https://docs.docker.com/install/linux/docker-ce/ubuntu/.

[2] The Github repository for Nvidia Docker (v2) is available at https://github.com/NVIDIA/nvidia-docker.

2.5   Cuda_tensorflow_opencv

Data Machines Corp. (DMC) has created a `cuda_tensorflow_opencv` container image by compiling a CUDA- and OpenMP-optimized OpenCV `FROM` the GPU-optimized TensorFlow container image. This image is designed to contain many tools often used by data scientists and to support machine learning research, with frameworks such as NumPy (https://www.numpy.org/), pandas (https://pandas.pydata.org/), and Keras (https://keras.io/).

DMC has made the `Dockerfile` and supporting files, including usage and build instructions, publicly available on its GitHub at https://github.com/datamachines/cuda_tensorflow_opencv. Building this container image is a long process. The initial attempt to auto-build the container on Docker Hub from the repository on GitHub took over four hours and was automatically canceled by the build system. On a 2.8 GHz quad-core 7th Gen i7, using an SSD, and running 8 concurrent `make`, it still takes 1 h (per `tag`) to build. As such, we have made available on our Docker Hub the final builds for different tags which can directly be used as `FROM` from further Docker containers images, at https://hub.docker.com/r/datamachines/cuda_tensorflow_opencv.

3   Using the Base Container

3.1   Testing Code from a Bash Terminal

The image tags follow the `cuda_tensorflow_opencv` naming order. As such, `9.0_1.12.0_4.1.0` refers to *CUDA 9.0*, *TensorFlow 1.12.0*, and *OpenCV 4.1.0*, and `10.0_1.13.1_3.4.6` refers to *CUDA 10.0*, *TensorFlow 1.13.1* and *OpenCV 3.4.6*. Docker images are also tagged with version information for the date (`YYYYMMDD`) of the `Dockerfile` against which they were built from, added at the end of the tag string (following a dash character) such that `9.0_1.12.0_4.1.0-20190605` matches the `Dockerfile` built on *June 5th, 2019*.

As of June 5th, 2019, the following tags are available on the Docker Hub: `9.0_1.12.0_3.4.6`, `9.0_1.12.0_4.1.0`, `10.0_1.13.1_3.4.6`, and `10.0_1.13.1_4.1.0`. The following shell script (`runDocker.sh`) will set up the X11 passthrough and give the user a root shell prompt, as well as mount the current directory as `/dmc`. If you want to run the base container as a non-root user, add `-u $(id -u):$(id -g)` to the `nvidia-docker` command line, but ensure that you have read/write/execute access to your working directories and files.

```
1  xhost +local:docker
2  XSOCK=/tmp/.X11-unix
3  XAUTH=/tmp/.docker.xauth
4  xauth nlist $DISPLAY | sed -e 's/^..../ffff/' | xauth -f
     $XAUTH nmerge -
5  nvidia-docker run -it --runtime=nvidia --rm -e DISPLAY=
     $DISPLAY -v $XSOCK:$XSOCK -v $XAUTH:$XAUTH -e XAUTHORITY
     =$XAUTH -v ${PWD}:/dmc --ipc host cuda_tensorflow_opencv
     :${CTO_TAG} /bin/bash
6  xhost -local:docker
```

To use it, the full tag of the container image should be passed as a `CTO_TAG` environment variable. For example, to use 9.0_1.12.0_4.1.0-20190605, run `CTO_TAG=9.0_1.12.0_4.1.0-20190605 ./runDocker.sh`. Note that `./` can be replaced by the location of `runDocker.sh` so that the user can mount its current working directory as `/dmc` in order to access local files. Once the tool is started, a bash shell is available to the researcher. By doing so, code can be placed in the mounted location, edited on the local system and transparently being used within the running container.

For example, if the user places a picture (named `pic.jpg`) in the `/dmc` directory, the following example script (naming it `display_pic.py3`) run as a container will display the picture on the user's X11 display.

```
1  import numpy as np
2  import cv2
3
4  img = cv2.imread('pic.jpg')
5  print(img.shape, " ", img.size)
6  cv2.imshow('image', img)
7  cv2.waitKey(0) & 0xFF
8  cv2.destroyAllWindows()
```

Because the user's directory is available within the running container, the user can keep altering and testing their code from a repeatable test framework.

By using this GPU-enabled container, it is possible to design and test CV and ML analytics and system code without having to setup an environment and modify this environment into an unstable condition. The use of a self-destructing (the `--rm` argument on the `nvidia-docker`) container image allows the use of a repeatable test framework.

Once the user is done using the repeatable test framework, it is then possible to integrate the desired content within a new container using the `cuda_tensorflow_opencv` container image as its `FROM`.

3.2 Integrating Darknet and Yolo V3 Python Bindings

A `cudnn_tensorflow_opencv` can be created from the base `cuda_tensorflow_opencv` by installing the required `cudnn` packages available from Nvidia (registration required, download the main/dev/doc deb files for cuDNN that can be retrieved from https://developer.nvidia.com/rdp/cudnn-download).

From there, a `FROM` hierarchy can be built so that

```
|ubuntu (*1)
|  |nvidia/cuda (*1)
|  |  |tensorflow:tensorflow (gpu) (*1)
|  |  |  |datamachines/cuda_tensorflow_opencv (*1) (*2)
|  |  |  |  |cudnn_tensorflow_opencv (*2)
|  |  |  |  |  |dmc_gpu_darknet_yolo34py (*2)
```

where *1 is a public repository and *2 a Docker image created for supporting video analytics.

To demonstrate a machine learning application, we propose to use an application of object detection and object classification, particularly the integration of an independent third-party, technological solution within our GPU-optimized container image. This leads us to use the Darknet[3] "You Only Look Once"[4] algorithm using Python bindings[5].

A `dmc_gpu_darknet_yolo34py:20190605` container image can be built using the following `Dockerfile`:

```
1   FROM cudnn_tensorflow_opencv:9.0_1.12.0_3.4.6-20190605
2
3   RUN mkdir /wrk \
4       && cd /wrk \
5       && git clone https://github.com/pjreddie/darknet \
6       && cd darknet \
7       && sed -i 's/GPU=0/GPU=1/;s/CUDNN=0/CUDNN=1/;s/OPENCV=0/
            OPENCV=1/;s/OPENMP=0/OPENMP=1/;s%-L/usr/local/cuda/
            lib64%-L/usr/local/cuda/lib64 -L/usr/local/cuda/lib64/
            stubs%' Makefile \
8       && make
9   ENV DARKNET_HOME /wrk/darknet
10  ENV LD_LIBRARY_PATH /wrk/darknet
11
12  ENV GPU 1
13  ENV OPENMP 1
14  ENV OPENCV 1
15  RUN cd /wrk \
16      && git clone https://github.com/madhawav/YOLO3-4-Py.git \
17      && cd YOLO3-4-Py \
18      && pip3 install pkgconfig \
19      && pip3 install cython \
20      && python3 setup.py build_ext \
21      && python3 setup.py install
22
23  WORKDIR /wrk
24  CMD /bin/bash
```

Within this container, it is possible to use Python code to:

```
1   # Load PyDarknet and import the Detector and Image functions
2   from pydarknet import Detector, Image
3   [...]
4   # Specify the Darknet YOLO parameters; adapting <> content to
        actual paths
5   net = Detector(<cfg_path>, <weights_path>, <data_path>)
6   [...]
7   frame = # function to obtain a frame
8   dframe = Image(frame) # convert it into a frame for the
        Detection algorithm
9   results = net.detect(dframe) # obtain all the candidates objects
10  for cat, score, bounds in results: # for each found object
        obtain
```

---

[3] (Open Source Neural Networks in C https://pjreddie.com/darknet/.

[4] YOLO v3 https://pjreddie.com/darknet/yolo/.

[5] https://pypi.org/project/yolo34py/.

```
11    # category, confidence score, bounding box (with x, y, h, w)
12    [...]
```

What makes this possible is the core Docker image that we built to support a reproducible and reusable high-performance solution for video analytics by creating "building blocks" container images, which are reusable and extensible in supporting machine learning on images/videos, and optimized for GPU.

Fig. 1. "You Only Look Once" running on a video file: processing frame per frame, detecting and classifying objects found using the available GPU

Using this method, we have performed an object detection on a video file, and displayed frame per frame the bounding box as well as the category name (see Fig. 1).

The result of this integration demonstrates the ease of abstraction of the GPU-optimized Docker Image it is built "FROM" (the CUDA + TensorFlow + OpenCV Docker Image), and performs object classification (with bounding boxes) on a video file at about 11 frames per second (fps) on an Nvidia GTX 1070. The same task performed on CPU-only took 17 s per frame (spf) (i.e. 0.06 fps), using 1x core of an i7 2.8 GHz processor. The same CPU-only test running on all 4x cores of the same processor still took 7 spf (i.e. 0.14 fps).

The Docker image hierarchy (i.e. cuda > tensorflow > opencv > cudnn > darknet + pydarknet) demonstrates why the "building blocks" approach is the right one to design a reproducible and reusable video streaming ML & CV HPC solution. Because the "building blocks" approach can be used as the foundation for novel analytics, it reduces the technical barrier of entry: a researcher can focus on the analytics, not the system deployment. Because they are Docker images, they can be moved from Linux host to Linux host without losing capabilities.

4   Conclusion

In this publication, we demonstrate the utility of containers to provide a testbed for researchers needing a repeatable, GPU-optimized base container for computer vision and machine learning. We have also introduced the reader to its use in interactive development, as well as presented an example of use as the base for more sophisticated video analytics.

As a component of an analytic researcher toolbox, it provides a building block toward sophisticated solutions and is a first iteration toward a reusable framework for Research & Development that enables collaboration.

It can be integrated within Kubernetes when using the `nvidia-docker` runtime (for more information, see https://kubernetes.io/docs/tasks/manage-gpus/scheduling-gpus/).

Further development for this container is planned, particularly its building off the core TensorFlow, independent of the TensorFlow Docker Hub provided container, as this container has a few CVEs that need to be addressed[6]. As this solution is also aimed as being used as an edge compute node, the integration within edge analytics compatible hardware is being investigated.

References

1. George A., et al.: TRECVID 2016: evaluating video search, video event detection, localization, and hyperlinking. In: Proceedings of TRECVID 2016. NIST, USA (2016). https://www-nlpir.nist.gov/projects/tvpubs/tv16.papers/tv16overview.pdf
2. Guan, H., et al.: MFC datasets: large-scale benchmark datasets for media forensic challenge evaluation. In: 2019 IEEE Winter Applications of Computer Vision Workshops (WACVW), pp. 63–72. IEEE (2019). https://www.nist.gov/publications/mfc-datasets-large-scale-benchmark-datasets-media-forensic-challenge-evaluation
3. Mariotti, K.: SARUS: an OCI-compliant container runtime for HPC. HPC-AI Advisory Council, April 3rd 2019. http://hpcadvisorycouncil.com/events/2019/swiss-workshop/pdf/030419/K_Mariotti_CSCS_SARUS_OCI_ContainerRuntime_04032019.pdf

---

[6] Because we are using older tagged version of *tensorflow* container, which is built from an older *ubuntu:16.04* base container, some security patches have not been applied to that older containers.

Software and Hardware Co-design for Low-Power HPC Platforms

Manolis Ploumidis[✉], Nikolaos D. Kallimanis, Marios Asiminakis,
Nikos Chrysos, Pantelis Xirouchakis, Michalis Gianoudis, Leandros Tzanakis,
Nikolaos Dimou, Antonis Psistakis, Panagiotis Peristerakis,
Giorgos Kalokairinos, Vassilis Papaefstathiou, and Manolis Katevenis

Foundation for Research and Technology – Hellas (FORTH), Heraklion, Crete, Greece
{ploumid,nkallima,marios4,nchrysos,pxirouch,yanoudis,ndimou,psistakis,
perister,george,papaef,kateveni}@ics.forth.gr

Abstract. In order to keep an HPC cluster viable in terms of economy, serious cost limitations on the hardware and software deployment should be considered, prompting researchers to reconsider the design of modern HPC platforms. In this paper we present a cross-layer communication architecture suitable for emerging HPC platforms based on heterogeneous multiprocessors. We propose simple hardware primitives that enable protected, reliable and virtualized, user-level communication that can easily be integrate in the same package with the processing unit. Using an efficient user-space software stack the proposed architecture provides efficient, low-latency communication mechanisms to HPC applications. Our implementation of the MPI standard that exploits the aforementioned capabilities delivers point-to-point and collective primitives with low overheads, including an eager protocol with end-to-end latency of $1.4\,\mu s$. We port and evaluate our communication stack using real HPC applications in a cluster of 128 ARMv8 processors that are tightly coupled with FPGA logic. The network interface primitives occupy less than 25% of the FPGA logic and only 3 Mbits of SRAM while they can easily saturate the 16 Gb/s links in our platform.

1 Introduction

With cluster computation power moving towards exascale, cost both in terms of installation and operation will play a significant role in future data centers and HPC clusters. This may impose a full system reconsideration from the ground up. More specifically, the processor, the memory hierarchy, the system interconnects and the system software may require fundamental changes to meet expectations for applications' performance.

With the end of Dennard's scaling, high-end computing chips turn to architectures that mix many, simple, RISC-like low-power processors with power-efficient accelerator units [6,7,17]. These heterogeneous chip multiprocessors are expected to use 3D-stacked DRAMs in order to improve their bytes-per-flop ratios. Along this direction, we need efficient interconnects to move data across system's distributed memories. These interconnects should be efficient not only

© Springer Nature Switzerland AG 2019
M. Weiland et al. (Eds.): ISC 2019 Workshops, LNCS 11887, pp. 88–100, 2019.
https://doi.org/10.1007/978-3-030-34356-9_9

among the chips of a blade, but also among the blades of a rack or across racks. An efficient interconnect should offer low latency and high throughput, and also issue multiple outstanding transactions in order to hide the memory latency and overlap the communication with computation.

However, efficient communication does not come for free. Traditional communication protocols deplete precious processor and memory cycles. More specifically, a common rule-of-thumb states that 1 GHz of CPU power is consumed per Gbit/s of (unidirectional) Ethernet-based traffic [12]. Additionally, by copying the message payload to intermediate buffers at network injection or reception time, the memory bandwidth is consumed needlessly and the caching subsystem is stressed. In order to offload the CPU from the overheads that the network protocols induce, two options are available. The first one is to deploy smart network interface cards (NICs), while the second one is to resort interconnects with memory semantics, e.g., InfiniBand [15] Aries [3]. These solutions rely on expensive hardware, since they have to support complex and continuously evolving operations. Moreover, such network interfaces have relatively big physical dimensions, e.g., a medium-sized PCIe network card. On the other side of the spectrum, cache-coherent memory interconnects implement intricate protocols in order to maintain consistency among caches [11]. These protocols are typically implemented in hardware, because they operate in the critical path of load and store instructions; nevertheless, typically they are very inefficient on simple copy operations due to protocol-induced overheads.

In this work, we propose simple but generic network interface primitives that can be integrated in the same chip with the main processor. In order to achieve low latency and low CPU overhead, the network interface supports *virtualized, user-level initiated, protected and reliable* bulk and synchronization-oriented transfers that completely bypass the kernel. Integrating the network interface in the same chip (or package) with the processors and the memory interconnect offers the possibility to use the same block both for on-chip and system level communication, thus saving cost and reducing the silicon area footprint. In our scheme, the network interface exploits he IOMMU unit of the processor to translate process-level virtual addresses to physical memory pages, thus avoiding the need for a separate, synchronized TLB inside the network interface card, as well as the need to pin the pages involved in communication, We handle the occasional page faults that may occur in RDMA transfers by retransmitting the failing packets in hardware.

In addition, we implement a library that allows user-level accesses to network interface primitives, and an MPI runtime that supports real HPC applications. The main characteristics of our communication stack are the following:

- The required hardware is simple enough to be integrated on the processor chip, but offers all the features needed for protected low latency communication and adequately supports complex communication mechanisms (e.g., MPI).
- Our communication protocols completely offload the CPU and bypass the kernel on the communication path, thus being suitable for low-power (RISC-like) processors.

– The proposed communication architecture is demonstrated through an efficient port of the MPI standard that implements point-to-point and collective primitives that exploit the hardware capabilities.

We have implemented the network interface primitives and the full network stack in a large HPC prototype consisting of ARM processors tightly coupled with the network interface (and other accelerators) implemented in the Zynq Ultrascale+ FPGAs. We run real HPC applications (e.g., LAMMPS [1]) on a 128-core cluster. Our results show that:

– Our implementation of the network interface blocks in Xilinx Ultrascale+ FPGA utilizes only 25% (70 K LUTS) of the available LUTS and 10% of the available BRAMS (3 Mbits).
– Our communication architecture is able to provide efficient communication mechanisms to HPC applications.
– The MPI implementation introduces low overheads, while the exploitation of the eager protocol gives us an end-to-end latency of just a bit more than 1 µs (see Sect. 5).
– MPI applications show almost linear scaling in a many real-world workloads.

The remainder of this paper is organized as follows. In Sect. 2, we describe our network interface primitives. In Sect. 3, we present the user-level library and the MPI port. Next, in Sect. 4 we describe our evaluation platform and our performance evaluation results. Finally, we conclude in Sect. 5 with discussions and future work items.

2   Network Interface Primitives

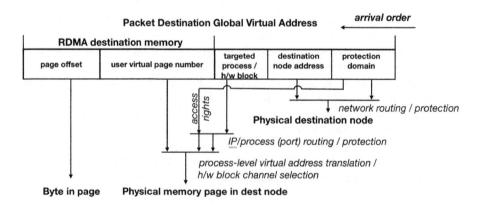

Fig. 1. The global virtual address space assumed in this work as carried on a network packet.

We consider an environment in which all memory locations belong to a Global Virtual Address Space (GVAS) and can be addressed by network packets. In our prototype, a GVAS address is 80 bits. The network interface provides mechanisms that allow to multiple software and hardware processes to initiate multiple concurrent transfers to mailboxes and processes address space (both uniformly addressable within our GVAS) without kernel involvment.

Figure 1 depicts an example of the GVAS, as used to specify the destination address of the first payload byte in an RDMA network packet. In order to access a location in the GVAS, a packet needs to specify a *protection domain id (PDID)*, 16 bits in our prototype, which is used by the hardware to safely check the initiator's access rights on particular GVAS locations. The PDIDs allow the administrator to create virtual groups of collaborating processes that share their virtual memory space, while protecting against unwanted accesses when we consolidate multiple such groups of processes on the platform. In order to shield against attacks, the PDID carried in network packets can only be set by network interface hardware, using registers set by systems software based on the process that requests a network channel (virtual interface).

The global virtual address of a packet additionally specifies a node ID, i.e. the physical location of the node in which the virtual location is contained. In our prototype, we have 22 bits node IDs, allowing 4M nodes, and 42 address bits for 4 Terabytes within each node. With 16-bits PDID, we can have up to 64K parallel instances of this deployment sharing the cluster. In principle, the node ID should also be virtual in order to allow process migration [10]. However, in our current prototype we assume a static mapping of GVAS node IDs to physical nodes – i.e. endpoints of the interconnect. Within the node, the GVAS expands further to identify a specific local port (3 bits in our prototype), such as a peripheral/accelerator or a (CPU) process with private memory space. Finally, the virtual address field can specify a channel (or virtual interface) of a peripheral or a byte in the virtual memory of a CPU or accelerator process (39 bits). Accesses to virtual locations from the network interface may be cacheable, reading memory locations that have updates present in caches or invalidating cache entries in case of writes.

Our network interface provides separate hardware primitives (i) for bulk data (RDMA) transfers and (ii) for latency-sensitive control messages.

Packetizers and Mailboxes: For fast notification (control) messages, we have built a *virtualized packetizer* and a *virtualized mailbox*. These blocks have been designed for latency-critical control messages. At the sending node, the virtualized packetizer offers 64 virtual interfaces (pages) that can be allocated to different threads and processes. Each page provides four (4) channels, where each channel can be used by the owner process to transfer a packet and monitor its execution by polling on specific bits of the page (i.e. load command). Each channel can be in one of the following states: ongoing, acknowledged, negatively acknowledged, timed out. A process acquires a page of the packetizer from a kernel driver. The driver writes into a special hardware register for this page the PDID of the requesting process, and returns to the process a virtual address which is mapped to the physical address of the packetizer page.

A transfer starts with the process filling up the payload of the transfer into the channel address using (posted) store commands, and is commenced when it writes the payload size and the destination address on a designated address of the channel. The hardware is responsible for creating a network packet that carries the user-defined payload and destination address, as well as the appropriate PDID. All hardware transactions additionally contain a unique transaction id that is filled up by the hardware and is used to match the end-to-end acknowledgements. A packetizer may target any location of the GVAS, such as the process virtual address or a virtual mailbox.

The virtualized mailbox is hardware block that consists of 64 virtual interfaces. The mailboxes keep their data in DRAM and in the L2 caches, but their tail pointers are maintained and updated by the hardware while their read pointers by the user-level libraries that read the data. Processes can acquire mailboxes from a kernel driver which associates each virtual interface with the PDID of the corresponding process group. When a packetizer sends a message to a virtualized mailbox, the receiving hardware checks the packet's PDID and tries to match it against that of the virtual mailbox, generating a NACK when these do not match. The mailbox may also drop a packet when it is full. Otherwise, the packet is enqueued into the virtual mailbox and an ACK is generated and routed to the issuing packetizer node. User processes can poll for new arrivals in their mailboxes by reading from a virtual addresses that has been memory-mapped to the physical address of their virtualized mailbox.

Simple RDMA: For large data transfers, we have built a simple virtualized RDMA engine, with coordinated units running at the sending (TX) and receiving (RX) endpoints. The RDMA engine implements an effective, hardware-level multi-path transport that provides reliability guarantees, allowing to completely bypass the kernel stack on I/O operations.

Every (Write or Read) RDMA operation transfers a message between two GVAS locations: the source, which in our implementation is always local to the TX engine that will realize the transfer, and the destination, which is local to the RX engine of the transfer. A detailed description of the hardware RDMA engine is subject of a future work item.

When running MPI applications, we can think that every process has its own virtual space, which is a subspace of the system-level GVAS. All memory accesses issued by the network interface go through a multi-channel I/O-MMU[1] to translate the virtual to physical addresses and to verify the access rights of the initiating processes using the PDID associated with a hardware channel or carried along a network packet. The I/O-MMU keeps a local translation lookaside buffer (TLB) and a page walker engine that runs through the page table of the targeted process to handle TLB misses. Page faults generate NACKs that are propagated to the source in order to retry the transaction.

---

[1] System MMU in the case of ARM processors.

3   HPC Prototype

This section provides a brief overview of the HPC prototype where the proposed software-hardware codesign was ported and evaluated. This prototype has been developed within the ExaNeSt project – for a more detailed description and the full potential of the project please refer to [9].

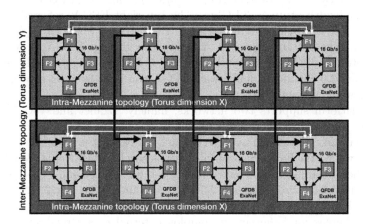

Fig. 2. HPC platform prototype used for porting and evaluating the proposed software-hardware codesign.

A high-level view of the prototype used in this study is depicted in Fig. 2. This currently consists of two mezzanines each one carrying four (4) *Quad FPGA Daughter Boards (QFDBs)* for a total of 32 FPGAs or 128 ARMv8 cores. The QFDBs, depicted through green boxes, are connected in a 2D Torus topology. The prototype is still growing in size – at the time of writing, it uses a 3D Torus topology to connect six (6) mezzanines, and, after the next planned update, it will reach 12 mezzanines, (48 QFDBs, 192 FPGAs, 512 ARM cores).

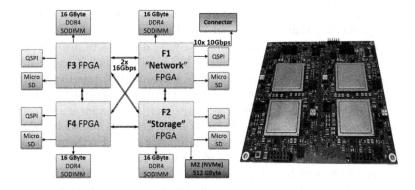

Fig. 3. QFDB block diagram and actual board.

As shown in Fig. 3, each QFDB provides four (4) interconnected FPGAs, a large amount of memory, and one SSD, within a small footprint (120 mm x 130 mm). The FPGAs are Xilinx Zynq Ultrascale+ devices (ZCU9EG), featuring four (4) ARM-A53, 16-GByte DDR4, along with a rich set of hard IPs and reconfigurable logic. Effectively, having two mezzanines, the prototype used for evaluation purposes in this study consists of 128 low-power ARMv8 cores.

There are two GTH transceivers (16 Gb/s each) for each FPGA pair, offering a total bandwidth of up to 32 Gbps. The top right FPGA, referred to as the Network FPGA, provides connectivity to the external world through ten (10) GTH links. The bottom right FPGA, named the Storage FPGA, provides connectivity to the NVMe memory through PS-GTR transceivers implementing a 4xPCIe Gen 2.0 channel. Finally, each FPGA can boot from an attached NOR flash, accessible through QSPI.

Our platform supports two networks, namely, Exanet and 10G Ethernet. Exanet is a custom packet-based hierarchical interconnect realized over high speed serial links, developed by FORTH and INFN (Istituto Nazionale di Fisica Nucleare) within the ExaNeSt project, using as baseline APENet [4]. Within each QFDB, there is an all-to-all connectivity, both for Exanet and Ethernet traffic, shown using black arrows among $F1$, $F2$, $F3$, and $F4$ in Fig. 2. As discussed above, in ExaNet we use a multi-dimensional Torus topology to connect the QFDBs, whereas for Ethernet, we employ external commercial switches with one 10G Ethernet interface per QFDB.

4   User-Level Communication Library

Part of the proposed architecture is a user-space API that allows user-level access to the hardware blocks described in Sect. 2, that is, a simple RDMA engine, virtualized packetizer and virtualized mailbox. The simplicity of the hardware blocks provided by the network interface allows for a minimal but powerfull user-space API.

The virtualized mailbox/packetizer hardware blocks that are exposed through the user space API allow the realization of user-level low-latency atomic message delivery. More precisely, this API gives to application threads the functionality for attaching a virtual interface of the virtualized mailbox and of the virtualized packetizer that reside on the local compute node. Notice that only the functionality for attaching/detaching the virtual interfaces involves the kernel of the operating system. Specifically, a kernel driver that is responsible for the mailbox hardware block exposes a set of hardware registers to threads and processes. With this set of hardware registers, the users can send and/or receive small messages to/from remote processes in a user-level manner. The provided API allows applications to atomically send messages of up to 64-bytes to any virtual interface (or process address) of any remote node. Furthermore, in case that a thread has acquired an interface of the virtualized mailbox, it is also able to receive messages sent by remote nodes in the same protection domain. The messages generated by the packetizer wait for an end-to-end acknowledgment, and can be retriggered in case of time-out.

The user-space API also allows applications or runtimes (such as the MPI implementation) to perform RDMA protected transfers with virtual local and remote addresses, without involving the kernel of the operating system. The API is quite minimal, providing calls for contructing a remote virtual address, inserting a descriptor, and for polling for completion. Both RDMA read and RDMA write operations are supported.

5 MPI Implementation over the Proposed Architecture

This section presents a partial implementation of the MPI standard, tunned to take advantage of the hardware design described in Sect. 2. This MPI implementation is realized on the HPC prototype described in Sect. 3, which has been developed in the ExaNeSt project [2]. From now on, we will refer to the proposed MPI implementation as *Exanest-MPI*. This MPI implementation is characterized as partial since it provides support for point-to-point and collective primitives while it does not support one-sided and MPI-IO communications. These primitives are delegated to an MPICH library (going over the Ethernet network) that is slightly modified to expose a communicators context ID – this is a 16-bit field needed to distinguish messages on different communicators.

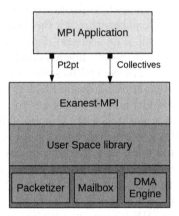

Fig. 4. Proposed co-design components.

In Fig. 4 we provide an overview of how Exanest-MPI exploits the proposed software-hardware co-design to provide an efficient MPI library. The hardware blocks that it relies on are the virtualized mailbox/packetizer and the RDMA engine. Access to these blocks is provided through the user-space library which gives user-level access to hardware blocks avoiding the kernel intervention. In short, the packetizers and mailboxes are exploited to relay control traffic, such as, message envelopes and MPI acknowledgments, in a low latency manner. For data transfers, we exploit the high throughput offered by the RDMA engine.

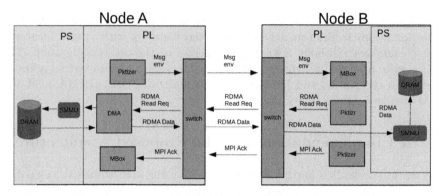

Fig. 5. Rendezvous protocol demonstrated through a pair of matching MPI_Send and MPI_Recv.

As far as point-to-point primitives are concerned, we have implemented both a rendezvous and an eager protocol. Figure 5 depicts the steps along with the hardware blocks involved in realizing the rendezvous protocol. Recall that multiple prototype nodes are arranged in a torus topology through a custom packet-based interconnect, where each node consists of four (4) Zynq FPGAs or 16 Armv8 cores. Inter-node traffic passes through the routers contributed by INFN within the ExaNeSt project [2]. The scenario depicted is as follows: a process running on node A issues an *MPI_Send* while a second process belonging to node B posts the matching receive. For control messages the low latency mechanism provided by the virtualized mailbox hardware block is used. In the above figure, process on node A uses the virtualized packetizer to send a message envelope to its peer process (arrows annotated with *Msg env* label in the above figure). Message envelopes for MPI messages typically contain the following information: *source*, *destination*, *tag*, and *communicator*. In our case, the message envelope also carries the buffer advertised by the process issuing the send operation. The message envelope is sent from a packetizer of node A to a mailbox in node B. As soon as the process on node B receives the message envelope in the virtualized mailbox used by the MPI library, it initializes an RDMA read from the remote virtual address extracted from the message envelope to the local virtual address described in the *MPI_Recv* call. The RDMA read requests is routed to node A, and is executed as an RDMA write operation by the RDMA TX engine. Note that reading (writing) data from (to) memory goes through the SMMU to translate virtual to physical addresses. When the RDMA read completes on node B, the process running on it will use a virtualized packetizer to send an MPI acknowledgment back to the peer process on node A[2].

---

[2] Note that, at the hardware level, the transfer has been separately acknowledged from the RX engine on node B to the TX engine on node A.

The low latency communication mechanism provided the packetizer and mailbox is also leveraged to implement an *eager protocol*. Messages of up to 32 bytes are sent through the packetizer without initializing an RDMA transfer.

In the current version of the MPI library discussed, almost all collective operations except for less frequently used ones are supported. The algorithms used to implement collective operations are the ones also used in MPICH and summarized in [16]. In the current MPI library version, for the case *MPI_Bcast*, *MPI_Reduce*, and *MPI_Allreduce*, the same algorithm is employed for small and large messages. Part of ongoing work is the validation of more efficient algorithms for the aforementioned primitives and large message sizes.

Evaluation

In this section we present the evaluation of the proposed communication architecture. Results are derived through both micro-benchmarks and a scientific MPI application triggering all components from all layers of the proposed co-design. Recall that Fig. 4 shows that point-to-point and collective MPI primitives are handled by Exanest-MPI using the proposed user-space communication library to exercise the implemented hardware blocks of the Exanet network.

In order to assess the performance of the proposed hardware and software blocks, the well known osu latency and osu allreduce micro-benchmark were used [14]. Two different sets of runs were performed for each of them. The first one uses the standard rendezvous protocol (Table 1) and the second one exploits the eager protocol available in Exanest-MPI (Table 1). For each set of runs, message size was set to 8 bytes and each run involved nodes at different distances starting from nodes in the same QFDB up to nodes that are 3 hops away. Note also that distance in terms of hop is only meaningful for the case of the ExaNet network (2D torus described in Sect. 3. Nodes that are 2 hops away in terms of ExaNet are connected through the saem Ethernet switch). Table 1 shows that the latency between nodes that are 1 hop away is almost higher than $6\,\mu s$ when no eager protocol is employed. However, eager protocol cuts down this latency to $1.5\,\mu s$. This is so because the eager protocol eliminates the overhead of the initialization of a DMA transaction whenever a packet of small size is transmitted. For processes that are placed in the same QFDB board, osu latency value becomes as low as $1.21\,\mu s$. As Table 1 also shows, ExaNest MPI outperfors MPICH utilizing TCP/IP over Ethernet (referred to as *standard MPICH* hereafter). Even for the case of 3 hops travelled for the case of ExaNest MPI, osu latency achieved by ExaNeSt MPI with eager protocol enabled is almost 20 times lower than the one achieved by standard MPICH. As this table also shows, for the case of the osu allreduce microbenchmark, ExaNest MPICH achives alomst 10 times lower latency than standard MPICH. The first reason for this performance benefit is that ExaNest MPI relies on the user-space API described in Sect. 4 which offers user-level access to the hardware blocks. In contrast with TCP/IP over Ethernet, the overhead of a system call is avoided. Secondly, the hardware blocks exploited by ExaNeSt MPI are part of the reconfigurable logic of each node (also discussed in Sect. 2) which means that communication does not share the CPU with computation as in the case of standard MPICH. There is ongoing work in order to lower the latency under the barrier of $1\,\mu s$.

Table 1. Osu latency and osu allreduce (usecs) with Exanest-MPI

ExaNet distance	Osu latency (8bytes)			Osu all reduce (8bytes)		
	No eager ExaNeSt MPI	Eager ExaNeSt MPI	TCP MPI	No Eager ExaNeSt MPI	Eager ExaNeSt MPI	TCP MPI
Intra-qfdb	4.97	1.21	37.2	19.13	6.69	70.5
Inter-qfdb (1 hop)	6.06	1.50	39.7	20.28	7.21	70.8
Inter-qfdb (2 hop)	7.47	1.75	39.4	21.41	7.71	69.8
Inter-qfdb (3 hop)	8.43	1.99	40.1	22.34	8.12	70.6

The proposed software-hardware co-design approach along with Exanest-MPI was also evaluated using the LAMMPS [1] scientific benchmark. LAMMPS is a state-of-the- art molecular dynamics code [13]. From the LAMMPS benchmark suite, the *rhodopsin* problem was selected. Different runs are obtained by varying the number of nodes (N) and the number of timesteps which are expresses as $N * 100$. For every *rhodopsin* run, 3 OpenMP threads were used. As in the case of the osu latency micro-benchmark, two different set of runs were performed, one using the standard rendezvous protocol and another exploiting the eager protocol available in Exanest-MPI. For each run Table 2(a) reports the number of timesteps per second that were achieved with higher values indicating better performance. This table also shows that the throughput achieved by the *osu_bibw* microbenchmark increases with message size.

Table 2. (a) LAMMPS performance (Timesteps/s) with Exanest-MPI (no eager protocol), (b) Osu bibw intra QFDB (Bandwidth (MB/s))

Num of FPGAs	no eager	eager
1	1.041	1.041
2	2.024	2.023
4	3.811	3.815
8	7.228	7.242
16	13.302	13.349
32	23.319	23.364

(a)

Msg size (bytes)	Bandwidth (MB/s)
8	7.29
64	24.90
256	88.88
1K	341.8
4K	863.8
16K	1100.3
1M	2221.0

(b)

6   Conclusions and Future Work

In this work, we described a hardware-software co-design for future low power processors. We have designed and implemented in hardware simple network interface primitives that are integrated close to the CPU, occupy less than 25% of a

Xilinx Ultrascale+ FPGA, and are suitable for bulk memory-to-memory transfers and for fast control messages. The hardware blocks are virtualized, and exploit the IO MMU to allow zero-copy, user-level initiated, reliable transfers, thus minimizing latency and the CPU overhead. On top of the NI primitives we derived an efficient MPI implementation that achieves a nearly $1\,\mu s$ OSU microbenchmark latency in a cluster of 128 ARM cores. Ongoing work includes deriving performance results on a liquid cooled version of the HPC platform described populated with 512 ARM cores.

Acknowledgments. This work is supported by the European Commission under the Horizon 2020 Framework Programme [8] for Research and Innovation through the EuroEXA project [5] (g.a. 754337), the EU H2020 FETHPC project Exanode (g.a. 671578) and the ExaNeSt project (g.a. 671553) [2].

References

1. LAMMPS Molecular Dynamics Simulator. Sandia National Laboratories. https://lammps.sandia.gov
2. The ExaNest project. European Exascale System Interconnect and Storage. GA-671553. www.exanest.eu
3. Alverson, B., Froese, E., Kaplan, L., Roweth, D.: Cray xc series network. Cray Inc., White Paper WP-Aries01-1112 (2012)
4. Ammendola, R., et al.: Apenet: a high speed, low latency 3d interconnect network. In: cluster, p. 481. Citeseer (2004)
5. EuroEXA: European Exascale System Interconnect and Storage. https://euroexa.eu/
6. Feldman, M.: Fujitsu switches horses for post-k supercomputer, will ride arm into exascale. Recuperado de (2016). https://www.top500.org/news/fujitsu-switcheshorses-for-post-k-supercomputer-will-ride-arm-intoexascale
7. Fu, H., et al.: The sunway taihulight supercomputer: system and applications. Sci. China Inf. Sci. **59**(7), 072001 (2016)
8. HORIZON 2020: The EU Framework Programme for Research and Innovation. https://ec.europa.eu/programmes/horizon2020/
9. Katevenis, M., et al., N.C.: The exanest project: Interconnects, storage, and packaging for exascale systems. In: 2016 Euromicro Conference on Digital System Design (DSD), pp. 60–67, August 2016. https://doi.org/10.1109/DSD.2016.106
10. Katevenis, M.G.: Interprocessor communication seen as load-store instruction generalization. In: The Future of Computing, essays in memory of Stamatis Vassiliadis. In: Bertels, K., et al. (eds.) Delft, The Netherlands. Citeseer (2007)
11. Katz, R.H., Eggers, S.J., Wood, D.A., Perkins, C., Sheldon, R.G.: Implementing a cache consistency protocol, vol. 13. IEEE Computer Society Press (1985)
12. Leitao, B.H.: Tuning 10gb network cards on linux. In: Proceedings of the 2009 Linux Symposium, pp. 169–185. Citeseer (2009)
13. LAMMPS Benchmark suite. http://lammps.sandia.gov/bench.html
14. OSU Micro-Benchmarks. http://mvapich.cse.ohio-state.edu/benchmarks/
15. Pfister, G.F.: An introduction to the infiniband architecture. High Perform. Mass Storage Parallel I/O **42**, 617–632 (2001)

16. Thakur, R., Rabenseifner, R., Gropp, W.: Optimization of collective communication operations in MPICH. Int. J. High Perform. Comput. Appl. **19**(1), 49–66 (2005). https://doi.org/10.1177/1094342005051521. http://dx.doi.org/10.1177/1094342005051521
17. Yokokawa, M., Shoji, F., Uno, A., Kurokawa, M., Watanabe, T.: The k computer: Japanese next-generation supercomputer development project. In: IEEE/ACM International Symposium on Low Power Electronics and Design, pp. 371–372. IEEE (2011)

Modernizing Titan2D, a Parallel AMR Geophysical Flow Code to Support Multiple Rheologies and Extendability

Nikolay A. Simakov[1] , Renette L. Jones-Ivey[1,2] , Ali Akhavan-Safaei[2] ,
Hossein Aghakhani[2] , Matthew D. Jones[1] , and Abani K. Patra[1,2(✉)]

[1] Center for Computational Research, University at Buffalo, Buffalo, NY, USA
abani@buffalo.edu
[2] Computational and Data-Enabled Sciences and Engineering, University at Buffalo,
Buffalo, NY, USA

Abstract. In this work, we report on strategies and results of our initial approach for modernization of Titan2D code. Titan2D is a geophysical mass flow simulation code designed for modeling of volcanic flows,
debris avalanches and landslides over a realistic terrain model. It solves
an underlying hyperbolic system of partial differential equations using
parallel adaptive mesh Godunov scheme. The following work was done
during code refactoring and modernization. To facilitate user input two
level python interface was developed. Such design permits large changes
in C++ and Python low-level while maintaining stable high-level interface exposed to the end user. Multiple diverged forks implementing different material models were merged back together. Data storage layout was
changed from a linked list of structures to a structure of arrays representation for better memory access and in preparation for further work on
better utilization of vectorized instruction. Existing MPI parallelization
was augmented with OpenMP parallelization. The performance of a hash
table used to store mesh elements and nodes references was improved by
switching from a linked list for overflow entries to dynamic arrays allowing the implementation of the binary search algorithm. The introduction
of the new data layout made possible to reduce the number of hash table
look-ups by replacing them with direct use of indexes from the storage
class. The modifications lead to 8–9 times performance improvement for
serial execution.

Keywords: Code refactoring · Python API · Geophysical mass flows

1 Introduction

Titan2D is a tool developed for simulation of granular flows over digital elevation models of natural terrain including volcanic flows, landslides, debris and

We gratefully acknowledge the support of NSF awards OAC 1339765.

© Springer Nature Switzerland AG 2019
M. Weiland et al. (Eds.): ISC 2019 Workshops, LNCS 11887, pp. 101–112, 2019.
https://doi.org/10.1007/978-3-030-34356-9_10

snow avalanches [9,11,13]. It is widely used by researchers and civil protection authorities for risk assessment and mitigation scenarios for these hazards.

The Titan2D code built on an earlier AMR infrastructure developed for fluid dynamics simulations using adaptive *hp* finite elements [7]. While this allowed rapid and reliable development, it also baked in design decisions in data structures and coding that were sub-optimal. Secondly, the wide adoption of the code based on its ability to use sophisticated computing methodologies like AMR and its application to many different physical contexts led to many versions and forks.

Many choices in the software design are motivated by how the computational problem is mapped to available hardware, therefore it is not surprising that many legacy applications do not operate optimally on modern systems. In the case of Titan2D many currently sub-optimal designs decisions were largely motivated by a file system input/output bottleneck caused by the inability to hold the whole topography in the available system memory. Since the I/O performance limitation disguised other inefficiencies, many design decisions favored ease of development or debugging. For example, a hash values lookup table (hash function based on space filling curve (SFC) ordering of cells) was used for accessing neighboring elements every time paying extra penalty for a search. However, it simplified the development as there is no need to track memory location of neighboring elements for each element and the performance penalty was way below that caused by poor filesystem performance. Nowadays most of the topological maps can fit into main memory and the element search penalty significantly degrades the overall performance.

Titan2D is open source and distributed through GitHub as source code and binaries. Code consists of over 50 thousand lines (generated using David A. Wheeler's SLOCCount) and is primarily written in C++, with new interface in Python and GUI written in Java. Titan2D is also available through an online resource for collaboration in volcanology research and risk mitigation called Vhub (vhub.org). It is a turnkey solution for running Titan2d. Since 2011 there were 650 unique users from 8 different counties (about 100 active users each year) executing more than 5 thousand simulation runs. Because GitHub does not provide enough statistic on utilization (it tracks cloning and visits for only two weeks), we cannot estimate the number of users who obtained code through GitHub and running it on their system. In our HPC center, all jobs executed Titan2D consume more than 2 million CPU hours (257 CPU years) since 2015 (tracking with XDMoD). Thus, performance and usability improvement benefit not only the developers' team and close affiliates but also other users as well.

In this work we report on our initial approach to modernize Titan2D. We replace the fixed format input with a Python interface, redesigned the data structure layout to benefit vectorized instructions, combined multiple forks under the same codebase, reduced hash table use with direct index use and introduced hybrid OpenMP/MPI parallelization. In the next section we briefly describe the Titan2D governing equation and numerical methods it uses to solve them. In the following sections we described our modifications in more detail.

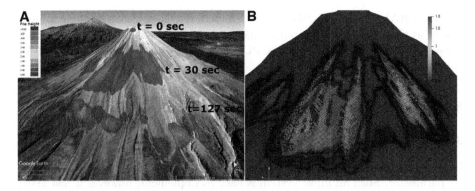

Fig. 1. Simulation of block and ash flows that have occurred at the Colima volcano, Mexico, during the 1991 year eruptive episode. **A**. Overlay of three snapshots from the simulation visualized with Google Earth. **B**. Illustration of adaptive grid used for same simulation, the snapshot corresponds to the middle region from *A*, visualized with ParaView.

2   Titan2D and Benchmark Problem

Titan2D is based upon a depth-averaged model for an incompressible continuum, a "shallow-water" granular flow. We will briefly review the functionality here; details of the modeling and numerical methodology may be found in the literature [9,11]. The conservation equations for mass and momentum are solved with different rheologies modeling the interactions between the grains of the media and between the granular material and the basal surface. The resulting hyperbolic system of equations is solved using an MPI parallel, adaptive mesh (see Fig. 1B for adaptive grid illustration), Godunov scheme. Titan2D also takes as input the topography maps in the form of Digital Elevation Models (DEM) and (where available) local information on basal resistance to the flow. Source codes, examples and Linux binaries are available at the Titan2D GitHub repository (https://github.com/TITAN2D).

Benchmark Problem. To measure the overall performance impact from our modifications, block and ash flow simulations on the Colima volcano, Mexico, (see Fig. 1) were done for the legacy and modernized versions. The simulations were done with Coulomb material model, first order method with AMR. The calculation was done for 10000 iterations totalling 2 min total flow time. The average number of elements was 141 thousand. This simulation corresponds to one from the Titan2D examples with increased space accuracy (number of cells across smallest pile axis increased from 16 to 32). This problem is of lower middle size. Number of users have done much larger computations while larger portion of users perform calculations on similar or smaller sizes. Thus, for the purpose of analysis this problem size exercises the code well. The legacy code was executed in MPI mode while modernized in OpenMP mode. Calculations were done on two systems: (1) desktop (Intel Core i7-9800X Skylake-X CPU, 8 cores, 3.80 GHz;

64 GB of RAM (4xDDR4-2800); 1TB SATA SSD) and (2) academic compute cluster at the Center for Computational Research, University at Buffalo, SUNY (Intel Xeon Gold 6130, Skylake-X CPU, 2x16 cores, 2.10 GHz; 192 GB of RAM; Isilon file-system).

3   Refactoring Strategies

3.1   Adopting a Python Interface

Legacy Titan2D has a fixed input file format, where each line specifies a particular parameter. Such an input system is easy to implement, however it has many drawbacks and lacks flexibility and is hard to extend to new models and options. Unused parameters still should be specified even when unused making software hard to maintain. Nevertheless, ease of implementation made this choice popular in older software especially given harder to find and steeper learning curves to other C/C++ implemented alternatives. In our modernization effort the fixed input format was replaced with a Python interface.

A Python interface to C++ applications provides many benefits. It is highly flexible and allows the implementation of multiple methods and models under the same codebase as well as a number of ways to extend the application. Its programmability allows the creation of higher-level simulations schemes like parameter search and better integration with a Graphical User Interface (GUI). It also has a number of ways to interface with programs and libraries written in C, C++ and Fortran. Due to these benefits Python is used in many scientific applications and chosen for modernization or to serve as "glue" for multiple legacy applications [5,6,8]. All this makes Python very popular and many modelers are familiar with it. It also has a large ecosystem of scientific libraries and applications. Thus, the implementation of the Titan2D Python interface would allow closer integration with that ecosystem and reuse of already developed software.

There are a number of ways for creating a Python API for C++ application. We choose to go with the Simplified Wrapper and Interface Generator (SWIG) since it provides automatic mapping of C++ classes and functions to Python. Such a mapping results in a Python API which closely follows C++ API. Due to the anticipation that the C++ API would change drastically during modernization, we chose two level design for Python interface: the low-level Python interface is automatically generated by SWIG and high-level is built on top of it and is exposed to the end user. This allows us to stabilize the user exposed high-level interface earlier while giving us the freedom of unrestricted modifications of underlying C++ and low-level Python interface.

Python programming language combined with C++ allows us to use the strengths of both languages. Python has significantly less boilerplate allowing fast prototyping and development while C++ can achieve high performance. Thus, using Python in performance non-critical places would lead to faster development. This way we also significantly improve user interaction by implementing extensive user input validation in the high-level Python layer.

3.2   Merging Multiple Forks

The rigidity of the fixed input format resulted in multiple Titan2D forks which differ in physical model or numeric method. Pressed by deadlines or the desire to test promising new models led some researchers to replace parts of code with a new implementation instead of extending the original code. This lead to multiple forks which largely differ only in few places where the new model replaced the original one. Because forks were branched at different times the forked version also differs in some core Titan2D classes and functions which were changed after the fork. Maintaining multiple forks implementing different methods in multiple places is a labor-intensive task even using modern tools with sophisticated branch merging routines. Another drawback of multiple forks is that improvements to core functionality in one fork do not automatically transfer to other forks. The Python interface provides the flexibility to keep multiple models under the same code base. In new Titan2D, the model and its parameter are specified by user using high-level Python interface and the parameters are propagated down to the C++ level. Because of forking at different times, code replacement for new models and lack of multi-model support in the original code an automatic merge was not possible. Consequently, the merging was done manually with heavy utilization of Integrated Developer Environment (IDE) code analysis tools and stand-alone difference visualization and merging tools.

The first merged fork was one implementing two-phase Pitman-Le material model [10] with the original single phase model. Due to the need to describe two separate phases this fork has significant differences with original Titan2D and the following strategy was used. First two branches were merged together into a single source code base and functionally similar parts were placed next to each within a conditional compilation if-else macro. That is, if the COULOMB_TWO_PHASE macro was defined the resulting code produced two phase Pitman-Le material model and the original single phase Coulomb model otherwise. Such single code base allows to see clearly all changes associated with merging fork and identify the best strategy to support both models without recompilation. To aid merging the visual differences and merge tool called Meld [4] was used. Next, the parameters needed for new models were identified and new model selection and parameters specification were implemented in Python with their propagation to the C++ level. Finally, the conditional compilation if-else macro was replaced either with conditions or separate functions depending on the amount and type of differences. Two other forks implementing Voellmy-Salm [2] and Pouliquen-Forterre [3,12] rheologies had very small and isolated changes and did not required as extensive work as the previously described merge. Briefly, the Python interface was extended to enable setting new parameters and propagate them to C++; next, several functions was converted from Fortran to C++, re-named and copied to master Titan2D. The converted Fortran function performed a computation for a single cell; thus it did not provide benefits of Fortran compiler optimization and converting to C++ inline function also allows to eliminate functional call and add space for further optimization.

The lesson learned: do not allow forks to diverge significantly; think about extensibility of the software and use modern tools for version control.

3.3   Changing Data Layout to for Modern CPU Architectures

Modern CPUs benefit greatly from vector instructions which require use of primitive data type arrays (e.g. arrays of integers or doubles) with stride of one for best results. Therefore, for performance reasons, Structure of Arrays (SoA) concept is more preferable than arrays of structure [1] which was often used due to better fit of object oriented design. The original Titan2d stores elements and nodes data in allocated on demand objects, the pointers to which are stored in hash tables with a linked list for overflow entries (Fig. 2A). This storage method closely resembles a linked list of structures and does not allow efficient use of vector instructions. Therefore, the first step was to redesign the data layout to a structure of arrays. Although it looks like an enormous amount of work requiring rewriting most of the code, taking advantage of C++ object-oriented design, data encapsulation strategy, modern refactoring tools, and regular expression substitution allows us to do it in a relatively short period of time.

The new data layout utilizes a structure of arrays approach. The hash table class was augmented with elements storage capability where the element's properties are stored as separate arrays and values with same array index belonging to the same element (Fig. 2B). To do a seamless transition, the original element class which stores the element properties values are transformed to an element properties accessor class which is a wrapper around new elements storage class and only stores the element index from the elements storage class. The element properties accessor class retains the same API as the original element properties class, allowing the existing functions to use new accessor class instead of old element class without any modifications as long as they do not access elements data directly but through getters and setters methods. Unfortunately, as is the case with many older transitional C to C++ codes even though getters and setters are present, they are not consistently utilized throughout the code. In addition, some of getters and setters operate on pointers. Therefore, prior to a transition to SoA, preparatory work needed to be done to ensure complete data encapsulation and work of getters and setters on proper data reference type.

The overall process of changing the data layout was as follow: (1) reinforce proper data encapsulation throughout the code, (2) create new elements storage class with necessary data manipulation infrastructure and old element class members transfer to new storage class, and (3) update the hot functions to use new storage class directly instead of the element accessor class.

Data Encapsulation Reinforcement. For each member of element and node class we ensure first that the proper data access interface is used. For example, accessor to class member *double state_vars[NUM_OF_STATE_VARS]* was *double* get_state_vars()* which essentially is almost the same as to use data directly and throughout the code it is used for both setting and getting. It was replaced with *double state_vars(const int idim) const* and *void state_vars(const int idim,* *const double value)*. Next the direct class members access was replaced with respective getters and setters methods. Manual refactoring for a large code is a tedious task. Fortunately the refactoring and code analyzing capabilities of modern IDEs significantly simplify interface transformation. NetBeans and Eclipse were used in this work. Unfortunately, these IDEs do not allow automatic conversion from direct members access to access through getters and setters. To aid this task the following strategy was used for each member of element and node classes: first using the IDEs refactoring tools the class member was renamed to a code-wide unique name to prevent accidental substitution during the next step, then the regular expression substitution was used to replace class member accesses with the proper getter or setter method. The IDEs regular expression substitution tool allows guided substitution throughout the whole code reducing changes for unintended substitution. The regression tests were run regularly to ensure that refactoring behaved as expected. Overall the described process is a labor intensive task, however it is tractable with proper tools and strategy.

Elements Content Storage Class. One of the key features of Titan2D is adaptive mesh refinement. This poses additional challenges on the elements properties storage class, due to the need to insert new elements as well as delete old elements. The linked structures on x86 architecture often have the best performance for this type of operation however their performance suffers during access to a small selection of their content due to a pseudo random access pattern. A structure of arrays approach offer better performance in the latter case but has worse performance for element insertion and deletion. With proper care this performance impact can be drastically reduced.

In the legacy implementation the elements are exclusively referred by their space filling curve (SFC) value. Without getting into detail the SFC function maps 2D coordinates to a single value and with adequate care for numeric accuracy such a mapping is unique. The elements are found through the hash table which uses truncated SFC values as the hash value. When iteration through all elements is needed it is done by iterating though all hash table entries. Thus, for elements insertion and removal one only needs to maintain the hash table and it is possible to use element appending in the elements properties storage class and delayed deletion. Elements are inserted only during the mesh refinement step and removed only during the coarsening step. For sequential storage of elements properties a new container class template, tivector, was created, it is similar to standard C++ std::vector class in that it pre-allocates internal arrays for larger number of entries (capacity) than requested (size) and reallocation happens only if new size exceeds the capacity. When a new element is created its properties are appended to corresponding tivectors and its mapping of SFC value to index is added to the hash table. This way the performance for new element insertion is comparable with a linked list implementation. For the element deletion it needs only be removed from hash table, the actual deletion from storage arrays can happen later in bulk. With the exception of mesh refinement and coarsening steps, the elements properties are stored ordered according to the elements SFC value. This is done in order to improve memory locality using

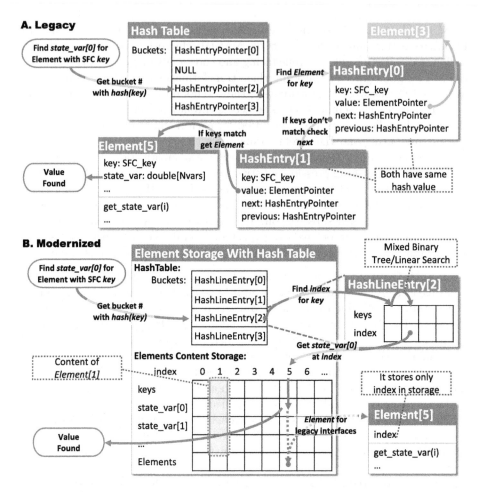

Fig. 2. Diagram showing search for state_var value of element with key SFC value. Another common operation is to cycle other all elements: in legacy version it was accomplished by looping through all linked hash entries for each hash bucket, in modernized version it is done by going through array of required data.

the locality property of SFC. Points with similar SFC values are located close to each other in 2D space. The SFC values are also used for load balancing during MPI runs. Actual element data deletion and reordering of new elements occurs only after both mesh refinement and coarsening steps are complete. Keeping track of new and removed elements allows us to use it during sorting step and reduce computational cost.

The migration to new element storage class was completed by removing all members from the old element class, adding the index of the element within the storage class and by changing the getters and setters to use the respective values from the storage class. The class member access method was implemented as an inline method allowing most modern compilers to replace the function call with direct class member access. The performance improvement due to changing the layout was 12.9%.

Updating the Hot Functions. The time-consuming functions were identified using Intel VTune profiler. In these functions the access to elements content were replaced with direct access to respective variables from the element content storage class. In most cases due to the unstructured grid the conditions for successful automatic vectorization were not met and thus we did not get significant performance improvement from this particular step. However, in the element storage class there is no strict requirements on the order of stored elements (the ordering by space filling curve values is done mainly for region distribution between MPI processes) and therefore in the future we may be able to reorder the elements to favor vectorized instructions.

3.4   Efficient Indexing for Elements/Nodes Addressing

As mentioned in the previous section, in the legacy implementation the elements are referenced by their SFC values and located through a hash table by their SFC value. The frequent hash table use for lookup presents a significant performance impact even for moderately sized simulations due to high amount of hash values collision (i.e. multiple entries have the same hash value). In the legacy Titan2D these collisions are resolved by a linear search through an overflow linked list of entries. Titan2D modernization replaces the overflow linked list entries with usage of standard C++ vectors for hash table buckets. This allows us to implement binary search with linear search at last level. This improvement gives us about 50% improvement in performance for large problems.

We also realized after the implementation of new elements properties storage class that we can use indexes from the storage class instead of SFC values and thus avoid the use of hash table in many cases. First, we implemented index search prior to getting into the PDE solving routines and later we implemented proper index handling during mesh refinement and coarsening.

3.5   Introducing OpenMP and Hybrid OpenMP/MPI Parallelization

Single core performance improvements have declined in recent years, resulting in an increasing number of core per node. It is common nowadays for HPC compute nodes to have half a hundred cores and many performance desktops have eight or more cores. Such high core counts and shared memory space make a multithreaded parallelization approach very attractive. Implementing parallel algorithms with OpenMP is relatively simple, although it can be challenging to achieve best possible performance. Therefore, we decided to go with hybrid OpenMP/MPI parallelization scheme and at first pay more attention to performance of pure OpenMP on a single node while ensuring that MPI parallelization is still working. Previously described modifications are mainly concerning single core performance and by adding OpenMP we following the strategy to maximize

single node performance prior moving to multi node runs. OpenMP parallelization was done for the most time-consuming parts of Titan2D. Such parts were
identified with Intel Vtune profiler. At our initial approach we largely add pragmas to implement parallel for loops (leaving room for future improvement with
more restructuring to take advantage of larger parallel regions, etc.). Due to
the large increase in performance of a single process the inefficiencies of MPI
implementation become a limiting factor for performance growth in MPI runs
to a degree that two MPI processes takes longer time to execute than a serial
run. It is not uncommon that improvements in one part of the program reveal
inefficiencies on other part as now they become a larger limiting factor.

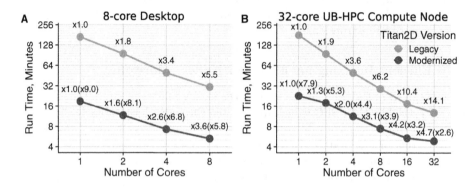

Fig. 3. Comparison of Titan2D performance as measure by execution time of Colima volcano benchmark between legacy and modernized version executed on **A** 8-core
desktop and **B** 32-core compute node from UBHPC cluster. The number for each
point shows the parallel scaling and the number in brackets shows speed-up from the
legacy version executed on same number of cores. Note the $\log_2 - \log_2$ scales. For this
benchmark, both Titan2D versions are limited to a single node.

4   Performance Improvement Evaluation

The overall effect of the modifications is shown in Fig. 3. Single core performance
is improved by 8 to 9 times, reducing calculation time from hours to tens of
minutes. OpenMP parallel run shows a very modest parallel scaling on a single
socket: the parallel speed-up is 3.6 on 8 cores, which is smaller than speed-up
of 5.5 demonstrated by legacy Titan2D (Fig. 3A). On a dual socket system the
OpenMP parallel speed-up starts to level-off on largest core count (Fig. 3C).
Interestingly, the speed-up on 2 cores is smaller for dual socket system, which is
most likely due to lack of NUMA awareness and no CPU affinity reinforcement.

The not so ideal parallel performance of the modernized version is mainly
due to a less than optimal implementation with OpenMP. To date we have
mainly concentrated on fork merge and data layout transformation. Still the
performance of modernized version on a single core of 8-core desktop is 64%
higher than the performance of the legacy version on all 8 desktop cores and for

the dual socket system 4 cores can perform better than the legacy code on the whole node (13% faster).

Table 1. Comparison of performance metrics obtained with Intel VTune profiler. Executed on eight cores, no. of elements and iterations were reduced for more tractable profiling.

Metric	Legacy	Modernized
Elapsed time, s	371.7	69.2
Instructions retired	4.28×10^{12}	1.41×10^{12}
Cycles per instruction rate (CPI)	2.84	1.50
DRAM bound, % of clockticks	60	20
Double precision GFLOPS	1.01	1.93
MPI busy wait time	0.8 s (0.2%)	
OMP parallel region, % of walltime		63.0%

Table 2. Comparison of hotspots obtained with Intel VTune profiler. Number of elements and interation was reduced for more tractable profiling.

Legacy	CPU time, s	Modernized	CPU time, s
HashTable::lookup	838.37	OMP barriers	187.88
MPI data moving	366.95	Integration step	34.08
Integration step	149.44	Slope calculation	30.38
Slope calculation	137.25	Edge states calculation	29.88
Statistics calculation	133.55	Z-direction flux calculation	15.49
Total CPU Time	2963.3	Total Time	517.1

The performance metrics, as well as hot spots obtained with Intel VTune profiler, is shown in Tables 1 and 2. As can be seen, the modernized version uses two times less instruction in part due to reducing hash table look-ups and improving its algorithm. The new version also has two times better cycles per instruction rate (CPI), that is it do twice more instruction per cycle and almost twice higher GFLOPS. In both cases, the floating point operation was not packed. The new version also reduces its memory bound. The current version still has high time for OpenMP barriers and on 63% parallel region. Therefore there is still space to improve OpenMP parallelization further.

5   Conclusions and Future Plans

Large amounts of work were done to bring Titan2D up-to-date. Introduction of a Python interface allows easier implementation of different material methods as well as numeric methods under the same source code. Merging several Titan2D forks together allows end users to use the same code for different models and discover which one suits their need. Redesign of the data layout provides better memory access and prepares the code foundation for future improvements. The current, modernized Titan2D, still largely does not use vectorized instructions, which is a non-trivial task for unstructured grids. We envision that proper ordering of elements within the storage class should allow us to implement a scheme which would benefit from vectorization. Still, modernized code already has significant performance improvement over the legacy version.

References

1. Soax: A generic c++ structure of arrays for handling particles in HPC codes. Comput. Phys. Communicat. 224, 325–332 (2018). https://doi.org/10.1016/J.CPC.2017.11.015
2. Christen, M., Kowalski, J., Bartelt, P.: Ramms: numerical simulation of dense snow avalanches in three-dimensional terrain. Cold Reg. Sci. Technol. 63(1–2), 1–14 (2010). https://doi.org/10.1016/J.COLDREGIONS.2010.04.005
3. Forterre, Y., Pouliquen, O.: Flows of dense granular media. Ann. Rev. Fluid Mech. 40(1), 1–24 (2008). https://doi.org/10.1146/annurev.fluid.40.111406.102142
4. Willadsen, K.: Meld: a Visual Diff and Merge Tool. http://meldmerge.org/
5. Krischer, L., et al.: ObsPy: a bridge for seismology into the scientific Python ecosystem. Comput. Sci. Discov. 8(1), 014003 (2015). https://doi.org/10.1088/1749-4699/8/1/014003
6. Ladwig, W.: wrf-python (version 1.2. 0). Boulder, Colorado (2017). https://doi.org/10.5065/D6W094P1
7. Laszloffy, A., Long, J., Patra, A.K.: Simple data management, scheduling and solution strategies for managing the irregularities in parallel adaptive HP finite element simulations. Parallel Comput. 26(13–14), 1765–1788 (2000). https://doi.org/10.1016/S0167-8191(00)00054-5
8. Marais, N.: Driving and extending legacy codes using python. IEEE Antennas Propag. Mag. 49(1), 140–148 (2007). https://doi.org/10.1109/MAP.2007.371002
9. Patra, A., et al.: Parallel adaptive numerical simulation of dry avalanches over natural terrain. J. Volcanol. Geothermal Res. 139(1–2), 1–21 (2005). https://doi.org/10.1016/J.JVOLGEORES.2004.06.014
10. Pitman, E.B., Le, L.: A two-fluid model for avalanche and debris flows. Phil. Trans. Roy. Soc. A: Math. Phys. Eng. Sci. 363(1832), 1573–1601 (2005). https://doi.org/10.1098/rsta.2005.1596
11. Pitman, E.B., Nichita, C.C., Patra, A., Bauer, A., Sheridan, M., Bursik, M.: Computing granular avalanches and landslides. Phys. Fluids 15(12), 3638–3646 (2003). https://doi.org/10.1063/1.1614253
12. Pouliquen, O., Forterre, Y.: Friction law for dense granular flows: application to the motion of a mass down a rough inclined plane. J. Fluid Mech. 453, 133–151 (2002). https://doi.org/10.1017/S0022112001006796
13. Takeuchi, Y., Nishimura, K., Patra, A.: Observations and numerical simulations of the braking effect of forests on large-scale avalanches. Ann. Glaciol. 1–9 (2018). https://doi.org/10.1017/aog.2018.22

Asynchronous AMR on Multi-GPUs

Muhammad Nufail Farooqi[1(✉)], Tan Nguyen[2], Weiqun Zhang[2],
Ann S. Almgren[2], John Shalf[2], and Didem Unat[1]

[1] Koç University, Istanbul, Turkey
mfarooqi14@ku.edu.tr
[2] Lawrence Berkeley National Laboratory, Berkeley, CA, USA

Abstract. Adaptive Mesh Refinement (AMR) is a computational and memory efficient technique for solving partial differential equations. As many of the supercomputers employ GPUs in their systems, AMR frameworks have to be evolved to adapt to large-scale heterogeneous systems. However, it is challenging to employ multiple GPUs and achieve good scalability in AMR because of its complex communication pattern. In this paper, we present our asynchronous AMR runtime system that simultaneously schedules tasks on both CPUs and GPUs and coordinates data movement between different processing units. Our runtime is adaptive to various machine configurations and uses a host resident data model. It helps facilitate using streams to overlap CPU-GPU data transfers with computation and increase device occupancy. We perform strong and weak scaling studies using an Advection solver on Piz Daint supercomputer and achieve high performance.

Keywords: Heterogeneous execution · Asynchronous runtime · Communication overlap · AMR

1 Introduction

Efficient utilization of computational resources and productivity of the domain scientists are the two main challenges faced for large-scale simulations. Adaptive mesh refinement (AMR) method is used for reducing computational and memory requirements and there are a number of frameworks [5,10,11,13,14,17] available for improving the productivity of the programmer. AMReX [3] is an example of such a framework designed to develop block-structured AMR applications. AMReX employs multiple levels of refinements to solve PDEs and uses a high resolution mesh at the area of interest where high accuracy is required. Astrophysics codes (e.g. CASTRO [2], Maestro [28], and Nyx [1]) and combustion codes (e.g. SMC [7], PeleLM [6]) are among the many research codes in-use today that are based on AMReX.

Currently, a quarter of Top500 supercomputers employ GPUs as the main processing power and scientific frameworks have to be evolved to adapt to heterogeneity available in the large-scale systems [21]. This heterogeneity trend in

© Springer Nature Switzerland AG 2019
M. Weiland et al. (Eds.): ISC 2019 Workshops, LNCS 11887, pp. 113–123, 2019.
https://doi.org/10.1007/978-3-030-34356-9_11

processor is expected to continue further in the next decade due to their power and performance advantage [4]. However, employing GPUs in an application is a challenging task for computational scientists. These complex machine architectures on the one hand provide us resources to accelerate computation, but they also demand a great deal of collaborative efforts to utilize resources at their full capacity both for developing new applications and porting existing ones. Thus, a runtime system targeting domain-specific optimizations can efficiently utilize the heterogeneous architectures.

In our prior work, we proposed an asynchronous AMR algorithm [8,9,15] that enables computation and communication overlap through asynchronous execution in AMR applications in a homogeneous multicore environment. In this work, we identify the challenges that arise while porting AMR applications on heterogeneous architectures and propose solutions to GPU programming in the context of AMR. To take advantage of both CPUs and GPUs, we employ hybrid execution where we deploy dynamic scheduling approach to perform computation on both CPUs and GPUs, simultaneously. The amount of work distributed among these computational units is based on their compute capability where a faster computational unit gets a larger fraction of the computational work. The device memory is scarce on GPU, and the AMR applications are data intensive therefore we choose a host-resident data model where all the data reside on the host while device memory is used as a cache. For CPU-GPU communication, we rely upon the managed memory where communication is automatically handled by the OpenACC runtime. To overlap the CPU-GPU data communication with computation, we leverage OpenACC streams. Application programmers can specify the number streams they intend to use, and the runtime will handle the scheduling of computation on these streams.

In summary, we make the following contributions:

- Asynchronous AMR execution on multiple GPUs and data transfer overlap with computation through streams
- Simultaneously scheduling of work on both CPU and GPU based on their compute capability
- Adaptation to various machine configurations in a multi-GPU environment and experiment results on CSCS's Piz Daint supercomputer, where we achieved scaling results comparable to the hand-tuned code variant.

2   Execution on Heterogeneous Architectures

In this section, we discuss the design and implementation details about the runtime support to address the challenges of enabling a multi-GPU execution of an AMR application. There are two essential optimizations to scale an AMR application on multi-GPU architectures. Firstly, the CPU-GPU data movement needs to be handled efficiently. Secondly, CPUs can be utilized for further performance gain; in other words, work can be split to execute both on the CPU and GPU simultaneously. Next, we present the data model and then the scheduler in our runtime to support execution in a multi-GPU environment.

2.1   Data Model and CPU-GPU Communication

Computation on GPU requires a task's relevant data to be present in its device memory that is limited in capacity. Thus, data needs to be moved back and forth between device and host memory, which poses a significant obstacle in scalability. Solutions both at hardware and software level are proposed to cope with the data transfer challenge [16, 19, 22]. At the hardware level, PCIe evolved from version 1.x with a bit rate of 2.5 GT/s per lane to version 4.x with 16 GT/s per lane and is expected to be 32 GT/s per lane in version 5.x [19]. A parallel data transfer technology NVLink 1.0 and 2.0 achieves 20 GT/s and 25 GT/s per lane, respectively. At the software level, initially, explicit data allocation and transfers were required to be carried out by the programmers. Unified virtual addressing was introduced to bring device and host memories under the same address space, enabling single pointer allocation [24]. Later on, unified memory technique added the automatic data migration support where data between CPU and GPU is moved either as a whole or page-wise depending on the underlying hardware support [18].

In literature [12, 20, 25, 26], there are two different data models used for GPUs, each of which has its advantages and disadvantages. First is GPU-resident data model [25, 26], where data used by computation on GPUs is always resident on device memory. In this model, only the communication data is copied to and from the host or other devices as required. Although this model puts less pressure on the CPU-GPU link, the problem size that can be used in the simulation is limited to the device memory, which makes it less suitable for applications that require a large amount of data for computation. Second is the host-resident data model [12, 20], where all data resides on the host, and device memory is used as a cache. The main issue with this model is the costly CPU-GPU data transfers. AMR applications being data intensive makes the GPU-resident data model less viable option as it would lead to underutilization of GPU due to the limited memory capacity. Let us consider the fastest supercomputer Summit: the GPU contribution in its compute power is ∼90% but its device to host memory ratio is ∼1:5. Thus a GPU-resident model can only utilize ∼17% out of the ∼90% GPU compute capacity on Summit. On the other hand, a host-resident model can better utilize Summit's GPU compute capacity.

The host-resident data model increases the load on CPU-GPU link. However, efficient CPU-GPU data transfers can reduce the effect of this increased load. CPU-GPU communication can be optimized using asynchronous data transfers where data copy of one task is overlapped with the computation of another task. This strategy can be implemented via CUDA/OpenACC streams and can be augmented with prefetching to improve the performance further. Our AMR runtime helps the application programmers create a number of streams and schedule computation on each stream, separately.

Furthermore, CPU-GPU data transfers can be carried out either manually using explicit data transfers or automatically with the help of unified memory. We chose to utilize unified memory (managed memory) because of two reasons. First, this would result in a low maintenance runtime as any changes in

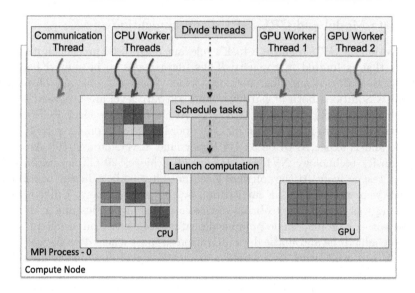

Fig. 1. Work scheduling on both CPU and GPU

the hardware architecture will not require modifications to the runtime. Second, hardware vendors are working hard to make the automatic data transfers efficient, e.g. hardware support for paging.

2.2   Scheduling on Heterogeneous Architectures

By default, our runtime schedules computation only on CPU. Within a process, the runtime divides CPU threads into communication and worker threads. Communication threads are responsible for intra-node and inter-node communication while worker threads perform the computation. Figure 1 shows a communication thread in red and worker threads in blue. The rectangle represents a task (subgrid), and colors within a rectangle represent tiles. When a task is scheduled on a CPU, the computation is distributed among worker threads through tiling where a few tiles within the subgrid are assigned to a thread [23,27]. All these worker threads are also responsible for pushing/pulling of communication data to/from the runtime.

Application programmers can explicitly turn on GPU support and specify the number of OpenACC streams in the proposed runtime. If the GPU support is turned on, then the runtime will schedule tasks for computation on both CPU and GPU. The runtime dedicates one CPU worker thread for each OpenACC stream to launch computation on GPU while the rest of the worker threads perform computation on CPU. The dedicated threads for GPU and CPU worker threads execute independently until all tasks are computed. Figure 1 shows scheduling of work on both CPU and GPU for three tasks (subgrids); one task executes on the CPU while the other two execute on the GPU

Task Graph Iterator:

```
for(TGIter tgi( tg ); tgi.isValid(); ++tgi){
  ExchangeGhost_receive(tgi, myMultiFab, ...)
  if(tgi.gpuTask)
    //compute_on_gpu(tgi, tgi.streamID)
  else
    //compute_on_cpu(tgi)
  ExchangeGhost_send(tgi, myMultiFab, ...)
}
```

Fig. 2. Asynchronous runtime's task graph iterator with support for GPUs

concurrently. The GPU worker thread launches computation of the entire sub-grid on the GPU, and the same thread is also responsible for pushing and pulling the communication data.

It is important to keep a balanced load distribution among CPUs and GPUs within a process. Load imbalance can result in inefficient use of computational units when some units are waiting idle while some are busy computing. The proposed asynchronous AMR algorithm employs an out-of-order task iterator. Thus, predicting a task being ready for scheduling is not possible and is dependent on the completion of its communication at runtime. For a balanced load distribution, ready tasks are kept in a single common queue instead of pre-distributing them among CPU and GPU. The ready task queue is accessed by a thread that schedules work on the CPU and all the threads launching work on the GPU. Whenever the CPU or GPU finishes a task, it can schedule the next task for computation from the ready queue. This will guarantee that a computational unit does not stay idle as long as there are ready tasks to be scheduled.

2.3   API

Figure 2 shows the runtime API to support execution on heterogeneous architectures. A member variable of the task graph iterator, *gpuTask*, is set if the current task is scheduled to run on the GPU. Programmer can use the iterator to check whether the current task is scheduled on CPU or GPU so that they can call the respective kernel. Relevant communication subroutines for CPU or GPU will be called automatically by the runtime without any intervention from the application programmer. Another member variable of the task graph iterator, *streamID*, contains the OpenACC stream ID for the current task scheduled on the GPU. Application programmers can use the *streamID* to implement OpenACC/CUDA streams for overlapping computation with data transfers. This interface enables an incremental acceleration with GPUs as we employ unified memory. The application programmer can provide GPU kernels either implemented using OpenACC or CUDA. The framework developers can implement communication subroutines for GPU and can modify them to increase performance without putting any extra burden on the application programmers.

Table 1. Machine specifications for Piz Daint

CPUs	Intel Xeon E5-2690 v3	GPUs	NVIDIA Tesla P100
Sockets	1	**GPUs/node**	1
Cores/socket	12	**GPU Peak DP Flops**	5 TF
Threads/core	2	**GPU Memory size**	16 GB
Clock Rate	2.6–3.5 GHz	**GPU Memory bandwidth**	520 GB/s
Main memory	64 GB	**CPU-GPU Interconnect**	PCIe 3.0
Memory bandwidth	68 GB/s	**System Interconnect**	Dragonfly

Table 2. Input configurations for heat Advection solver on Piz Daint

MPI processes per node	2	Refinement levels	2
OpenMP threads per MPI process	12	**Subcycling iterations**	2
OpenMP threads per core	2	**Refinement ratio**	2
Fab size	64^3	**Tile size**	$64 \times 4 \times 2$
Mesh size for R-T (level 0)			
(1–8)-Nodes (Strong Scaling/Weak Scaling)		$512 \times 256 \times 256$	
16-Nodes (Weak Scaling)		$512 \times 512 \times 256$	
32-Nodes (Weak Scaling)		$512 \times 512 \times 512$	
64-Nodes (Weak Scaling)		$1024 \times 512 \times 512$	

2.4   Multi-GPU Support

We employ MPI to support multi-GPU execution. In terms of the number of GPUs and CPUs, machine configurations can vary widely. Our runtime is flexible and can be easily configured to execute an application on different machine configurations. On each node, the runtime detects the number of GPU devices and exclusively binds one device per MPI process on that node if the number of devices is equal to the number of MPI processes per node. In a scenario where the number of GPUs per node are less than the number of processes per node, the runtime enables Multi Process Service (MPS) support so that multiple MPI processes can share a GPU. The current implementation does not support multiple GPUs within a single process. If there are fewer MPI processes than GPUs, some of the GPUs will not be used. Our host-resident data approach eliminates the need for explicit GPU-GPU communication because the device memory is used as a cache. A task's data is moved to the device for computation and then moved back to host after computation. The required communication, if any, is carried out between the hosts.

3   Evaluation

For performance analysis, we use the heat Advection solver [9] on Piz Daint located at Swiss National Supercomputing Centre, Lugano, Switzerland. The machine specifications are shown in Table 1. Computational kernels of the advection solver for execution on GPU were implemented using OpenACC. The input configurations for performance studies are shown in Table 2.

We present six code variants: ① *CPU* ② *GPU-Manual* ③ *GPU-Managed* ④ *Hybrid-Manual* ⑤ *Hybrid-Managed-S1* ⑥ *Hybrid-Managed-Prefetching-S1*, where for work scheduling we use three modes CPU, GPU and *Hybrid*. In the CPU mode all computation is scheduled on CPU cores. The GPU mode schedules all computation on GPU and the *Hybrid* mode simultaneously schedules computation on both CPU cores and GPU. CPU-GPU data transfers are performed either manually or through managed memory. In *Manual*, all the required data between CPU-GPU are explicitly handled through OpenACC data directives that initiate transfers on first touch either by host or device. In *Managed* memory, data transfers are handled automatically by the underlying CUDA runtime that transfers a page between CPU and GPU memories using page fault mechanism. *Hybrid-Managed-Prefetching* adds prefetching hints to start CPU-GPU data transfers beforehand. The $S1$ or $S2$ suffix indicates the number of OpenACC streams used. Advection solver contains very low computation compared to communication. Therefore, for performance comparison, we increase the amount of computation by recomputing a subgrid twice (2x) and four times (4x) when it is scheduled for computation. All these code variants use our runtime.

Figure 3 shows the strong scaling performance for all implementations using up to 8 Piz Daint nodes. We use single node CPU within each x-compute group as a baseline for that group. The CPU version uses all the 12 cores (24 hyperthreads) of the node. As shown in the figure the performance of GPU increases as we increase the amount of computation and *Hybrid-Manual* performs the best among all implementations. *Managed memory* could not beat the manually tuned data transfers but its performance improves with streams and prefetching. The code variant with managed memory, prefetching and 2 streams approaches to the performance of *Hybrid-Manual* for 4x-compute. This shows that using managed memory with prefetching and multiple streams can attain performance comparable to the manual version for compute intensive applications.

Weak scaling results on 64 nodes are shown in Fig. 4. We remove OpenACC single stream code variant to simplify the figure. *Hybrid-Manual* again performs the best among all implementations where as *Hybrid-Managed-Prefetching-S2* is the second best. The time/iteration scales almost linearly for all code variants as we weak scale. As evidenced by the strong and weak results, the runtime successfully schedules work among different types of computational resources and balances the load based on their performance.

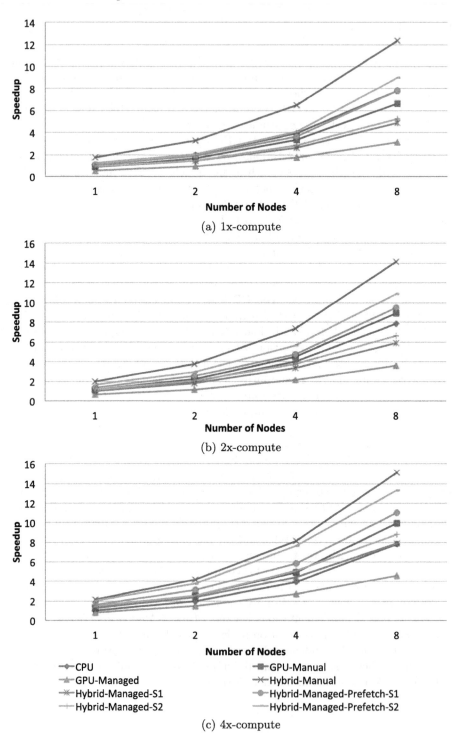

(a) 1x-compute

(b) 2x-compute

(c) 4x-compute

Fig. 3. Strong scaling comparison of different implementations and amount of computation on CSCS.

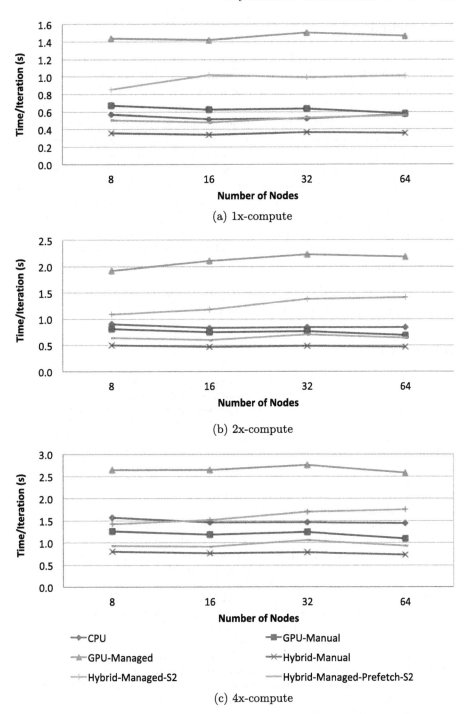

(a) 1x-compute

(b) 2x-compute

(c) 4x-compute

Fig. 4. Weak scaling comparison of different implementations and amount of computation on CSCS.

4   Conclusions

This paper presents multi-GPU extension of our previous work on asynchronous runtime for AMR applications. For heterogeneous architectures, we choose a host resident data model because device memory is limited and AMR application are data intensive. The host resident model requires extensive data transfers but the runtime has a provision to exploit streams for possible overlap of CPU-GPU communication with computation. We devise a work scheduling technique to efficiently use all computational units on a machine based on their compute capacity. We compare the performance of 6 code variants on the Piz Daint supercomputer. The results show that the code variant using automatic memory transfers with prefetching and multiple streams can reach the performance of a hand-tuned code. Future work can further optimize communication overlap by sending a task's data to GPU before scheduling the task but after completion of its dependent communication, which will eliminate the need for adding prefetching hint in the code.

Acknowledgements. This work was supported by a grant from the Swiss National Supercomputing Centre (CSCS) under project d87.

References

1. Almgren, A., Bell, J.B., Lijewski, M., Lukic, Z., Andel, E.V.: Nyx: a massively parallel amr code for computational cosmology. APJ **765**, 39 (2013)
2. Almgren, A.S., et al.: CASTRO: a new compressible astrophysical solver. I. Hydro-dynamics and self-gravity. Astrophys. J. **715**, 1221–1238 (2010)
3. AMReX: Block-structured AMR framework. https://ccse.lbl.gov/AMReX/index.html
4. Ang, J., et al.: In: 2014 Hardware-Software Co-Design for High Performance Computing (2014)
5. Colella, P., et al.: Chombo software package for AMR applications design document. Technical report, LBNL (2003)
6. Day, M.S., Bell, J.B.: Numerical simulation of laminar reacting flows with complex chemistry. Combust. Theory Model. **4**(4), 535–556 (2000)
7. Emmett, M., Zhang, W., Bell, J.B.: High-order algorithms for compressible reacting flow with complex chemistry. Combust. Theory Model. **18**(3), 361–387 (2014). https://doi.org/10.1080/13647830.2014.919410
8. Farooqi, M.N., Nguyen, T., Zhang, W., Almgren, A.S., Shalf, J., Unat, D.: Phase asynchronous AMR execution for productive and performant astrophysical flows. In: SC18: International Conference for High Performance Computing, Networking, Storage and Analysis, pp. 880–893 (2018)
9. Farooqi, M.N., Unat, D., Nguyen, T., Zhang, W., Almgren, A.S., Shalf, J.: Non-intrusive AMR asynchrony for communication optimization. In: Euro-Par 2017: Parallel Processing - 23rd International Conference on Parallel and Distributed Computing, Santiago de Compostela, Spain, August 28 - September 1, 2017, Proceedings, pp. 682–694 (2017)
10. Fryxell, B., et al.: Flash: an adaptive mesh hydrodynamics code for modeling astro-physical thermonuclear flashes. Astrophys. J. Suppl. Ser. **131**(1), 273 (2000)

11. Goodale, T., et al.: The cactus framework and toolkit: design and applications. In: Palma, J.M.L.M., Sousa, A.A., Dongarra, J., Hernández, V. (eds.) VECPAR 2002. LNCS, vol. 2565, pp. 197–227. Springer, Heidelberg (2003). https://doi.org/10.1007/3-540-36569-9_13

12. Humphrey, A., Meng, Q., Berzins, M., Harman, T.: Radiation modeling using the Uintah heterogeneous CPU/GPU runtime system. In: Proceedings of the 1st Conference of the Extreme Science and Engineering Discovery Environment: Bridging from the eXtreme to the Campus and Beyond. pp. 4:1–4:8. XSEDE 2012 (2012)

13. MacNeice, P., Olson, K.M., Mobarry, C., de Fainchtein, R., Packer, C.: PARAMESH: a parallel adaptive mesh refinement community toolkit. Comput. Phys. Commun. **126**(3), 330–354 (2000)

14. Meng, Q., Humphrey, A., Berzins, M.: The Uintah Framework: a unified heterogeneous task scheduling and runtime system. In: 2012 SC Companion: High Performance Computing, Networking Storage and Analysis, pp. 2441–2448 (2012)

15. Nguyen, T., Unat, D., Zhang, W., Almgren, A., Farooqi, N., Shalf, J.: Perilla: metadata-based optimizations of an asynchronous runtime for adaptive mesh refinement. In: Proceedings of the International Conference for High Performance Computing, Networking, Storage and Analysis, SC 2016, pp. 81:1–81:12. IEEE Press, Piscataway (2016)

16. NVLink. https://www.nvidia.com/en-us/data-center/nvlink/

17. O'Shea, B.W., et al.: Introducing Enzo, an AMR Cosmology Application. Adaptive Mesh Refinement - Theory and Applications, pp. 341–349 (2004)

18. Unified Memory on Pascal and Volta. http://on-demand.gputechconf.com/gtc/2017/presentation/s7285-nikolay-sakharnykh-unified-memory-on-pascal-and-volta.pdf

19. PCIe. https://pcisig.com/specifications/pciexpress/

20. Schive, H.Y., Tsai, Y.C., Chiueh, T.: Gamer: A graphic processing unit accelerated adaptive-mesh-refinement code for astrophysics. Astrophys. J. Suppl. Ser. **186**(2), 457–484 (2010)

21. Top500. https://top500.org

22. Unified memory. https://devblogs.nvidia.com/unified-memory-cuda-beginners/

23. Unat, D., et al.: Tida: high-level programming abstractions for data locality management. In: High Performance Computing - 31st International Conference, ISC High Performance 2016, Frankfurt, Germany, June 19–23, 2016, Proceedings, pp. 116–135 (2016)

24. Unified Virtual Addressing. https://devblogs.nvidia.com/unified-memory-in-cuda-6/

25. Wahib, M., Maruayama, N.: Data-centric GPU-based adaptive mesh refinement. In: Proceedings of the 5th Workshop on Irregular Applications: Architectures and Algorithms, IA3 2015, pp. 3:1–3:7 (2015)

26. Wahib, M., Maruyama, N., Aoki, T.: Daino: a high-level framework for parallel and efficient AMR on GPUs. In: Proceedings of the International Conference for High Performance Computing, Networking, Storage and Analysis, SC 2016, pp. 53:1–53:12. IEEE Press, Piscataway (2016)

27. Zhang, W., Almgren, A., Day, M., Nguyen, T., Shalf, J., Unat, D.: Boxlib with tiling: an adaptive mesh refinement software framework. SIAM J. Sci. Comput. **38**(5), S156–S172 (2016). https://doi.org/10.1137/15M102616X

28. Zingale, M., Almgren, A.S., Bell, J.B., Malone, C.M., Nonaka, A.: Astrophysical applications of the maestro code. J. Phys. Conf. Ser. **125**(1), 012013 (2008). http://stacks.iop.org/1742-6596/125/i=1/a=012013

Batch Solution of Small PDEs
with the OPS DSL

Istvan Z. Reguly[1,2(✉)], Branden Moore[3], Tim Schmielau[3], Jacques du Toit[3],
and Gihan R. Mudalige[2]

[1] Faculty of Information Technology and Bionics, Pázmány Péter Catholic
University, Budapest, Hungary
`reguly.istvan@itk.ppke.hu`
[2] University of Warwick, Department of Computer Science, Coventry, UK
`g.mudalige@warwick.ac.uk`
[3] Numerical Algorithms Group Ltd., Oxford, UK
{`branden.moore,tim.schmielau,jacques`}`@nag.co.uk`

Abstract. In this paper we discuss the challenges and optimisations
opportunities when solving a large number of small, equally sized discre-
tised PDEs on regular grids. We present an extension of the OPS (Oxford
Parallel library for Structured meshes) embedded Domain Specific Language, and show how support can be added for solving multiple systems,
and how OPS makes it easy to deploy a variety of transformations and
optimisations. The new capabilities in OPS allow to automatically apply
data structure transformations, as well as execution schedule transformations to deliver high performance on a variety of hardware platforms. We
evaluate our work on an industrially representative finance simulation on
Intel CPUs, as well as NVIDIA GPUs.

Keywords: Domain Specific Language · Stencil computations ·
Batching

1 Introduction

Traditional imperative programming languages, such as C/C++ and Fortran,
still dominate computational sciences. However, these were designed for a single
thread of execution in mind together with a flat memory model. In contrast,
modern hardware provides massive amounts of parallelism, billions of threads
in large-scale machines, at multiple levels (such as multiple cores, each with
wide vectors), and a multi-level memory hierarchy or even several discrete memory spaces on a single system. Such hardware complexity need to be carefully
considered for their efficient utilisation.

To allow access to new hardware features, new programming models and
extensions are being introduced - the list is far too long, but the prominent
models and extensions include MPI [6], OpenMP [4], CUDA [17] and OpenCL
[21]. Newer models also come to light with new hardware such as the introduction of OpenACC for NVIDIA GPUs and the most recent announcement of

© Springer Nature Switzerland AG 2019
M. Weiland et al. (Eds.): ISC 2019 Workshops, LNCS 11887, pp. 124–141, 2019.
https://doi.org/10.1007/978-3-030-34356-9_12

the OneAPI model from Intel for their upcoming Xe GPUs. Such diversity in both hardware, as well as programming approaches, presents a huge challenge to computational scientists; how to productively develop code that will then be portable across different platforms *and* perform well on all of them. The problem appears to have no solution in the general sense, and research instead focuses on narrowing the scope, and targeting smaller problem domains. A practical concept here is the idea of *separation of concerns*; separate the description of what to compute from how to actually do it. The challenge then is to design a programming interface that is wide enough to support a large set of applications, but it is also narrow enough that a considerable number of assumptions can be made, and parallel execution, as well as data movement, can be organised in a variety of ways targeting different hardware.

The separation of concerns approach yields a layer of abstraction that also separates computational scientists, who use these tools, from the parallel computing experts who develop these tools, whose goal is to apply transformations and optimisations to codes using this abstraction - which given all the assumptions can be much more powerful than in the general case (i.e. what general purpose compilers can do). Domain Specific Languages in high performance computing narrow their focus on a set of well defined algorithmic patterns and data structures - OPS is one such DSL, embedded in the C/C++ and the Fortran languages. OPS presents an abstraction for describing computations on regular meshes - and application written once with the OPS API can then be automatically translated to utilise various parallel hardware using MPI, OpenMP, CUDA, OpenCL, and OpenACC.

There is a rich literature of software libraries and DSLs targeting high performance computing with the goal of performance portability. Some of the most prominent ones include KOKKOS [3] and RAJA [7], which are C++ template libraries that allow execution of loops expressed using their STL-like API on CPUs and GPUs. They also support the common Array-of-Structures to Structure-of-Arrays data layout transformation. Their approach however is limited by having to apply optimisations and transformations at compile-time, and the inability to perform cross-loop analysis (though support for task graphs has been introduced, but that is not directly applicable to the problem we study here). The ExaStencils project has also developed the ExaSlang DSL which is capable of data layout transformations and some limited execution schedule transformations [12], however their approach also does not consider batching, or the kind of cross-loop analysis and transformations that our work does.

OPS was designed to tackle a moderate number of large structured meshes, where there is sufficient parallelism within each mesh. However, there is a class of applications where computations need to be carried out on a large number of small structured meshes. This algorithmic pattern is prevalent in computational finance, where predictions need to be made given a large set of different initial conditions or other parameters. Similarly, a large fraction of computations in Adaptive Mesh Refinement (AMR) computations execute the same computations on a collection of small structured blocks. With these application domains in mind, in this paper we present an extension of the OPS abstraction that makes it practically trivial to extend an OPS application computing on a single PDE system to compute on multiple systems of the same size. We are also introducing a number of optimisations and transformations specific to situations where multiple systems are present, and expose these to the user so the most performant combination can be found easily - without requiring changes in the code. Specifically we make the following contributions:

- Extend the OPS abstraction to accommodate multiple systems.
- Introduce a number of data layout and execution schedule transformations applicable to the solution of multiple systems.
- We develop an industrially representative financial application, and evaluate our work on Intel CPUs and NVIDIA GPUs.

The rest of the paper is organised as follows: Sect. 2 describes the OPS framework, Sect. 3 describes the extension of the OPS abstraction and the transformations and optimisations developed for batching. Section 4 describes the test application and the results, and finally Sect. 5 draws conclusions.

2 The OPS DSL

The Oxford Parallel library for Structured meshes (OPS), is a DSL embedded into C/C++ and Fortran [19]. It presents an abstraction to its users that lets them describe *what* to compute on a number of structured blocks, without specifying *how* – the details of data movement and the orchestration of parallelism are left entirely to the library, thereby achieving separation of concerns.

The abstraction allows the user to define blocks (`ops_block`) and describe their dimensionality (2D/3D, etc.), which serves to group datasets (`ops_dat`) together - these have specific extents, user-defined boundary regions, and an underlying datatype. Extents are defined by datasets rather than the blocks to allow for staggered grids and multigrid. When multiple blocks are defined, their datasets can be connected by user-defined halos (`ops_halo`). The user then defines a number of access patterns, or stencils (`ops_stencil`), that describe the pattern of access to neighbouring elements during computations later on. This information is sufficient to initialise and distribute data across different memory spaces and over MPI. The computations are then described as a parallel iteration on a given N dimensional range, executing a user-defined kernel (defined as a C or Fortran function pointer) at each point, accessing datasets using predefined stencils, also specifying the method of access (read/write). The parallel loop construct is `ops_par_loop`, with datasets passed wrapped in `ops_arg_dat` arguments. Mesh invariant values can be passed using the `ops_arg_gbl` argument to the parallel loops, and reductions with the `ops_arg_reduce` argument, passing in a reduction handle (`ops_reduction`), which can be queried separately. For a full description of the API, please refer to the user documentation [1].

A specific example for a parallel loop is shown in Fig. 1 - the user-defined kernel is always written from the perspective of a single iteration on the mesh,

```
1  user-defined kernel function
2 id kernel(cost ACC<double> &in, ACC<double> &out) {
3   out(0,0) = (in(0,0) + in(1,0) + in(-1,0) +
4                   in(0,1) + in(0,-1))/5.0;
5
6 .
7 t range[] = {1, 99, 1, 499};
8 s_par_loop(kernel, "smooth", block, 2, range,
9      ops_arg_dat(in, 1, S2D_5pt, "double", OPS_READ),
10     ops_arg_dat(out, 1, S2D_00, "double", OPS_WRITE));
```

Fig. 1. An example for an OPS parallel loop

with data passed in through the templated **ACC** wrappers, which allow access through the overloaded parentheses operator. The only requirement regarding the user-defined kernel is that the order in which OPS iterates through the mesh must not change the end result within machine precision. This description avoids the specification of parallelism and how data gets to the user-defined kernel - the goal of OPS is to facilitate efficient parallelisation and data movement on a variety of hardware architectures, with different parallel programming models.

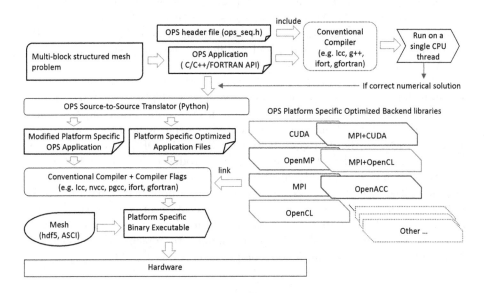

Fig. 2. The workflow for developing an application with OPS

An OPS application written once with its high-level API can immediately be compiled with a traditional compiler and tested for correctness using a header file sequential implementation of **ops_par_loop**. OPS uses an "active-library" approach to parallelising on different targets; while its API looks like that of a traditional software library, it uses a combination of code generation and back-end libraries. The full OPS build system is shown in Fig. 2. The code generation step takes the user's code, looking for calls to ops_par_loop, and parses them, gathering all information into internal data structures, that are then passed to a set of code generators targeting parallel programming methods such as OpenMP, CUDA, OpenCL, OpenACC, etc., which essentially generate the boilerplate code around the user-defined kernel, managing parallelism and data movement. These can then be compiled with target-specific compilers, and linked to the backend libraries of OPS that manage distributed and/or multiple memory spaces, and execution schedules.

During the initialisation and set-up phase of an application all mesh data is handed to OPS, and can later only be accessed through API calls. Temporaries and working arrays can be automatically allocated by OPS. While obviously limiting, it allows OPS to take full control of data management and movement. This has a number of advantages; the most prominent is the automatic distribution of data over MPI, and the management of halo exchanges - OPS is capable of running on distributed memory machines without any changes to user code, and can scale up to hundreds of thousands of cores and thousands of GPUs [11,15]. Multiple memory spaces can also be handled automatically - such as up/downloading data to/from GPUs. The layout of data itself can also be changed with the cooperation of backend logic and code generation - a simple example is the Array-of-Structures to Structure-of-Arrays conversion, which involves the transposition itself (and changed access patterns for MPI communications) in the backend, and a different indexing scheme in the ACC data wrappers handed to the user-defined kernels.

OPS having full control over the data has another key advantage; the ability to re-schedule to order of computations - not just within a single parallel loop, but across multiple ones. The execution of an OPS application can be though of as a series of transactions that access data in clearly defined ways, and unless the control flow of the user code between calls to the OPS API is affected by data coming out of OPS, it can be perfectly reproduced. This leads to the lazy execution mechanism in OPS; calls to the OPS API are recorded and stored in a queue (without actually executing them), up to a point where data has to be returned to the user. This then triggers the execution of computations in the queue, giving OPS the ability to make transformations on an intra- and inter-loop level. We have previously used this mechanism to implement cache-blocking tiling on CPUs [18], and out-of-core computations on GPUs [20].

3   Batching Support in OPS

The key need tackled in this work is that of *batching*; the same computations have to be done on not just one structured block, but a large number of them. The computations are identical except for the data that is being computed on. This of course presents trivial parallelisation opportunities, and allowing for such computations in most computations is easily done. The challenge lies in achieving high performance on a variety of hardware, which may require significant data layout and execution schedule transformations - and being able to do all this without needing changes to the high level user code.

The most trivial ways to implement solving multiple systems is to either surround the entire computational code with an iteration across different systems, or just smaller code regions (such as each computational loop). This is a natural way of coding, because it allows describing computations on a single system, and the surrounding code just passes in data for different systems. This is the approach used in most existing software - perhaps most commonly in Adaptive Mesh Refinement (AMR) codes [14,26]. The approach of surrounding several computational steps with a loop over systems is also naturally cache-friendly on CPUs, but can pose under-utilisation problems, particularly on GPUs. Loop structures with some of the common options are shown in Fig. 3.

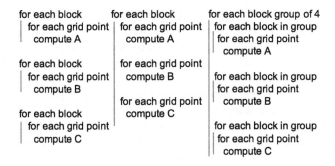

Fig. 3. Examples of loop structure formulations when solving multiple systems

More specifically with small individual systems, there may be considerable overheads in carrying out a computational step - such as getting full vectorisation, good utilisation of prefetch engines on CPUs, or kernel launches on GPUs. This is something OPS also suffers from - the generated boilerplate code that executes and feeds the user-defined kernel has non-negligible costs, which can become significant when executing on very small blocks (100–1000 grid points). Task scheduling systems [2,16] are also affected by this.

Another trivial approach is to extend the problem to a higher dimension, packing systems next to one another - e.g. packing multiple 2D systems into a 3D grid. While this does reduce the aforementioned overheads, it is less cache-friendly on CPUs, and may require significant code refactoring.

The challenge of appropriately arranging data for efficient execution, and scheduling computations to minimise overheads and improve data locality is highly non-trivial on any given platform, and is further complicated by the need for performance portability across multiple platforms. No implementation should therefore tie itself to a particular data structure or execution structure - this is what drove us to extend the OPS abstraction to support batching.

3.1   Extending the Abstraction

Our goals in designing extension of the abstraction were twofold: (1) a minimally intrusive change that makes it easy to extend existing applications, and (2) to allow for OPS to apply a wide range of optimisations and transformations to data layout and execution schedule.

First, we extend `ops_block` with an additional `count` field, which indicates the total number of systems. All datasets defined on these blocks will be extended to store data for each system. Furthermore, reductions need to return values of each system separately, therefore reduction handles, `ops_reduction`, were extended with a `count` field as well. The way computations in OPS are expressed is unchanged - loops are written as if they only operated on a single system. This extension allows for describing problems that are trivially batched.

However, there are situations, particularly when using iterative solvers, when certain systems no longer need to be computed upon, but others do. This necessitates the introduction of APIs that enable or disable the execution of certain systems. OPS adds two APIs - `ops_par_loop_blocks_all()` to indicate that computations following this point need to be carried out on all systems (which is also the default behaviour), and `ops_par_loop_blocks_predicate(block, flags)`, which takes an array of flags to indicate which systems to execute and which ones to skip in following calls to `ops_par_loop`.

Semantically, the newly introduced support for multiple systems in OPS means that each `ops_par_loop` will be executed for each system, and each reduction will compute results for each system separately, returning an array of results (through `ops_reduction_result`, indexed in the same order as the systems are. From the perspective of the user, execution is done in a "bulk synchronous" way - whenever an API call is used to get data out of OPS (such as the result of a reduction), data for all the systems is returned.

In summary, an existing single-block application can be extended to work on multiple systems with the following steps:

- Specify the number of systems when declaring an `ops_block`,
- Receive multiple reduction results from OPS, one for each system,
- Optionally, add the loop over blocks API calls, particularly when over time some systems are to be omitted from the calculations.

3.2   Execution Schedule Transformation

The two most trivial ways to execute multiple systems, as discussed above, is (1) for each `ops_par_loop` to introduce an extra loop over the different systems, and (2) to execute all `ops_par_loop` operations to the first system in one go, then to the second system, etc. On the level of loopnests, this maps down to having an extra loop over systems just above each spatial loop nest, or to have this loop over systems surround the whole computational code.

The first approach is trivial to implement in OPS as well, and it is indeed what the sequential header-file implementation does. It is also the preferred option for running on GPUs - launching a large grid of blocks and threads mitigates kernel launch costs. It is however not optimal on CPUs because while individual systems may fit in cache, all of them likely do not, leading to poor cache locality between subsequent ops_par_loop operations. Parallelisation on the CPU using OpenMP happens across the different systems, for each ops_par_loop separately, which also leads to unnecessary synchronisation points.

The second approach relies on the lazy execution scheme in OPS - as the code executes, loops are queued instead of being executed, and once execution is triggered, OPS iterates through all the systems, and within this iteration, all the parallel loops in the queue, passing each one the current system. CPU parallelisation is then done across different systems using OpenMP, which improves data locality between subsequent parallel loops and also removes thread synchronisation overheads. This optimisation can be enabled by defining the OPS_LAZY preprocessor macro.

When the memory footprint of a single system is small, and/or when efficient execution requires it (overheads of executing a single loop on a single system, as discussed above, e.g. efficient vectorisation on CPUs), one can create smaller batches of systems, and execute them together, thereby mitigating overheads, and making better use of caches. This is also facilitated by the lazy execution mechanism in OPS, in a similar way to the second approach described above, by passing batches of systems to each parallel loop in the queue. This number can be passed as a runtime argument to the application (OPS_BATCH_SIZE), and optionally the same preprocessor macro can be defined to make this size a compile-time constant, which enables further optimisations by the compiler.

3.3   Data Layout Transformation

The performance of computations can be significantly affected by how data is laid out and how it is accessed, and whether it aligns with the execution schedule. Considering that OPS owns all the data, it is free to make transformations to layout, and work with the generated code and the data accessor objects of OPS (ACC<>), so from the perspective of the user-defined kernel, these transformations are completely transparent. Given the wide array of options and target architectures, we have chosen to make these transformation options hyper-parameters - specifiable at compile- and/or run-time.

OPS expects data that is read in by the user to be passed to it when datasets are declared. Such data is supposed to follow a column major layout, and be contiguous in memory; for example for a 2D application $x\_size \times y\_size \times \#systems$. OPS can then arbitrarily swap the axes, or even break them into multiple parts.

We first introduce the batching dimension parameter - i.e. which dimension of the $N + 1$ dimensional tensor (N for spatial dimensions of an individual system, $+1$ the different systems) storing data should be used for the different systems. We have implemented code in OPS that can perform an arbitrary change of axes on input data. There are two obviously useful choices; the last dimension - the way data is given to OPS in the first place - or the first dimension, so values at the same grid point from different systems are adjacent to each other:

$\#systems \times x\_size \times y\_size$.... The batching dimension can be set by defining the OPS_BATCHED preprocessor macro to the desired dimension index.

Keeping the batching dimension as the last dimension will keep data from the same system contiguous in memory, which lead to good data locality, but may lead to unaligned memory accesses when accessing adjacent grid points. It also means that the lowest level of parallelisation - vectorisation on CPUs, and adjacent threads on GPUs - will be on the first spatial dimension. For small systems, this may lead to underutilisation, and cause issues for auto-vectorisation.

Setting the batching dimension to be the first one makes auto-vectorisation in particular easier, as the loop over the batching dimension becomes trivially parallelisable, all accesses become aligned, and with large system counts, the utilisaiton of vector units will be high as well. It does however mean slightly more indexing arithmetic; for example in 2D, accessing a neighbour with a (i, j) offset yields the $i * \#systems + j * x\_size * \#systems$ computation. This change in indexing scheme is done in the implementation of the ACC data wrapper, and is applied at compile time. This layout also leads to jumps in memory addresses when accessing neighbouring grid points, and accessing non-contiguous memory when executing only a subset of all systems (batched execution schedule).

Finally, in situations where data locality is to be exploited, which prefers a layout with batching dimension being the last one, and vectorisation efficiency also to be improved, which prefers the layout with the batching dimension being the first one, we can use a hybrid of the two. OPS can break up the dimension of different systems into two - by forming smaller batches of systems (e.g. 4 or 8). This yields the following layout for 2D: $batch\_size \times x\_size \times y\_size \times \#systems/batch\_size$, which can be trivially extended to higher dimensions. The batch size can be set to a multiple of the vector length on CPUs, ensuring perfect utilisation of vector units, and sized so the memory footprint fits a certain level of cache. OPS allows this parameter to be set at compile time, using the OPS_HYBRID_LAYOUT macro, allowing for better compiler optimisations - e.g. if $batch\_size$ is a power of two, integer multiplications can be replaced with bit shifts, and also no loop peeling is required for generating vectorised code.

3.4 Alternating Direction Implicit Solver

The base OPS abstraction requires that all computations are order-independent - that is, the manner in which OPS iterates through the mesh and calls the user-defined kernel, does not affect the end result. This is a reasonable requirement for most explicit methods, however many implicit methods are not implementable because of this. The alternating direction implicit (ADI) method (see e.g. [9] and the references therein) is very popular in structured mesh computations - it involves an implicit solve in alternating dimensions. We have introduced support for tridiagonal solvers (banded matrices with non-zeros on, above and below the diagonal), for which the need arises naturally from stencil computations. Tridiagonal solves are then applied in different spatial dimensions. We integrate a library which supports CPUs and GPUs [13], and write simple wrappers in OPS to its API calls; the user has to define the datasets that store the coefficients below, on, and above the diagonal, plus the right hand side, and specify the solve direction. Then, there is trivial parallelism in every other dimension, and the integrated library is additionally capable of parallelising the solution of individual systems as well using the parallel cyclic reduction (PCR) algorithm [24].

The tridiagonal solver library has a number of different implementations for solving systems that are laid out in the contiguous direction (X) - when solving many of these systems in parallel, the challenge is that their coefficients do not lend themselves to "coalesced" memory reads - which is a problem on GPUs in particular. The library offers five options for GPUs;

0. Transpose the data using CUBLAS, and perform a Y-direction solve, then transpose the solution back,
1. Each thread works on a different system and carries out non-coalesced reads,
2. Load data in a coalesced way into shared memory, and transpose it there
3. Load data in a coalesced way and use warp shuffle operations to transpose it,
4. Load data in a coalesced way and use warp shuffle operations to transpose it, and use a hybrid Thomas-PCR algorithm to expose parallelism within a single system.

Fitting this solver in our batched extension is a matter of adding an extra dimension to the data, and solving in the appropriate dimension. When data layout is changed, the solve dimension is changed accordingly - e.g. when the batching dimension is 0, X solves become Y solves. A call to this library is represented just like any other ops_par_loop, and can be inserted into the queue during lazy execution. The wrapper takes care of selecting the correct solve dimension when the data layout is re-arranged, and passing the correct extents so the desired systems are solved.

4   Evaluation

In this section, we evaluate our work on an industrially representative computational finance application. While it does not exercise all the newly introduced features, it does help demonstrate the productivity achieved through OPS of extending support to multiple systems, and exploring the optimisation space.

4.1   The Application

In contemporary financial mathematics, *stochastic local volatility* (SLV) models (see e.g. [22]) constitute state-of-the-art models to describe asset price processes, notably foreign exchange rates. The model is specified via a stochastic differential equation

$$dX_t = (r_d - r_f - 1/2L^2(X_t, t)V_t)dt + L(X_t, t)\sqrt{V_t}dW_t^1 \tag{1}$$
$$dV_t = \kappa(\eta - V_t)dt + \xi\sqrt{V_t}dW_t^2$$
$$dW_t^1 dW_t^2 = \rho dt$$

for constants $r_d, r_f, \kappa, \eta, \xi$ and ρ and positive function L. W^1 and W^2 are two independent standard Brownian motions. Note that X above is in log-space, so can be positive or negative. The process V however cannot be negative.

Using standard results from stochastic analysis, it follows that the price V of any financial contract written on X with payoff f at time 0 is given by the PDE

$$[h]0 = V_t + \tfrac{1}{2}L^2(x,t)vV_{xx} + (r_d - r_f - \tfrac{1}{2}L^2(x,t)v)V_x \qquad (2)$$
$$+ \tfrac{1}{2}\xi^2 vV_{vv} + \kappa(\eta - v)V_v + L(x,t)\xi v\rho V_{xv}$$

subject to the initial condition $V(0, x, v) = f(x)$ for all x and all $v \geq 0$. Usually Dirichlet or so-called "zero gamma" boundary conditions are imposed as well. The PDE (2) is usually solved with finite differences and time integration is via an ADI time stepper, for example Modified Craig-Sneyd or Hundsdorfer-Verwer (see e.g. [10] and [8,23]).

In [25] a finite difference solver was developed for this problem, and this solver has been ported to OPS. The solver is fairly standard, using second order finite differences on non-uniform grids and a first order upwind stencil at the $v = 0$ boundary. It uses the Hundsdorfer-Verwer (HV) method for time integration. In financial applications the initial condition f is often non-smooth, and is typically smoothed out with a few (2 or 4) fully implicit backward Euler steps (so-called "Rannacher smoothing" in the finance literature) before switching to an ADI method. The solver in [25] has this capability, but it is also possible to turn these steps off and only use the HV stepper. Practitioners often do this when the non-smoothness in f is not too severe. In our example of a European call option, the non-smoothness in the initial condition $f(x) = \max\{\exp(x) - K, 0\}$ is fairly benign. We therefore switch off the Rannacher stepping and only use HV time integration.

Computing the prices of financial options is important, however an arguably more important task is risk management. Banks manage risk by hedging options. Heuristically this is done by taking a first order Taylor series approximation of the option price with respect to all parameters which depend on market data. Banks therefore require derivative estimates of V with respect to many of the parameters in the model, which means that not only one option price is sought, but many prices, arising from pretty much identical PDEs (2) with slightly different coefficients.

In addition, regulators are requiring banks to do comprehensive "What if" scenario analyses on their trading books. These require getting option prices in various "stressed" market conditions and seeing what the bank's exposure is. These market conditions again translate to solving (2) with different sets of coefficients.

A single option contract may therefore need to be priced between 20 and 200 times (depending on various factors) each day to meet trading and regulatory requirements. Banks trade thousands of options, large international banks can trade hundreds of thousands of options. This translates to a massive computational burden in order to manage the bank's trading risk.

Lastly, banks frequently trade very similar options, which translate computationally to many instances of (2) on the same (or similar) grids, but with different initial conditions or coefficients. There is therefore an ample supply of small, more or less identical PDE problems that can be batched together.

4.2 Experimental Set-Up

We solve the SLV problem on a range of grid sizes and numbers of systems (batch size). The exact grid sizes are shown in Table 1, including the memory footprint of a single system, as well as the system counts that were considered. In a financial context, these problems range from tiny (50×50) to typical (200×50 or 200×100) to the large (500×500). Typical batch sizes are between 50 and 200, large would be around 400 to 600, and beyond this the batch sizes are probably unrealistic for *identical* PDE systems with different coefficients.

Table 1. Problem sizes and system counts (batch size) considered - each problem size X-V pair was evaluated with all listed system counts

Problem size X	50	100	100	200	200	200	300	300	400	400	500	500
Problem size V	50	50	100	50	100	200	150	300	200	400	250	500
Memory footprint (MB)	0.43	0.86	1.70	1.71	3.4	6.8	7.6	15.2	13.5	26.9	21.1	42.1
System count	1	48	96	144	200	248	296	400	600	800	1000	

The first workstation has an Intel(R) Xeon(R) Silver 4116 CPU with 12 cores per socket, running at 2.10 GHz, which has 32 KB of L1 cache, 1 MB of L2 cache per core, and 16 MB of L3 cache. The system has 96 GB of DDR4 memory across 12 memory modules to utilise all channels. The machine is running Debian Linux version 9, kernel version 4.9.0. We use the Intel Parallel Studio 18.0.2, as well as GCC 8.1.0. All tests use a single socket of the workstation with 24 OpenMP threads to avoid any NUMA effects - the STREAM benchmark shows a 62 GB/s achievable bandwidth on one socket.

The second workstation houses an NVIDIA Tesla P100 GPU (16 GB, PCI-e) - it has an Intel(R) Xeon(R) E5-2650 v3 CPU with 10 cores per socket, running at 2.30 GHz. The system is running CentOS 7, kernel version 3.10.0, and we used CUDA 10 (with a GCC 5.3 host compiler) to compile our codes. The Babel STREAM benchmark [5] shows an achievable bandwidth of 550 GB/s.

Considering that our application has an approximately 1.25 flop/byte ratio, it is bound by memory bandwidth - thus the key metric that we evaluate is achieved bandwidth. We report "effective bandwidth"; based on algorithmic analysis we calculate the amount of data moved by each computational step by adding up the sizes of the input and output arrays, neglecting any additional data movement due to having to store intermediate results (which may be affecting some tridiagonal solver algorithms).

Most of our results show performance based on timing the purely computational part of the code, which does not include start-up costs such as reading data from a file, or even the data layout transformation (where applicable) - this is discussed separately at the end of Sect. 4.3.

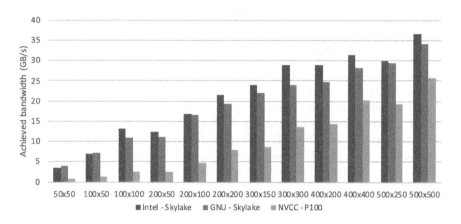

Fig. 4. Bandwidth on Skylake CPU and P100 GPU when solving a single system

4.3   Results

First, we discuss baseline results that do not use the new API of OPS, and solve only a single system. The results are shown in Fig. 4; due to the small size of individual systems, utilisation is low, but increases steadily with larger systems. On the CPU, it does reach 58% of peak bandwidth at the largest problem, but on the P100 GPU these sizes are still far too small to efficiently use the device. For completeness, here we show performance achieved with both the Intel and the GNU compilers – the latter is 5–15% slower, and this difference is observed on later tests as well, which we omit for space reasons.

Next, we discuss the effect of optimisations at the other extreme, having 1000 systems. Results are shown in Fig. 5. The two basic strategies use flat OpenMP parallelism - here each `ops_par_loop` is extended with an extra loop over the different systems and parallelised over the outermost loop using OpenMP. The two variants of this scheme are when data is laid out in a way so values from subsequent systems are in the last dimension (Dim 2 - $x\_size \times y\_size \times \#systems$), or in the first dimension (Dim 0 - $\#systems \times x\_size \times y\_size$). Results clearly show the advantage of the Dim 2 layout, which consistently achieves 45–50 GB/s, or 72–80% of peak, as opposed to the 35–40 GB/s achieved by the Dim 0 layout. This is in part due to the Intel compilers having vectorised all the loops regardless of layout, and the loss in parallel efficiency when executing remainder loops being negligible.

When enabling execution schedule transformations, relying on the lazy execution functionality of OPS, we can specify a Batchsize parameter - the number of systems to be solved together by a single thread. There are then combined

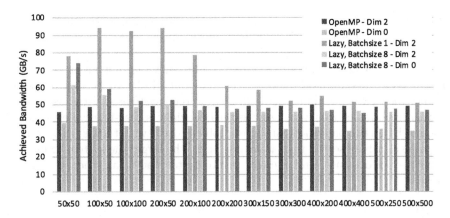

Fig. 5. Achieved bandwidth on the Skylake CPU when using different optimisations, solving 1000 systems

with various data layouts, the two that are applicable here is the original Dim 2 layout, and the hybrid batched layout in Dim 0 ($batch\_size \times x\_size \times y\_size \times \#systems/batch\_size$) - the flat Dim 0 layout causes non-contiguous memory accesses when solving groups of systems separately, and performs poorly, therefore it is not shown in this figure.

Two obvious choices for the Batchsize parameter are 1 - where the Dim 2 and hybrid Dim 0 layouts are actually the same, and a Batchsize that matches the vector length of the CPU, which in this case is 8 (512 bit vector length with 64 bit doubles). For the Dim 2 layout smaller batch sizes may be useful to mitigate any overheads in executing an ops_par_loop on a given system. For the Dim 0 layout having fewer systems in a batch would result in the underutilisation of vector units, because the innermost loop (which is being vectorised) is over different systems.

For our application, which has a considerable memory footprint for each system, and is primarily bandwidth-limited, the performance of these combinations is driven by how efficiently they can use the cache. At the largest problems it is clear, that not even a single system fits in cache, therefore the performance is bound by DDR4 bandwidth, and the different approaches are within 10% of each other - the lazy execution variant is the fastest due to having fewer synchronisations than the flat OpenMP version. At smaller problem sizes however, the Batchsize = 1 version performs the best, achieving over 90 GB/s, well above the DDR4 bandwidth; this is due to the data for a single system still fitting in cache. The memory footprint of individual systems is shown in Table 1 - considering that on this CPU, each core has approximately 2.3 MB of L2+L3 cache, the drop in performance above system sizes of 200×50 matches the cache capacity. At the smallest problem size, the caching effect is still observable on the Batchsize = 8 versions (8 systems of size 50×50 have a memory footprint of 3.4 MB), but performance quickly falls below the DDR4 bandwidth when moving to larger problems. It should also be noted, that at Batchsize = 8, the Dim 0 layout always outperforms the Dim 2 layout, thanks to more efficient vectorisation. This suggests that on applications which have fewer data per grid point, this strategy may perform the best.

The number of systems to be solved is also an important factor to performance. Figure 6 shows the best performance out of the various optimisation options above, when running with 48, 200, or 1000 systems - system counts in-between are omitted from this figure as the behaviour is near-linear. Performance is bound by DDR4 bandwidth at larger problem sizes even at low system counts. It can be clearly observed that at smaller sizes, the larger the system count, the better the performance - in large part due to better load balance across different threads.

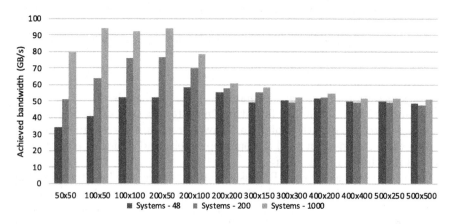

Fig. 6. Achieved bandwidth on the Skylake CPU when solving different numbers of systems

Finally, we evaluate performance on an NVIDIA Tesla P100 GPU. Here the range of options in terms of execution schedule and data layout transformations are more limited - cache locality cannot be reasonably exploited between subsequent CUDA kernel launches. This leaves us with the two layouts where the batching dimension is either the first or the last one (denoted as Dim 0 or Dim 2). However, the tridiagonal solver library exposes a number of algorithmic options for solving in the contiguous (X) dimension. There are no such options for solving in the Y or Z directions, as data accesses are naturally coalesced when adjacent threads solve adjacent systems. Figure 7 shows the results - Trid #0–4 denote the different X solve algorithms. While at smaller problem sizes, performance is affected by underutilisation, performance quickly reaches the 270–300 GB/s levels (50–55% of peak) for the two fastest options; when batching in Dim 0, and when using the Hybrid Thomas-PCR tridiagonal solver algorithm with register shuffles during the X solves for the Dim 2 layout.

The data layout transformations in particular have non-negligible overheads - OPS usually makes a copy of the user-supplied data even when no transformation is necessary to e.g. pad data in the X direction to a multiple of the cache

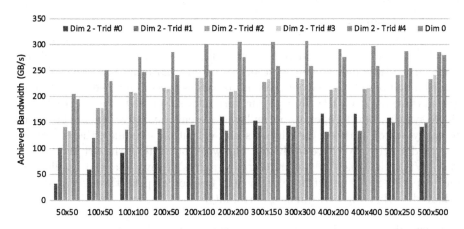

Fig. 7. Achieved bandwidth on the P100 GPU when using different optimisations, solving 1000 systems

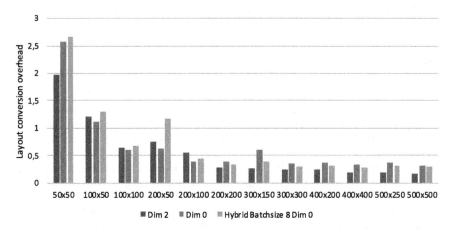

Fig. 8. Overhead of data layout conversion relative to the cost of a single time iteration, when using 200 systems.

line length. This transformation is parallelised by OPS using OpenMP, and its overhead is reported. Here, we show the overhead in relative terms compared to the time it takes to execute a single time iteration (for our tests we execute 10 time iterations). Figure 8 shows the overhead of the conversion from the default Dim 2 layout as the user provides the input, when using 200 systems - relative to the cost of a single time iteration. Clearly, the larger the system size the less the overhead, and it stabilises around the 0.25–0.35 time iteration cost. Conversion to Dim 0, or the hybrid layout is inevitably less efficient because of the strided memory accesses when writing data.

5   Conclusions

In this paper we have considered the challenge of performing the same calculations on multiple independent systems on various hardware platforms. We discussed a number of data layout options, as well as execution schedules, and integrated these into the OPS library. Our work allows users to trivially extend their single-system code to operate on multiple systems, and gives them the ability to easily switch between data layouts and execution schedules, thereby granting productivity. We have evaluated our work on state-of-the art Intel CPUs and NVIDIA GPUs, and an industrially representative financial application. Our experiments demonstrate that a high fraction of peak throughput can be achieved - delivering performance portability.

Acknowledgements. István Reguly was supported by the János Bolyai Research Scholarship of the Hungarian Academy of Sciences. Project no. PD 124905 has been implemented with the support provided from the National Research, Development and Innovation Fund of Hungary, financed under the PD_17 funding scheme. Supported by the ÚNKP-18-4-PPKE-18 new National Excellence Program of the Ministry of Human Capacities.

References

1. OPS Library (2014). https://github.com/OP-DSL/OPS
2. Bauer, M., Treichler, S., Slaughter, E., Aiken, A.: Legion: expressing locality and independence with logical regions. In: SC'12: Proceedings of the International Conference on High Performance Computing, Networking, Storage and Analysis, pp. 1–11. IEEE (2012)
3. Carter Edwards, H., Trott, C.R., Sunderland, D.: Kokkos. J. Parallel Distrib. Comput. **74**(12), 3202–3216 (2014). https://doi.org/10.1016/j.jpdc.2014.07.003
4. Chandra, R., Dagum, L., Kohr, D., Menon, R., Maydan, D., McDonald, J.: Parallel Programming in OpenMP. Morgan Kaufmann, San Francisco (2001)
5. Deakin, T., Price, J., Martineau, M., McIntosh-Smith, S.: Evaluating attainable memory bandwidth of parallel programming models via babelstream. Int. J. Comput. Sci. Eng. **17**(3), 247–262 (2018)
6. Gropp, W., Thakur, R., Lusk, E.: Using MPI-2: Advanced Features of the Message Passing Interface. MIT press, Cambridge (1999)
7. Hornung, R.D., Keasler, J.A.: The RAJA portability layer: Overview and status. Technical report, Lawrence Livermore National Lab. (LLNL) (9 2014). https://doi.org/10.2172/1169830
8. Hundsdorfer, W.: Accuracy and stability of splitting with stabilizing corrections. Appl. Numer. Math. **42**(1–3), 213–233 (2002)
9. In't Hout, K., Welfert, B.: Stability of adi schemes applied to convection-diffusion equations with mixed derivative terms. Appl. Numer. Math. **57**(1), 19–35 (2007)
10. In't Hout, K., Welfert, B.: Unconditional stability of second-order adi schemes applied to multi-dimensional diffusion equations with mixed derivative terms. Appl. Numer. Math. **59**(3–4), 677–692 (2009)

11. Jammy, S.P., Mudalige, G.R., Reguly, I.Z., Sandham, N.D., Giles, M.: Block-structured compressible navier-stokes solution using the ops high-level abstraction. Int. J. Comput. Fluid Dyn. **30**(6), 450–454 (2016). https://doi.org/10.1080/10618562.2016.1243663

12. Kronawitter, S., Kuckuk, S., Köstler, H., Lengauer, C.: Automatic data layout transformations in the exastencils code generator. Mod. Phys. Lett. A **28**(03), 1850009 (2018)

13. László, E., Giles, M., Appleyard, J.: Manycore algorithms for batch scalar and block tridiagonal solvers. ACM Trans. Math. Softw. **42**(4), 31:1–31:36 (2016). https://doi.org/10.1145/2830568. http://doi.acm.org/10.1145/2830568

14. MacNeice, P., Olson, K.M., Mobarry, C., De Fainchtein, R., Packer, C.: Paramesh: a parallel adaptive mesh refinement community toolkit. Comput. Phys. Commun. **126**(3), 330–354 (2000)

15. Mudalige, G.R., Reguly, I.Z., Giles, M.B., Mallinson, A.C., Gaudin, W.P., Herdman, J.A.: Performance analysis of a high-level abstractions-based hydrocode on future computing systems. In: Jarvis, S.A., Wright, S.A., Hammond, S.D. (eds.) PMBS 2014. LNCS, vol. 8966, pp. 85–104. Springer, Cham (2015). https://doi.org/10.1007/978-3-319-17248-4_5

16. Nath, R., Tomov, S., Dongarra, J.: An improved magma gemm for fermi graphics processing units. Int. J. High Perform. Comput. Appl. **24**(4), 511–515 (2010)

17. Nvidia, C.: Programming guide (2010)

18. Reguly, I.Z., Mudalige, G.R., Giles, M.B.: Loop tiling in large-scale stencil codes at run-time with OPS. IEEE Trans. Parallel Distrib. Syst. **29**(4), 873–886 (2018). https://doi.org/10.1109/TPDS.2017.2778161

19. Reguly, I.Z., Mudalige, G.R., Giles, M.B., Curran, D., McIntosh-Smith, S.: The ops domain specific abstraction for multi-block structured grid computations. In: 2014 Fourth International Workshop on Domain-Specific Languages and High-Level Frameworks for High Performance Computing, pp. 58–67, November 2014. https://doi.org/10.1109/WOLFHPC.2014.7

20. Siklosi, B., Reguly, I.Z., Mudalige, G.R.: Heterogeneous cpu-gpu execution of stencil applications. In: 2018 IEEE/ACM International Workshop on Performance, Portability and Productivity in HPC (P3HPC), pp. 71–80, November 2018. https://doi.org/10.1109/P3HPC.2018.00010

21. Stone, J.E., Gohara, D., Shi, G.: Opencl: a parallel programming standard for heterogeneous computing systems. Comput. Sci. Eng. **12**(3), 66 (2010)

22. Tataru, G., Fisher, T.: Stochastic local volatility. Quantitative Development Group, Bloomberg Version 1(February 5) (2010)

23. Verwer, J.G., Spee, E.J., Blom, J.G., Hundsdorfer, W.: A second-order rosenbrock method applied to photochemical dispersion problems. SIAM J. Sci. Comput. **20**(4), 1456–1480 (1999)

24. Wang, H.: A parallel method for tridiagonal equations. ACM Trans. Math. Software (TOMS) **7**(2), 170–183 (1981)

25. Wyns, M., Du Toit, J.: A finite volume-alternating direction implicit approach for the calibration of stochastic local volatility models. Int. J. Comput. Math. **94**(11), 2239–2267 (2017)

26. Zingale, M., et al.: Meeting the challenges of modeling astrophysical thermonuclear explosions: castro, maestro, and the amrex astrophysics suite. In: Journal of Physics: Conference Series, vol. 1031, p. 012024. IOP Publishing (2018)

Scalable Parallelization of Stencils Using MODA

Nabeeh Jumah[1(✉)] and Julian Kunkel[2]

[1] Universität Hamburg, Hamburg, Germany
Jumah@informatik.uni-hamburg.de
[2] University of Reading, Reading, UK
j.m.kunkel@reading.ac.uk

Abstract. The natural and the design limitations of the evolution of processors, e.g., frequency scaling and memory bandwidth bottlenecks, push towards scaling applications on multiple-node configurations besides to exploiting the power of each single node. This introduced new challenges to porting applications to the new infrastructure, especially with the heterogeneous environments. Domain decomposition and handling the resulting necessary communication is not a trivial task. Parallelizing code automatically cannot be decided by tools in general as a result of the semantics of the general-purpose languages.

To allow scientists to avoid such problems, we introduce the *Memory-Oblivious Data Access (MODA)* technique, and use it to scale code to configurations ranging from a single node to multiple nodes, supporting different architectures, without requiring changes in the source code of the application. We present a technique to automatically identify necessary communication based on higher-level semantics. The extracted information enables tools to generate code that handles the communication. A prototype is developed to implement the techniques and used to evaluate the approach. The results show the effectiveness of using the techniques to scale code on multi-core processors and on GPU based machines. Comparing the ratios of the achieved GFLOPS to the number of nodes in each run, and repeating that on different numbers of nodes shows that the achieved scaling efficiency is around 100%. This was repeated with up to 100 nodes. An exception to this is the single-node configuration using a GPU, in which no communication is needed, and hence, no data movement between GPU and host memory is needed, which yields higher GFLOPS.

Keywords: HPC · Scalability · Parallel programming · Stencils

1 Introduction

In modern computing technology, the processing speed on a single processor core reached its limit. Therefore, parallelism of multiple cores within a node and inter-node communication via high-speed networks is required to satisfy

© Springer Nature Switzerland AG 2019
M. Weiland et al. (Eds.): ISC 2019 Workshops, LNCS 11887, pp. 142–154, 2019.
https://doi.org/10.1007/978-3-030-34356-9_13

performance demanding applications. For example, developers of earth system modeling software demand higher-resolution grid as they provide more accurate results from a scientific perspective.

The task of rewriting software to scale on multiple nodes is challenging for scientists. It requires distributing the data (domain decomposition [10]) and balancing of the computational load between the nodes and handling the communication. Other considerations and particularly portability should be taken into account, e.g. communicating data residing on device memory when running kernels on GPUs differs from data existing on host memory.

Stencils include access to fields at spatially-neighboring points. This leads to accessing memory multiple times to get field data to load stencil points. Normally, memory access with general-purpose languages indices defines explicitly where the data resides in memory. Such characteristic stems from the design of the general-purpose languages, which carries the semantics of access to local memory.

An important aspect of the move from the local memory to the distributed memories on multi-node machines is locating and accessing data. Generally, with general-purpose languages and explicit memory indices, developers need to keep in mind the domain decomposition and to keep track of the mapped partition of the problem domain to the local memory, and use the indices to access the right data elements. So, mapping the global position of a data element (with respect to the global problem domain) to the right indices in the local memory should be tracked by the developers. Furthermore, developers need to identify the necessary communication between the nodes, and hence write code to prepare the necessary data and handle the exchange to make the data that resides on a remote memory accessible through the local memory.

To avoid the necessity of architecture-specific code inside applications, and to ease the development of new applications, the parallelization should be handled semi-automatically by tools and libraries. Unfortunately, the semantics of the general-purpose languages do not provide compilers with the necessary information to make such decisions.

The **main contribution** of this work is the introduction of the Memory-Oblivious Data Access (MODA) technique to replace local-memory-bound explicit data access; it consists of a technique to extract the necessary semantics from the source code to automatically generate code to handle parallelization of stencil computations on multiple nodes, in addition to shared-memory parallelization.

MODA allows using the same source code on different run configurations including shared and distributed memory, and different architectures. It requires application source code to be written with higher-level semantics. As a prototype we utilize the GGDML [9] language extensions, which allow mixing general-purpose code with additional higher-level semantics to describe stencil computations. GGDML extends the grammar of a programming language with higher semantics that bypasses the architectural differences and provides performance portability [7]. This allows our solution to support performance portability and fit different architectures.

This article is structured as follows: a review of related work is done in Sect. 2, the technique and the methodology are described in Sect. 3, an evaluation of the technique is discussed in Sect. 4, and we conclude the text with Sect. 5.

2   Related Work

The natural limits of the single processors necessitate to seek for methods, strategies, and tools to support performance demanding applications and simplifying the parallelization.

Manual Parallelization. With this strategy, the developer adjusts the code to integrate parallelization strategies explicitly in the code which means that application logic is mixed with code fragments that control the parallelization. This is an old strategy, for example, in the early times of concurrent computing, [4] applied explicit domain decomposition to run large-scale scientific software applications on concurrent computers, both on distributed and shared memory systems. Domain decomposition was decided by the developers within the code. Compilers are then used to build the code for the target architecture as provided by the developers. This explicit decomposition was successful on different machines, and allows for near-optimal performance.

In fact, in the 1980's many publications were released concerning strategies to apply domain decomposition to parallel computing for various application domains. Domain decomposition of stencil computations represented an important research direction in the evolution of parallel computing technologies. For example, [1] discussed a solution that handles domain decomposition and the necessary interactions between the resulting regions to parallelize elliptic problems. Also, [2] used a domain decomposition strategy to develop a Poisson solver using parallel machines. These are examples among other many suggested solutions at that time. A comparison of domain decomposition strategies was made in [11].

Even in the recent years, many papers are published that parallelize a specific problem manually solving different problems using the recent advances in the computing infrastructure. For example, [14] proposes a communication model to handle data exchange on reconfigurable clusters. Another example, [6] used a domain decomposition strategy to strong scale a solver of the Lattice Quantum Chromodynamics on the KNC Xeon Phi co-processor, which highly reduces the time to solution.

Data-Structure Libraries. Exascale applications will need to access data which resides on another node. To support such applications, some efforts provide solutions at the data-structure level. DASH [5] is an ongoing work (under the Smart-DASH project) to provide data structures that account for node-level parallelism.

Code Generation. Besides to the evolution of the strategies to apply domain decomposition, another direction in research was taken to support parallelization, and hence simplify the developers' task regarding domain decomposition. Instead of manual coding, tools generate code to solve a problem, including domain decomposition and communication. This is possible because code generators generate code for a problem among a specific family of computations, e.g., elliptical PDE solvers. Code generators use a specification of a problem and generate code to solve that particular problem. This technique is used in many efforts including [3,13] to generate code for stencil computations. Tools with specific goals, e.g., YASK [15] use code generation to generate optimized code for parallel computing. YASK allows to explore the performance of a stencil on Xeon and Xeon Phi processors, where optimal parameters can be identified for a specific problem (stencil). The ExaStencils [12] project also generates the necessary code based on an abstract higher-level problem specification. ExaStencils is an ongoing project to support multi-grid solutions of stencils counting for the expected exascale computing infrastructures.

In **our work**, we suggest a technique in which higher semantics are extracted from the source code, and used to transform the code to enable domain decomposition and data communication between nodes. Tools identify the necessary communication based on user-defined extensions, which are integrated into a general-purpose language. Those extensions provide Memory-Oblivious Data Access which resolves targeting the actual data location in memory, whether local or remote.

Using our approach, we simplify scaling code to support modern multi-node configurations using the same source code that is used for a single node. In comparison to previous efforts, scientists do not need to manually parallelize their modeling code. Nor do they need to care about calling any libraries to handle domain decomposition or communication or keeping track of such details. Tools infer all needed details from the language extensions. Compared to code generation techniques, developers can still define their indices (which serve and fit the needs of their application) instead of using explicit memory and array semantics or using a predefined set of problem-family-specific constructs, e.g. expressions to solve PDEs assuming a rectangular grid.

3   Methodology

In our approach, the computations are written using a general-purpose language (GPL) extended by language constructs that blend into the GPL. We use GGDML (General Grid Definition and Manipulation Language [9]) language extensions for this purpose. GGDML provides an adaptable set of language extensions to support application needs. The DSL syntax and behavior can be adjusted through configuration files [7] that guide the high-level code transformation procedures. This is prepared based on the needs of the specific application or domain.

With this approach, a big chunk of the code can be kept, except for some small replacements: Loop control code is written with GGDML iterator. The body of

Listing 1.1. Example GGDML access operator definitions

```
east_neighbor():    XD=$XD+1
north_neighbor():   YD=$YD+1
west_neighbor():    XD=$XD−1
south_neighbor():   YD=$YD−1
```

the loop is modified by replacing the indices with user-defined extensions and removing the loop structures. The semantics of the GGDML language extensions allow the tools to identify the necessary communication.

3.1   MODA and User-Defined Indices

As discussed, array notation and memory access semantics in general-purpose languages define explicitly the location of data in local memory, which obligates the developers to keep track of mapping data from global domain to distributed memories and handle communication to guarantee access to the right data through local memory when needed. Here comes the role of MODA, where we use GGDML language extensions to access data. With GGDML indices, the source code does not include explicit memory locations that depend on machine semantics. On the contrary, GGDML indices reflect spatial relationships. Thus, developers do not need to know if the neighboring grid cell is in the local memory or in a remote one.

In fact the GGDML indices serve other purposes. As they hide the real location of the data in memory, they allow using different data layouts. Different memory layouts could achieve different performance on different architectures or problems. A study to show the impact was published in [8].

To cope with different application needs, e.g., collocated vs. staggered, regular vs. icosahedral grids, triangular vs. hexagonal vs. rectangular cells, GGDML allows users to define access operators to specify indices. Index adaptability to application needs allows to define halo patterns and identify the necessary communication. An example definition of a GGDML index is illustrated in Listing 1.1. The example shows definitions of access operators to refer to the four neighboring cells around a cell in a regular rectangular grid; as mentioned, the definition is provided by the user and can be adjusted to any problem.

3.2   Using GGDML Indices

To illustrate the flexibility in the definition of access operators, take as example a simple collocated rectangular grid. If we want to write a simple Laplacian kernel using GGDML, we can use the access operators shown in Listing 1.1 inside a configuration file that we use to process our application code. In the source code we can write the following kernel (Listing 1.2). In this kernel, we could access the four neighboring cells using the spatial relationships, which we define to fit our application.

Assume in another application we need to use a staggered grid to compute the divergence at the centers of the grid cells based on flux values which reside on the

Listing 1.2. Example GGDML code using access operators

```
// Traverse the cells of the grid
foreach c in grid{
    f_H_new[c] = f_H[c] * W1                    +
                 (f_H[c.east_neighbor() ]  +
                  f_H[c.north_neighbor()]  +
                  f_H[c.west_neighbor()  ]  +
                  f_H[c.south_neighbor()]
                 ) * W2;
}
```

Listing 1.3. Example GGDML code using access operators in a staggered grid

```
// Traverse the cells of the grid
foreach c in grid{
        // Use GGDML access operators east_edge & west_edge
        //   to refer to the U edges of the cell
        float df = (f_F[c.east_edge()] −
                    f_F[c.west_edge()]) / dx;

        // Use GGDML access operators north_edge & south_edge
        //   to refer to the V edges of the cell
        float dg = (f_G[c.north_edge()] −
                    f_G[c.south_edge()]) / dy;

        f_HT[c] = df + dg;
}
```

edges between the grid cells. In this case, we can add a new set of access operators
to support this second application, e.g., *east_edge*, *north_edge*, *west_edge*, and
south_edge. Using those access operators, the kernel can be written as shown
in Listing 1.3. The new access operators define new spatial relationships that
allowed access to the cell edges.

Looking at both applications, a user (or better scientific programmer) could
define the necessary access operators that serve the application, where spatial
relationships are used, while no information regarding where the data is located
in memory are mentioned. The source code in both applications doesn't explicitly
state whether the data is in the local memory or stored remotely.

3.3   Communication Identification

The developers responsibility to track data location, to communicate data
between nodes, and to use the right memory indices to access data locally is
shifted to the tools through the semantics of the GGDML extensions. Depending on the domain decomposition method, an access operator leads to identify
the needed communication if any. For example, *north_edge* is sufficient to let a
tool know that the data of the edges should be communicated when the edges of a
set of cells reside on a different node when dividing the surface into sub-domains.
To do this, we suggest an algorithm (Algorithm 1) to infer some information from
the AST and use this information to generate the necessary code to handle the
communication.

```
/* traverse the iterator AST                                    */
foreach AST_node in iterator_subtree do
    /* if the node is an expression to access a field data       */
    if AST_node is a field_access_expression then
        /* get field name, list of indices, and access type      */
        field_name ← get_field_name(AST_node);
        access_type ← get_access_type(AST_node);        /* e.g., read */
        index_node_list ← get_index_node_list(AST_node);
        /* iterate over the access indices                        */
        foreach index_node in index_node_list do
            /* use indices to identify necessary communication    */
            if is_GGDML_index(index_node) then
                /* build a list of access operators               */
                AO_list ← fetch_access_operator_list(index_node);
                /* check all access operators if they require halo
                   exchange                                       */
                foreach AO in AO_list do
                    if is_access_operator_a_probable_halo_exchange_reason(AO)
                    then
                        add_entry_to_needed_halo_exchange_list(AO, field_name,
                        access_type);
                    end
                end
            end
        end
    end
end
/* check redundancies and dependencies                           */
analyse_and_rebuild_needed_halo_exchange_list();
/* generate code to handle communication                        */
generate_code_halo_pattern_communication_code();
```
Algorithm 1: Necessary communication detection algorithm

In this algorithm, we look for data access expressions and process all the access operators used to access data. This processing includes checking if the access operator corresponds to a halo pattern. Information is logged in a list about the variable, e.g., whether we need to read some halo region from a different node. This list is further processed to analyze dependencies and redundancies to optimize communication. Finally, code is generated to handle the communication. The generated code includes the necessary data preparations and calls to communication library routines, e.g. MPI_Isend or MPI_Irecv.

To demonstrate the work of the algorithm and the techniques, lets take a look at the example code shown in Listing 1.3. For this code, we apply a domain decomposition of the Y dimension, where a set of consecutive X-rows is stored on a node and processed on it. Based on this domain decomposition and the relationships between the cells and their edges, the expression $f\_G[c.north\_edge()]$ means an X-row of edges (the halo/south-most row) should be communicated

Listing 1.4. Generated communication sections from example code in Listing 1.3

```
if (mpi_world_size > 1) {
    comm_tag++;
    int pp = mpi_rank != 0 ? mpi_rank - 1 : mpi_world_size - 1;
    int np = mpi_rank != mpi_world_size - 1 ? mpi_rank + 1 : 0;

    MPI_Isend(f_G[0], GRIDX + 1, MPI_FLOAT, pp, comm_tag,
              MPI_COMM_WORLD, &mpi_requests[0]);

    MPI_Irecv(f_G[local_Y_Eregion], GRIDX + 1, MPI_FLOAT,
              np, comm_tag, MPI_COMM_WORLD, &mpi_requests[1]);

    MPI_Waitall(2, mpi_requests, MPI_STATUSES_IGNORE);
}
```

Listing 1.5. Generated data copy from example code in Listing 1.3

```
for (int j = 0; j < local_Y_Eregion; j++) {
    f_F[j][GRIDX] = f_F[j][0];
}
```

from the node that is responsible for the north neighborhood. Our implementation generated the MPI code in Listing 1.4 to handle the needed communication.

Some data access expressions imply the need to access halo data which resides on the same node, which does not need MPI communication. In this case a normal data copy can be done. For example, the access operator *east_edge* in the expression $f\_F[c.east\_edge()]$ and the mentioned domain decomposition case means the cells at the rightmost column needs to access their right edges. In this application we use periodic boundaries, in which the rightmost edge of a row is itself the leftmost one. This means, copying those edges allows the rightmost cells to access edges using the same computational kernel. Again our implemented tool generates the following code (Listing 1.5) to copy the data of those halo edges.

After the necessary data is ready in memory on the processing node to execute the computation, the compute kernel can be run. To improve this in lengthy communication cases, the communication code time can be overlapped with the computation time, given that inner regions do not depend on the data that should be communicated. In this case, the computation of the outer region (which depends on halo data) should start after the communication is finished. The computation kernel that is generated from the example code in Listing 1.3 is shown in Listing 1.6.

4 Evaluation

In this section, we show some results achieved using the discussed techniques. Experiments were done on single nodes and multiple nodes, multi-core processors and GPUs were involved in the experiments.

4.1   Test Application

The test application is a solver of the shallow water equations on a two-dimensional regular grid with cyclic boundary conditions[1]. The application applies the finite difference method with an explicit time stepping scheme. Eight kernels are included in which flux, velocities, surface level are computed besides to tendencies in each time step.

Listing 1.6. Generated computing code from example code in Listing 1.3

```
for (size_t blk_start = (0); blk_start < (GRIDX); blk_start += 20000) {
    size_t blk_end = GRIDX;
    if ((blk_end - blk_start) > 20000) blk_end = blk_start + 20000;
    #pragma omp parallel for
    for (size_t YD_index = (0); YD_index < local_Y_Cregion; YD_index++) {
        #pragma omp simd
        for (size_t XD_index= blk_start; XD_index < blk_end; XD_index++){
            {
                float df = (f_F [YD_index][XD_index + 1] -
                            f_F [YD_index][XD_index]) / dx;
                float dg = (f_G [YD_index + 1][XD_index] -
                            f_G [YD_index][XD_index]) / dy;
                f_HT [YD_index][XD_index] = df + dg;
            }
        }
    }
}
```

4.2   Test System

The multi-core processor experiments are run on dual socket Broadwell nodes on the machine Mistral at the German Climate Computing Center (DKRZ). The processors are Intel(R) Xeon(R) CPU E5-2695 v4 with 2.10 GHz. We used the Intel (18.0.2) C compiler and the IntelMPI (2018.1.163) library.

The GPU experiments are run on the nodes on the machine 'Piz Daint' at the Swiss National Supercomputing Center (CSCS). The GPUs are Tesla P100 with 16 GB memory and PCIe interconnect to the host. We used the PGI (17.7.0) C compiler and the MPICH (7.6.0) library.

4.3   Experiments

We used GGDML with the C language to write our code. Configuration files were prepared to guide the code translation into C with OpenMP for multi-core processors, and C with OpenACC for GPUs. Optimization procedures were applied during the translation process, e.g., blocking, to exploit the features, e.g., caching, of the processing units. Parallelization on the node resources, i.e., the cores of the multi-core processors and the threads and SMs on GPUs, was applied using OpenMP and OpenACC.

---

[1] The code is available at https://github.com/aimes-project/ShallowWaterEquations/.

Translating the source code for the Broadwell and running it on a single node shows near optimal use of the processor. The application (and the kernels) runs with around 80% of the processor's memory bandwidth (measurement with the 'stream_sp_mem_avx' benchmark from the 'Likwid' tools measured 67 GBytes/s). This code uses caches optimally, where minimal data movement between memory and processor is needed. Minimizing the movement of the data in a memory-bound code means the code runs with about an optimal performance.

Using the defined access operators to generate communication code, allows us to run the same source code on multiple nodes. Using our implementation of the technique, we generated the necessary MPI code to handle halo exchange. Running the code on different numbers of nodes we could scale the code to more resources. We use multiples of ten, up to hundred nodes. The results are shown in Fig. 1.

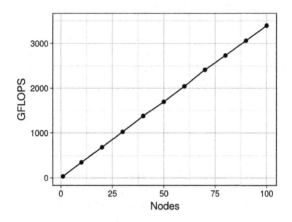

Fig. 1. Scaling on multiple Broadwell nodes

Translating the source code for the P100 GPU and running it on a single node shows near optimal use of the GPU. The application (and the kernels) runs with around 80% of the GPU's memory bandwidth (measurement with a CUDA STREAM benchmark yielded about 498 GB/s). This code uses caches and warps optimally, where minimal data movement between the device memory and the executing GPU threads is done. This means the code runs with about an optimal performance.

Using the access operators again we generated the application code that includes the necessary communication code, which allowed to run the same source code on multiple nodes with GPUs. We generated the necessary MPI code to handle halo exchange, besides to the OpenACC code. The application scaled to multiple nodes with GPUs. Again we use multiples of ten, up to hundred nodes. The results are shown in Fig. 2.

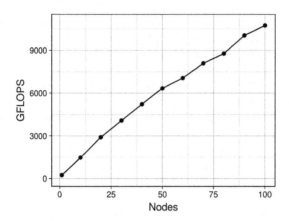

Fig. 2. Scaling on multiple nodes with P100 GPUs

To distribute the work between the running resources, both on multi-core processors and on GPUs, the problem domain is decomposed into local domains that reside on each node. Contiguous lines of the grid are given to each local domain. While the domain decomposition strategy maximizes load balance between nodes, other on-node considerations are taken into account. Data reuse, and distribution over cores/threads were maximized with blocking and on-node parallelization.

5   Summary

In this paper, we introduced the MODA technique to allow access to data while having no information about where the data is located or whether it is on the local memory or on a remote one. We used the GGDML set of language extensions to access data based on spatial relationships rather than memory location. The GGDML extensions allowed to describe an application in a single (unified) source code, this code could be translated to different target different architectures. We used a technique to extract information through the higher-level semantics to identify the necessary communication to exchange data between the nodes, or even copy data on the local memory. We demonstrated the use of MODA and the GGDML language extensions to write the kernels in two kinds of grids; collocated and staggered. That was possible as a result of the design of GGDML, in which users define access operators. User-defined access operators enable the adaptability of the GGDML extensions to support application-specific needs. We described an algorithm to extract the necessary information from the source code and generate the necessary communication code and hence scale the code, which is not aware of sequential or parallel execution, to use resources on multiple nodes.

We showed the generated inter-node communication code and on-node data copy code which were generated from the example staggered grid kernel. We also showed the results of experiments executed on a test application, which was written with GGDML and C language. The results show that the discussed techniques scale the same source code that can be used for a single node (or even sequential code) to run on multiple nodes. Two architectures were included in our experiments, multi-core processors, and GPUs.

We have a list of todos for future work. We have already implemented some improvements to prepare data to optimize communication, e.g. packing data residing on GPU's device memory, but there are still some work to be done to study and implement interfering communication with computing in more complex computations. Also, improvements towards more flexible and improved preparation of communication code fragments will be published soon, including the flexibility to switch communication libraries, e.g. use GASPI is an alternative to MPI.

Acknowledgements. This work was supported in part by the German Research Foundation (DFG) through the Priority Programme 1648 Software for Exascale Computing SPPEXA (GZ: LU 1353/11-1). We also thank the Swiss National Supercomputing Center (CSCS), who provided access to their machines to run the experiments. We also thank Prof. John Thuburn – University of Exeter, for his help to develop the code of the shallow water equations.

References

1. Bjørstad, P.E., Widlund, O.B.: Iterative methods for the solution of elliptic problems on regions partitioned into substructures. SIAM J. Numer. Anal. **23**(6), 1097–1120 (1986)

2. Chan, T.F., Resasco, D.C.: A domain-decomposed fast Poisson solver on a rectangle. SIAM J. Sci. Stat. Comput. **8**(1), s14–s26 (1987)

3. Christen, M., Schenk, O., Burkhart, H.: PATUS: a code generation and autotuning framework for parallel iterative stencil computations on modern microarchitectures. In: 2011 IEEE International Parallel & Distributed Processing Symposium, pp. 676–687. IEEE (2011)

4. Fox, G.C.: Domain decomposition in distributed and shared memory environments. In: Houstis, E.N., Papatheodorou, T.S., Polychronopoulos, C.D. (eds.) ICS 1987. LNCS, vol. 297, pp. 1042–1073. Springer, Heidelberg (1988). https://doi.org/10.1007/3-540-18991-2_62

5. Fürlinger, K., et al.: DASH: data structures and algorithms with support for hierarchical locality. In: Lopes, L., et al. (eds.) Euro-Par 2014. LNCS, vol. 8806, pp. 542–552. Springer, Cham (2014). https://doi.org/10.1007/978-3-319-14313-2_46

6. Heybrock, S., et al.: Lattice QCD with domain decomposition on Intel® Xeon Phi™ co-processors. In: Proceedings of the International Conference for High Performance Computing, Networking, Storage and Analysis, pp. 69–80. IEEE Press (2014)

7. Jum'ah, N., Kunkel, J.: Performance portability of earth system models with user-controlled GGDML code translation. In: Yokota, R., Weiland, M., Shalf, J., Alam, S. (eds.) ISC High Performance 2018. LNCS, vol. 11203, pp. 693–710. Springer, Cham (2018). https://doi.org/10.1007/978-3-030-02465-9_50

8. Jumah, N., Kunkel, J.: Automatic vectorization of stencil codes with the GGDML language extensions. In: Proceedings of the 5th Workshop on Programming Models for SIMD/Vector Processing, WPMVP 2019, pp. 2:1–2:7. ACM, New York (2019)

9. Jumah, N., Kunkel, J.M., Zängl, G., Yashiro, H., Dubos, T., Meurdesoif, T.: GGDML: icosahedral models language extensions. J. Comput. Sci. Technol. Updates 4(1), 1–10 (2017)
10. Keyes, D.E.: Domain decomposition: a bridge between nature and parallel computers. Technical report, Institute for Computer Applications in Science and Engineering Hampton VA (1992)
11. Keyes, D.E., Gropp, W.D.: A comparison of domain decomposition techniques for elliptic partial differential equations and their parallel implementation. SIAM J. Sci. Stat. Comput. 8(2), s166–s202 (1987)
12. Lengauer, C., et al.: ExaStencils: advanced stencil-code engineering. In: Lopes, L., et al. (eds.) Euro-Par 2014. LNCS, vol. 8806, pp. 553–564. Springer, Cham (2014). https://doi.org/10.1007/978-3-319-14313-2_47
13. Maruyama, N., Nomura, T., Sato, K., Matsuoka, S.: Physis: an implicitly parallel programming model for stencil computations on large-scale GPU-accelerated supercomputers. In: Proceedings of 2011 International Conference for High Performance Computing, Networking, Storage and Analysis, p. 11. ACM (2011)
14. Niu, X., Coutinho, J.G.F., Luk, W.: A scalable design approach for stencil computation on reconfigurable clusters. In: 2013 23rd International Conference on Field programmable Logic and Applications, pp. 1–4. IEEE (2013)
15. Yount, C., Tobin, J., Breuer, A., Duran, A.: YASK–yet another stencil kernel: a framework for HPC stencil code-generation and tuning. In: 2016 Sixth International Workshop on Domain-Specific Languages and High-Level Frameworks for High Performance Computing (WOLFHPC), pp. 30–39. IEEE (2016)

Comparing High Performance Computing Accelerator Programming Models

Swaroop Pophale[(✉)], Swen Boehm, and Verónica G. Vergara Larrea

Oak Ridge National Laboratory, Oak Ridge, USA
{pophaless,boehms,vergaravg}@ornl.gov

Abstract. Accelerator devices are becoming a norm in High Performance Computing (HPC). With more systems opting for heterogeneous architectures, portable programming models like OpenMP and OpenACC are becoming increasingly important. The SPEC ACCEL 1.2 benchmark suite consists of comparable benchmarks in OpenCL, OpenMP 4.5, and OpenACC 2.5 that can be used to evaluate the performance and support for programming models and frameworks on heterogeneous platforms. In this paper we go beneath the normative metric of performance times and look at the individual kernels to study the usage, strengths, and weaknesses of the two prevalent portable heterogeneous programming models, OpenMP and OpenACC. From our analysis we identify that benchmarks like MRI-Q, SP and BT have better performance using OpenACC, while benchmarks like MiniGhost, LBM and LBDC do consistently better with the OpenMP programming model across super-computers like Titan, and Summit. We deep dive into the kernels of select four benchmarks to answer questions like: Where does the benchmark spend most of its cycles? What is the parallelization strategy used? Why is one programming model more performant than the other? By identifying the similarities and differences we want to contrast between the benchmark implementation strategies in the SPEC ACCEL 1.2 benchmarks and provide more insights into the OpenMP and OpenACC programming models.

1 Introduction

The SPEC ACCEL benchmarks are written and maintained by members of Standard Performance Corporation (SPEC) High Performance Group (HPG) and are written in a performance portable manner. The SPEC ACCEL 1.2 suite

This manuscript has been authored by UT-Battelle, LLC, under contract DE-AC05-00OR22725 with the US Department of Energy (DOE). The US government retains and the publisher, by accepting the article for publication, acknowledges that the US government retains a nonexclusive, paid-up, irrevocable, worldwide license to publish or reproduce the published form of this manuscript, or allow others to do so, for US government purposes. DOE will provide public access to these results of federally sponsored research in accordance with the DOE Public Access Plan (http://energy.gov/downloads/doe-public-access-plan).

© Springer Nature Switzerland AG 2019
M. Weiland et al. (Eds.): ISC 2019 Workshops, LNCS 11887, pp. 155–168, 2019.
https://doi.org/10.1007/978-3-030-34356-9_14

includes a collection of benchmarks that cover a variety of common HPC algorithms. SPEC ACCEL consists of 19 OpenCL benchmarks that are based on the Parboil Benchmark (University of Illinois at Urbana-Champaign) and the Rodinia benchmark (University of Virginia) and 15 benchmarks for OpenMP 4.5 and OpenACC 2.5, that are based on the NAS Parallel benchmarks, SPEC OMP 2012 and benchmarks derived from HPC applications. The benchmarks in the suite can provide insights about the quality of different implementations of the OpenMP and OpenACC compilers and runtime environments. We have tested them to evaluate the extent of support available for new OpenMP 4.5 features on leadership computing systems like Titan [7] and Summit [2]. Comparing performance portability across different architectures and implementations provides insight to the application programmers/users as to the readiness of the systems. This is especially true for Summit where the implementations are still under development. Although programming models like OpenMP are designed to be platform agnostic, architectural differences can have a profound effect on performance. Users can then compare functionality and performance across a range of architectures and implementations of OpenMP and OpenACC.

In this paper, we document results from running the SPEC ACCEL 1.2 benchmark suite on Titan and Summit to see the current status of support and performance afforded by current OpenMP and OpenACC implementations. We perform experiments to capture the changing landscape of OpenMP 4.5 support and look deeper into the specific kernels that are the key performance bottlenecks. We also take a closer look at that subset of SPEC ACCEL benchmark kernels to determine which factors account for the performance difference. We look at the performance profiles and focus on the kernels/sub-routines that take the most time. Understanding the different strategies used by OpenMP and OpenACC is an exercise in finding equivalence, analyzing productivity and understanding the level of user intervention required to gain most of the benefits afforded by the programming model.

2   Motivation

In this study, we look into the different benchmark kernels with the objective of highlighting and investigating the differences and similarities between the two programming models, OpenMP and OpenACC. Fundamentally, OpenMP has been identified as prescriptive while OpenACC claims to be descriptive in their approach. Prescriptive model of programming requires very tight semantics and implementations must provide the exact behavior promised. While descriptive models describe the objective and leave more room for the implementations to work towards this objective. Looking at the benchmark kernels allows us to investigate real cases and analyze if the differences stemming from the specification are only in the semantics or the actual implementations. If a lot of implementation defined features are in play, the behavior of the kernels and the performance changes accordingly. For example, the maximum number of threads created per team is implementation defined in OpenMP. The user has the option to specify

Table 1. Successes and failures of running the SPEC ACCEL 1.2 benchmarks on different architectures with OpenMP 4.5 and OpenACC. The compiler versions used are: On Summit: PGI 18.3, XL V16.1.0, Clang/LLVM (ykt branch), GCC 7.2 (gomp branch), on Titan Cray CCE 8.7.0, PGI 18.4

	Summit (NV100 GPU)					Titan (K20X GPU)	
	XL	PGI	GCC		Clang	PGI	CCE
	OMP	ACC	ACC	OMP	OMP	ACC	OMP
Stencil	✓	✓	✓	✓	✓	✓	✓
LBM	✓	✓	✓	✓	✓	✓	✓
MRI-Q	✓	✓	✓	✗RE	✓	✓	✓
MD	✓	✓	✓	✗RE		✓	✗RE
PALM	✗RE	✓	✓	✗RE		✗CE	✗CE
EP	✓	✓	✓	✗VE	✓	✓	✓
CLVRLEAF	✓	✓	✓	✗RE		✓	✗VE
CG	✓	✓	✓	✗VE	✗RE	✓	✓
SEISMIC	✓	✓	✓	✗RE		✓	✗RE
SP F	✓	✓	✓	✗RE		✓	✗RE
C	✓	✓	✓	✗RE	✓	✓	✓
MiniGhost	✓	✓	✓	✗RE		✗CE	✗RE
LBDC	✓	✓	✓	✓		✓	✗RE
Swim	✓	✓	✓	✗RE		✓	✗RE
BT	✓	✓	✓	✗RE	✓	✓	✓
Passed	14	15	15a	3	6	13	7

a GCC/OpenACC only offloads 4 out of the 15 benchmarks, the remaining 11 benchmarks utilize the CPU.
VE: Verification error
RE: Runtime error
CE: compile error

a `thread_limit` clause that gives an upper bound to the implementation defined value for the number of threads per team. A user can request a given number of threads for a parallel region via the `num_threads` clause. Another example of an implementation dependent behavior can be observed in the LLVM compiler, which defaults to `schedule(static,1)` for the parallel loops when executed inside a target region that is offloaded to a GPU.

On Summit, the world's fastest supercomputer [8], vendors are still in the process of providing full support for the OpenMP 4.5 programming model. Through this work we want to also provide a temporal snapshot of the programming models support on Summit. Table 1 shows the number of benchmarks that compile and execute correctly with different OpenMP and OpenACC implementations. Figure 1 compares the best performance time for OpenACC vs. OpenMP on Summit and Titan with latest versions of the OpenMP implementations from IBM.

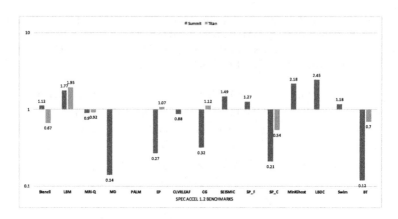

Fig. 1. OpenMP's performance improvement over OpenACC.

As it happens, there is not a single vendor or compiler implementation that provides both OpenMP and OpenACC implementation with the same degree of success and, as such, the comparisons across different vendors may, at first sight, seem unfair. But it is our experience that applications will choose the fastest implementation and in that respect comparing the best of OpenMP and OpenACC gives a fair assessment, as we expect these implementations on the same platform to have exploited similar architectural features.

For this work the relative speed up is calculated by dividing the best OpenACC timing by the best OpenMP for individual benchmarks on a particular platform. The benchmarks scoring above the threshold line (at 1) indicate better performance with OpenMP programming model, while those scoring in the negative Y axis direction indicate that they perform better with OpenACC programming model. For Titan we use PGI's OpenACC and Cray's OpenMP implementations while for Summit (Power9 + NVIDIA V100 GPU) we compare PGI's OpenACC 2.5 with XL's OpenMP 4.5.

We see that the MRI-Q, SP (C version) and BT benchmark have better performance using OpenACC, while the LBM, MiniGhost, and LBDC benchmark do consistently better with the OpenMP programming model across Titan and Summit. Based on the analysis in Fig. 1 we take a more detailed look into benchmarks BT, SP, LBM, and LBDC as they show distinct and pronounced performance advantage with one of the programming models.

3   Related Work

Previous work has compared the performance of the SPEC ACCEL benchmark suite codes when using different programming models including OpenCL, OpenACC, and OpenMP 4.x. In [4], the three different programming models are used to compare performance of OpenACC on two different GPU devices, and OpenMP on the Intel Xeon Phi coprocessor. At the time, only the Intel compiler provided support for the OpenMP 4.0 accelerator model. Since then,

GNU, LLVM, and XL compilers have added support for this model. In addition, the PGI compiler has added support to self-offload using OpenACC which has enabled testing of the PGI compiler on Intel Xeon Phi based architectures.

In [5], Juckeland et al., provide a detailed overview of the effort required to port the SPEC ACCEL benchmark suite from the OpenACC programming model to the OpenMP 4.5 accelerator programming model. The work highlights the differences between each programming model. For example, in OpenACC, the developer can briefly describe the intended parallelism of a region and the runtime takes care of executing it. In OpenMP, however, the developer explicitly specifies the type of parallelism and those choices often have a measurable impact on the performance of the code. Converting a code from one programming model to another can be a fairly straightforward change [5,9]. However, porting a code to achieve the best performance can be a challenging task.

This work builds upon the results observed in [3], which includes an evaluation of the SPEC ACCEL benchmark suite across five compilers on three distinct architectures including Percival [1], Titan [7], and Summit [2].

4   Analysis

Here we take a closer look at the SPEC ACCEL benchmark kernels to determine what factors account for the performance difference. Since the benchmarks claim that they were created with performance portability in mind, the created kernels are functionally equivalent. Here we first present the profiling results as analyzed and displayed by the NVIDIA Visual Profiler [6]. From these profiles we pick the kernels that the most time to see how they differ in the two programming models. There exists a large number of variables in the determination of the exact cause of the performance difference, hence we follow the standard performance analysis criteria and analyze the kernels taking the maximum wall-clock time as they have the most impact on the performance of the benchmark. Figure 2 shows the timing profile of the GPU for the OpenMP version of the BT benchmark. We see that the kernels that take the maximum time for BT OpenMP version are from functions x_solve, y_solve, and z_solve, which account for 24% each of the total GPU time. Similarly, Fig. 3 shows the timing profile of the GPU for

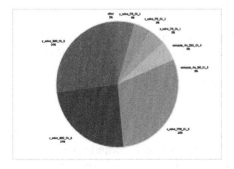

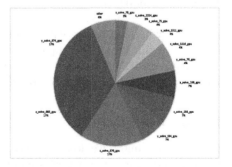

Fig. 2. BT OpenMP calls profiled.   **Fig. 3.** BT OpenACC calls profiled.

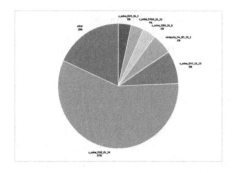

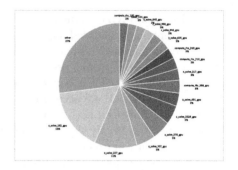

Fig. 4. SP OpenMP calls profiled.   **Fig. 5.** SP OpenACC calls profiled.

the OpenACC version of the benchmark. The 51% of the total GPU processing time is evenly spread across x_solve, y_solve, and z_solve functions. The *other* category includes cumulative timings of kernels that take less than 1% of the total time. Figures 4 and 5 show the GPU profiles for SP benchmark's OpenMP and OpenACC versions. For OpenMP version of the benchmark we see that 57% of the GPU time is utilized by one invocation of the kernel from y_solve function while for the OpenACC version we see a trend of little contributions from all calls take relatively uniform times except kernels from the function x_solve. The *other* category includes cumulative timings of kernels that take less than 2% of the total time.

For the LBC and LBDC benchmarks we see that all of the GPU time is spent on a single invocation of a kernel. The details are presented in the Table 2.

Table 2. GPU profile for LBC and LBDC benchmarks.

Benchmark	Kernel	No. of invocations	OpenMP Avg. duration (μs)	OpenACC Avg. duration (μs)
LBM	StreamCollide	5000	3.100844	6.120061
LDBC	relax_collstream	5000	1.903010	2.003094

5   Discussion

In the following section we will discuss the kernels identified in Sect. 4 for the different benchmarks. We compare and contrast the differences in OpenMP and OpenACC constructs used in these kernels and throw some light on the relative performance based on additional profiles collected for these specific kernels.

5.1   BT Benchmark

For BT benchmark we look at the x_solve kernel and compute_rhs. Since y_solve and z_solve are very similar to x_solve our analysis on x_solve is applicable for the other two. Listing 5.1.1 and 5.1.2 lists the kernel for x_solve.

The OpenMP version the directive `target teams distribute parallel for` is short for `target` followed by `teams distribute parallel for`. The `teams` construct creates a league of thread teams and the master thread of each team executes the region. The `distribute parallel` loop construct specifies that the for loop with iterator "j" can be executed in parallel by threads from teams from different contention groups. The `for` loop enclosed by `omp simd` indicates that the loop can be lowered where multiple iterations of the loop can be executed by multiple SIMD lanes.

Listing 5.1.1. BT Kernel for x_solve (__xl_x_solve_1709_OL_6)

```
707    ...
708    #pragma omp target teams
           distribute parallel for
           private(i,k)
709    for (j = 1; j <= gp12; j++) {
710        for (i = 1; i <= isize-1;
               i++) {
711            #pragma omp simd
                   private(pivot,coeff)
712            for (k = 1; k <= gp22;
                   k++) {...}
713        }
714    }
715    ...
```

Listing 5.1.2. BT Kernel for x_solve

```
679    ...
680    #pragma acc kernels loop
681    for (k = 1; k <= gp22; k++) {
682        for (j = 1; j <= gp12; j++)
               {
683            for (i = 1; i <=
                   isize-1; i++) {...}
684        }
685    }
686    ...
```

Listing 5.1.3 shows the parallelization strategy implemented by the PGI compiler. The OpenACC version marked the loop nest with the kernel directive and leaves it to the compiler to analyze the loop and pick the right schedule for the loops. We see that OpenACC is more descriptive, there is more freedom for the compilers to apply parallelization techniques. In this case the PGI compiler decided to pick a gang and vector schedule of the "k" loop, a gang schedule for the "j" loop and a sequential schedule for the "i" loop.

Listing 5.1.3. PGI Compiler Parallelization Strategy for x_solve

```
1    681, Loop is parallelizable
2    682, Loop is parallelizable
3    683, Loop carried dependence of rhs,lhsX prevents parallelization
4         Loop carried backward dependence of rhs,lhsX prevents
              vectorization
5         Inner sequential loop scheduled on accelerator
6         Accelerator kernel generated
7         Generating Tesla code
8    681, #pragma acc loop gang, vector(128) /* blockIdx.x threadIdx.x */
9    682, #pragma acc loop gang /* blockIdx.y */
10   683, #pragma acc loop seq
```

More insights can be obtained from the profiles in Figs. 6 and 7. The key parameters to look at there are the Grid Size and the Block Size as they together indicate the level of parallelism achieved. In addition the number of registers per thread and shared memory affects the performance, as threads share a finite number of registers and shared memory. The performance gain from increased occupancy (block size) may be outweighed by the lack of registers per thread. Inadequate registers will mean access to local memory more often, which is more expensive.

__xl_x_solve_l709_OL_6	
Queued	n/a
Submitted	n/a
Start	1.176 s (1,176,282,928 ns)
End	1.333 s (1,333,471,139 ns)
Duration	157.188 ms (157,188,211 ns)
Stream	Stream 40
Grid Size	[1280,1,1]
Block Size	[256,1,1]
Registers/Thread	255
Shared Memory/Block	952 B
Launch Type	Normal
▼ Occupancy	
Theoretical	12.5%
▼ Shared Memory Configuration	
Shared Memory Requested	96 KiB
Shared Memory Executed	96 KiB
Shared Memory Bank Size	4 B

x_solve_683_gpu	
Queued	n/a
Submitted	n/a
Start	1.073 s (1,072,826,178 ns)
End	1.084 s (1,083,724,217 ns)
Duration	10.898 ms (10,898,039 ns)
Stream	Default
Grid Size	[1,100,1]
Block Size	[128,1,1]
Registers/Thread	64
Shared Memory/Block	0 B
Launch Type	Normal
▼ Occupancy	
Theoretical	50%
▼ Shared Memory Configuration	
Shared Memory Requested	96 KiB
Shared Memory Executed	96 KiB
Shared Memory Bank Size	4 B

Fig. 6. BT benchmark x_solve OpenMP calls profiled.

Fig. 7. BT benchmark x_solve OpenACC calls profiled

For the OpenMP version, the GPU schedule is 1280 for the grid size and 256 for the thread block size. The register usage was 255. Overall this loopnest achieved a total of 12.5% GPU occupancy. On the other hand, for the OpenACC version, the GPU schedule for the loop nest was 100 grid size and 128 for the thread block size. The register usage per thread was 64 with no shared memory per file. This scheduled achieved a higher GPU occupancy of 50% than the OpenMP version. This is one of the primary reasons that the OpenACC version of the **loopnest** performed 14.4x faster than the OpenMP version. Another reason from the programming models point of view is that the OpenMP SIMD construct is not able to vectorize the loop iterations and serial execution further reduces performance. The OpenMP benchmark would benefit from having architecture specific code paths for further performance gain.

Listing 5.1.4. BT Kernel for compute_rhs (__xl_compute_rhs_l261_OL_4)

Listing 5.1.5. BT Kernel for compute_rhs

```
259 ...
260 #pragma omp target teams
          distribute parallel for
          private(vijk,vp1,vm1,i,j,k)
261 for (k = 1; k <= gp22; k++) {
262     for (j = 1; j <= gp12; j++)
        {
263         #pragma omp simd
              private(vijk,vp1,vm1)
264         for (i = 1; i <= gp02;
              i++) {...}
265     }
266 }
267 ...
```

```
262 ...
263 #pragma acc kernels loop
264 for (k = 1; k <= gp22; k++) {
265     for (j = 1; j <= gp12; j++)
        {
266         for (i = 1; i <= gp02;
              i++) {...}
267     }
268 }
```

Listing 5.1.6. PGI Compiler Parallelization Strategy for compute_rhs

```
1  264, Loop is parallelizable
2  265, Loop is parallelizable
3  266, Loop is parallelizable
4      Accelerator kernel generated
5      Generating Tesla code
6      264, #pragma acc loop gang /* blockIdx.y */
7      265, #pragma acc loop gang, vector(4) /* blockIdx.z threadIdx.y */
8      266, #pragma acc loop gang, vector(32) /* blockIdx.x threadIdx.x */
```

__xl_compute_rhs_l261_OL_4

Queued	n/a
Submitted	n/a
Start	1.109 s (1,108,877,216 ns)
End	1.142 s (1,142,043,597 ns)
Duration	33.166 ms (33,166,381 ns)
Stream	Stream 26
Grid Size	[1280,1,1]
Block Size	[640,1,1]
Registers/Thread	96
Shared Memory/Block	952 B
Launch Type	Normal
▼ Occupancy	
Theoretical	31.2%
▼ Shared Memory Configuration	
Shared Memory Requested	96 KiB
Shared Memory Executed	96 KiB
Shared Memory Bank Size	4 B

Fig. 8. BT benchmark compute_rhs OpenMP calls profiled.

compute_rhs_266_gpu

Queued	n/a
Submitted	n/a
Start	1.059 s (1,059,472,930 ns)
End	1.06 s (1,059,993,085 ns)
Duration	520.155 µs
Stream	Default
Grid Size	[4,100,25]
Block Size	[32,4,1]
Registers/Thread	56
Shared Memory/Block	0 B
Launch Type	Normal
▼ Occupancy	
Theoretical	56.2%
▼ Shared Memory Configuration	
Shared Memory Requested	96 KiB
Shared Memory Executed	96 KiB
Shared Memory Bank Size	4 B

Fig. 9. BT benchmark compute_rhs OpenACC calls profiled

Listing 5.1.4 and 5.1.5 shows the OpenMP and OpenACC version of another `loopnest` in the `rhs` kernel of BT. We look at this kernel specifically because it takes 6% of the total time in the OpenMP version but about 1% in the OpenACC benchmark. Here both versions have the same code structure. No loop interchanged was done by the programmer. All the loops are parallel. The benchmark employs the OpenMP SIMD directive to the innermost loop. The OpenACC version of the loop uses the kernels directive and lets the compiler apply the loop schedules (Figs. 8 and 9).

Listing 5.1.6 is the output from the PGI compiler for the OpenACC `loop nest`. We can see that OpenACC applies gang and vector schedules for the three loops in the loopnest. As a result it gets a $4 \times 100 \times 25$ schedule for the grid and 32×4 schedule for the `threadblock` size. The occupancy is of 56.2%. The OpenMP version, on the other hand, has a schedule of 1280×1 for the grid and 640×1 for the same `threadblock`. The occupancy for OpenMP version is 31.2%. Low occupancy results in poor instruction issue efficiency and since there are not enough eligible warps, the latency between dependent instructions is more obvious. As a result, using default settings for both the versions of the benchmark, more threads were spawned in the OpenACC version leading to 63x better performance. This is the direct result of OpenACC compiler picking a better schedule for the loops.

5.2   SP Benchmark

In Listings 5.2.1 and 5.2.2 we compare OpenMP and OpenACC versions of the SP benchmark. We see that the outer loop is parallelized using OpenMP `target teams distribute parallel for` combined directive and using kernels, respectively. The OpenACC version parallelizes the "k" and "i" loop with gang vector schedules.

The loop schedule selected by OpenACC was $5 \times 40 \times 1$ grid size and $32 \times 4 \times 1$ thread block. OpenMP selected a $2 \times 1 \times 1$ grid size and $128 \times 1 \times 1$ thread block. The GPU occupancy for OpenACC was 50% and for OpenMP 31.2%. The 135x faster performance using OpenACC can be contributed to (1) better occupancy and (2) optimum registers per thread. In spite of OpenMP benchmark having shared memory between CPU and GPU and more registers per thread, the default block size was not the optimum size. This is an important aspect and leads to degraded performance due to inadequate resources per thread (Figs. 10 and 11).

Listing 5.2.1. SP Kernel for y_solve using OpenMP

```
763   ...
764   #pragma omp target teams
          distribute parallel for
          private(i,j,k,m,fac1,j1,j2)
765   for (k = 1; k <= gp2-2; k++) {
766      for (j = 0; j <= gp1-3;
             j++) {
767         j1 = j + 1;
768         j2 = j + 2;
769         for (i = 1; i <= gp0-2;
                i++) {
770            ...
771            for (m = 0; m < 3;
                  m++) {...}
772            ...
773            for (m = 0; m < 3;
                  m++) {...}
774            ...
775            for (m = 0; m < 3;
                  m++) {...}
776         }
777      }
778   }
779   ...
```

Listing 5.2.2. SP Kernel for y_solve using OpenACC

```
643   ...
644   #pragma acc kernels loop
645   for (k = 1; k <= gp2-2; k++) {
646      for (j = 0; j <= gp1-3;
             j++) {
647         j1 = j + 1;
648         j2 = j + 2;
649         for (i = 1; i <= gp0-2;
                i++) {
650            ...
651            for (m = 0; m < 3;
                  m++) {...}
652            ...
653            for (m = 0; m < 3;
                  m++) {...}
654            ...
655            for (m = 0; m < 3;
                  m++) {...}
656         }
657      }
658   }
659   ...
```

Listing 5.2.3. PGI's Parallelization Stratergy for y_solve

```
643   645, Loop is parallelizable
644   646, Loop carried dependence of lhsY prevents parallelization
645        Loop carried backward dependence of lhsY prevents vectorization
646        Loop carried dependence of rhs prevents parallelization
647        Loop carried backward dependence of rhs prevents vectorization
648   649, Loop is parallelizable
649        Accelerator kernel generated
650        Generating Tesla code
651        645, #pragma acc loop gang, vector(4) /* blockIdx.y threadIdx.y */
652        646, #pragma acc loop seq
653        649, #pragma acc loop gang, vector(32) /* blockIdx.x threadIdx.x */
654        653, #pragma acc loop seq
655        658, #pragma acc loop seq
656        663, #pragma acc loop seq
```

__xl_y_solve_l765_OL_24

Queued	n/a
Submitted	n/a
Start	2.183 s (2,183,209,865 ns)
End	2.334 s (2,333,694,638 ns)
Duration	150.485 ms (150,484,773 ns)
Stream	Stream 35
Grid Size	[2,1,1]
Block Size	[128,1,1]
Registers/Thread	86
Shared Memory/Block	916 B
Launch Type	Normal
▼Occupancy	
Theoretical	31.2%
▼Shared Memory Configuration	
Shared Memory Requested	96 KiB
Shared Memory Executed	96 KiB
Shared Memory Bank Size	4 B

Fig. 10. SP benchmark compute_rhs OpenMP calls profiled.

y_solve_649_gpu

Queued	n/a
Submitted	n/a
Start	2.441 s (2,441,456,011 ns)
End	2.443 s (2,442,565,604 ns)
Duration	1.11 ms (1,109,593 ns)
Stream	Default
Grid Size	[5,40,1]
Block Size	[32,4,1]
Registers/Thread	64
Shared Memory/Block	0 B
Launch Type	Normal
▼Occupancy	
Theoretical	50%
▼Shared Memory Configuration	
Shared Memory Requested	96 KiB
Shared Memory Executed	96 KiB
Shared Memory Bank Size	4 B

Fig. 11. SP benchmark compute_rhs OpenACC calls profiled

5.3   LBM Benchmark

The OpenACC and OpenMP version of LBM are almost identical. Since the entire subroutine is called, we do not include the code listing. The OpenMP version uses the `target` combined directive and the OpenACC version uses parallel loop. In this case both versions use the same schedule 10157×1 for grid block and 128×1 for `threadblocks`. However, we observe that the OpenMP version is 2X faster than the OpenACC version. Contributing factors include (1) GPU shared memory, and (2) the number of registers per thread (3x as those in the OpenACC versions) (Figs. 12 and 13).

__xl_LBM_performStreamCollide_l159_OL_1

Queued	n/a
Submitted	n/a
Start	997.516 ms (997,516,434 ns)
End	1.001 s (1,000,590,913 ns)
Duration	3.074 ms (3,074,479 ns)
Stream	Stream 20
Grid Size	[10157,1,1]
Block Size	[128,1,1]
Registers/Thread	122
Shared Memory/Block	896 B
Launch Type	Normal
▼Occupancy	
Theoretical	25%
▼Shared Memory Configuration	
Shared Memory Requested	96 KiB
Shared Memory Executed	96 KiB
Shared Memory Bank Size	4 B

Fig. 12. LBM benchmark OpenMP kernel details.

LBM_performStreamCollide_195_gpu

Queued	n/a
Submitted	n/a
Start	755.546 ms (755,546,152 ns)
End	761.619 ms (761,619,310 ns)
Duration	6.073 ms (6,073,158 ns)
Stream	Stream 19
Grid Size	[10157,1,1]
Block Size	[128,1,1]
Registers/Thread	56
Shared Memory/Block	0 B
Launch Type	Normal
▼Occupancy	
Theoretical	56.2%
▼Shared Memory Configuration	
Shared Memory Requested	96 KiB
Shared Memory Executed	96 KiB
Shared Memory Bank Size	4 B

Fig. 13. LBM benchmark OpenACC kernel details.

5.4   LBDC Benchmark

Table 2 shows that relax_collstream subroutine is invoked 5000 times by both OpenMP and OpenACC versions of the LBDC benchmarks. The OpenMP benchmark uses the combined construct `target teams distribute parallel do simd` to offload the computation loop to the GPU. This allows for a `team` of threads to, in parallel, execute `simd` instructions when possible.

The corresponding code for the OpenACC version depicted in Listing 5.4.2 uses a simple OpenACC parallel loop. Since the OpenMP code has been better optimized to use vectorization through SIMD construct we see up to 2.5X performance improvement on Summit. The sub-routine details highlighted in Figs. 14 and 15 show that though most other parameters are identical OpenMP uses 900 B of GPU shared memory. This leads to better data access patterns leading to better execution times for the OpenMP version.

Listing 5.4.1. LBDC OpenMP Offloading of relax_collstream

```
1  !$omp target ! present(f_now,f_nxt,send)
2  !$omp teams distribute parallel do simd
       private(f_tmp_NE,f_tmp_N,...,feq_common)              &
3  !$omp    shared(omega_h,asym_omega_h,f_now,f_nxt,n_cells,omega,send)
4     do i_ct = 1, n_cells
5        f_tmp_NE = f_now( F_IDX(i_ct,Q19_NE) )
6        ...
7        f_tmp_S  = f_now( F_IDX(i_ct,Q19_S ) )
8  ...
9  !$omp end target
```

Listing 5.4.2. LBDC OpenACC Offloading of relax_collstream

```
1  !$acc parallel loop present(f_now,f_nxt,send)
2     do i_ct = 1, n_cells
3        ...
4  ...
5     end do
```

__xl__mod_relax_NMOD_relax_collstream_l47_OL_1	
Queued	n/a
Submitted	n/a
Start	1.457 s (1,456,545,867 ns)
End	1.458 s (1,458,423,488 ns)
Duration	1.878 ms (1,877,621 ns)
Stream	Stream 20
Grid Size	[25669,1,1]
Block Size	[128,1,1]
Registers/Thread	64
Shared Memory/Block	900 B
Launch Type	Normal
▼Occupancy	
Theoretical	50%
▼Shared Memory Configuration	
Shared Memory Requested	96 KiB
Shared Memory Executed	96 KiB
Shared Memory Bank Size	4 B

relax_collstream_48_gpu	
Queued	n/a
Submitted	n/a
Start	747.049 ms (747,048,905 ns)
End	749.05 ms (749,049,783 ns)
Duration	2.001 ms (2,000,878 ns)
Stream	Stream 19
Grid Size	[25669,1,1]
Block Size	[128,1,1]
Registers/Thread	64
Shared Memory/Block	0 B
Launch Type	Normal
▼Occupancy	
Theoretical	50%
▼Shared Memory Configuration	
Shared Memory Requested	96 KiB
Shared Memory Executed	96 KiB
Shared Memory Bank Size	4 B

Fig. 14. LBDC benchmark OpenMP kernel details.

Fig. 15. LBDC benchmark OpenACC kernel details.

6   Conclusion

In this paper we highlight the differences in the much used HPC accelerator programming models - OpenMP and OpenACC through the in depth analysis of the SPEC ACCEL 1.2 benchmarks suite. Both OpenACC and OpenMP versions of each benchmark followed similar parallelization strategies at the directive level, save some vectorization hints through OpenMP's SIMD directives. However, OpenACC gives more freedom to the compiler to accelerate their `loopnests`. OpenMP leaves all the choices to the user because of its more prescriptive nature. As a result, in many cases, OpenACC picks better schedules than what a programmer or OpenMP implementation allows because OpenACC relies on compiler optimization technology to generate their directives. This shows that OpenACC needs good compiler implementations as most of the choices are left to the implementation.

Another factor is the number of active blocks on the GPU device. This contributes to the occupancy of the device. We have seen that low occupancy results in poor instruction issue efficiency (BT and SP). In such cases there are not enough eligible warps to hide latency between dependent instructions. When occupancy is at a sufficient level to hide latency, increasing it further may degrade performance due to the reduction in resources per thread (as seen for LBM). For better performance as well as optimal use of resources an early step of kernel performance analysis must check occupancy and observe the effects on kernel execution time when running at different occupancy levels.

OpenMP can mimic OpenACC behavior by tuning to the parameters selected by the OpenACC compilers. However, the OpenMP implementations are becoming more sophisticated and sometimes support optimizations that are not supported by OpenACC compilers, such as GPU shared memory. We saw this case where the loop schedules were identical for OpenMP and OpenACC implementations of LBDC but OpenMP version took advantaged of GPU shared memory and thus performed better.

Acknowledgement. This material is based upon work supported by the U.S. Department of Energy, Office of Science, Office of Advanced Scientific Computing Research, under contract number DE-AC05-00OR22725. This research used resources of the Oak Ridge Leadership Computing Facility at the Oak Ridge National Laboratory, which is supported by the Office of Science of the U.S. Department of Energy under Contract No. DE-AC05-00OR22725. We would like to thank Dr. Oscar Hernandez from ORNL for his guidance and support during the writing of this manuscript.

References

1. Percival quickstart guide. https://www.olcf.ornl.gov/percival-quickstart-guide/
2. Summit: Scale new heights. Discover new solutions. https://www.olcf.ornl.gov/summit/
3. Boehm, S., Pophale, S., Vergara Larrea, V.G., Hernandez, O.: Evaluating performance portability of accelerator programming models using SPEC ACCEL 1.2 benchmarks. In: Yokota, R., Weiland, M., Shalf, J., Alam, S. (eds.) ISC High Performance 2018. LNCS, vol. 11203, pp. 711–723. Springer, Cham (2018). https://doi.org/10.1007/978-3-030-02465-9_51
4. Juckeland, G., Grund, A., Nagel, W.E.: Performance portable applications for hardware accelerators: lessons learned from SPEC ACCEL. In: 2015 IEEE International Parallel and Distributed Processing Symposium Workshop, pp. 689–698, May 2015. https://doi.org/10.1109/IPDPSW.2015.26
5. Juckeland, G., et al.: From describing to prescribing parallelism: translating the SPEC ACCEL OpenACC suite to OpenMP target directives. In: Taufer, M., Mohr, B., Kunkel, J.M. (eds.) ISC High Performance 2016. LNCS, vol. 9945, pp. 470–488. Springer, Cham (2016). https://doi.org/10.1007/978-3-319-46079-6_33

6. NVIDIA: NVIDIA Visual Profiler. https://developer.nvidia.com/nvidia-visual-profiler
7. Oak Ridge National Lab: Titan supercomputer. https://www.olcf.ornl.gov/titan/
8. Top 500: Top 500: June 2018. https://www.top500.org/lists/2018/06/
9. Wienke, S., Terboven, C., Beyer, J.C., Müller, M.S.: A pattern-based comparison of OpenACC and OpenMP for accelerator computing. In: Silva, F., Dutra, I., Santos Costa, V. (eds.) Euro-Par 2014. LNCS, vol. 8632, pp. 812–823. Springer, Cham (2014). https://doi.org/10.1007/978-3-319-09873-9_68

Tracking User-Perceived I/O Slowdown via Probing

Julian Kunkel[1]([⊠]) and Eugen Betke[2]

[1] University of Reading, Reading, UK
j.m.kunkel@reading.ac.uk
[2] DKRZ, Hamburg, Germany
betke@dkrz.de

Abstract. The perceived I/O performance of a shared file system heavily depends on the usage pattern expressed by all concurrent jobs. From the perspective of a single user or job, the achieved I/O throughput can vary significantly due to activities conducted by other users or system services like RAID rebuilds. As these activities are hidden, users wonder about the cause of observed slowdown and may contact the service desk to report an unusual slow system.

In this paper, we present a methodology to investigate and quantify the user-perceived slowdown which sheds light on the perceivable file system performance. This is achieved by deploying a monitoring system on a client node that constantly probes the performance of various data and metadata operations and then compute a slowdown factor. This information could be acquired and visualized in a timely fashion, informing the users about the expected slowdown.

To evaluate the method, we deploy the monitoring on three data centers and explore the gathered data for up to a period of 60 days. A verification of the method is conducted by investigating the metrics while running the IO-500 benchmark. We conclude that this approach is able to reveal short-term and long-term interference.

Keywords: Parallel file systems · Performance analysis · Latency

1 Introduction

HPC centres are highly motivated to improve efficiency and utilization of their systems. The estimation of the current system state is often based on a few metrics, which are continuously observed by a monitoring system.

Although, basic metrics are sufficient for identification of the most typical problems, they are less suitable for special tasks, e.g., one major difficulty for the file system state assessment is that many I/O metrics depend on both: application behavior and file system state. In case of non-obvious I/O issues, i.e., when all metrics looks good except I/O performance, it's not easy to say what is the cause just by looking at them. Understanding the quality of the file system health

© Springer Nature Switzerland AG 2019
M. Weiland et al. (Eds.): ISC 2019 Workshops, LNCS 11887, pp. 169–182, 2019.
https://doi.org/10.1007/978-3-030-34356-9_15

and quantifying its performance is another challenge. Users may wonder if the subjective experienced performance ("today the system is very slow") is actually true and, particularly, when jobs are aborted since the I/O phases take subjectively longer than normal[1]. This may lead to additional queries for the help-desk – which might be busy to resolve an issue. Knowing that the observed file system behavior is monitored and already classified as "slow" due to a degraded system state has a prospect to help users (but also staff) to understand the situation and reduce the queries.

To be able to identify the misbehaving component, it is beneficial to have a reliable metric that refers to file system only, i.e., it must be independent from any application. It would be also beneficial to quantify current file system state and to measure reaction to different I/O workloads. The latter specially useful to assess recurring I/O-intensive tasks such as backup of data.

The **key contribution** of this paper is the introduction of a systematic I/O performance monitoring using a probe with low intrusion and the investigation of means to derive a user-understandable slowdown factor.

The paper is structured as follows: First, we discuss related work in Sect. 2. Next, in Sect. 3, we discuss the methodology that we use for this work. The experimental results are presented in Sect. 4. Finally, the work is concluded in Sect. 5.

2   Related Work

There are various monitoring systems for cluster activities. Darshan [2,3] is an open source I/O characterization tool for post-mortem analysis of HPC applications' I/O behavior. Its primary objective is to capture concise but useful information with minimal overhead. Statistics are captured in a bounded amount of memory per process as the application executes. When the application shuts down, it is reduced, compressed, and stored in a unified log file. Utilities included with Darshan can then be used to analyze, visualize, and summarize the Darshan log information. Because of Darshan's low overhead, it is suitable for system-wide deployment on large-scale systems. In this deployment model, Darshan can be used not just to investigate the I/O behavior of individual applications but also to capture a broad view of system workloads for use by facility operators and I/O researchers.

In [9] Uselton and Wright claim that conventional I/O performance analysis based on transferred data volume and bandwidth doesn't provide reliable information about the state of file systems. They investigate a new metric called file system utilization (FSU) that takes into account the number and the size of disk I/O operations. A mathematical I/O transaction model brings all parameters together. On NERSC's Hopper Cray XE6 system they detect a busy file system with FSU, even if I/O performance indicates an idle state. This approach requires a complicated setup, that captured and collects I/O data from client and server nodes.

---

[1] When the specified job walltime limit is hit, jobs are terminated.

A machine learning approach for anomaly detection was investigated by Tuncer et al. in [8]. This approach targets two aspects. First, data reduction by mapping large raw time series to a few relevant statistics. Second, automatic anomaly detection and classification with machine learning algorithms. With sufficient data, a model can be adapted to several anomaly types, e.g. hardware issues, memory leaks, system health status. In the experiments on a HPC cluster and a public cloud the resulting ML-model a high accuracy (F-score higher than 0.97). Probably, the biggest challenge of this approach the machine learning technology. Creation of well trained models requires a lot of expertise in this area.

The LASSi Tool [7] captures I/O behavior and computes risk metrics that are related to application's I/O behavior. While this is similar to the goal of this approach, the interpretation of the synthetic LASSi metrics is difficult.

Sometimes developers or users utilize the principle of performance regression testing, i.e., to run an application periodically and measure the performance development while developing the code further. Typically this serves the purpose of identifying introduced performance issues but it is sometimes also used to identify slowdown in the system. For instance, in [10] the authors run benchmarks with Jenkins periodically to monitor system health. In [6], IOR is run daily to track the performance behavior. Additionally, performance of I/O motifs is analyzed over time.

This information is targeted to the data center staff and able to track changes in long-term system behavior (e.g., after updates), while our probing approach addresses the user side focusing on giving feedback of the perceived system load in a timely fashion.

3   Methodology

To quantify the user-slowdown, we periodically gather the response time from the client side and then apply statistics to reduce data points to meaningful metrics.

3.1   Probing

An accurate analysis of client-perceived response time can be done by running probes on a compute node periodically; a probe executes a small I/O operation. We assume that the response time of the probe is representative for similar I/O operations during the time of execution.

As the file system performance depends on the type of the operation performed, in this paper, we cover several data and metadata patterns as follows: **Data I/O**: a block of 1 MB is read and written each at different random locations in a large file. **Metadata**: the operations create, stat, read, and delete of small files (3901 Byte) are executed on a pool of files, i.e., the number of files of the pool remains identical as each iteration accesses the oldest created file and deletes it, and then creates a new file.

These six operations are executed sequentially periodically by the probing tool and the response time is measured for each operation individually. We use the dd tool to measure data I/O latency and for metadata the MDWorkbench [4] – this test allows to iterate on a working set for regression testing. The purpose of this process is not to mimic the behavior of a parallel application but to probe the system performance from the user-side – this is the performance a user would see.

Discussion. The frequency of the polling could be adjusted to minimize the impact on the file system – we use 1 s as the generated load with 2 MB/s and 5 metadata operations/s is negligible. Instead of running sequentially, the tests could be run in parallel or by spawning one thread for each operation. However, this would increase the load of the file system when the file system is already overloaded and makes it more difficult to assess the results as the measurements interfere with each other.

Running such a tool requires additional compute resources and storage capacity. Firstly, to reduce the impact of caching, it is required that a sufficiently large file is pre-created (exceeding the memory of the client) and that the pool of files is sufficiently large. Additionally, a file should be spread across all servers and storage media. Depending on the system configuration, a random I/O operation may access only a single server or storage media. As the probing frequency is very high, we claim this is still representative for storage systems with 100 servers – to increase the accuracy for large systems, multiple I/O probes could be executed, one per server.

The probing tool could run as a service on a maintenance node, on compute nodes, or on shared/interactive nodes. As additional I/O operation performed on the probing server (e.g., by users) influences the response time, for most accurate results, the probing tool should be run on a compute node exclusively – which implies some costs. Our experiments have shown that deployment on a shared node still produces meaningful results.

3.2   Data Reduction Using Statistics

When measuring small I/O requests, the response time is expected to vary frequently between two consecutive measurements but also statistics of longer sequences of measurements differ. The former is caused by short events like concurrent accesses, cache misses, or network congestion, while sequences of measurements are impaired by the long-term effects we are interested in.

In order to report meaningful slowdown metrics for longer intervals, high-frequent changes must be dampened. A typical approach is to compute the mean value in an interval. The arithmetic mean, however, is sensitive to outliers, therefore, we explore the use of various statistics particularly, the median, and the 90% and 95%-quantiles. Reporting the statistics for a quantile allows to understand the fraction of I/O operations that are slowed down in a certain interval, e.g., reporting a waiting time of 0.1 s for the 90%-quantile means that 90% of the operations are faster and 10% are slower than 0.1 s. Depending on the intended service level agreement with users, this is more appropriate than reporting high means caused by single stragglers.

3.3 Computing the Slowdown

Generally, we could define the user-perceived slowdown of a particular operation naturally as the observed response time of the operation divided by the expected response time: $s = \dfrac{t_{observed}}{t_{expected}}$. Thus, the reported slowdown is a factor by which I/O is expected to take longer. An issue is the robust determination of $t_{expected}$. A production system is typically experiencing slowdown over an empty system. This might confuse users to see that a system is typically slow by 3x, sometimes by 5x. Therefore, we define $t_{expected}$ as median of all observed values (for the specific operation)[2]. The reported slowdown is then computed based on the statistics for each interval.

4 Evaluation

4.1 Test Systems

JASMIN is the national data analysis facility of the UK for the European climate and earth system modelling community [5]. For each file system a 200 GB file is precreated a pool of 200k files for MDWorkbench. The script is run exclusively on one node and after 20 h the job is restarted; as there are many nodes available, typically a host runs only one or two 20 h periods during the 60 days of recording.

Archer is the UK national supercomputing service[3] consisting of a 4,920 node Cray XC30 utilizing the Sonexion Lustre storage. The file system used for testing provides 1.6 PB of capacity on 14 OSSs and 56 OSTs. For each file system a 200 GB file is precreated and a pool of 200k files for MDWorkbench. The jobs are executed on one of two interactive nodes that are shared with the users.

Mistral the High Performance Computing system for Earth system research (HLRE-3), is DKRZ's supercomputer. The HPC system has a peak performance of 3.14 PetaFLOPS and consists of approx. 3,300 compute nodes, 100,000 compute cores, and 266 TB of memory. The total capacity of two Lustre file systems attached to the system is 54 PB (lustre01: 21 PB and lustre02: 33 PB). All components are using FDR Infiniband interconnect.

For each file system a 1.3 TB file is precreated and a pool of 100k files for MDWorkbench. During the experiments the I/O-Probing tool runs on a login node, sharing the system with other users. The tool is executed on an interactive node that is shared with the users.

---

[2] The value could be updated periodically in a sliding window to cover the typical operational conditions or it could utilize other statistics than the median.

[3] http://www.archer.ac.uk.

4.2   Probing Tool

Our first measurements are done with a BASH script, that implements the behavior from Sect. 3.1. On systems with older kernels, we encountered an issue with frequent forking of probes in new processes. Over long time period, it causes high CPU load and makes compute nodes unresponsible. Therefore, we created a tool – I/O-Probing[4] that exhibits the same behavior; it is a single process solution written in C programming language. With corresponding program parameters it emulates the behavior of the script. It is using the sophisticated functions from MDWorkbench to get reliable response times and to calculate statistics. In the read/write test, the I/O-Probing tool accesses a large file with random patterns using POSIX `read64()`/`write64()`.

4.3   Timeseries of Individual Measurements

First, we investigate the gathered data for JASMIN on various levels of detail starting from individual measurements. Figure 1 shows the response time of each individual probe on two file systems for a duration of 10 min. It can be observed that the performance on the home directory is very predictable for all operations, as this is a PureStorage system and not used for parallel data production, this is expected. The 1 MB read operations express two bands of accesses, one around 0.1 ms and one around 10 ms – the latter are caused by disk accesses while the former is caused by caching on client or server[5].

The work file system is at the beginning also robust but after 1.5 min, the behavior changes, a fraction of operation is now 10–100 times slower (stat and delete remains low). As only isolated operations are slow, this is likely caused short-period load on the data and metadata servers.

4.4   Host Variability

As hosts are typically connected identically to the storage, it is expected that the reported response time is independent from the node, where the script is executed. This is important as we assume that the observed response time on the probing host is similar to the response time on other (non-monitored) hosts.

We verified this by running the script on JASMIN in parallel on five different nodes for a period of one hour covering at least 2,000 measurements of each metric per host. The obtained statistics are visualized in Fig. 2 as boxplot. Most metrics are indistinguishable for the different hosts and the systematic difference in behavior between home and work directory is observable. However, the first and third quartile for the write and read performance are slightly different and so is the median for Host 5. Still, we assume that the metrics are robust as different nodes observe them similarly.

---

[4] https://github.com/joobog/io-probing.
[5] To minimize this, the precreated file size could have been increased.

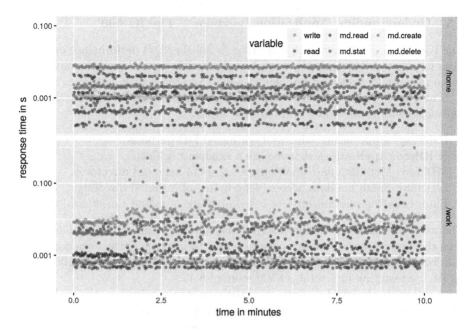

Fig. 1. Jasmin every data point for 10 min from one node

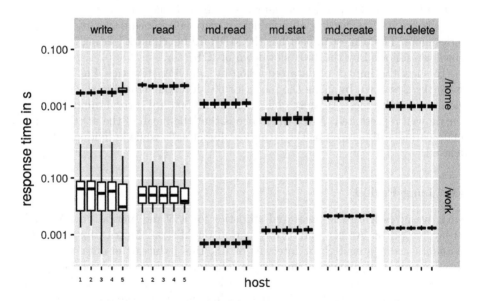

Fig. 2. Jasmin boxplot statistics from five different hosts

4.5   Understanding Application Behavior – The IO-500

The IO-500 [1] is a benchmark suite that establishes I/O performance expectations for naive and optimized access; a single score is derived from the individual measurements and released publicly in a list to foster the competition.

The IO-500 is built on the standard benchmarks MDTest and IOR[6] and represents various metadata and data patterns:

- IOREasy: Applications with well optimized I/O patterns
- IORHard: Applications that require a random workload
- MDEasy: Metadata and small object access in balanced directories
- MDHard: Small file data access (3901 bytes) of a shared directory
- Find: Locating relevant objects based on name, size and timestamp

The workloads are executed in a script that first performs all write phases and then the read-phases to minimize cache reuse. To investigate the behavior of the risk for running applications, we executed the IO-500 benchmark on 100 nodes on Archer resulting in a total IO-500 score of 8.45.

As they are designed to be part of the user-side monitoring, the probes are run concurrently with the benchmark (and any other I/O operation) and, in case of server-side contention, the latency is expected to increase. The response time of the probe is shown in Fig. 3(a) correlating directly to the slowdown in Fig. 3(b) – note that the slowdown factor is still computed based on the median for the 30 day period. In many cases, the influence of a metadata or data heavy benchmark is directly observable; for metadata benchmarks, the response varies more. The biggest impact has the MDHard benchmark leading to a 1000x slowdown followed by the 100x slowdown of IOREasy.

To show the impact of data reduction by applying statistics, Fig. 3(c) computes the slowdown by using the mean for 60 s intervals reducing the noise and short-term influences. As most phases of the IO-500 are several minutes, these remain well represented. A key difference is that the mean of the stat() call of a 60 s period still behaves as the mean for all stat calls while individual calls are delayed.

4.6   Long-Period

Next, we investigate the measured statistics for a 60 day period on JASMIN, 30 day period on Archer and 18 day period on Mistral. Metrics for data and metadata are aggregated for intervals of 4 h; this reduces the data points for visualization, and allows to investigate long-term influences on performance. The observed performance statistics for various access types and the three data centers are shown in Fig. 4 and selected timelines in Fig. 5. Note that the observations differ significantly between the three data centers and between file systems.

---

[6] https://github.com/hpc/ior.

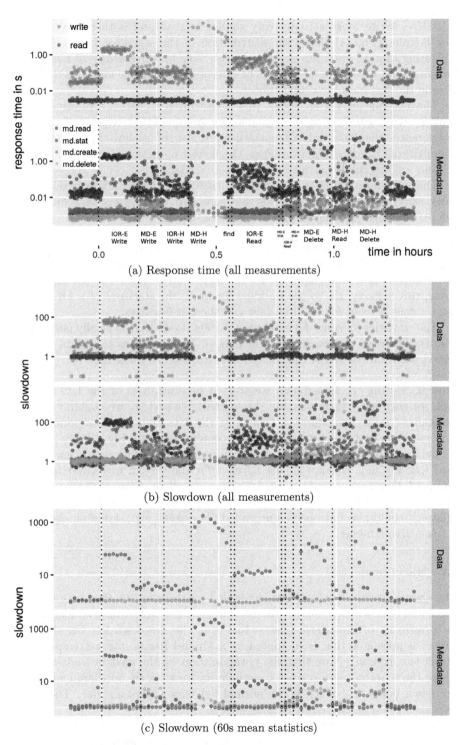

Fig. 3. IO-500 on Archer with annotated phases

JASMIN. Write looks actually very similar to read and is therefore omitted. The boxplot (Fig. 4a) shows the distribution of the statistics for the 60 days; indicating that all statistics including mean vary by three orders of magnitude for work and by 10–100x for home. The interquartile distance indicates that 50% of time the statistics are rather robust.

The timeline in Fig. 5a shows that consecutive statistics typically exhibit similar behavior indicating that some longer-running I/O-heavy activity creates interference. The 95% and 99% quantiles are less robust but tell us something about the distribution of performance; the slowest operation of a 4 h period takes at least a few seconds but also sometimes 10–100 s!

The metadata statistics (Fig. 4b) indicates that the metadata performance varies stronger. The timeline reveals that consecutive accesses often achieve similar performance (not shown due to space constraints).

Archer. The timeline for metadata probing is shown in Fig. 5b (the data timeline is not so interesting for work). A weekly slowdown of the small read and delete operations is observable (similarly for the large read accesses too, not shown) on home, this is likely due to the backup. On work, the statistics of a 4 h interval stays robust, except for the first days and the last few days.

The statistics for some 4 h intervals are 100x slower than typically (see Fig. 4c and d). The read statistics with a median of 5 ms indicates that data is often served not from the HDD; the 200 GB files still lead to cache hits.

Mistral. During the experiment we started two instances of the I/O-Probing tool, for each file system one. On the lustre01 file system, we couldn't observe anomalies (results are omitted). Generally, the data and metadata performance is worse compared to the two other data centers (compare Fig. 4).

On lustre02, there is one 27x slowdown compared to typical performance for read (see Fig. 5c). It takes almost 6.5 days for the system to recover from the I/O load. One reason could be an I/O intensive chained job, that was running on a shared SLURM partition as shared partitions allow for a runtime up to 7 days. It could also have been a degraded file system, e.g., server outage in the active-active fail-over.

4.7   Slowdown

The computation of a slowdown factor and presentation to the users was the main goal of this article. As we discussed in Sect. 3.3, longer interval length lead to a smearing of short-term effects. In Fig. 6, the slowdown for JASMIN and Archer is presented that is computed on a 4 h and 10 min interval, respectively (using the median). Note that the normalization by the median leads to cases where the reported performance is actually faster than the median, and thus a slowdown below 1 – which is the normal behavior – is observable. These fast responses could be caused by caching effects.

By looking at the graphs, the expected slowdown of the I/O could be determined, for example, a slowdown of 10 can be seen for read operations on JASMIN

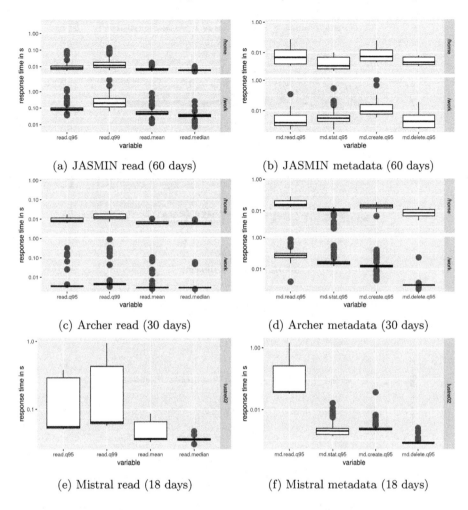

(a) JASMIN read (60 days)   (b) JASMIN metadata (60 days)

(c) Archer read (30 days)   (d) Archer metadata (30 days)

(e) Mistral read (18 days)   (f) Mistral metadata (18 days)

Fig. 4. Statistics for 4 h intervals

for several 4 h periods. Remember, the slowdown for a given type of operation quantifies the expected slowdown compared to normal operation. Thus, for I/O, the reading/writing is expected to take x times longer than normal. This is expected to be true for small application runs. However, I/O intense hero runs are expected to cause the I/O slowdown. The impact of running them on other applications is the cause of the experienced slowdown factor.

Generally, the effects on JASMIN take longer and are well visible, while the work directory on Archer exhibits mostly short-term bursty behaviors that is invisible in 4 h intervals. The home directory exhibits a slowdown of 3 during the weekly service activities. We conclude that by setting the interval length appropriately, short-term and long-term influences can be detected and communicated to the user.

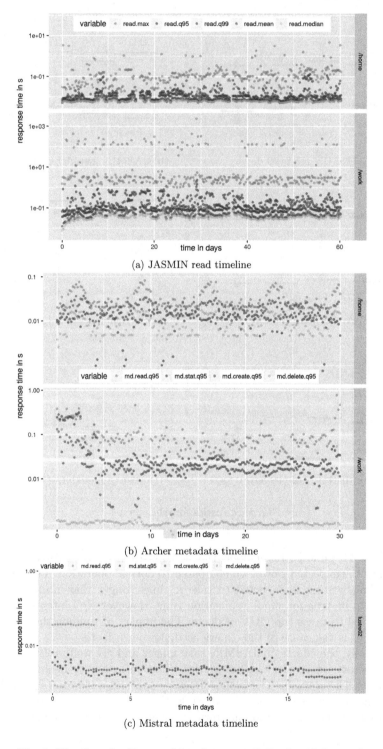

(a) JASMIN read timeline

(b) Archer metadata timeline

(c) Mistral metadata timeline

Fig. 5. Timelines for Data or Metadata – statistics for 4 h intervals

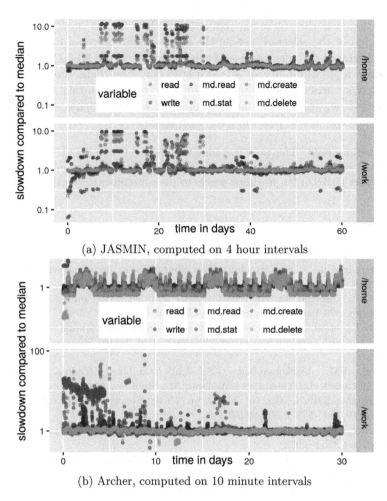

(a) JASMIN, computed on 4 hour intervals

(b) Archer, computed on 10 minute intervals

Fig. 6. Computed slowdown compared to median

5   Conclusion

In this article, we introduced an approach to monitor the system performance and derive the user-experienced slowdown by constantly running small I/O probes. This allows users and data center experts to investigate and track system performance over time but also to quantify the slowdown compared to normal operation. The slowdown factor is expected to correspond to the delay of parallel applications for data bound and metadata bound applications. The data could be feed into a monitoring system such as Grafana allowing stakeholders to investigate the slowdown in a timely fashion – for instance, helpdesk employees can answer the question if the storage is currently overloaded.

A key issue is the statistical reduction of the sampled data, depending on the selection of the selected metric, the effect on the user can be investigated. We demonstrated the effectiveness of this approach on the IO-500 workload and showed the high variability of 4-h statistics for three data centers. We were particularly surprised to see small individual I/Os that can take up to 100 s.

In the future, we will combine this approach with additional server-side data and user-utilization and perform long-term studies.

Acknowledgements. This work was supported by the UK National Supercomputing Service, ARCHER funded by EPSRC and NERC. We thank the German Climate Computing Center (DKRZ) for providing access to their machines to run the experiments.

References

1. Bent, J., Kunkel, J., Lofstead, J., Markomanolis, G.: IO500 Full Ranked List, Supercomputing 2018 (Corrected), November 2018. https://www.vi4io.org/io500/list/19-01/start
2. Carns, P.: Darshan. In: High Performance Parallel I/O. Computational Science Series, pp. 309–315. Chapman & Hall/CRC (2015)
3. Carns, P., et al.: Understanding and improving computational science storage access through continuous characterization. ACM Trans. Storage (TOS) **7**(3), 8 (2011)
4. Kunkel, J.M., Markomanolis, G.S.: Understanding metadata latency with MDWorkbench. In: Yokota, R., Weiland, M., Shalf, J., Alam, S. (eds.) ISC High Performance 2018. LNCS, vol. 11203, pp. 75–88. Springer, Cham (2018). https://doi.org/10.1007/978-3-030-02465-9_5
5. Lawrence, B., et al.: The JASMIN super-data-cluster. arXiv preprint arXiv:1204.3553 (2012)
6. Lockwood, G.K., Snyder, S., Wang, T., Byna, S., Carns, P., Wright, N.J.: A year in the life of a parallel file system. In: Proceedings of the International Conference for High Performance Computing, Networking, Storage, and Analysis, p. 74. IEEE Press (2018)
7. Sivalingam, K., Richardson, H., Tate, A., Lafferty, M.: LASSi: metric based I/O analytics for HPC. In: SCS Spring Simulation Multi-Conference (SpringSim 2019), Tucson, AZ, USA (2019)
8. Tuncer, O., et al.: Diagnosing performance variations in HPC applications using machine learning. In: Kunkel, J.M., Yokota, R., Balaji, P., Keyes, D. (eds.) ISC 2017. LNCS, vol. 10266, pp. 355–373. Springer, Cham (2017). https://doi.org/10.1007/978-3-319-58667-0_19
9. Uselton, A., Wright, N.: A file system utilization metric for I/O characterization (2013)
10. Voss, J., Garcia, J.A., Cyrus Proctor, W., Todd Evans, R.: Automated system health and performance benchmarking platform: high performance computing test harness with Jenkins. In: Proceedings of the HPC Systems Professionals Workshop, HPCSYSPROS 2017, pp. 1:1–1:8. ACM, New York (2017)

A Quantitative Approach to Architecting All-Flash Lustre File Systems

Glenn K. Lockwood$^{(\boxtimes)}$, Kirill Lozinskiy, Lisa Gerhardt, Ravi Cheema,
Damian Hazen, and Nicholas J. Wright

Lawrence Berkeley National Laboratory, Berkeley, CA 94720, USA
{glock,klozinskiy,lgerhardt,rcheema,dhazen,njwright}@lbl.gov

Abstract. New experimental and AI-driven workloads are moving into the realm of extreme-scale HPC systems at the same time that high-performance flash is becoming cost-effective to deploy at scale. This confluence poses a number of new technical and economic challenges and opportunities in designing the next generation of HPC storage and I/O subsystems to achieve the right balance of bandwidth, latency, endurance, and cost. In this work, we present quantitative models that use workload data from existing, disk-based file systems to project the architectural requirements of all-flash Lustre file systems. Using data from NERSC's Cori I/O subsystem, we then demonstrate the minimum required capacity for data, capacity for metadata and data-on-MDT, and SSD endurance for a future all-flash Lustre file system.

Keywords: Architecture · Lustre · Flash

1 Introduction

The conventional wisdom of I/O subsystem design in high-performance computing (HPC) are rapidly changing as a result of the broadening scope of HPC beyond traditional modeling and simulation. The emergence of applying artificial intelligence (AI) at scale is showing promise as a completely new means to extract new insights from huge bodies of scientific data [13,14]. Concurrently, there has been an explosion of high resolution detectors available to experimental and observational scientific communities [5,18] which can produce scientific data at unprecedented rates [3,20]. These workloads do not simply perform I/O to save and load the state of their calculation synchronously; rather, they are often marked by having to process volumes of data that far exceed the amount of memory available on their processing elements. Furthermore, the amount of computations they perform are often dictated by the contents of the data they are processing and cannot be determined *a priori*. As a result, the I/O patterns of these emerging workloads differ from those of traditional checkpoint-restart and do not perform optimally on today's production, disk-based parallel file systems.

© Springer Nature Switzerland AG 2019
M. Weiland et al. (Eds.): ISC 2019 Workshops, LNCS 11887, pp. 183–197, 2019.
https://doi.org/10.1007/978-3-030-34356-9_16

Fortunately, the cost of flash-based solid-state disks (SSDs) has reached a point where it is now cost-effective to integrate flash into large-scale HPC systems to work around many of the limitations intrinsic to disk-based high-performance storage systems [6,11,19]. The current state of the art is to integrate flash as a *burst buffer* which logically resides between user applications and lower-performing disk-based parallel file systems. Burst buffers have already been shown to benefit experimental and observational data analysis in a multitude of science domains including high-energy physics, astronomy, bioinformatics, and climate [5,7,14,17,24].

However such burst buffers often enable high performance by exposing additional complexity to users. For example, DataWarp burst buffers offer a separate ephemeral namespace into which data must be staged in or out using non-standard APIs, while Infinite Memory Engine offers only eventual consistency between data written to flash and data on the backing file system. It is ultimately the responsibility of users to track the tier (flash or disk) in which their most up-to-date data resides. This incentivizes a return to a single high-performance storage tier, and the dropping cost of SSDs [9] are expected to once again give rise to a single, high-performance storage tier that has the performance of a burst buffer but the capacity of a traditional disk-based parallel file system [12,15].

In practice, balancing performance, capacity, resilience, and cost requires a system architecture driven by several goals:

- The capacity of the file system must be "just enough" for the aggregate workload to ensure that flash, which is still expensive on a cost-capacity basis, is not over- or underprovisioned for capacity
- The SSD media must be of sufficient endurance to meet the service requirements of the workload without being overprovisioned for unrealistically high endurance levels, as this adds to overall cost
- All available performance features for low latency I/O with Lustre must be effectively provisioned for and usable by the workload

Meeting these goals requires a quantitative understanding of the I/O workload that will run on the target storage system to ensure that the most critical portions of the system architecture receive the most investment.

In this work, we present a series of analytical methods by which the requirements of a future all-flash file system can be quantitatively defined. We then use telemetric data collected from a reference production storage system to inform the minimum and maximum values required to achieve an optimal balance of capacity and value on a future all-flash parallel file system. However, we do *not* address I/O performance in this work because we expect that the absolute throughput of first-generation all-flash parallel file systems will be limited by software, not flash media, when they are initially deployed. It follows that the absolute performance of these systems will steadily increase with successive software improvements over the service lives of these all-flash file systems, making performance prediction difficult and highly dependent on software architecture, not system architecture.

2   Methods

The goal of this work is to define models through which the design space surrounding several key dimensions of parallel file system architecture can be quantified. These models project the requirements of a notional future parallel file system by combining data from an existing reference parallel file system with parameters that describe the future system. For simplicity, we refer to the model inputs as coming from the *reference* system, and the model outputs as describing the requirements for a *new* system. To illustrate the efficacy of these models, we then apply data collected from the I/O subsystem of Cori, a Cray XC-40 system deployed at NERSC, to derive the requirements for a notional all-flash Lustre file system that will be deployed with Perlmutter, NERSC's next-generation system.

The reference system is Cori, a Cray XC-40 system comprised of 9,688 compute nodes with Intel Xeon Phi 7250 processors and 2,388 compute nodes with Intel Xeon E5-2698 v3 processors. Cori's I/O subsystem has two tiers: a disk-based Lustre file system and an all-flash DataWarp burst buffer. The precise configurations of these two storage tiers are described in Table 1.

Table 1. Description of reference system

Tier (file system)	Capacity	Peak bandwidth	#Data servers	#Drives
Burst buffer (DataWarp)	1.84 PB	1,740 GB/s	288	1,152
Scratch (Lustre)	30.5 PB	717 GB/s	248	10,168

We rely on the Lustre Monitoring Tool (LMT) [21] to quantify the I/O requirements imposed on the reference file system by NERSC's production workload. LMT reports the total number of bytes read and written to each Lustre object storage target (OST) since the time each object storage server (OSS) was last rebooted on a five-second interval. To understand how the file system's fullness increases, we run the standard Lustre `lfs df` command every five minutes to archive a consistent view each OST's fullness.

To characterize the utilization of the burst buffer tier on Cori, we use the Intel Data Center SSD Tool [2] to collect device-level data including the total bytes read and written to each SSD by the host DataWarp server and the total bytes read and written to the underlying NAND. The device-level read and write activity from the host is a close approximation of the aggregate user workload because user I/O is simply striped across devices without additional parity in DataWarp. Comparing the host- and NAND-level I/O volumes also allows us to explicitly calculate the aggregate write amplification factor (WAF = NAND bytes written/host bytes written) of each SSD over its service life.

We obtain the distribution of file and inode sizes from a MySQL database populated using the Robinhood policy engine [8] version 3.1.4. This database contains the results of scanning the Lustre namespace from a Lustre client and inserting records that catalog the POSIX metadata fields intrinsic to each inode. For each type of inode, we build histograms of inode size with exponentially increasing bins such that bin i contains the number of inodes with size S such that $2^{i-1} < S \leq 2^i$.

3   File System Capacity

To determine the minimum required capacity, C^{new}, for the storage subsystem of a new HPC system, we use a simple growth model that uses empirical measurements from the reference HPC system's compute and storage subsystems. This model is expressed as

$$C^{\text{new}} = \text{SSI} \cdot \left(\frac{\lambda_{\text{purge}}}{\text{PF}} \right) \cdot \left(\frac{\partial C^{\text{ref}}}{\partial t} \right) \tag{1}$$

where

1. SSI is the Sustained System Improvement [4], a metric incorporating both performance and throughput improvement of the new system relative to the reference system
2. $(\lambda_{\text{purge}}/\text{PF})$ encapsulates the numerical description of the anticipated data retention policy of the new file system
3. $(\partial C^{\text{ref}}/\partial t)$ is daily growth rate observed on the reference file system

We use SSI to account for the fact that a system with a higher capability or throughput will be able to consume and generate data at a proportionally higher rate. For example, a workflow that can execute $3\times$ faster on the new system will be able to produce three times as much useful output in a fixed amount of time relative to the reference system assuming no other changes.

The $(\lambda_{\text{purge}}/\text{PF})$ term represents a data management policy whose terms can be interpreted in several different ways. λ_{purge} is a measure of time that reflects either the periodicity of purge cycles or the time after which files are eligible to be purged. PF is the fraction of total file system capacity to be reclaimed after each purge or the fraction fullness of the file system above which files become eligible for purging. These two terms provide enough flexibility to capture the most common approaches to purging. For example, files not touched in more than λ_{purge} days will be purged if doing so will aid in driving down file system fullness below $(100 \times \text{PF})\%$. As with any numerical expression of a data retention policy though, it cannot capture the effects of ill-intentioned users who touch files to make them ineligible for purge, the effects of excluding certain projects from purge, or other purge exceptions that manifest in real production systems. As such, this may be a liberal estimate what the true production data retention policy may be and should be specified with these uncertainties in mind.

The rate at which the reference file system grows, $(\partial C^{\text{ref}}/\partial t)$, is the most challenging term to calculate rigorously. In practice, the growth rate of file systems is a function of many variables including user diversity (some scientific workflows must retain more data than others [1]), time of year (conference deadlines and allocation expiration dates are often preceded by high utilization), and system age (improvements to system stability and usability encourage longer-term data retention). As such, correctly parameterizing $\left(\partial C^{\mathrm{ref}}/\partial t\right)$ requires institutional knowledge of both the technological and sociological factors intrinsic to the reference system.

To determine $\left(\partial C^{\mathrm{ref}}/\partial t\right)$ for our reference system, we first define the *daily growth* for day d as the difference between the capacity used on day d and $d-1$. We further constrain this daily growth metric by stating that it is undefined for days when there was a net reduction in file system fullness. In doing so, we minimize the effects of center-wide policies on daily growth by disregarding days during which significant amounts of user data were being purged.

To avoid biasing our analysis with the low growth rates often experienced during the earlier months of a system's service life, we also define an arbitrary cutoff date before which all daily growth measurements are discarded. For this study, we chose the cutoff to be exactly two years before the day on which the daily growth data were collected for this study to ensure that we captured the growth contributions of a broad range of projects that run at NERSC. In addition, our choice to align the sample period with a calendar year ensures that we capture the full range of sociological effects (such as conference deadlines) that may cause users to behave differently over the course of their year-long allocations.

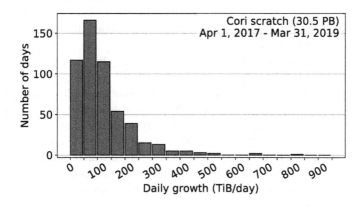

Fig. 1. Distribution of daily growth of Cori's scratch file system.

Figure 1 shows the resulting distribution of this daily growth metric and reflects a median growth of 104 TB/day and a mean daily growth of 133 TB/day. The long tail of this distribution indicates that there are periods throughout the year when significant amounts of data are either generated within or imported to NERSC, and these outlying days should not be ignored when projecting future requirements. As a result, we choose to use the mean daily growth rather than the median as the basis for $\left(\partial C^{\mathrm{ref}}/\partial t\right)$.

We define the new system's data retention policy such that data older than 28 days is subject to purge, and each purge interval aims to remove or migrate 50% of the total file system capacity. Furthermore, the SSI for our new system is anticipated be between 3× and 4× that of the reference system. Given this range of anticipated SSI, Eq. 1 gives the minimum required usable capacity C^{new} as being between 22 PB and 30 PB.

Although this is a wide range, Eq. 1 provides a means to understand how tradeoffs can be made between user convenience (via a more generous data retention policy) and usable capacity. Similarly, the flexibility of the SSI metric also defines how changes to system capability, throughput, and application optimizations will affect storage system capacity requirements. Thus, it is possible to decide where in this range the target storage system capacity should be based on how a facility weighs each of these factors given a fixed budget.

4   Drive Endurance

The flash cells within SSDs can be rewritten a finite number of times before they are no longer able to reliably store data, and as a result, SSDs are only warranted for a finite number of drive writes per day (DWPD) over their service life. Since HPC file systems have historically been subject to write-intensive workloads [10,22], the endurance requirements of SSDs in HPC environments have been a cause of concern. To date, most large-scale flash deployments in HPC have resorted to using extreme-endurance SSDs (5–10 DWPD for a five-year period) to ensure that the SSDs do not fail before the end of the overall system's service life [11,19].

This comes at a steep cost, though; for example, the Trinity supercomputer at Los Alamos National Laboratory employs a burst buffer comprised of drives configured to endure 10 DWPD instead of the factory default of 3 DWPD [11]. This is achieved by reserving 20% of each SSD's usable capacity for wear leveling. If this extreme level of endurance is not truly required though, reducing the drives' endurance from 10 DWPD to 3 DWPD would provide an additional 25% usable capacity at no added cost. To determine the optimal balance of cost and endurance for HPC workloads, we use an analytical model (Eq. 2) that uses file system-level load data and sources of write amplification to define the minimum required DWPD for an all-flash file system.

$$\text{DWPD}^{\text{new}} = \text{SSI} \cdot \text{FSWPD}^{\text{ref}} \cdot \text{WAF} \cdot \left(\frac{1}{\chi}\right) \left(\frac{N^{\text{ref}}}{N^{\text{new}}}\right) \left(\frac{c^{\text{ref}}}{c^{\text{new}}}\right) \left(\frac{R^{\text{ref}}}{R^{\text{new}}}\right) \quad (2)$$

where

1. SSI is the sustained system improvement as defined in Sect. 3
2. FSWPD^{ref} is the reference file system's total write volume expressed in units of file system writes per day
3. WAF is the write amplification factor that results from factors intrinsic to the application workload and file system implementation

4. χ is the fraction of Lustre capacity available after formatting, typically ranging from 0.95 to 0.97
5. N^{ref} and N^{new} are the number of drives in the reference and new systems
6. c^{ref} and c^{new} are the per-drive capacities in the reference and new systems
7. R^{ref} and R^{new} are the code rates of the reference and new systems

Figure 2 shows the distribution of daily write workloads on the reference file system over a period of two years measured using LMT. As with the growth rates presented in Sect. 3, there is a long tail of days that experience abnormally high write volumes which reflect the use of the file system as a data processing capability and should not be discarded. We therefore choose to use the mean, not median, FSWPD value of 0.024 FSWPD.

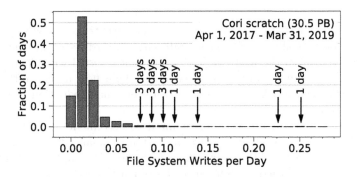

Fig. 2. Distribution of file system writes per day to the Cori scratch file system. 1 FSWPD = 30.5 PB of writes per day. Nonzero fractions in the tail are annotated in absolute days.

The WAF term accounts for the fact that writes smaller than a full RAID stripe require the RAID subsystem to (1) read the stripe blocks that will be modified, (2) make the modification to those blocks, (3) recalculate parity on P blocks, and (4) write a minimum of $P + 1$ blocks back to the underlying media.[1] This read-modify-write penalty is a function of the anticipated workload; if all applications buffer their writes such that only full-stripe writes are issued to the SSDs, this term is effectively 1.0.

We do not directly monitor I/O transfer sizes on the Cori file system which prevents us from quantifying WAF. However, we can estimate WAF from the SSDs in the reference system's burst buffer, shown in Fig. 3 The NERSC burst buffer workload results in WAFs ranging from 1.35 to 10.15, and the median and 95th percentile are $\text{WAF}_{50} = 2.68$ and $\text{WAF}_{95} = 3.17$, respectively. Although the drives showing extremely high WAFs (>5) appear to be cause for concern,

---

[1] We do not consider write amplification caused by garbage collection internal to the SSDs since drive endurance is warranted on the basis of host-initiated write load, not total write load to NAND.

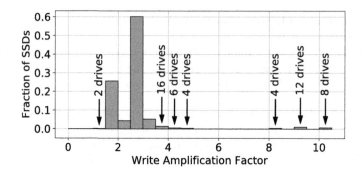

Fig. 3. Distribution of SSD WAFs on the Cori Burst buffer after approximately 3.4 years in service

these outliers are actually a result of drives that see extremely low use. Because SSDs must periodically rewrite pages internally regardless of weather data is written to them from the host, there is a constant internal write load on SSDs which becomes dominant in the presence of very light host usage. In the case of Fig. 3, all SSDs with WAF >5 belong to a development partition of the burst buffer that is not in production.

The χ and R terms in Eq. 2 are required to account for the fact that the formatted capacity of a reliable Lustre file system is smaller than the aggregate storage device capacity. The coding rates R^{ref} and R^{new} capture differences in write amplification caused by different ratios of parity overheads in the systems' RAID schemes. χ accounts for additional minor capacity overheads such as the root file system of each Lustre OSS. The N and c terms are required to account for differences in the actual file system capacity of the reference file system and new file system, as a single file system write to a small reference file system represents only a fraction of a file system write to a larger new file system.

We choose values that are optimistic (SSI = 3.0, $R^{\mathrm{new}} = 10/12$, and WAF = 2.68) and pessimistic (SSI = 4.0, $R^{\mathrm{new}} = 8/10$, and WAF = 3.17) to determine the minimum and maximum required DWPD, respectively. Because the specific hardware geometry for a new file system (N^{new} and c^{new}) may not be defined at the time of requirements definition, we note that $\chi \cdot N^{\mathrm{new}} \cdot c^{\mathrm{new}} \cdot R^{\mathrm{new}} \approx C^{\mathrm{new}}$ and reduce Eq. 2 to

$$\mathrm{DWPD}^{\mathrm{new}} \approx \mathrm{SSI} \cdot \mathrm{FSWPD}^{\mathrm{ref}} \cdot \mathrm{WAF} \cdot \frac{N^{\mathrm{ref}} \cdot c^{\mathrm{ref}} \cdot R^{\mathrm{ref}}}{C^{\mathrm{new}}} \tag{3}$$

Given that $R^{\mathrm{ref}} = 8/10$, $N^{\mathrm{ref}} = 10168$, and $c^{\mathrm{ref}} \approx 4$ TB, we find that $\mathrm{DWPD}^{\mathrm{new}}_{\mathrm{min}} = 0.28$ and $\mathrm{DWPD}^{\mathrm{new}}_{\mathrm{max}} = 0.33$. From this, it becomes very clear that extreme-endurance SSDs are unnecessary for HPC workloads that resemble those of the reference system, and even 1 DWPD leaves significant headroom for increased wear from unanticipated new workloads.

5   Metadata Configuration

Lustre's Data-on-MDT (DOM) feature allows the first S_0 bytes of every file to be stored on the same storage devices as their file metadata. This introduces several major benefits for small-file access:

1. Lock traffic is reduced since data and metadata are colocated
2. File size can be determined without sending RPCs to OSSes
3. Small file I/O interferes much less with large-file I/O on OSTs

However, DOM adds additional complexity to system design because MDT capacity must now account for both the capacity required to store inodes and the capacity required to store small files' contents. The precise definition of what constitutes a "small" file is also site-configurable, meaning that system architects must define both the required MDT capacity, C^{MDT}, and the threshold for storing small files exclusively on the MDT, S_0.

Thus, we define a model for the required MDT capacity as the sum of the capacity required by DOM to store the first S_0 bytes of every file (C^{DOM}) and the capacity required to store inodes[2] (C^{inode}) in Eq. 4.

$$C^{\mathrm{MDT}} = C^{\mathrm{DOM}} + C^{\mathrm{inode}} \qquad (4)$$

The required MDT capacity for a new system is invariably a function of the expected file size distribution on that new system. It is not sufficient to parameterize such a model on the average file size alone because file size distributions on HPC systems are almost always skewed towards small files [16, 22, 23], and small changes to the mean file size could represent a significant change to where the optimal DOM size threshold should be. As shown in Fig. 4, this is true of the reference system where 95% of the files comprise only 5% of the capacity used. As a result, both C^{DOM} and C^{inode} are a function of the probability distribution of file size, P_i^{file}, shown in Fig. 4.

5.1   MDT Capacity Required by DOM

To calculate C^{DOM}, we first convert the probability distribution of file sizes P_i^{file} into a mass distribution of data M_i^{data} for the new file system using Eq. 5.

$$M_i^{\mathrm{data}} = P_i^{\mathrm{file}} \cdot C^{\mathrm{new}} \qquad (5)$$

Because P_i^{file} is expressed as a discrete histogram rather than a density function, Eq. 5 requires that we assume all files in each bin i have an average mass that lies between the minimum and maximum size of the bin, $S_{i,\mathrm{min}}$ and $S_{i,\mathrm{max}}$. For example, if the bin bounded by (1024 bytes, 2048 bytes] contains 512 files, we can only say that the total mass lies between 512.5 KiB (if all 512 files are

---

[2] Strictly speaking, we define C^{inode} to include the MDT block allocated for inodes *and* additional data blocks that may be required to store, for example, large numbers of directory entries.

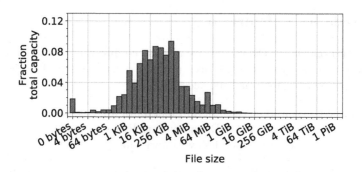

Fig. 4. Probability distribution of file size on the reference system in January 2019.

of size $S_{i,\min} = 1025$ bytes) and 1 MiB (if all 512 files are of size $S_{i,\max} = 2048$ bytes). Thus, M_i^{data} is actually a set of mass distributions that result from assuming different average file sizes for each bin when applying Eq. 5. Hereafter, we acknowledge this by referring to the set of mass distributions as $\boldsymbol{M}_i^{\text{data}}$. We use this set of distributions to attribute uncertainty to all subsequent calculations derived from $\boldsymbol{M}_i^{\text{data}}$ and explicitly calculate

- $M_i^{\text{data,min}}$ which assumes all files in i have size $S_{i,\min}$
- $M_i^{\text{data,max}}$ which assumes all files in i have size $S_{i,\max}$
- $M_i^{\text{data,avg}} = 1/2 \cdot (M_i^{\text{data,min}} + M_i^{\text{data,max}})$

From $\boldsymbol{M}_i^{\text{data}}$, we can then estimate file count distributions of the new file system, $\boldsymbol{N}_i^{\text{file}}$, using Eq. 6.

$$\boldsymbol{N}_i^{\text{file}} = \boldsymbol{M}_i^{\text{data}}/\boldsymbol{S}_i \qquad (6)$$

$\boldsymbol{N}_i^{\text{file}}$ is a set of distributions due to the dependence of Eq. 6 on $\boldsymbol{M}_i^{\text{data}}$ and $\boldsymbol{S}_i$, both of which are themselves sets of distributions. Thus, as with $\boldsymbol{M}_i^{\text{data}}$, we carry forward the minimum, maximum, and average file count distribution using Eq. 7.

$$\begin{aligned} N_i^{\text{file,min}} &= M_i^{\text{data,min}}/S_i^{\max} \\ N_i^{\text{file,max}} &= M_i^{\text{data,max}}/S_i^{\min} \\ N_i^{\text{file,avg}} &= M_i^{\text{data,avg}}/S_i^{\text{avg}} \end{aligned} \qquad (7)$$

With an estimate of the number of files and their sizes for the new file system, we can now calculate the range of capacities required for DOM, $\boldsymbol{C}^{\text{DOM}}$, with Eq. 8.

$$\boldsymbol{C}^{\text{DOM}} = \sum_i^{S_i \leq S_0} \left(\boldsymbol{N}_i^{\text{file}} \cdot \boldsymbol{S}_i\right) + \sum_i^{S_i > S_0} \left(\boldsymbol{N}_i^{\text{file}} \cdot S_0\right) \qquad (8)$$

Thus, this gives us a way to determine the capacity required for DOM as a function of the DOM threshold S_0 that carries forward ranges of uncertainty intrinsic to our dependence on sets of discrete distributions.

5.2 MDT Capacity Required for Inodes

The MDT capacity required to store inodes, C^{inode}, follows a similar approach. By default, Lustre reserves 4 KiB of MDT capacity for every inode, but there are cases where an inode can consume significantly more capacity. Figure 5 shows the probability distribution of non-file inodes' masses on the reference system and demonstrates this phenomenon. In the most extreme case, a single directory requires nearly 1 GiB of MDT capacity as a result of it containing over eight million child inodes.

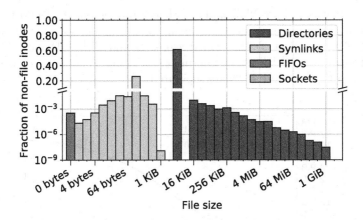

Fig. 5. Probability distribution of inode sizes on NERSC's Cori file system in January 2019. This diagram does not show block or character device inode types because none were present at the time of data collection. Break in y scale intended to contrast small numbers of large directory inodes with the predominant 4 KiB inode size.

To ensure that such extreme requirements are not lost when calculating the MDT inode capacity requirements, we explicitly calculate the inode size distribution for every inode type (directories, symbolic links, etc.) based on the file size distributions N_i^{file} derived from Eq. 6. Equation 9 demonstrates this derivation for the directory size distribution; the process is the same for all non-file inode types.

$$N_i^{\text{dir}} = N_i^{\text{file}} \cdot \frac{N_i^{\text{ref,dir}}}{N_i^{\text{ref,file}}} \tag{9}$$

The inode size distribution reported by Robinhood can be misleading as a result of the difference between an inode's apparent size (as returned by `stat(2)`) and its block consumption. To ensure that inodes of small apparent size do not underrepresent the true inode capacity requirements, we assume that each inode whose apparent size is less than 4 KiB actually requires a full 4 KiB block. Thus, we calculate the total mass of these inodes using Eq. 10.

$$C^{\text{inode}} = \sum_i \left[\max\left(\boldsymbol{S}_i, 4096\right) \cdot \sum_j \boldsymbol{N}_i^j \right] \tag{10}$$

This equation gives the total mass of all bins i for all inodes of type j with the constraint that all inodes must consume at least one block and therefore be at least 4 KiB in size.

5.3   Overall MDT Capacity

We now evaluate $C_{\min}^{\text{MDT}}$, $C_{\max}^{\text{MDT}}$, and $C_{\text{avg}}^{\text{MDT}}$ as a function of the DOM threshold size S_0 using Eq. 4. Figure 6 shows the result of this model for a target capacity $C^{\text{new}} = 30$ PB from Sect. 3. The shaded regions bound $C^{\text{MDT,min}}$ and $C^{\text{MDT,max}}$, and the black line is $C^{\text{MDT,avg}}$. Furthermore, the components of this uncertainty attributed to $\boldsymbol{C}^{\text{DOM}}$ and $\boldsymbol{C}^{\text{inode}}$ are separated.

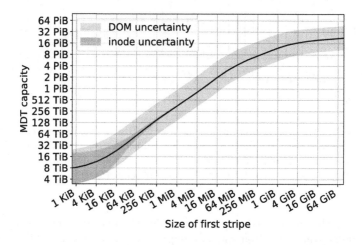

Fig. 6. Required MDT capacity as a function of S_0. Shaded area bounded by the minimum and maximum estimated requirements dictated by the DOM component and the inode capacity component of MDT capacity. Note that, in practice, the DOM component size cannot be smaller than the minimum Lustre stripe size. At the time of writing, the minimum DOM component size is 64 KiB.

The sigmoidal shape of C^{MDT}'s dependence on the DOM threshold S_0 is a result of two competing factors. For very small S_0, the large number of small files simply does not consume a large amount of DOM capacity so there are only modest increases in C^{DOM} in this region. For very large S_0, the great majority of files are stored entirely within the MDT and only a small number of very large files are increasing the C^{DOM} requirements.

The region between the two extremes of small and large DOM thresholds leaves considerable room for optimization though. For example, doubling the

MDT capacity from 512 TiB to 1 PiB allows a fourfold increase in S_0. The cost-per-bit for an MDT is typically higher than that for an OST due to different parity configuration (e.g., $5+5$ parity on an MDT vs. $8+2$ on an OST), but this increased cost comes with better IOPS performance.

If one assumes that C^{DOM} is proportional to cost and S_0 is proportional to IOPS performance, Fig. 6 becomes a price-performance curve as well. In this context, the behavior for $S_0 \to C^{\text{new}}$ suggests that the benefit of increasing S_0 above several GiB is not an optimal configuration for price/performance. Thus, while a Lustre file system entirely comprised of MDTs with DOM could be possible in principle, its performance improvements would likely not justify its cost when compared to a Lustre file system with a judiciously chosen S_0.

6   Conclusion

We have presented methods by which workload data from a reference file system can be used to determine the best balance of cost, performance, and usability along several dimensions. We then quantified the relationship between factors including purge policy, growth rate, and file size distribution and design space parameters surrounding an all-flash file system such as data capacity, SSD endurance, and metadata configuration. As the economics of flash continue to displace hard disk drives from high-performance storage tiers, such analytical methods will become increasingly important for future system deployments.

Acknowledgments. The authors would like to thank John Bent, Andreas Dilger, and the anonymous reviewers for their valuable feedback on this work. This material is based upon work supported by the U.S. Department of Energy, Office of Science, under contract DE-AC02-05CH11231. This research used resources and data generated from resources of the National Energy Research Scientific Computing Center, a DOE Office of Science User Facility supported by the Office of Science of the U.S. Department of Energy under Contract No. DE-AC02-05CH11231.

References

1. APEX Workflows Whitepaper. Tech. Rep., Los Alamos National Laboratory, Lawrence Berkeley National Laboratory, and Sandia National Laboratories (2016). https://www.nersc.gov/assets/apex-workflows-v2.pdf
2. Intel SSD Data Center Tool (2017). https://www.intel.com/content/www/us/en/support/articles/000006289
3. Alewijnse, B., et al.: Best practices for managing large CryoEM facilities. J. Struct. Biol. **199**(3), 225–236 (2017). https://doi.org/10.1016/j.jsb.2017.07.011. https://linkinghub.elsevier.com/retrieve/pii/S1047847717301314
4. Austin, B., et al.: A metric for evaluating supercomputer performance in the era of extreme Heterogeneity. In: 2018 IEEE/ACM Performance Modeling, Benchmarking and Simulation of High Performance Computer Systems (PMBS), pp. 63–71. IEEE (November 2018). https://doi.org/10.1109/PMBS.2018.8641549, https://ieeexplore.ieee.org/document/8641549/

5. Bhimji, W., et al.: Extreme I/O on HPC for HEP using the burst buffer at NERSC. J. Phys. Conf. Ser. **898**, 082015 (2017). https://doi.org/10.1088/1742-6596/898/8/082015. https://iopscience.iop.org/article/10.1088/1742-6596/898/8/082015

6. Bhimji, W., et al.: Accelerating science with the NERSC burst buffer early user program. In: Proceedings of the 2016 Cray User Group, London (2016). https://cug.org/proceedings/cug2016_proceedings/includes/files/pap162.pdf

7. Daley, C.S., Ghoshal, D., Lockwood, G.K., Dosanjh, S., Ramakrishnan, L., Wright, N.J.: Performance characterization of scientific workflows for the optimal use of burst buffers. In: Future Generation Computer Systems (December 2017). https://doi.org/10.1016/j.future.2017.12.022, http://linkinghub.elsevier.com/retrieve/pii/S0167739X16308287

8. Declerck, T.M.: Using Robinhood to purge data from Lustre file systems. In: Proceedings of the 2014 Cray User Group, Lugano, CH (2014). https://cug.org/proceedings/cug2014_proceedings/includes/files/pap157.pdf

9. Fontana, R.E., Decad, G.M.: Moore's law realities for recording systems and memory storage components: HDD, tape, NAND, and optical. AIP Adv. **8**(5), 056506 (2018). https://doi.org/10.1063/1.5007621. http://aip.scitation.org/doi/10.1063/1.5007621

10. Gunasekaran, R., Oral, S., Hill, J., Miller, R., Wang, F., Leverman, D.: Comparative I/O workload characterization of two leadership class storage clusters. In: Proceedings of the 10th Parallel Data Storage Workshop (PDSW 2015), pp. 31–36. ACM Press, New York (2015). https://doi.org/10.1145/2834976.2834985, http://dl.acm.org/citation.cfm?doid=2834976.2834985

11. Hemmert, K.S., et al.: Trinity: architecture and early experience. In: Proceedings of the 2017 Cray User Group (2017)

12. Bent, J., Settlemeyer, B., Grider, G.: Serving data to the lunatic fringe: the evolution of HPC storage. Login **41**(2), 34–39 (2016). https://www.usenix.org/publications/login/summer2016/bent

13. Joubert, W., et al.: Attacking the opioid epidemic: determining the epistatic and pleiotropic genetic architectures for chronic pain and opioid addiction. In: Proceedings of the International Conference for High Performance Computing, Networking, Storage, and Analysis, pp. 57:1–57:14, SC 2018. IEEE Press, Piscataway (2018). http://dl.acm.org/citation.cfm?id=3291656.3291732

14. Kurth, T., et al.: Exascale deep learning for climate analytics. In: Proceedings of the International Conference for High Performance Computing, Networking, Storage, and Analysis, pp. 51:1–51:12, SC 2018. IEEE Press, Piscataway (2018). http://dl.acm.org/citation.cfm?id=3291656.3291724, arXiv:1810.01993

15. Lockwood, G.K., et al.: Storage 2020: a vision for the future of HPC storage. Tech. rep., Lawrence Berkeley National Laboratory, Berkeley (2017). https://escholarship.org/uc/item/744479dp

16. Lockwood, G.K., Wagner, R., Tatineni, M.: Storage utilization in the long tail of science. In: Proceedings of the 2015 XSEDE Conference: Scientific Advancements Enabled by Enhanced Cyberinfrastructure (2015). https://doi.org/10.1145/2792745.2792777, http://dl.acm.org/citation.cfm?id=2792777

17. Regier, J., et al.: Cataloging the visible universe through Bayesian inference at petascale. In: 2018 IEEE International Parallel and Distributed Processing Symposium (IPDPS), pp. 44–53 (May 2018). https://doi.org/10.1109/IPDPS.2018.00015

18. Standish, K.A., et al.: Group-based variant calling leveraging next-generation supercomputing for large-scale whole-genome sequencing studies. BMC Bioinf. **16**(1), 304 (2015). https://doi.org/10.1186/s12859-015-0736-4. http://www.biomedcentral.com/1471-2105/16/304

19. Strande, S.M., et al.: Gordon: design, performance, and experiences deploying and supporting a data intensive supercomputer. In: Proceedings of the 1st Conference of the Extreme Science and Engineering Discovery Environment: Bridging from the eXtreme to the Campus and Beyond, pp. 3:1–3:8, XSEDE 2012. ACM, New York (2012). https://doi.org/10.1145/2335755.2335789
20. Thayer, J., et al.: Data systems for the linac coherent light source. J. Appl. Crystallogr. **49**(4), 1363–1369 (2016). https://doi.org/10.1107/S1600576716011055. http://scripts.iucr.org/cgi-bin/paper?S1600576716011055
21. Uselton, A.: Deploying server-side file system monitoring at NERSC. In: Proceedings of the 2009 Cray User Group (2009)
22. Vazhkudai, S.S., et al.: GUIDE: a scalable information directory service to collect, federate, and analyze logs for operational insights into a leadership HPC facility. In: Proceedings of the International Conference for High Performance Computing, Networking, Storage and Analysis on - SC 2017, pp. 1–12 (2017). https://doi.org/10.1145/3126908.3126946, http://dl.acm.org/citation.cfm?doid=3126908.3126946
23. Wang, F., Sim, H., Harr, C., Oral, S.: Diving into petascale production file systems through large scale profiling and analysis. In: Proceedings of the 2nd Joint International Workshop on Parallel Data Storage & Data Intensive Scalable Computing Systems - PDSW-DISCS 2017, pp. 37–42. ACM Press, New York (2017). https://doi.org/10.1145/3149393.3149399, http://dl.acm.org/citation.cfm?doid=3149393.3149399
24. Weeks, N.T., Luecke, G.R.: Optimization of SAMtools sorting using OpenMP tasks. Cluster Comput. **20**(3), 1869–1880 (2017). https://doi.org/10.1007/s10586-017-0874-8

MBWU: Benefit Quantification for Data Access Function Offloading

Jianshen Liu[1(✉)], Philip Kufeldt[2(✉)], and Carlos Maltzahn[1(✉)]

[1] University of California, Santa Cruz, Santa Cruz, CA 95064, USA
{jliu120,carlosm}@ucsc.edu
[2] Seagate, Longmont, CO 80303, USA
philip.kufeldt@seagate.com

Abstract. The storage industry is considering new kinds of storage devices that support data access function offloading, i.e. the ability to perform data access functions on the storage device itself as opposed to performing it on a separate compute system to which the storage device is connected. But what is the benefit of offloading to a storage device that is controlled by an embedded platform, very different from a host platform? To quantify the benefit, we need a measurement methodology that enables apple-to-apple comparisons between different platforms. We propose a Media-based Work Unit (MBWU, pronounced "MibeeWu"), and an MBWU-based measurement methodology to standardize the platform efficiency evaluation so as to quantify the benefit of offloading. To demonstrate the merit of this methodology, we implemented a prototype to automate quantifying the benefit of offloading the key-value data access function.

Keywords: MBWU · Performance quantification · Function offloading · Efficiency evaluation · Data access function

1 Introduction

Benefit quantification is critical in value assessment of offloading data access functions from traditional host platforms to embedded platforms that are expected to serve beyond the role of transitional storage devices. Though a couple of frameworks focusing on breaking down the offloading complexity [7,15] have been proposed in recent research, the fundamental question regarding how much can be saved from offloading a given data access function to an embedded platform has not been addressed. The challenge is whether to offload a data access function depends not only on the characteristics of workloads, which essentially are the function calls organized in some pattern, but also on the performance of the storage media with which the data access function interacts. In practical environments, hardware platforms and workloads of interest may differ significantly; solutions of benefit quantification focusing on specific functions [9,23] or using simplified evaluation models [1,12] may not apply to a different

© Springer Nature Switzerland AG 2019
M. Weiland et al. (Eds.): ISC 2019 Workshops, LNCS 11887, pp. 198–213, 2019.
https://doi.org/10.1007/978-3-030-34356-9_17

function. Furthermore, since different storage media have significantly different requirements on the bandwidth of various platform resources, the optimal placement of data access functions in terms of the platform efficiency can be dramatically different. We propose a Media-Based Work Unit (MBWU, pronounced "MibeeWu") and developed an MBWU-based measurement methodology for the purpose of standardizing the efficiency comparison for different platforms running a given workload over a specific storage media. By evaluating the efficiency of each platform in terms of its cost ($/MBWU), power (kW/MBWU), and space (m³/MBWU), we can quantify the benefit of offloading a data access function from traditional host platforms to embedded platforms. We have implemented a prototype for evaluating key-value data management function offloading and generated instructive results from our experiment. We discuss MBWU as well as this measurement methodology in detail in Sect. 2.

Starting from Active Disks [11,14,17,18,22], moving high-selectivity data access functions to storage devices gains increasing research interest mainly because of the conceivable benefits [10] such as reducing the size of data transmission between hosts and storage devices, reducing total power consumption, increasing overall resource utilization, and simplifying the application design by leveraging high-level storage semantics. For example, key-value smart storage devices can substitute the translation layers from key-value down to physical block address, which includes a key-value to file translation in the front, a file to logical block address translation in the middle, and a logical block address to physical block address translation at the bottom. Besides these benefits, energy consumption is thought to be another major saving from offloading functions to storage devices. For example, Choi et al. [3] identified more than 3x energy efficiency with 80% compute offloaded for data-intensive applications.

Though various benefits have been studied, the storage industry remains conservative when adding data access functions to storage devices. The main barrier is that extra processing required in the storage device increases the cost of the device. Since applications run on system platforms, we believe an increase in storage device does not necessarily increase the overall platform cost. Considering the variety of workloads and the diversity of hardware, we need a systematic and reproducible methodology to quantify the overall benefit of offloading any given data access function to embedded platforms.

2   The MBWU-Based Methodology

2.1   Background

The emergence of various storage technologies has changed the regular formula for constructing storage infrastructure. Historically, this formula was built around hiding the latency of storage devices using caching. However, innovations of recent NAND and storage-class memory technologies (e.g., V-NAND [8], 3D XPoint [25]) have altered the cost-optimal placement of various software and hardware resources [19,21] since storage media of different performance impose different demands for the bandwidth of CPU, memory, network, and storage interface. For example, applications may want memory closer to computation for slow storage media because hiding data access latency is important, while the applications may want storage closer to computation for fast media because high-speed networking fabrics and data buses are expensive. With more domain-specific processing units (e.g., GPU, Google TPU [27], FPGA) taking over computations from host CPUs, the storage industry asks itself the same question: What should be done to improve the cost-efficiency of utilizing a specific storage media for data access? In terms of the placement of data access functions, the specific question is: For a given workload, can offloading a data access function from host platforms to storage devices reduce the overall cost per performance when the workload uses the same storage media?

2.2 What Is MBWU

Host platforms and embedded platforms differ significantly in cost, usage, performance, power, and form factor. To compare the cost per performance of different platforms, we need to have a reference point to normalize the performance value generated from heterogeneous platforms so that these normalized values are directly comparable. The reference point is required to be **platform-independent** but **media- and workload-dependent**. The reasons are as follows:

- **platform-independence:** The reference point should be platform-related hardware independent. Otherwise, the normalized performance value of a platform may not be able to represent the efficiency of the platform utilizing a specific storage media under a workload. For example, if the reference point relates to a specific CPU architecture, then the normalization for the performance of a platform using a different CPU is skewed by the efficiency difference caused by the different CPUs.
- **media-dependence:** Since the cost-optimal placement of functions is sensitive to types of storage media, the reference point should be media-dependent so that we can always normalize the performance of different platforms to the efficiency of utilizing a specific storage media. For this to work, all the different platforms under test should use the same type of storage media for performance evaluation.
- **workload-dependence:** From an application point of view, the performance of a platform is the amount of work the platform can do in a unit of time. To measure the amount of work done, we need to define a unit of work as the reference point so that the performance of different platforms can be normalized to the number of units they can perform. Since different workloads have different work definitions, the unit of work should be measured in workload operations (WOs). Hence, the reference point is workload-dependent.

The combination of platform-independence and media-dependence indicate that the reference point can only be media-based. We call this media-based and workload-dependent reference point **MBWU** and define it as the highest number of workload operations per second (WOPS) a given workload on a specific storage media can achieve with all external caching effects eliminated/disabled. In this definition, workload operations should not be simply interpreted as block I/Os. For key-value operations as the workload, a WO is a GET, PUT, or DELETE. For file operations as the workload, a WO is a read or write. On the other hand, we use the term storage media to express a configuration of storage devices. For example, a storage media can be a device with six flash chips, or a device that combines a spinning media, two flash components, and some non-volatile random-access memory. The MBWU definition has no requirement on what the storage media should look like, which means our MBWU-based measurement methodology is seamlessly applicable to different types of storage media. In the following sections we use the two terms *storage media* and *storage device* interchangeably. Finally, since an MBWU only depends on a specific storage media and a given workload, its WOPS should only be throttled by a specific storage media. Platform-related system resources like CPU, memory, and network can throttle the WOPS when measuring an MBWU. Resources like memory can also enhance the WOPS when the data access is from memory instead of storage devices. A throttled or enhanced WOPS number is not an MBWU because it is platform-dependent.

Once an MBWU is measured, the performance of a platform can be measured by its maximum MBWUs under the same workload. The greater number of MBWUs a platform can generate, the higher performance the platform is. The efficiency of a platform can then be evaluated based on the cost, power, and space of this platform. For example, if the platform can generate M MBWUs, cost-efficiency of the platform (\$/MBWU) can be calculated by $\frac{cost(plat)}{M}$. Similarly, the power-efficiency of the platform (kW/MBWU) can be calculated by $\frac{amp \cdot volt}{1000 \cdot M}$, where *amp* and *volt* are the current and voltage of the platform respectively when it was generating M MBWUs. Space-efficiency of the platform (m^3/MBWU) can be calculated in a corresponding manner by $\frac{volume(plat)}{M}$.

The MBWU-based measurement methodology is intended to be used by storage device and storage system designers to assess whether to pair a given function to a specific storage media. It is not intended to be used to evaluate online methods during production workloads, because ensuring the workloads are the same for different platforms is difficult.

2.3   How to Measure MBWU(s)

Measuring an MBWU for a given workload that uses a specific storage media is different from measuring MBWUs for a platform except that the storage media and workload should be the same in these two measurements. To measure a single MBWU, we need a capable host to drive the peak performance of a given workload running on a single storage device with all external caching effects disabled. Since high-selectivity workloads are primarily I/O bound, looking for such a host is not difficult. The process of measuring MBWUs for a platform is to measure the maximum steady-state WOPS of the same workload running on the platform with normal caching configuration. The goal of this measurement is to evaluate what is the maximum WOPS that is eventually limited by the platform-related resources instead of storage devices. One way to push the WOPS to the limit is to replicate the workload on multiple storage devices. Once we have the value of the maximum WOPS, the MBWUs of this platform is equal to this value divided by a single MBWU. Figure 1 is an example to show the general relationship between the number of MBWUs and the number of storage devices. The increment of MBWUs brought by an additional storage device decreases as the device number increases until finally no increment exists on the total MBWUs. The final stable MBWUs is the MBWUs of this platform for the workload. One reason for the diminishing MBWUs increment shown in the figure is the increasing average CPU cycles on a single data read due to the increasing system memory pressure.

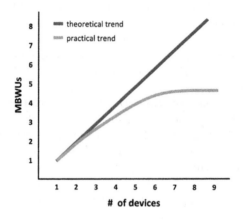

Fig. 1. Relationship between the number of MBWUs and the number of storage devices

In addition to resources like CPU, memory, and network, the real estate issue is another important platform-related bottleneck. For example, a limitation on the available hardware connectors may limit the number of storage devices that can be attached to a platform, thus throttling the MBWUs of a platform as well. We have seen this type of limitation in our experiment (Sect. 3).

2.4 Evaluation Prototype

We chose key-value data management as a function to be offloaded in our study. The design goal of the evaluation prototype was to provide a framework to demonstrate the merit of our MBWU-based measurement methodology by automatically generate reproducible values that represent the benefit of offloading the key-value data management function for a given workload. Key-value data management is a typical high-selectivity function due to the massive amount of data needed to move back and forth between different levels of data representation in response to various operations in data management. For example, we used RocksDB [2] as the key-value engines to run YCSB [4] workload A. We saw up to

6x traffic amplification between the key-value data received by the RocksDB (red dashed line) and the final data written out to the underlying block devices (red solid line) (Fig. 2). Though we used the key-value function as an example, there is nothing to prevent the MBWU-based measurement methodology from being applied to other functions, such as read/write functions in the file system and SELECT/PROJECT functions in the database management system.

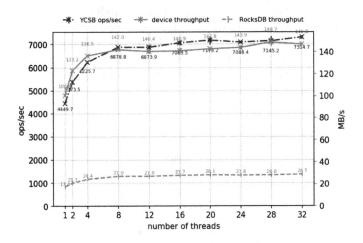

Fig. 2. Amplification of key-value data traffic (Color online figure)

Our prototype starts with pre-conditioning for NAND-based storage devices used to store workload data. This process is necessary as it relates to whether reproducible results are possible. In the prototype, the pre-conditioning is implemented following SNIA performance test specification [20]; it purges the devices followed by performing a workload independent pre-conditioning process. After the storage devices are pre-conditioned, a number of RocksDB daemons are started and waiting for connection requests from YCSB. Storage devices, RocksDB daemons, and the YCSB processes are in a one-to-one relationship. Therefore, the number of RocksDB daemons is identical to the number of YCSB processes. The RocksDB daemon is implemented using Java RMI technology [24]. It exposes all public interfaces (e.g., *open()*, *close()*, *get()*, *put()*, *delete()*) of a RocksDB object to network securely by binding this object to an RMI registry (Fig. 3). We have ported the RocksDB daemon program to support not only x86 and x86_64, but also aarch64 platforms since most embedded platforms use ARM-based processors. A YCSB process looks up the corresponding RocksDB object from a specified RMI registry and requests to create a RocksDB instance on the host of the registry by issuing an *open()* remote call. This call gives the RocksDB object the location of a RocksDB options file, which defines the shape of the internal LSM [6] tree and all the data migration policies for key-value data management. Having a consistent RocksDB options file for different platforms avoids using a "platform optimized" configuration file generated by RocksDB by default. Once RocksDB instances are successfully created, YCSB can start filling instances with initial key-value records to support later read/write operations. The data operation requests generated by YCSB are simply passed down by calling the exposed RocksDB interfaces. To ensure the final underlying LSM trees are consistent on platforms of different performance, we added an option to our prototype to control the speed of data loading. Slowing down the loads gives RocksDB instances enough system resources to finish regular data compaction and compression for keeping LSM trees stable. Finally, when the initial data are loaded, YCSB starts to run the workload specified by a parameter file with which the target workload is defined. YCSB offers various options to customize a workload: from the total number of operations, to request distribution, to the ratio between reads and writes, and so on. A high-level evaluation process of our prototype is shown in Fig. 4.

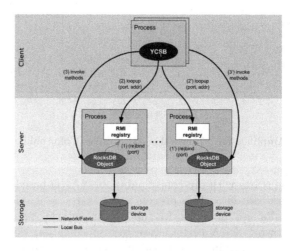

Fig. 3. Call graph of RocksDB RMI server

Depending on the configuration of a platform, the storage devices that RocksDB instances see can either be physical storage devices at local or network storage devices managed by any storage disaggregation protocol such as iSCSI [26] and NVMe-oF [13]. The purge process, however, will always take place on the physical storage devices. We discuss different storage configurations and how they affect the cost-efficiency of a platform in Sect. 3.

Measuring MBWUs requires identifying which system resource is the bottleneck. Our prototype will automatically monitor and record utilization of CPU, memory, device I/O, network, and power for platforms during the whole evaluation process. At the end of a measurement, the prototype extracts all useful information from these logs and generates a platform resource utilization report for the target workload.

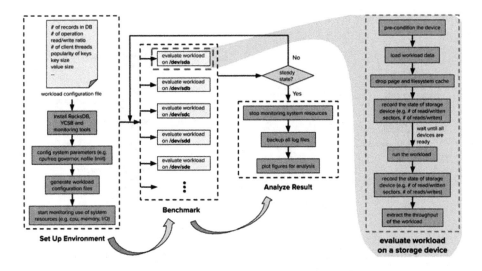

Fig. 4. A high-level view of the evaluation process

3   Evaluation

The purpose of the evaluation is to demonstrate the use of our evaluation prototype discussed above for quantifying the benefit of offloading the key-value data management function from traditional host platforms to embedded smart key-value platforms. A smart key-value platform exposes a key-value interface instead of a block interface.

3.1   Infrastructure

Figure 5 shows the basic components of the two platforms we set up for comparison. For the traditional platform, RocksDB runs on the host and stores data on either direct-attached storage devices or network storage devices. For the embedded platform, RocksDB runs on a single board computer (SBC) named ROCKPro64 [16]. This SBC, together with two adapters and a block storage device, creates a smart key-value storage device that clients can interact with through a key-value interface.

3.2   Test Setup and Results

To better understand where the benefit of offloading come from and how much savings occur regarding benefit, we have designed a set of tests involving three-stages (Fig. 6). Each test was a different setup with different placement of either software or hardware components. We used the following workload in all tests. The key size is 16 bytes, and the value size is 4 KiB. The read/write ratio is 50/50 following a Zipf [28] distribution for data accessing. Finally, the total size of dataset is 40 GiB.

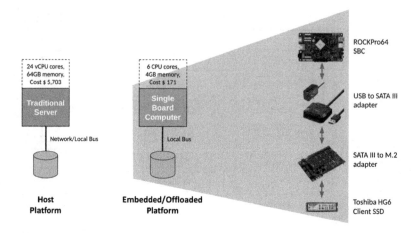

Fig. 5. Configuration of our host platform and embedded platform

The first tests were integrated tests. Both YCSB and RocksDB ran within platforms and access data from direct-attached storage devices. The purpose of these tests was to reveal the benefit of leveraging cost-effective hardware to provide the function of a key-value data store. The first step was to measure the value of an MBWU. This measurement process went from using one YCSB thread to generate the defined key-value workload to using 32 YCSB threads for concurrent request generation. The reason we stopped at 32 threads relates to the use of SATA SSDs in our experiment. SATA interface provides a single command queue for a depth of up to 32. This feature suggests there is no need to use more than 32 threads to generate requests if the request generation is

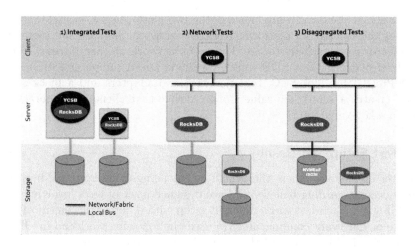

Fig. 6. Three-stage test setup

not slower than the request consumed by the underlying storage device. Figure 2 shows that the YCSB throughput was mostly stable with more than 20 threads. Considering the amplification factor between the traffic generated by YCSB and the traffic to the underlying storage device, we thought there was no need to test with more than 32 threads. However, if the evaluation regards faster storage devices such as NVMe SSDs, we may need to increase the thread number corresponding to the capability of the storage interface to measure an MBWU. In our results, we saw the YCSB reaches peak throughput with 32 threads on the host platform. We ensured this throughput was the MBWU by carefully examining the resource utilization report generated by our evaluation prototype. Once a single MBWU is measured, we can measure the MBWUs for the two platforms. Our host platform can host up to eight SSDs because it has limited hardware connectors. The workload performance with eight SSDs, as expected, was neither limited by the CPU nor the memory. As discussed previously, the real estate issue is one type of system bottlenecks. This type of bottleneck causes the other system resources to be underutilized; thus, it is conceivable that it increased the values of all three metrics ($/MBWU, kW/MBWU and m^3/MBWU) for this platform. Under this restriction, our host platform can generate six MBWUs. Figure 7 shows the evaluation results of the host platform. We skipped some data points in this and some of the following figures as we believed that those values could not be the peak performance numbers according to the trends. We applied the same measurement methodology to the embedded platform, and the results are shown in Fig. 8. Limited by CPU performance of this platform, it can only generate 0.5 MBWU with a single SSD. After platform MBWUs are measured, we can compare these platforms using any of the three MBWU-based metrics. We saw that the embedded platform reduced the $/MBWU by 64% compared to processing the same key-value workload on the host platform. At the same time, this platform reduced the kW/MBWU by 39.6% as well. These optimistic results show that it is worth offloading the key-value data management function to the embedded platform due to the significant saving from the hardware. Specifically, compared with the expensive and powerful resources used in the host platform, the cost reduction of the less powerful resources used in the embedded platform is greater than the performance reduction of these resources. In other words, it simply emphasizes the fact that improving the system performance through scaling out is much more cost-effective than through scaling up.

In network tests, YCSB sent key-value requests through network as opposed to through local bus in the integrated tests. The introduction of network traffic may have different impacts on different platforms depending on the availability of computing resources and the amount of network traffic. For our host platform, since its throughput performance was not CPU or memory bound in the integrated tests, adding the overhead to process network packets has lower performance impact than the embedded platform where its CPU was already the performance bottleneck for the defined key-value workload. Therefore, the purpose of the network tests was to evaluate how the introduction of this front-end network affected the benefit results we obtained from the integrated tests. Figures 9

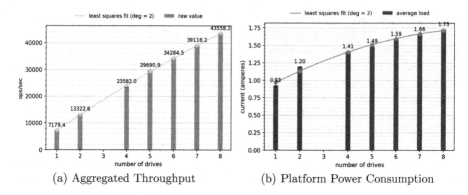

(a) Aggregated Throughput   (b) Platform Power Consumption

Fig. 7. Integrated test: performance of the host platform with different number of storage devices

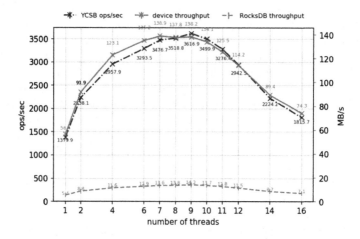

Fig. 8. Integrated test: evaluation for the embedded platform

and 10 respectively show the results of our host platform and embedded platform for these tests. Based on the results, the host platform can generate 5.2 MBWUs, and the embedded platform can generate 0.37 MBWUs. With these numbers, we again compared the two platforms using the $/MBWU and the kW/MBWU metrics. We saw that the embedded platform saved 57.86% of $/MBWU compared to processing the same key-value workload on the host platform. For energy consumption, the embedded platform can reduce the kW/MBWU by 45.9% as well. The reduction of benefit on $/MBWU is expected since the performance degradation on the embedded platform is greater than the performance degradation on the host platform. Similarly, the percentage of energy saving was increased because the host platform utilized additional system resources for network traffic processing, which raised its total power consumption. For the embedded platform, it had already enabled all system resources to process the workload. In other words, the embedded platform was already under the peak power consumption no matter whether it was required to deal with network traffic.

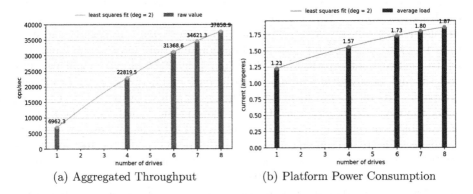

(a) Aggregated Throughput   (b) Platform Power Consumption

Fig. 9. Network test: performance of the host platform with different number of storage devices

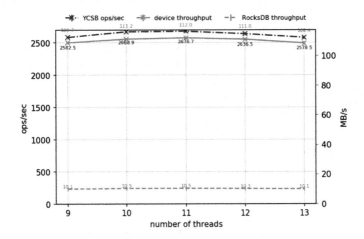

Fig. 10. Network test: evaluation for the embedded platform

Storage disaggregation is known for simplifying and reducing the cost of storage management. It requires additional expense on network infrastructure as the data lives remotely. The faster the storage devices, the higher network bandwidth is required. Hiding the data management traffic within storage devices is especially attractive in this context due to the high amplification factor for data access—6x amplification means more than 5x extra expense on the network to support the bandwidth that is not directly relevant to user applications. In the case of key-value data management function, data amplification comes from data compaction and compression that frequently happen behind the scenes of client applications. In the last test setup, we simulated an environment with disaggregated storage devices to evaluate how much we can save from removing the back-end network requirement for data management traffic. The host and storage devices are connected using iSCSI. Our host platform exactly captured the cost overhead resulting from the data amplification. On the one hand, the built-in network interface card (NIC) in our host platform was unable to support the high bandwidth requirement of the back-end network; we had to install a capable NIC on it, which increased the cost of this platform. On the other hand, the new NIC occupied a PCIe slot causing the reduction of the number of available connectors for storage devices to 4. This reduction exacerbated the unbalance of system resource utilization on this platform and resulted in a lower MBWUs number that the platform can generate, thus decreasing the platform efficiency represented by the three MBWU-based metrics. It is worth mentioning that keeping the system resource utilization in balance for transitional platforms is practically untraceable. In the HPC environment, the ratios between different components in a traditional platform (e.g., the ratio between the number of CPU cores and the number of NICs, and the ratio between the size of memory and the number of storage devices) were designed at the time of purchase according to the requirements of expected workloads. However, the change of workloads is difficult to predict; should that change, the system resource utilization could easily become unbalanced. Figure 11 shows the performance results of our host. In disaggregated tests, the host platform could generate only 3.28 MBWUs. The number of MBWUs of the embedded platform is the same as in the network tests since its setup is the same. By putting all these numbers together, the embedded platform can save 73.4% of \$/MBWU and 70.7% of kW/MBWU if we choose not to use the host platform to process the target key-value workload.

4   Related Work

Choi et al. [3] evaluated the energy efficiency of scale-in clusters that support in-storage processing using computation and data-movement energy models. Do et al. [5] suggested offloading selected query processing components to smart SSDs. The comparisons were conducted based on raw performance metrics such as elapsed time and energy in Joules, and did not involve any cost comparison. Floem [15] is a programming system that aims to accelerate NIC applications development by providing abstractions to ease NIC-offloading design. Biscuit [7] is a near-data processing framework. It allows developers to write data-intensive programs to be offloaded onto storage devices. Both Floem and Biscuit are similar to our evaluation prototype in that they provide a way to trial and error instead of modeling, which is helpful given the complexity of real-world hardware environment. Our MBWU-based measurement methodology differs from all the previous research in that it focuses on quantifying the benefit of offloading alternatives.

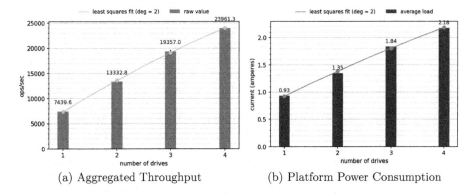

(a) Aggregated Throughput   (b) Platform Power Consumption

Fig. 11. Disaggregated test: performance of the host platform with different number of storage devices

5   Conclusion

Host platforms and embedded platforms differ greatly in resource allocations and placements, causing the cost per performance to be significantly different under the same workload. To quantify the benefit of offloading a given data access function to an embedded platform, we proposed a novel MBWU-based measurement methodology. The core of this methodology is to construct an MBWU as a workload-dependent and media-based reference point and use the MBWU to normalize the performance of different platforms such that the performance values of these platforms are directly comparable. It is the direct comparability that enables us to perform apple-to-apple efficiency comparisons for different platforms. Our evaluation prototype releases the power of this methodology and automates the evaluation process for quantifying the benefit of offloading the key-value data management function under a customized workload. Our next step is to evaluate the benefit of offloading other types of data access functions, such as data decryption/encryption functions, database select/project functions, and other data management functions. We believe this measurement methodology will be a useful tool as it fills the need for benefit quantification in current in-storage computing development.

References

1. Boboila, S., Kim, Y., Vazhkudai, S.S., Desnoyers, P., Shipman, G.M.: Active flash: out-of-core data analytics on flash storage. In: 2012 IEEE 28th Symposium on Mass Storage Systems and Technologies (MSST), pp. 1–12. IEEE (2012)
2. Borthakur, D.: Under the hood: building and open-sourcing RocksDB. Facebook Engineering Notes (2013)
3. Choi, I.S., Kee, Y.S.: Energy efficient scale-in clusters with in-storage processing for big-data analytics. In: Proceedings of the 2015 International Symposium on Memory Systems, pp. 265–273. ACM (2015)

4. Cooper, B.F., Silberstein, A., Tam, E., Ramakrishnan, R., Sears, R.: Benchmarking cloud serving systems with YCSB. In: Proceedings of the 1st ACM Symposium on Cloud Computing, pp. 143–154. ACM (2010)

5. Do, J., Kee, Y.S., Patel, J.M., Park, C., Park, K., DeWitt, D.J.: Query processing on smart SSDs: opportunities and challenges. In: Proceedings of the 2013 ACM SIGMOD International Conference on Management of Data, pp. 1221–1230. ACM (2013)

6. Dong, S., Callaghan, M., Galanis, L., Borthakur, D., Savor, T., Strum, M.: Optimizing space amplification in RocksDB. In: CIDR, vol. 3, p. 3 (2017)

7. Gu, B., et al.: Biscuit: a framework for near-data processing of big data workloads. In: ACM SIGARCH Computer Architecture News, vol. 44, pp. 153–165. IEEE Press (2016)

8. Kang, D., et al.: 256 Gb 3 b/cell v-NAND flash memory with 48 stacked WL layers. IEEE J. Solid-State Circ. **52**(1), 210–217 (2016)

9. Kang, Y., Kee, Y.S., Miller, E.L., Park, C.: Enabling cost-effective data processing with smart SSD. In: 2013 IEEE 29th Symposium on Mass Storage Systems and Technologies (MSST), pp. 1–12. IEEE (2013)

10. Kang, Y., et al.: Towards building a high-performance, scale-in key-value storage system. In: Proceedings of the 12th ACM International Conference on Systems and Storage, pp. 144–154. ACM (2019)

11. Keeton, K., Patterson, D.A., Hellerstein, J.M.: A case for intelligent disks (IDISKs). ACM SIGMOD Rec. **27**(3), 42–52 (1998)

12. Kim, S., Oh, H., Park, C., Cho, S., Lee, S.W.: Fast, energy efficient scan inside flash memory SSDs. In: Proceeedings of the International Workshop on Accelerating Data Management Systems (ADMS) (2011)

13. Minturn, D.: NVM express over fabrics. In: 11th Annual OpenFabrics International OFS Developers' Workshop, Monterey, CA, USA (2015)

14. Ouyang, J., Lin, S., Hou, Z., Wang, P., Wang, Y., Sun, G.: Active SSD design for energy-efficiency improvement of web-scale data analysis. In: Proceedings of the 2013 International Symposium on Low Power Electronics and Design, pp. 286–291. IEEE Press (2013)

15. Phothilimthana, P.M., Liu, M., Kaufmann, A., Peter, S., Bodik, R., Anderson, T.: Floem: a programming system for NIC-accelerated network applications. In: 13th USENIX Symposium on Operating Systems Design and Implementation (OSDI 2018), pp. 663–679 (2018)

16. PINE64: ROCKPro64 4 GB Single Board Computer, February 2019. https://www.pine64.org/?product=rockpro64-4gb-single-board-computer

17. Riedel, E., Gibson, G.: Active disks-remote execution for network-attached storage. Technical report, School of Computer Science, Carnegie-Mellon University, Pittsburgh (1997)

18. Riedel, E., Gibson, G., Faloutsos, C.: Active storage for large-scale data mining and multimedia applications. In: Proceedings of 24th Conference on Very Large Databases, pp. 62–73. Citeseer (1998)

19. Shulaker, M.M., et al.: Three-dimensional integration of nanotechnologies for computing and data storage on a single chip. Nature **547**(7661), 74 (2017)

20. Thatcher, J., Kim, E., Landsman, D., Fausset, M., Jones, A.: Solid state storage performance test specification v2.0.1. Technical report, SNIA, Feburary 2018

21. Theis, T.N., Wong, H.S.P.: The end of Moore's law: a new beginning for information technology. Comput. Sci. Eng. **19**(2), 41 (2017)

22. Tiwari, D., et al.: Active flash: towards energy-efficient, in-situ data analytics on extreme-scale machines. In: Presented as Part of the 11th USENIX Conference on File and Storage Technologies (FAST 2013), pp. 119–132 (2013)
23. Wang, J., Park, D., Kee, Y.S., Papakonstantinou, Y., Swanson, S.: SSD in-storage computing for list intersection. In: Proceedings of the 12th International Workshop on Data Management on New Hardware, p. 4. ACM (2016)
24. Wikipedia Contributors: Java remote method invocation – Wikipedia, the free encyclopedia (2018). https://en.wikipedia.org/w/index.php?title=Java_remote_method_invocation&oldid=859953202. Accessed 5 June 2019
25. Wikipedia Contributors: 3d xpoint – Wikipedia, the free encyclopedia (2019). https://en.wikipedia.org/w/index.php?title=3D_XPoint&oldid=902944964. Accessed 1 July 2019
26. Wikipedia Contributors: iSCSI – Wikipedia, the free encyclopedia (2019). https://en.wikipedia.org/w/index.php?title=ISCSI&oldid=896076870. Accessed 5 June 2019
27. Wikipedia Contributors: Tensor processing unit – Wikipedia, the free encyclopedia (2019). https://en.wikipedia.org/w/index.php?title=Tensor_processing_unit&oldid=898169944. Accessed 9 June 2019
28. Wikipedia Contributors: Zipf's law – Wikipedia, the free encyclopedia (2019). https://en.wikipedia.org/w/index.php?title=Zipf%27s_law&oldid=890450623. Accessed 10 June 2019

Footprinting Parallel I/O – Machine Learning to Classify Application's I/O Behavior

Eugen Betke[1][(✉)] and Julian Kunkel[2][(✉)]

[1] DKRZ, Hamburg, Germany
betke@dkrz.de
[2] University of Reading, Reading, UK
j.m.kunkel@reading.ac.uk

Abstract. It is not uncommon to run tens of thousands of parallel jobs on large HPC systems. The amount of data collected by monitoring systems on such systems is immense. Checking each job individually by hand, e.g., for identification of high workloads or detection of anomalies, is infeasible. Therefore, we are looking for an automated approach.

Many automated approaches are looking at job statistics over the entire job run time. Information about different activities during the job execution is lost. In our work, we partition the collected monitoring data for each job into a sequence of smaller windows for which we analyze the I/O behavior. Then, we convert the sequence to a footprint vector, where each element shows how often this behavior occurs. After that, the footprint dataset is classified to identify applications with similar I/O behavior. The classes are interpreted by a human which is the only non-automatic step in the workflow.

The contribution of this paper is a data reduction technique for monitoring data and an automated job classification method.

1 Introduction

Modern HPC systems involve a complex interaction between many hardware and software components. To get information about the system health and utilization powerful monitoring systems are deployed and constantly improved. Basically, monitoring systems share the same principle: (1) Collectors capture utilization metrics from HPC components in a fixed interval. (2) Analysis tools access data for visualization and statistic computation.

They may utilize various visualization and statistical tools that process monitoring data, and aggregate it to an appropriate and understandable representation. These systems allow a detailed look at the current system state. Advanced features allow archiving of job data, set alerts and expose the data to users.

Daily, tens of thousands of jobs can be executed on modern HPC systems, producing an immense amount of monitoring data. These data contain a lot of useful and interesting information but it is a challenging task to evaluate all these data with human power only. Therefore, these systems require new tools for automatic evaluation.

© Springer Nature Switzerland AG 2019
M. Weiland et al. (Eds.): ISC 2019 Workshops, LNCS 11887, pp. 214–226, 2019.
https://doi.org/10.1007/978-3-030-34356-9_18

In respect to I/O, storage is known to be not very well utilized on many systems. As data is crucial for operation and storage an expensive part of HPC systems, data centers are interested in its efficient usage. The good news is that many workflows have often hidden optimization potential there, that is waiting to be discovered and utilized. For example, a workload manager can launch non-interfering applications together (e.g., I/O intensive and CPU-intensive applications), troublemakers can be isolated and problems can be communicated to users. Applications, with bad I/O behavior can be identified and optimized. A more predictable I/O could make application runtime predictable and provide a better user experience. A deep insight in the current systems and understanding of the problem could be helpful for designing future system.

This paper is structured as follows. We start with the related work in Sect. 2. Then, in Sect. 3 we introduce the DKRZ monitoring systems and explain how I/O metrics are captured by the collectors. In Sect. 4 we describe the data reduction and the machine learning approaches and do an experiment in Sects. 5 and 6. Finally, we finalize our paper with a summary in Sect. 8.

2   Related Work

Advanced HPC monitoring systems collect data from different sources and convert them into an understandable representation. Then, they compute statistics, correlate data from multiple system levels and visualize them. This allows a deep understanding of the system, application I/O profiling and anomaly detection. Often, a portion of this data, which doesn't require a deep domain knowledge, is exposed to users. Many monitoring systems work in this way, e.g., Beacon [11], XDMoD [5], or the DKRZ monitoring system [1]. Many more tools to capture and analyse I/O behavior are described in [3].

An automated workload characterization on storage was investigated in [2]. This approach includes a monitoring infrastructure, that collects storage-specific metrics from arriving I/O requests. Based on the captured data, a workload model, that represents the main aspects of I/O-intensive applications, is created. Experiments with predictive models for I/O performance and variability are conducted in [4,6,10].

A machine learning approach for anomaly detection was investigated by Tuncer et al. in [8]. This approach targets two aspects. First, data reduction by mapping large raw time series to a few statistics. Second, automatic anomaly detection and classification with machine learning algorithms. With appropriate data, a model can be adapted for detection of different anomaly types, e.g., hardware issues, memory leaks, system health status. In the experiments on an HPC cluster and a public cloud, a trained machine learning model shows a high accuracy (F-score higher than 0.97).

In [7] Seo et al. are classifying I/O traces with a data-mining approach to build a software for flash translation layer (FTL) on SSDs, with intention to improve I/O performance and to increases hardware lifetime. The traces consist of sequences of I/O requests, where each I/O request contains the logical block address, access type and number of pages to read/write. In the pre-processing step, each trace is reduced to a small and well-optimized feature vector. Then, a data set of these vectors is used for classification and training of a prediction model.

Job runtime and I/O prediction were done in PRIONN [9]. PRIONN is a neural network that is trained with constant size 1D or 2D images, that in turn are derived from variable length job scripts. This representation allows using deep learning algorithms. In the experiments on a real HPC this approach works with 75% mean and 98% median accuracy. It is also able to predict around 50% of the data bursts.

In contrast to existing work, we segment the job data into windows of activity that are characterized and investigate unsupervised methods for the analysis.

3   DKRZ Monitoring

DKRZ maintains a monitoring system that gathers various statistics from the "Mistral" HPC system, that has 3,340 compute nodes, 24 login nodes, and two Lustre file systems (lustre01 and lustre02) that provide a capacity of 52 Petabyte. The monitoring system is made up of open source components such as Grafana, OpenTSDB, and Elasticsearch but also includes a lightweight self-developed data collector, that captures continuously node statistics – we decided to implement an own collector when analyzing the overhead of existing approaches. Additionally, the monitoring system obtains various meta-information from the Slurm workload manager and injects selected log files. A schematic overview is provided in Fig. 1. The data is aggregated and visualized by a Grafana web interface, which is available to all DKRZ users: Mainly, that are three type of information about login nodes, user jobs, and queue statistics.

In the first place, a monitoring service gives the users an overview of the current state of the system, the current load of login nodes and Slurm partitions. For each single machine, a detail view also provides information (incl. historical data) about system load, memory consumption, and Lustre statistics. Job monitoring is enabled by default in a coarse-grained mode, but the functionality can be extended by Slurm parameters. With appropriate parameters, the monitoring system can gather information about CPU usage and frequency, memory consumption, Lustre throughput, and network traffic for each compute node. DRKZ also runs XDMoD on compute nodes for viewing historical job information as well as real-time scientific application profiling.

3.1   Metrics

In our experience, collecting many metrics from thousands of nodes in short time intervals creates a noteworthy overhead (exceeding 1%). Additionally, over time, monitoring data occupies a significant amount of data space. For a relatively large system like Mistral this is of particular concern – it would take at least 800 GiB to record a single metric with a 1s interval for one year on all nodes. Therefore, we reduced the number of captured metrics to a minimum.

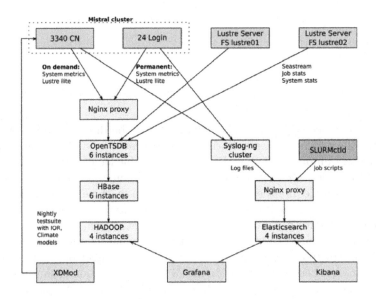

Fig. 1. Monitoring components.

To avoid much overhead, metadata and I/O metrics are selected in the following way: (1) Similar metadata counters are combined into three different groups: read, modification and other accesses. They create and unlink counters are captured separately. The exact group compositions and metric names are listed in Listing 1. (2) For I/O we just capture a set counters. The read_*, write_* and seek counters provide the basic information about file system access performed by the application. We also include the osc_read_*, osc_write_*, because the Lustre client transforms the original file system accesses, made by the application, to Lustre specific accesses – for instance by utilizing the kernel cache. This can have a significant impact on I/O performance (e.g., when many small I/O accesses are created but coalesced). The metrics are listed in Listing 2.

These metrics are collected in a 5 s interval for both file systems and send in JSON format to the Elasticsearch database.

4   Methodology

From the monitoring system we can map jobs to hosts and can extract a time series per host for the job runtime.

```
Source files: /proc/fs/lustre/llite/lustre*-*/stats
md_read = getattr + getxattr + readdir + statfs + listxattr + open + close
md_mod = setattr + setxattr + mkdir + link + rename + symlink + rmdir
md_other = truncate + mmap + ioctl + fsync + mknod
md_file_create = create
md_file_delete = unlink
```

Listing 1. Metadata metrics captured on compute nodes for lustre01 and lustre02.

```
Source files: /proc/fs/lustre/llite/lustre*-*/read_ahead_stats
osc_read_bytes , osc_read_calls
osc_write_bytes , osc_write_calls
read_bytes , read_calls
write_bytes , read_calls
seek
```

Listing 2. I/O metrics captured on compute nodes for lustre01 and lustre02.

However, machine learning algorithms can not be directly trained with the raw data collected from our monitoring system because most algorithms require a fixed number of inputs, but the job data is of variable length: Firstly, the job run times are variable. Secondly, jobs can run on any number of nodes producing one time series per node. In order to process them with machine learning algorithms, we convert them into a suitable fixed length representation. A pleasant side effect of the following data pre-processing step is data reduction.

In the first step, we split the job runtime in equal length windows. Since a parallel job can run on several nodes, we obtain a number of 2D segments for each metric. A schematic illustration of a 3×4 segmentation is shown in Fig. 2.

In the next step, the segments are converted to $N \times N$ matrices ($N = $ length(v) = 12 in our case), by computing statistics for each segment on runtime and nodes using the stats() function in Eq. (1).

The conversion process for a segment is shown in Fig. 3. Firstly, the stats() function is applied to all segment rows line by line, i.e., a statistics for each host's time series is computed removing the variability of job lengths. Then, stats() is applied to all columns of the intermediate result, i.e., a single statistics is computed across all hosts making the statistics independent of the number of hosts. The latter statistics is particularly relevant for large jobs. Finally, for each job and each metric we get a sequence of $N \times N$ matrices.

$$\text{stats}\left(\vec{v}\right) = (\min, \max, \text{mean}, q01, q10, q05, q25, q50, q75, q90, q95, q99) \qquad (1)$$

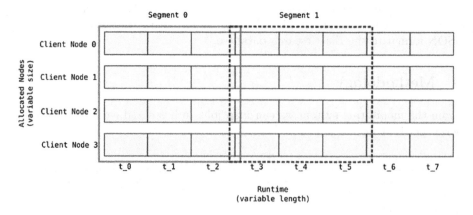

Fig. 2. Example of a job running on four nodes for eight time units and the resulting 3×4 segmentation.

In our experiments, we don't use the **seek** metric, i.e., we use the remaining 13 metrics (see Listings 1 and 2). On the whole, there are 12 stats (x-axis) · 12 stats (y-axis) · 13 metrics = 1872 statistics for each segment. A schematic representation of a statistic matrix that contains these values is given in Fig. 3. On this pre-processing stage, we have a sequence of statistic matrices.

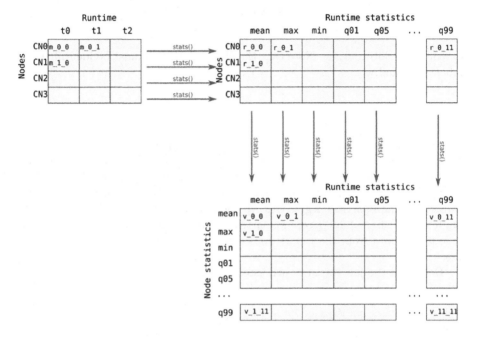

Fig. 3. Conversion of a 3 × 4 segment to a statistic matrix.

Our goal is to convert the sequences to fixed size vectors, called footprints according to Eq. (2), where each element represents a kind of I/O behavior.

In the first step, we do the segmentation and create statistics matrices for all jobs. Then, we put them in a data pool, and group them by means of a clustering algorithm. The statistics in the same group are labeled with the same I/O class. After the identification of I/O classes, we compute footprints for each job, i.e., statistics which tell us how often the I/O classes occur in a job. In the last step, we use the clustering algorithm again to group the footprints to identify different types. (See Sect. 6.2 for details.)

$$\text{footprint}(\text{jobid}) = \vec{v}_{\text{jobid}} \tag{2}$$

with $\vec{v}$ is a fixed length numeric vector

A generic example in Fig. 4 illustrates the basic idea: from a single footprint, we can compute the exhibition of four different I/O behaviors to a different

$$\text{footprint}(14400233) = \begin{pmatrix} IO1 : 20\% \\ IO2 : 10\% \\ IO3 : 30\% \\ IO4 : 50\% \end{pmatrix} \quad \begin{array}{l} \text{IO1: Metadata intensive} \\ \text{IO2: Using I/O node} \\ \text{IO3: Highly parallel I/O} \\ \text{IO4: No I/O} \end{array}$$

Fig. 4. Footprint example.

extent of the job runtime. Note that the classes IO1–IO4 must be identified and labeled manually.

5   Test Data

For evaluation, we downloaded a data set for a time period of 5 days, from 2018-12-07 to 2018-12-13. It contains data of 70846 jobs. 33193 (47%) of them are jobs from `compute` and `compute2` Slurm partitions with exit status `COMPLETED`. These are used for our evaluation. Jobs not considered where either faulty, or short jobs run on the small partitions `gpu`, `miklip` and `minerva`. Additionally, omitted jobs are from the `shared` and `prepost` partitions are shared by several users, so that monitoring data from these partitions can not be assigned unambiguously to a job.

Details of the job statistics are listed in Table 1.

Table 1. Dataset statistics of 70846 jobs captured on Mistral supercomputer in the time period of 5 days.

JOBS	EXIT STATUS
1,026	CANCELLED
63,636	**COMPLETED**
5,753	FAILED
3	NODE_FAIL
426	TIMEOUT

(a) Exit status statistics

JOBS	SLURM PARTITION
37,989	**compute,compute2**
241	gpu
828	miklip
34	minerva
31,752	shared,prepost

(b) Slurm statistics

5.1   Data Preparation

The time series of the job are split in 10 min large segments and converted to fixed size matrices, as described in the previous section. The leftovers at the end of job data and jobs that are smaller than 10 min are discarded. Finally, we apply the log10 function to all values, e.g., as a 10x increase in a statistics adds one to the distance. This shortens the distance from far-away classes and allows clustering algorithms to combine neighbouring classes instead of grouping all observations similar to the maximum together and the rest. Theoretically, this pre-processing step would make it easier to recognize outlier classes, which are present in this data set.

After processing the monitoring data, we obtain around 128,000 statistics matrices. Out of convenience, these segment statistics are deflated to 1D-representation and stored row-wise in a file. The created dataset contains all statistics (1872 columns) and statistics matrices (around 128,000 rows). In further course of the paper use this representation for visualization and refer to them as samples.

6   Evaluation

6.1   I/O Behavior Classification

In the training phase, we feed a kMeans algorithm with 100,000 randomly selected samples from the dataset and obtain a model that can recognize 8 classes of I/O behavior. Table 2 shows the clustering result.

The resulting classes are quite different. We could describe only two of them, IO0 (Normal I/O) and IO3 (Intensive I/O). Five random samples for IO0 and IO3 are visualized in Figs. 5a and b to give the reader an impression of the I/O behavior of each class. Arguably, the third and fourth example from the class IO0 still performs some read and write calls but with little data, while IO3 shows a consistently high activity.

On the x-axis, metric names represent the whole set of segment statistics, e.g., `bytes_read` is a collective term for all statistics that were calculated statistics matrices for `bytes_read`. That are min, max, mean values and quantiles (q01, q05, q10, q25, q50, q75, q90, q95, q99) for nodes and runtime, i.e., 144 values/metric. Due space restrictions, we do not label them all, but show only the metric names. Values on the y-axis are scaled to a range between 0 and 1 for each statistic individually. This scaling was done only for the purpose of the visualization. It allows to consider all statistics in one picture.

Table 2. I/O class distribution.

I/O class	Size		Description
	# of segments	in %	
IO0	117239	91.28	No I/O, Typical I/O, ...
IO1	552	0.43	
IO2	13	0.01	
IO3	471	0.37	Intensive I/O
IO4	1404	1.09	
IO5	8738	6.8	
IO6	5	0.0	
IO7	19	0.01	

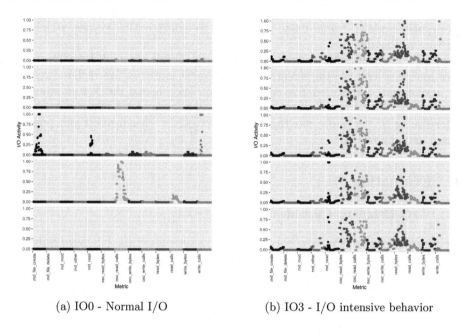

(a) IO0 - Normal I/O   (b) IO3 - I/O intensive behavior

Fig. 5. Five randomly selected individual segments (y-axis) of the identified classes.

IO0 represents non-I/O or typical storage usage class. With 91,28%, this is by far the largest class of all. Probably, several classes were combined into one large class. Formation of such a large class helps to isolate outliers classes with extremely poor or intensive I/O performance.

IO3 shows an increased read I/O performance and large number of metadata reads. Both can interfere with each other, e.g., metadata and storage access are done sequentially one after each other, and neither I/O performance, nor meta data access can achieve full speed. Nevertheless, as we see later, this I/O class represents I/O intensive behavior.

The description and labeling by experts of other classes are difficult and requires further investigations. That becomes particularly apparent when the jobs are visualized individually. In Fig. 5a we can see that the kMeans algorithm puts at least three different I/O behavior classes into the IO4 class. The same observation we could made for IO0 and IO5. This is at least hint, that the number of clusters was too small.

The samples in other classes are classes are similar and even for IO0 and IO3 we can not be sure, that they represent only one I/O pattern. Precise description can be done only by understanding of the rules of the trained model – it must be decomposed and analyzed after each training. In practice this task is quite burdensome and very difficult to apply, hence we do not consider this approach to be beneficial by itself. We will look for alternatives in our further research.

```
io_sequence(14496682) =
[2 3 3 2 2 3 2 2 3 1 3 2 1 4 4 1 0 0 0 1 1 1 1 1 1 1 1 1 1 1 1 1 1 1 1 1 1
 1 1 1 1 1 1 1 1 1 1 1 1 1 1 1 1 1 1 1 1 1 1 5 5 5 6 6 6 7 7 7 7 7]

footprint(14496682) =  [3, 44, 6, 5, 2, 3, 4, 5]
footprint_norm(14496682) = [0.04, 0.61, 0.08, 0.07, 0.03, 0.04, 0.06, 0.07]
```

Listing 3. Sequence of I/O classes.

6.2   Footprinting

After the first clustering pass, the time series can be represented as a sequence of the eight generated I/O classes. An example is shown in Listing 3. This sequence is still variable length and is not suitable for most machine learning algorithms. Therefore, we do another data reduction by counting I/O classes and obtain another fixed length vector, called (absolute) footprint. We also do a normalization of the vector, i.e., each value is divided by the sum of vector elements, i.e., in a normalized footprint the sum of vector elements is 1. Examples are given in Listing 3. Doing this for each job data, we obtain a new dataset consisting of 20,704 normalized footprints.

To group similar jobs we apply kMeans algorithm a second time on the footprint dataset and obtain a footprint classifier for 8 *job classes*. The footprints are visualized in Fig. 6. As we can see, IO0 dominates in FP0 and IO3 in FP2. From this observation we conclude that FP0 represents jobs with low I/O activity and FP2 represents I/O intensive jobs. Unfortunately, without a precise description of other I/O classes we can not provide a reasonable description of the remaining footprint classes.

Table 3. Footprint statistics. I/O intensive jobs with score ≥ 6 and ≥ 7 were identified manually. (Class size percentage refers to total number of jobs. I/O intensive job percentage refers to class size.)

Class	Class size		Job score ≥ 6		Job score ≥ 7	
	# of jobs	in %	# of jobs	in %	# of jobs	in %
FP0	16003	77.29	5	0.03	0	0.00
FP1	2605	12.58	20	0.77	2	0.08
FP2	404	1.95	395	97.77	0	0.00
FP3	65	0.31	1	1.54	0	0.00
FP4	160	0.77	58	36.25	0	0.00
FP5	440	2.13	0	0.00	0	0.00
FP6	164	0.79	8	4.88	0	0.00
FP7	863	4.17	0	0.00	0	0.00

7   Manual Identification of I/O Intensive Jobs

For verification, we identify manually the I/O intensive jobs. In the first step, we visualize the average performance of all metrics in density plots and determine thresholds for normal, high and critical performance values. This is a highly subjective assessment without any consideration other factors, but for validation it is sufficient to pick a set of most I/O intensive jobs from our dataset. Then, we use the thresholds to label job performance, i.e., values for normal performance are labeled 0, values for high performance are labeled with 1 and for critical performance are labeled with 2. After that, for each job we obtain 13 labels. The sum of these labels is the resulting job score. The distribution is visualized in Fig. 7.

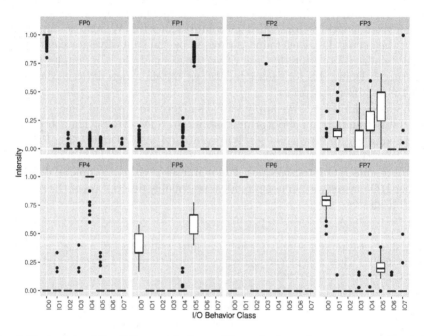

Fig. 6. Footprints of the different job classes. For each class, the percentage of each IO class is shown.

According to the definition, the jobs with a high score are I/O intensive. The complete distribution is shown in Table 3. We pick jobs with high job scores and compare them with the previous results.

For job score ≥ 7 there are 2 jobs. Both of them are located in the FP1 class, where IO5 dominates. IO5 contains several I/O subclasses, one of them is metadata sensitive. A closer look on both jobs reveals, that they are metadata intensive. This explain why kMeans put them in the FP1 class, but it is also a hint, that the amount of I/O classes should be increased.

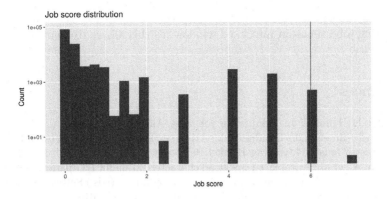

Fig. 7. Score distribution. Red line shows 99.8-quantile. (Color figure online)

For job score ≥6 there are 487 jobs. Surprisingly, 97.77% of FP2 class are these I/O intensive jobs, and FP2 class identifies 81.1% of them. Hence, the automatically determined classes cover the most I/O-intensive jobs well, albeit it requires a manual step to first label them accordingly.

8   Summary and Conclusion

In this paper, we utilize an unsupervised machine learning approach to analyse internal I/O behavior of parallel jobs. The basic idea of the approach is to generate footprints of the jobs by splitting a timeseries of I/O metrics for a job into fixed windows and compute statistics per host and time window. Then, the kMeans algorithm is used to generate classes for each window, then the time series of a job is converted into a time series of classes and reduced to a vector that contains how often the classes occur during the job runtime. The different jobs are classified by running kMeans on the resulting time series creating a single class for each job. We then explore the result of the approach on a week's data of the Mistral supercomputer.

It turned out, that the most challenging part is to describe the automatically generated I/O classes, that are found by the clustering algorithm. We could identify three of eight of them: "normal I/O", "intensive I/O" and "other I/O", whereby "other I/O" is a container for I/O classes, that are not clear what they represent.

Surprisingly, applied to our small data set, the manual labeling lead to the situation that I/O intensive applications could be identified with a precision of 97% and a recall of 81%. However, the approach is still not completely automated and there is uncertainty in determining the number of relevant IO classes and job classes. Another weakness of this approach is that it gives no answer to the question, if it this approach works generally and how decision rules can be extracted and used for I/O class description.

As we found the unsupervised labeling not optimal, we are investigating to replace that portion of the workflow with a semi-manual labeling that is more easily comprehensible. We will keep the basic idea of the workflow, i.e., segmenting job execution into fixed window, as this allows to identify phases of I/O activity.

References

1. Betke, E., Kunkel, J.: Monitoring von Ein-/Ausgabe am DKRZ (2017). https://zki2.rz.tu-ilmenau.de/fileadmin/zki/Arbeitskreise/SC/webdav/web-public/Vortraege/Jena2017/vortrag-Kunkel-Betke.pdf
2. Busch, A., et al.: Automated workload characterization for I/O performance analysis in virtualized environments. In: Knoop, J., Zdun, U. (eds.) Software Engineering 2016, pp. 27–28. Gesellschaft für Informatik e.V., Bonn (2016)
3. Julian, K., et al.: Tools for analyzing parallel I/O. In: Yokota, R., Weiland, M., Shalf, J., Alam, S. (eds.) ISC High Performance 2018. LNCS, vol. 11203, pp. 49–70. Springer, Cham (2018). https://doi.org/10.1007/978-3-030-02465-9_4
4. Madireddy, S., et al.: Machine learning based parallel I/O predictive modeling: a case study on lustre file systems. In: Yokota, R., Weiland, M., Keyes, D., Trinitis, C. (eds.) ISC High Performance 2018. LNCS, vol. 10876, pp. 184–204. Springer, Cham (2018). https://doi.org/10.1007/978-3-319-92040-5_10
5. Palmer, J.T., et al.: Open XDMoD: a tool for the comprehensive management of high-performance computing resources. Comput. Sci. Eng. **17**(4), 52–62 (2015). https://doi.org/10.1109/MCSE.2015.68. ISSN 1521–9615
6. Schmid, J., Kunkel, J.: Predicting I/O performance in HPC using artificial neural networks. Supercomput. Front. Innov. **3**(3), 19–33 (2016). http://superfri.org/superfri/ article/view/105. ISSN 2313–8734
7. Seo, B., et al.: IO workload characterization revisited: a data-mining approach. IEEE Trans. Comput. **63**(12), 3026–3038 (2014). https://doi.org/10.1109/TC.2013.187. ISSN 0018–9340
8. Tuncer, O., et al.: Diagnosing performance variations in HPC applications using machine learning. In: Kunkel, J.M., Yokota, R., Balaji, P., Keyes, D. (eds.) ISC 2017. LNCS, vol. 10266, pp. 355–373. Springer, Cham (2017). https://doi.org/10.1007/978-3-319-58667-0_19. ISBN 978-3-319-58667-0
9. Wyatt II, M.R., et al.: PRIONN: predicting runtime and IO using neural networks. In: Proceedings of the 47th International Conference on Parallel Processing (ICPP 2018) (2018). ISBN 978-1-4503-6510-9
10. Xie, B., et al.: Predicting output performance of a petascale supercomputer. In: Proceedings of the 26th International Symposium on High-Performance Parallel and Distributed Computing, HPDC 2017, Washington, DC, USA, pp. 181–192. ACM (2017). https://doi.org/10.1145/3078597.3078614. ISBN 978-1-4503-4699-3
11. Yang, B., et al.: End-to-end I/O monitoring on a leading supercomputer. In: 16th USENIX Symposium on Networked Systems Design and Implementation (NSDI 2019), pp. 379–394. USENIX Association, Boston (2019). https://www.usenix.org/conference/nsdi19/presentation/yang. ISBN 978-1-931971-49-2

Adventures in NoSQL
for Metadata Management

Jay Lofstead[1]([✉])[ORCID], Ashleigh Ryan[1,2], and Margaret Lawson[1,3]

[1] Sandia National Laboratories, Albuquerque, NM, USA
gflofst@sandia.gov
[2] Georgia Institute of Technology, Atlanta, GA, USA
[3] University of Illinois, Urbana-Champaign, IL, USA

Abstract. This paper describes an attempt to use a NoSQL database engine to manage custom metadata using a rich query interface as motivating and descriptive examples of what kind of functionality is desired. While the difficulties are numerous, a number of important considerations for how and when to use this alternative technology were revealed as well as some initial performance numbers showing the performance impact of those choices.

Keywords: Metadata · NoSQL · Cassandra · Spark

1   Introduction

As technology and computing are rapidly advancing, so is the amount of data we see being produced by scientific processes and experiments. Extreme-scale scientific simulations and observations are an excellent example of this, where the data produced by a large simulation run can be on the order of hundreds of terabytes. As the amount of data being produced by these experiments is increasing, so is the amount of time scientists must spend working to sift through said data in order to find the relatively minuscule quantities of interest.

Previous work available as open source, EMPRESS [11,12,19], has explored how to use an embedded relational database engine deployed as a service to store user-defined custom metadata tags at various levels in the data hierarchy. For example, a tag can be added at the run, timestep, variable, or some region of a variable level. Each tag has associated with it some value that is stored as a blob. If the end-user does all of the decoding of this blob, then this is an easily workable solution. Unfortunately, users see that a maximum value or region is stored in the blob and they want to run a query that uses that value to further reduce the data selected. This is a reasonable demand, but it is harder than it might appear when using the rigidly structured relational database model.

More specifically, by using custom metadata classes with potentially an attached blob representing a specific quantity or set of quantities, scientists can track the presence or absence of these metadata classes across entire or subdivisions of simulations. In a weather simulation, for example, this kind of capability

M. Weiland et al. (Eds.): ISC 2019 Workshops, LNCS 11887, pp. 227–239, 2019.
https://doi.org/10.1007/978-3-030-34356-9_19

enables scientists to query for the presence or absence of a storm within a particular simulation domain region. It does this using metadata tags attached to the data chunks written by each process. For example, the scientist may ask whether storms exist at timestep 1 of the simulation and be given a list of data chunks where storms have been tagged. While this is a boon for data analysis, a major question remains: what if the scientist wanted more detail? What if they wanted to know, for example, when the storms in timestep 1 crosses a particular region? This is where the limitation of such a system becomes noticeable. Because the metadata is stored in key-value pairs where the values are stored as blobs, it is impossible to do value-based queries without first decoding the blobs into discrete values.

While it is possible to make a relational database model and set of tables to represent the various possible values for these custom attributes, the complexity is high and the potential for errors and/or still having hard limits makes this a difficult idea. Instead, using the generic promise of a NoSQL database, such as a columnar database, may be a better solution. Conceptually, and naively, a columnar NoSQL database would offer the ability to add arbitrary additional columns, one or more per custom attribute, each strongly typed (or effectively strongly typed). This paper explores the potential to manage metadata through a NoSQL database rather than the traditional file system extended attributes or file format (e.g., ADIOS [15] or HDF5 [4]).

This paper explores the challenges in using a NoSQL database to enable more detailed queries, thus giving scientists the ability to quickly and efficiently locate points or regions of interest based on arbitrary criteria. This will be incredibly useful in extreme-scale simulations in particular, where manually locating areas of interest takes a significant amount of time. Imagine, for example, a simulation of nuclear fusion. Here, scientists often find relatively cool spots that are believed to be a major source of instability within the reaction. Now, these scientists can simply ask for a list of all the points where the temperature is below a certain degree rather than having to sift through all of the data themselves. Instead of having to parse a database blob, we can have the database itself process the query against the actual values, ideally radically reducing the time to search against these values.

We believe that a NoSQL database will provide the most promising results due to their allowing table schema to be easily modified and allowing querying based on column values. This would mean we could avoid the rigid table structure of relational databases and easily support many different value types within a single metadata table. The core challenge we face with this project is how to take the raw, theoretical potential of a columnar, NoSQL database and leverage that to support the custom metadata activities offered by EMPRESS. Getting this to work was far from easy and led to many interesting insights into the nature of these tools and the kinds of operations we need to perform for large scale modeling and simulation (modsim) data analysis tasks.

As this paper explores, numerous technological issues make this a far more challenging problem to explore than one might expect. The limited platform

Internet access and user-space-only software install access renders much of the advice on how to get these systems running impossible. Along with preliminary results, a detailed discussion of the challenge of bringing in scale out cloud tools into a restricted scale up environment are discussed.

The rest of this paper is organized as follows. First is a brief look at related work in Sect. 2 to understand how NoSQL databases have been used in modsim environments. A brief discussion of the metadata model we are attempting to represent is in Sect. 3. Next is a discussion of the general approach and design in Sect. 4. Following this in Sect. 5 is the evaluation we were able to perform. Finally, in Sect. 6 are conclusions and future work.

2   Related Work

SoMeta [21], a system that uses a hash-based approach for indexing objects based on user provided names. This is a key-value approach to custom metadata that relies on the user knowing the key or forcing the user to do a table scan to find the potential object of interest.

MDHIM [6] offers a different key-value approach largely focused on data rather than metadata. Similarly, Faodel [23] offers a key-value service intended for transient data storage without consideration for rich metadata.

HDF5 [4], ADIOS [16], PnetCDF [13], and NetCDF [3,17] all offer the ability to annotate data. HDF5's hierarchical model allows annotations down to a single variable level or at any granularity up to the entire file. PnetCDF and NetCDF adopt a more limited approach where the user can annotate the file as a whole, but not more detailed elements. ADIOS is a bit of a hybrid in that it offers the data characteristics that can be used to annotate a single process group's data, but does not offer more detailed or arbitrary data annotation capabilities.

The richest capabilities have been demonstrated by EMPRESS [11,12]. With the open source release [10] making leveraging that work easier, we are able to steal much of those test cases to explore a potentially better approach.

3   Metadata Model

EMPRESS uses a conceptual metadata model to support domain independent, extensible, user-defined metadata and to provide a wide range of metadata operations efficiently. This metadata model also makes EMPRESS easy to use since it is based on runs, timesteps and variables, high-level constructs that application scientists are accustomed to.

3.1   Basic Metadata

Basic metadata captures the structure of a simulation output and simple metadata about the various components. Basic metadata is composed of three categories: (application) runs, timesteps (individual writes or data outputs), and variables (such as temperature or pressure). The basic run structure that

EMPRESS assumes is a hierarchical one. A simulation may be run one or more times, and each run is composed of timesteps. Each timestep is composed of variables. The variables and number of variables output may differ for each timestep. This basic metadata structure is domain-independent and allows users a great deal of flexibility.

3.2 Custom Metadata

Custom metadata refers to attributes (user-defined metadata objects) and their associated tags (user-defined labels for attributes). A tag indicates what kind of metadata is being stored. An attribute can be viewed as an instance of a particular tag that is associated with a basic metadata object. Attributes can be associated with an entire run, timestep, or a subset of a variable. Each attribute is associated with a user-defined tag and a value, which can be of any data type. Variable attributes also store the global spatial coordinates of the variable subset they refer to. For example, a scientist could add a "maximum" attribute with value $10 K$ onto the "temperature" variable from X:[75,80], Y[60,80], Z[300,325]. Thus, EMPRESS provides substantial flexibility and extensibility through its user-defined tags and attributes.

4 Design

The general approach to the problem at hand was to find a potential NoSQL database based on a list of requirements and assure that it could perform six basic sample queries, which we believe to be indicative of its ability to perform all the necessary queries we predict scientists might want to ask. The six basic queries are motivated from the Six Degrees of Scientific Data [14] paper. Those queries were selected based on discussions with application scientists. Additional queries were added based on the custom metadata idea and the various places where those tags can be applied.

In addition to these, we have added queries like, "What timesteps have a particular custom metadata tag?" and "What is the x value for a given variable?"

Ultimately, we want to support the full suite of queries from the EMPRESS relational model version in a NoSQL version as well as adding queries like, "What are the timesteps where the *max* custom attribute has a value greater than 500?" and "What are the timesteps where a *storm* custom attribute appears in this 3-D region?"

Trying to get NoSQL to work on a scale up platform proved challenging. We present a series of four major challenges we addressed and discuss the implications of what we learned on using these and other cloud/scale out style tools in a limited scale up environment.

4.1 What Has the Right Features to Be Worth Testing?

With the plethora of NoSQL databases available, choosing the right one to evaluate required a feature evaluation to determine which one was likely to offer the right combination of features while still being able to be run on an isolated cluster without a direct Internet connection. Since we are not machine administrators and wish this to be client deployable software, requiring root access is not an acceptable option. While running in an isolated environment is less common, plenty of environments wish to ensure their scaled computing does not accidentally leak sensitive information to the Internet or have those resources be affected by Internet traffic and choose to isolate these resources for greater performance and security stability.

To evaluate the potential databases, we selected several different options and explored what their license terms and features to support arbitrary column creation are, among other attributes. Our evaluation criteria are the following. First, we require open source software because we give away our work as open source and do not wish to burden potential users with any proprietary licensing concerns. Second, we mainly looked at columnar databases given our intuition that these are likely the right model, but also looked at a key-value store. We know that primarily we will use an in memory model, but we need to have a level of fault tolerance for long term data life. However, we do not wish to be tied to having to write to a persistent storage mechanism unnecessarily. Finally, the query language gives us a view into the difficulty of programming to the system. The various options explored are described in Table 1.

Table 1. Databases evaluated

Database	Free open source	Columnar key-value	Fault tolerance	General language
Apache Accumulo [1]	✓	Columnar	Write ahead + HDFS-based	Java
Cassandra [8]	✓	Columnar	Replication	Cassandra Query Language
Druid [22]	✓	Columnar	Replication + HDFS backup	JSON over HTTP
Dynamo [2]	X	Key-value	S3	AWS API
Hbase [25]	✓	Columnar	HDFS	Java API
Vertica [9]	X	Columnar	Varies	SQL

Results. Ultimately, the best potential choice, not surprisingly was one of the columnar databases. In particular, we chose Cassandra [8]. The ability to store data in memory or use replication for fault tolerance was sufficient. The Cassandra Query Language offers a subset of SQL that seemed sufficient for our needs. A close second choice was Hbase [7]. The native Java API was not ideal for a portable system and the HDFS storage required additional tools we wished to avoid. While Java may be the ideal tool, our system administrators do not wish to support Java on our clusters making deploying Java-based code an entirely user handled situation. The integrated Hadoop connection offered a different avenue to implement some more complex queries, should the default API prove insufficient.

Bottom Line: While Cassandra can work since we can get all of the source code for all of the nearly countless dependencies and can build it all, it is far from an easy solution. Containers can simplify this, but it requires that we build a container with all of these dependencies. We do not have permission to install these packages natively. The active community to get help for Cassandra was seen as a potential advantage or tie breaker. Getting help from active users and admins would make this far easier to get it working. Hbase is also a viable alternative, but we did not investigate it as part of this effort. We expect that it has a similarly complex dependency tree that will make building the code to deploy on the cluster difficult. Other efforts [24] suggest that getting Hbase to run may be easier, with the right support tools.

4.2 What Is It Going to Take to Get It All Working at All?

Cassandra itself is theoretically fine. The challenge was trying to install it. There are three problem sets we encountered while trying to get this working.

Problem 1: Install Software?! The normal build and deployment process for Cassandra, or any of these tools, is to do a `sudo apt-get install` x of the dependent packages and the voila, it works. Installed software on our clusters is tightly controlled. Using the procedure is impossible. Instead, we have to get source code and manually build each dependency, in order, and then we can build Cassandra. This is far from unique. Our previous experience trying to get Ceph's RADOS to build in user space on our clusters took weeks to work out. In this case, we ultimately worked through the list and managed to get it all built properly. While for production use system administrators will spend the time to build dynamic deployments using technologies like containers, the complexity of building from scratch rather than using the automatic dependency handling installer is still present. Systems like Spack [5] offer help in building these tools for use in a dynamic environment. However, these tools, not being typically used in the scale up computing environment, will likely require generating Spack recipes to address the build issues.

Problem 2: Run as a Service?! As is typical for tools like databases, the typical installation is as a system service that continually runs in the background. This is another impossible requirement. Our typical storage tools, such as Lustre, also all work like this. It is not an unreasonable requirement–except when you want to deploy it dynamically and fully in user space. This makes it challenging for a few reasons. First, our scheduler assumes that anything that runs on a compute node uses MPI. While this requirement will relax over time, it is a current requirement. We would have to wrap Cassandra in an MPI application and have it fork out the Cassandra process to enable it. There is an upside to this. DataStax [20] has a C++-language API for programmatically accessing Cassandra and it works well in this environment. The TCP/IP requirement is not deadly as we can run TCP over IB instead.

Problem 3: Replication Is Nearly Required?! While Cassandra has a configuration file that allows specifying the number of replicas for a particular deployment, that setting is not always observed. We had a week-long problem solving hunt that ultimately came down to that setting not being respected. Instead, we had to programmatically tell Cassandra that there are no other replicas and to not look for them. This is clearly a bug in Cassandra, but is a general condition of cloud tools. Rather than resilience using checkpoint/restart, cloud tools rely on replicas to continue to operate in the face of failures. The additional resource requirement is something the scale up environment cannot readily afford. With single tasks that use the entire platform, reserving two-thirds of it so that we can have 3 replicas is not reasonable. We would want a machine three times the size instead–something we cannot afford on a variety of metrics.

Results. Cloud tools have a strong assumption in their design and implementation that they are on an open cluster that uses TCP/IP where the software can be installed natively and that Internet access is available from everywhere trivially. This last requirement was made clear when we realized that on startup, Cassandra digs through the list of dependent packages it uses and then goes to the Internet to look for updated versions to try to keep things up to date. This is specifically something we do not want. We would want stability for our tools so that we know that what we have configured will work. Ultimately, we had to disable the checking and take a cached set of dependent tool versions and install that in our home directory to make Cassandra happy and work.

Bottom Line: The assumed environment causes numerous headaches. With significant effort, it is possible to make things work in our different environment, but it is not a trivial task. The assumption of Internet access everywhere, the ability to install locally, TCP/IP being the networking employed, and replicas 'R' us all require explicit efforts to work around.

4.3   Can We Make Our Queries Work with Any Performance?

Now that we have a barely working system, the main functionality we want answered can be addressed. There are two main problems we address to answer this question.

Problem 1: Limits on New Columns? The variety of open source tools and libraries have exploded over the years. One observation is that part of the source of this explosion is that team splintering causes a code fork and a new project with an unrelated name is created. In other cases, if a tool or library does not offer feature 'x', a new tool is created optimized to work for this function. This latter case describes our experience with Cassandra. While there are clearly other columnar databases, Cassandra is very limited in what it can support for queries. For example, there is a hard-coded model such that the basic columns are indexed and queries against them are optimized. Any additional columns added are assumed to be something that will be access based on the basic columns. This is problematic.

The key functionality we are trying to enable are queries like, "what timesteps have a temperature where the max value ≥ 500?" This clearly requires selecting timesteps based on the max value column we presumably have added as a custom metadata item. The result is that Cassandra uses a table scan on the new column to find those that meet the ≥ 500 requirement. This is exactly what we are trying to avoid. Clearly this is a less than ideal implementation for our needs. Other tools all suffer from similar hyper-specialization that has allowed these tools to be the exactly best choice for the scenarios they cover. For our case, we want a rich query capability that requires extensive, rather than strictly limited, functionality.

Problem 2: Can We Avoid Table Scans? Hbase has a built-in Map-Reduce engine. Our initial evaluation determined that this was an extra feature we probably didn't need. However, Cassandra can hook together with Spark [26] to achieve the same end. This eliminates the need to switch to Hbase, but it adds another software stack and the dependency tree it requires.

Results. The narrow functionality offerings on tools that, at a surface level, seem general, causes false starts until the situation is really understood well. Once the situation is understood, that the tools each have a narrow niche where they work well, more detailed evaluation can be done to determine if it is possible to perform the desired operations with the selected tool.

The Cassandra-Spark connection, while it can work, has a hidden limitation. Spark gets its performance by caching the results from each stage so that subsequent operations can use the processed data rather than having to re-process data. The hidden limitation is that Spark, when it runs out of memory, silently throws away these cached results and just loses performance [18]. The memory limitation is based on memory allocated to the Java runtime rather than the node itself making it harder to determine if the cache flushing has been done or not. Allocating all of a node's memory to Spark also cannot work since Cassandra also needs space and it ends up essentially doubling the memory requirement for storing the data.

Bottom Line: Getting things to work is only the first part of the battle. The real challenge is finding a tool that has a broad enough functionality base to make the tool worth using. The strict limits on what columns an index can be applied to give optimized queries was unexpected, but has turned out to be a common sort of limitation that requires more detailed reading rather than selecting solely based on the tool description.

4.4 Battle Scars and Lessons for Our Next Battle Against Scale Out Computing Tools

Given the problems described above, getting these tools to work may be more trouble than they are worth. The incompatibilities and difficulty in getting solutions that offer performant functionality may not even be possible. Three specific problems have to be addressed.

Problem 1: Can This Work with Performance at All? There is not a performance option without wasting large amounts of memory and making sure that Spark does not silently flush the cache. Some functionality simply does not exist. For example, performing a query based on the presence or absence of a value in a column REQUIRES a table scan. There is no other option for a non-base column. While using a Bloom filter may be able to indicate the absence of a value without error, it cannot address the presence check. These limitations make achieving performance essentially impossible.

Problem 2: Can the Software Co-exist on Scale up Platforms? Even with the various issues trying to get the software working, it is possible to eventually work through all of the dependencies and the networking issues and make things work. If a system administrator would be willing to address these limitations by installing software as a base part of the system, things can be vastly easier. Deploying in containers can help, but the size and complexity can be a problem and the assumption that things are running as services may make using a container problematic. While professional system administrators routinely work through these issues based on user demands, the building, packaging, installation, and runtime requirements are but one factor to consider when trying to bring scale out tools into the scale up environment.

Problem 3: Is There a Way to Get What We Want? It is possible to work around the software installation issues, for the most part. It is possible, given sufficient memory and carefully configured software to get reasonable performance (memory scan rather than a storage scan and data parsing). These issues are really hard, but not insurmountable.

Results. Given the goal of trying to port EMPRESS from SQLite, an embedded relational database, to Cassandra, a columnar NoSQL database, the result is a failure. The challenges from the software installation to the query limitations to the work around to the software architecture assumptions we have to work around all add up to an unworkable solution.

Bottom Line: What this work has not shown is that the idea of using a NoSQL database is bad. It has shown that if we want to use such a tool, we need to develop one that works for our environment. Given the existing tools and the unproven research or production use benefits, retrofitting a relational database is the most efficient solution.

5 Evaluation

Since we managed to get a basic setup created, an initial, limited evaluation is performed to get an idea if this idea is really worth pursuing given the high up front cost.

To evaluate the implementation, tests are performed on a single desktop workstation. While this is not an "at scale" implementation, it is sufficient to show how this can work for file per process workloads. Alternative workloads that use an N-1 pattern will require further exploration.

The testing environment is a Dell Precision 3420 SFF tower. It has an Intel Core i7-6700 CPU @ 3.40 GHz, 32 GB RAM, and a 256 GB ATA SAMSUNG SSD SM87 for storage. It is running Ubuntu 16.04 LTS - 64-bit.

Each test writes a single application run with 3 timesteps. Each timestep is composed of a set of 10 3D variables. Variables used in this evaluation include temperature, pressure, and density among others. Each of these variables is distributed across the processes using a 3D domain decomposition, so that each process writes a regular hyper-rectangle (a "chunk") per variable that is .04 GB large. This size is chosen so that each process writes 10% of its total RAM per timestep, which is a typical amount. 10 tags are used, each of which has a set frequency that determines what percentage of chunks it is associated with. These tags include "blobs" (a scientific name for spatial phenomena), annotations, ranges, and maximum and minimum. The blobs have a Boolean value (indicating presence or absence of a particular feature), the maximum and minimum have a double value (like the associated data), the notes have text values, and the ranges have values that are a pair of integers. On average, 2.6 attributes are written per chunk (per variable, per timestep). A full discussion of the tags are available in our previous work [11]. For each timestep, the global maximum and minimum for the "temperature" variable are written as timestep attributes and the maximum and minimum across all timesteps are inserted as run attributes.

Mimicking our production runtime restrictions set by our users, we need to run with the smallest footprint possible. Any resources used for hosting these services will be scrutinized with the thought of how much more compute could be done with those resources compared to the value generated. This eliminates the ability to use more than a single replica for data storage and makes many of the performance configurations typically used by these scale out tools impossible to leverage.

5.1 Insert Time

To evaluate how well the Cassandra/Spark setup works, we ran 10 tests as described above (3 timesteps, 10 vars, $10 \times 10 \times 10$ processes). We placed timing measurements to identify various pieces of overhead so we could quantify how long each different kind of insert operation takes. The results are presented in Table 2.

Overall, the results are reasonable for inserts. The initial database setup time of about 1.6 s is a one-time cost at startup. The table creation cost of 2.5 s is also a one-time startup cost. While 5 s is not fast, since this is a one-time cost, we think it is something that users may be willing to accept.

The data insertion time is significantly faster. In all cases, it will be a combination of the first two times (0.015 s) with statistically little additional time for the other attributes. Even with the skew to the maximum, given the frequency, these numbers are not terrible. Since they can be batched and done asynchronously, this may be acceptable time as well.

Table 2. Performance results

Test	Mean (secs)	Min (secs)	Max (secs)
Spark setup	1.46	1.41	1.50
Create table description	0.208	0.165	0.355
Instantiate table	2.217	2.107	2.277
Insert basic info	0.008	0.005	0.211
Insert basic attributes	0.007	0.005	0.208
Insert other attributes	0.013	0.006	1.356

5.2 Query Time

We ran out of time to complete the query tests. However, we can describe the difficulty and the cost overheads we expect.

The initial schema setup required by a NoSQL database, particularly those that do not allow joins, is essentially a fully denormalized form. While this is not inherently bad, it does have some serious drawbacks. First, the amount of redundant data is significant. Instead of using a foreign key to a separate table that lists the various attributes, it has to include it in every row. For example, the run, timestep, and variable name must all be repeated with every row.

Second, the vast areas of `null` values should offer more compact storage, but we don't know for sure.

6   Conclusion and Future Work

The evaluation revealed challenges and performance issues of NoSQL when used as a general purpose database tool for scale up computing. In particular, while SQL databases offer a general purpose solution, NoSQL databases are highly optimized for a few operations. If your need can fit within the functionality of a NoSQL database, superior performance can be achieved. The challenges for end users to attempt to use these scale out technologies, particularly in a strongly security conscious environment that limits software installs, are difficult to overcome.

Given the experience of this exploration, it suggests that using existing solutions may be a better option. For example, using the NoSQL database is an attempt to avoid a complex relational database schema. While it is certainly possible to create a sufficiently rich relational schema, the complexity will make it fragile and more difficult to extend and maintain. However, an end user can relatively easily create such a schema and have no issues deploying it within a tight security regime. The costs involved with testing, developing, and deploying the NoSQL solution outweigh the costs of using the proven technology in a more complex way.

For future work, determining if other technology families can be used effectively by end users in the secured scale up environment will be pursued. The financial pressures of having two different infrastructures (scale out and scale up) will force finding ways to make this merger feasible.

References

1. Apache: Apache Accumulo (2018). http://accumulo.apache.org. Accessed 18 Dec 2018
2. Baron, J., Kotecha, S.: Storage options in the AWS cloud. Amazon Web Services, Washington DC, Technical report (2013)
3. Edward Hartnett, E., Rew, R.K.: Experience with an enhanced NetCDF data model and interface for scientific data access. In: 24th Conference on IIPS (2008)
4. Folk, M., Heber, G., Koziol, Q., Pourmal, E., Robinson, D.: An overview of the HDF5 technology suite and its applications. In: Proceedings of the EDBT/ICDT 2011 Workshop on Array Databases, pp. 36–47. ACM (2011)
5. Gamblin, T., et al.: The spack package manager: bringing order to HPC software chaos. In: Proceedings of the International Conference for High Performance Computing, Networking, Storage and Analysis, p. 40. ACM (2015)
6. Greenberg, H., Bent, J., Grider, G.: MDHIM: a parallel key/value framework for HPC. In: HotStorage (2015)
7. Khetrapal, A., Ganesh, V.: Hbase and hypertable for large scale distributed storage systems. Dept. of Computer Science, Purdue University, pp. 22–28 (2006)
8. Lakshman, A., Malik, P.: Cassandra: structured storage system on a P2P network. In: Proceedings of the 28th ACM Symposium on Principles of Distributed Computing, p. 5. ACM (2009)
9. Lamb, A., et al.: The vertica analytic database: C-store 7 years later. Proc. VLDB Endow. 5(12), 1790–1801 (2012)

10. Lawson, M.: EMPRESS Metadata Management System (2018). https://github. com/mlawsonca/empress. Accessed 18 Dec 2018
11. Lawson, M., Lofstead, J.: Using a robust metadata management system to accelerate scientific discovery at extreme scales. In: Proceedings of the 3rd Joint International Workshop on Parallel Data Storage & Data Intensive Scalable Computing Systems. ACM (2018)
12. Lawson, M., et al.: Empress: extensible metadata provider for extreme-scale scientific simulations. In: Proceedings of the 2nd Joint International Workshop on Parallel Data Storage & Data Intensive Scalable Computing Systems, pp. 19–24. ACM (2017)
13. Li, J., et al.: Parallel NetCDF: a high-performance scientific I/O interface. In: 2003 ACM/IEEE Conference on Supercomputing, p. 39, November 2003. https://doi. org/10.1109/SC.2003.10053
14. Lofstead, J., et al.: Six degrees of scientific data: reading patterns for extreme scale science IO. In: Proceedings of the 20th International Symposium on High Performance Distributed Computing, HPDC 2011, pp. 49–60. ACM (2011). http:// doi.acm.org/10.1145/1996130.1996139
15. Lofstead, J., Zheng, F., Klasky, S., Schwan, K.: Adaptable, metadata rich IO methods for portable high performance IO. In: Proceedings of IPDPS 2009, Rome, Italy, 25–29 May 2009
16. Lofstead, J.F., Klasky, S., Schwan, K., Podhorszki, N., Jin, C.: Flexible IO and integration for scientific codes through the adaptable IO system (ADIOS). In: Proceedings of the 6th International Workshop on Challenges of Large Applications in Distributed Environments, pp. 15–24. ACM (2008)
17. Rew, R., Hartnett, E., Caron, J., et al.: NetCDF-4: software implementing an enhanced data model for the geosciences. In: 22nd International Conference on Interactive Information Processing Systems for Meteorology, Oceanograph, and Hydrology (2006)
18. Sahin, S., Cao, W., Zhang, Q., Liu, L.: JVM configuration management and its performance impact for big data applications. In: 2016 IEEE International Congress on Big Data (BigData Congress), pp. 410–417. IEEE (2016)
19. Sevilla, M.A., et al.: Tintenfisch: file system namespace schemas and generators. In: The 10th USENIX Workshop on Hot Topics in Storage and File Systems (HotStorage 2018) (2018)
20. Stax, D.: DataStax Cassandra Connector (2018). https://www.datastax.com/. Accessed 18 Dec 2018
21. Tang, H., Byna, S., Dong, B., Liu, J., Koziol, Q.: SoMeta: scalable object-centric metadata management for high performance computing. In: 2017 IEEE International Conference on Cluster Computing (CLUSTER), pp. 359–369. IEEE (2017)
22. Tschetter, E.: Introducing Druid (2012). http://druid.io/blog/2012/10/24/ introducing-druid.html. Accessed 18 Dec 2018
23. Ulmer, C.D., et al.: Faodail: enabling in situ analytics for next-generation systems. Technical report, Sandia National Lab. (SNL-NM), Albuquerque, NM (United States) (2017)
24. Indiana University: IndexedHbase (2019). http://salsaproj.indiana.edu/Indexed HBase/HBguide.html. Accessed 14 June 2019
25. Vora, M.N.: Hadoop-hbase for large-scale data. In: 2011 International Conference on Computer Science and Network Technology (ICCSNT), vol. 1, pp. 601–605. IEEE (2011)
26. Zaharia, M., et al.: Apache spark: a unified engine for big data processing. Commun. ACM **59**(11), 56–65 (2016)

Towards High Performance Data Analytics for Climate Change

Sandro Fiore[1]([✉])[iD], Donatello Elia[1,2][iD], Cosimo Palazzo[1][iD],
Fabrizio Antonio[1][iD], Alessandro D'Anca[1][iD], Ian Foster[3][iD],
and Giovanni Aloisio[1,2][iD]

[1] Euro-Mediterranean Center on Climate Change Foundation, Lecce, Italy
sandro.fiore@cmcc.it
[2] University of Salento, Lecce, Italy
[3] University of Chicago & Argonne National Laboratory, Chicago, USA

Abstract. The continuous increase in the data produced by simulations, experiments and edge components in the last few years has forced a shift in the scientific research process, leading to the definition of a fourth paradigm in Science, concerning data-intensive computing. This data deluge, in fact, introduces various challenges related to big data volumes, formats heterogeneity and the speed in the data production and gathering that must be handled to effectively support scientific discovery. To this end, High Performance Computing (HPC) and data analytics are both considered as fundamental and complementary aspects of the scientific process and together contribute to a new paradigm encompassing the efforts from the two fields called High Performance Data Analytics (HPDA). In this context, the Ophidia project provides a HPDA framework which joins the HPC paradigm with scientific data analytics. This contribution presents some aspects regarding the Ophidia HPDA framework, such as the multidimensional storage model, its distributed and hierarchical implementation along with a benchmark of a parallel in-memory time series reduction operator.

Keywords: HPDA · Climate change · Scientific data analysis · Storage model · Multidimensional data

1 Introduction

Scientific research has been experiencing a shift over the last few years due to the enormous increase of data produced by simulations, experiments, edge components, etc. which has led to the definition of a fourth paradigm in Science concerning data-intensive computing [7]. The deluge of data, however, poses several challenges that must be tackled accordingly to cope with bigger data volumes, heterogeneous formats and different frequency in data generation. To fully support data-intensive scientific applications, High Performance Computing (HPC) and data analytics are both deemed as fundamental and complementary aspects of the scientific process [21], providing together a new paradigm for

© Springer Nature Switzerland AG 2019
M. Weiland et al. (Eds.): ISC 2019 Workshops, LNCS 11887, pp. 240–257, 2019.
https://doi.org/10.1007/978-3-030-34356-9_20

eScience named High Performance Data Analytics (HPDA). Related to that, in the current scientific landscape, the Ophidia project provides a HPDA framework joining HPC paradigms with scientific data analytics approaches. This paper describes key aspects of the Ophidia HPDA framework, such as the multidimensional storage model design and the related distributed and hierarchical implementation across multiple, heterogeneous physical resources; additionally, it also presents a benchmark of a key analytical operator for parallel, in-memory time series reduction.

The rest of this paper is organized as follows. After the review of some key challenges for scientific data analysis in Sects. 2 and 3 presents some of the main aspects of the Ophidia project like its internal storage model and partitioning/distribution schema design and implementation. Section 4 presents a time series reduction benchmark, while Sect. 5 presents state of the art projects in the scientific data analytics area. Finally, Sect. 6 draws the main paper conclusions and describes future work.

2   Main Challenges

By reviewing a previous work presented at BDEC [2], we summarize some key challenges [1,3,10,18] for addressing scientific data analytics at scale. In particular, we (i) discuss the need to review the *scientific data analysis workflow* (*shifting from client to server-side approaches*), and (ii) highlight *storage, data management and metadata-related challenges*.

The workflow commonly used in production for scientific discovery has traditionally been based on the *search, locate, download and analyze* steps, typically performed on a researcher's desktop. Such workflow could not scale for several reasons including (i) ever-larger scientific datasets, (ii) time- and resource- consuming data downloads, and (iii) increased problem size and complexity requiring bigger computing facilities. Server-side approaches have helped address challenges related to the analysis of very large datasets, keeping data produced from simulations or gathered from observations close to the data center facilities.

As regards the *storage*, new storage models are essential to support datacube-oriented analytics. New data organizations are needed to better fit the intrinsic datacube model of n-dimensional data. Data partitioning and distribution can enable parallelism, whereas indexing, replication, and caching can improve execution efficiency and throughput. In a multidimensional space, dimensional data independence - where the storage model should be independent of the number of dimensions - should be clearly addressed to provide the right level of separation of concerns.

Finally, *metadata* represents a valuable source of information for data description, data search & discovery as well as for properly (from a semantics perspective) running scientific tasks. In this regard, with the shift towards server-side approaches, it becomes extremely relevant to support, in close proximity to the compute and data storage facilities available in a data center: (i) metadata management capabilities to index datasets and support datasets search & discovery,

(ii) provenance metadata capture and collection for describing the flow of analytics operators in scientific data analysis experiments; (iii) integration of information linking cross-related digital objects (using PIDs), (iv) the creation of new community-oriented tools to enrich metadata and provide, at the same time, a way to move this process towards much more open, multi-level and collaborative forms, targeting Open Science-oriented approaches.

3   The Ophidia Project

In the eScience landscape, the Ophidia project [11,12] provides a HPDA framework joining HPC paradigms with scientific data analytics approaches. Primarily exploited in the climate domain, it provides a domain-agnostic architectural design, which makes it suitable for any scientific domain dealing with multidimensional data formats [15]. A complete architectural overview of Ophidia is reported in [14].

Ophidia provides in-memory, parallel, server-side data analysis & I/O, an internal storage model and a hierarchical data organization to manage large amounts of multidimensional scientific data. The multidimensional storage model and related implementation aspects are presented in Sect. 3.1.

Array-based functionalities ("primitives") as well as datacube kernels ("operators") represent two levels through which end-users can operate on scientific data performing analytics tasks. Such aspects are discussed in detail in Sect. 3.2.

3.1   Multi-dimensional Storage Model

The objective of addressing efficient climate data management inherently leads to the key challenges of properly dealing with scientific multidimensional data. To achieve this goal, Ophidia implements a storage model leveraging the datacube abstraction from the well-known On-Line Analytical Processing (OLAP) systems in the databases field.

In such a context, a datacube consists of several measures representing numerical values that can be analyzed over the available dimensions. The multidimensional data model exists in the form of star, snowflake or galaxy schema. The Ophidia storage model [14] (see Fig. 1) builds on top of the classic star schema. In such a schema, the data warehouse implementation consists of a large central table (the *fact* table) that contains all the data and a set of smaller tables (*dimension* tables), one for each dimension. The dimensions can also define *hierarchies*, which represent a convenient way to organize the information according to their level of aggregation; a very common example is the time dimension, which can represent information at various levels of aggregations (e.g. *hours ->days ->months*, etc.).

In Fig. 1, the fact table is represented with the Dimensional Fact Model (DFM) [17], a conceptual model for data warehouse (see Fig. 1a). The example shows one fact table (FACT) with four dimensions (dim1, dim2, dim3, and dim4), where the last dimension is modeled through a 4-level concept hierarchy (lev1, lev2, lev3, lev4), and a single measure (measure). This schema can be easily used to map a NetCDF file produced, for example, by a global climate simulation, where the four dimensions correspond to *latitude, longitude, depth,* and *time,* while the measure can represent the *air temperature.* The classic Relational-OLAP (ROLAP) logical model can then be used to implement the star schema (see Fig. 1b).

In terms of storage model, Ophidia implements a two-step-based evolution of the star schema. The first step introduces the support for array-based data types (see Fig. 1c), by merging multiple rows into a single binary array. Rows are merged according to one or more dimensions. In this way, an array contains the values of the measure related to all the possible configurations of these dimensions. The second step performs the mapping of the set of foreign keys (*fks*) (see Fig. 1d), related to the remaining subset of dimensions, to a single new key. Thus, a multidimensional array can be managed using single tuple (e.g., an entire time series) identified by one key (a numerical ID). It is worth noting that, thanks to this second step, the Ophidia storage model is *independent of the number of dimensions,* unlike the classic ROLAP-based implementation. Hence, the system implements a key-value schema (i) supporting n-dimensional data management, (ii) exhibiting data locality, and (iii) reducing disk space occupancy.

A combination of values of m dimensions ($m < n$) is mapped through a numerical function onto the key attribute: $ID = f(fk\_dim_1, fk\_dim_2, \ldots, fk\_dim_m)$; the corresponding dimensions are defined in Ophidia as *explicit dimensions.* The array attribute manages the other n-m dimensions, called *implicit dimensions.*

The ID key is defined as a sequential integer positive number computed with the following function (1).

$$ID = \sum_{j=i}^{m} S_j fk_j, \text{ with } S_j = \prod_{i=j+i}^{m} size(d_i) \; \forall \; j = 1, \ldots, m-1 \text{ and } S_m = 1 \quad (1)$$

where m is the number of explicit dimensions, $(fk_1, fk_2, \ldots, fk_m)$ is the particular configuration of dimension indexes and $size(d_j)$ is the size of the *j-th* dimension.

In our example, latitude, longitude and depth could be the explicit dimensions, whereas time would be the implicit one (in this case 1-D array). The mapping onto the Ophidia key-array storage model would therefore result in a single table with two attributes:

- an ID attribute: $ID = f(fk_{latitudeID}, fk_{longitudeID}, fk_{depthID})$ as a numerical data type;
- an array-based attribute, managing the implicit dimension time, as a binary data type.

In terms of implementation, several traditional RDBMSs allow data to be stored as a binary data type, by exploiting for instance the string data type (as CHAR, BINARY, BLOB, TEXT types), but they do not provide a way to manage the array as a native data type. The reason is that the available binary data type does not look at the binary array as a vector, but rather as a single binary block. Therefore, we have designed and implemented a comprehensive set of array-based primitives to manage the arrays stored in Ophidia according to its internal storage model.

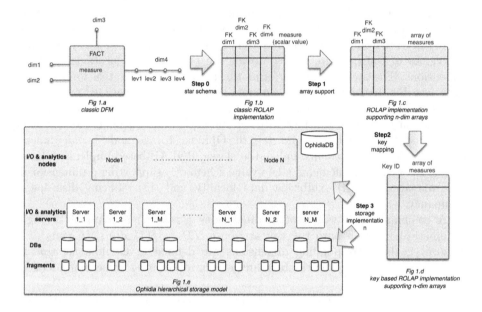

Fig. 1. Ophidia storage model and implementation

With regard to the physical mapping onto the storage systems (see Fig. 1e), Ophidia horizontally partitions this very long table into several *fragments* to efficiently handle big datacubes on the physical file system. This fragmentation is driven by the underlying resources following a hierarchical approach composed of four different levels, as shown in Fig. 1:

- Level 0: multiple Ophidia I/O & analytics nodes (multi-host);
- Level 1: multiple instances of Ophidia I/O & analytics servers on the same node (multi-server);
- Level 2: multiple instances of databases on the same IO & analytics server (multi-DB);
- Level 3: multiple fragments on the same database (multi-table).

The total number of fragments associated with a datacube is the product of these four parameters, which represents key settings for fragments distributions. Fine tuning of these parameters is out of the scope of this paper and will be discussed in more detail in a future work.

Finally, from an end-user perspective, the logical/virtual file system hosting the datacube objects is defined as a *cube space* (see Fig. 2) in Ophidia (as opposed to the physical file system associated with files) due to the datacube abstraction delivered to the users. Related to this, there is a set of operators that specifically allows copying, moving, deleting and listing datacubes and folders in the cube space. Metadata information (like that stored in the header of scientific data, e.g. NetCDF) is separately stored into the OphidiaDB, i.e., the Ophidia system catalog.

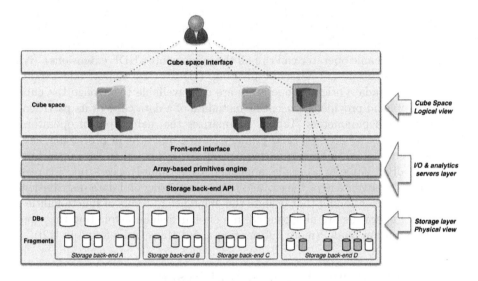

Fig. 2. Cube space abstraction and physical storage implementation/mapping

3.2   Array-Based Primitives and Parallel Operators

At the I/O and analytics server level (see Fig. 2), Ophidia provides an array-based engine and a set of array-based primitives as Structured Query Language (SQL) extensions relying on the User-Defined Functions (UDF) approach. About 100 primitives have been implemented. Among others, the available array-based functions allow the performance of data sub-setting, data aggregation (i.e., max, min, avg), array concatenation, algebraic expressions and predicate evaluation. We note that multiple plugins can be nested to implement a single and more complex task (e.g., aggregating by sum a subset of the entire array). Bit-oriented plugins have also been implemented to manage binary datacubes. The array-based processing is performed by the I/O and analytics servers engine, which supports the management of n-dimensional array structures both at the data type and primitives levels. An in-depth view of the array-based primitives has been discussed in a previous work [14].

Additionally,

- through the storage back-end API, the I/O and analytics servers can transparently interface to different storage back-ends such as POSIX-like file system, object stores, relational DBMSs and memory. As the main focus of Ophidia is the support of in-memory analytics, the default 'storage back-end' is *memory*.
- on GPU-equipped nodes, the I/O and analytics servers can run some primitives available as a CUDA-based implementation.

From a datacube abstraction perspective, the Ophidia HPDA platform provides several MPI-based parallel operators to manipulate (as a whole) the entire set of fragments associated with a datacube. Some relevant examples include: (i) data sub-setting (slicing and dicing), (ii) data aggregation, (iii) array-based primitives (the same operator can run all the implemented UDF extensions), (iv) datacube duplication, (v) datacube pivoting, (vi) NetCDF-import and export. Still, some metadata-oriented operators are also available to manage the cube space objects and provide the scientific metadata of a data cube or its partitioning/distribution parameters. Table 1 summarizes the main types of operators, by classifying them based on their primary feature and type of processing; as it can be noted, metadata operators are sequential, as opposed to data operators, which are all available in a parallel implementation (multi-process/multi-thread based) to take advantage of the storage-level partitioning and data distribution.

It is worth mentioning that despite the difference in terms of functionalities, the parallel operators are all executed in a similar fashion, exploiting the same runtime execution model (more information about this can be found in [12]).

4   Benchmark and Experimental Results

This section describes a benchmark defined for the performance evaluation and scalability of the Ophidia framework when running a typical data reduction analysis operator (*OPH_REDUCE2*). Although Ophidia provides several classes of operators, as shown in Table 1, the *OPH_REDUCE2* is one of the most used and interesting in terms of parallel data processing; it addresses array-based data reduction to compute statistical indicators such as, among others, maximum, minimum, average and standard deviation.

In this respect, the computation of the average value of the time series for each point in a 3-dimensional spatial domain (e.g. latitude, longitude and pressure level) is considered, under different data partitioning and distribution settings. While previous works have addressed coarse-grain, application-level and end-user perspective scenarios by primarily focusing on scientific use cases (i.e., workflows) for climate indicators [9] and multi-model analysis [13], the goal of the benchmark proposed in this paper is to provide key insights into largely used core Ophidia operators. In this respect, the *OPH_REDUCE2* is one of the best candidates because it relates to statistical analysis, which is very common in any scientific data analysis.

Table 1. Main Ophidia operator classes

Class	Processing type	Operator(s)
I/O	Parallel	-Data import (OPH_IMPORTNC, OPH_IMPORTFITS) -Data export (OPH_EXPORTNC) -Append data from files to datacubes (OPH_CONCATNC) -Generate random data (OPH_RANDUCUBE)
Time series processing	Parallel	-Apply generic time series transformation (OPH_APPLY)
Datacube reduction	Parallel	-Reduction over the implicit dimensions (OPH_REDUCE) -Reduce time series based on concept hierarchies (OPH_REDUCE2) -Reduction over the explicit dimensions (OPH_AGGREGATE)
Datacube subsetting	Parallel	-Subset data based on dimension coordinates or indexes (OPH_SUBSET)
Datacube combination	Parallel	-Compare different cubes (OPH_INTERCUBE) -Merge multiple cubes (OPH_MERGECUBES)
Datacube structure manipulation	Parallel	-Split the fragments (OPH_SPLIT) -Merge fragments together (OPH_MERGE) -Change dimension order/type (OPH_ROLLUP, OPH_DRILLDOWN, OPH_PERMUTE)
Datacube/file system management	Sequential	-Delete a datacube (OPH_DELETE) -Manage virtual file system (OPH_FOLDER) -Browse real file system (OPH_FS)
Metadata management	Sequential	-Metadata management (OPH_METADATA) -Provenance exploration (OPH_CUBEIO) -Datacube info (OPH_CUBESCHEMA)
Datacube exploration	Sequential	-Datacube exploration (OPH_EXPLORECUBE) -File exploration (OPH_EXPLORENC)

It should be noted that the benchmark is not intended to be large-scale per se, but rather to provide some key insights into the scalability of the *OPH_REDUCE2* operator from a performance standpoint on a Terabyte-scale. The large-scale scientific data analysis scenario that can be targeted with Ophidia is not about running a single operator on a Petabyte-scale datacube, but rather several operators in the same analysis (i.e., workflows) on hundreds/thousands of Terabyte-scale datacubes. In this respect, the Terabyte-scale performance metrics addressed in the paper turn out to be very good indicators of the scalability of a core Ophidia data reduction operator.

4.1 Benchmark Definition

As stated above, the main focus of this benchmark is to evaluate the scalability of data reduction operations. In particular, the *OPH_REDUCE2* parallel operator has been tested to compute the average value of each time series stored in the input datacube.

An example of the Ophidia command used to run the *OPH_REDUCE2* operator is described as follows (more details about the *OPH_REDUCE2* operator available options can be found on the online Ophidia documentation[1]):

```
oph_reduce2 operation=avg;dim=time;ncores=10;nthreads=10;
    cube=<input_cube>;
```

The declarative statement presented above shows: (i) the type of reduction operation (*avg*); (ii) the reduction dimension (*time*); (iii) the number of MPI processes (set to 10 *ncores*); (iv) the number of threads for each process (set to 10 *nthreads*); and (v) the input datacube (*input_cube*).

In this benchmark, three tests have been identified and set up to evaluate the behaviour of Ophidia under different settings, with the aim of providing multiple insights from different perspectives.

1. *Strong scalability.* This test case aims to evaluate the platform scalability by measuring the *OPH_REDUCE2* execution time on a fixed problem size while increasing the number of executed parallel tasks, from 1 to 100.
2. *Weak scalability.* In this test, the *OPH_REDUCE2* operator is executed by scaling up the data size along with the number of used parallel tasks, from 1 to 100; only the data size for a unit of computation is fixed.
3. *Array-oriented.* This test aims to evaluate the performance of the framework while increasing the length of the binary array, with fixed data partitioning and number of parallel tasks.

It is worth mentioning that, in order to better adapt the data size used for the experiments, while trying to maximize the amount of memory used from the environment, the input datacubes have been derived from random data. The *OPH_RANDCUBE2* operator has been used to manually tune the datacube structure and populate it with random values (generated through a first order autoregressive model). The maximum problem size used is actually slightly different in the various tests due to datacube structure and fragmentation requirements. An example of the *OPH_RANDCUBE2* statement used during the tests to generate a random-data datacube is:

```
oph_randcube2 exp_dim=lat|lon|plev;exp_dim_size
    =1200|800|24;imp_dim_size=11680;imp_dim=time;measure=
    tas;nfrag=240;ntuple=19200;nhost=5;algorithm=
    auto_reg_first_order;
```

Such command is very flexible, providing the end users with multiple options to model and create a datacube. In this case, a 4d (*lat, lon, plev, time*) datacube is created with a total number of $1200 \times 800 \times 24 \times 11680$ tas elements (*float* type), stored in 240 (*nfrag*) fragments, each one storing 1.92×10^4 (*ntuples*) tuples and distributed across 5 (*nhost*) nodes running the native in-memory I/O & analytics servers. The first three dimensions (*lat, lon, plev*) are the explicit

---

[1] OPH_REDUCE2 documentation http://ophidia.cmcc.it/documentation/users/operators/OPH_REDUCE2.html.

ones (*exp_dim*) in the datacube, whereas time is the implicit or array-based one (*imp_dim*); tas is the name used to refer to the climate air temperature variable.

The main metrics measured during the tests include the *execution time* and the *data size*; other metrics derived from these include:

- *efficiency* is the percentage rate of the sequential execution time over the parallel execution time divided by the computation units (in the *strong scalability* test) or the rate of sequential execution time with respect to the parallel time (in the *weak scalability* test);
- *processing throughput* is the rate of input data processed with respect to the execution time and it is measured as GB/s.

4.2   Test Environment

The benchmark has been performed in a real data center setting, on a dedicated cluster designed for in-memory analytics, hosted at the CMCC SuperComputing Centre in Lecce (Italy).

The cluster is composed of five fat nodes, individually equipped with 256 GB of main memory, 1TB of local disk and 2 Intel Xeon processors (2×10 cores), for a total of 100 physical cores. These nodes are used for the execution of the native Ophidia in-memory I/O & analytics servers.

The storage is shared across the five nodes, which are connected together through a high-speed network (10Gb/s). The shared storage exploits a GlusterFS file system[2] distributed over five disks with about 60TB of total raw disk capacity. The official 1.4.0 release of Ophidia has been deployed on the cluster.

4.3   Experimental Results and Discussion

Multiple runs of the *OPH_REDUCE2* operator have been executed for each configuration of the three tests and the average time has been considered in the results hereafter. It is important to mention that all average values feature a 95% confidence interval whose maximum relative error is at most 7%.

Strong Scalability. In this first test case, the datacube size has been fixed to about 1TB, consisting of approximately 2.7×10^{11} floating point values organized into 2.3×10^7 time series (1.17×10^4 elements each one). At the storage level, the data has been partitioned into 1200 fragments evenly distributed over the five I/O & analytics servers, each one running on a single node and managing around 200 GB of data/node. The partitioning parameters have been defined to ensure that the number of fragments processed by each task is always well balanced while scaling up the number of parallel tasks from 1 to 100.

---

[2] GlusterFS documentation https://docs.gluster.org/en/latest/.

The size of the resulting output datacube is approximately 90 MB (18 MB/node, 4 order of magnitude smaller than the input datacube, but with the same degree of fragmentation). Table 2 shows a summary of the results obtained from this test, which include speedup, efficiency and data reduction throughput.

Table 2. Summary of results for the strong scalability test. In this case, the data size is constant (1TB) as well as the partitioning parameters (1200 fragments, 5 nodes, 1 I/O & analytics server/node).

Number of tasks	Execution time [s]	Efficiency [%]	Throughput [GB/s]
1	1290.8	100	0.8
10	144.3	89.4	6.9
20	73	88.5	13.7
40	35.5	90.8	28.2
60	23.4	91.8	42.9
80	19.5	82.7	51.4
100	17.6	73.2	56.8

The first row of the table provides the results of a sequential computation, while the others show the results for parallel processing. The number of tasks has been increased up to 100 to show the behaviour of the operator up to the full utilization of the cluster resources. Figure 3a provides a graphical representation of the efficiency and data reduction throughput (GB/s).

As it can be clearly seen, the efficiency is stable around 90% up to 60 tasks, going down to 73% only when the cluster resources are fully utilized. The best case exhibits an execution time of 17.6 s, which corresponds to 56.8 GB/s of processed data. Finally, besides the analytics performance evaluation, the benchmark shows how the distributed storage model implementation efficiently scales up with the problem size over multiple nodes, allowing to tackle larger-scale scenarios. This is actually something that would not be feasible (from a scalability standpoint) on a single host.

Weak Scalability. In this second test, the data size has been increased along with the number of tasks used to run the data reduction (average) operation. With respect to the previous test, since the data size and partitioning change over the different runs, the number of fragments per task has been fixed to 1 to make the results evaluation easier. Each fragment contains about 2.8×10^9 floating point values organized into 2.4×10^5 elements time series (1.17×10^4 elements each) for a total of 10.4 GB of data.

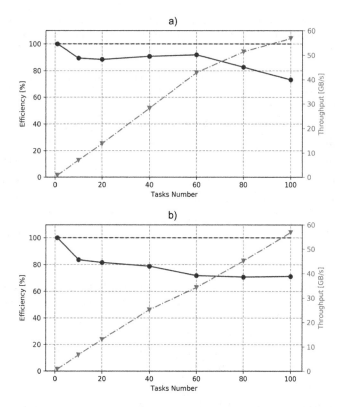

Fig. 3. Results of the strong (a) and weak (b) scalability tests. Efficiency is plotted with the full line, while data reduction throughput is plotted with the dashed line. The straight dashed line represents the ideal efficiency.

The *OPH_REDUCE2* operator has been executed by scaling up the number of fragments together with the parallel tasks up to 100 (i.e., 1.04 TB). In this test, the number of servers has been increased together with the data size. In particular, a single I/O & analytics server has been used for the first three configurations (i.e., 1, 10, 20), while 2, 3, 4 and 5 servers have been used for the other configurations. Through this setup, it has been possible to exploit the full resources provided by the cluster.

Table 3 provides an overview of the results of this test. The execution time and the total problem size have been measured for each run; based on them, we also inferred efficiency and processing throughput metrics.

In this case, as also highlighted in the plot in Fig. 3b the efficiency remains over 80% when the executed task remains bounded to one node, whereas it slightly decreases down to 70% when the computation runs over multiple nodes. This is related to the additional overhead required to manage a larger set of tasks running on multiple nodes. This experiment shows how the processing exhibits a good level of scalability over multiple nodes thanks also to the underlying distributed storage model and partitioning schema (the drop in performance

Table 3. Summary of results for the weak scalability test. In this case, the data size per task is constant (10.4 GB) while the number of tasks and fragments is scaled up from 1 to 100.

Tasks (fragments)	I/O & Analytics nodes	Execution time [s]	Efficiency [%]	Throughput [GB/s]	Data size [GB]
1	1	13.1	100	0.8	10.4
10	1	15.7	83.6	6.7	104.4
20	1	16.1	81.6	13.0	208.9
40	2	16.6	78.8	25.1	417.7
60	3	18.3	71.8	34.4	626.6
80	4	18.5	70.7	45.1	835.4
100	5	18.4	71.2	56.7	1044.3

is about 10% from 1 to 5 nodes, which corresponds to 2.3 s in our test). The execution time remains between 13 and 18.5 s, while the processing throughput peaks to almost 57 GB/s. The scalability of the storage model implementation is further demonstrated in the plot (see Fig. 3b), which highlights that the efficiency does not degrade as more resources are added; after the initial slowdown, it actually remains stable to around 70%.

Array-Oriented. In this test, the data partitioning parameters, as well as the number of tasks, have been kept constant while increasing the number of elements stored in the binary arrays (together with the total problem data size). Similarly to the previous test, the number of fragments per task has been set to one, hence the data has been split into 100 fragments, consisting of 2.3×10^5 time series each. Again, five nodes individually running an Ophidia in-memory I/O and analytics server have been exploited for this test. The execution time of the *OPH_REDUCE2* operator has been computed with a fixed number of tasks (i.e., 100), while increasing the array length by one order of magnitude each time, from 12 to 1.2×10^4 values (i.e., 1.03 TB). The data reduction throughput has also been computed for each array configuration. Table 4 reports a summary of the results for this test.

The results confirm the benefits of the array-based organization in the Ophidia storage model implementation (which inherently takes full advantage of the data locality) from a processing performance standpoint. As it can be seen from Table 4, the throughput can be greatly improved, with the same amount of resources, just by increasing the array length.

To sum up, the results show that data partitioning and distribution jointly with the parallel processing approach implemented in Ophidia provide good performance under both strong and weak scalability conditions. Moreover, the array-oriented physical data organization proves to be extremely efficient (super linear) in the management of (very) long time series.

Table 4. Summary of results for the array-oriented test.

Array length	Execution time [s]	Throughput [GB/s]	Data size [GB]
12	1.8	0.6	1
120	2.1	4.9	10.3
1200	3.9	26.4	103
12000	18.9	54.5	1030

5   Related Work

Data analytics in eScience requires solutions able to manage and process large-scale data, taking into account several aspects, such as (i) the multi-dimensional nature of the datasets, (ii) the relevance of metadata for analysis purposes and (iii) the peculiarities of domain-specific algorithms.

The tools typically used for scientific data processing/analysis are client-side and operate mostly sequentially. Their inherent design does not make them particularly suited to target huge amounts of data. Indeed, such tools do not rely on distributed data storage and parallel processing, often failing for the lack of hardware resources (primarily RAM) on the execution node. To give some examples in the climate change domain, tools like CDO [22], NCO [26], ICCLIM[3], NCL[4] are successfully and largely adopted, very well-known, but unfortunately they are not designed to straightforwardly meet large data volume requirements and scenarios.

SciDB [8,24] and Rasdaman [4–6] are eScience-oriented projects aimed at addressing the above issues. SciDB is actually a distributed non-relational DBMS supporting full ACID properties and based on a multi-dimensional array oriented data model. Its set of statistical and linear algebra operations can be easily extended with user-defined types and user-defined functions. SciDB has been effectively used for data analysis in various scientific domains [23]. Rasdaman ("raster data manager") is an array database designed to store and query massive multi-dimensional arrays-based data, like images, simulation and sensors from various scientific domains. Similarly to Ophidia, they rely on n-dimensional arrays and offer a server side and declarative approach, although Ophidia is rather a framework centered around the datacube abstraction, providing an HPC-based environment for parallel data processing, metadata/provenance management and OLAP. Furthermore, Ophidia relies on a custom imperative-declarative approach to specify operations and implements interfaces for the creation and execution of high-level Python-based applications (through Ophidia python bindings, PyOphidia[5]) and scientific workflows.

---

[3] ICCLIM (Indice Calculation CLIMate) https://icclim.readthedocs.io/en/latest/intro.html.
[4] NCAR command language https://www.ncl.ucar.edu/.
[5] PyOphidia - Conda Forge https://anaconda.org/conda-forge/pyophidia.

Some efforts focusing on the extension of general purpose systems to support more scientific-oriented data analytics and formats have also recently emerged in literature. In particular, the well-known Spark parallel computing framework has been extended in various projects. SciSpark [20,25], for example, extends the Spark framework with the Scientific Resilient Distributed Dataset (sRDD), a distributed in-memory array structure for multi-dimensional data designed to support scientific data structures and algorithms. In particular, it targets the weather and climate change domains providing features to read data in parallel directly from HDF [16] and NetCDF file formats and a common interface to multiple linear algebra libraries. Another similar example is ClimateSpark [19], which also extends Spark to support climate change data analysis by defining an extension of RDD, called ClimateRDD, i.e., an immutable in-memory distributed collection of climate data chunks capable of managing multi-dimensional arrays. The system also provides some domain-specific transformations performed in parallel. These tools provide better support for scientific analysis, with respect to general purpose frameworks, while exploiting the power of the Spark programming and computing framework. However, differently from Ophidia, these solutions have not been originally designed for HPDA, using a parallel shared I/O and HPC-based computation model, or do not yet provide full support for domain-specific metadata management.

Another effort that is currently in the spotlight in the scientific community is Dask[6], a flexible library for parallel computing in Python. Eco-systems like Pangeo[7] are exploiting Dask for parallel climate data analysis. With respect to Dask, Ophidia includes (i) a very flexible and robust I/O layer (thus providing both compute- and storage-level capabilities), (ii) a more integrated approach with HPC-based parallel paradigms (i.e. MPI, OpenMP).

6   Conclusions

In the eScience landscape, the Ophidia project provides a High Performance Data Analytics framework joining HPC paradigms with scientific data analysis approaches to tackle large-scale parallel climate change data analysis. The core aspects of Ophidia, such as its storage model design and related distributed and hierarchical implementation across multiple physical storage resources are presented. Additionally, the experimental results (e.g., parallel efficiency and throughput) about a key analytical operator for data reduction, executed under different experimental setups (i.e., data partitioning and distribution conditions), are also discussed. Still, a specific benchmark of time series data reduction provides some insights in terms of scalability, efficiency and throughput of Ophidia. In particular, the results show how the Ophidia data distribution and partitioning enable the parallel data reduction operator to scale up to the full capacity of our cluster (more than 70% in all the cases analyzed). As a future work, a large-scale benchmark running on Marenostrum (PRACE Tier0 machine at

---

[6] Dask, library for dynamic task scheduling https://dask.org.

[7] Pangeo. A community platform for big data geoscience. https://pangeo.io/.

Barcelona Supercomputing Center) to evaluate the performance results of other classes of Ophidia operators (e.g., I/O), as well as a set of selected end-users applications, will be performed in the context of the ESiWACE Center of Excellence on Weather and Climate Simulations in Europe project[8]. Additionally, Ophidia will be further extended to support the Earth System Data Middleware[9] interface, developed in the ESiWACE project, to enable advanced scenarios at extreme-scale, like scalable in-situ visualization on HPC machines of global, high-resolution climate change simulation datasets.

Acknowledgments. This work was supported in part by the EU H2020 Excellence in SImulation of Weather and Climate in Europe (ESiWACE) project (Grant Agreement 675191). Moreover, the authors would like to acknowledge Antonio Aloisio for his editing and proofreading work on this paper.

References

1. Aloisio, G., Fiore, S.: Towards exascale distributed data management. Int. J. High Perform. Comput. Appl. **23**(4), 398–400 (2009). https://doi.org/10.1177/1094342009347702
2. Aloisio, G., Fiore, S., Foster, I., Williams, D.: Scientific big data analytics challenges at large scale. Proceedings of Big Data and Extreme-scale Computing (BDEC) (2013)
3. Asch, M., et al.: Big data and extreme-scale computing: pathways to convergence-toward a shaping strategy for a future software and data ecosystem for scientific inquiry. Int. J. High Perform. Comput. Appl. **32**(4), 435–479 (2018). https://doi.org/10.1177/1094342018778123
4. Baumann, P., Dehmel, A., Furtado, P., Ritsch, R., Widmann, N.: The multidimensional database system RasDaMan. SIGMOD Rec. **27**(2), 575–577 (1998). https://doi.org/10.1145/276305.276386
5. Baumann, P., Dehmel, A., Furtado, P., Ritsch, R., Widmann, N.: Spatio-temporal retrieval with RasDaMan. In: Proceedings of the 25th International Conference on Very Large Data Bases, VLDB 1999 pp. 746–749. Morgan Kaufmann Publishers Inc., San Francisco (1999). http://dl.acm.org/citation.cfm?id=645925.671513
6. Baumann, P., Furtado, P., Ritsch, R., Widmann, N.: The RasDaMan approach to multidimensional database management. In: Proceedings of the 1997 ACM Symposium on Applied Computing, SAC 1997, pp. 166–173. ACM, New York (1997). https://doi.org/10.1145/331697.331732
7. Bell, G., Hey, T., Szalay, A.: Beyond the data deluge. Science **323**(5919), 1297–1298 (2009). https://doi.org/10.1126/science.1170411
8. Brown, P.G.: Overview of sciDB: large scale array storage, processing and analysis. In: Proceedings of the 2010 ACM SIGMOD International Conference on Management of Data, SIGMOD 2010, pp. 963–968. ACM, New York (2010). https://doi.org/10.1145/1807167.1807271

---

[8] The ESiWACE Center of Excellence on Weather and Climate Simulations in Europe project https://www.esiwace.eu/.

[9] ESiWACE Earth System Data Middleware https://github.com/ESiWACE/esdm.

9. D'Anca, A., et al.: On the use of in-memory analytics workflows to computer science indicators from large climate datasets. In: 2017 17th IEEE/ACM International Symposium on Cluster, Cloud and Grid Computing (CCGRID), pp. 1035–1043, May 2017. https://doi.org/10.1109/CCGRID.2017.132

10. Dongarra, J., et al.: The international exascale software project roadmap. Int. J. High Perform. Comput. Appl. **25**(1), 3–60 (2011). https://doi.org/10.1177/1094342010391989

11. Elia, D., et al.: An in-memory based framework for scientific data analytics. In: Proceedings of the ACM International Conference on Computing Frontiers, CF 2016, pp. 424–429. ACM, New York (2016). https://doi.org/10.1145/2903150.2911719

12. Fiore, S., et al.: Ophidia: a full software stack for scientific data analytics. In: 2014 International Conference on High Performance Computing Simulation (HPCS), pp. 343–350, July 2014. https://doi.org/10.1109/HPCSim.2014.6903706

13. Fiore, S., et al.: Distributed and cloud-based multi-model analytics experiments on large volumes of climate change data in the earth system grid federation ecosystem. In: 2016 IEEE International Conference on Big Data (Big Data), pp. 2911–2918, December 2016. https://doi.org/10.1109/BigData.2016.7840941

14. Fiore, S., D'Anca, A., Palazzo, C., Foster, I.T., Williams, D.N., Aloisio, G.: Ophidia: toward big data analytics for escience. In: Proceedings of the International Conference on Computational Science, ICCS 2013, Barcelona, Spain, 5–7 June 2013, pp. 2376–2385 (2013). https://doi.org/10.1016/j.procs.2013.05.409

15. Fiore, S., et al.: Big data analytics on large-scale scientific datasets in the INDIGO-DataCloud project. In: Proceedings of the Computing Frontiers Conference, CF 2017, pp. 343–348. ACM, New York (2017). https://doi.org/10.1145/3075564.3078884

16. Folk, M., Heber, G., Koziol, Q., Pourmal, E., Robinson, D.: An overview of the HDF5 technology suite and its applications. In: Proceedings of the EDBT/ICDT 2011 Workshop on Array Databases. AD 2011, pp. 36–47. ACM, New York (2011). https://doi.org/10.1145/1966895.1966900

17. Golfarelli, M., Rizzi, S.: Data Warehouse Design: Modern Principles and Methodologies, 1st edn. McGraw-Hill Inc., New York (2009)

18. Gray, J., Liu, D.T., Nieto-Santisteban, M., Szalay, A., DeWitt, D.J., Heber, G.: Scientific data management in the coming decade. SIGMOD Rec. **34**(4), 34–41 (2005). https://doi.org/10.1145/1107499.1107503

19. Hu, F., et al.: ClimateSpark: an in-memory distributed computing framework for big climate data analytics. Comput. Geosci. **115**, 154–166 (2018). https://doi.org/10.1016/j.cageo.2018.03.011

20. Palamuttam, R., et al.: SciSpark: applying in-memory distributed computing to weather event detection and tracking. In: 2015 IEEE International Conference on Big Data (Big Data), pp. 2020–2026, October 2015. https://doi.org/10.1109/BigData.2015.7363983

21. Reed, D.A., Dongarra, J.: Exascale computing and big data. Commun. ACM **58**(7), 56–68 (2015). https://doi.org/10.1145/2699414

22. Schulzweida, U.: CDO user guide - version 1.9.6 (2019). https://code.mpimet.mpg.de/projects/cdo/embedded/cdo.pdf

23. Stonebraker, M., Brown, P., Becla, J., Zhang, D.: SciDB: a database management system for applications with complex analytics. Comput. Sci. Eng. **15**(3), 54–62 (2013). https://doi.org/10.1109/MCSE.2013.19

24. Stonebraker, M., Brown, P., Poliakov, A., Raman, S.: The Architecture of SciDB. In: Bayard Cushing, J., French, J., Bowers, S. (eds.) SSDBM 2011. LNCS, vol. 6809, pp. 1–16. Springer, Heidelberg (2011). https://doi.org/10.1007/978-3-642-22351-8_1

25. Wilson, B., et al.: SciSpark: highlyinteractive in-memory science data analytics. In: 2016 IEEE InternationalConference on Big Data (Big Data), pp. 2964–2973, December 2016. https://doi.org/10.1109/BigData.2016.7840948

26. Zender, C.S.: Analysis of self-describing gridded geoscience data with netCDF Operators (NCO). Environ. Model. Softw. **23**(10), 1338–1342 (2008). https://doi.org/10.1016/j.envsoft.2008.03.004

An Architecture for High Performance Computing and Data Systems Using Byte-Addressable Persistent Memory

Adrian Jackson[1]([✉]), Michèle Weiland[1], Mark Parsons[1], and Bernhard Homölle[2]

[1] EPCC, The University of Edinburgh, Edinburgh, UK
a.jackson@epcc.ed.ac.uk
[2] SVA System Vertrieb Alexander GmbH, Paderborn, Germany

Abstract. Non-volatile and byte-addressable memory technology with performance close to main memory has the potential to revolutionise computing systems in the near future. Such memory technology provides the potential for extremely large memory regions (i.e. >3 TB per server), very high performance I/O, and new ways of storing and sharing data for applications and workflows. This paper proposes hardware and system software architectures that have been designed to exploit such memory for High Performance Computing and High Performance Data Analytics systems, along with descriptions of how applications could benefit from such hardware, and initial performance results on a system with Intel Optane DC Persistent Memory.

Keywords: Non-volatile memory · Persistent memory · System architecture · Systemware · NVRAM · B-APM

1 Introduction

There are a number of new memory technologies that are impacting, or likely to impact, computing architectures in the near future. One example of such a technology is so called high bandwidth memory, already featured on Intel's latest many-core processor, the Xeon Phi Knights Landing [1], and NVIDIA's latest GPU, Volta [2]. These contain MCDRAM [1] and HBM2 [3] respectively, memory technologies built with traditional DRAM hardware but connected with a very wide memory bus (or series of buses) directly to the processor to provide very high memory bandwidth when compared to traditional main memory (DDR channels).

This has been enabled, in part, by the hardware trend for incorporating memory controllers and memory controller hubs directly onto processors, enabling memory to be attached to the processor itself rather than through the motherboard and associated chipset. However, the underlying memory hardware is the same, or at least very similar, to the traditional volatile DRAM memory that is still used as main memory for computer architectures, and that remains attached to the motherboard rather than the processor.

M. Weiland et al. (Eds.): ISC 2019 Workshops, LNCS 11887, pp. 258–274, 2019.
https://doi.org/10.1007/978-3-030-34356-9_21

Non-volatile memory, i.e. memory that retains data even after power is turned off, has been exploited by consumer electronics and computer systems for many years. The flash memory cards used in cameras and mobile phones are an example of such hardware, used for data storage. More recently, flash memory has been used for high performance data input/output (I/O) in the form of Solid State Disk (SSD) drives, providing higher bandwidth and lower latency than traditional Hard Disk Drives (HDD).

Whilst flash memory can provide fast I/O performance for computer systems, there are some drawbacks. It has limited endurance when compare to HDD technology, restricted by the number of modifications a memory cell can undertake and thus the effective lifetime of the flash storage [29]. It is also generally more expensive than other storage technologies. However, SSD storage, and enterprise level SSD drives, are heavily used for I/O intensive functionality in large scale computer systems because of their random read and write performance capabilities.

Byte-addressable random access persistent memory (B-APM), also known as storage class memory (SCM), NVRAM or NVDIMMs, exploits a new generation of non-volatile memory hardware that is directly accessible via CPU load/store operations, has much higher durability than standard flash memory, and much higher read and write performance. B-APM, with its very high performance access characteristics, and vastly increased capacity (compared to volatile memory), offers a potential hardware solution to enable the construction of a compute platform that can support high-performance computing (HPC) and high-performance data analytics (HPDA) use cases, addressing some of the performance imbalance systems currently have between memory and I/O performance.

In this paper, we outline the systemware and hardware required to provide such a system, and discuss preliminary performance results from just such a system. We start by describing persistent memory, and the functionality it provides, in more detail in Sect. 2. In Sect. 3 we discuss how B-APM could be exploited for scientific computation or data analytics. Following this we outline our systemware architecture in Sect. 4. We finish by presenting performance results on a prototype system containing Intel Optane DC Persistent memory, in Sect. 5, discussing related work in Sect. 6, and summarise the paper in the final section.

2 Persistent Memory

B-APM takes new non-volatile memory technology and packages it in the same form factor (i.e. using the same connector and dimensions) as main memory (SDRAM DIMM form factor). This allows B-APM to be installed and used alongside DRAM based main memory, accessed through the same memory controller. As B-APM is installed in a processor's memory channels, applications running on the system can access B-APM directly in the same manner as main memory, including true random data access at byte or cache line granularity. Such an access mechanism is very different to the traditional block based approaches used for current HDD or SSD devices, which generally requires I/O to be done using blocks of data (i.e. 4 KB of data written or read in one operation), and relies on expensive kernel interrupts and context switches.

The first B-APM technology to make it to market is Intel's Optane DC Persistent^{TM} memory [5]. The performance of this B-APM is lower than main memory (with a latency $\sim$5–10x that of DDR4 memory when connected to the same memory channels), but much faster than SSDs or HDDs. It is also much larger capacity than DRAM, around 2–5x denser (i.e. 2–5x more capacity in the same form factor, with 128, 256, and 512 GB currently available DIMMs).

2.1   Data Access

This new class of memory offers very large memory capacity for servers, as well as long term persistent storage within the memory space of the servers, and the ability to undertake I/O in a new way. B-APM can enable synchronous, byte level, direct access (DAX) to persistent data, moving away from the asynchronous block-based file I/O applications currently rely on. In current asynchronous I/O user applications pass data to the operating system (OS) which then use driver software to issue an I/O command, putting the I/O request into a queue on a hardware controller. The hardware controller will process that command when ready, notifying the OS that the I/O operation has finished through an interrupt to the device driver.

B-APM, on the other hand, can be accessed simply by using a load or store instruction, as with any other memory operation from an application or program. However, because B-APM can provide persistence functionality (allowing data to be accessible after power loss), some further considerations are required if persistent is to be guaranteed. Applications must also ensure stored data has been flush from the volatile CPU caches and has arrived on the non-volatile medium (using new cache flush commands and fence instructions to ensure stores are ordered ordered before subsequent instructions) before they can confirm data has been persisted (although this flush may only be required to the memory controller, rather than the non-volatile medium, if using enhanced power supply functionality [6]).

With B-APM providing much lower latencies than external storage devices, the traditional I/O block access model, using interrupts, becomes inefficient because of the overhead of context switches between user and kernel mode (which can take thousands of CPU cycles [30]). Furthermore, in the future it may become possible to implement remote persistent access to data stored in the memory using RDMA technology over a suitable interconnect. Using high performance networks has the potential to enable access to data stored in B-APM in remote nodes faster than accessing local high performance SSDs via traditional I/O interfaces and stacks inside a node.

Therefore, it is possible to use B-APM to greatly improve I/O performance within a server; increase the memory capacity of a server; or provide a remote data store with high performance access for a group of servers to share. Such storage hardware can also be scaled up by adding more B-APM memory in a server, or adding more nodes to the remote data store, allowing the I/O performance of a system to scale as required. The use of B-APM in compute nodes also removes competition for I/O resources between jobs in a system, isolating application I/O traffic and removing the performance fluctuations associated with I/O users often experience on shared HPC systems [25]. However, if B-APM is provisioned in the servers, there must be software support for managing data within the B-APM. This includes moving data as required for the jobs running on the system, and providing the functionality to let applications run on any server and still utilise the B-APM for fast I/O and storage (i.e. applications should be able to access B-APM in remote nodes if the system is configured with B-APM only in a subset of all nodes).

As B-APM is persistent, it also has the potential to be used for resiliency, providing backup for data from active applications, or providing long term storage for databases or data stores required by a range of applications. With support from the systemware, servers can be enabled to handle power loss without experiencing data loss, efficiently and transparently recovering from power failure and resuming applications from their latest running state, and maintaining data with little overhead in terms of performance.

2.2   B-APM Modes of Operation

Ongoing developments in memory hierarchies, such as the high bandwidth memory in Xeon Phi manycore processors or NVIDIA GPUS, have provided new memory models for programmers and system designers. A common model that has been proposed includes the ability to configure main memory and B-APM in two different modes: Single-level and Dual-level memory [8].

Single-level memory, or SLM, has main memory (DRAM) and B-APM as two separate memory spaces, both accessible by applications, as outlined in Fig. 1. This is very similar to the Flat Mode [7] configuration of the high bandwidth, on-package, MCDRAM in Intel Knights Landing processor. The DRAM is allocated and managed via standard memory API's such as *malloc* and represent the OS visible main memory size. The B-APM is be managed by programming APIs and presents the non-volatile part of the system memory. In order to take advantage of B-APM in SLM mode, systemware or applications have to be adapted to use these two distinct address spaces.

Dual-level memory, or DLM, configures DRAM as a cache in front of the B-APM, as shown in Fig. 2. Only the memory space of the B-APM is available to applications, data being used is stored in DRAM, and moved to B-APM when no longer immediately required by the memory controller (as in standard CPU caches). This is very similar to the Cache Mode [7] configuration of MCDRAM on KNL processors.

This mode of operation does not require applications to be altered to exploit the capacity of B-APM, and aims to give memory access performance at main memory speeds whilst providing access to the large memory space of B-APM. However, exactly how well the main memory cache performs will depend on the specific memory requirements and access pattern of a given application.

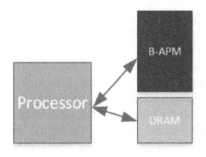

Fig. 1. Single-level memory (SLM) configuration using main memory and B-APM

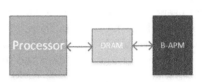

Fig. 2. Dual-level memory (DLM) configuration using main memory and B-APM

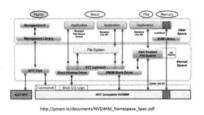

Fig. 3. PMDK software architecture

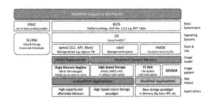

Fig. 4. Software stack exploiting B-APM in compute nodes

Furthermore, persistence of the B-APM contents cannot be longer guaranteed, due to the volatile DRAM cache in front of the B-APM, so the non-volatile characteristics of B-APM are not exploited. A hybrid mode is also supported, where only a part of the B-APM is used to extend the main memory and the remaining part is used for persistent operations. The sizes of B-APM used for memory extension and persistent memory can be set flexibly.

2.3 Non-volatile Memory Software Ecosystem

The Storage Networking Industry Association (SNIA) have produced a software architecture for B-APM with persistent load/store access, formalised in the Linux Persistent Memory Development Kit (PMDK) [9] library. This approach re-uses the naming scheme of files as traditional persistent entities and maps the B-APM regions into the address space of a process (similar to memory mapped files in Linux). Once the mapping has been done, the file descriptor is no longer needed and can be closed. Figure 3 outlines the PMDK software architecture. Figure 4 details the software architecture we are considering for systems exploiting B-APM for HPC and HPDA work, which will be discussed in more detail in Sect. 4.

3   Opportunities for Exploiting B-APM for Computational Simulations and Data Analytics

Reading data from and writing it to persistent storage is usually not the most time consuming part of computational simulation applications. Analysis of common applications from a range of different scientific areas shows that around 5–20% of runtime for applications is involved in I/O operations [10,11]. It is evident that B-APM can be used to improve I/O performance for applications by replacing slower SSDs or HDDs in external filesystems. However, such a use of B-APM would be only an incremental improvement in I/O performance, and would neglect some of the significant features of B-APM that can provide performance benefits for applications.

Firstly, deploying B-APM as an external filesystem would require provisioning a filesystem on top of the B-APM hardware. Standard storage devices require a filesystem to enable data to be easily written to or read from the hardware. However, B-APM does not require such functionality, and data can be manipulated directly on B-APM hardware simply through load/store instructions. Adding the filesystem and associated interface guarantees (i.e. POSIX interface [12]) adds performance overheads that will reduce I/O performance on B-APM.

Secondly, an external (to the compute nodes) B-APM based filesystem would require all I/O operations to be performed over a network connection (see Fig. 5). This would limit the maximum performance of I/O to that of the network between compute nodes and the nodes the B-APM is hosted in, and expose application I/O performance to the variations associated with a shared external resource, however fast it is.

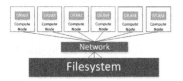

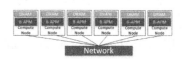

Fig. 5. Current external storage for HPC and HPDA systems

Fig. 6. Internal storage using B-APM in compute nodes for HPC and HPDA systems

Our vision for exploiting B-APM for HPC and HPDA systems is to incorporate the B-APM into the compute nodes, as outlined in Fig. 6. This architecture allows applications to exploit the full performance of B-APM within the compute nodes they are using, by enabling access to B-APM through load/store operations at byte-level granularity, as opposed to block based, asynchronous I/O. Incorporating B-APM into compute nodes also has the benefit that I/O capacity and bandwidth can scale with the number of compute nodes in the system. Adding more compute nodes will increase the amount of B-APM in the system and add more aggregate bandwidth to I/O/B-APM operations.

For example, current memory bandwidth of a HPC system scales with the number of nodes used. If we assume an achievable memory bandwidth per node of 200 GB/s, then it follows that a system with 10 nodes has the potential to provide 2TB/s of memory bandwidth for a distributed application, and a system with 10000 nodes can provide 2PB/s of memory bandwidth. If an application is memory bandwidth bound and can parallelise across nodes then scaling up nodes in this fashion clearly has the potential to improve performance. For B-APM in nodes, and taking Intel®Optane DC persistent memory (DCPMM) as an example, we have measured 40 GB/s of memory bandwidth per node (read and write) or 80 GB/s (read) for the STREAMS benchmark using DCPMM (two sockets), then scaling up to 10 nodes provides 400 GB/s of (I/O) memory bandwidth and 10000 nodes provides 400 TB/s of(I/O) memory bandwidth. For comparison, the Titan system at ORNL has a Lustre file system with 1.4TB/s of bandwidth [26] and they are aiming for 50 TB/s of burst buffer [28] I/O by 2024 [27]. Furthermore, there is the potential to optimise not only the performance of a single application, but the performance of a whole scientific workflow, from data preparation, simulations, data analysis and visualisation. Optimising full workflows by sharing data between different stages or steps in the workflow has the scope to completely remove, or greatly reduce, data movement/storage costs (and associated energy costs) for large parts of the workflow altogether. Leaving data in-situ on B-APM for other parts of the workflow can significantly improve the performance of analysis and visualisation steps at the same time as reducing I/O costs for the application when writing the data out.

Finally, the total runtime of an application can be seen as the sum of its compute time, plus the time spent in I/O. Greatly reduced I/O costs therefore also has the beneficial side effect of allowing applications to perform more I/O within the same total cost of the overall application run. This will enable applications to maintain I/O costs in line with current behaviour whilst being able to process significantly more data. Furthermore, for those applications for which I/O does take up a large portion of the run time, including data analytics applications, B-APM has the potential to significantly reduce runtime.

3.1   Potential Caveats

However, utilising internal storage is not without drawbacks. Firstly, the benefit of external storage is that there is a single namespace and location for compute nodes to use for data storage and retrieval. This means that applications can run on any compute nodes and access the same data as it is stored external to the compute nodes. With internal storage, this guarantee is not provided, data written to B-APM is local to specific compute nodes. It is therefore necessary for applications to be able to manage and move data between compute nodes, as well as to external data storage, or for some systemware components to undertake this task, to reduce scheduling restrictions on applications sharing a system with a finite set of compute nodes.

Secondly, B-APM may be expensive to provision in all compute nodes. It may not be practical to add the same amount of B-APM to all compute nodes, meaning systems may be constructed with islands of nodes with B-APM, and islands of nodes without B-APM. Therefore, application or systemware functionality to enable access to remote B-APM and to exploit/manage asymmetric B-APM configurations will be required. Both these issues highlight the requirement for an integrated hardware and software (systemware) architecture to enable efficient and easy use of this new memory technology in large scale computational platforms.

4   Systemware Architecture

Systemware implements the software functionality necessary to enable users to easily and efficiently utilise the system. We have designed a systemware architecture that provides a number of different types of functionality, related to different methods for exploiting B-APM for large scale computational simulation or data analytics.

From the hardware features B-APM provides, our analysis of current HPC and HPDA applications and functionality they utilise, and our investigation of future functionality that may benefit such applications, we have identified a number of different kinds of functionality that the systemware architecture should support:

1. Enable users to be able to request systemware components to load/store data in B-APM prior to a job starting, or after a job has completed. This can be thought of as similar to current burst buffer technology. This will allow users to be able to exploit B-APM without changing their applications.
2. Enable users to directly exploit B-APM by modifying their applications to implement direct memory access and management. This offers users the ability to access the best performance B-APM can provide, but requires application developers to undertake the task of programming for B-APM themselves, and ensure they are using it in an efficient manner.
3. Provide a filesystem built on the B-APM in compute nodes. This allows users to exploit B-APM for I/O operations without having to fundamentally change how I/O is implemented in their applications. However, it does not enable the benefit of moving away from file based I/O that B-APM can provide.
4. Provide an object, or key value, store that exploits the B-APM to enable users to explore different mechanisms for storing and accessing data from their applications.
5. Enable the sharing of data between applications through B-APM. For example, this may be sharing data between different components of the same computational workflow, or the sharing of a common dataset between a group of users.
6. Ensure data access is restricted to those authorised to access that data and enable deletion or encryption of data to make sure those access restrictions are maintained

7. Provide different memory modes if they are supported by the B-APM hardware.
8. Enable job scheduling on the system that can optimise performance or energy usage by utilising B-APM functionality

The systemware architecture we have defined appear to have a large number of components and significant complexity, however the number of systemware components that are specific to a system that contains B-APM is relatively small. The new or modified components we have identified are required to support B-APM in a large scale, multi-user, multi-application, compute platforms are as follows; *Job Scheduler*, *Data Scheduler*, *Object Store*, and *Filesystems*. There are a number of object stores under development, of which some are focussed on efficiently exploiting B-APM hardware, such as DAOS [21] and dataClay [22]. As such we will not focus on object stores in this paper. Likewise, there are a plethora of filesystems that could be deployed on the hardware, both as local filesystems on each node (i.e. ext4) or as distributed filesystems spanning compute nodes (i.e. GekkoFS [33]). We will utilise some filesystems to test performance but not focus on the specifics of filesystems in this paper.

4.1   Job Scheduler

As the innovation in our proposed system is the inclusion of B-APM within nodes, one of the key components that must support the new hardware resource is the job scheduler. Job schedulers, or batch systems, are used to manage, schedule, and run user jobs on the shared resource that are the compute nodes. Standard job schedulers are configured with the number of nodes in a system, the number of cores per node, and possibly the amount of memory or whether there are accelerators (like GPUs) in compute nodes in a system. They then use this information, along with a scheduling algorithm and scheduling policies, to allocate user job request to a set of compute nodes. Users submit job requests specifying the compute resources required (i.e. number of nodes or number of compute cores a job will require) along with a maximum runtime for the job. This information is used by the job scheduler to accurately, efficiently, and fairly assign applications to resources.

Adding B-APM to compute nodes provides another layer of hardware resource that needs to managed by the job scheduler. As data can persist in B-APM, and one of our target use cases is the sharing of data between applications using B-APM, the job scheduler needs to be extended to both be aware of this new hardware resource, and to allow data to be retained in B-APM after an individual job has finished. This functionality is achieved through adding workflow awareness to the job scheduler, providing functionality to allow data to be retained and shared through jobs participating in the workflow, although not indefinitely [24]. The job scheduler also needs to be able to clean up the B-APM after a job has finished, ensuring no data is left behind or B-APM resources consumed, unless specifically as part of a workflow. Job schedulers already do support assigning resources to jobs, in the form of burst buffer allocations.

They also can support workflows, with users able to specify dependencies between jobs submitted or running on a system. However, currently no schedulers support workflow locality, the association of specific nodes with workflow jobs, as is required when sharing data residing in compute nodes. The allocation of burst buffer resources through scheduler functionality also does not provide support for the local nature of data in B-APM, relying on the external nature of burst buffer placements in the storage hierarchy.

Furthermore, as the memory system can have different modes of operation, a supporting job scheduler will need to be able to query the current configuration of the memory hardware, and be able to change configuration modes if required by the next job that will be using a particular set of compute nodes. There are job schedulers that do have support for querying and modify hardware configurations, such as Slurm functionality to support different KNL processor configurations. However, the configuration of B-APM is significantly more complex that KNL MCDRAM, and requires the use of multiple system tools or interfaces to ensure valid memory configurations can be achieved. This requires significant extra on-node scheduler functionality for a job scheduler.

Finally, efficiently allowing users to exploit this new hardware resource will require data aware and energy aware scheduling algorithms. These will utilise the job scheduler's awareness of B-APM functionality and compute job data requirements, and enable scheduling compute tasks to data rather than moving data to compute tasks (as is currently done with external filesystems), or moving data between compute nodes or external filesystems as required to maximise the utilisation or efficiency of the overall system.

4.2   Data Scheduler

The data scheduler is an entirely new component, designed to run on each compute node and provide data movement and shepherding functionality. This include functionality to allow users to move data to and from B-APM asynchronously (i.e. pre-loading data before a job starts, or moving data from B-APM after a job finishes), or between different nodes (i.e. in the case that a job runs on a node without B-APM and requires B-APM functionality, or a job runs and needs to access data left on B-APM in a different node by another job). To provide such support without requiring users to modify their applications we implement functionality in the data scheduler component. This component has interfaces for applications to interact with, and is also for job scheduler component on each compute node. Through these interfaces the data scheduler can be instructed to move data as required by a given application or workflow.

5   Performance Evaluation

To evaluate the performance and usability of our architectures we benchmarked on a prototype HPC system with B-APM installed in the compute nodes. We used a range of different benchmarks, from synthetic workflows, through large scale applications, and I/O benchmarks such as IOR [38].

Table 1. Synthetic workflow benchmark using Lustre or B-APM in a compute node

Component	Target	Runtime (seconds)
Producer	Lustre	197
Consumer	Lustre	112
Producer	B-APM	133
Consumer	B-APM	60

Table 2. OpenFOAM workflow benchmark using Lustre or B-APM with data staging

Workflow phase	Lustre	B-APM
Decomposition	1352	1323
Data-staging	–	51
Solver	747	95

Test System and Setup: All experiments were conducted using a prototype system composed of 34 compute nodes. Each node has two Intel® Xeon® Platinum 8260M CPU running at 2.40 GHz (i.e. 48 physical cores per node), 192 GiB of DDR4 RAM (12 × 16 GB DIMMs) and 3 TBytes of DCPMM memory (12 × 256GB DCPMM DIMMs). A single rail Intel® Omni Path network connects the compute nodes through a 100 Gbps switch, as well as to a 270 TB external Lustre filesystem with 6 OSTs. The compute nodes are running Linux CentOS 7.5 and we use Slurm for job scheduling. To manage and configure the DCPMM we use Intel's *ipmctl* and Linux's *ndctl* [37] tools. Version 1.05 of the PMDK toolkit is installed, along with the Intel 19 compiler suite, and Intel's MPI and MKL libraries.

Synthetic Workflow: We created a synthetic workflow benchmark that contains two components, a producer and a consumer of data. These components can be configured to produce and consume a number of files of different sizes, but then do no work other than reading or writing and verifying data. We ran this benchmark either targeting the Lustre filesystem or the B-APM in the compute node, and also using the job scheduler integration and data scheduler component to maintain data in B-APM between workflow component execution. Table 1 outlines the performance achieved when producing and consuming 200 GB (10 × 20 GB files) of data for each configuration. Each benchmark workflow ran 5 times and we report the mean time to complete the benchmark. Performance varied by <15% across runs when using Lustre and <2% when using B-APM. When using B-APM we ran a job that reads and writes 200 GB of data between workflow components on the same node to ensure caching does not affect performance. Benchmarks were compiled using the Intel 19 compiler with the -O3 flag.

Benchmarking using Lustre was configured with the producer and consumer processes on two separate compute nodes to ensure that I/O caching locally did not affect measured runtimes. For the benchmark using B-APM we ran using the same node for producer and consumer, communicating data through the B-APM in the node. We can see from the Table 1 using B-APM storage gives ≈45% faster overall runtime (172 vs 309 s) for the workflow compared to using Lustre.

Application Workflow: OpenFOAM [35] is a C++ library that provides computational fluid dynamics functionality that can easily be extended and modify by users. It is parallelised with MPI and is heavily used in academia and industry for large scale computational simulations. It often requires multiple stages to complete a simulation, from preparing meshes and decomposing them for the required number of parallel processes, to running the solver and processing results. It also, often, undertakes large amounts of I/O, reading in input data and producing data for analysis. It is common that the different stages require differing amounts of compute resources, with some stages only able to utilise one node, and others (such as the solver) requiring a large number of nodes to complete in a reasonable amount of time. OpenFOAM generally creates a directory per process that will be used for the solver calculations, necessitating significant amounts of I/O operations for a large simulation. It is also often useful to save data about the state of the simulation every timestep or every few timesteps. Given these features, OpenFOAM is a good target for both workflow functionality and improved I/O performance through node-local I/O hardware.

To evaluate the performance of our architectures using OpenFOAM we ran a low-Reynolds number laminar-turbulent transition modeling simulation of the flow over the surface of an aircraft [34], using a mesh with ≈43 million mesh points. We decomposed the mesh over 20 nodes enabling 960 MPI processes to be used for the solver step (picoFOAM). The decomposition step is serial, takes 1105 s, and requires 30 GB of memory.

We ran the solver for 20 timesteps, and compared running the full workflow (decomposing the mesh and then running the solver) entirely using the Lustre filesystem or using node-local B-APM with data staging between the mesh decomposition step and the solver. The solver produces 160 GB of output data when run in this configuration, with a directory per process. Running the solver using Lustre required 747 s, whereas running the solver using node-local B-APM storage required 95 s, more than seven times faster (see Table 2). Using node-local storage needs a redistribution of data from the storage on the single compute node used for decomposing the mesh to the 20 nodes needed for the solver. This data copy took 51 s, so even if not overlapped with other running tasks this approach would provide improved performance compared to directly using Lustre, more so when run for a full simulation, which would require many thousands of timesteps meaning the initial cost of copying the data would be negligible.

IOR: Finally, we ran the IOR benchmark on the prototype system using the GekkoFS distributed filesystem. We ran the filesystem on 10 compute nodes, and ran 10 IOR clients per compute node, give a total of 100 IOR processes. We tested both IOR with a single file per process (FPP), and IOR with a shared file (SF) for all processes. For the FFP benchmark each process is writing or reading 8.2GB per file. For the SF benchmark each process is writing 222000 blocks containing 47008 bytes each.

Table 3 presents the performance achieved using 10 nodes using the GekkoFS distributed filesystem exploiting B-APM. We can see that using a single file

Table 3. 10 node IOR performance using B-APM and GekkoFS

Benchmark	Bandwidth (GB/s)
FPP write	24
SF write	3
FPP read	27
SF read	7

per process, read and write bandwidth as around 24–27 GB/s. The bandwidth achieved using a shared file for all processes is low, at 3 GB/s for write and 7 GB/s for read (the B-APM is slower for writing than it is for reading). However, these tests are run with a prototype version GekkoFS using only TCP/IP for communication between the nodes, and only the B-APM on a single socket per node meaning communication performance and NUMA effects have reduced the achieved performance.

6   Related Work

There are existing technological solutions that are offering similar functionality to B-APM and that can be exploited for high performance I/O. E.g. Memory mapped files, which allows copy files into main memory and therefore byte level CPU instructions to modify data. In fact, the use of B-APM by the PMDK library is based on the memory mapped file concept and therefore allows an easy transition from this well-known I/O handling into the B-APM future. The major difference with B-APM usage is that it does not perform any I/O operations, only memory operation, removing the requirement for context switches, buffers management, programming scatter/gather lists, I/O interrupt handling and wait for external I/O devices to complete and ensure persistence (e.g. msync). A pointer to the requested B-APM address space is all that is required for CPU instructions to operate on persistence memory, and the use of the cflush instruction to ensure persistence of data.

In comparison the NVMe protocol requires thousands of CPU instructions to read data from the device or to make data persistent. In addition, even the fastest NVMe devices such as Intel's NVMe Optane SSD or Samsung Z-NAND require tens of microseconds to respond while B-APM based on DCPMM will respond in 100 s of nanoseconds. This is especially true for access to small amounts of data located at random data locations in memory. With larger amounts of data, the overall performance effect is smaller (the proportion of I/O operation on the total amount of data is smaller), but traditional I/O still necessitates copying to buffers and I/O page caches instead of working directly on the data. B-APM is a natural fit for CPU operations to manage persistent data compared to the device driven block I/O traditional storage media requires.

We are proposing hardware and systemware architectures in this work that will integrate B-APM into large scale compute clusters, providing significant I/O performance benefits and introducing new I/O and data storage/manipulation features to applications. Our key goal is to create systems that can both exploit the performance of the hardware and support applications whilst they port to these new I/O or data storage paradigms.

Indeed, we recognise that there is a very large body of existing applications and data analysis workflows that cannot immediately be ported to new storage hardware (for time and resource constraint reasons). Therefore, our aims in this work are to provide a system that enables applications to obtain best performance if porting work is undertaken to exploit B-APM hardware features, but still allow applications to exploit B-APM and significantly improve performance without major software changes.

7   Summary

This paper outlines a hardware and systemware architecture designed to enable the exploitation of B-APM hardware directly by applications, or indirectly by applications using systemware functionality that can exploit B-APM for applications. This dual nature of the system provides support for existing application to exploit this emerging memory new hardware whilst enabling developers to modify applications to best exploit the hardware over time.

The system outlined provides a range of different functionality. Not all functionality will be utilised by all applications, but providing a wide range of functionality, from filesystems to object stores to data schedulers will enable the widest possible use of such systems. We are aiming for hardware and systemware that enables HPC and HPDA applications to co-exist on the same platform.

Whilst the hardware is novel and interesting in its own right, we predict that the biggest benefit in such technology will be realised through changes in application structure and data storage approaches facilitated by the byte-addressable persistent memory that will become routinely available in computing systems.

In time it could possible to completely remove the external filesystem from HPC and HPDA systems, removing hardware complexity and the energy/cost associated with such functionality. There is also the potential for volatile memory to disappear from the memory stack everywhere except on the processor itself, removing further energy costs from compute nodes. However, further work is required to evaluate the impact of the costs of the active systemware environment we have outlined in this paper, and the memory usage patterns of applications.

Moving data asynchronously to support applications can potentially bring big performance benefits but the impact such functionality has on applications running on those compute node needs to be investigated. This is especially important as with distributed filesystems or object stores hosted on node distributed B-APM such in-node asynchronous data movements will be ubiquitous, even with intelligent scheduling algorithms. We have demonstrated significant performance improvements using B-APM for applications and synthetic benchmarks, showing 7–8x performance improvements for a I/O intensive CFD solver, even using the slower file-based, rather than byte-access, I/O functionality.

Acknowledgements. The NEXTGenIO project[1] and the work presented in this paper were funded by the European Union's Horizon 2020 Research and Innovation programme under Grant Agreement no. 671951. All the NEXTGenIO Consortium members (EPCC, Allinea, Arm, ECMWF, Barcelona Supercomputing Centre, Fujitsu Technology Solutions, Intel Deutschland, Arctur and Technische Universität Dresden) contributed to the design of the architectures.

References

1. Sodani, A.: Knights landing (KNL): 2nd Generation Intel Xeon Phi Processor. In: IEEE Hot Chips 27 Symposium (HCS). IEEE, January 2015
2. NVIDIA Volta. https://www.nvidia.com/en-us/data-center/volta-gpu-architecture
3. Jun, H., et al.: HBM (high bandwidth memory) DRAM technology and architecture. In: 2017 IEEE International Memory Workshop (IMW), pp. 1–4 (2017)
4. Turner, A., Simon, M.-S.: A survey of application memory usage on a national supercomputer: an analysis of memory requirements on ARCHER. In: Stephen, J., Steven, W., Simon, H. (eds.) PMBS 2017. LNCS, vol. 10724, pp. 250–260. Springer, Cham (2018). https://doi.org/10.1007/978-3-319-72971-8_13, http://www.archer. ac.uk/documentation/white-papers/memory-use/ARCHER_mem_use.pdf
5. Hady, F.T., Foong, A., Veal, B., Williams, D.: Platform storage performance with 3D XPoint technology. Proc. IEEE **105**(9), 1–12 (2017). https://doi.org/10.1109/JPROC.2017.2731776
6. NVDIMM Messaging and FAQ: SNIA website. Accessed Nov 2017. https://www.snia.org/sites/default/files/NVDIMM%20Messaging%20and%20FAQ%20Jan%2020143.pdf
7. Report on MCDRAM technology from Colfax Research. https://colfaxresearch.com/knl-mcdram/
8. Intel Patent on multi-level memory configuration for nonvolatile memory technology. https://www.google.com/patents/US20150178204
9. pmem.io. http://pmem.io/
10. Layton, J.: IO pattern characterization of HPC applications. In: Mewhort, D.J.K., Cann, N.M., Slater, G.W., Naughton, T.J. (eds.) HPCS 2009. LNCS, vol. 5976, pp. 292–303. Springer, Heidelberg (2010). https://doi.org/10.1007/978-3-642-12659-8_22
11. Luu, H., et al.: A multiplatform study of I/O behavior on petascale supercomputers. In: Proceedings of the 24th International Symposium on High-Performance Parallel and Distributed Computing (HPDC 2015), pp. 33–44. ACM, New York (2015). https://doi.org/10.1145/2749246.2749269
12. IEEE Std 1003.1-2008 (Revision of IEEE Std 1003.1-2004) - IEEE Standard for Information Technology - Portable Operating System Interface (POSIX(R))
13. Schwan, P.: Lustre: building a file system for 1000-node clusters. In: Proceedings of the 2003 Linux Symposium, vol. 2003 (2003)
14. Schmuck, F., Haskin, R.: GPFS: a shared-disk file system for large computing clusters. In: Proceedings of the 1st USENIX Conference on File and Storage Technologies (FAST 2002), Article 19. USENIX Association, Berkeley (2002)
15. Introduction to BeeGFS. http://www.beegfs.io/docs/whitepapers/Introduction_to_BeeGFS_by_ThinkParQ.pdf

---

[1] www.nextgenio.eu.

16. Sun, J., Li, Z., Zhang, X.: The performance optimization of Lustre file system. In: 2012 7th International Conference on Computer Science and Education (ICCSE), Melbourne, VIC, pp. 214–217 (2012). https://doi.org/10.1109/ICCSE.2012.6295060

17. Choi, W., Jung, M., Kandemir, M., Das, C.: A scale-out enterprise storage architecture. In: IEEE International Conference on Computer Design (ICCD) (2017). https://doi.org/10.1109/ICCD.2017.96

18. Lin, K.-W., Byna, S., Chou, J., Wu, K.: Optimizing fastquery performance on lustre file system. In: Szalay, A., Budavari, T., Balazinska, M., Meliou, A., Sacan, A. (eds.) Proceedings of the 25th International Conference on Scientific and Statistical Database Management (SSDBM), Article 29, 12 p. ACM, New York (2013). https://doi.org/10.1145/2484838.2484853

19. Carns, P., et al.: Understanding and improving computational science storage access through continuous characterization. In: Proceedings of the 2011 IEEE 27th Symposium on Mass Storage Systems and Technologies (MSST 2011), pp. 1–14. IEEE Computer Society, Washington (2011). https://doi.org/10.1109/MSST.2011.5937212

20. Kim, J., Lee, S., Vetter, J.S.: PapyrusKV: a high-performance parallel key-value store for distributed NVM architectures, SC, vol. 57, no. 14, pp. 1–57 (2017)

21. Lofstead, J., Jimenez, I., Maltzahn, C., Koziol, Q., Bent, J., Barton, E.: DAOS and friends: a proposal for an exascale storage system. In: International Conference for High Performance Computing, Networking, Storage and Analysis, pp. 585–596, Salt Lake City (2016). https://doi.org/10.1109/SC.2016.49

22. Martí, J., Queralt, A., Gasull, D., Barceló, A., Costa, J.J., Cortes, T.: Dataclay: a distributed data store for effective inter-player data sharing. J. Syst. Softw. **131**, 129–145 (2017). ISSN 0164–1212, https://doi.org/10.1016/j.jss.2017.05.080

23. Tejedor, E., et al.: PyCOMPSs: parallel computational workflows in Python. Int. J. High Perform. Comput. Appl. **31**(1), 66–82 (2017). First Published August 19, 201, https://doi.org/10.1177/1094342015594678

24. Farsarakis, E., Panourgias, I., Jackson, A., Herrera, J.F.R., Weiland, M., Parsons, M.: Resource Requirement Specification for Novel Data-aware and Workflow-enabled HPC Job Schedulers, PDSW-DISCS17 (2017). http://www.pdsw.org/pdsw-discs17/wips/farsarakis-wip-pdsw-discs17.pdf

25. Weiland, M., Jackson, A., Johnson, N., Parsons, M.: Exploiting the performance benefits of storage class memory for HPC and HPDA Workflows. Supercomput. Front. Innov. **5**(1), 79–94 (2018). https://doi.org/10.14529/jsfi180105

26. ORNL Titan specification. http://phys.org/pdf285408062.pdf

27. Anantharaj, V., Foertter, F., Joubert, W., Wells, J.: Approaching exascale: application requirements for OLCF leadership computing, July 2013. https://www.olcf.ornl.gov/wp-content/uploads/2013/01/OLCF_Requirements_TM_2013_Final1.pdf

28. Daley, C., Ghoshal, D., Lockwood, G., Dosanjh, S., Ramakrishnan, L., Wright, N.: Performance characterization of scientific workflows for the optimal use of burst buffers. Future Gener. Comput. Syst. (2017). https://doi.org/10.1016/j.future.2017.12.022

29. Mielke, N.R., Frickey, R.E., Kalastirsky, I., Quan, M., Ustinov, D., Vasudevan, V.J.: Reliability of solid-state drives based on NAND flash memory. Proc. IEEE **105**(9), 1725–1750 (2017). https://doi.org/10.1109/JPROC.2017.2725738

30. Li, C., Ding, C., Shen, K.: Quantifying the cost of context switch. In: Proceedings of the 2007 Workshop on Experimental Computer Science (ExpCS 2007), Article 2. ACM, New York (2007). https://doi.org/10.1145/1281700.1281702

31. Liu, N., et al.: On the role of burst buffers in leadership-class storage systems. In: 2012 IEEE 28th Symposium on Mass Storage Systems and Technologies (MSST), pp. 1–11, San Diego (2012). https://doi.org/10.1109/MSST.2012.6232369

32. Petersen, T.K., Bent, J.: Hybrid flash arrays for HPC storage systems: an alternative to burst buffers. In: High Performance Extreme Computing Conference (HPEC) 2017. IEEE, pp. 1–7 (2017)

33. Vef, M.-A., et al.: GekkoFS - a temporary distributed file system for HPC applications. In: Proceedings of the 2018 IEEE International Conference on Cluster Computing (CLUSTER), Belfast, 10–13 September 2018

34. Matej, A., Gregor, V., Nejc, B.: Cloud-based simulation of aerodynamics of light aircraft. https://hpc-forge.cineca.it/files/CoursesDev/public/2015/Workshop_HPC_Methods_for_Engineering/cloud_based_aircraft.pdf

35. Jasak, H.: OpenFOAM: open source CFD in research and industry. Int. J. Naval Architect. Ocean Eng. **1**(2), 89–94 (2009). issn 2092-6782

36. IPMCTL. https://github.com/intel/ipmctl

37. NDCTL - Utility library for managing the libnvdimm (non-volatile memory device) sub-system in the Linux kernel. https://github.com/pmem/ndctl

38. IOR. https://github.com/LLNL/ior

Mediating Data Center Storage Diversity in HPC Applications with FAODEL

Patrick Widener[1]([✉]), Craig Ulmer[2], Scott Levy[1], Todd Kordenbrock[3],
and Gary Templet[3]

[1] Center for Computing Research, Sandia National Laboratories,
Albuquerque, NM, USA
patrick.widener@sandia.gov
[2] Scalable Modeling and Analysis Systems, Sandia National Laboratories,
Livermore, CA, USA
[3] Perspecta, Inc., Chantilly, VA, USA

Abstract. Composition of computational science applications into both
ad hoc pipelines for analysis of collected or generated data and into
well-defined and repeatable workflows is becoming increasingly popular. Meanwhile, dedicated high performance computing storage environments are rapidly becoming more diverse, with both significant amounts
of non-volatile memory storage and mature parallel file systems available. At the same time, computational science codes are being coupled
to data analysis tools which are not filesystem-oriented. In this paper,
we describe how the FAODEL data management service can expose different available data storage options and mediate among them in both
application- and FAODEL-directed ways. These capabilities allow applications to exploit their knowledge of the different types of data they may
exchange during a workflow execution, and also provide FAODEL with
mechanisms to proactively tune data storage behavior when appropriate. We describe the implementation of these capabilities in FAODEL
and how they are used by applications, and present preliminary performance results demonstrating the potential benefits of our approach.

Keywords: Workflow · Composition · Data management · Scalability

1 Introduction

Traditionally, I/O for data storage in high-performance computing applications
(especially computational science simulations) has almost always meant data
transfer from node DRAM to a parallel file system (PFS) such as Lustre or
GPFS. That traditional arrangement has been destabilized in a number of ways:

- Impedance mismatches, between the rates at which application data is generated (through simulation of physical phenomena or capture from external sources) and the available bandwidth to stable storage provided by
  datacenter-scale PFS, have not abated.

SAND2019-6668C.

- Available PFS solutions in many cases require application-specific configuration and tuning, and continue to be a major source of resilience issues.
- Partly as a response to the above points, the storage hierarchy continues to grow deeper and more complex. Potential layers include local and remote memory (e.g., on package high bandwidth memory, DRAM, nonvolatile memory (NVM), 3D-stacked DRAM); compute area Storage Class Memories such as burst buffers; parallel file systems; campaign storage; and archival storage. Each level in the hierarchy has its own operational tradeoffs that users must understand to efficiently leverage the underlying storage resources in their application.
- The influence of data movement between host and accelerator memories, and the desire to maintain zero-copy performance as that data must be moved to stable storage, has increased the influence of APIs such as OpenACC [1] and Kokkos [7].

Additionally, the abstractions commonly available to application developers will not support the development and deployment of future exascale systems. Several important trends in application design and deployment are highly dependent on the availability of high-performance and semantically-flexible I/O services:

- *Coupled Simulation Codes:* Increasingly, important scientific simulations require multiple physical models to be evaluated simultaneously. To leverage existing software, one way to combine these physical models is to run each model independently and map the output of one physical model to the input for another, and vice-versa. In this way, physical models that are captured by independent executables exchange information about the state of the simulated system as the simulation progresses. Achieving high performance for these coupled simulation codes requires the availability of services that facilitate the efficient exchange of data between multiple physical models. Moreover, programmer efficiency is dependent on simple and robust mechanisms for exchanging data between coupled simulation codes.
- *Complex Workflows:* Analysis of scientific simulation data commonly requires processing by a sequence of several specialized analysis tools; the output of one is the input for the next. The analysis tools that comprise these workflows include: mesh generation and mesh refinement tools, preconditioners, uncertainty quantification tools, simulation frameworks, solvers, and visualization/analysis tools. Workflow management tools have typically exchanged data via a parallel filesystem. However, the PFS I/O bandwidth limitations throttle severely the amount of work that can be done, while the gap between compute speed and IO bandwidth continues to increase.
- *Asynchronous Many-Task (AMT) Programming Models:* AMT programming models (e.g., Legion [4], Charm++ [14], and Uintah [10]) are designed to allow compilers and the associated AMT runtimes to manage the complexities that arise due to performance variation and resource heterogeneity [18]. Moreover, the asynchronous nature of these models allows them to overcome many of the

performance costs that are borne by bulk synchronous parallel (BSP) codes on extreme-scale systems. However, these characteristics of AMT applications mean that predicting where a task may execute is not straightforward. As a result, AMT runtimes have commonly relied on the parallel filesystem to facilitate access to applications. Because of the costs associated with parallel filesystem access, the performance of AMT-based applications will be highly dependent on the ability of AMT runtimes to leverage the entire storage hierarchy to provide AMT tasks with efficient access to application variables.

- *Beyond POSIX storage:* Many widely used tools from the high-performance data analytics (HPDA) space are oriented toward data storage without using traditional file system interfaces. Apache's Spark [9] toolset is an exemplar of this approach. Spark relies on data access capabilities provided by the non-POSIX APIs of sources like HDFS, Cassandra, and others which may themselves rely on traditional filesystems to varying extents but do not expose those interfaces to their users. As HPDA becomes a more popular component of workflows, sharing data in a single data center with HPDA tools means finding ways to coexist with their data management strategies.
- *Resilience:* The dominant approach to fault tolerance is checkpoint/restart. Minimizing the performance impact of checkpoint/restart requires services that provide efficient access to persistent storage resources. Moreover, while checkpoints have traditionally been stored in parallel filesystems, techniques for leveraging the entire storage hierarchy have begun to grow in importance, *cf.* [16].

FAODEL [19] provides a set of data movement, storage, and management services designed to address these challenges for next-generation HPC applications and workflows. FAODEL's advantages include:

- *Programmer efficiency:* presenting application programmers with a single interface for data movement lowers the burden on application programmers, reduces development costs, and lowers the risk of mistakes as programmers attempt to master multiple interfaces to data movement services.
- *Shared optimization:* because FAODEL provides data movement services through a unified interface, optimization and validation of shared components can provide performance benefits in multiple data movement scenarios.
- *Aggregated storage resources:* because FAODEL provides a unified interface to multiple levels of the storage hierarchy, it can dynamically make decisions that allow it to avoid storage resources that are slow or have high energy costs unless absolutely necessary (e.g., avoiding the parallel filesystem in favor of node-local storage: DRAM, SSDs, NVRAM).

In this paper, we describe recent work which expands upon the last of these advantages. Specifically, we describe how FAODEL allows applications to choose, in a semantically appropriate manner, different persistent storage destinations for different subsets of the data they produce or exchange with other applications. These decisions are typically driven by a tradeoff space that encompasses the available storage hardware, the locality properties of the data in question, and whether other tools requiring specific data management are being used. This kind of tradeoff space is already not uncommon: data center managers seek to leverage existing power and cooling installations; same-platform deployment of both HPC and HPDA applications is becoming a priority; and as stated above increasingly diverse storage hierarchies are now in wide deployment.

Our discussion is structured as follows. Section 2 briefly recaps the structure of FAODEL, with emphasis on the Kelpie service within which our work described here is implemented. Section 3 describes our implementation of mediated storage within Kelpie. Sections 4 and 5, discuss related work and conclude our discussion, respectively.

2   FAODEL Background

We briefly discuss relevant components of the FAODEL service in this section. An overview of the relationships between the software components that comprise FAODEL is shown in Fig. 1. A more detailed description of other FAODEL components can be found in [20]. High-level components that are most relevant to application developers in the remainder of this section.

2.1   Kelpie

Kelpie provides a *key/blob* abstraction to facilitate flexible data exchange between different executables (e.g., a simulation application and applications

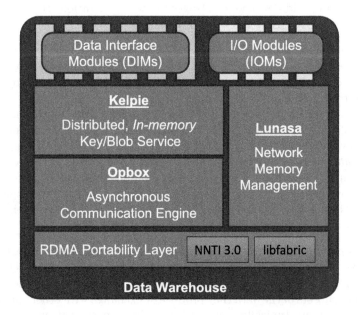

Fig. 1. Software architecture overview of FAODEL.

for visualization and analysis). A *key* is a programmer-defined text string that allows the programmer to attach semantic significance to the associated data: a *blob*. Although a key may attach programmer-cognizable meaning (and possibly structural information) to a blob, Kelpie is entirely ignorant of any meaning attached to keys or blobs.

Independent processes can exchange data in Kelpie by simply exchanging keys. The semantics of the keys exchanged may be *implicit*, the processes involved in the exchanges are unaware of the keys' semantics, or *explicit*, the processes involved in the exchange can extract meaning from the key. For example, a programmer may construct a key by encoding metadata (e.g., the application name, run number, iteration number, and variable name) that describes the contents of the associated blob. Based on shared knowledge of the key's encoding, the recipient of a key can extract the metadata from the key to inform its handling of the blob.

A key abstraction in Kelpie is represented by `Pool` objects. Each `Pool` object represents a collection of resources (e.g., nodes) that support a key/blob store. A `Pool` supports three basic operations: *Publish*, *Want*, and *Need*. *Publish* allows the user to add a key/blob pair to the `Pool`. *Want* and *Need* allow the user to request the blob associated with a key in the `Pool`. The distinction between the two is that *Want* is a non-blocking operation and *Need* is a blocking operation.

2.2   I/O Management (IOM) Modules

One of the services provided by Kelpie is to allow users to request the transfer of key/blob data to persistent storage. The interface between Kelpie and persistent storage resources (e.g., NVRAM, parallel filesystem, databases) is managed by I/O Management (IOM) modules. IOMs are built on high-level APIs (e.g., POSIX-compliant filesystems, HDF5, LevelDB) that provide access to the underlying storage resources. Each `Pool` is associated with an IOM that provides access to a particular storage resource interface (e.g., POSIX, HDF5).

FAODEL provides applications with services for transferring data to storage resources throughout the system's storage hierarchy. Each tier in the storage hierarchy provides different access characteristics that are leveraged by different use cases.

Various types of storage resources are accessible through Kelpie's IOM modules:

- **Distributed memory.** Distributed memory provides access to the collective DRAM (conventional DRAM devices and 3D-stacked DRAM devices) within the application's hardware allocation. Relative to other storage resources, distributed memory provides low-latency, high-bandwidth storage. RDMA transfers allow for efficient access to remote memory resources. Distributed memory can be used by AMT runtimes to store and exchange application variables and by coupled codes to exchange simulation data.
- **Local persistent storage.** Local persistent storage resources include SSDs and NVRAM. Locality varies by system. In some cases, persistent storage may

be available on each compute node, other systems may provide per-chassis or per-rack persistent storage resources. Local persistent resources can be leveraged as part of a checkpoint/restart solution (*cf.* [16]). Similarly, because these devices typically provide much more storage capacity than volatile memory (i.e., DRAM), they may also be used in support of *in situ* analytics.

- **Burst buffers.** Recent HPC systems such as the Cray XC40 (deployed at Los Alamos National Laboratory and the National Energy Research Scientific Computing Center) and the IBM CORAL system provide fast non-volatile storage colloquially referred to as *burst buffers*. These resources are made available to compute nodes via vendor-specific libraries (e.g., Cray DataWarp) and integrated via high-speed interconnects.

- **Archival storage.** In most systems, the principal archival storage resources are provided by a parallel filesystem. Archival storage provides high-latency, low-bandwidth access to high-capacity storage devices (e.g., hard disks).

3   Mediating Storage Using Kelpie Object Naming

Applications use the Kelpie interface to specify data they wish to store, retrieve, or exchange with other applications using the service. Like in other key-value stores, applications can use Kelpie's key structure to represent a namespace whose components have semantics appropriate to those applications and to application-to-application interactions. In this way, the namespace can convey important information about the data being exchanged and help developers reason about the structure of the problem being addressed.

Our work here explores the use of the Kelpie namespace to reflect information about how Kelpie handles data storage. A common conceptual distinction in computational workflows is the notion of a *control plane* of metadata about the current problem being solved and a *data plane* of result data from simulation or analysis. The difference between these two is the amount of data and how it is used. The control plane typically comprises larger numbers of smaller data items which are more frequently used. This use case is well supported by storage on solid-state media where reads and random access are advantaged. Volume data comprising smaller numbers of larger data sets, conversely, is better suited to bulk parallel file systems which are optimized for this case. An orthogonal case which also can be addressed here is when certain data must be shared with other applications that do not rely on file system interfaces, instead using byte-addressable interfaces or relying on services such as NoSQL databases.

We describe in this section how we support the annotation of Kelpie object namespaces with enough information for Kelpie to perform *storage mediation*. In this way, determination of persistent storage destinations for data can be based (to varying degree) on how that data is named. This provides multiple benefits. Applications can structure the namespace to hint to Kelpie about the relative "shape" of their data (signaling metadata vs. result data, for example). A partition of the namespace can be dedicated to storage via non-POSIX methods, allowing other workflow components to better understand which data is being produced for which purposes. Also, our approach provides mechanisms for Kelpie to either cooperate with application-structured namespaces (and the implied storage hints), weigh those hints alongside internal considerations which need not be exposed to applications, or restructure or even ignore application namespace partitioning entirely.

3.1   Kelpie Architectural Considerations

Kelpie Namespaces. Kelpie implements different key indices; for the purposes of our discussion we concern ourselves with its distributed hash table (DHT) implementation (its details are similar to implementations in other KV stores). Kelpie's API provides either a one- or two-dimensional namespace. In practice, this allows applications to easily separate 2-dimensional data (row vs. column) for efficient distributed indexing. A Kelpie key can be anything serializable to a string. For a one-dimensional Kelpie keyspace, a hierarchical tree-based name structure (similar to that used in POSIX file systems) can be defined. This is the type of namespace we consider in this work.

Kelpie Persistent Storage. FAODEL (of which Kelpie is a component) is designed as a memory-to-memory data management system, where running Kelpie instances on separate nodes cooperate in DHTs by storing and providing data in node memory. However, Kelpie also supports persistent storage of data to satisfy resilience requirements or to relieve pressure on node memory allocations. This persistent storage is managed by Kelpie's *I/O management* (IOM) subsystem. Each Kelpie instance has associated with it an IOM object which provides access to a particular kind of persistent storage. IOM types include file system storage supported by POSIX and HDF5 APIs, lightweight KV storage implemented in LevelDB [11,12], and the Apache Cassandra column-oriented database [8,15].

3.2   Annotating the Kelpie Namespace

Applications interact with Kelpie through a `Pool` object, issuing *Want*, *Need*, and *Publish* operations for data objects located at given points in the namespace managed by the `Pool`. We did not want to change this interaction for existing Kelpie clients, so we added an aggregation object called `Metapool`. A `Metapool` mimics the interface of a `Pool`, allowing clients to use it in the same manner. Calls to this interface are delegated to a collection of `Pools` which are managed by the `Metapool` (Fig. 2). A newly created `Metapool` cannot be used until it this collection of `Pools` is provided.

Applications using a `Metapool` acquire `Pool` objects in the normal manner. Each `Pool` object is registered with the `Metapool` along with a C++ function closure or *lambda* whose function signature is `bool fn(const std::string& keystr)`. Each call to the `Metapool` object's *Publish*, *Want*, or *Need* methods takes the key string (supplied as a required parameter) and searches through the

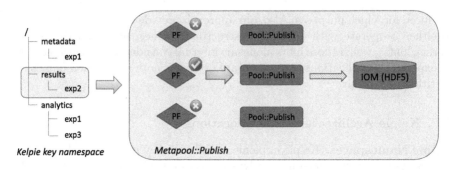

Fig. 2. A *Publish* operation makes data available at a particular location in the Kelpie namespace. Using the `Metapool` object, the location is examined to determine which of the managed `Pools` should handle the request. Each `Pool` can be configured with a different persistent storage strategy through its IOM component, giving applications a means of selecting their preferred storage approach. In a hypothetical example depicted here, the application makes large experimental result data available at */results/exp2*, and its `Metapool` has been configured to delegate management for data under */results* to a `Pool` whose persistent storage method is the HDF5 library.

collection of `Pools` in order of their registration, calling the associated function closure for each registered `Pool`. The first function closure called that returns `true` indicates that its paired `Pool` is the one which should be delegated this call from the `Metapool` object. This results in, for example, a *Publish* operation being delegated to a particular `Pool`, which has an IOM subsystem targeted at a particular kind of storage (HDF5 vs POSIX vs LevelDB, etc.).

This arrangement gives application developers a great deal of flexibility in partitioning the namespace. For example, assume two `Pools` are in use, P1 and P2. P1 is registered with the `Metapool` using a function closure that returns `true` if the given key string has a prefix of `/metadata'` and is configured to store data persistently using LevelDB. In similar fashion, P2 is registered using a function closure returning `true` for keys prefixed by `/results`, and is configured to store data persistently using HDF5 (Fig. 3). Under this arrangement, the application can store control plane information using the `/metadata` key prefix and exploit lightweight storage for that data. This would of course depend as well on how LevelDB was configured, and in this scenario configuring LevelDB to use locally accessible NVRAM would be appropriate. The end effect is that of a single namespace available through and managed by the `Metapool` object, which after configuration provides data persistence to different storage targets without any additional intervention by the application (Fig. 4).

3.3   Service-Initiated Mediation

The `Metapool` implementation also provides Kelpie with the means of mediating the configuration of `Pools` requested by an application. Since Kelpie manages the collection of `Pools`, it can introduce changes to `Metapool` handing at run

```
hdf5_dht = kelpie::Connect( "ref:/myapp/results" );
leveldb_dht = kelpie::Connect( "ref:/myapp/metadata" );
cassandra_dht = kelpie::Connect( "ref:/myapp/analytics" );

metapool.Manage( hdf5_dht,
[]( const kelpie::Key& k ) {
  if( k.K1.size() < 9 ) return false;
  if( k.K1.substr( 0, 8 ) != "/results" ) return false;
  return true;
} );

metapool.Manage( leveldb_dht,
[]( const kelpie::Key& k ) {
  if( k.K1.size() < 10 ) return false;
  if( k.K1.substr( 0, 9 ) != "/metadata" ) return false;
  return true;
} );

metapool.Manage( cassandra_dht,
[]( const kelpie::Key& k ) {
  if( k.K1.size() < 11 ) return false;
  if( k.K1.substr( 0, 10 ) != "/analytics" ) return false;
  return true;
} );
```

Fig. 3. An example of configuring the Metapool object from client code. The application supplies lambda functions to the Metapool object through the Manage method, associating each with a particular Kelpie Pool.

time, in response to changing system or workflow conditions. Different strategies that Kelpie can employ for such service-initiated mediation include:

- *Weighting partition function responses.* If the local Kelpie configuration has enough information about local storage configuration, it might be appropriate to assign different weights to the filter functions registered with the Metapool (as opposed to the nominal situation where the first true response is considered 100% authoritative. This could prove useful in a case where a Kelpie application configured for one data storage environment is ported to a different environment.
- *Changing IOM configuration at runtime.* Different storage targets can be assigned as a workflow execution evolves, and additional targets might be added as a form of load balancing.
- *Disregarding partition function responses entirely.* At times it may make sense to disregard the application's suggested namespace partitioning entirely and route data to a specific storage configuration. This also might be useful in the case of porting a Kelpie application to a new storage environment.

3.4   Performance Considerations

In its current state, our work is a *usability* contribution, not a performance-improvement contribution. There are several aspects to this. Metapool operations impose an extra overhead on top of normal FAODEL Pool operations, dominated by the $O(n)$ search through all managed Pools for a Pool matching a

```
for( int i = 0; i < 25; i++ ) {
  kelpie::Key k;

  k.K1( "/metadata/" + random_string( 10 ) );

  lunasa::DataObject ldo( 0, 256, lunasa::DataObject::AllocatorType::eager );
  metapool.Publish( k, ldo );
}

for( int i = 0; i < 25; i++ ) {
  kelpie::Key k;

  k.K1( "/results/" + random_string( 10 ) );

  lunasa::DataObject ldo( 0, 256 * 1e6, lunasa::DataObject::AllocatorType::eager );
  metapool.Publish( k, ldo );
}
```

Fig. 4. An example of using the `Metapool` object to publish data to Kelpie. The application need not do anything except use the designated namespace partition for each "kind" of data it intends to publish. The `Metapool` uses the previously-supplied namespace partition functions to decide how to route the *Publish* request.

given namespace partitioning. There are obvious algorithmic and data-structure enhancements to `Metapool` which could address this, but this can be managed directly by the application through the degree of partitioning it implements. Apart from that, I/O performance will be governed by the performance of the chosen storage backend, over which FAODEL has no control.

The contribution of the `Metapool` concept, from a performance standpoint, is the degree of control it provides to applications in matching their data to the characteristics of available storage backends. We expect this to be a foundation for future performance advantages for applications using FAODEL. Instead of having to explicitly partition the data namespace according to (well-informed, to be sure) assumptions about data usage, policy-driven or machine learning approaches could be introduced to automatically micro-manage the partitioning (and consequently the IOM layer and associated storage modalities). This possibility underscores our choice of a service mediator like FAODEL as a beneficial place for such decisions, rather than performing them at the storage layer or embedding them in applications.

4   Related Work

One of the first efforts to apply semantics to hierarchical namespaces was the Intentional Naming System [2], which introduced the principle of naming what applications are interested in, as opposed to where to find them (*e.g.,* locating services by their internet hostnames). Active Names [21] was another early effort to couple resource location and naming semantics. Another example is the Proactive Directory Service [5], which allowed applications to add user-defined behavior and data management to partitions of a shared namespace. Our work takes inspiration from these projects, giving applications tools to overlay semantics associated with how data should be persistently stored onto the shared key namespace offered by Faodel.

Many scientific simulations have the potential to generate vast quantities of output data. Domain scientists rely on sophisticated analysis and visualization to make sense of these data. Efficient use of these tools requires robust data management services to find and access output datasets. Pavlo et al. [17] compare the use of MapReduce and Parallel Database Management Systems (DBMS) for analyzing large volumes of data. For both of these approaches, data is stored and exchanged through the filesystem. SENSEI [3] defines a generic data model to facilitate the transfer of data between simulation and analysis tasks. Their generic data model is intended to simplify the process combining a simulation code with different kinds of analysis.

HPC systems have recently experienced significant growth in the depth of their storage hierarchy. SSDs, NVRAM, and 3D-stacked DRAM are all becoming increasingly common. Because each level of the hierarchy represents a different set of tradeoffs (and possibly also, different programming interfaces), application developers face an increasingly complex set of choices when decided where their data should reside. UNITY [13] provides a single interface for applications to access all levels of storage hierarchy. Data Elevator [6] provides a transparent mechanism for moving data among different layers of the storage hierarchy. Specifically, the authors describe and demonstrate their approach to moving data between burst buffers and the parallel file system.

5   Conclusion

As modern extreme computing environments evolve, flexible solutions for managing data exchanges between the applications they host will be necessary. In this paper, we have described a set of modifications to the FAODEL data management framework which allow applications to mediate among available data storage services. By partitioning the namespace provided by the Kelpie key-value service within FAODEL, applications can indicate, based on their knowledge of how data will be used, where subsets of the data they manage are best stored. We anticipate that this type of capability will prove useful in data centers where applications must make use of a set of common storage systems and services instead of being able to supply their own custom configurations. We also expect workflows which couple HPC and HPDA tasks to benefit from Kelpie's ability to persistently store data in formats suitable for off-the-shelf services without requiring explicit application data transformation or reformatting. We are working to expand the functionality of Kelpie's `Metapool` interface as well as to more fully characterize its performance with production-scale workflows.

References

1. The OpenACC application programming interface, November 2018. http://openacc-standard.org

2. Adjie-Winoto, W., Schwartz, E., Balakrishnan, H., Lilley, J.: The design and implementation of an intentional naming system. In: Proceedings of the Seventeenth ACM Symposium on Operating Systems Principles, SOSP 1999, pp. 186–201. ACM, New York (1999). https://doi.org/10.1145/319151.319164
3. Ayachit, U., et al.: The SENSEI generic in situ interface. In: Workshop on In Situ Infrastructures for Enabling Extreme-Scale Analysis and Visualization (ISAV), pp. 40–44. IEEE (2016)
4. Bauer, M., Treichler, S., Slaughter, E., Aiken, A.: Legion: expressing locality and independence with logical regions. In: Proceedings of the International Conference on High Performance Computing, Networking, Storage and Analysis, p. 66. IEEE Computer Society Press (2012)
5. Bustamante, F., Widener, P., Schwan, K.: Scalable directory services using proactivity. In: Proceedings 2002 ACM/IEEE Conference on Supercomputing. ACM/IEEE, Baltimore, November 2002
6. Dong, B., et al.: Data elevator: low-contention data movement in hierarchical storage system. In: 2016 IEEE 23rd International Conference on High Performance Computing (HiPC), pp. 152–161. IEEE (2016)
7. Edwards, H.C., Trott, C.R., Sunderland, D.: Kokkos: enabling manycore performance portability through polymorphic memory access patterns. J. Parallel Distrib. Comput. **74**(12), 3202–3216 (2014). https://doi.org/10.1016/j.jpdc.2014.07.003. http://www.sciencedirect.com/science/article/pii/S0743731514001257. Domain-Specific Languages and High-Level Frameworks for High-Performance Computing
8. The Apache Software Foundation: Apache cassandra (2018). https://cassandra.apache.org/. Accessed 10 May 2018
9. The Apache Software Foundation: Apache spark - unified analytics engine for big data (2018). https://spark.apache.org/. Accessed 10 May 2018
10. Germain, J.D.d.S., McCorquodale, J., Parker, S.G., Johnson, C.R.: Uintah: a massively parallel problem solving environment. In: 2000 Proceedings the Ninth International Symposium on High-Performance Distributed Computing, pp. 33–41. IEEE (2000)
11. Ghemawat, S., Dean, J.: LevelDB, a fast and lightweight key/value database library by Google (2014)
12. google: Github - google/leveldb: Leveldb is a fast key-value storage library written at Google that provides an ordered mapping from string keys to string values (2018). https://github.com/google/leveldb. Accessed 10 May 2018
13. Jones, T., et al.: Unity: unified memory and file space. In: Proceedings of the 7th International Workshop on Runtime and Operating Systems for Supercomputers (ROSS 2017), p. 6. ACM (2017)
14. Kale, L.V., Krishnan, S.: Charm++: a portable concurrent object oriented system based on C++. ACM SIGPLAN Not. **28**, 91–108 (1993)
15. Lakshman, A., Malik, P.: Cassandra: a decentralized structured storage system. SIGOPS Oper. Syst. Rev. **44**(2), 35–40 (2010). https://doi.org/10.1145/1773912.1773922
16. Moody, A., Bronevetsky, G., Mohror, K., de Supinski, B.R.: Design, modeling, and evaluation of a scalable multi-level checkpointing system. In: Proceedings of the 2010 ACM/IEEE International Conference for High Performance Computing, Networking, Storage and Analysis, pp. 1–11. IEEE Computer Society (2010)
17. Pavlo, A., et al.: A comparison of approaches to large-scale data analysis. In: Proceedings of the 2009 ACM SIGMOD International Conference on Management of Data, pp. 165–178. ACM (2009)

18. Pébaÿ, P., et al.: Towards asynchronous many-task in situ data analysis using legion. In: 2016 IEEE International Parallel and Distributed Processing Symposium Workshops, pp. 1033–1037. IEEE (2016)
19. Ulmer, C., et al.: Faodel: data management for next-generation application workflows. In: Proceedings of the 9th Workshop on Scientific Cloud Computing, p. 8. ACM (2018)
20. Ulmer, C., et al.: Faodel: data management for next-generation application workflows. In: Proceedings 9th Workshop on Scientific Cloud Computing, Science Cloud 2018. ACM, June 2018
21. Vahdat, A., Dahlin, M., Anderson, T., Aggarwal, A.: Active names: flexible location and transport of wide-area resources. In: Proceedings USENIX Symposium on Internet Technology and Systems, October 1999

Predicting File Lifetimes with Machine Learning

Florent Monjalet[✉] and Thomas Leibovici

CEA/DAM, Ollainville, France
{florent.monjalet,thomas.leibovici}@cea.fr

Abstract. In this article, we show how machine learning methods, namely random forests and convolutional neural networks, can be used to predict file lifetimes from their absolute path with a high reliability in an HPC filesystem context. The file lifetime is defined in this article as the time between the creation of the file and the last time it is read. Such results can be applied to the design of smart data placement policies, especially for hierarchical storage systems.

Keywords: Machine learning · Deep learning · HSM · Data placement

1 Introduction

In order to store more data overall while retaining high performances, storage systems tend to be multi-tiered, with *top* tiers being faster but smaller in capacity (*e.g.* flash drives) than *bottom* tiers. These *bottom* tiers can be more capacitive at equivalent cost, but with poorer performance (*e.g.* the latency of a tape library). By being able to predict precisely which file will be accessed in the future or not, the usable capacity of a given tier can be augmented at no financial cost. For example, retaining all the files for at least one month on a *top* tier is a waste of useful storage if 50% of them are not accessed anymore in practice.

Finer prediction than a simple LRU[1] eviction can also be done by manually inspecting how the files are accessed, deducing patterns for files that are unlikely to be accessed in the future and automating their eviction this way. For example, an administrator may notice that /scratch/user1/job1/**/*.log files are written for one day, and read for maximum one week.

In this paper, we attempt to predict the probable lifetime of a file given its metadata using machine learning algorithms, namely random forests and convolutional neural networks. We try to evaluate the efficiency of such an approach and examine its pros and cons for this problem. In our approach, we only use the path of the file as an input for the prediction, for two main reasons:

- In our case, the path already contains the name of the group and user that produced the file – our method could be adapted for situations where this is not the case;

---

[1] Least Recently Used.

© Springer Nature Switzerland AG 2019
M. Weiland et al. (Eds.): ISC 2019 Workshops, LNCS 11887, pp. 288–299, 2019.
https://doi.org/10.1007/978-3-030-34356-9_23

– As this work is still in its early stages, we want to get the maximum efficiency with the minimal information. Doing so can allow to measure the actual benefits of using additional metadata in the future.

Reliably predicting file lifetimes can allow to build smarter data placement policies in heterogeneous (and particularly hierarchical) storage systems, such as the ones encountered in the SAGE2 [1] project, without needing any human intervention.

2   Specifying the Problem and Building the Models

2.1   Problem Specification

Our model has the following input and output:

– **Input:** a full path (*e.g.* `/scratch/group/user/project1/dir/file.ext`).
– **Output:** a duration, what we call the lifetime of the file.

Depending on the data the algorithm is trained on, this lifetime can be the estimated duration between:

– the creation of a file and the last time it will be read;
– the creation of a file and the last time it will be written;
– the last time a file was written and the last time it will be read.

The whole method presented thereafter is not specific to any of these cases, although in this article we will use the first definition: the time between the creation of a file and the last time it will be read. Experimentally, results for these three lifetime definitions are very similar on this dataset.

Another important aspect of this problem is that we want to avoid underestimations. Underestimating a file lifetime may trigger a spurious *top* tier eviction followed by an access to this file soon after, resulting in a performance penalty. In addition to predicting accurately file lifetimes, we also focus on minimizing the underestimations, which results in maximizing the amount of usable predictions.

2.2   Dataset

The dataset consisted in around 5,000,000 files with associated creation time, last modification time and last access times. This data was extracted from the Robinhood Policy Engine [6] database of one of the production Lustre filesystems of the TGCC[2]. These three timestamps allow to retrieve any of the three durations discussed previously.

During training, a random sample of 70% of the dataset was used for training and the remaining 30% for validation, giving a good idea of the generalization

---

[2] http://www-hpc.cea.fr/en/complexe/tgcc.htm.

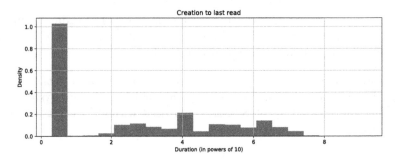

Fig. 1. Lifetime distribution in the dataset (45.80% are less than 10 s)

potential of the model. As a comparison, Sect. 3 also shows results when training on 95% of the dataset and validating on 5%.

As can be seen on Fig. 1, the dataset is highly imbalanced, with 45.80% of the lifetimes being less than 10 s. This means that special care must be taken to ensure that the model accuracy is consistent across all the lifetime value space, and not only for most represented lifetimes.

On this filesystem, these 45.80% files represent approximately 4 PB over a total of 10 PB, meaning that being able to determine early on that these files can be sent to a *bottom* tier would save about 40% of the *top* tier capacity.

2.3   Data Preprocessing

Paths. The machine learning algorithms used in this work only work on fixed size, potentially multidimensional, arrays of numbers. Therefore, paths cannot be fed directly into the algorithm: they have to be transformed into arrays of numbers. There are many ways of performing this operation, but the one we opted for is summed up in Fig. 2 and based on similar research [7].

	\0	\0	/	b	a	c	/	b	c	eof
\0	1	1	0	0	0	0	0	0	0	0
eof	0	0	0	0	0	0	0	0	0	1
/	0	0	1	0	0	0	1	0	0	0
a	0	0	0	0	1	0	0	0	0	0
b	0	0	0	1	0	0	0	1	0	0
c	0	0	0	0	0	1	0	0	1	0

Fig. 2. Path preprocessing overview

First, all the input paths are left padded with '\0' (or truncated) to be exactly 256 characters long, giving a fixed size input for our algorithm. Left aligning the paths allows to keep the file name part in case of a truncature (if the path is more than 256 characters long). In our dataset, only 1% of the paths are longer than 256 characters.

Next, each character has to be transformed into a number or array of numbers in a way that properly expresses the semantic of a path. For example, transforming a path into an array of the corresponding ASCII codes, as follows, yields some problems:

```
"/foo/bar" -> [47, 102, 111, 111, 47, 98, 97, 114]
```

The main issue with this transformation is that the distance between the letter 'a' and the letter 'c' is twice the distance between the letter 'a' and the letter 'b', which means that for the algorithm (working on numbers), 'a' may be seen as more *like* 'b' than *like* 'c'. This does not properly translate the properties of characters in a path.

A more proven approach is to represent each character as a *one-hot* vector, as is done in [7]. Such a vector is of dimension A (A being the size of the alphabet, the number of different characters supported), its value being 1 at the index of the given character and 0 elsewhere, as shown in Fig. 2. In this representation, each character is at the same distance of all the others, and each character vector is orthogonal to all the others.

In our dataset, 103 distinct characters are seen, adding a special EOF (end marker), \0 (for padding) and <UNDEF> for unrecognized characters, our alphabet size is 106. Therefore, after padding and *one-hot* vectorization, each path is transformed into a 256×106 matrix.

This method was selected over other known approaches (such as *tf-idf*[3] on n-grams) because it exposes the data as unprocessed as possible to the algorithm, letting it learn on the raw data rather than preprocessed data. Our choice is also motivated by [5], that shows that character level convolutional neural network can outperform all other known methods for text classification.

Durations. Durations are scaled logarithmically ($log_{10}(duration)$) to reflect that the nature of error on the durations is multiplicative and not additive. Intuitively, a difference of 10^6 s is negligible for a long duration such as 10^9 s but very important for a short duration such as 1 s. However, a $\times 10$ multiplication has the same importance, no matter the value of the duration.

Making the algorithm work on properly scaled durations also allows to better use standard *loss* functions and yields a better convergence of the model. The algorithm therefore predicts $log_{10}(estimated\_duration)$, which can then be turned back into a standard duration by exponentiation.

---

[3] Term Frequency - Inverse Document Frequency, in this case the frequency of an n-gram in a path divided by the logarithm of the inverse of the frequency of this n-gram in the whole corpus of paths.

2.4   Models

Two models will be presented here: random forest and convolutional neural network. The former is a traditional machine learning model, whereas the later is a deep learning model.

Random Forest Regressor Model. As a point of comparison to the convolutional network based algorithm, several regressors from the Sckit Learn [2] machine learning framework were tested. Among them, the random forest regressor gave the best result – this is why it is presented here as a less computationally intensive alternative to convolutional neural networks.

Random forests consist in a set of decision trees, each tree being trained on a different subset of the input. As a result, random forests tend to be resilient to small changes in the input.

The algorithm used was `sklearn.ensemble.RandomForestRegressor`, with 16 estimators and all other parameters left to the defaults of `sklearn` v0.20.2. Experiments showed that increasing the number of estimators did not yield significant accuracy improvements.

For memory occupation reasons and simplicity of implementation, the actual implementation did not perform the *one-hot* vectorization, just transforming characters into their ASCII codes. Experiments on smaller datasets with *one-hot* vectorization did not show any improvement for random forests, probably due to the way decision trees handle the input data.

Convolutional Neural Network Model

Architecture
The architecture has been inspired by usual practice in image recognition rather than natural language processing, as paths tend to be built more as sequences of patterns (or patterns of patterns) than natural language. While paths such as `/home/user/project/run53/logs/foo.log` can help getting this intuition, it has also been shown by previous research, such as the *eXpose* paper[4].

The architecture is a simplified version of *eXpose* [7], sharing similarities with the VGG [8] family of networks (see Fig. 3) and consists of:

- An embedding layer mapping each 106 dimension character vector into a 32 dimension vector. In the output space (32 dimensions), characters are not expected to be equidistant anymore: the embedding will learn to map interchangeable characters to close points in this space. This layer helps the network to be more resilient to irrelevant path modification (*e.g.* replacing 2001 by 2002).
- Two convolution and pooling layers for automated feature extraction. These layers are expected to learn and recognize relevant patterns from the input paths.

---

[4] *eXpose: A Character-Level Convolutional Network with Embeddings For Detecting Malicious URLs, File Paths and Registry Keys*, Joshua Saxe and Konstantin Berlin.

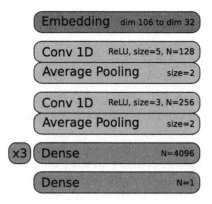

Fig. 3. Convolutional Neural Network Architecture

- Several fully connected layers that compute the regression (estimation of the duration value) from the features extracted by previous layers.

The exact composition of the network (embedding output dimension, convolution and fully connected layers parameters) have been experimentally explored and tuned to perform well on this problem.

Loss

The loss function determines how a given error on the prediction affects the weights of the network during the learning phase. For this application, we selected two different losses with different properties: *logcosh* and *quantile N* loss [4]. The network predicts logarithms of lifetimes, therefore in the subsequent equations, the error is defined as:

$$err = log_{10}(predicted\_lifetime) - log_{10}(true\_lifetime) \qquad (1)$$

$$= log_{10}\left(\frac{predicted\_lifetime}{true\_lifetime}\right) \qquad (2)$$

- The *logcosh* loss gives a very good accuracy profile while being resilient to outliers (anomalies in the dataset). The formula is the following:

$$logcosh\_loss(err) = log(cosh(err))$$

- The *quantile N* loss (also called *tilted loss*) penalizes unevenly positive and negative errors. Various values of N have been tried, *quantile99* ($N = 99$) yielded the most interesting results. Concretely, this quantile loss means that *underestimations* of file lifetime are 99 times more penalized than overestimation, leading the network to be trained to overestimate rather than underestimate. The formula is the following (in this equation, a negative error is an underestimation):

$$quantile99\_loss(err) = max(0.01 \times err, -0.99 \times err)$$

3   Results

3.1   Evaluation Methodology

Both methods have been evaluated in two situations:

- Training on a random sample representing 70% of the dataset and evaluating on the remaining 30% – this setup allows to measure how well the model can generalize;
- Training on 95% of the dataset and evaluating on the remaining 5% – this setup allows to see whether training on more data improves accuracy significantly or not. This may also be more representative of real workloads, where the amount of files created in a day is small compared to the amount of files created before this day.

In this section, the term *accuracy* is defined as the percentage of prediction that are less than a factor $10^{threshold}$ away from the truth. More formally, with $\{P_1, P_2, ..., P_N\}$ the predictions and $\{T_1, T_2, ..., T_N\}$ the associated true lifetime values:

$$accuracy(threshold) = \frac{|\{i \in [1, N] \text{ such as } |log_{10}\left(\frac{T_i}{P_i}\right)| < threshold\}|}{N}$$

Concretely, $accuracy(1)$ is the percentage of prediction that are less than a factor 10^1 away from the truth, and $accuracy(0.1)$ the percentage that is less than a factor $10^{0.1}$ away from the truth.

The accuracies presented hereafter are always on the validation set only, *i.e.* on data on which the network never trained.

3.2   Training Times and Model Sizes

To obtain the results presented here:

- **Random Forest Regressor** (from `sklearn` [2]):
  - Trained approximately 5 min on 24 CPU. Training more cannot yield more accuracy.
  - The serialized model is about 1.2 GB.
- **Convolutional Neural Network** (implemented with `tensorflow` [3]):
  - Trained approximately 1.5 h on 4 NVidia Tesla V100-SXM2-16 GB (100 epochs) for each loss. Training more may marginally increase the accuracy, and training less may still yield a satisfactory accuracy: the accuracy improvement decays almost exponentially with training time. Reducing the fully connected layer sizes could reduce the training time at the cost of a slightly lower accuracy.
  - The serialized model is about 377 MB, this could also be optimized by reducing the fully connected layer sizes, at the cost of a slightly lower accuracy.

Table 1. Result summary for all the tested algorithm with 70%–30% learning (best performances are emphasized).

70%–30%	Random Forest	CNN (*logcosh*)	CNN (*quantile99*)
accuracy(1)	96.47%	**98.79%**	94.59%
accuracy(0.1)	86.81%	**91.57%**	66.47%
underestimations	10.55%	36.62%	**0.68%**
underest. > ×10	1.78%	0.63%	**0.12%**

Table 2. Result summary for all the tested algorithm with 95%–5% learning (best performance are emphasized).

95%–5%	Random Forest	CNN (*logcosh*)	CNN (*quantile99*)
accuracy(1)	96.75%	**99.03%**	94.69%
accuracy(0.1)	87.21%	**93.26%**	70.42%
underestimations	9.54%	24.83%	**0.94%**
underest. > ×10	1.78%	0.50%	**0.09%**

3.3 Accuracy

Table 1 sums up the results for all the tested algorithms: random forest, convolutional neural network with logcosh loss and with quantile99 loss.

- The accuracy is defined in Sect. 3.1.
- The underestimations row is the percentage of predictions that were below the truth. As stated in Sect. 2.1, avoiding underestimations is a crucial aspect of solving this problem properly.
- The underest. > ×10 row is the percentage of predictions that are at least 10 times less than the truth. Concretely, this is the percentage of "spurious predictions", predictions that may induce a performance loss, even when taking a ×10 margin.

Table 2 shows the same metrics when training on 95% of the dataset and evaluating on 5%. Although the results are slightly better, they are not *drastically* better, showing that the algorithms were already able to generalize very well in the 70%–30% case. This result may be specific to the regularity of our dataset, but the TGCC hosts projects and users from various communities (including genomics, climatology, astrophysics and various industrial partners); we therefore believe it to be representative of a typical HPC filesystem storing user computation data.

For all three methods, the accuracy and underestimation rate seem good enough for practical applications:

- In the case of a data placement policy based on lifetimes, the CNN with *quantile99* loss will be preferred, since it provides a very low rate of underestimation with a decent accuracy (see the "accuracy(1)" row).

- If lifetime accuracy is more important than the underestimation rate, the CNN with *logcosh* will be preferred.
- If available computational resources are low or the dataset is very large, random forest may be preferred for its very good computational cost over accuracy ratio.

Manual investigation showed that most of the significant prediction errors for the convolutional neural networks fell into two categories:

- **Outliers:** these cases are anomalies, behaving in an inconsistent way. It can for example be a file that is manually accessed long after its creation despite the fact that all other similar files in the training set are not.
- **Ambiguities:** for a given path, multiple lifetimes are likely. For example, the training set contains an ensemble E of similar paths, where half of them are short lived and half of them is long lived. When predicting the lifetime corresponding to a path similar to the ones in E, the algorithm cannot decide accurately its lifetime (a human would not do better). The *quantile99* loss tends to deal more gracefully with these cases by predicting the longest lifetime when the case is ambiguous.

We believe the CNN results to be very close to the theoretical maxima (in terms of accuracy and underestimations), *i.e.* the best possible guess given the information in the training set, although this is hard to evaluate objectively.

3.4   Error and Accuracy Distribution

As mentioned in Sect. 2.2, global accuracy is not sufficient to determine the quality of the prediction. Figure 4 shows the *accuracy*(1) and underestimation rate across all the lifetime orders of magnitude, for random forest and convolutional neural network.

These figures show that the accuracy is well balanced over the whole spectrum of values, with an exception in one point where there is not enough data to train the model properly: around 10^2, as can be verified with Fig. 1. The *quantile99* accuracy is better for high values, which is expected as it favors overestimations.

The underestimation rate is rather well balanced as well, but less stable than accuracy.

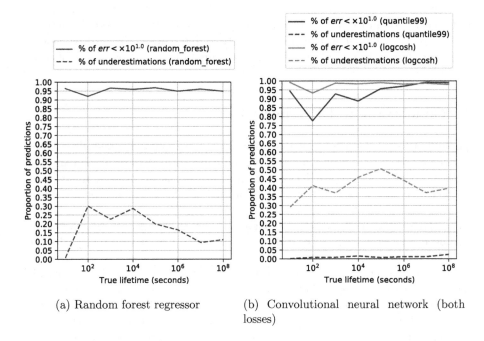

(a) Random forest regressor

(b) Convolutional neural network (both losses)

Fig. 4. Accuracy and underestimation across lifetime values

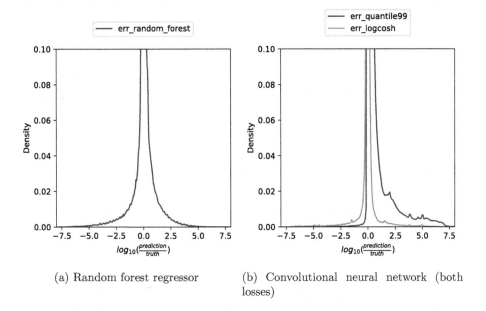

(a) Random forest regressor

(b) Convolutional neural network (both losses)

Fig. 5. Error distribution (0 is no error, <0 is underestimation)

Figure 5 shows the error distribution for each method, 0 signifying "no error". Random forest and CNN with *logcosh* loss errors are well centered around 0, whereas CNN with *quantile99* loss is heavily tilted toward the positive side of the error, illustrating the fact that underestimations are avoided as much as possible.

4   Conclusion and Perspectives

These first results suggest that our approach is very viable for metadata based lifetime estimation of files, making it a good candidate for data placement optimization. However, this kind of algorithm only works properly if it has been trained with a dataset representative of production data (which can be the production data itself at a given point in time) and can give unpredictable results on metadata that look nothing like what it has been trained on. It may therefore need to be regularly retrained to keep up with new patterns in paths and associated lifetimes.

To gain better confidence in the predictions, a solution could be to train several algorithms independently and combine their predictions to estimate the lifetime of a file and an associated confidence index. A special case of this approach would be to train several neural network (or one network with several outputs) with different *quantile losses* (1, 10, 25, 50, 75, 90 and 99 for example) giving something akin to a probability function for the lifetime of a path.

The XGBoost algorithm could also be investigated, as it could yield similar results as random forest if tuned properly, but with the advantage of specifying a custom loss. This custom loss could be *quantile99*, potentially making XGBoost another more computationally efficient alternative to the convolutional neural network, with the same interesting overestimation bias that was achieved with *quantile99*.

The next step of this work would probably be to implement a policy-based on lifetime estimation on a production filesystem and estimate the actual gain yielded and the amount of prediction errors that could have been avoided with classic strategies.

References

1. Sage2. http://sagestorage.eu/content/sage2-overview
2. Scikit learn. https://scikit-learn.org
3. Tensorflow. https://www.tensorflow.org
4. Abeywardana, S.: Deep quantile regression (2018). https://towardsdatascience.com/deep-quantile-regression-c85481548b5a
5. Conneau, A., Schwenk, H., Barrault, L., Lecun, Y.: Very deep convolutional networks for text classification. In: Proceedings of the 15th Conference of the European Chapter of the Association for Computational Linguistics: Volume 1, Long Papers, Valencia, Spain, pp. 1107–1116. Association for Computational Linguistics, April 2017. https://www.aclweb.org/anthology/E17-1104

6. Leibovici, T.: Robinhood policy engine. https://github.com/cea-hpc/robinhood
7. Saxe, J., Berlin, K.: eXpose: a character-level convolutional neural network with embeddings for detecting malicious urls, file paths and registry keys. CoRR abs/1702.08568 (2017). http://arxiv.org/abs/1702.08568
8. Simonyan, K., Zisserman, A.: Very deep convolutional networks for large-scale image recognition. CoRR abs/1409.1556 (2014). https://arxiv.org/abs/1409.1556

An I/O Analysis of HPC Workloads on CephFS and Lustre

Alberto Chiusole[1]⬤, Stefano Cozzini[1,2]([✉])⬤, Daniel van der Ster[3],
Massimo Lamanna[3], and Graziano Giuliani[4]⬤

[1] eXact Lab s.r.l., via Beirut 2, 34151 Trieste, Italy
[2] CNR-IOM c/o SISSA, Via Bonomea 265, 34136 Trieste, Italy
cozzini@iom.cnr.it
[3] CERN, Geneva 23, Switzerland
[4] ICTP, Strada Costiera 11, 34151 Trieste, Italy

Abstract. In this contribution we compare the performance of the
Input/Output load (I/O) of a High-Performance Computing (HPC)
application on two different File Systems: CephFS and Lustre; our goal is
to assess whether CephFS could be considered a valid choice for intense
HPC applications. We perform our analysis using a real HPC workload,
namely RegCM, a climate simulation application, and IOR, a synthetic
benchmark application, to simulate several I/O patterns using different
I/O parallel libraries (MPI-IO, HDF5, PnetCDF). We compare writing
performance for the two different I/O approaches that RegCM implements: the so-called spokesperson or serial, and a truly parallel one. The
small difference registered between the serial I/O approach and the parallel one motivates us to explore in detail how the software stack interacts
with the underlying File Systems. For this reason, we use IOR and MPI-
IO hints related to Collective Buffering and Data Sieving to analyze
several I/O patterns on the two different File Systems.

Finally we investigate Lazy I/O, a unique feature of CephFS, which
disables file coherency locks introduced by the File System; this allows
Ceph to buffer writes and to fully exploit its parallel and distributed
architecture. Two clusters were set up for these benchmarks, one at CNR-
IOM and a second one at Pawsey Supercomputing Centre; we performed
similar tests on both installations, and we recorded a four-times I/O performance improvement with Lazy I/O enabled.

Preliminary results collected so far are quite promising and further
actions and new possible I/O optimizations are presented and discussed.

Keywords: Ceph · Lustre · HPC · RegCM · Lazy I/O · Performance

1 Introduction

The storage component of an HPC infrastructure is becoming more and more
relevant in dictating the performance of the whole system: the time spent in

© Springer Nature Switzerland AG 2019
M. Weiland et al. (Eds.): ISC 2019 Workshops, LNCS 11887, pp. 300–316, 2019.
https://doi.org/10.1007/978-3-030-34356-9_24

performing I/O is, in many cases, the real bottleneck of many scientific applications. For this reason storage complexity at both hardware and software level is increasing, and the correct tuning of all the layer involved is not an easy task. Moreover, together with a standard File System approach, an object storage solution is also often needed in flexible HPC infrastructures which need to cope with the increasingly large data requirements. In this context, Ceph, a well-established object storage solution for virtualization platforms, can be used also as the primary File System in an HPC infrastructure; there are several advanced features in Ceph that make it worth to test it in a true HPC environment, and compare it against standard and well-known solutions, e.g., a Lustre File System.

The main goal of this on-going work is thus to evaluate CephFS (the File System layer provided by Ceph) on several HPC workloads and compare the results so obtained against a more traditional Lustre File System. We are interested in understanding whether CephFS can be used as a proper parallel and distributed File System specifically for HPC applications. In addition, we want to understand the behavior of different I/O layers with respect to the underlying File System, in order to identify interesting optimizations that could be applied to HPC applications, to obtain the best performance out of CephFS.

The Ceph installation we tested in this study is deployed at CERN, Switzerland, and is based on Ceph version 13.2.5, codename "Mimic". The overall infrastructure is composed of 402 OSDs on 134 host servers: on each host are installed three 1 TiB SSD disks. The overall storage capacity available is therefore around 200 TiB. Replica factor is set to 2 and there are two active-active MDS nodes with 64 GB RAM each. This installation provides storage capabilities to an HPC cluster composed of more than 100 computational nodes (only 32 available for our experiments), each mounting 2 Intel E5-2630 v4 CPUs, for a total of 20 physical cores per node. The Ceph OSDs are co-located on computing nodes, which are interconnected by FDR InfiniBand network and 10 Gbit Ethernet; applications use InfiniBand for low latency messaging, while Ceph is configured to communicate over Ethernet. The infrastructure is colloquially known as "hyper-converged", because computing power and the Ceph storage service are served by the same physical hosts.

Results obtained at CERN are compared against the ones obtained on C3HPC, a small HPC facility managed by eXact lab, Trieste, Italy, where a Lustre File System is installed; the computational nodes are 15 (but only 8 available for our experiments), each of them equipped with 2 Intel Xeon E5-2697 v2 CPUs, for a total of 24 cores per node (only 20 cores per node were actually used, to maintain the same numbers used on the CERN infrastructure). The Lustre File System is composed of two I/O servers and 4 different OSTs for a total of 24 TiB of available space. The Metadata server uses SSD technology to reduce the response time. The network among computational nodes and storage nodes is a QDR InfiniBand connection. The two storage infrastructure are quite different in size, however both of them are production platform: in particular C3HPC runs routinely climate/weather simulations and therefore this should be considered as our starting point for the comparison. We also note that both File

Systems are used in production: results reported can therefore be affected and perturbed by concurrent activity of other users.

This paper is organized as follows: in Sect. 2 we give an overview of the RegCM [1] package, then we present our benchmarking methodology and the results so far obtained; in the next Section we present a few experiments performed by means of IOR [6] and we discuss them along with some results, on the basis of data collected from RegCM. In Sect. 4 we present Lazy I/O, a POSIX extension designed for HPC and implemented by CephFS; promising benchmark improvements are reported and discussed. Finally, in Sect. 5 we briefly summarize the work done and we infer some possible new experiments to perform in the future.

2   RegCM Benchmarking Analysis

2.1   RegCM Description

RegCM [1] is a state-of-the-art regional climate model developed by ICTP, Trieste, Italy. The application simulates climate evolution over a region of the Earth, using boundary conditions provided by a Global Climate Model (GCM), in order to estimate with high physical and temporal resolution a possible model of climate evolution over the target regional domain.

The time integration domain is a 3D box, typically with a large number of horizontal points defining the domain extension over the Earth surface and with a small number of vertical levels into the atmosphere. The simulation loads into memory the 3D grid of initial conditions taken from the driving GCM and then proceeds to evolve it over time, relaxing the model internal solution at the boundary towards the external solution. Time dependent boundary condition are thus constantly read while simulation proceeds. The time varying Boundary Conditions (BC) are interpolated in advance from any of the global model simulations available. During the computation phase RegCM saves into multiple files all the climate variables, at user configurable time periods; a production run can last for days or even weeks, producing Terabytes of output data.

RegCM requires a stack of scientific software libraries common to most atmospheric models applications. The parallel Fortran90 code implements a 2D domain decomposition by means of MPI; the I/O stack is based on the NetCDF library, a de-facto standard for earth sciences code: since version 4.0, NetCDF can be built on top of the HDF5 library (NETCDF4-HDF5), which extends its saving capabilities by providing parallel I/O access, not available in the previous-generation NetCDF 3 interface. A different and independent implementation of NetCDF called PnetCDF [2] has been developed starting from NetCDF 3, and is based on MPI-IO collective operations: the two versions can be used almost interchangeably.

A typical RegCM simulation requires the user to prepare an input model using some provided pre-processing utilities. The most important input is the ICBC (Initial Condition Boundary Condition) set of files, which contains the result of a global simulation over the region that RegCM will simulate, containing data for the whole period of simulation. The dimension of the ICBC input files could easily reach several terabytes in a common simulation run. The model is configured to save multiple variables in multiple files (ATM, RAD, SRF, STS) using different output frequencies for different variables, usually set at 6 h by default. The amount of output data can be more than double the input data, and for this reason in this study we focus mainly on writing performance.

RegCM can be used with two different patterns to perform its I/O operations: in the serial mode (the so-called "spokesperson approach"), all processes send their portion of data to a single collector process, which writes the results to file serially; in the parallel writing mode, all processes concurrently write to the same NetCDF file using collective operations, provided by either the HDF5 or the PnetCDF libraries.

2.2 Benchmarking Methodology and Space of Parameters

The main goal of our benchmarking work is focused on determining three different aspects of the performance of RegCM:

- compare I/O performance among different I/O software stacks (MPI and I/O stack libraries) and hardware architectures, in order to outline the optimal environment for the code;
- compare the serial and parallel approach to I/O against all the different software stacks presented in the previous analysis;
- compare the role of the underlying File Systems (CephFS and Lustre) with respect to the above analysis.

The workload we use in these tests comes from a real simulation dataset: we simulate a high horizontal (11 km) resolution for a domain extended over the European continent: the grid is $500 \times 500 \times 23$ (width, depth and height of the 3D grid to evolve).

With respect to a standard RegCM run we just limit the temporal extension of the evolution phase: we perform one single day of simulation (from 1990-06-01 to 1990-06-02), and we tuned the application to save all the variables in output files every hour to increase the I/O activity of the code.

We originally used RegCM version 4.7.1 but then we moved to version 4.7.3.4, always using Intel compiler version 18.0.3; Intel MPI 2018.3.222 and OpenMPI 3.1.2 as MPI layers; NetCDF C 4.6.3 and NetCDF Fortran 4.4.4 to save files according to the NetCDF standard, and HDF5 1.10.4 and PnetCDF 1.11.0 to provide parallel I/O capabilities to the NetCDF file format.

The RegCM source code at version 4.7.1 that was initially used was able to take advantage of only some specific calls from the PnetCDF interface, when compiled with `--enable-parallel-nc`; since the latest release, with tag 4.7.3.4[1], full PnetCDF support is included, and can be enabled by applying `--enable-pnetcdf` at the configure.

---

[1] https://github.com/ictp-esp/RegCM/releases/tag/4.7.3.4.

Table 1. Software stack used by RegCM.

Application layer	RegCM 4.7.1/4.7.3.4		
NetCDF library	NetCDF C 4.6.3 + NetCDF Fortran 4.4.4		PnetCDF 1.11.0 (RegCM 4.7.3.4)
Parallel I/O backend	HDF5 1.10.4	PnetCDF 1.11.0	
MPI communication	Intel MPI 18.0.3		
	OpenMPI 3.1.2		

In Table 1 we report the different implementations tested; a total of 6 different combinations of RegCM were built and compared in this study, namely Intel MPI with HDF5 (IH), Intel MPI with partial PnetCDF support (IP, on RegCM 4.7.1), Intel MPI with full PnetCDF support (IFP), OpenMPI with HDF5 (OH), OpenMPI with partial PnetCDF support (OP, on RegCM 4.7.1), OpenMPI with full PnetCDF support (OFP). We name the six binaries with two letter acronyms to allow an easier discussion of the results obtained.

Compared to other open-source MPI libraries, where the File System drivers are included at compile-time by enabling the corresponding flag, Intel MPI comes already built with all drivers, which can then be enabled at run-time by using environment variables[2]. We executed mpirun with the options -env I_MPI_EXTRA_FILESYSTEM on -env I_MPI_EXTRA_FILESYSTEM_LIST lustre during the runs performed with the Intel MPI library, but we did not notice any improvement from the runs performed on builds compiled without the flag; the Intel MPI library may have introduced an automatic mechanism to recognize the File System used and automatically apply optimizations.

2.3 RegCM Benchmarking Analysis Results

We first performed a RegCM strong scalability analysis in order to assess the role of the different software stacks on different File Systems. We executed RegCM on the CERN HPC facility, on a number of nodes varying from 1 to 32 (in power of 2), for all the six RegCM binaries discussed above and presented in Table 1, and using both the serial and the parallel I/O approaches; the timings were recorded at least 2 times, and the best performing results were taken into consideration, because the File System was already in production and was shared with other users.

Referring to Fig. 1 we can observe the following: RegCM scales more than linearly up to 8 nodes on both cluster and with both MPI libraries: this is thanks to an efficient memory hierarchy exploitation of the RegCM code. On 16 nodes (320 processors) and with the Intel MPI builds on CephFS, performance decreases slightly for the build with partial PnetCDF support (IP), while IH and IFP continue to scale linearly; on 32 nodes (640 processors) all the 3 Intel MPI-based implementations cannot scale linearly anymore, but IFP maintains a

---

[2] https://www.mcs.anl.gov/projects/romio/2014/06/12/romio-and-intel-mpi/.

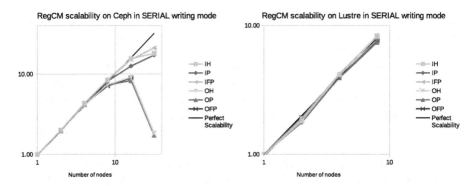

Fig. 1. RegCM scalability on CephFS (left, from 1 to 32 nodes) and Lustre (right, from 1 to 8 nodes) with Serial I/O.

promising increasing trend in performance. Such behavior is again expected: on a large number of processors the domain decomposition algorithm starts to be dominated by MPI communication times and not by actual computation, due to the shrinking of the subdomain.

What is actually surprising is that the performance of all the OpenMPI-based builds (OH, OP and OFP) on 16 and 32 nodes clearly shows a dramatic slowdown: this is due to the OpenMPI library not being able to deal with such large number of processors on our specific workload, often crashing and interrupting execution; the data point on 32 nodes for the OFP build was not collected due to the constant crashes.

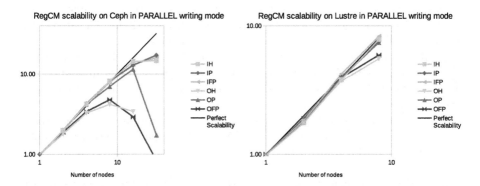

Fig. 2. RegCM scalability on CephFS (left, from 1 to 32 nodes) and Lustre (right, from 1 to 8 nodes) with Parallel I/O.

Figure 2 reports parallel writing results on RegCM, similar to the serial approach: the Intel MPI-based builds scale perfectly linear up to 8 nodes on CephFS, then IH and IFP continue scaling linearly at 16 nodes; on 32 nodes, all the builds generally slow down, but the PnetCDF-based builds do not suffer like the HDF5 build, which does not report an improvement compared to the 16 nodes execution. OP is the only OpenMPI build able to sustain an almost linear scalability up to 16 nodes; the OH and OFP builds immediately produce bad results, then deeply collapsing at 16 and 32 nodes, as well as the OP build on 32 nodes. Due to the constant crashes, the timing of the OH build on 32 nodes was not collected.

On Lustre at C3HPC we can see that the OH build starts diverging from the linear scalability line on 8 nodes, probably due to the MPI algorithms provided by OpenMPI not optimized for HDF5 algorithms when performing parallel I/O.

Figure 3 presents the performance of the 2 best performing binaries (IH and IFP) on both HPC architectures when using parallel I/O: there is a slightly better result for parallel writing mode on 8 and 16 nodes on CephFS at CERN, which becomes interesting on 32 nodes, because IH is no more capable to scale, while IFP scales better; also in the runs on Lustre at C3HPC we can appreciate that the build based on PnetCDF produces a slightly better scalability plot, although there is a low number of processors.

The difference between the HDF5 and the PnetCDF builds is not negligible: we can appreciate that all the 4 builds using PnetCDF maintain almost the same performance regardless of the writing mode, while the builds based on HDF5 perform very well in serial mode, but tend to be slower when performing parallel I/O, probably due to internal communication algorithms used, not as efficient as those implemented by PnetCDF.

The general similarity between serial and parallel runs is probably caused by locks introduced by the File System when multiple processes simultaneously open a file in write mode: the locks cause parallel writes to become synchronous to preserve file coherency, as expected by all POSIX-compliant File Systems. Therefore the synchronous writing induced by the File System is performance-wise comparable to the serial/"spokesperson" approach, despite a user may expect the parallel version to be faster, because uses multiple writers. An interesting solution to this constraint is discussed in detail in Sect. 4.

Similar scalability results have been obtained also on C3HPC, despite the older generation of Intel CPUs installed: almost perfect scalability up to 4 nodes, and slightly less than perfect with 8 nodes; unfortunately, no more than 8 nodes were available during our tests.

To better understand the surprisingly absence of performance in case of parallel I/O and in particular the very similar timings in parallel writing for both PnetCDF and HDF5 implementation a in-depth further analysis is therefore needed.

In particular we want to understand the underlying details of our software stack and its interaction with the underlying File System. This is discussed in the next Section.

Our benchmarking analysis on RegCM application, despite not yet complete, does give us interesting information that we can summarize as follows: CephFS does not hinder the I/O performance of the application with respect to a Lustre File System. The I/O stack used by the application behaves correctly as well and no major issues are reported with the underlying File System.

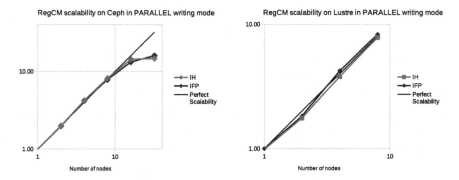

Fig. 3. RegCM parallel I/O performance for HDF5 and PnetCDF: left CephFS, right Lustre.

3 Analysis of Several MPI-IO Hints with IOR

3.1 IOR Introduction and Benchmark Setup

We are now interested in evaluating only the I/O performance of both File Systems and to understand the effect of the two MPI-IO hints, which are "suggestions" that the user can pass to the MPI-IO layer of an MPI application, to tune several parameters, according to the different hardware and software solutions a File System is built upon. We are interested in understanding the effect of such hints on different I/O layers (MPI-IO, HDF5 and PnetCDF) used in the software stack of RegCM; we expected to see some differences among MPI-IO hints on the several I/O patterns typical of RegCM and other HPC applications.

We used IOR [6] (Interleaved-Or-Random) is an open-source I/O generator tool, to study several combinations of the 2 most relevant MPI-IO hints with various access patterns, similarly to [3] and [5]: Collective Buffering (controlled by hints `romio_cb_write` and `romio_cb_read`) and Data Sieving (`romio_ds_write` and `romio_ds_read`). IOR can apply MPI-IO hints at runtime, by reading them from a configuration file or from environment variables[3]. We tested nine combinations of the hints (see Table 2) controlling the Collective Buffering (CB) and Data Sieving (DS) algorithms, the same used in [3].

For these benchmarks, IOR version 3.2.0 was compiled with the same I/O software stack used for RegCM.

The Collective Buffering optimization (also called two-phase I/O) aims to improve performance when multiple MPI processes execute noncontiguous requests to the File System. When operating in a parallel application, MPI processes often request several portions of the same file: if the MPI-IO implementation is made aware of the requests pattern, multiple requests to the File System for the same region can be avoided. The approach used by ROMIO is to

---

[3] Refer to "How do I use hints?" in the FAQ of the project: https://ior.readthedocs.io/en/latest/userDoc/faq.html.

Table 2. The 9 different configurations of MPI-IO hints analysed.

MPI-IO hints config number	romio_cb_write/ romio_cb_read	romio_ds_write/ romio_ds_read
1	enable	enable
2	enable	disable
3	enable	auto
4	disable	enable
5	disable	disable
6	disable	auto
7	auto	enable
8	auto	disable
9	auto	auto

perform collective I/O at the client level, inside the MPI layer, which is portable across File System vendors.

When performing collective reads, each process broadcasts the offsets of the range it needs to read; then all the portions are summed together to obtain the largest amount of data to read from file. The first phase of the operation means that all the processes involved retrieve one part of the whole segment; in the second phase, each process goes asking data to the process that obtained it in the first phase and, at the same time, it serves data other processes need, all using point-to-point non-blocking MPI operations.

When writing, the two-phase I/O is basically inversed; in the first phase, the processes communicate together to collect contiguous portions of data to be written, while in the second phase the actual writing is performed. It is interesting to notice that, since in the first phase the processes collected all the portions of data to be written, there is no need to introduce locks on the file to avoid race conditions, and therefore the writing could be performed in parallel; it is important to note that the File System needs to cooperate in order not to insert locks.

The two-phase I/O abstraction could actually introduce an overhead due to the MPI communication required to organize the collection of segments: moreover, modern distributed File Systems often already provide similar optimizations internally, which could clash with the collective buffering implementation.

Data Sieving is the second main optimization available in ROMIO and similar implementations; it aims to reduce the number of requests to the File System, by merging together multiple noncontiguous requests into a single one. Using data sieving, the latency can be reduced, with the drawback of reading more data than originally needed: a smart implementation can attenuate this phenomenon, by applying data sieving only when holes between regions are close enough, and apply normal I/O when the regions are too scattered. Data Sieving can be applied also for writes, using a read-modify-write approach and file locks at specific offsets. Most File Systems provide caching mechanisms and often implement read-ahead strategies, which could actually reduce the effect of data sieving.

When reading Table 2, we can group the 9 configurations into 3 sub-categories: the first 3 configurations (hints configurations: 1, 2, 3) where the RW hints for Collective Buffering are explicitly enabled, the next 3 (hints configurations: 4, 5, 6) where CB is explicitly disabled, and the last 3 configurations (7, 8, 9) where the MPI-IO implementation can choose whether to enable CB or not (which is the default behavior adopted by all MPI implementations).

We also varied the MPI-IO hints related to Data Sieving, forcing them to be enabled (hints configuration: 1, 4, 7), disabled (hints configurations: 2, 5, 8) or set to `automatic` (hints 3, 6, 9), to let the implementation decide whether to apply it (the default behavior).

The configuration of hints labeled by number 9 in Table 2 (where all the hints values are set to `automatic`) represents the behavior of the MPI-IO implementation when no hints are explicitly set, and can be considered the baseline of performance for the following tests.

We performed two different benchmarks using IOR on the two File Systems: we first used a single, relatively small, 20 GiB test file, roughly the same amount of data written by RegCM in a single day of simulation. Our goal here is to measure the overhead associated in coordinating efforts among many processors, because the amount of data to write becomes negligible on a large number of processors. In the second test we increased the total test file by a factor of ten to reach 200 GiB, to better balance the coordination operation against the writing phase. We remark that cache and buffers effects are minimized in both cases due to usage of `-e` flag which performs an `fsync` at file closing.

In both experiments we keep constant the output file size and we make each processor write a chunk of the global file; we execute the benchmark ranging from 1 node with 20 processes (where each core writes 1 GiB and 10 GiB, respectively for the 20 and 200 GiB test file) up to 32 nodes (where each of the 640 processors writes only 32 and 320 MiB, respectively for the two test files). We always used the same transfer size of 2 MiB in all the IOR tests, the same adopted in [3], which is defined in IOR as the amount of data to be transferred in a single I/O call; this means that all reads and writes are performed in chunks of 2 MiB each. We see little difference between the 20 GiB and 200 GiB cases: this is likely due to the fact that the coordination phase is dominating in both cases; we therefore discuss here in details only the 20 GiB test file size.

We collected measurements for both CephFS at CERN and Lustre at C3HPC in Table 3: the table reports the writing performance obtained on 20 GiB test file for the three of I/O backends (MPI-IO, HDF5 and PnetCDF) on 4, 8, 16 and 32 nodes (80 to 640 processors) on CephFS, and 2 4, 8, nodes on Lustre.

Being the Lustre setup much smaller than the hyper-converged Ceph installation, raw bandwidth results collected were generally one order of magnitude smaller than those obtained on CephFS at CERN, but we are not interested in absolute performance but rather on the difference in performance between the

Table 3. Writing performance for IOR on a 20 GiB test file on CephFS and Lustre.

	File System						
	CephFS at CERN				Lustre at C3HPC		
Number of processors	80	160	320	640	40	80	160
MPI-IO write							
Hint 1	38.00	67.90	105.99	145.47	118.69	115.08	–
Hint 2	37.38	64.57	96.60	140.80	132.65	133.42	–
Hint 3	38.39	65.81	100.11	141.45	130.02	130.06	–
Hint 4	3093.66	3378.77	3763.28	3130.25	346.60	289.27	196.05
Hint 5	3192.76	3351.80	3527.81	3163.44	341.28	330.48	215.76
Hint 6	3268.91	3438.99	3993.69	3195.81	306.69	290.73	247.73
Hint 7	744.84	1126.31	1083.58	1387.34	301.07	308.47	221.06
Hint 8	791.18	1179.27	872.02	1368.01	301.30	183.08	227.24
Hint 9	799.78	1178.31	849.05	1284.46	309.70	289.26	236.93
HDF5 write							
Hint 1	–	39.51	68.60	97.80	114.29	126.21	–
Hint 2	–	39.82	65.68	96.21	119.31	109.21	–
Hint 3	–	39.34	64.64	94.07	95.45	124.02	–
Hint 4	423.06	567.40	816.07	1206.80	256.25	287.57	201.68
Hint 5	490.81	717.83	1052.07	1258.99	283.89	249.26	200.19
Hint 6	436.32	694.24	854.59	1167.77	280.03	283.03	210.35
Hint 7	446.23	698.46	865.17	1240.44	287.01	229.19	183.50
Hint 8	514.56	770.26	1136.30	1330.69	302.07	223.25	219.11
Hint 9	422.38	690.01	1036.81	1245.88	244.96	250.36	204.23
PnetCDF write							
Hint 1	–	39.54	69.55	106.07	127.70	124.47	–
Hint 2	–	39.31	65.19	95.02	120.60	113.04	–
Hint 3	–	38.95	63.24	96.17	119.89	86.76	–
Hint 4	553.78	662.54	919.87	1182.61	297.92	265.47	234.77
Hint 5	571.14	758.55	1045.32	1295.07	317.64	253.04	227.05
Hint 6	580.24	883.59	1158.90	1235.74	293.60	314.74	221.21
Hint 7	549.71	857.16	1150.99	1129.65	267.45	299.37	246.28
Hint 8	574.27	830.25	1143.79	1199.30	325.46	223.45	244.00
Hint 9	550.83	870.79	1115.57	1229.15	276.37	282.19	251.31

different configurations. From all the results collected we can differentiate three clearly marked levels of bandwidth: a slow level is identified in the first group of hints (1, 2, 3) on all the backend APIs, a medium bandwidth for the third group of hints (7, 8, 9) on all APIs and also for the second group of hints (4, 5, 6) with HDF5 and PnetCDF APIs; the highest speed is achieved with the second group of hints (4, 5, 6) when using the MPI-IO backend API.

This initial difference could be explained by the difference in the I/O software libraries used by most HPC applications and studied in this paper: MPI-IO is the simplest I/O mode, while HDF5 and PnetCDF require more computation and process intercommunication to setup metadata and arrays of the correct dimensions, and are probably the reasons why are both slower than MPI-IO when explicitly disabling CB (hints 4, 5 and 6). We can clearly see that second group of hints (4, 5, 6) performs really well when writing MPI-IO (reaching 3.1 GB/s and 3.7 GB/s in bandwidth speed with 640 processors on the 20 and 200 GiB test files, respectively).

Similarly to what was reported on other File Systems in [3], we discovered that the default hints configuration (number 9 in Table 2, with all hints set to automatic), produces low I/O performance with regard to reads with both MPI-IO and HDF5 APIs, while with PnetCDF it matches the same speed reached by hints 4, 5 and 6.

As clearly seen with the first 3 MPI-IO hints in Table 2 (forcing the use of Collective Buffering), produced very low I/O bandwidth performance results, therefore we soon discarded them and did not collect all the data points on the CephFS and Lustre File Systems. We obtained an almost constant I/O bandwidth measurement with CB disabled or when left to its automatic value, for all the three API available (MPI-IO, HDF5 and PnetCDF): Lustre registered around 0.3 GB/s when writing with 1, 2 and 4 nodes, while it slightly decreased to 0.25 GB/s with 8 nodes.

We can summarize the analysis performed on MPI-IO hints by saying that disabling Collective Buffering when using collective operations on the CephFS led to interesting improvements in I/O bandwidth writing performance.

Changing hints related to DS did not produce any impact on I/O bandwidth performance: this kind of optimization may be actually already implemented by most distributed File Systems, and may explain the absence of improvements we noticed in the different hint configurations.

Disabling Collective Buffering (hints 4, 5, 6) produces interesting improvements on CephFS: in particular when using MPI-IO we registered a 3x performance increase in writes; the same MPI-IO hint configuration (CB disabled) causes instead a decrease in performance on Lustre.

4   Unlock Write Buffers in CephFS with Lazy I/O

In this final section we investigated an interesting feature provided by the latest version of CephFS, called lazy I/O (or O_LAZY), proposed as a POSIX extension specifically for HPC, and included in the stable release since version 14, codename "Nautilus", released in March 2019.

CephFS adheres to the POSIX standard whenever possible and reasonable [7], but it diverges slightly to improve performance. Most modern network File Systems (e.g., NFS), and also many local File Systems (e.g., XFS, ext4), do not entirely comply to the POSIX standard: nevertheless, CephFS behaves similarly to a local File System, by ensuring that file coherency is maintained across all the client nodes; most software applications cannot notice the difference between CephFS and a local File System.

File coherency can be defined as the capability of a File System to maintain file replicas synchronized across storage nodes, so that clients always work on the most recent version of a file. To ensure file coherency, CephFS (along with Lustre and other distributed File Systems) allows a single process to write at a time: this constraint is put in place to avoid an inconsistent state in the resulting file, but forces the I/O to become synchronous, thus wasting the advantage of having multiple parallel disks.

Lazy I/O relaxes file coherency to provide parallel I/O performance, especially significant in HPC applications: when this mode is enabled on a file, writes are not saved to disk until `lazyio_propagate`, `fsync` or `close` are explicitly called, and reads are not consistent with other writers until `lazyio_synchronize` is executed. This feature can be enabled [8] by manipulating an open file descriptor using ioctl, allowing CephFS to apply buffered writes; applications need to handle the file coherency internally, and cannot rely on the file consistency usually granted by the File System. This POSIX extension allows the user to take advantage of the parallel architecture of a distributed File System.

Lazy I/O mode has to be used with a carefully designed data accessing policy, in order not to leave files in inconsistent states. File-consistency is usually assured in HPC applications by using external synchronization libraries, such as MPI; a strategy usually applied by many HPC applications preallocates a file with size multiple of the number of processors, then uses collective calls (MPI-IO, HDF5, PnetCDF) to make each process write its portion of data at its specific offset.

4.1 Performance Evaluation of Lazy I/O

Lazy I/O was included as a stable feature in Ceph 14: the Ceph installation at CERN was version 13, therefore we could not use it for this analysis. We studied the possible performance improvements of this feature on two small ad hoc Ceph test clusters.

The first tests on Lazy I/O were performed on a small Ceph cluster created on 2 servers installed at the CNR-IOM computing facility in Trieste, Italy: each storage node was equipped with 1 Intel E5-2620 v4 CPU and 2×2 TB NVMe devices: 2 dedicated nodes with 20 physical cores each simulated computing nodes (Hyper-Threading/Simultaneous Multi-Threading was enabled but unused); an Ethernet connection of 1 Gbit was available to connect storage and client nodes.

A second Ceph cluster composed of 6 servers was made available at Pawsey Supercomputing Centre in Perth, Western Australia; each storage node was equipped with 1 AMD EPYC 7351 CPU with 16 physical cores (Simultaneous Multi-Threading unused), 1 Intel P4600 NVMe and a 100 Gbps Ethernet connection. In this setup, the storage servers were also acting as clients.

The replica factor of both Ceph clusters was left at its default value of 2, so each file was always replicated and available on at least 2 Ceph OSDs.

We created a File System storing both data and metadata on the NVMe devices, and we mounted it with three different strategies: the kernel client mount option (available in the Linux kernel since version 2.3.64), a normal FUSE mount, and a different FUSE mount with the Ceph option `client_force_lazyio=true` enabled. The option used for the second FUSE mount forces every file to be opened in Lazy I/O mode; unfortunately this debug option is available only for the FUSE mount. The FUSE mount introduces a relevant overhead compared to the kernel mount due to its user space implementation, but it allowed us to quickly test the behavior of Lazy I/O in CephFS, by adding a single-line option in the Ceph configuration.

On both clusters we used IOR 3.2.0, built with a software stack similar to the benchmarks performed on the Ceph hyper-converged infrastructure at CERN, to simulate the I/O patterns of RegCM. The software stack used to build IOR on CNR-IOM infrastructure was Intel 18.0.3 with Intel MPI 2018.3.222, while at Pawsey we used GCC 8.2.0 and MPICH 3.3 (which Intel uses as code-base to produce their optimized Intel MPI library); on both clusters HDF5 1.10.4 and PnetCDF 1.11.0 were used as I/O backends to IOR.

Similarly to the tests performed at CERN, the tests at CNR-IOM had a fixed total file size, which were 2 and 20 GiB, similar to the amount generated by RegCM; the more processors used, the less amount of I/O each one generates.

At the Pawsey installation, each process was given a fixed amount of data to generate, set at 256 MiB, causing the total test file size to change with the number of processes. The tests reported were executed with 48 and 96 processors, creating files of 12 and 24 GiB, respectively.

Based on the results obtained in the previous section we decided to focus only on hints 4, 5 and 6.

4.2   Results Obtained

From the results obtained at CNR-IOM and at Pawsey, presented in Table 4, we can appreciate an improvement of an order of magnitude between the normal FUSE mount and the FUSE mount with the Lazy I/O option. In both test-beds, the asynchronous writes (using Lazy I/O) on the FUSE mount produced better results than the synchronous writes on the kernel mount.

Many data points were not collected at Pawsey on the 24 GiB test file on the FUSE mount due to the continuous crashes; 96 processors accessing resources simultaneously with the slow FUSE protocol may be the cause.

Unfortunately, IOR does not come with an option to enable LAZY I/O on-demand, so we were unable to test performance improvement directly on the kernel mount option; a patch is currently being developed, with the aim to propose it to the IOR development community and possibly include such option

Table 4. Lazy I/O writing performance in MiB/s; the total file size was static during each run at CNR-IOM, while the total file size at Pawsey was variable, being 256 MiB times the number of processors.

Mount option	Backend API	MPI-IO hint configurations	Cluster			
			CNR-IOM		Pawsey	
			2 GiB	20 GiB	12 GiB (48 procs)	24 GiB (96 procs)
Kernel	MPI-IO	Hint 4	179.21	217.49	3194.19	3550.32
		Hint 5	174.43	216.44	2477.83	3443.75
		Hint 6	173.74	220.16	2110.56	3582.70
	HDF5	Hint 4	153.88	182.11	1243.42	941.28
		Hint 5	158.17	174.53	700.76	945.49
		Hint 6	163.93	186.01	1596.26	1099.42
	PnetCDF	Hint 4	120.90	182.57	817.00	815.06
		Hint 5	161.95	189.07	742.15	946.26
		Hint 6	163.65	187.16	674.49	858.06
FUSE	MPI-IO	Hint 4	43.08	43.06	488.26	–
		Hint 5	44.73	41.62	490.71	–
		Hint 6	45.72	43.14	492.92	–
	HDF5	Hint 4	36.58	19.36	343.18	–
		Hint 5	42.38	29.00	445.02	–
		Hint 6	36.52	19.40	343.50	–
	PnetCDF	Hint 4	42.75	28.82	452.43	–
		Hint 5	43.15	29.83	452.75	–
		Hint 6	43.35	29.74	453.76	–
FUSE with Lazy	MPI-IO	Hint 4	192.68	205.90	3385.60	3406.92
		Hint 5	198.55	214.39	3306.59	3429.71
		Hint 6	190.17	212.66	3285.65	3433.21
	HDF5	Hint 4	197.61	195.25	1682.36	1964.43
		Hint 5	240.31	220.36	3496.83	3454.82
		Hint 6	192.72	193.85	1665.83	1999.34
	PnetCDF	Hint 4	238.46	222.27	3618.39	–
		Hint 5	244.99	223.48	3694.40	–
		Hint 6	222.57	224.16	3517.74	–

in future versions of IOR. The FUSE mount option allowed us to quickly perform some benchmarks, but its usage introduced a significant slowdown compared to the kernel mount, which represents the best mount option available for CephFS.

The two test clusters examined are not exa-scale storage installations, due to the limited nodes available and the slow network available (at the CNR-IOM cluster), but the performance improvement measured with Lazy I/O is certainly promising for HPC applications working on parallel File Systems and using high level I/O libraries such as HDF5 and PnetCDF.

We can conclude that Lazy I/O mode can greatly improve bandwidth writing performance, and could become a valid motivation to choose Ceph over other File Systems to provide storage to an HPC infrastructure.

We plan to provide RegCM with Lazy I/O capability, and a patch is being designed together with the main developer of the application: RegCM already uses standard parallel I/O libraries and employs an embarrassingly parallel approach to save files, which makes applying Lazy I/O trivial.

5   Conclusions

In this paper we present some preliminary results of our investigation on the feasibility of using Ceph as an alternative solution for I/O intensive HPC workloads; despite this investigation being still a work in progress, some interesting results are emerging, and a discussion deserves to be carried out with the aim to identify further lines of research.

Our preliminary results indicate that CephFS fits perfectly with the RegCM I/O load, and there are no significant differences with respect to a Lustre File System. This promising result hides however a wealth of different and not so clear behaviors once we analyze in more depth the I/O stack RegCM requires. When writing with the serial approach, we noticed that HDF5 scales perfectly, while PnetCDF tends to be slower, but still scales well; when performing parallel I/O, HDF5 loses the serial advantage, while PnetCDF maintains the same scalability seen in the serial writing mode.

This motivated us to explore in more detail the behavior of the I/O stack libraries by means of IOR, a I/O benchmarking tool: the results are showing an improvement of performance of CephFS compared to Lustre when using MPI-IO and disabling Collective Buffering, as reported in Sect. 3.

Such results give us some suggestions about future investigations to better understand the overall behavior of RegCM. We consider it is worth to patch RegCM to allow the user to pass MPI-IO hints to the MPI layer, in particular those identified in our IOR analysis could reduce the execution time of RegCM simulations.

Although the Lustre installation at C3HPC is very small (only 2 I/O servers compared to the 402 available at CERN) we consider both the RegCM and the IOR tests valuable and relevant, because the goal of this contribution was to understand the actual scalability obtainable from a Ceph solution, also for small HPC production clusters such as C3HPC.

Lazy I/O mode results are already promising, although further measurements and tests are needed; Lazy I/O could corrupt data if the application relies on file-consistency (i.e. expecting a POSIX-compliant standard): we compared the output files produced by RegCM on the different mounts, and the only difference found was the timestamp applied during file creation; this makes us confident of the integrity of the resulting files for our application when using Lazy I/O and a synchronization library such as MPI.

We are now currently developing a patch to RegCM to apply Lazy I/O and completely exploit the parallel capabilities of CephFS.

Based on the results of this paper we identified two different approaches to improve I/O performance of RegCM, depending on the presence or not of a write buffering feature (like Lazy I/O) on the File System: in the former, the best solution would be to use RegCM with HDF5 in serial writing mode, which scales linearly up to 16 nodes, as presented in the benchmarks of Sect. 2; in the latter, a build with the PnetCDF library could be used: it provides optimized parallel I/O performance, while Lazy I/O removes locks on multiple writers, thus fully exploiting the parallel capabilities of CephFS.

Acknowledgments. We thank Luca Cervigni, Pawsey Supercomputing Centre, for the opportunity to collaborate and extract Lazy I/O timings from their Ceph test cluster.

We thank Pablo Llopis, CERN, for all the precious HPC support provided.

References

1. Giorgi F., Coppola E., Solmon F., Mariotti L.: RegCM4: model description and preliminary tests over multiple CORDEX domains. Clim. Res. **52**, 7–29 (2011). https://doi.org/10.3354/cr01018. The RegCM versions used in this study are available in the release page of the project on GitHub: https://github.com/ictp-esp/RegCM/releases
2. Li, J., et al.: Parallel netCDF: a scientific high-performance I/O interface. In: The Proceedings of ACM/IEEE Conference on Supercomputing, pp. 39, November 2003. Project web-site: https://parallel-netcdf.github.io. Accessed 22 July 2019
3. Wauteleta, P., Kestener, P.: Parallel IO performance and scalability study on the PRACE curie supercomputer, Partnership For Advanced Computing in Europe (PRACE), Technical report, September 2009
4. Thakur, R., Ross, R., Lusk, E., Gropp, W., Latham, R.: Users Guide for ROMIO: A High-Performance, Portable MPI-IO Implementation. http://citeseerx.ist.psu.edu/viewdoc/download?rep=rep1&type=pdf&doi=10.1.1.218.9852
5. Wautelet, P.: Parallel I/O experiments on massively parallel computers. In: SciComP 17 Conference, Paris, May 2011. http://www.idris.fr/docs/docu/IDRIS/IDRISioscicomp2011.pdf
6. IOR benchmark project on GitHub. https://github.com/hpc/ior. Accessed 22 July 2019
7. CephFS documentation about POSIX compliance. http://docs.Ceph.com/docs/mimic/Cephfs/posix/. Accessed 22 July 2019
8. CephFS documentation about Lazy I/O feature. http://docs.Ceph.com/docs/master/Cephfs/lazyio/. Accessed 22 July 2019
9. Carns, P., et al.: Understanding and improving computational science storage access through continuous characterization. In: Proceedings of 27th IEEE Conference on Mass Storage Systems and Technologies (MSST 2011) (2011). http://www.mcs.anl.gov/uploads/cels/papers/P1859.pdf. Project web-site: https://www.mcs.anl.gov/research/projects/darshan/

Enabling Fast and Highly Effective FPGA Design Process Using the CAPI SNAP Framework

Alexandre Castellane$^{(\boxtimes)}$ and Bruno Mesnet$^{(\boxtimes)}$

OpenCAPI and CAPI SNAP Enablement IBM France, 1 Rue de la Vieille Poste,
34006 Montpellier, France
{alexandre.castellane,bruno.mesnet}@fr.ibm.com

Abstract. The CAPI SNAP (Storage, Network, and Analytics Programming) is an open source framework which enables C/C++ as well as FPGA programmers to quickly create FPGA-based accelerated computing that works on server host data, as well as data from storage, flash, Ethernet, or other connected resources. The SNAP framework is based on the IBM Coherent Accelerator Processor Interface (CAPI). From POWER8 with CAPI1.0, to POWER9 with CAPI2.0 and Open-CAPI, programmers can have access to a very simple framework to develop accelerated applications using high speed and very low latency interfaces to access an external FPGA. With SNAP, no specific hardware skill is required to port or develop an application and then accelerate it. Even more, a cloud environment is being offered as a cost effective, ready-to-use environment for a first-time right experience as well as a deeper development so that it can be achieved with very little investment.

Keywords: Innovative hardware/software co-design · Processor architecture · Chip multiprocessors · Custom and reconfigurable logic · Solutions for parallel programming challenges · Parallel programming languages · Libraries · Models and notations · Alternative and specialized parallel operating systems and runtime systems

1 Introduction

Software engineers are looking for means to compensate for Moore's law not being observed anymore. While GPUs are providing obvious mean to accelerate processes, FPGA, "Field Programmable Gate Array" can offer very good acceleration performances.

Once coupled to a server they can provide very efficient manners to share high computation tasks between software and hardware, provided that the data link is efficient.

Text analytics [1] or regular expression matching [2] or even implementation of neural networks [3] are few examples of proven successful FPGA-server combinations.

The usual objections to FPGA usage are their relative complexity, specific skills requirements or bad Return On Investment. Skills required to know the details of their hardware and long design times have been common in past decades.

© Springer Nature Switzerland AG 2019
M. Weiland et al. (Eds.): ISC 2019 Workshops, LNCS 11887, pp. 317–329, 2019.
https://doi.org/10.1007/978-3-030-34356-9_25

In this paper, we present a use case of using CAPI SNAP to enable the fast and effective acceleration of a SHA3 cryptographic key calculation function coded in C language into a FPGA. Work was performed in **11 working days** with a result showing an **acceleration factor of 35 versus running on a server with multi-threaded CPUs.** No modification of the code of the algorithm itself, was necessary. No specific FPGA knowledge or specific tools was necessary.

After reviewing what FPGA technology provides, we will then explore the CAPI interface. We will present what **"OpenPower"**, a consortium created around IBM's POWER Processor technology has set up in terms of development environment allowing to popularize the use of this technology.

We will then be able to see some details and results of an actual opensource SHA3 calculation implementation.

2   The FPGA Technology

2.1   A FPGA, a Component Programmed for YOUR Function

These 4 letters "FPGA" stand for "Field Programmable Gate Array" and designate a **reprogrammable component**. As shown in Fig. 1 it contains combinational logic (logical gates OR, AND, XOR, adders, multipliers) but also memory and inputs/outputs. These elements repeated a vast number of times, are distributed using an interconnection matrix which allows to connect all these resources together.

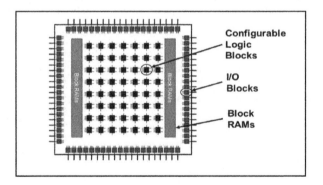

Fig. 1. Typical FPGA content.

Thanks to this, we will be able to create "customized" logical functions that are perfectly optimized for the function you want to outsource or accelerate. This concept is very important to understand because, unlike a processor (CPU or GPU), we do not adapt the "function to be executed" to the logic but **we build the logic for the "function to be executed".** By extension, we can easily understand, that according to the size taken by the logic, we can easily **duplicate** this logic to parallelize the processing as many times as the FPGA can contain duplications! Once the logic is built, the FPGA is programmed, and the users can execute the programmed function until they decide to reprogram this FPGA.

2.2 Choosing the Right FPGA

These FPGAs, first introduced in 1985 by Xilinx, not only contain more and more logic and memory at every new generation but may also contain very specific resources such as ARM processors, DSPs, or very high-speed links. Even if the top two manufacturers of FPGAs are Xilinx and Intel FPGA (formerly Altera), the diversity comes mainly from the card manufacturers using these FPGAs. Indeed, we can find an almost unlimited number of cards adapted to all possible standards depending on the usage we need. The FPGA cards that are used in servers will for example be connected to a PCIe slot and contain either a lot of memory (2 TB Flash) or connectors to interface with the outside world: network, disks, etc. (see Fig. 2) The choice of the FPGA and its associated card, are essentially determined by the resources needed by the function we are porting to the FPGA.

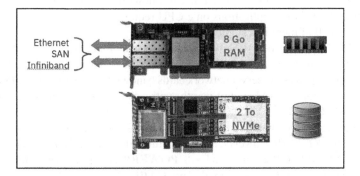

Fig. 2. FPGA offers path to the external world.

2.3 Programming a FPGA in C/C++ Language…at Last!

Understanding what a FPGA is, and how to choose it is one thing. **Programming** it is another one … and this has been a blocking point to use FPGA for years! Up to now, only "hardware" developers were able to code these components. Indeed, High-level Hardware Description Language (HDL) languages such as Verilog or VHDL was mandatory to describe the basic logic. On top of that language, all the logic needs then to be connected and then synchronized by a clock. This requires extremely specific skills very far from usual software coder knowledge.

Many companies have tried to build "compilers" or create new languages (SystemC, OpenCL, etc.) to allow application coders to use FPGAs efficiently, but they all "describe hardware" rather than "code software". For the past two years, we have finally begun to see "C/C++ code converters to HDL". These tools called HLS (High Level Synthesis) are much more than a simple language translator, because they essentially **analyze sequential code** by understanding the dependencies between the inputs and outputs of the functions **to be able to parallelize** the algorithm. This converter needs to target the FPGA specific resources so that the overall design takes up the least possible space in the component. The clocking of the logic is also checked at this level to ensure that the "timing" of the FPGA will be met. This ensures that the logic is fully synchronous otherwise the user may experience some unexpected bad results! These HLS tools are mainly delivered by FPGA manufacturers (Intel, Xilinx) or component design tools (Cadence, Mentor Graphics).

2.4 Improve the Whole "Storage - Network - CPU" Chain

It is interesting to highlight **for important aspects of FPGA** that are much different compared to classical CPU implementations:

- The **processor frequency** is 3 or 4 GHz while a GPU is clocked at about 1 GHz where FPGA runs at much lower frequency, in the 250 MHz range. The fact that we can create 'user' logic and duplicate it will allow to gain performance despite this lower frequency. N multiplications on a CPU require N clock cycles while a FPGA can perform all of them in a single clock cycle!
- The FPGA allows data to be stored in the card's local memory or get them directly from its external connectors. This can help bypassing the server network card to **reduce** latency, but also saves the server network cards bandwidth. Integrating an FPGA is not limited to "offload" a task but improves the entire chain **"external storage - network – memory – CPU"**.
- All external cards today mainly use the PCIe interface which is Gen3, and even Gen4 supported by POWER9. However, PCIe has a limited theoretical bandwidth of 8 GBps on Gen3 × 8 and 16 GBps with Gen4 × 8. **POWER9** has also a very **high bandwidth – low latency new interface named OpenCAPI** which use a 25 Gbps OpenCAPI Link and that gives an effective 22 GBps data flow with half the latency we had using PCIe Gen3 interface!
- A key point to have in mind also is that a FPGA, depending on the workload may offer **much better power consumption/performance ratio**, than GPUs or even CPUs.

2.5 The FPGA, More Performance but Too Many Constraints!

To summarize, a card containing an FPGA allows to:

- **Offload** a program usually running on the CPU, and therefore reduce the use of CPU time,
- **Accelerate** the offloaded function by optimized and parallelized logic,
- Take **advantage** of additional resources available on the FPGA board, thus reducing the use of server resources
- **Reduce** power consumption by optimizing the entire execution chain.
- Be programmed with advanced software languages such as C/C++

However the FPGA being outside the server implies **new constraints** which are not to be underestimated:

- Management of **data flows** to/from the external card. *This is an additional task to be coded in the calling application.*
- Management of **additional resources** brought by the FPGA card and unknown to the server. *This additional task must be coded in the function implemented in the FPGA.*
- Using a **card device driver** requires CPU time but also server memory resources.
- Tight dependency between the "hardware" function considered as a **slave** of the calling application.

3   With CAPI the FPGA Becomes a Processor Peer

3.1   The Solution Provided by CAPI

CAPI SNAP addresses these 4 last essential points so that a software developer can now:

- Use a FPGA with identical rights than all server processors. This means direct and consistent access to the server memory, autonomy, etc.
- Completely release the CPU and the memory used by the device driver as soon as the processing is offloaded.
- Speed up the code without learning a new language,
- Port the code with as little modification as possible

The developed solution is composed of 3 distinct elements:

- An **interface** integrated into processor chip which provides to an external card the rights to access the server memory as any of the processors of the server, and this without the need to use a software device driver. This interface named **CAPI** (Coherent Accelerator Processor Interface) was developed as part of the OpenPower foundation for the first time for the IBM POWER8 processor and has been improved for the POWER9 processor (available since the end of 2017). This ensure **coherency of the data** since no duplication of them are done by any software device driver.
- A "**framework**" allowing to give to software programmers a simple development environment so that they can port their applications to a FPGA card with logic built from their algorithm. **SNAP** (Storage, Networking, Analytics Programming) is an open-source framework addressing FPGA-based cards.
- A **FPGA card** PCIe based with different resources depending on the needs of the function to accelerate (Flash 2 TB, 4 GB of DDR4, 8 GB of DDR3, 2 ports 40 Gbps QSFP+, etc.).

A comparison between this FPGA approach and others can be summarized in Table 1.

Table 1. Accelerator types classification 1

	Separate private memory	Coherent shared memory
PCIe peripheral interconnect	Alpha data board 5 Microsoft catapult 6	IBM CAPI 9
Processor interconnect	N/A	Intel altera HARP (QPI) 7 Convey HC-1 (FSB) 8

3.2 CAPI/OpenCAPI Performances

Following SHA3 example is mainly using the FPGA internal logic using the bare mini-mum exchanges required to run a pure calculation task. What about memory exchanges? It is well known they can drastically reduce the overall FPGA task efficiency. The time required to read or store server memory information is critical. Pure PCI (non CAPI) techniques exist to manage moving data in big bursts. The goal is to avoid small data transfers which are considered very inefficient. However this requires extra architecture to prepare such large movements. **CAPI/OpenCAPI technology is removing these drawbacks, while offering full coherency**. It allows FPGA to access server memory just like any core would do, without requiring neither extra cache to synchronize data, nor software device driver. FPGA can operate as a master, meaning it can read or store data into server memory by itself without requiring any CPU operation.

OpenCAPI Link's offer bandwidth as high as 22 GBps on 8 lanes. This is obtained by reducing the overhead. High bandwidth is not only excellent on latest OpenCAPI technology, but also latency has been reduced. OpenCAPI can offer less than 400 ns total round trip latency which is overperforming on the market today.

Figures 3 and 4 present the performances of CAPI/OpenCAPI in terms of bandwidth and latency.

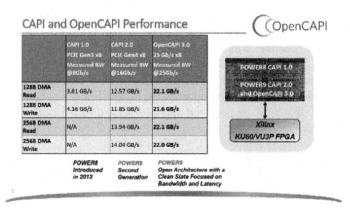

Fig. 3. CAPI/OpenCAPI bandwidth and latency results

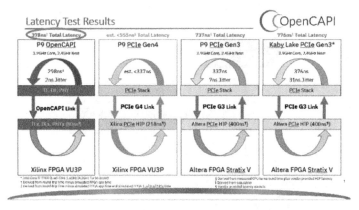

Fig. 4. CAPI/OpenCAPI bandwidth and latency results

3.3 A Partnership Development

This framework, developed in collaboration with IBM and its OpenPower partners, made possible to assemble the best technologies to achieve this innovative and powerful solution in an open-source environment. Figure 5 shows the main contributors of this ecosystem.

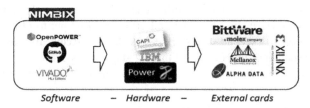

Fig. 5. SNAP ecosystem: from FPGA to cloud.

This simple and powerful solution is finally offered to application developers thanks to the integration of:

- the **CAPI interface** of the POWER processor
- an **FPGA**
- functions being programmed in C/C ++ thanks to **Vivado HLS**, the only HLS tool that we found that can be used without hardware skills,
- simple access the various resources, thanks to our **SNAP framework** containing APIs on application side and logic on the FPGA side that simplifies interfacing with this external card.

Fig. 6. Unique combination offering unprecedented FPGA acceleration solution.

4 SNAP Flow or How to Port a Function to a FPGA

4.1 Identify the Function to Port

Specifically, when a function within an application is identified as taking a **significant part of the CPU time** or is seen as a **bottleneck** of an execution chain, it is advisable to see how to optimize it. In a first step, all efforts will be put to offload it from the server to the FPGA. In a second step, work will be done to **accelerate** it and get superior results. Before spending time on any of these 2 steps, users can very quickly evaluate the processing time that they can expect of their function executed on a FPGA.

4.2 Porting the Function to the FPGA

CAPI/OpenCAPI interface provides to the FPGA a direct access to the memory of the server. Remember that the function in the FPGA just needs to know the address where the data are located, and it will go and fetch the data by itself without the help of the application and of a driver. This will ease the porting of the function since data are fetched when needed and not copied to the FPGA memory by default.

This porting will be done in 4 phases:

(1) **Separation** of the "function to offload" from the "calling application". Then integration of the application and this "software" function into the SNAP framework.
(2) **Adaptation** of the "function to offload" from "software" to "hardware". Then simulation in the SNAP environment with a model of the CAPI/OpenCAPI interface of the POWER processor
(3) **Execution** of the "hardware" "function to offload". Then performance measurement on a FPGA Card plugged in an IBM POWER Systems Server
(4) Code **optimization** to get the best performance.

Note that the "software" function is executed on the CPU, as opposed to the "hard-ware" function that is run on the FPGA. These 2 functions are intentionally kept in parallel to measure comparative performances but also to make it easier to locate and debug any errors that may be encountered.

4.3 SNAP Environment

Once the open-source SNAP framework 10 is installed, the function in C/C++ to be offloaded is first **compiled** with Xilinx's "Vivado HLS" tool which will generate HDL code describing the FPGA understandable logic. Some compilation issues may happen due to some constraints, mainly due to the lack of operating system on the FPGA and access to data in memory. This will require some adaptations in code: circumvent system calls, replace dynamic allocations of memory by fixed allocation, etc.

Once compiled the code of the function, it is necessary to **adapt the application** so that it can interface with the function. In other words, the application will have to call a function which may be anywhere on a FPGA card. Indeed, the SNAP framework can effectively manage several cards per server but also several "actions" by cards. SNAP will so first initiate once the discovery of all cards of a system to get and handle he list of all the actions available in the server. This is mandatory to assign, or queue, a request made by an application to access an action.

The code of the application must therefore contain the **attachment** of the **card** and the **action** as follows:

```
card = snap_card_alloc_dev(device, VENDOR_ID, DEVICE_ID);
action = snap_attach_action(card, HELLOWORLD_ACTION_TYPE,
     (SNAP_ACTION_DONE_IRQ | SNAP_ATTACH_IRQ), timeout);
.../...
snap_detach_action(action);
snap_card_free(card);
```

The interfacing between the calling application and the function is done through 2 channels:

- a **register structure** to exchange asynchronously a limited number of parameters (**MMIO**) and
- the **memory area** of the server to exchange a large amount of data. Only the address of this zone will be given in the registers.

4.4 APIs to Facilitate the Management of the FPGA

The very limited number of APIs allows you to exchange as below:

```
    /* to read and write a FPGA register through input or output
structures */
mjob_in->chk_in = chk_in_value;
mjob_out->chk_out = 0x0;

snap_job_set(cjob,     mjob_in,     sizeof(*mjob_in),     mjob_out,
sizeof(*mjob_out));

    /* to send the server memory area address where data are lo-
cated */
snap_addr_set(&mjob->out, addr_out, size_out, type_out, FLAGS);

/* to start the function in the FPGA */
rc = snap_action_sync_execute_job(action, &cjob, timeout);
```

Let's keep in mind that the function in the FPGA is completely autonomous. The paradigm of passing arguments to a function, moving data to the function and waiting for the result before progressing further has changed with CAPI. Indeed, the application has just now to **configure** the function by setting some registers and just tell the function to **start**. The results will be available directly in server memory when the application needs it. The application can be informed by an **interrupt** that the job is completed **or read the status** of the execution in the function registers, **or** also **poll** the result availability in the server memory.

4.5 Architecture Built Around Testing

To easily help localizing an issue, a three steps SNAP process has been setup, as shown on Fig. 6. Each step of the flow allows to make simple modifications that can be checked to secure progress. Note that Xilinx development tools are not yet available on POWER, hence X86 server usage for first steps.

Once this code is compiled, it can be simulated to verify that these changes did not alter the functionality of the code. The test of this code is then like the test of a classic C code with "printf", but the coder can also very easily check the exchanges between the application and the function by adding a "trace" option before the call of the application.

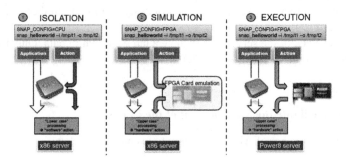

Fig. 7. Three steps process to externalize an action.

```
SNAP_TRACE=0xF     snap_helloworld -i t1 -o t2
.../...
R   hw_snap_mmio_write32(0x22c4010, f100, f0020100)
R   hw_snap_mmio_write32(0x22c4010, f104, 0)
R   hw_snap_mmio_write32(0x22c4010, f108, c0febabe)
R   hw_snap_mmio_write32(0x22c4010, f10c, deadbeef)
R   hw_snap_mmio_read32(0x22c4010, f000, 6) 0
.../...
```

The final code, which is the binary program of the function executed into the FPGA, can then be generated and executed.

Today, (in addition to traditional HDL languages,) the language supported by the SNAP framework is C/C ++ thanks to Xilinx's "Vivado HLS" tool. There is research being done in order to support other languages such as Go, but C/C ++ often remains as the standard that today allows to have a multitude of gateways from/to other languages such as Java with JNI, Arrow from Apache and many others.

5   SHA3 Example

Now that you have a good overview of SNAP, we will demonstrate its application on an actual example of implementing a SHA3 benchmark [11] coded in C [12] and porting it on SNAP. The whole process was run in less than 3 working weeks (11 working days) on a KU60 Xilinx FPGA available on a AlphaData ADKU3 board [13], running on a POWER8 server. The different steps and associated schedule have been summarized in the following Table 2:

Table 2. SHA3 Porting Steps

Sponge code porting into SNAP and optimizing	2-Mar	3-Mar	4-Mar	5-Mar	6-Mar	7-Mar	8-Mar	9-Mar	10-Mar	11-Mar	12-Mar	13-Mar	14-Mar	15-Mar	16-Mar
Have Sponge code synthesized without SNAP	x	x													
Integrate Sponge with SNAP and get a first performance result					x	x									
Performance measurements on FPGA and CPU							x	x	x			x	x	x	x
Optimize Sponge code (speed, area, loops...)						x	x	x	x			x	x	x	x

The first step was to successively compile the C code with the HLS C compiler. After having corrected some few lines to circumvent system calls and replaced dynamic memory allocation, we were able to measure the latency of the mathematical function.

The first latency measurement of the function was 438×4 ns $= 1.75$ µs. As the whole benchmark is made of 65,536 by 100,000 by 24 loops, this means that this SHA3 function requires 76.57 h to compute 6.553.600.000 keys without optimization!

Multiple experiments using specific compiler directives names (like *"#pragma HLS PIPELINE"* to avoid serializing processes [14]) were tested in various locations, to understand where, in the C code, we could get better performance results while monitoring the size of the logic created by the compiler for the algorithm. Very quickly, we were able to find that adding this directive was reducing the latency by a factor 219, meaning that the whole SHA3 mathematical function could be done in 8 ns (versus 1.75 µs). This timing of the elementary loop is related to the numbers of clocks ticks required for task execution and is a deterministic value.

As this result was promising enough, we started inserting the code through the SNAP flow and formalism. This example was basic enough to not move any data to/from the FPGA, so we just had to define the registers to pass calculation parameters and get some key results enough to manage and monitor the benchmark. Figure 7 shows the main blocs of the SHA3 Acceleration (Fig. 8).

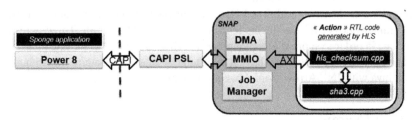

Fig. 8. PSL (P8) or CAPI-BSP (P9) interconnects SNAP and server

Once all the C code inserted into SNAP, we were able to check that the "8 ns latency" found during first evaluation was still met. The second step was to identify the loops that could be parallelized. Adding a directive "#pragma HLS UNROLL factor = 32" [14] constrained the main loop to be duplicated 32 times, meaning able to process the function 32 times in parallel (hence the KU060-32 name of the part). This value of 32 was determined by the maximum size of the logic we were able to put in the FPGA. The new performance measured was now down to … 43 s (versus 76.57 h)!

Some performances tests were performed using multi-threading on the 160 threads of a 20-core server. Table 3 shows results. The last lines shows a factor 35 gain for FPGA compared to CPU computation under heavy load.

Table 3. SHA3 FPGA vs multithread computation comparison

	slices/32	CPU (antipode) 20 cores - 160 threads	FPGA speedup vs CPU
	FPGA KU060-32//	System P	
Computed keys	(msec)	(msec)	
100 000	21	669	31
200 000	21	676	32
400 000	21	819	38
800 000	21	925	43
1 600 000	21	1 018	47
3 200 000	22	1 260	57
12 800 000	85	3 460	41
409 600 000	2 715	95 975	35
819 200 000	5 429	190 347	35
3 276 700 000	21 709	754 198	35
6 553 600 000	43 418	1 505 790	35

Note that until 32 parallel computation blocks are used the time required is stable, but absolute performance suffers.

Depending on the code and the data move, performance can really be outstanding. Thanks to the whole SNAP environment, a quick evaluation and porting can be done. This prevents spending too much time on tuning an algorithm in the FPGA.

6 Conclusion

We have presented a complete FPGA acceleration enablement path based on a simple calculation example. This path relies on HLS, CAPI/OpenCAPI and SNAP framework whose details have been discussed to allow software engineers to discover and efficiently use this technology on OpenPower architectures.

More information on: **ibm.biz/powercapi_snap** or https://developer.ibm.com/linuxonpower/capi/snap/.

Question or information: write to: **capi@us.ibm.com**.

References

1. Peltenburg, J., van Straten, J., Brobbel, M., Hofstee, H.P., Al-Ars, Z.: Supporting columnar in-memory formats on FPGA: the hardware design of fletcher for apache arrow. In: Hochberger, C., Nelson, B., Koch, A., Woods, R., Diniz, P. (eds.) ARC 2019. LNCS, vol. 11444, pp. 32–47. Springer, Cham (2019). https://doi.org/10.1007/978-3-030-17227-5_3
2. https://github.com/open-power/snap/tree/master/actions/hls_scatter_gather
3. Diamantopoulos, D., et al.: Energy efficient coherent transprecision accelerators—the bidirectional long short-term memory neural network case (2018) https://doi.org/10.1109/coolchips.2018.8373077
4. Choi, Y.K., et al.: A quantitative analysis on microarchitectures of modern CPU-FPGA platforms. In: 2016 53nd ACM/EDAC/IEEE Design Automation Conference (DAC). IEEE (2016)
5. SDAccel development environment. http://www.xilinx.com/products/design-tools/software-zone/sdaccel.html
6. Putnam, A., et al.: A reconfigurable fabric for accelerating large-scale datacenter services. In: ISCA (2014)
7. Intel, Intel quickpath interconnect fpga core cache interface specification
8. Brewer, T.M.: Instruction set innovations for the convey hc-1 computer. IEEE Micro **2**, 70–79 (2010)
9. Stuecheli, J., et al.: CAPI: a coherent accelerator processor interface. IBM J. Res. Dev. **59**(1), 7:1–7:7 (2015)
10. SNAP github website. https://github.com/open-power/snap
11. Very small, readable implementation of the SHA3 hash function. https://github.com/mjosaarinen/tiny_sha3
12. SHA3 SNAP implementation. https://github.com/open-power/snap/tree/master/actions/hls_sponge
13. Alpha-Data ADM-PCIE-KU3 board information. http://www.alpha-data.com/dcp/products.php?product=adm-pcie-ku3
14. Vivado Design Suite User Guide - High-Level Synthesis. https://www.xilinx.com/support/documentation/sw_manuals/xilinx2018_3/ug902-vivado-high-level-synthesis.pdf

Scaling the Summit: Deploying the World's Fastest Supercomputer

Verónica G. Vergara Larrea$^{(\boxtimes)}$, Wayne Joubert, Michael J. Brim,
Reuben D. Budiardja, Don Maxwell, Matt Ezell, Christopher Zimmer,
Swen Boehm, Wael Elwasif, Sarp Oral, Chris Fuson, Daniel Pelfrey,
Oscar Hernandez, Dustin Leverman, Jesse Hanley, Mark Berrill,
and Arnold Tharrington

National Center for Computational Sciences, Oak Ridge National Laboratory,
Oak Ridge, TN, USA
`vergaravg@ornl.gov`

Abstract. Summit, the latest flagship supercomputer deployed at Oak Ridge Leadership Computing Facility (OLCF), became the number one system in the TOP500 [17] list in June 2018 and retained its top spot in the November 2018 list. An extensive acceptance test plan was developed to evaluate the unique features introduced in the Summit architecture and system software stack. The acceptance test also includes tests to ensure that the system is reliable, stable, and performant.

Keywords: Large-scale system testing · High performance computing

1 Introduction

The United States Department of Energy's Collaboration of Oak Ridge, Argonne, and Livermore National Laboratories (CORAL) project started in 2012 with the goal to procure and deploy up to three pre-exascale systems by 2018. These systems were designed to provide world-class speed and capability to the computing community, advance the Department of Energy's mission, and achieve a necessary step towards exascale.

© Springer Nature Switzerland AG 2019
M. Weiland et al. (Eds.): ISC 2019 Workshops, LNCS 11887, pp. 330–351, 2019.
https://doi.org/10.1007/978-3-030-34356-9_26

Oak Ridge National Laboratory (ORNL) and Lawrence Livermore National Laboratory (LLNL) selected IBM POWER-based systems with NVIDIA accelerators, and Argonne National Laboratory (ANL) selected an Intel-based system.

In June 2018, ORNL's system, Summit [15], became the fastest supercomputer in the world as measured by the TOP500 [17] organization. The Summit system not only achieved the highest High Performance Computing Linpack Benchmark (HPL) number, but also took the top spot in the 10th HPCG Performance list [1], and the number three spot in the Green 500 [9] November 2018 list. Furthermore, five of six SC18 Gordon Bell award finalists used Summit, including the two winners.

Due to the scale and complexity of the Summit system, the Oak Ridge Leadership Computing Facility (OLCF) developed a thorough acceptance test (AT) plan that both verified performance targets of individual hardware as well as determined the system's readiness to support the OLCF's user programs by conducting tests of all major components of the system software stack. The AT plan includes four distinct test elements: hardware test (HW), functionality test (FT), performance test (PT), and stability test (ST).

In this work, we describe the multi-month process of the Summit deployment which includes acceptance test plan design, test development and validation, Summit's acceptance phases, and the description of several issues, lessons learned, and best practices uncovered along the way.

2 System Architecture

2.1 Summit

The Summit supercomputer consists of 4,608 AC922 compute nodes each with two 22-core POWER9 (P9) processors and six NVIDIA Tesla V100 (Volta) GPUs. NVLink 2.0 buses with 50 GB/s peak bandwidth connect each POWER9 to three V100s, and each of the three GPUs to one another (see Fig. 1 for connection details). The V100 GPU peak single (double) precision performance is approximately 14 (7) TF, and peak memory bandwidth is 900 GB/s. Each node contains 512 GB DDR4 main memory, and each GPU has 16 GB HBM2 memory. The nodes are connected to two rails of a Mellanox EDR InfiniBand fat tree interconnect. Each node includes a 1.6 TB NVMe device for use as node-local storage. For shared storage Summit is connected to Alpine, the center-wide GPFS file system.

2.2 File Systems

Two different file systems were used during acceptance test: Alpine Test and Development System (AlpineTDS) and Alpine. AlpineTDS was deployed to provide a sandbox environment for testing software, firmware, and configuration changes before they are applied to the main production file system, Alpine. AlpineTDS consists of an IBM Elastic Storage Server (ESS) GL4, which is the basic building block for Alpine. There are 77 GL4s deployed and configured as

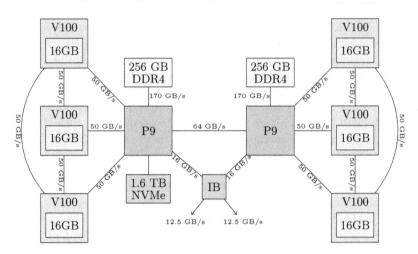

Fig. 1. Summit node architecture

a single POSIX namespace in Alpine. AlpineTDS is a standalone system and is configured as a separate POSIX namespace.

Each GL4 has four 106-port disk enclosures, connected to two Network Shared Disk (NSD) I/O servers with POWER9 CPUs. The NSD servers act as a failover pair. The disk enclosures are connected to NSD servers via 12 Gbps SAS links. Each GL4 has 422 10 TB Near-Line SAS disks. These are organized in two Redundancy Groups (RG), each with 211 disks. The software-based distributed parity RAID services (GPFS Native RAID engine - GNR) running on the NSD servers use an 8+2 RAID 6 scheme built atop of these RGs.

AlpineTDS provides roughly 3 PB usable capacity and performs at around 35 GB/s for large-block sequential read and write I/O operations. Alpine provides 250 PB usable capacity and performs at 2.5 TB/s for large-block sequential reads and writes.

To streamline the Summit acceptance activities, AlpineTDS was deployed and configured first and presented to Summit as a POSIX mountpoint. This allowed more time to properly deploy, configure, test, and validate the Alpine file system without impeding Summit acceptance activities.

3   Acceptance Test

In addition to Summit, the last two supercomputers that the OLCF has successfully deployed, Jaguar [20] and Titan [25], have been ranked number one on the TOP500 [17] list. Summit's acceptance test followed the same methodology used for both Titan and Jaguar. The objective for any OLCF acceptance is to develop a set of tests that represent the current OLCF application portfolio and that can adequately simulate the expected production workload.

Summit's acceptance was conducted in two phases: (i) Summit Phase 1 (SP1) included 1,080 compute nodes (60 racks) and was completed in December 2017;

and (ii) Summit Phase 2 (SP2) used the full system (256 racks) and was completed in November 2018. Concurrent to both phases, we also executed acceptance of the AlpineTDS and Alpine GPFS file systems.

The AT plan includes four distinct test elements: hardware test (HW), functionality test (FT), performance test (PT), and stability test (ST). SP1 included the following elements: HW, FT, and 3-day ST. SP2 included the following elements: HW, FT, PT, and 14-day ST. AlpineTDS was used for SP1 and for the FT of SP2. Alpine was used for PT and ST of SP2.

Each AT element has specific entry and exit criteria that must be successfully met before the next element can begin. At the entry to each AT element, all compute nodes that will be used in testing must be online and available. In addition, during an AT element, the system software must remain unchanged.

Throughout acceptance, any issue or test failure encountered is documented and a bug is filed with the vendor. The severity of each issue is classified following the definitions shown in Table 1. If a Severity 1 or Severity 2 issue is opened during an AT element, the element cannot be concluded until a fix or workaround is identified.

Table 1. Defect severity classification

Severity level	Priority	Description
Severity 1	Highest	Complete failure of the system, a subsystem, or a unit within the system. Application results that fail to meet correctness criteria
Severity 2	High	Service is partially interrupted or impaired with significant impact to the AT. Any Sev 1 problems that can be circumvented
Severity 3	Medium	A problem that impacts specific tests but that does not interfere with the AT. Node failures that cause a running job to terminate abnormally
Severity 4	Low	A problem that has little or no impact on users and can be bypassed easily

Hardware Test (HW). The HW consists of complete hardware diagnostics executed by the vendor to ensure that individual parts meet the manufacturer's specifications. The results from HW are provided to ORNL staff for review and archival. The HW element includes diagnostics designed to measure the performance of each POWER9 CPU and each V100 GPU on the system. As part of HW, the vendor also executes the High Performance Computing Linpack Benchmark (HPL) benchmark [29].

The HW also verifies that telemetry data from various components is available. It is critical to be able to monitor power, temperature, and utilization of the system in real-time in order to automatically adjust different support systems (e.g., water temperature, chillers). For that reason, during HW we also verify that telemetry data can be collected with reasonable performance.

The HW also includes system administration tasks commonly needed in production. First, the full system is rebooted twice to ensure that it can be put back into production in a reasonable amount of time. Then, a collection of multi-node jobs, each running a simple MPI application, is started until the entire system is occupied. A node failure is then simulated, and the test is considered successful if the failure only impacts the job that was allocated on that node. Finally, the HW also includes thermal protection and emergency power off (EPO) tests.

Functionality Test (FT). The FT demonstrates that basic hardware and software functionality meet essential requirements. The FT includes tests to evaluate the functionality of the application launcher, the scheduler and resource manager, advanced network features, burst buffer, compilers, math and I/O libraries, MPI implementation, and tools. To accomplish this goal a set of benchmarks, mini-applications (miniapps), and real-world applications is used. These were selected to ensure high coverage of features commonly used by scientific application developers. Table 2 summarizes the codes used during the FT phase and each code's test objectives.

During FT, each code is compiled with each applicable compiler. Then, a single job for each unique test is submitted. Once each test has completed successfully at least once, the entire set of tests is launched continuously for a period of at least 8 hours. During that period, any job failure is investigated and classified. The test phase is considered complete if there are no job failures, or in the event that there are failures, if the root cause for each failure has been identified and a remediation or a fix exists.

Performance Test (PT). The PT demonstrates that the system hardware and software meet performance and scalability requirements of the CORAL Benchmarks suite [3] defined in the contract with the vendor.

During PT, each test is executed in isolation to minimize disruptions or activity on the system that could negatively impact performance. For that reason, only a subset of test codes is used for this AT element. Individual performance metrics are collected for each test and later used to measure runtime variability under a realistic workload during the ST.

In addition, the results obtained for the CORAL Benchmarks from the vendor at HW are verified to ensure that the reported metrics are reproducible, and the scalability requirements in the contract were met. Table 8 summarizes the figures of merit obtained for each individual benchmark.

Stability Test (ST). The ST demonstrates stability across a mix of simulated code development activity and production simulations. The OLCF test harness [31] is used to fill the entire system with test jobs that vary in terms of

Table 2. FT benchmarks, miniapps, and applications

Test	Description
ALCF MPI Benchmarks	MPI bandwidth and latency
AMG[a]	Parallel algebraic multigrid solver for linear systems
CAM-SE[a]	Atmospheric climate modeling code
CUDA & GPU Direct tests	CUDA, CUDA Fortran, CUDA MPS, and GPU Direct
Chroma	QCD application
E3SM (formerly ACME)	Energy Exascale Earth System Model
GTC[d]	Gyrokinetic 3D particle-in-cell application
HACC[b,d]	Extreme-scale cosmological simulation application
Intel MPI Benchmarks	MPI bandwidth and latency
LAMMPS	Molecular dynamics application
LSMS[b,c]	Locally Self-consistent Multiple Scattering application
LULESH[a]	Shock hydrodynamics miniapp
MCB[a]	Monte Carlo benchmark
Minisweep	Radiation transport miniapp with OpenMP 3.1 and CUDA support
NAMD[a,c,d]	Molecular dynamics application
NUCCOR kernels	Nuclear physics miniapp; DLA operations using: LAPACK, OpenBLAS, ESSL; programming models: OpenMP 3.1, OpenMP 4.5, OpenACC
Nekbone[b]	Simulates Nek5000
NVLink Tests	CPU↔GPU, GPU↔GPU bandwidth
NWCHEM[d]	Computational chemistry application
OpenMP 3.1 verification and validation	OpenMP 3.1 specification
OpenMP 4.5 verification and validation	OpenMP 4.5 specification

(*continued*)

Table 2. (*continued*)

Test	Description
OpenACC verification and validation	OpenACC specification
Profugus	Radiation transport miniapp; proxy application for Shift
QBOX[b]	First-principles molecular dynamics application
QMCPACK[a,d]	Quantum Monte Carlo simulation code
ScaLAPACK tests	Parallel dense linear algebra (DLA) operations
SNAP[a]	Proxy application for PARTISN
SPEC OMP2012	OpenMP 3.1 functionality and performance
SPEC ACCEL ACC suite	OpenACC 1.0 functionality and performance
SPEC ACCEL OMP suite	OpenMP 4.5 functionality and performance
STRIDE	Stress test for the memory subsystem
STREAM & GPU-STREAM	Measures memory bandwidth
UMT[a]	Radiation transport mimniapp
XRayTrace	Ray propagation miniapp; uses: C++11 threads, OpenMP, OpenACC, CUDA

[a] CORAL Throughput benchmark.
[b] CORAL Scalable benchmark.
[c] CORAL benchmark and upstream versions used.
[d] CAAR version was not used as it was in development.

number of nodes used and runtime. The executable for each test is built on the system right before its job is submitted, which mirrors normal user behavior. The mixed workload includes benchmarks, miniapps, and real scientific applications selected from the OLCF portfolio.

ST is executed continuously for a predetermined length of time. For Summit Phase 1, a 72 hours ST was executed. For Summit Phase 2, which included the full system, ST was required to be executed for 336 hours without any Severity 1 or Severity 2 failures. ST requires the following criteria:

- **Pass rate:** 95% of jobs executed complete successfully.
- **Correctness:** 100% of jobs that complete must produce correct results.
- **Availability:** 95% of resources must be available at least 90% of the time.

4   Alpine Acceptance

A large-scale file system deployment and acceptance is a complex effort and requires careful resource planning to manage the internal (file system specific) and external dependencies (network and clients). Alpine is no exception considering the sheer number of components: 32,494 disks, 154 NSD servers, and 40 InfiniBand top-of-rack (TOR) and 10 Ethernet switches.

To simplify the acceptance process the deployment and acceptance team divided the work into manageable subgroups, where the same acceptance tests can be run in parallel in a repetitive manner over multiple subgroups. Each subgroup consisted of eight GL4s arranged in four racks. A series of basic functionality tests was conducted on each subgroup. These included configuring and verifying RGs and building individual and standalone POSIX namespaces on each GL4. Once each namespace was verified for correctness, the performance of each GL4 was tested and verified for sequential and random write and read I/O patterns followed by a metadata test.

Individual performance tests on each GL4 allowed the team to quickly build a performance profile and establish a baseline for comparing each unit's performance. Often, lower performance of a storage unit is a clear indication of a fault within the unit, and it is common for a storage system to have multiple faults at initial deployment. After identifying and clearing out faults on units, the team scaled up the namespace on each subgroup independently. This was the team's first scale up experience with IBM Spectrum Scale technology. Performance tests were again conducted on each subgroup to make sure there were no problems at each scaling level.

After enough subgroups were scaled up and verified for performance, a larger scale namespace was built consisting of half of the available storage hardware. Again, performance was measured and verified to ensure that the scaling results were within expected parameters. Finally, after all subgroups were cleared of problems, a full-scale namespace was built on all Alpine hardware. Correctness was tested and verified. Using roughly 600 Summit compute nodes, the first full-scale performance test was conducted, using sequential and random I/O workloads for write and read operations with 32 MB and 16 MB I/O sizes. The metadata performance with 32 KB write operations and file creation performance on a single shared directory were also tested according to the acceptance test plan.

Lastly, a 2-week stability test was conducted to make sure Alpine was able to stay operational under load and ride out any errors without a downtime. This test overlapped with Summit's ST. During this period, a known I/O pattern was issued from a limited number of Summit compute nodes while the remaining nodes generated a regular production I/O workload against Alpine during execution of acceptance codes.

Table 3 shows the results of Alpine acceptance testing. As shown in Table 3, the file I/O performance at scale was satisfactory. Improvements to metadata performance are expected in late 2019.

Table 3. Summary of Alpine at-scale acceptance performance testing.

Acceptance test description	Results
Sequential IOR write/read for 20 min	2.476 TB/s write (mean)
	2.723 TB/s read (mean)
Random IOR write/read for 20 min	2.381 TB/s write (mean)
	3.072 TB/s read (mean)
32 KiB creates for 20 min using IOR	607.007K creates/s (mean)
Run mdtest for 20 s in single shared directory	25.465K creates (mean)
Run IOR on a single node single thread for 20 min	10.126 GB/s write (mean)
	6.404 GB/s read (mean)
Run IOR on a single node multi thread for 20 min	13.708 GB/s write (mean)
	14.415 GB/s read (mean)

5 Summit Phase 2 Acceptance

Summit Phase 2 acceptance (SP2) included all acceptance test elements: HW, FT, PT, and a 336 hours ST. In this section, we describe the each element and present a summary of the results obtained.

5.1 Hardware Test (HW)

The vendor completed the delivery and installation of all 4,608 compute nodes on August 4, 2018. On August 30, 2018 the IBM HPC Software Stack (HPC SW) that was targeted for acceptance was released. The HPC SW included the full stack as shown in Table 4.

Table 4. IBM HPC software stack evolution

Feature	Product	Aug. 2018	Dec. 2018	Production	Vendor
Batch Scheduler	Spectrum LSF	10.1.0.6	10.1.0.6[b]	10.1.0.7[a]	IBM
	Job Step Manager	10.2.0.7	10.2.0.10	10.2.0.11	IBM
MPI Library	Spectrum MPI	10.2.0.7	10.2.0.10	10.2.0.11	IBM
Math Libraries	ESSL	6.1.0.1	6.1.0.2	6.1.0.2	IBM
Compilers	XL C/C++	16.1.0	16.1.1-1	16.1.1-2	IBM
	XL Fortran	16.1.0	16.1.1-1	16.1.1-2	IBM
	PGI	18.7	18.10-1	19.1	PGI
	clang[c]	5.X	5.X	5.X	IBM
	GCC	4.8.5	4.8.5	4.8.5	RedHat
CUDA Support	CUDA Toolkit	9.2.148.1-1	9.2.148.1-1	9.2.148.1-1	NVIDIA
	CUDA Driver	396.47	396.64	396.64	NVIDIA
Parallel File System	Spectrum scale (GPFS)	5.3.1 eFix 14	5.0.1-2 efix 7	5.0.1-2 efix 8	IBM

[a] CAAR version was not used as it was in development.
[b] Patched version.
[c] IBM branch.

5.2   Functionality Test (FT)

There are two types of tests in FT: ones that must be executed successfully on every single compute node, and those that must be executed successfully at least once. The set of "every node" tests includes GPU specific tests to evaluate correct functionality of NVLink, GPU_Direct, CUDA libraries, MPI benchmark tests, and memory bandwidth tests for both CPU and GPU memory.

Once the "every node" tests were completed and we verified that the hardware was healthy, we continued to execute the full set of FT tests.

GPU Tests: To verify that both the accelerator hardware (V100s) and the accelerator software (CUDA Driver and CUDA Toolkit) were functioning correctly, we used tests derived from samples included in the CUDA Toolkit 9.0 release. The CUDA tests executed are shown in Table 5.

Table 5. Tests used from samples provided with CUDA Toolkit 9.0.

Feature	Samples test
CUDA	UnifiedMemoryStreams, UnifiedMemoryStreams_GPU_Direct, asyncAPI, batchCUBLAS, concurrentKernels, conjugateGradient, cppIntegration, cudaOpenMP, inlinePTX_nvrtc, radixSortThrust, simpleCUFFT_MGPU, simpleHyperQ, simpleIPC, simpleMPI_MPS, simpleMultiCopy, simpleP2P
GPU Direct	Collective, Pingpong, Stencil
NVLink	p2pBandwidthLatencyTest, simpleP2P, bandwidthTest

Some of the samples were modified to use Multi-Process Service (MPS), CUDA Fortran, GPU Direct, and managed memory. The GPU Direct tests uncovered an issue that prevented direct device-device communication due to the use of cgroups to delineate resource sets. Without this capability, applications cannot take advantage of the fast NVLink interconnect. To work around this issue, the -step_cgroup n option had to be used when submitting a batch job to disable job step cgroups. Then, the CUDA_VISIBLE_DEVICES environment variable was needed to assign GPUs to specific tasks in the job. A fix for this issue is expected in the upcoming software stack release.

The NVLink tests measure data transfer bandwidth and latency for GPU-to-GPU and GPU-to-CPU memory copies, which we refer to as "device-device" and "host-device" respectively. Both forms of memory copies utilize the NVLink 2.0 buses that connect the V100 GPUs and POWER9 CPU, and cross-socket data copies additionally traverse the CPU X-Bus. To fully evaluate node functionality, a variety of GPU memory copy operation modes were used, including with/without peer-to-peer (P2P) for device-device copies and with/without unified memory (UVA) for host-device copies. The programs p2pBandwidthLatencyTest and simpleP2P were used for device-device tests, and bandwidthTest for host-device tests. The host-device test was modified to support unified memory using the cudaMallocManaged() memory allocation API. Although these tests were primarily functionality oriented, they were also useful for understanding relative performance of the various memory copy modes. As expected, direct copies using CUDA were faster than using UVA, and for device-device copies, P2P reduced latency and provided a substantial performance boost. The performance baselines for the tests were 46 GB/s per direction for device-device P2P copies, and 240 GB/s for host-device CUDA copies involving all six GPUs. The tests were also useful for identifying misbehaving hardware, such as slow GPUs/HBM, misconfigured P2P, and occasionally stray processes leftover from previous jobs that were not properly removed.

MPI Tests: To evaluate the Spectrum MPI implementation we used the Intel MPI Benchmarks (IMB) [10] to verify correct functionality and measure the performance provided by this new implementation. In addition, we used an in-house developed benchmark called kickstart to measure application launch time.

IMB test results identified performance issues that caused early timeouts, particularly at scale when using a high number of processes per node (PPN). Upgrades to the stack allowed successful resolution of several performance issues.

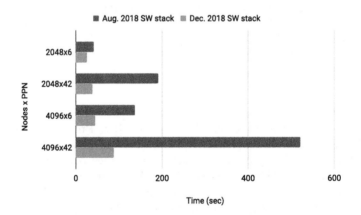

Fig. 2. Application launch times on Summit.

Figure 2 shows a comparison of the results obtained from running kickstart on Summit using the initial acceptance stack versus the next release. Initially, the job step launcher did not allow full system jobs to launch at a reasonable time. The Dec. 2018 SW stack resolved these performance issues.

In addition, with the Aug. 2018 SW stack, we observed that job steps could not be launched when using 168 PPNs (the maximum value possible that utilizes all hardware threads). The root cause was tracked down to a bug in PMIx which caused the job step to fail.

Memory Bandwidth Tests: The stream [14] and gpu-stream [13] functionality tests measure memory bandwidth for four basic computational kernels with streaming vector access patterns: copy, scale, sum, and triad. All four patterns exercise both streaming loads and stores. These tests ensure that each node meets our specified bandwidth targets: 266 GB/s for CPU memory (all patterns), 765 GB/s for GPU copy/scale, and 810 GB/s for GPU sum/triad. For CPU memory bandwith gathered using stream, the test used a single process per node with 42 OpenMP threads (i.e., one thread per CPU core across both sockets). GPU memory bandwith was measured by the CUDA implementation of gpu-stream, which ran with one process per GPU.

InfiniBand Network Tests: Acceptance of the InfiniBand network helped validate the proposed performance of the network and identify several issues resulting in the replacement of equipment and software updates. Most notably, we used MPIGraph [11] to test the aggregate system bandwidth when Adaptive Routing is enabled. MPIGraph uses a single rank per node measuring send and receive bandwidth in a ring communication pattern. The ring monotonically increases the rank distance after each phase until all ranks have communicated with every other rank. The output from MPIGraph shows bandwidth measured from/to all nodes. Using tools to visualize this bandwidth over successive runs it became clear that particular senders and receivers had distinct performance bottlenecks imposing upon their measurements. Using the exact locations of the nodes participating, we identified that a particular switch was underperforming, leading to the replacement of this switch. Subsequent measurements showed improved performance and the elimination of the performance degradations. Our results show that Summit's network can achieve a bisection bandwidth of 95 TiB/s. The latency experiments showed a latency of 1.3 μs for 0B messages, 3.54 μs for 4 KB messages, and 12.67 μs for 64 KB messages.

Another area of improvement identified in network acceptance was in the measurement of hardware accelerated collectives. Using collective benchmark suites including the OSU Microbenchmarks and the ALCF MPI Benchmark suite, we validated that the hardware accelerated collectives met performance targets. Our testing identified several issues including performance degradation and application crashes associated with Spectrum MPI and the Mellanox HCOLL library. The Spectrum MPI implementation contains its own software collective library that must be bypassed in order to use SHARP collectives. In one particular case we found that using 32 or more PPN at large scale resulted in consistent application segmentation faults. Working with our vendors we have mostly remedied these functionality and performance related issues.

Ethernet Network Tests: During Summit's installation, we started noticing intermittent network performance issues. As the number of nodes increased, the problem became worse. Testing confirmed that traffic going from the compute nodes (1 GigE) to the management hosts (10/40 GigE) worked as expected. However, traffic from the management hosts to the compute nodes would intermittently hang and timeout. Packet captures confirmed that data from the management nodes was not reaching the compute nodes.

The Mellanox SX 1024 switches that were originally installed only had 4.6 MB buffers. The 10 GigE ports on these switches are allocated a maximum of 64 KB [33]. This limit was generating a large amount of microbursts. Network microbursts are difficult to detect and can result in dropped packets when buffers are exhausted. These can occur with network oversubscription, speed mismatches, unicast and broadcast flooding. These Ethernet switches did not have adequate buffers to handle microbursts and would frequently drop packets. Ultimately, they were replaced with switches that had larger buffers.

System Software Tests: Given that several components of the IBM HPC SW stack were brand new and developed specifically for the CORAL systems, close coordination and testing with IBM was needed to stabilize the products.

The batch workload manager and job launcher work together to allocate and limit compute resources and are key components to system management and usability. IBM's Spectrum Load Sharing Facility (LSF) provides workload management. The LSF development team worked closely with the OLCF to test and modify the existing LSF product to ensure functionality requirements were met. For example, as part of the OLCF leadership computing mandate, batch jobs requesting large portions of the system's compute resources are prioritized above jobs requesting smaller portions of the system's compute resources. The LSF development team was able to provide a method that, when combined with a submission script maintained by the OLCF, allows batch job limits and priorities to be placed on a batch job based on its requested amount of nodes. To help control batch queue throughput, the center limits the number of jobs each project member can have in a running state as well as an eligible to run state. Batch jobs are considered to be in a running state when LSF has allocated the requested compute resources. Batch jobs considered to be in an eligible to run state have not been allocated, but are eligible for allocation as resources become available. LSF developers created a limit named ELIGIBLE_PEND_JOBS that enforces a limit on the number of batch jobs eligible for execution. The center utilizes the new limit to control the number of eligible batch jobs each user may have per project at any given time. Similar functionality to limit the number of simultaneous running batch jobs already existed in LSF through the JOBS limit. Through testing, the center discovered that queued jobs over the set limit were not considered for allocation, but still gained priority for queue wait time. The center worked with LSF developers to add a configurable limit, INELIGIBLE, to the LSF product. When set, the flag prevents queued batch jobs over the JOBS limit from gaining wait priority.

The application launcher used on Summit is IBM's Job Step Manager (JSM). JSM provides the jsrun command which is the only mechanism provided to launch job steps on the compute nodes. During AT, we identified the need to specify specific and often irregular task and thread layouts on the compute nodes. In response to our feedback, JSM developers provided new functionality via the

Extended Resource Format (ERF) [5] file that allows users to create a custom mapping file to specify task and thread placements. OLCF worked closely with developers to help design the map file's structure and functionality.

Compiler Tests: Several compiler tool chains are available on Summit and were evaluated as part of acceptance: IBM XL C/C++ and Fortran, PGI, GNU, and clang. Testing for the various compilers focused on support for directives-based programming models for both CPU (OpenMP) and GPU offloading (OpenACC and OpenMP 4.5). OpenACC offloading was evaluated using the OpenACC 2.5 test suite [12,24]. Support for OpenMP on the CPU was tested using the OpenMP 3.1 test suite [28,32] while OpenMP GPU offloading was tested using a development snapshot of the OpenMP 4.5 offloading testing suite [23,30]. Table 6 shows compiler support and test results for the various compilers available on Summit.

Table 6. Compiler directives test results

Compiler	OMP-CPU		OMP-Offloading		OpenACC	
	Support	Results	Support	Results	Support	Results
PGI-C/C++	Y	95.93%	N/A	–	Y	99.4%
PGI-Fortran	Y	88.54%	N/A	–	Y	
XL-C/C++	Y	94.31%	Y	86.00%	N/A	–
XL-Fortran	Y	86.46%	Y	N/A	N/A	–
Clang-C/C++	Y	96.58%	Y	94.00%	N/A	–
GNU-C/C++	Y	95.93%	N/A	–	N/A	–
GNU-Fortran	Y	88.54%	N/A	–	N/A	–

Testing used GA versions of the PGI and XL compilers at the time of testing. The Clang compiler is based on Clang version 3.8 with patches that have since been mostly ported to the mainline Clang public repository. For the GNU compiler, we used version 6.3. We tested CPU OpenMP directives using varying numbers of threads. The numbers reported in Table 6 represent results using 8 OpenMP threads. It should be noted that even though the XL Fortran compiler supports OpenMP offloading, no Fortran version of the test suite was available at the time, so this capability was not exercised. Also, OpenACC offloading in the GNU compiler is available in more recent versions than that used for acceptance testing. We have deployed a version of GCC with OpenACC offloading on Summit (using the `openacc-gcc-8` development branch [8]).

The Standard Performance Evaluation Corporation (SPEC) releases a variety of standardized benchmarks that are widely used to evaluate the performance of computer systems. For Summit acceptance two SPEC benchmark suites, SPEC OMP2012 and SPEC ACCEL, were used to evaluate the different compilers.

SPEC OMP2012 measures the performance of OpenMP 3.1 applications using fourteen benchmark applications. The SPEC ACCEL suite measures the performance of accelerator-based systems using a set of computationally intensive applications, and supports OpenCL, OpenACC and OpenMP 4.5.

For the evaluation, "base" runs were produced following SPEC rules. All benchmarks were built using the compiler versions listed in Table 4 using common optimization flags. The benchmarks were run with both the test and train problem sizes, and three iterations of the reference problem sizes. All metrics presented in this section are measured estimates (i.e., SPEC scores normalized to a baseline reference system measurement), and higher scores indicate better performance. Table 7 summarizes the results for the benchmarks. It is notable that the XL and PGI compilers are both successfully compiling the Spec OMP suite and their respective scores are close. The Spec ACCEL suite is passing compilation for the PGI compiler. The XL compiler failed compilation of one benchmark (551.ppalm). The Table includes data for a run of the benchmark in early February 2018. This shows a) the progress the compiler teams have made and b) the overall performance improvement of the software stack. It is notable, that the ACCEL benchmark shows significant variance between PGI and XL versions of the suite.

Table 7. Measured estimates for SPEC OMP and ACCEL using PGI and XL.

SPEC OMP			SPEC ACCEL					
Benchmark	PGI	XL	PGI			XL		
	18.7	16.1.0	Benchmark	18.1*	18.7	Benchmark	13.1.7*	16.1.0
350.md	4.65	3.82	303.ostencil	6.67	12.4	503.postencil	4.106	10.7
351.bwaves	7.25	0.69	304.olbm	10.2	12.7	504.polbm	4.53	5.80
352.nab	2.61	2.64	314.omriq	8.9	31.3	514.pomriq	4.65	17.4
357.bt331	6.82	8.09	350.md	13.6	25.7	550.pmd	CE	1.49
358.botsalgn	3.26	2.54	351.palm	2.84	3.06	551.ppalm	CE	CE
359.botsspar	1.41	1.32	352.ep	7.76	11.1	552.pep	0.856	1.29
360.ilbdc	3.15	3.43	353.clvrleaf	7.98	12.0	553.pclvrleaf	CE	18.3
362.fma3d	3.49	3.48	354.cg	7.9	12.9	554.pcg	2.35	7.13
363.swim	7.45	7.57	355.seismic	5.29	13.1	555.pseismic	2.11	6.07
367.imagick	5.42	4.40	356.sp	6.74	11.7	556.psp	CE	22.1
370.mgrid	5.11	5.51	357.csp	RE	13.5	557.pcsp	RE	8.82
371.applu	8.77	7.77	359.miniGhost	6.85	9.79	559.pmniGhost	CE	2.64
372.smithwa	6.22	3.00	360.ilbdc	6.5	11.3	560.pilbdc	1.08	21.0
376.kdtree	1.61	1.94	363.swim	4.1	5.87	563.pswim	CE	3.54
			370.bt	RE	16.1	570.pbt	RE	6.70

*Results from February 2018
CE Compile error
RE Runtime error

Math Libraries: Two test codes were used to evaluate vendor and third party libraries of critical importance to applications at the OLCF (for further details see [19]). First, the ScaLAPACK test was used to validate functionality and correctness of the ScaLAPACK library for a variety of compiler choices and underlying BLAS dense linear algebra libraries. Second, the nuccor_kernels test evaluates a large number of combinations of compilers (XL, PGI, GNU, LLVM), parallelism models (OpenMP, OpenACC, CUDA), and BLAS libraries (ESSL variants, MAGMA, LAPACK, CUBLAS). The main focus of these tests was functionality and correctness; performance was primarily evaluated by other tests such as the CORAL applications.

I/O Libraries: Although I/O libraries are implicitly tested using applications and miniapps, reports of possible performance issues from CAAR development teams prompted us to include two I/O-specific miniapps in the AT. FLASH I/O [7] recreates the primary data structure of the full application FLASH [6] and measures only the I/O portion. Chimera I/O mimics the I/O subroutines of Chimera [21] by using parallel HDF5 to collectively write output files from multiple processes, with each process writing the sub-domain it owns. Using both miniapps, we identified very slow performance for parallel HDF5 with a single-shared file. A subsequent Spectrum MPI update included a newer version of ROMIO that, coupled with necessary tuning hints, improved parallel HDF5 performance significantly.

OLCF Application Tests: After reviewing the set of applications that were actively used on Titan, we selected applications that represented a diverse set of algorithmic patterns, programming models, programming languages, and math and I/O libraries. The application set used in [19] was augmented to provide full coverage for these requirements (see Table 2).

Debugger and Profiler Tests: Arm DDT is the primary parallel debugger used in production at OLCF. The FT criteria for DDT includes starting the debugger at 20% of full-system scale within five minutes and performing basic debugging operations, such as setting breakpoints at various source locations and inspecting local variables. For this test we used DDT's `offline` capability that permits non-interactive debugging in batch jobs, with output captured in a log file. GenASiS [22] was used as the target application, using several test cases and varied PPN. Early test attempts failed to start DDT consistently at scale within a reasonable amount of time, due to what appeared to be a hang. Subsequent updates to the software stack resolved this problem. The DDT test also uncovered an issue with CUDA debugging which caused breaking at kernel launches to take many seconds per kernel. As DDT in offline mode automatically breaks at all kernel launches by default, applications with many kernel launches appeared non-responsive. We disabled this behavior while the issue is being resolved.

The nvprof tests exercise the profiler in a variety of operational modes, using both single-host and multi-host applications. We verified the ability of nvprof to generate traces, profiles, and analysis metrics for regular CUDA programs, as well as applications using OpenMP and OpenACC directives. Additionally, we evaluated support for profiling MPS and MPI applications. By engaging NVIDIA, we identified unsupported modes that were not properly documented (i.e., limitations for "application replay" mode), as well as a bug that produced incorrect profiling results when running multiple nvprof instances concurrently on a node. A fix for this bug is included in the CUDA 10.1 release.

5.3   Performance Test (PT)

To ensure that the system was able to meet contractual performance from the CORAL Benchmarks as well as deliver adequate performance for real-world applications, several tests were executed in isolation. The subset of tests included all the CORAL Scalable Science and Throughput Benchmarks and the applications shown in Table 2 selected from the OLCF portfolio.

As part of PT, the scalable and throughput CORAL benchmarks were executed to measure their individual figures of merit (FOMs). For the scalable benchmarks, each code was executed on a quiet system at near full system scale. Each throughput benchmark requires 192 nodes. In order to measure the throughput FOMs, 22 job steps of the same benchmark were executed simultaneously to fill up the system. Table 8 summarizes the results obtained when executed on a quiet system.

Table 8. CORAL scalable and throughput benchmarks FOMs obtained on Summit.

CORAL benchmark		RFP baseline FOM	Measured FOM	Speedup
Scalable	LSMS	3.39E+00	3.01E+01	8.88
	QBOX	5.31E+09	3.65E+10	6.87
	HACC	1.06E+09	1.01E+10	9.53
	Nekbone	1.58E+09	1.10E+10	6.96
Throughput	CAM-SE	4.44E−01	1.12E+00	2.52
	UMT	2.58E+11	5.87E+11	2.28
	AMG	4.50E+10	3.15E+11	7.00
	MCB	3.23E+10	4.56E+11	14.12
	QMCPACK	2.29E+05	1.86E+06	8.12
	NAMD	1.55E+00	8.01E+00	5.17
	LULESH	1.12E+07	2.89E+08	25.80
	SNAP	2.21E+02	9.76E+02	4.42

NAMD is a classical molecular dynamics application and part of the CORAL Throughput benchmarks. NAMD is both compute and communication intensive with random memory access. For acceptance testing, multiple copies of 192-node NAMD jobs were run concurrently to fill up the system. Each run was required to meet the contractual performance target.

We encountered several issues with NAMD during the acceptance period. Because it is communication and memory intensive, NAMD's performance is sensitive to process placement on the node. We also identified a bug in CHARM++'s PAMI back-end which is used on Summit [2]. This bug caused a race condition manifested by occasional hangs on application exit. When the scheduler eventually killed the job due to its time limit, stray processes were often left on the node that degraded the node's performance until they were cleaned up. NAMD was able to meet its performance target following the resolution of these issues.

While verifying the CORAL benchmarks, we observed Nekbone test performance using 4,560 nodes was 48–71% slower than expected. A single node screen was developed to narrow down the cause, which helped identify specific nodes in this degraded state. The root cause was found to be a firmware bug that was leaving the PCIe bus improperly trained [18], resulting in degraded bandwidth. This issue was addressed in the December 2018 HPC SW stack update.

5.4   Stability Test (ST)

In order to simulate a realistic workload on the full system, we used the OLCF Test Harness [31]. The harness submits the full set of tests developed for acceptance as individual jobs in the batch queue. The code or application used for a given test is built before submission to simulate code development activities. The harness records whether a given test instance builds successfully, is submitted to the batch queue successfully, and is executed successfully.

The ST started on Oct. 25, 2018 and was executed continuously for 2 weeks (336 h). Over 29,000 individual tests were executed out of which 97.77% completed successfully. Figure 3 shows a distribution of the types of failures encountered during ST. Intermittent performance failures were observed in NAMD,

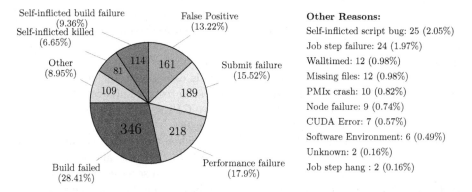

Fig. 3. Failure distribution for SP2 ST (336-hour period).

Chroma, RayTrace, CAM-SE, nvlink, and stream tests. For some of the applications, the performance failures exceeded the acceptable runtime variability criteria. In addition, 339 build failures occurred because the temporary license used with the IBM XL compiler expired. The IBM applications team determined that the two failures marked as unknown at the conclusion of ST were caused by a race condition in LULESH. In addition to job failures, all ST hardware failures were closely monitored. As shown in Fig. 4, we encountered a hardware failure that terminated a job every 28 hours on average. For this reason, we set the maximum allowed walltime on Summit to be 24 hours.

6 Lessons Learned

With each successive leadership class system the OLCF has launched, the number of tests in the acceptance test suite has continued to rise. This is inevitable insofar as node and system complexity and heterogeneity are continually increasing, requiring more testing.

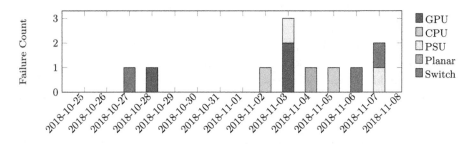

Fig. 4. Number of catastrophic job failures due to a CPU, GPU, power supply unit (PSU), motherboard (Planar), or switch issue for SP2 ST (336-h period).

Deploying Summit involved switching to a different vendor for the OLCF's top computing system as well as using brand new components for parts of the system software stack, e.g., IBM's JSM, CSM, and Spectrum MPI. Close interactions with the vendor starting early in the project were key to the successful deployment of features required by OLCF users.

When selecting tests for a new system, it is essential to include codes that check for exact bit-for-bit correctness. Two of such tests, Minisweep and CoMet, allowed us to identify and replace two defective GPUs. Both tests were incorporated to the "every node" tests set for this reason.

The results of AT show that in some cases, when the system is fully loaded, runtime variability can exceed the desired threshold. This was alleviated by dedicating one core on each POWER9 processor to system services. While isolating additional cores per socket could further reduce variability and increase I/O bandwidth, this will result in reduced throughput for applications. To effectively use the GPUs, applications require as many cores as available.

Testing revealed that releasing the GPFS daemon from the isolated cores can provide up to ~22 GB/s of I/O bandwidth. In cases where applications are I/O limited, it can be beneficial to use the locally-developed `maximizegpfs` LSF option.

Benchmarks and applications are both necessary to provide full coverage for acceptance testing. One is not a substitute for the other. In the case of parallel HDF5 and MPI-IO libraries, although the file system acceptance used benchmarks that utilized these libraries under the hood, performance issues were not discovered until we ran an application test. This is due to the fact that benchmarks' access patterns are not equivalent to those of real applications. The former is likely written to get the best performance the system is capable of providing. The latter is written to fulfill the need of the application.

When designing a network, the nature of all of the applications, and directions of traffic flows and their speeds must be well understood and inform the hardware selection. Vendors should include detailed information on buffer sizes and how buffers are allocated to ports in their data sheets. We should stress test any new network gear for congested paths, large amounts of broadcast traffic, and mixed speeds. This should be done throughout the system's deployment. We should validate network monitoring features in any new gear to verify if it is capable of alerting and monitoring microbursts, latency, buffer usage, quality of service and any dropped data.

7   Science on Summit

All thirteen Center for Accelerated Application Readiness (CAAR) applications selected for Summit successfully achieved their performance targets.

The Summit Early Science Program generated tremendous interest, with 65 letters of intent, 48 full proposals and 33 early access awards. Notably, 12 of the intent letters featured a machine learning component, reflecting high interest in using Summit's machine learning capabilities for scientific discovery.

Of the five 2018 ACM Gordon Bell finalists using Summit, all projects used mixed precision, four projects used the Volta GPU Tensor Cores, and four projects used some form of machine learning. In particular, the CoMet computational genomics application achieved 2.36 ExaOps of mixed precision performance out of the peak achievable Summit performance of 3.2 ExaOps. This was the world's first application to break the ExaOp barrier, with real-world applications such as finding genetic causes of diseases like opioid addiction [26]. The Tensor Cores were also successfully used to develop a half-precision version of the DeepLabv3+ neural network used to detect extreme weather patterns. DeepLabv3+ was able to achieve 1.13 ExaOps of peak performance [27] on Summit.

Summit was put in production in January 2019, and currently supports 30 projects for the DOE Innovative and Novel Computational Impact on Theory and Experiment (INCITE) program [4], as well as other projects delivering new science outcomes.

8 Conclusions

Deploying a system of Summit's scale requires close collaboration between the vendor and the center. OLCF and IBM worked together to identify and fix issues encountered during Summit's installation and acceptance testing. Thanks to this collaboration, we were able to provide direct feedback to IBM development teams in the early stages of deployment.

The OLCF designs a thorough AT plan to help determine if the system is ready for production workloads. As presented here, several issues that impacted functionality and performance of applications were addressed. The issues found and lessons learned from executing the AT have been translated into documentation and examples [15, 16]. This information will be helpful for users starting to run on Summit.

Summit, with 4,608 compute nodes and 27,648 V100 GPUs, is currently ranked first in the TOP500 [17] and the HPCG list [1]. Its top-three ranking in the Green500 list [9] also reflects its energy efficiency. In its short lifetime, Summit has already proven to be a prolific scientific instrument. Projects working on climate analytics [27] and bioinformatics [26] have leveraged Summit's mixed-precision Tensor Cores to break the ExaOp barrier.

Acknowledgement. The authors would like to thank the entire IBM CORAL team for their efforts towards a successful deployment and acceptance of the Summit system.

This research used resources of the Oak Ridge Leadership Computing Facility, which is a DOE Office of Science User Facility supported under Contract DE-AC05-00OR22725.

References

1. 10th HPCG Performance List. https://www.hpcg-benchmark.org/custom/index. html?lid=154&slid=298
2. Charm++ Bug # (1988). https://charm.cs.uiuc.edu/redmine/issues/1988
3. CORAL Benchmark Codes. https://asc.llnl.gov/CORAL-benchmarks
4. DOE Leadership Computing: INCITE. http://www.doeleadershipcomputing.org/
5. Extended resource file format. https://www.ibm.com/support/knowledgecenter/ en/SSWRJV_10.1.0/jsm/10.2/base/erf_format.html
6. Flash center for comptational sciecne. http://flash.uchicago.edu/site/flashcode/
7. Flash i/o benchmark routine - parallel hdf 5. http://www.ucolick.org/~zingale/ flash_benchmark_io/
8. GCC8 openacc development branch. https://github.com/gcc-mirror/gcc/tree/ openacc-gcc-8-branch
9. Green 500. https://www.top500.org/green500
10. Intel MPI Benchmarks User Guide. https://software.intel.com/en-us/imb-user-guide
11. mpiGraph. https://github.com/LLNL/mpiGraph
12. OpenACC Test Suite. https://github.com/OpenACCUserGroup/OpenACCV-V
13. STREAM, for lots of devices written in many programming models. https://github. com/UoB-HPC/BabelStream
14. STREAM: Sustainable Memory Bandwidth in High Performance Computers. https://www.cs.virginia.edu/stream

15. Summit: Scale new heights. Discover new solutions. https://www.olcf.ornl.gov/summit/
16. Summit System User Guide: Known Issues. https://www.olcf.ornl.gov/for-users/system-user-guides/summit/summit-user-guide/#known-issues
17. Top 500. https://top500.org
18. TS001460803: "slow nodes" observed with nekbone tests
19. Experiences Evaluating Functionality and Performance of IBM POWER8+ Systems, October 2017
20. Bland, A.S., Joubert, W., Kendall, R.A., Kothe, D.B., Rogers, J.H., Shipman, G.M.: Jaguar: the world's most powerful computer system-an update. Cray Users Group (2010)
21. Bruenn, S.W., et al.: Chimera: a massively parallel code for core-collapse supernova simulation. arXiv e-prints arXiv:1809.05608, September 2018
22. Cardall, C.Y., Budiardja, R.D.: Genasis basics: object-oriented utilitarian functionality for large-scale physics simulations (version 2). Comput. Phys. Commun. **214**, 247 – 248 (2017).https://doi.org/10.1016/j.cpc.2016.12.019, http://www.sciencedirect.com/science/article/pii/S0010465517300097
23. Diaz, J.M., Pophale, S., Hernandez, O., Bernholdt, D.E., Chandrasekaran, S.: OpenMP 4.5 validation and verification suite for device offload. In: de Supinski, B.R., Valero-Lara, P., Martorell, X., Mateo Bellido, S., Labarta, J. (eds.) IWOMP 2018. LNCS, vol. 11128, pp. 82–95. Springer, Cham (2018). https://doi.org/10.1007/978-3-319-98521-3_6
24. Friedline, K., Chandrasekaran, S., Lopez, M.G., Hernandez, O.: OpenACC 2.5 validation testsuite targeting multiple architectures. In: Kunkel, J.M., Yokota, R., Taufer, M., Shalf, J. (eds.) ISC High Performance 2017. LNCS, vol. 10524, pp. 557–575. Springer, Cham (2017). https://doi.org/10.1007/978-3-319-67630-2_39
25. Joubert, W., et al.: Accelerated application development: the ORNL Titan experience. Comput. Electr. Eng. **46** (2015).https://doi.org/10.1016/j.compeleceng.2015.04.008
26. Joubert, W., et al.: Attacking the opioid epidemic: determining the epistatic and pleiotropic genetic architectures for chronic pain and opioid addiction. In: Proceedings of the International Conference for High Performance Computing, Networking, Storage, and Analysis, SC 2018, Piscataway, NJ, USA, pp. 57:1–57:14. IEEE Press (2018). http://dl.acm.org/citation.cfm?id=3291656.3291732
27. Kurth, T., et al.: Exascale deep learning for climate analytics. In: Proceedings of the International Conference for High Performance Computing, Networking, Storage, and Analysis, p. 51. IEEE Press (2018)
28. OpenMP Validation and Verification Suite: OpenMP validation suite. https://github.com/sunitachandra/omp-validation
29. Petitet, A., Whaley, R.C., Dongarra, J., Cleary, A.: High performance linpack (2018). https://www.netlib.org/benchmark/hpl
30. Pophale, S., Diaz, J.M., Hernandez, O., Bernholdt, D., Chandrasekaran, S.: OpenMP 4.5 Validation and Verification Suite for Device Offload. https://crpl.cis.udel.edu/ompvvsollve/
31. Tharrington, A.N.: NCCS regression test harness, version 00, September 2015. https://www.osti.gov//servlets/purl/1232564
32. Wang, C., Chandrasekaran, S., Chapman, B.: An OpenMP 3.1 validation testsuite. In: Chapman, B.M., Massaioli, F., Müller, M.S., Rorro, M. (eds.) IWOMP 2012. LNCS, vol. 7312, pp. 237–249. Springer, Heidelberg (2012). https://doi.org/10.1007/978-3-642-30961-8_18
33. Warner, J.: Mellanox switches. https://people.ucsc.edu/~warner/Bufs/mellanox

Parallelware Tools: An Experimental Evaluation on POWER Systems

Manuel Arenaz[1,2(✉)] and Xavier Martorell[3,4]

[1] University of A Coruna, A Coruña, Spain
[2] Appentra Solutions, A Coruña, Spain
manuel.arenaz@appentra.com
[3] Computer Architecture Department, Universitat Politécnica de Catalunya,
Barcelona, Spain
[4] Computer Sciences Department, Barcelona Supercomputing Center,
Barcelona, Spain
xavier.martorell@bsc.es

Abstract. Static code analysis tools are designed to aid software developers to build better quality software in less time, by detecting defects early in the software development life cycle. Even the most experienced developer regularly introduces coding defects. Identifying, mitigating and resolving defects is an essential part of the software development process, but frequently defects can go undetected. One defect can lead to a minor malfunction or cause serious security and safety issues. This is magnified in the development of the complex parallel software required to exploit modern heterogeneous multicore hardware. Thus, there is an urgent need for new static code analysis tools to help in building better concurrent and parallel software. The paper reports preliminary results about the use of Appentra's Parallelware technology to address this problem from the following three perspectives: finding concurrency issues in the code, discovering new opportunities for parallelization in the code, and generating parallel-equivalent codes that enable tasks to run faster. The paper also presents experimental results using well-known scientific codes and POWER systems.

Keywords: Static code analysis · Quality assurance and testing ·
Detection of software defects · Concurrency and parallelism ·
Parallelware tools · OpenMP · Tasking · POWER systems

1 Introduction

Static code analysis tools are highly specialized to detect one or more defects, typically categorized into similar types of defects. These tools fulfill a group of specific needs of software developers. It is only recently that heterogeneous multicore systems have been adopted in a wide-range of hardware in industrial sectors such as automotive, wireless communication and embedded vision. Therefore it is increasingly important to develop new static code analyses that address the

© Springer Nature Switzerland AG 2019
M. Weiland et al. (Eds.): ISC 2019 Workshops, LNCS 11887, pp. 352–360, 2019.
https://doi.org/10.1007/978-3-030-34356-9_27

fundamental problem of concurrency, which means that many tasks running at the same time on the same hardware can lead to unpredictable and incorrect behaviour. Identifying and fixing issues related to concurrency and parallelism is one of the most time-consuming and costly aspects of parallel programming. However, static code analysis tools that detect defects related to parallel programming are at a very early stage.

This papers presents an experimental evaluation of Appentra's Parallelware static code analysis tools on POWER systems, which go beyond the state of the art by addressing the problem of concurrency and parallelism from three different perspectives: finding concurrency issues in the code, discovering new opportunities for parallelization in the code, and generating parallel-equivalent code that enables tasks to runs faster. In the rest of the paper, Sect. 2 describes the current set of Parallelware tools, namely, the Parallelware development library, Parallelware Analyzer (BETA) and Parallelware Trainer. Next, Sect. 3 presents early results from the analysis of the SNU NPB Suite [6], a C version of the NAS Parallel Benchmarks [5], using POWER systems available at the Jülich Supercomputing Centre and at Appentra headquarters. Finally, Sect. 4 presents conclusions and future work.

2   Parallelware Tools

Appentra is a Deep Tech global company that delivers products based on the Parallelware technology [1,4], a unique approach to static code analysis for concurrent and parallel programming. It is based on an engine for the detection of parallel patterns such as forall, scalar reduction, sparse forall and sparse reduction. These patterns are used to detect software issues related to concurrency and parallelism, discover parallelism and generate parallel-equivalent code. The current portfolio of tools based on Parallelware technology is as follows:

- **Parallelware developer library**, which offers the static code analysis capabilities of the Parallelware technology. It provides an Application Program Interface (API) that is the basis of Parallelware Analyzer and Parallelware Trainer, and that is designed to enable the integration in third-party software development tools. It supports the C programming language, the OpenMP 4.5 [8] and OpenACC 2.5 [7] directive-based parallel programming interfaces, and the multithreading, offloading and tasking parallel programming paradigms.
- **Parallelware Analyzer (BETA)** [3] is designed to speed up the development of parallel applications and to enforce best practice in parallel programming for heterogeneous multicore systems. It helps software developers by finding software defects early in the parallelization process and thus increases productivity, maintainability and sustainability. It is available as a set of command-line tools to enable compatibility with Continuous Integration and DevOps platforms.
- **Parallelware Trainer** [3] is an interactive, real-time code editor that enables scalable, interactive teaching and learning of parallel programming, increasing

productivity and retention of learning. It is available for Windows, Linux and MacOS operating systems.

3   Experimental Results

This section presents experimental results obtained on POWER systems using Parallelware tools. More specifically, Sect. 3.1 presents the report generated by Parallelware Analyzer and Sect. 3.2 presents experimental results of codes parallelized using Parallelware Trainer.

3.1   Report Generated Using Parallelware Analyzer

The report shown in Table 1 was generated by the Parallelware Analyzer tool after analyzing codes written in the C programming language from the SNU NPB Suite [5,6] benchmarks (NPB-SER-C and NPB-OMP-C implementations). The structure of the report is as follows: *Benchmark*, the software application; *Files*, number of source code files; *SLOC*, source lines of code calculated by the *sloccount* tool; *Time*, runtime of the Parallelware Analyzer tool in milliseconds; *Software issues*, number of issues found in the code related to concurrency and parallelism; and *Opportunities*, number of loops found in the code that have opportunities for parallelization using multithreading and SIMD paradigms. The last row of the table provides total numbers for all the analyzed benchmarks.

The current tool setup reports five software issues related to concurrency and parallelism: *Global*, use of global variables in the body of a function; *Scope*, scalar variables not declared in the smallest scope possible in the code; *Pure*, pure functions free of side effects not marked by the programmer; *Scoping*, variables in an OpenMP parallel region without an explicit data scoping; and *Default*, OpenMP parallel region without the *default(none)* clause. More information about each one of them can be found in the Appentra Knowledge website [2]. The tool also reports two types of opportunities for parallelization: *Multi*, outer loops that can be parallelized with the multithreading paradigm; and *SIMD*, inner loops that can be parallelized with the SIMD paradigm.

Parallelware Analyzer successfully analyzed a total of 192 source files of code, containing 39890 lines of code written in the C programming language, in less than 13 s. In terms of software issues related to concurrency and parallelism, the tools detected a total of 296 uses of global variables in the body of functions. There are 2082 declarations of scalars in a scope bigger than necessary. Moreover, a total of 9 pure functions that are free of side effects but not marked as such were found. Finally, 329 variables with an implicit datascoping and 117 OpenMP parallel regions having a default one were detected. In terms of opportunities for parallelization, a total of 312 outer loops and the same number of inner loops can be parallelized using the multithreading and SIMD paradigms respectively.

Table 1. Parallelware Analyzer report.

Benchmark	Files	SLOC	Time (ms)	Software issues					Opportunities	
				Global	Scope	Pure	Scoping	Default	Multi	SIMD
NPB3.3-SER-C/BT	17	2608	557.97	13	143	0	0	0	24	44
NPB3.3-SER-C/CG	3	521	143.69	3	20	1	0	0	13	10
NPB3.3-SER-C/DC	11	2725	430.67	10	0	3	0	0	13	0
NPB3.3-SER-C/EP	2	175	88.61	1	0	0	0	0	2	0
NPB3.3-SER-C/FT	7	625	238.77	4	0	1	0	0	0	0
NPB3.3-SER-C/IS	2	463	69.3	4	0	0	0	0	4	0
NPB3.3-SER-C/LU	19	2389	739.86	15	298	0	0	0	29	59
NPB3.3-SER-C/MG	3	873	648.68	11	2	0	0	0	4	2
NPB3.3-SER-C/SP	19	2056	683.6	19	381	0	0	0	28	91
NPB3.3-SER-C/UA	13	5576	2181.73	53	163	0	0	0	77	69
NPB3.3-SER-C/common	0	296	174.19	0	0	0	0	0	0	0
NPB3.3-SER-C/config	0	0	28.71	0	0	0	0	0	0	0
NPB3.3-SER-C/sys	1	759	182.71	2	0	0	0	0	0	0
NPB3.3-SER-C	97	19066	6168.48	135	1007	5	0	0	194	275
NPB3.3-OMP-C/BT	17	2693	568.03	13	144	0	41	9	8	4
NPB3.3-OMP-C/CG	3	627	171.77	5	20	1	16	5	9	3
NPB3.3-OMP-C/DC	11	2754	425.05	10	0	3	0	0	13	0
NPB3.3-OMP-C/EP	2	198	92.4	1	0	0	4	3	0	0
NPB3.3-OMP-C/FT	3	649	163.39	12	0	0	10	8	0	0
NPB3.3-OMP-C/IS	2	634	88.15	6	4	0	7	4	4	0
NPB3.3-OMP-C/LU	20	2542	778.31	17	295	0	55	9	5	0
NPB3.3-OMP-C/MG	3	923	662.07	11	2	0	19	10	4	2
NPB3.3-OMP-C/SP	19	2147	693.33	19	381	0	45	13	8	4
NPB3.3-OMP-C/UA	14	6549	2749.03	65	229	0	132	56	67	24
NPB3.3-OMP-C/bin	0	0	29.25	0	0	0	0	0	0	0
NPB3.3-OMP-C/common	0	349	178.34	0	0	0	0	0	0	0
NPB3.3-OMP-C/config	0	0	28.47	0	0	0	0	0	0	0
NPB3.3-OMP-C/sys	1	759	179.29	2	0	0	0	0	0	0
NPB3.3-OMP	95	20824	6806.88	161	1075	4	329	117	118	37
Totals	192	39890	12975.36	296	2082	9	329	117	312	312

3.2 Report Generated Using Parallelware Trainer

The Parallelware Trainer tool was used to automatically generate several parallel versions of a code that computes the Mandelbrot sets. Four parallel versions of Mandelbrot are considered in this work: *Sequential*, serial version (see Listing 1.1, ignoring the OpenMP directives); *Multithreading*, OpenMP version using multithreading paradigm (see Listing 1.1, which contains directives *#pragma omp parallel for*); *Taskwait*, parallel version using OpenMP 3.0 tasking paradigm (see Listing 1.2, which contains directives *#pragma omp task* and *#pragma omp taskwait*); *Taskloop*, parallel version using OpenMP 4.5 tasking paradigm (see Listing 1.3, which contains directives *#pragma omp taskloop*). It should be noted that a software engineer with little experience used the tool to generate and test all the parallel versions for correctness and performance in less than one hour.

Experiments were conducted on two POWER systems: a compute node of the *Juron* supercomputer at Jülich Supercomputing Centre and the *Appentra server* available at Appentra's headquarters. In Juron, the hardware setup of each compute node consists on a IBM S822LC system with 2x 10-core SMT8 POWER8NVL CPUs, offering a total of 160 threads. It provides a *CentOS Linux 7 (AltArch)* Linux operating system with a GCC 4.8.5 compiler. In Appentra server, the hardware setup consists on a RaptorCS Talos II system equipped with an 8-core SMT4 POWER9 processor, offering a total of 32 threads. It runs a *Debian 10 (buster)* Linux with a GCC 8.3.0 compiler. In both systems, GCC compiler flags were used as follows: -O2 for sequential execution and -fopenmp -O2 for OpenMP-enabled parallel execution.

Listing 1.1. OpenMP-enabled parallel version of Mandelbrot using multi-threading paradigm. Parallel code automatically generated by Parallelware Trainer.

```
int mandelbrot(int max_iter, int height, int width,
        double **output, double real_min, double real_max,
        double imag_min,
                double imag_max) {
    double scale_real = (real_max - real_min) / width;
    double scale_imag = (imag_max - imag_min) / height;

    #pragma omp parallel default(none) shared(height,
            imag_min, max_iter, output, real_min, scale_imag,
            scale_real, width)
    {
    #pragma omp for schedule(auto)
    for (int row = 0; row < height; row++) {
        for (int col = 0; col < width; col++) {

            double x0 = real_min + col * scale_real;
            double y0 = imag_min + row * scale_imag;

            double y = 0, x = 0;
            int iter = 0;
            while (x * x + y * y < 4 && iter < max_iter)
                {
                double xtemp = x * x - y * y + x0;
                y = 2 * x * y + y0;
                x = xtemp;
                iter++;
            }
            output[row][col] = iter;
        }
    }
    } // end parallel
    return 0;
}
```

Table 2. Execution times (in seconds) and speedups of Mandelbrot in Juron (2x 10-core SMT8 POWER8 processors) and in Appentra's POWER server (8-core SMT4 POWER9) for problem size of 20000.

Version	No. Threads	Juron		Appentra's server	
		Time (secs)	Speedup	Time (secs)	Speedup
Sequential	4	89.50	1	178.92	1
Multithreading	4	32.85	2.72	37.94	4.72
Taskwait	4	23.30	3.84	24.38	7.34
Taskloop	4	133.31	0.67	37.99	4.71
Sequential	8	89.52	1	178.92	1
Multithreading	8	31.77	2.82	38.96	4.59
Taskwait	8	17.91	4.99	21.57	8.29
Taskloop	8	143.22	0.63	38.82	4.61
Sequential	16	89.51	1	178.93	1
Multithreading	16	14.42	6.21	20.96	8.54
Taskwait	16	7.67	11.67	12.02	14.89
Taskloop	16	86.44	1.04	20.99	8.53
Sequential	32	89.51	1	178.93	1
Multithreading	32	8.57	10.45	10.93	16.37
Taskwait	32	4.97	19.01	6.31	28.36
Taskloop	32	99.93	0.89	11.05	16.19
Sequential	64	89.52	1	178.92	1
Multithreading	64	4.24	21.11	7.80	22.94
Taskwait	64	2.60	34.43	6.33	28.27
Taskloop	64	86.45	1.04	7.70	23.24
Sequential	80	89.53	1		
Multithreading	80	3.50	25.58		
Taskwait	80	2.34	38.26		
Taskloop	80	86.45	1.04		
Sequential	128	89.51	1		
Multithreading	128	2.59	34.56		
Taskwait	128	1.64	54.58		
Taskloop	128	86.46	1.04		
Sequential	160	89.53	1		
Multithreading	160	2.53	35.39		
Taskwait	160	1.60	55.96		
Taskloop	160	86.42	1.04		

Listing 1.2. OpenMP-enabled parallel version of Mandelbrot using tasking paradigm of OpenMP version 3.0 (task/taskwait). Parallel code automatically generated by Parallelware Trainer.

```
int mandelbrot(int max_iter, int height, int width,
        double **output, double real_min, double real_max,
        double imag_min,
                    double imag_max) {
    double scale_real = (real_max - real_min) / width;
    double scale_imag = (imag_max - imag_min) / height;

    #pragma omp parallel default(none) shared(height,
            imag_min, max_iter, output, real_min, scale_imag,
            scale_real, width)
    #pragma omp single
    {
    for (int row = 0; row < height; row++) {
    #pragma omp task
    {
        for (int col = 0; col < width; col++) {
            ...
            output[row][col] = iter;
        }
    } // end task
    }
    #pragma omp taskwait
    } // end parallel
    return 0;
}
```

Listing 1.3. OpenMP-enabled parallel version of Mandelbrot using tasking paradigm of OpenMP version 4.5 (taskloop). Parallel code automatically generated by Parallelware Trainer.

```
int mandelbrot(int max_iter, int height, int width,
        double **output, double real_min, double real_max,
        double imag_min,
                    double imag_max) {
    double scale_real = (real_max - real_min) / width;
    double scale_imag = (imag_max - imag_min) / height;

    #pragma omp parallel default(none) shared(height,
            imag_min, max_iter, output, real_min, scale_imag,
            scale_real, width)
    #pragma omp single
    {
    #pragma omp taskloop
    for (int row = 0; row < height; row++) {
        for (int col = 0; col < width; col++) {
            ...
            output[row][col] = iter;
        }
    }
    } // end parallel
    return 0;
}
```

Table 2 shows the runtimes and speedups for a problem size of 20000. Its structure is as follows: *Version*, serial or parallel version of the code, one of *Sequential, Multithreading, Taskwait* and *Taskloop*; *No. Threads*, number of OpenMP threads; *Time*, runtime in seconds, and *Speedup*, speedup calculated with respect to the sequential version, for each POWER system. The *Taskwait* version is the fastest code both in Juron (maximum speedup is 56 for 160 threads) and Appentra's POWER9 server (maximum speedup above 28 for 32 and 64 threads). The *Multithreading* version is also fast, but the speedup is below *Taskwait* because the OpenMP code generated by Paralellware Trainer includes the clause *schedule(auto)* which defaults to *schedule(static)*. Note that since the workload of Mandelbrot is not constant, different threads are assigned different workloads. Therefore, *schedule(static)* is not the better choice and should be replaced by *schedule(static,1)* or *schedule(dynamic)*. Finally, note that the *Taskloop* version does not scale with the number of threads. This needs to be further investigated as we expected *Taskloop* to also decrease the execution time on both systems.

4   Conclusions and Future Work

Preliminary results show evidences that Parallelware tools have the potential to help software developers to build better quality parallel code. On the one side, Parallelware Analyzer was used to evaluate the SNU NPB Suite, a C implementation of the NAS Parallel Benchmarks. The static code analysis capabilities of Parallelware technology reported the existence of data scoping issues in the codes as well as the existence of pure functions which were not marked as such to provide additional hints to the compiler. Additionally, the tool also reported the existence of sequential loops that could be parallelized using the multithreading and SIMD paradigms.

On the other side, Parallelware Trainer provides a GUI that facilitates the generation of parallel version of a code, as well as the testing of those version for correctness and performance. In less than one hour, a software engineer with little experience in parallel programming generated several OpenMP-enabled parallel versions of the Mandelbrot algorithm using multithreading and tasking paradigms. Performance tests showed significant speedups on both Juron and Appentra POWER systems.

As future work, we plan to further develop Parallelware tools to support C++ and Fortran, as well as other task-based parallel versions tuned for execution on GPUs and FPGAs. We also plan to extend the number of software issues related to concurrency and parallelism detected by the Parallelware tools and run them on a wider set of scientific and engineering software.

Acknowledgements. This work has been partly funded from the Spanish Ministry of Science and Technology (TIN2015-65316-P), the Departament d'Innovació, Universitats i Empresa de la Generalitat de Catalunya (MPEXPAR: Models de Programació i Entorns d'Execució Parallels, 2014-SGR-1051), and the European Union's Horizon 2020 research and innovation program through grant agreements MAESTRO (801101) and EPEEC (801051). The authors gratefully acknowledge the access to the Juron system at Jülich Supercomputing Centre.

References

1. Andión, J., Arenaz, M., Rodríguez, G., Touriño, J.: A novel compiler support for automatic parallelization on multicore systems. Parallel Comput. **39**(9), 442–460 (2013)
2. Appentra. Defects and Recommendations for Concurrency and Parallelism (2019). https://www.appentra.com/knowledge
3. Appentra. Parallelware tools (2019). http://www.appentra.com
4. Arenaz, M., Touriño, J., Doallo, R.: XARK: an extensible framework for automatic recognition of computational kernels. ACM Trans. Program. Lang. Syst. (TOPLAS) **30**(6), 32:1–32:56 (2008)
5. Bailey, D., et al.: The NAS parallel benchmarks - summary and preliminary results. In: Proceedings of the 1991 ACM/IEEE Conference on Supercomputing, Supercomputing 1991, pp. 158–165. ACM (1991)
6. Center for Manycore Programming, Seoul National University (SNU). SNU NPB Suite (2013). http://aces.snu.ac.kr/software/snu-npb/
7. OpenACC Architecture Review Board. The OpenACC Application Programming Interface, Version 2.5, October 2015. http://www.openacc.org
8. OpenMP Architecture Review Board. OpenMP Application Program Interface, Version 4.5, November 2015. http://www.openmp.org

Performance Evaluation of MPI Libraries on GPU-Enabled OpenPOWER Architectures: Early Experiences

Kawthar Shafie Khorassani[✉], Ching-Hsiang Chu[✉], Hari Subramoni[✉], and Dhabaleswar K. Panda[✉]

Department of Computer Science and Engineering, The Ohio State University, Columbus, OH 43210, USA
{shafiekhorassani.1,chu.368}@osu.edu, {subramon,panda}@cse.ohio-state.edu

Abstract. The advent of Graphics Processing Unit (GPU)-enabled OpenPOWER architectures are empowering the advancement of various High-Performance Computing (HPC) applications from dynamic modular simulation to deep learning training. GPU-aware Message Passing Interface (MPI) is one of the most efficient libraries used to exploit the computing power on GPU-enabled HPC systems at scale. However, there is a lack of thorough performance evaluations for GPU-aware MPI libraries to provide insights into the varying costs and benefits of using each one on GPU-enabled OpenPOWER systems. In this paper, we provide a detailed performance evaluation and analysis of point-to-point communication using various GPU-aware MPI libraries including SpectrumMPI, OpenMPI+UCX, and MVAPICH2-GDR on Open-POWER GPU-enabled systems. We demonstrate that all three MPI libraries deliver approximately 95% of achievable bandwidth for NVLink communication between two GPUs on the same socket. For inter-node communication where the InfiniBand network dominates the peak bandwidth, MVAPICH2-GDR and SpectrumMPI attain approximately 99% achievable bandwidth, while OpenMPI delivers close to 95%. This evaluation is useful to determine which MPI library can provide the highest performance enhancement.

Keywords: OpenPOWER · MPI · GPU · NVLink · RDMA

1 Introduction

With an increasing demand for higher computing power for end applications, the adoption of GPU is becoming more prevalent in the HPC community [25]. This is an obvious trend in the recent Top500 supercomputer list [5], where 126 out of 500 supercomputers, i.e., 25.2%, are equipped with NVIDIA GPUs (8.4% higher than the previous year). This is further demonstrated by the fact that #1 Summit and #2 Sierra (as of Nov '18) are adopting a GPU-enabled

© Springer Nature Switzerland AG 2019
M. Weiland et al. (Eds.): ISC 2019 Workshops, LNCS 11887, pp. 361–378, 2019.
https://doi.org/10.1007/978-3-030-34356-9_28

OpenPOWER architecture with high-speed interconnects, including NVIDIA NVLink [13,21] and InfiniBand networks [22].

On the software side, MPI is a standard programming model for developing parallel applications in the HPC community. The MPI standard provides high-level primitives for application developers to hide the complexity of handling data movement through various interconnects under different configurations, e.g., non-uniform memory access (NUMA) effect. Compute Unified Device Architecture (CUDA), which is an extension of C/C++, is the parallel computing platform to harness GPU's high-bandwidth memory (HBM) and massive parallelism. To efficiently perform parallel computing tasks on multiple GPU nodes, the concept of CUDA-aware MPI [28] has been introduced and widely adopted in many production MPI libraries. It is worth noting that an intelligent CUDA-aware MPI implementation, which leverages the cutting-edge hardware technologies, can *transparently* provide significant performance improvement to the end applications [23,24]. As a result, the use of MPI for parallel applications significantly increases productivity and improves performance.

The advent of the GPU-enabled OpenPOWER systems not only brings new opportunities, but also introduces additional challenges due to the variety of interconnects. Many studies have been presented to provide the performance evaluation on an OpenPOWER system from different angles [7,10,19,27]. However, the performance of CUDA-aware MPI libraries on GPU-enabled Open-POWER architectures remains ambiguous due to the lack of thorough and comprehensive performance evaluations. The broad research question is: **Can the state-of-the-art MPI libraries fully leverage the various interconnects on GPU-enabled OpenPOWER architectures?** To the best of our knowledge, this is the first work to provide a comprehensive evaluation of multiple CUDA-aware MPI libraries and make the following contributions:

- Evaluate the state-of-the-art CUDA-aware MPI libraries in a systematic manner on Sierra-like and Summit OpenPOWER Systems
- Present comprehensive evaluation results with various configurations to understand the achievable performance of MPI libraries through different interconnects
- Provide insight into the expected performance of MPI libraries for the end applications

We elaborate on the importance and motivation of having a comprehensive evaluation of MPI performance on GPU-enabled OpenPOWER systems in Sect. 2. Section 3 describes the necessary background knowledge related to this work. The experimental setup is thoroughly detailed, including information on the hardware and software used in Sect. 4. To conclude, we present the evaluation results with various configurations and provide a thorough analysis of how the results compare to each other based on the context in Sects. 5 and 6.

2   Motivation

With advancement in technology and an ever more prevalent interest in parallel computing, it has become increasingly vital to optimize communication libraries such as MPI. Optimizing MPI communication entails being able to handle upgraded performance requirements in an increasingly efficient manner. On a GPU-enabled OpenPOWER system, as exhibited in Fig. 1, there are four primary interconnects being deployed: (1) NVLink between CPU and GPU and between GPUs, (2) X-Bus between two IBM POWER9 (P9) processes, i.e., NUMA nodes, (3) Peripheral Component Interconnect express (PCIe) between CPU to Mellanox InfiniBand EDR Host Channel Adapter (HCA), and (4) Infini-Band networks between multiple OpenPOWER nodes. This architecture with such powerful interconnects undeniably entails a performance boost [27]. On the other hand, it also poses a great challenge to MPI library developers to optimize communication protocols for the different data paths that can be selected between a pair of processes. The data path(s) selected varies in different use cases to provide the best performance.

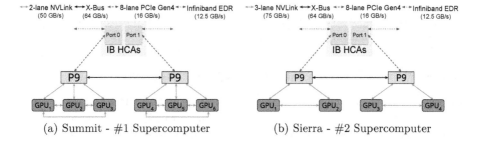

(a) Summit - #1 Supercomputer   (b) Sierra - #2 Supercomputer

Fig. 1. Hardware configuration of cutting-edge OpenPOWER GPU-enabled systems

Although previous studies provide a detailed evaluation of the achievable performance of various interconnects on the OpenPOWER systems [19,27], it is unclear whether the state-of-the-art CUDA-aware MPI can achieve the peak performance that underlying interconnects provide when moving data within GPUs, between GPUs, between CPU and GPU and between GPU nodes. Table 1 presents the theoretical and achievable peak bandwidth of various interconnects on OpenPOWER systems (refer to Sects. 4 and 5 for experimental configurations). Based on the table, the achievable bandwidths range from 85.43% to 94.56% of theoretical peak bandwidths due to the overhead of hardware, firmware and software protocols, and other factors like cache effect. It is critical to understand how much overhead the CUDA-aware MPI implementations have when using various interconnects and how it would reflect to the end applications. Through generating a comprehensive evaluation and analysis, we can develop knowledge about the MPI libraries that can obtain the highest bandwidth closest to the theoretical peak bandwidth of all interconnects in an OpenPOWER

GPU-enabled system. By understanding the performance, restrictions, and draw-backs of different CUDA-aware MPI implementations, we generate a thorough analysis of the factors that need to be considered in future adjustments to the communication libraries and end applications.

Table 1. Theoretical and achievable peak bandwidth of data movement over interconnects in a sierra-like and summit OpenPOWER systems

	GPU HBM2	Sierra-Like System		Summit		X-Bus	InfiniBand EDR
		3-lane NVLink2 CPU-GPU	3-lane NVLink2 GPU-GPU	2-lane NVLink2 CPU-GPU	2-lane NVLink2 GPU-GPU		
Theoretical Peak Bandwidth (Uni-directional)	900 GB/s	75 GB/s	75 GB/s	50 GB/s	50 GB/s	64 GB/s	12.5 GB/s
Achievable Peak Bandwidth (Uni-directional)	768.91 GB/s	68.78 GB/s	70.56 GB/s	45.9 GB/s	47 GB/s	58.01 GB/s	11.82 GB/s
Fraction of Peak	85.43%	91.7%	91.81%	91.8%	94%	90.64%	94.56%

3   Background

In this section, we describe background information related to the content of the analysis and evaluation performed.

3.1   GPU and NVIDIA GPUDIRECT Technology

General-purpose GPU has been widely adopted in the HPC community due to its high bandwidth memory and ultra-high throughput of computing. The cutting-edge NVIDIA Tesla Volta V100 GPU has 16 GB HBM2 with theoretically 900 GB/s bandwidth [21] for 80 streaming multiprocessors and 4 copy engines. GPUDirect technology provided by NVIDIA enables faster handling of compute-intensive applications through the various features it provides. These features range from peer-to-peer memory access and transfers between GPUs to improving bandwidth and reducing latency through remote direct memory access (RDMA). GPUDIRECT RDMA allows the third-party devices, e.g., Mellanox InfiniBand HCA, to access GPU memory without intervention from the CPU, reducing the overhead of additional memory copies. Direct memory access enables copying data between the memory of GPUs on the same PCIe bus or NVLink. Through GPUDirect technology, a pinned buffer shared by the GPU and third party devices eliminates the need to copy memory multiple times in CUDA host memory [20].

3.2   Message Passing Interface

MPI is a programming paradigm often used in parallel applications that provides a mechanism for processes to communicate with each other. This communication can happen in different forms: point-to-point, one-sided, or collective. These various communication patterns involve a different number of processes communicating with each other and various restrictions on synchronization between the processes involved. The ability to apply the MPI standard to heterogeneous systems has evolved with support for inter-process and intra-process communication through the CUDA-aware feature. CUDA-aware MPI enables communication between the host and the GPU, further optimizing applications by introducing this level of GPU support. Some modern MPI libraries that provide support for CUDA-aware MPI include SpectrumMPI, OpenMPI (with and without UCX), and MVAPICH2.

SpectrumMPI, provided by IBM, is a default CUDA-aware MPI library deployed on many OpenPOWER systems including Summit and Sierra, as previously mentioned. This library takes advantage of various optimizing schemes such as GPUDirect RDMA and CUDA Inter-process communication (IPC) to enhance the efficiency of GPU based communication.

OpenMPI is a CUDA-aware library implementation of MPI with similar support for GPU based point-to-point and collective communication as noted above [14,17]. **Unified Communication X (UCX)** is an open-source communication framework for HPC applications and also supports CUDA-aware point-to-point communication [6]. It was developed as a result of a collaboration between academia, government, and industry and presents an optimized communication layer for MPI. It is often recommended to build and use OpenMPI with UCX support for GPU-based communication.

MVAPICH2 is an MPI library implementation with support for Infiniband, Omni-Path, Ethernet/iWarp, and RoCE. Various versions of the library include additional features for a more specific application of the library [3]. MVAPICH2-GDR is optimized with features to support clusters with NVIDIA GPUs and is used for GPU-enabled HPC and deep learning applications [8,11,12]. It exploits the advantages of GPUDirect RDMA to optimize data movement between nodes and to offload communication between GPUs on clusters with NVIDIA GPUs [23,24]. It is also enhanced with support for OpenPOWER with NVLink interconnect, CUDA-aware managed memory, and MPI-3 one-sided communication, among many features.

4 Experimental Setup

In this section, we elaborate on the hardware and software environment used in our evaluation. We also describe the methods used to evaluate MPI libraries in various configurations. The experiments were conducted on a GPU-enabled OpenPOWER system similar to the one presented in Fig. 1(b). Each node is equipped with two NUMA nodes, where each one has a 22-core IBM POWER9 and 2 NVIDIA Volta GPUs. Each NUMA node has 128 GB system memory, and each GPU has 16 GB HBM. The nodes run Red Hat Enterprise Linux Server release 7.5 with a kernel version of 4.14.0-49.18.1. Mellanox OFED 4.3, NVIDIA driver version 418.39 and CUDA toolkit 9.2.148 are used on all nodes.

In this paper, we first present the achievable peak bandwidth of interconnects based on benchmarks using the low-level primitives. Next, we conduct a performance evaluation of CUDA-aware MPI libraries to perform the data movement through desired interconnects between MPI processes.

Evaluating Achievable Native Performance of Interconnects. To build a proper baseline, i.e., upper bound, we use different software tools to obtain the achievable bandwidth of various interconnects as shown in Table 1. Each tool performs the corresponding data movement 1,000 times, and we report the average in this paper. The following points summarize the details of the tests:

1. NVLink between CPU and GPU: We used a modified *bandwidthTest* test from NVIDIA CUDA sample to obtain the bandwidth of NVLink between CPU and GPU by performing multiple *cudaMemcpyAsync* back-to-back between system memory to GPU memory (i.e., with copy type *cudaMemcpyDeviceToHost* and *cudaMemcpyHostToDevice*).
2. GPU HBM2 and NVLink between GPUs: Similarly, we used the *simpleIPC* test from NVIDIA CUDA sample to fork two CPU processes to perform data transfer within one GPU and between GPUs to measure the bandwidth of HBM2 and NVLink, respectively, (i.e., with copy type *cudaMemcpyDeviceToDevice* with CUDA P2P feature enabled).
3. X-Bus: STREAM benchmark [15] is used to measure the bandwidth of accessing system memory from the CPU. We manually bind the memory and CPU on different NUMA nodes by using *numactl* tool to measure the achievable bandwidth of X-Bus.
4. InfiniBand: We use an *ib_read_bw* test in InfiniBand Verbs Performance Tests [2] to measure the bandwidth of the IB network by moving data between two physical nodes. To have a comprehensive and fair analysis, we measured two data movement paths: (1) from system memory to remote system memory, and (2) from one GPU to remote GPU memory using GPUDirect RDMA technology.

Evaluating MPI-Level Performance. The OSU Micro-benchmark (OMB) suite is a benchmark used to evaluate the performance of various MPI libraries. Bureddy et al. [9] extend OMB to support evaluating point-to-point, multi-pair, and collective communication on GPU clusters. This extended version of OMB includes latency, bandwidth, and bidirectional bandwidth benchmarks for point-to-point communication. Each of these tests takes two parameters to indicate the location of the buffers being passed into the communication at different processes. The buffer can either be on the device, i.e., GPU, or on the host. The various configurations of the buffer locations at each rank determine whether the benchmark is evaluating inter-node or intra-node communication on the host, on the device, or between the host and the device.

In this work, we use OMB v5.6.1 and focus on the evaluation of point-to-point communication and report the most representative metrics including latency, uni-directional bandwidth, and bi-directional bandwidth. The latency test is performed in a ping-pong manner by using MPI_Send and MPI_Recv primitives. In the uni-directional bandwidth configuration, a set number of back-to-back messages are sent from the sender by calling MPI_Isend. The sender then waits for a reply from the receiver after receiving all the messages by calling MPI_Waitall. To receive the data, it uses MPI_Irecv on the receiver process. The bi-directional bandwidth benchmark is different than the bandwidth benchmark in that it measures the maximum overall bandwidth between the two processes. It does this through sending back-to-back messages from both the sender and the receiver and waiting for both processes to send a reply only after obtaining all the messages.

To evaluate data movement on different interconnects, we used the environment variable *CUDA_VISIBLE_DEVICES* to force MPI processes to select the desired GPU(s). This can be summarized as follows:

1. (Section 5.1) Evaluating NVLink between GPUs (NVLink GPU-GPU): This is a common case where each CPU process uses different physical GPUs, and NVLink is available between GPUs. We use *CUDA_VISIBLE_DEVICES=0,1* to make only two GPUs, which are connected by the NVLink, visible to MPI processes and processes can bind to different GPUs.

2. (Section 5.2) Evaluating HBM2 (GPU HBM2): Resulting from Multi-Process Service (MPS) capabilities in NVIDIA GPUs, multiple processes can be using the same GPU concurrently. This proves to be a benefit in scenarios where a single process cannot fully utilize the GPU compute capacity. To evaluate this scenario, we set the environment variable *CUDA_VISIBLE_DEVICES = 0* to make only one GPU visible to all processes; this results in all MPI processes using the same GPU through MPS transparently.

3. (Section 5.3) Evaluating NVLink between CPU and GPU (NVLink CPU-GPU): In a heterogeneous system, applications may exploit both CPU and GPU to maximize the parallelism. This is where a CPU process may require transfer of data from system memory to a GPU owned by another CPU process. In this case, we place two MPI processes on the same NUMA node; thus, a NVLink is available between CPU and GPU.

4. (Section 5.4) Evaluating X-Bus and NVLink (X-Bus): In a multi-GPU system, communication between GPUs across NUMA node is inevitable. To evaluate this scenario, we use *CUDA_VISIBLE_DEVICES = 0,3* to make two GPUs, which physically reside on different NUMA nodes, visible to the MPI processes.

5. (Section 5.5) Evaluating GPU transfer across nodes via InfiniBand network (Infiniband): MPI processes are launched on different nodes. By default, each MPI process selects the first discovered GPU in the same socket (GPU 0 in our case).

In this paper, we evaluated the following three CUDA-aware MPI libraries: (1) SpectrumMPI 10.3.0.01, which is the default library installed on the OpenPOWER system (labeled *SpectrumMPI*) [1], (2) OpenMPI 4.0.1 + UCX 1.6

(labeled *OpenMPI+UCX*) [4], and (3) MVAPICH2-GDR 2.3.2 pre-release version (labeled *MVAPICH2-GDR*) [3]. We ran the experiments with settings recommended by the user guides provided by the MPI libraries.

5   Evaluation and Analysis

In this section, we present the experimental results based on the environmental setup described in Sect. 4 and provide an analysis of these results. There are five primary scenarios presented: (1) Communication through NVLink between GPUs, (2) Communication through GPU HBM2, (3) Communication through NVLink between CPU and GPU, (4) Communication through NVLink and X-Bus, and (5) Communication through InfiniBand Network. Note that we only present the most representative results to avoid repetition.

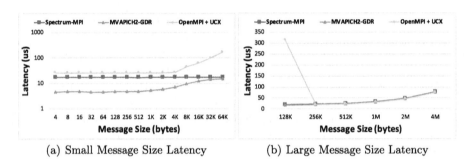

(a) Small Message Size Latency   (b) Large Message Size Latency

Fig. 2. Latency comparison of MPI libraries on moving data between GPUs on the same socket (i.e., via NVLink interconnect) on a Sierra-like system

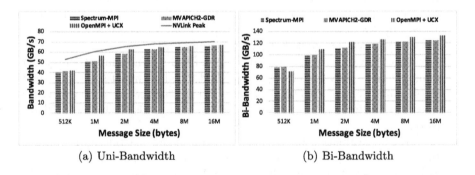

(a) Uni-Bandwidth   (b) Bi-Bandwidth

Fig. 3. Bandwidth comparison of MPI libraries on moving data between GPUs on the same socket (i.e., via NVLink interconnect) on a Sierra-like system

5.1   Communication Through NVLink Between GPUs

One MPI process using one single GPU is the most common configuration for MPI+CUDA applications. Here, we bind MPI processes to two GPUs with NVLink connection on the same socket to evaluate if MPI libraries can efficiently utilize the NVLink. Figure 2 shows a comparison of the MPI libraries through communication via the NVLink interconnect. MVAPICH2 outperforms SpectrumMPI by a factor of up to 4 for message sizes up to 32KB for latency and outperforms OpenMPI by a factor of up to 5. Both SpectrumMPI and MVAPICH2 libraries generally depict the same range for bandwidth and bi-bandwidth. These bandwidth numbers are close to the theoretical peak bandwidth of NVLink as shown in Fig. 3. OpenMPI is relatively within a similar range for uni-bandwidth but slightly outperforms the other libraries for bi-bandwidth, whereas latency is higher than both comparing libraries from message sizes between 4 and 126 KB. Similar trends are also observed on the Summit system for latency in Fig. 4. In contrast to the 75 GB/s theoretical peak bandwidth on a Sierra-like OpenPOWER System, the theoretical peak for uni-directional bandwidth on the Summit system is 50 GB/s as depicted in Fig. 5.

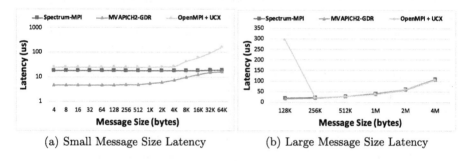

(a) Small Message Size Latency   (b) Large Message Size Latency

Fig. 4. Latency comparison of MPI libraries on moving data between GPUs on the same socket (i.e., via NVLink interconnect) on Summit system

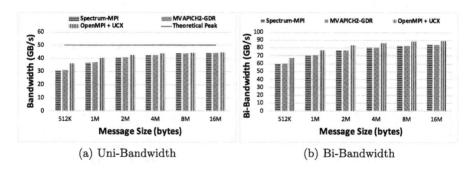

(a) Uni-Bandwidth   (b) Bi-Bandwidth

Fig. 5. Bandwidth comparison of MPI libraries on moving data between GPUs on the same socket (i.e., via NVLink interconnect) on Summit system

5.2   Communication Through GPU HBM2

To evaluate the performance of MPI libraries when moving data within a GPU, i.e., through GPU's HBM2, we map two MPI processes into the same GPU. Figure 6 depicts a comparison of latency obtained from SpectrumMPI, OpenMPI, and MVAPICH2-GDR for moving data within a single GPU. MVAPICH2-GDR drastically outperforms SpectrumMPI for message sizes between 1 byte and 16 KB then depicts similar latency behavior for larger message sizes. The latency provided by OpenMPI is also drastically higher than MVAPICH2 and SpectrumMPI for large message sizes. The same communication pattern is also compared for bandwidth and bidirectional bandwidth in Fig. 7. MVAPICH2 outperforms SpectrumMPI for both bi-directional bandwidth and uni-directional bandwidth, while OpenMPI does not have comparable bandwidth numbers for any of the large message sizes. After profiling further to determine the cause of this performance, we found that OpenMPI does not use CUDA IPC for intra-node, intra-GPU communication, unlike MVAPICH2-GDR and SpectrumMPI. However, all MPI libraries can only achieve about half of the peak bandwidth provided by the GPU HBM2, which is 768.91 GB/s. We suspect this is due to the limitation of GPU's MPS feature when sharing a single GPU with multiple processes, i.e., the bandwidth of GPU memory is also shared. Additionally, the bidirectional bandwidth is only slightly higher and sometimes lower than the uni-directional bandwidth because it already reaches the peak in one direction.

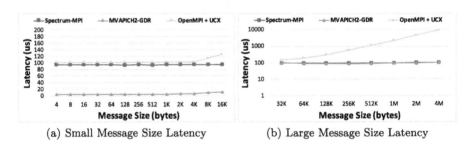

(a) Small Message Size Latency   (b) Large Message Size Latency

Fig. 6. Latency comparison of MPI libraries on moving data within one single GPU on a Sierra-like system

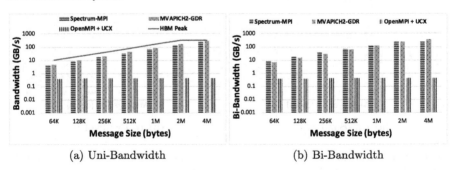

(a) Uni-Bandwidth   (b) Bi-Bandwidth

Fig. 7. Bandwidth comparison of MPI libraries on moving data within one single GPU on a Sierra-like system

5.3   Communication Through NVLink Between CPU and GPU

In a hybrid application, it is common to utilize the computing power of both
CPU cores and GPUs. Therefore, data transfer from system memory to another
process's GPU memory may be required. To evaluate such a scenario, we perform the tests on two MPI processes, where one process uses a communication
buffer on system memory, and the communication buffer of another process is on
GPU memory (i.e., Host-to-Device communication). Figure 8 provides a latency
comparison of Host-to-Device communication between the MPI libraries. For
small message sizes, MVAPICH-GDR and OpenMPI perform in a similar range
while SpectrumMPI is up to 10× higher. SpectrumMPI also depicts a jump in
latency between 2 KB and 8 KB message sizes.

As shown in Fig. 9, the achievable uni-directional peak bandwidth of SpectrumMPI, OpenMPI, and MVAPICH2-GDR are 21.74 GB/s, 23.63 GB/s, and
26.84 GB/s, respectively. Clearly, none of the MPI libraries efficiently utilize the
NVLink between CPU and GPU as they are only able to attain between 31% to
39% achievable peak bandwidth. MVAPICH2-GDR may push the data through

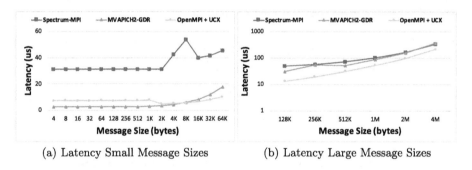

(a) Latency Small Message Sizes   (b) Latency Large Message Sizes

Fig. 8. Latency comparison of MPI libraries on moving data from the Host to the
Device on a Sierra-like system

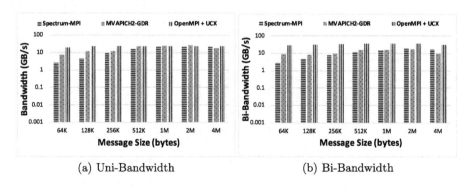

(a) Uni-Bandwidth   (b) Bi-Bandwidth

Fig. 9. Bandwidth comparison of MPI libraries on moving data from the Host to the
Device on a Sierra-like system. The peak achievable uni-directional bandwidth in this
case is approximately 68.78 GB/s.

InfiniBand HCA as their peak uni- and bi-bandwidth are close to the peak bandwidth 8-lane PCIe Gen4 provides. Based on these results, we can conclude that
the current CUDA-aware MPI libraries do not have good locality support to
efficiently move data between CPU and GPU. Similar results can be expected
for Device-to-Host communication, which is not shown to avoid repetition.

5.4 Communication Through NVLink and X-Bus

Similar to Sect. 5.1, communication can happen between GPUs without direct connection via NVLink. On a GPU-enabled OpenPOWER system, the data needs
to be moved not just through NVLink between CPU and GPU but also through
X-Bus between the NUMA nodes. Figure 10 displays a latency comparison where
the data is being moved between GPUs on different sockets. Compared to Fig. 2,
we can see that latency is similar for small messages but significantly higher for
large messages. This indicates that the X-bus becomes the performance bottleneck when moving data across sockets. Figure 11 indicates that SpectrumMPI
and MVAPICH2-GDR can achieve comparable uni-bandwidth and bi-bandwidth,
where OpenMPI is 25% lower than the peak bandwidth that can be attained. However, the peak bandwidth MPI libraries can achieve is only around 80% of achiev-

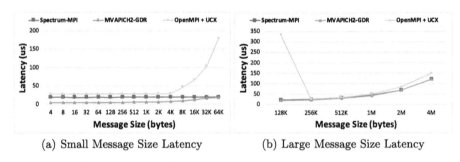

(a) Small Message Size Latency   (b) Large Message Size Latency

Fig. 10. Latency comparison of MPI libraries on moving data between GPUs on different sockets on a Sierra-like system

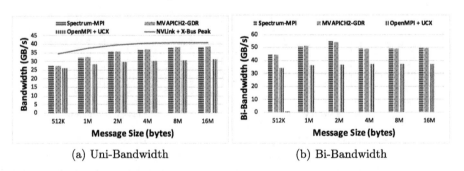

(a) Uni-Bandwidth   (b) Bi-Bandwidth

Fig. 11. Bandwidth comparison of MPI libraries on moving data between GPUs on
different sockets on a Sierra-like system

able bandwidth of X-bus as exhibited in Table 1. We observed that it is because these MPI libraries rely on moving GPU-resident data using CUDA driver or run-time APIs. In this case, it is using CUDA IPC feature since peer-to-peer access is possible across the socket due to the Address Translation Service provided by NVLink2 technology. However, CUDA IPC can only achieve around 41 GB/s, which is only 64% of theoretical peak bandwidth, when data needs to be moved across NUMA-node. Taking this into account, SpectrumMPI and MVAPICH2-GDR are both achieving within a range of 80% to 95% of achievable peak band-width over the various message sizes shown. Nevertheless, the bidirectional band-width shown in Fig. 11(b) indicates that MPI libraries are not able to fully utilize the bi-directional X-bus.

5.5 Communication Through InfiniBand Network

Moving GPU-resident data across nodes is common for HPC applications in order to achieve higher performance at scale. It is critical to understand if MPI libraries can saturate the bandwidth provided by InfiniBand networks. Here, we conducted latency, uni- and bi-bandwidth tests between two GPU nodes. Figure 12 provides a latency comparison of inter-node communication between the MPI libraries. As can be seen, MVAPICH2-GDR and OpenMPI provide the lowest latency across all message sizes. The latency of SpectrumMPI increases at 256 KB after steadily maintaining latency about 30% higher than that of OpenMPI and MVAPICH2-GDR.

In terms of bandwidth as shown in Fig. 13(a), it indicates that the libraries are leveraging both IB EDR adapters, i.e., so-called multi-rail support, efficiently in the system to achieve almost twice peak bandwidth of a single IB EDR, i.e., single-rail. The bandwidth and bi-bandwidth shown in Fig. 13(b) reveals a performance degradation issue in OpenMPI when the message size is larger than 2 MB. Spectrum-MPI achieves approximately 50% of the bandwidth achieved by OpenMPI and MVAPICH2-GDR until 1 MB message size.

By default, multi-rail support is not enabled for GPU resident data when using OpenMPI+UCX, therefore, HCA selection is crucial at run-time in order to achieve comparable performance to that of MVAPICH2-GDR and SpectrumMPI.

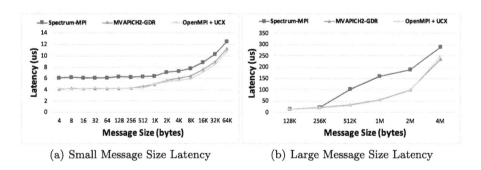

(a) Small Message Size Latency   (b) Large Message Size Latency

Fig. 12. Latency comparison of MPI libraries on moving data between GPU Nodes on a Sierra-like system

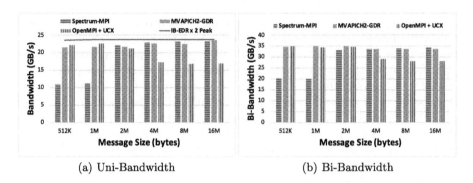

(a) Uni-Bandwidth   (b) Bi-Bandwidth

Fig. 13. Bandwidth comparison of MPI libraries on moving data between GPU nodes on a Sierra-like system

6   Discussion

Based on the experiments presented above, Table 2 summarizes the peak bandwidth the CUDA-aware MPI libraries can achieve over various interconnects on a GPU-enabled OpenPOWER system. It is worth noting that the achievable peak bandwidths of HBM2 and X-Bus are further reduced due to the overhead or limitation of the CUDA driver when inter-process communication is involved, e.g., MPS and CUDA IPC.

As show in Table 2 SpectrumMPI, OpenMPI+UCX, and MVAPICH2-GDR provide 99.20%, 95.40%, and 99.70% achievable peak bandwidth, respectively, for inter-node communication by utilizing the achievable bandwidth of two IB EDR adapters. This can significantly improve the performance of HPC applications at scale. All three libraries achieve in the range of 31% to 39% of the NVLink which is available to be used when moving data between system and GPU memory.

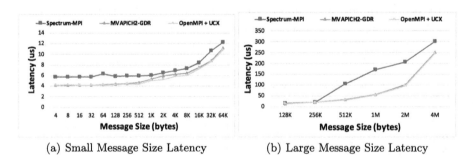

(a) Small Message Size Latency   (b) Large Message Size Latency

Fig. 14. Latency comparison of MPI libraries on moving data between GPU Nodes on Summit system

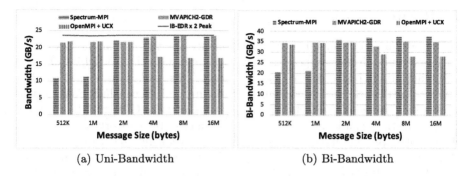

(a) Uni-Bandwidth   (b) Bi-Bandwidth

Fig. 15. Bandwidth comparison of MPI libraries on moving data between GPU nodes on Summit system

This is an open performance issue for all CUDA-aware MPI libraries. Finally, both SpectrumMPI and MVAPICH2-GDR outperform OpenMPI + UCX when the communication is limited by HMB2 or when the communication is through NVLink and X-Bus.

Through the results and analysis presented in Sect. 5, we highlight the several limitations of the existing MPI libraries on the OpenPOWER architectures as follows:

1. Limited bandwidth of HBM2 when sharing a memory
2. Host-to-Device and Device-to-Host communications are not efficiently utilizing NVLink
3. MPI Libraries are not able to fully utilize the bi-directional X-bus
4. Multi-rail support is a pertinent feature for high-performance GPU-to-GPU communication

It is worth noting that these limitations may become the performance bottleneck of collective operations as many collectives are implemented based on the point-to-point primitives. To address these limitations, the CUDA-aware MPI libraries need to be further optimized with new features and designs under different communication patterns.

Table 2. Summary of achievable peak bandwidth of MPI libraries and fraction of peak over Interconnects on a Sierra-like GPU-enabled OpenPOWER System

	GPU HBM2	3-lane NVLink2 CPU-GPU	3-lane NVLink2 GPU-GPU	X-Bus	InfiniBand EDR×2
SpectrumMPI	329 GB/s	21.74 GB/s	67.14 GB/s	39.16 GB/s	23.45 GB/s
	(36.55%)	(31.61%)	(95.20%)	(94.60%)	(99.20%)
OpenMPI+UCX	0.457 GB/s	23.63 GB/s	67.22 GB/s	31.77 GB/s	22.55 GB/s
	(0.05%)	(34.35%)	(95.40%)	(76.73%)	(95.40%)
MVAPICH2-GDR	390.88 GB/s	26.84 GB/s	67.15 GB/s	39.28 GB/s	23.56 GB/s
	(43.43%)	(39.02%)	(95.30%)	(94.97%)	(99.70%)

7 Related Work

In [18], Mojumder et al. generate a performance analysis of training Deep Neural Networks with peer-to-peer data transfer and with the NVIDIA Collective Communications library on a DGX-1 system. This analysis was used to identify any bottlenecks in the system architecture and to conclude that various factors such as the neural network architecture, and the GPU-to-GPU communication method can heavily influence performance. In the work done by Acun et al. [10], a parallel molecular dynamics application referred to as Nanoscale Molecular Dynamics (NAMD) is optimized for enhancement in performance on the IBM Newell platform (Power9 processors and NVIDIA Volta V100 GPUs). Various approaches were incorporated to achieve improved performance including improving GPU offload efficiency, load balancing, and vectorizing NAMD routines on Power9.

In [16], Li et al. evaluate the various modern GPU interconnects including: PCIe, NVLink, NV-SLI, NVSwitch and GPUDirect, on various systems to develop an analysis of their impact on multi-GPU application performance. They determine that GPU communication efficiency is heavily influenced by selecting a correct GPU combination. Talle et al. [26] contrast the performance of a PCIe based GPU interconnect with NVIDIA's NVLink interconnect to determine the performance impact each can entail. They use NVIDIA DGX-1 and Cirrascale GX8 to develop this comparison, leading them to conclude that DGX-1 is attributed with higher performance due to the additional links and higher per-link bandwidth associated with the NVLinks.

8 Conclusion

With enhancing GPU-enabled OpenPOWER architectures, HPC applications are achieving higher performance through exploiting the various features that enable such efficiency. CUDA-aware MPI is the communication standard that is able to exploit these features. In order to optimize HPC applications, take advantage of the enhanced support provided, and achieve peak performance, we need detailed evaluation of the most efficient communication libraries to use.

In this paper, the following three MPI libraries: SpectrumMPI, OpenMPI, and MVAPICH2-GDR were evaluated based on the latency, uni-directional bandwidth, and bi-directional bandwidth of point-to-point communication. The evaluation results show that all three MPI libraries deliver approximately 95% of achievable bandwidth for NVLink communication between two GPUs on the same socket. Most notably, for inter-node communication where the InfiniBand network determines the peak bandwidth, MVAPICH2-GDR and SpectrumMPI attain approximately 99% achievable bandwidth, while OpenMPI delivers close to 95%. Through our evaluation of these MPI libraries on GPU-enabled OpenPOWER architectures, we witnessed varying performance associated with each library based on the interconnects selected.

Finally, we have identified the following performance limitations for the state-of-the-art CUDA-aware MPI libraries: (1) communication between the CPU and

GPU is not utilizing NVLink efficiently, (2) the bi-directional X-bus is not fully utilized by the MPI libraries, and (3) bandwidth is limited when MPI processes are sharing the GPU. In the future, we plan to conduct a comprehensive evaluation to include MPI collectives for GPU-resident data on OpenPOWER systems and their impact on applications.

References

1. IBM Spectrum MPI version 10.3. https://www.ibm.com
2. Infiniband Verbs Performance Tests. https://github.com/linux-rdma/perftest. Accessed 26 Oct 2019
3. MVAPICH: MPI over InfiniBand, Omni-Path, Ethernet/iWARP, and RoCE. http://mvapich.cse.ohio-state.edu/features/
4. Open MPI: Open Source High Performance Computing. https://www.open-mpi. org
5. TOP 500 Supercomputer Sites. http://www.top500.org
6. Unified Communication X. http://www.openucx.org/. Accessed 26 Oct 2019
7. Ashworth, M., Meng, J., Novakovic, V., Siso, S.: Early application performance at the hartree centre with the OpenPOWER architecture. In: Taufer, M., Mohr, B., Kunkel, J.M. (eds.) ISC High Performance 2016. LNCS, vol. 9945, pp. 173–187. Springer, Cham (2016). https://doi.org/10.1007/978-3-319-46079-6_13
8. Awan, A.A., Bédorf, J., Chu, C.H., Subramoni, H., Panda, D.K.: Scalable distributed DNN training using TensorFlow and CUDA-aware MPI: characterization, designs, and performance evaluation. In: The 19th Annual IEEE/ACM International Symposium in Cluster, Cloud, and Grid Computing (CCGRID 2019) (2019)
9. Bureddy, D., Wang, H., Venkatesh, A., Potluri, S., Panda, D.K.: OMB-GPU: a micro-benchmark suite for evaluating MPI libraries on GPU clusters. In: Träff, J.L., Benkner, S., Dongarra, J.J. (eds.) EuroMPI 2012. LNCS, vol. 7490, pp. 110–120. Springer, Heidelberg (2012). https://doi.org/10.1007/978-3-642-33518-1_16
10. Pearson, C., Chung, I.-H., Sura, Z., Hwu, W.-M., Xiong, J.: NUMA-aware data-transfer measurements for power/NVLink multi-GPU systems. In: Yokota, R., Weiland, M., Shalf, J., Alam, S. (eds.) ISC High Performance 2018. LNCS, vol. 11203, pp. 448–454. Springer, Cham (2018). https://doi.org/10.1007/978-3-030-02465-9_32
11. Chu, C.H., Hamidouche, K., Venkatesh, A., Banerjee, D.S., Subramoni, H., Panda, D.K.: Exploiting maximal overlap for non-contiguous data movement processing on modern GPU-enabled systems. In: 2016 IEEE International Parallel and Distributed Processing Symposium (IPDPS), pp. 983–992, May 2016
12. Chu, C.H., et al.: Efficient and scalable multi-source streaming broadcast on GPU clusters for deep learning. In: 46th International Conference on Parallel Processing (ICPP-2017), August 2017
13. Foley, D., Danskin, J.: Ultra-performance pascal GPU and NVLink interconnect. IEEE Micro 37(2), 7–17 (2017). https://doi.org/10.1109/MM.2017.37
14. Gabriel, E., et al.: Open MPI: goals, concept, and design of a next generation MPI implementation. In: Kranzlmüller, D., Kacsuk, P., Dongarra, J. (eds.) EuroPVM/MPI 2004. LNCS, vol. 3241, pp. 97–104. Springer, Heidelberg (2004). https://doi.org/10.1007/978-3-540-30218-6_19
15. McCalpin, J.D.: STREAM: sustainable memory bandwidth in high performance computers (2019). https://www.cs.virginia.edu/stream/. Accessed 26 Oct 2019

16. Li, A., et al.: Evaluating modern GPU interconnect: PCIe, NVLink, NV-SLI, NVSwitch and GPUDirect. CoRR abs/1903.04611 (2019). http://arxiv.org/abs/1903.04611

17. Luo, X., Wu, W., Bosilca, G., Patinyasakdikul, T., Wang, L., Dongarra, J.: ADAPT: an event-based adaptive collective communication framework. In: Proceedings of the 27th International Symposium on High-Performance Parallel and Distributed Computing, HPDC 2018, pp. 118–130. ACM, New York (2018). https://doi.org/10.1145/3208040.3208054

18. Mojumder, S.A., et al.: Profiling DNN workloads on a volta-based DGX-1 system. In: 2018 IEEE International Symposium on Workload Characterization (IISWC), pp. 122–133, September 2018. https://doi.org/10.1109/IISWC.2018.8573521

19. Moreno, R., Arias, E., Navarro, A., Tapiador, F.J.: How good is the OpenPOWER architecture for high-performance CPU-oriented weather forecasting applications? J. Supercomput., April 2019. https://doi.org/10.1007/s11227-019-02844-3

20. NVIDIA: NVIDIA GPUDirect. https://developer.nvidia.com/gpudirect. Accessed 26 Oct 2019

21. NVIDIA: NVIDIA Tesla V100 GPU Architecture (2019). https://images.nvidia.com/content/volta-architecture/pdf/volta-architecture-whitepaper.pdf. Accessed 26 Oct 2019

22. Pfister, G.F.: An introduction to the infiniband architecture. High Perform. Mass Storage Parallel I/O **42**, 617–632 (2001)

23. Potluri, S., Hamidouche, K., Venkatesh, A., Bureddy, D., Panda, D.K.: Efficient inter-node MPI communication using GPUDirect RDMA for InfiniBand clusters with NVIDIA GPUs. In: 2013 42nd International Conference on Parallel Processing (ICPP), pp. 80–89. IEEE (2013)

24. Shi, R., et al.: Designing efficient small message transfer mechanism for inter-node MPI communication on InfiniBand GPU clusters. In: 2014 21st International Conference on High Performance Computing (HiPC), pp. 1–10, December 2014

25. Stone, J.E., Hynninen, A.-P., Phillips, J.C., Schulten, K.: Early experiences porting the NAMD and VMD molecular simulation and analysis software to GPU-accelerated OpenPOWER platforms. In: Taufer, M., Mohr, B., Kunkel, J.M. (eds.) ISC High Performance 2016. LNCS, vol. 9945, pp. 188–206. Springer, Cham (2016). https://doi.org/10.1007/978-3-319-46079-6_14

26. Tallent, N.R., Gawande, N.A., Siegel, C., Vishnu, A., Hoisie, A.: Evaluating on-node GPU interconnects for deep learning workloads. In: Jarvis, S., Wright, S., Hammond, S. (eds.) PMBS 2017. LNCS, vol. 10724, pp. 3–21. Springer, Cham (2018). https://doi.org/10.1007/978-3-319-72971-8_1

27. Vazhkudai, S.S., et al..: The design, deployment, and evaluation of the CORAL pre-exascale systems. In: Proceedings of the International Conference for High Performance Computing, Networking, Storage, and Analysis, SC 2018, pp. 52:1–52:12. IEEE Press, Piscataway (2018). http://dl.acm.org/citation.cfm?id=3291656.3291726

28. Wang, H., Potluri, S., Bureddy, D., Rosales, C., Panda, D.K.: GPU-aware MPI on RDMA-enabled clusters: design, implementation and evaluation. IEEE Trans. Parallel Distrib. Syst. **25**(10), 2595–2605 (2014). https://doi.org/10.1109/TPDS.2013.222

Exploring the Behavior of Coherent Accelerator Processor Interface (CAPI) on IBM Power8+ Architecture and FlashSystem 900

Kaushik Velusamy$^{(\boxtimes)}$, Smriti Prathapan, and Milton Halem

University of Maryland Baltimore County, Baltimore, MD, USA
{kaushikvelusamy,smritip1,halem}@umbc.edu
https://carta.umbc.edu/

Abstract. The Coherent Accelerator Processor Interface (CAPI) is a general term for the infrastructure that provides high throughput and low latency path to the flash storage connected to the IBM POWER 8+ System. CAPI accelerator card is attached coherently as a peer to the Power8+ processor. This removes the overhead and complexity of the IO subsystem and allows the accelerator to operate as part of an application. In this paper, we present the results of experiments on IBM FlashSystem900 (FS900) with CAPI accelerator card using the "CAPI-Flash - IBM Data Engine for NoSQL Software" Library. This library provides the application, a direct access to the underlying flash storage through user space APIs, to manage and access the data in flash. This offloads kernel IO driver functionality to dedicated CAPI FPGA accelerator hardware. We conducted experiments to analyze the performance of FS900 with CAPI accelerator card, using the Key Value Layer APIs, employing NASA's MODIS Land Surface Reflectance dataset as a large dataset use case. We performed Read and Write operations on datasets of size ranging from 1MB to 3TB by varying the number of threads. We then compared this performance with other heterogeneous storage and memory devices such as NVM, SSD and RAM, without using the CAPI Accelerator in synchronous and asynchronous file IO modes of operations. The asynchronous mode had the best performance on all the memory devices that we used for this study. In particular, the results indicate that FS900 & CAPI, together with the metadata cache in RAM, delivers the highest IO/s and OP/s for read operations. This was higher than just using RAM, along with utilizing lesser CPU resources. Among FS900, SSD and NVM, FS900 had the highest write IO/s. Another important observation is that, when the size of the input dataset exceeds the capacity of RAM, and when the data access is non-uniform and sparse, FS900 with CAPI would be a cost-effective alternative.

Keywords: CAPI · Accelerators · Heterogeneous storage · NVM · Flash · SSDs

© Springer Nature Switzerland AG 2019
M. Weiland et al. (Eds.): ISC 2019 Workshops, LNCS 11887, pp. 379–396, 2019.
https://doi.org/10.1007/978-3-030-34356-9_29

1   Introduction

Emerging needs as we approach for exascale computing bring new challenges related to heterogeneous computing which requires intensive analysis of massive and dynamic data. These new data challenges require us to move from conventional processing to new paradigms to better exploit and optimize the IO system architecture to support these needs [2]. The increase in computational bandwidth brings a massive increase in memory bandwidth requirements. High bandwidth memory (HBM) [3] enabled FPGA accelerators address these challenges to provide a large memory bandwidth. The use of accelerators as co-processors is the most prevalent way to achieve performance gains to compensate for the slowdown of Moore's Law. However, there are limiting factors in this approach such as (1) device driver overheads (2) operating system code path length (3) and CPU overhead required in managing the IO requests. Coherent Accelerator Processor Interface (CAPI) was developed to address these challenges, where an accelerator is attached coherently as a peer to the CPU through its IO physical interface [1].

This method significantly increases the performance of the accelerator when compared to the traditional IO model. The performance of a CAPI attached heterogeneous storage device is drastically improved by reducing the overhead of the device driver in the operating system. It also allows direct memory access to the underlying storage without the calls to the device driver and without any intervention from the operating system thereby, reducing the code path length.

Our goal is to understand and analyze the performance capabilities of Power8+ CAPI infrastructure through FlashSystem900 (FS900) and compare it with the other heterogeneous memory devices without CAPI. For this experiment, we use the Key Value (KV) Layer (ArkDB) APIs provided by IBM CAPI-Flash library [4]. The CAPIFlash library provides a multiple of 4K block access to the flash. Our benchmark application uses this facility provided by the library to read a 4K block for the values. Our benchmark results directly relate to real-world application performance. Apart from obtaining the peak performance (IO/s, OP/s and Time) of the heterogeneous storage devices, we also focus on storage and computational efficiency.

This paper makes the following contributions:

- Analyze the performance of the CPU threads for read/write workload on IBM FS900 with CAPI and compare it to RAM, NVM and SSD (Without CAPI) using the CAPIFlash library's synchronous and asynchronous modes of communication.
- Analyze the time taken to completion with varying threads, optimal IO/s (Input Output per second) and OP/s (OPerations per second) of heterogeneous storage devices.
- Analyze the impact of CPU usage in handling the IO requests in heterogeneous storage systems when using CAPIFlash library.
- Provide a performance evaluation of IBM FS900 with CAPI and RAM without CAPI when the input dataset size exceeds the capacity of RAM (1 TB).

The paper is organized as follows. Section 2 presents the background, featuring the enhancements that adding CAPI to the architecture brings. Section 3 details the library used in our experiments - CAPIFlash Library Design, from the kernel to the API. Section 4 describes the Test Bed and System Configuration. Section 5 explains the Experimental Setup and the Benchmark. The Performance Results are presented in Sect. 6. Related works are discussed in Sect. 7, followed by the conclusions and the summary in Sect. 8.

2 Background

The main problem we encounter with traditional flash storage is the CPU overhead leading to stranded IOs [5]. There was a CPU overhead in managing the IO requests as it flows through the CPU to the storage device. Even with the multi-core architecture, more CPUs are needed to handle the IO request. This results in the wastage of significant portions of the available CPUs that are tied to the IO overhead, rather than doing the useful computations. For applications that require high computational power, multi-core processors often do not suffice to provide high performance. The use of hardware accelerators such as GPUs, ASICs, and FPGAs can provide increased performance for massively parallel programmable architectures for a wide range of applications.

On each Power8+ processor, there is one CAPI interface called Coherent Accelerator Processor Proxy (CAPP). The PCIe Host Bridge (PHB) on the processor connects to the PCIe IO links. The CAPP unit together with PHB acts as memory coherence, data transfer, interrupt, and address translation agents on the Symmetric Multi Processor (SMP) interconnect fabric for PCIe-attached accelerator [6]. This FPGA accelerator has a Power Service Layer (PSL) which provides address translation and system memory cache for the Accelerator Function Unit (AFU) and is connected to the Power8+ processor chip by the PCIe link. The combination of PSL, PCIe link, PHB, and CAPP enhance the capabilities of AFUs. AFUs operate coherently on the data in memory, as peers of other caches in the system.

An application which runs on the processor core has a virtual address space on the memory for performing IO with other devices attached to the processor. In a heterogeneous compute cluster without CAPI, a hardware accelerator such as an FPGA is attached using a PCIe. This leads to having many separate copies of the data, thereby adding overhead to using the FPGA. Since the copies of the data reside in different memory address spaces, any changes that were made to the data by the application would not be coherent with that on the FPGA.

With CAPI FPGA attached to a PCIe, the PSL layer is used to access shared memory regions and cache areas as though they were a processor in the system. This ability enhances the performance of the data access and simplifies the programming effort to use the storage device. Instead of treating the hardware accelerator as an IO device, it is treated as a co-processor, which eliminates the requirement of a device driver to perform communication and the need for Direct Memory Access that requires system calls to the operating system (OS) kernel.

By removing these layers, the data transfer operation requires much fewer clock cycles in the processor, improving the IO performance [9].

Hence with CAPI, there are fewer overheads in IO, thereby minimizing thousands of instructions. All the data is coherently managed by the hardware. Furthermore, an FPGA accelerator can now act as an additional core in the server with a coherent memory. CAPI enables many heterogeneous memory devices to coherently attach to the Power8+ processors, facilitating an environment to connect various high bandwidth IO devices [8]. By using CAPI, terabytes of the flash storage array can be attached to the Power8+ CPU via an FPGA. CAPI enables applications to get direct access to the hardware storage (a large flash array) with reduced IO latency and overhead, thereby increasing the read/write performance compared to the standard IO-attached flash storage [5]. CAPI also eliminates the context switch penalties caused by interrupts. All these benefits enable CAPI to provide a hybrid computing environment. For more information on the Coherent Accelerator Processor Interface on Power8+ Processor chip refer to the CAPI user manual [7].

3   CAPIFlash Design

In the Linux kernel, the Coherent Accelerator Interface (CXL) is designed to allow the coherent connection of accelerators (FPGAs and other devices) to a Power processor [11]. Through LibCXL, the user-space applications can directly communicate to a device (network or storage) bypassing the typical kernel/device driver stack. The CXL flash adapter driver enables direct access to flash storage for a userspace application. Applications which need access to the CXL Flash from the user space should use the CAPIFlash library. More information about the interfacing between CXL and the CAPIFlash is provided in [10].

The CAPIFlash library IBM Data Engine for NoSQL – Integrated Flash Edition [4] was built on Power8 systems with CAPI. This library helps to create a new tier of memory by attaching up to 57 terabytes of auxiliary flash memory to the processor. This library provides two sets of public APIs for reading and writing to the physical address space on the flash device: 1. Cflash - Block Layer APIs and 2. ArkDB - Key Value (KV) Layer APIs. Our benchmark is focused mainly on the ArkDB KV layer APIs. The ArkDB KV layer API provides synchronous and asynchronous read/write requests to the flash memory.

The send and receive operations to the KV Store (ArkDB) on the intended device (FS900, RAM, NVM, SSD) can be either synchronous or asynchronous. In synchronous operation, with a read/write request, the operation is initiated, following which the process is blocked and the system waits for the completion of the process. During this time, the ArkDB threads store and retrieve the data from the KV database instance (ArkDB) on the intended devices through CAPI.

In an asynchronous operation, the processes run in non-blocking mode. It initiates the operation and does not wait for the completion to start the next operation. The caller would discover the completion of the operations later by polling the ArkDB. Since the processes are non-blocking in asynchronous message passing setup, some computations can be performed when the message is in transit, thereby allowing more parallelism.

4 Test Bed and System Configuration

In this work, the following storage devices have been used for performance analysis using the CAPI infrastructure. Flash memory, as a storage technology, is available in multiple forms, such as IBM FS900 or PCIe NVMe-SSD or a standard SSD product with a hard disk form factor.

4.1 CAPI Adapter

The PCIe3 LP CORSA CAPI fibre channel Flash Accelerator x8 adapter (FC EJ16; 04CF) (Nallatech 385A72 with Intel Altera) FPGA accelerator card (with two 4 GB DDR3), acts as a co-processor for the Power8+ processor. This is designed to offload CPU access to external fiber channel flash storage [12]. The adapter requires a direct-attach, point-to-point 8Gb fiber channel link to external storage, such as IBM FS900 [12]. This FPGA accelerator card includes the CAPI PSL, AFU [7] and interfaces to fiber channel IO ports to allow direct memory access to an IBM Flash System [5]. The EJ1K CAPI flash accelerator leverages the ability to provide high throughput, low latency connection to flash memory to address the scaling problems found in typical flash deployments [5]. The clock rate of the PCIe bridge is 33 MHz.

4.2 IBM FlashSystem 900

FS900 uses FPGA based flash arrays without involving processors and is cost effective when compared to DRAM [11]. The flash memory in the IBM FS900 has higher performance due to hardware only data path whereas a traditional SSD based flash memory is typically limited by the software processing. The IBM FS900 is connected to the CAPI accelerator through a fiber channel. This storage device is configured at RAID 5 and has a usable capacity of 20 TB. It also enables a distributed random-access memory and allows massive data parallelism. FS900 has persistent memory whereas RAM does not. The maximum 4 KB IOPS 100% random read is 1,100,000 and 100% random write is 600,000.

We used one CAPI accelerator card, which has two ports, with the World Wide Port Name (WWPN) for each port mapped to a single volume. The KV experiments on the IBM FS900 were performed by setting the two volumes of FS900 (each 10 TB) in superpipe mode. This enables hardware acceleration, with the CPU offloading IO to the device.

4.3   NVM and SSD

NVMe is a host controller interface and a storage protocol, designed to accelerate the speed of data transfer using the PCIe bus, through processor-based storage solutions. It can read/write NAND flash memory to deliver the full potential of non-volatile memory in PCIe-based solid-state storage devices. The NVM in Power8+ system uses PCIe3, 3.2 TB NVMe Flash x4 adapter CCIN non-volatile memory controller (HGST Inc Ultrastar SN100) series with Non-Volatile Memory Express (NVMe) SSD. For the PCIe Interconnect, each POWER8 processor has 32 PCIe lanes running at 9.6 Gbps full-duplex. The theoretical bandwidth is: 32 lanes × 2 processors × 9.6 Gbps × 2 = 153.6 GB/s [9].

The Samsung SATA SSD (MZ7LM3T8HCJM) used in the S822LC system has a capacity of 3.840 TB with a form factor of 2.5″ inches. This SSD use a V-NAND technology and has a data transfer rate of 600 MBps. There are 2 SSDs in this Power8+ system and are connected to the integrated SATA controller in the motherboard.

4.4   RAM

RAM in the IBM Minsky system has a total capacity of 1 TB. The Power8+ S822LC computing server provides 8 DIMM memory slots each with 128 GB, allowing for a maximum system memory of 1024 GB DDR3 ECC at 1333 MHz. Each Power8+ processor has four memory channels running at 9.6 Gb/s capable of reading 2 Bytes and writing 1 byte at a time. The total theoretical memory bandwidth is: 4 channels * 9.6 Gb/s * 3 Bytes = 115.2 GB/s per processor module [9].

4.5   Processor

This CAPI enabled system S822LC server has two 64-bit IBM Power8+ processors with 10 cores each with 8 threads/core, running at a clock rate of 4 GHz. This system runs Ubuntu OS (version - 16.04.5 LTS) on the PPC64LE architecture. It has a 64 KB D cache, 32KB I cache, 512 KB private L2, 8 MB L3 per core (96M)on a 22 nm chip. The processor to memory bandwidth is 170 GB/s per socket i.e. 340 GB/s per system and IO bandwidth of 64 GB/s simplex. Each Power8+ processor has 2 memory controller. Each memory controller has a two buffer L4 cache and each of them are connected to four RAM DIMM slots [9]. POWER8+ is a revised version of the original 12-core POWER8 from IBM. The main new feature is the support for Nvidia's bus technology NVLink, connecting up to four NVLink devices directly to the chip. IBM removed the "A Bus and PCI interfaces" for SMP connections to other POWER8 sockets and replaced them with NVLink interfaces.

5 Experimental Setup and Benchmark Overview

5.1 Dataset

The input data used for this work is NASA's MODIS (MODerate-resolution Imaging Spectrometer) Terra/Aqua Surface Reflectance data [13]. Surface reflectance is the amount of light reflected by the surface of the earth. In addition to the geo-location coordinates, the data contains several fields collected every 5 min at 250 m, 500 m and 1 km resolution as 8-bit, 16-bit or 32-bit signed float/integer types. A sample structure for a refined subset of this dataset is shown in Table 1. The data attributes that are of interest for this study are: Key, Value4, Value5 and Value6 with each entity of size 8 Bytes with a total of 32 Bytes per row in the input data. In our experiments, the dataset ranges from 10 million KV pair records (543 MB) to 100 billion KV pair records (3.1 TB).

Table 1. Data fields in the MODIS Surface Reflectance dataset

Key	Value 1	Value 2	Value 3	Value 4	Value 5	Value 6
No:	Latitude	Longitude	Day	Band 1	Band 2	Band 3
1	80.647079	34.720413	67	-28672	-28672	-28672
2	80.658272	34.457428	67	-28672	-28672	-28672
.	..	..	..	..	..	..

5.2 Performance Metrics

Some of the performance metrics used for this experiment are as follows. OP/s is the number of Set(write)/Get(read) operations per second submitted by the CAPIFlash library. IO/s or IOPS is the number of IO operations per second. Read time/Write time is the time taken to complete entire reading/writing of data (in seconds).

5.3 CAPI Flash Parameters

The following are the important parameters used for evaluating this benchmark; 1. Hcount, 2. Threads, 3. Queue Depth, 4. Metadata Cache.

The CAPIFlash library provides access to the flash in multiples of 4K blocks. The hcount (-h) parameter is a calculation of how the KV pairs fit into a physical 4K block [4]. This, in turn, provides a more balanced allocation of storage space, thereby increasing the performance and storage efficiency. Hcount is calculated by dividing 4K by (32 (Bytes per KV entry in the dataset) + 8 Bytes (metadata)). Hence, a value of 100 would give the best performance for a dataset where each record is of 32 Bytes. The value 100 in this calculation means that the read/write operations would be performed on 100 KV pairs in parallel in a given 4K block. The value of `hcount` is calculated as the total number of KV pairs in the input data divided by 100 in this example. The total memory allocated in Bytes (*inuse*) would then be close to the Bytes written to the KV instance (*actual*), thus providing an optimal storage efficiency.

There are two different threads with regards to this benchmark: 1. application threads and 2. ArkDB threads. Each read/write is an operation submitted by application thread(s) to the ArkDB, and then the application threads poll the ArkDB for their completion. There is a maximum number of operations that can be queued to the ArkDB. The maximum value for `QueueDepth` (QD) is 1024 with a default of 400. The queued operations are then submitted by the ArkDB threads to the storage media. QD represents the number of ArkDB operations which may run in parallel.

In synchronous mode, an application thread sends a command (read/write) and waits for completion while the ArkDB threads do the work. As a result, one thread can do $QD = 1$. More threads are required to handle a greater value of QD. In asynchronous mode, each operation submitted adds to the QD. A certain QD is required to reach the maximum bandwidth of the card. In asynchronous mode, with more threads, more CPU is used. The threads can be increased until the maximum performance is obtained. In asynchronous mode, one thread may submit any number of operations ($QD = N$) and then check for the completion of each command. The ArkDB threads do the database side of the work. Too many ArkDB threads increase CPU usage without increasing `OP/s` and reduce the overall performance. Hence finding an optimal thread for the peak performance is important. The threads mentioned in the remainder of the experiment are the ArkDB threads. The number of threads can be passed in as an input parameter which specifies the total ArkDB threads.

FS900 can be used either with `MetaDataCache` turned on or off. This allows a part of the RAM to be used as a cache for the data access to the FS900. Note that, the number of IO/s for FS900 which are greater than 400 K are from the ArkDB cache hits, which is RAM. In order to get the maximum performance for the benchmark, all FS900 experiments were run with ArkDB metadata cache hits (RAM) enabled unless specified.

5.4   Benchmark Application

The benchmark application used, runs a simple read/write operation to the KV store (ArkDB) on the intended devices (FS900, RAM, NVM, SSD) using the KV layer APIs of the CAPIFlash library. Only FS900 uses the CAPI accelerator card in the real IO mode, whereas NVM and SSD do not use the CAPI accelerator and are configured in the file IO mode. When the benchmark application requests to run to a file on NVM or SSD, the Block API diverts to the file before reaching the CAPI card [5]. When the benchmark application requests to run on RAM, then the ArkDB API diverts the calls to RAM, before reaching the CAPI card. The CAPI card is not used when running the application to RAM. FS900 experiments were run with enabling the metadata cache (RAM). When an ArkDB operation gets a hit on the ArkDB metadata cache, the call does not go to the CAPI card or FS900. When the maximum bandwidth of a single Corsa CAPI card reaches 380K IO/s, any OP/s higher than 380K, are due to the ArkDB cache hits. We ran the KV R/W experiments by varying the threads from 1 to 128 and QD = 400 in both synchronous and asynchronous modes to find out the peak performance of each device. Finally, we summarize the overall read/write performance for all storage devices. The CAPIFlash library version used in this experiment is 5.0.2706.

6   Performance Results

6.1   Performance of Write Operations

The results of Write performance of FS900, RAM, NVM and SSD for a dataset of 10 million KV pairs (0.5 GB) are in Fig. 1. In synchronous Write IO/s graph, for FS900, NVM and SSD, there was a plateau in the graph between 0.4 million to 0.8 million IO/s after 10 threads, with FS900 giving the maximum IO/s out of the three devices. For RAM, after 40 threads, the IO/s plateaued around 3.25 million after 40 threads. A similar trend was observed in the synchronous OP/s graph. With asynchronous Write IO/s graph, increasing the number of threads increased the IO/s performance in RAM until 5 million IO/s. There was little variation in the case of FS900, SSD and NVM. A similar trend was observed in the asynchronous OP/s graph. In the case of analyzing the time to completion for read/write operations, having a lower value is better. For write operations, the optimal threads for all devices were found around 30 threads. After 30 threads, each of the devices plateaued around a band of certain time regions without decreasing much time. From Fig. 1 for write operations, it is clear that the best performance was found in the following order: RAM, FS900, NVM and SSD. Asynchronous mode was able to give the peak performance. RAM consumed more numbers of threads to reach peak IO/s and OP/s, whereas for FS900, 10 threads were enough to reach the peak performance and lowest completion time. The performance in asynchronous mode was found to be better since the computations do not block the process to wait for its completion, as opposed to synchronous mode. In asynchronous mode, the ArkDB threads continue the computations while the messages are in transit and this approach allows more parallelism. The main advantage of FS900 with CAPI is the use of lesser CPU resources (if CPU threads are crucial to the application). Throughout the write operation, it is observed that using too many ArkDB threads decreases performance without increasing IO/s or OP/s and reduces the latency. For write operations, SSD and NVM showed similar performances as FS900.

6.2   Performance of Read Operations

Figure 2 depicts the performance comparison on all the devices for reading 10 million KV pairs. For synchronous mode, the read IO/s for all devices lie around 1.5 million to 4.5 million, whereas in asynchronous mode, increase in threads

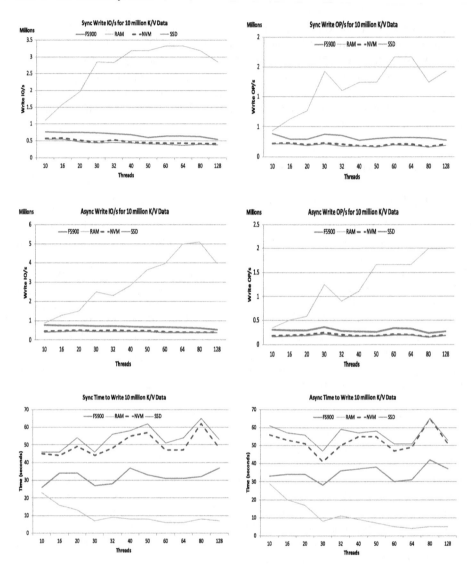

Fig. 1. Write performance for FS900, RAM, NVM and SSD

almost gave a linear increase in read IO/s. In synchronous mode, FS900, NVM and SSD gave the maximum read IO/s compared to RAM. In the case of asynchronous, FS900 gave the maximum performance of 17 million IO/s. SSD and NVM at 10 million IO/s and RAM at 6 million IO/s. For OP/s, FS900 performed better than RAM in both synchronous and asynchronous modes. FS900 took less time to complete the read operation in comparison with RAM. This was possible even with lesser number of threads. Based on our analysis, RAM is well suited for write-intensive workloads. For read operations, FS900 was found to be bet-

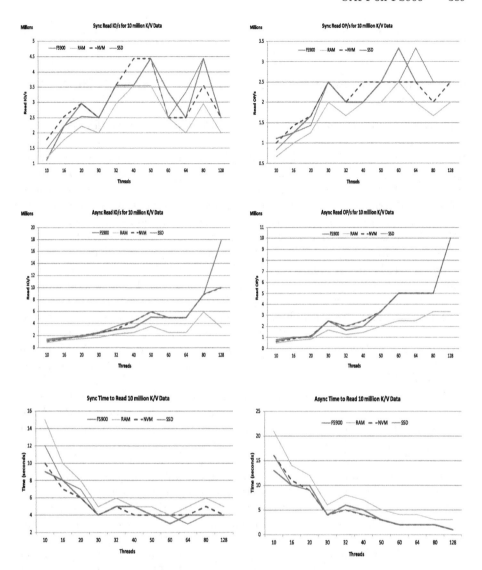

Fig. 2. Read performance for FS900, RAM, NVM and SSD

ter than RAM. Having a RAM of large capacity comes at a higher overall cost. Similar or near to RAM performance could be achieved with FS900 at a lesser cost [11]. CAPI facilitates attaching terabytes of the flash storage array to the Power8+ CPU with reduced IO latency and overhead compared to a standard IO-attached flash storage. FS900 with CAPI, when using the RAM metadata cache, performed 2x as many read operations in synchronous mode and 3x in asynchronous mode. The lower performance of RAM may be due to the CPU overhead required in managing IO operations. Without metadata cache, FS900 gave a steady 380K IO/s in both the modes consistently for all threads above 10.

6.3 Summary of Read Write Performance of RAM, FS900, NVM and SSD

The peak R/W performance for 10 million KV pairs on all the devices is summarized in Fig. 3. The best values of read and write OP/s, IO/s and time are compared for all the devices. RAM outperformed all the other devices for write in terms of OP/s, IO/s and completion time. Hence for write-intensive applications, RAM would provide the best performance. Although RAM performed the best for write operations, FS900 provided the highest IO/s for reads. To read 10 million KV pairs, FS900 had the peak IO/s and lowest read completion time. RAM was 2x slower than the other devices in asynchronous mode and 1.3x slower in synchronous mode. After 128 threads, the performance plateaued.

Based on the above analysis, we chose an optimal thread (40), QD (400) and compared the performance of synchronous and asynchronous modes on all devices for 30 million KV pairs (1.6 GB dataset) and the results are shown in Figs. 4 and 5. Here, we also show the difference in the performance between FS900 with meta data cache (WMC) enabled and without meta data cache (WoMC). For all the devices, asynchronous mode gave the peak performance and the lowest completion time, with FS900 giving the peak read IO/s compared to other devices.

Figures 6 and 7 details the CPU utilization (% CPU and SYS % CPU) for 30 million KV pairs. The graphs start with a straight line indicating the Write operation. The change in the slope of the line indicates that the write operation is completed and the Read operation has begun. This second part of the line indicates the CPU consumption during read operation. The series lines end at different times for different devices, indicating the faster completion time. With regards to % CPU consumption, FS900 in asynchronous is found to be an efficient choice next only to RAM. Considering the fact that FS900 gives the peak performance with IO/s and OP/s, this minimal difference in CPU consumption can be eliminated. With % SYS CPU consumption, the time spent on running kernel space system process, FS900 asynchronous with metadata cache enabled is found to be an optimal choice, especially for reads. The reason for the limited CPU consumption is due to the fact that, the total number of instructions per IO is reduced with CAPI. This leads to significant improvement in processor time spent in managing the IO. This, in effect, frees up processing resources for actual compute work and not just moving around data [5].

6.4 Performance of ark_nextN API

A normal read (without NextN) calls ark_get API for each key in the ArkDB to return the value for the key, and these operations are done in parallel based on QD. Whereas, the ark_nextN API returns each key and not its value in the ArkDB, in a psuedo-random order, one operation at a time. The ark_next API

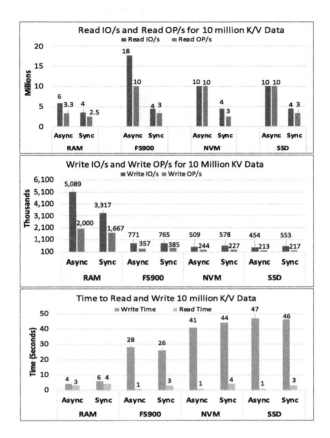

Fig. 3. Peak performance of FS900, RAM, NVM and SSD for 10 Million KV dataset

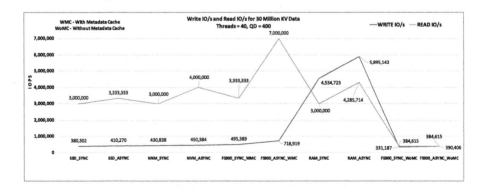

Fig. 4. IO/s performance of FS900, RAM, NVM and SSD for 30 Million KV dataset

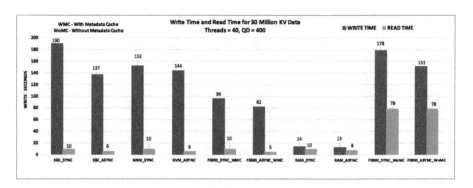

Fig. 5. Read Time and Write Time of FS900, RAM, NVM and SSD for 30 Million KV dataset

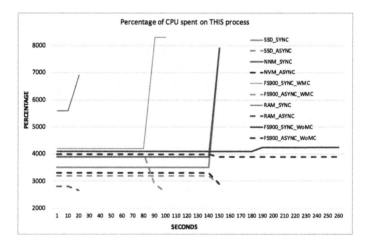

Fig. 6. CPU% used by the application process for 30 million KV dataset

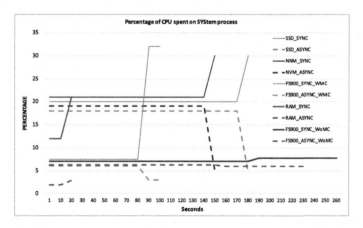

Fig. 7. CPU% used by the system process for 30 million KV dataset

reads one KV pair at a time for each 4K reads. ark_nextN API gets "N" keys at a time for each 4K reads in the ArkDB store. For the dataset in this study: key = 8 Bytes and values = 24 Bytes. This is about 100x faster for just reading the keys.

Table 2. Performance of ark_ nextN API for SSD, NVM, RAM, FS900 in Asynchronous Mode for 100 million (5 GB) KV dataset

Device	G Value	Write			Read		
		OP/s	IO/s	Time (seconds)	OP/s	IO/s	Time (seconds)
SSD	1	39,840	326,236	251	6,086	48,861	1,643
	1000	40,000	356,924	250	5,250	42,148	2
NVM	1	41,152	367,205	243	6,644	53,341	1,505
	1000	41,152	367,205	243	5,250	42,148	2
FS900	1	285,714	727,040	35	4,411	7,832	2,267
	1000	294,117	748,424	34	3,973	5,772	23
RAM	1	588,235	1,496,848	17	86,956	154,396	115
	1000	555,555	1,413,689	18	91,385	132,769	1

With $G = 1$ vs $G = 1000$, there was around 800x improvement on read time from SSD and NVM and 100x improvement for FS900 and RAM. Table 2 also indicates that, even though the read IO/s and OP/s was not the maximum or the optimal for the device. We were able to reduce the time-taken by a huge margin with ark_nextN API. This was also the reason why we focused on getting the peak IO/s and OP/s rather than the time taken to completion.

6.5   Large Experiments Results

Using a CAPI Interface, FS900 performs better for read operations than the other devices, including RAM. This becomes highly advantageous when the dataset size is very large. Table 3 shows the results of the performance experiments on larger datasets (120 GB, 954 GB, 1500 GB and 3 TB). The OP/s and IO/s for FS900 were almost consistent, irrespective of the dataset size. In the case of RAM, the performance of read/write OP/s and IO/s increased by around 1.5 times until the dataset size is less than the size of RAM (1 TB). When the dataset size gets larger than the size of RAM, RAM can have cache misses and the virtual memory manager would be using the system disk for swapping, thereby increasing the paging and latency. At this stage, we observed a drastic decrease in the performance of IO/s and OP/s for RAM. For the dataset with 100 billion KV pairs (3.17 TB), FS900 provided a steady 380K IO/s for 71 h.

In general, RAM would be faster for most of the operations, but it comes with a limited capacity (1 TB). FS900 has 20 TB of storage and can also persist

Table 3. Large Experiments Results

Device	Dataset size	Write			Read		
		OP/s	IO/s	Time (seconds)	OP/s	IO/s	Time (seconds)
FS900	120 GB	166,223	331,259	18,048	358,808	381,680	8,361
	954 GB	179,750	357,695	138,386	383,222	383,222	64,910
	1.5 TB	188,628	375,354	210,148	383,822	383,822	103,277
	3.17 TB	189,564	377,477	515,391	382,732	382,732	255,270
RAM	120 GB	2,941,176	5,861,339	1,020	4,716,981	5,017,660	636
	954 GB	3,539,413	7,043,255	7,028	5,327,693	5,327,693	4,669
	1.5 TB	2,149,267	4,283,774	16,936	2,576,991	2,576,991	14,125

the data. The effectiveness of FS900 with CAPI comes into picture only when the dataset size is very large compared to the size of RAM. The CAPI 2.0 in Power9 makes use of the PCIe Gen4 and provides double the performance.

7 Related Works

There are various studies on benchmarking and evaluating heterogeneous storage systems. Apache Cassandra Optimized durable commit log using CAPI-Flash [14] focuses on durable logging on flash using Power8 CAPI-Flash. Their CAPI-Flash commit log showed a 107% better throughput in write-only workloads compared to Cassandra's durable alternative.

Our work is the first to study the performance of the FS900 with CAPI accelerator card through CAPIFlash read write benchmark. We also evaluated the performance by varying the threads and other parameters of the CAPIFlash library and compared it with RAM, SSD and NVM without using the CAPI accelerator. We evaluated the read time/write time, OP/s and IO/s of RAM, SSD, NVM and FS900 with both synchronous and asynchronous modes. We also found the optimal CPU threads and other parameters of the CAPIFlash library to attain a peak performance. These results for different memory devices, and their communication modes when using CAPIFlash library, will be helpful for developers in estimating their applications design choices.

8 Conclusions

In this paper, we examined the performance of the FS900 with CAPI accelerator card through a basic read/write benchmark and compared it to various heterogeneous storage devices. The asynchronous mode on all devices gave the best results with IBM FS900, giving the highest read IO/s. We were able to achieve peak performance on FS900 with CAPI, using a lesser number of threads. This enables the CPU resources to be efficiently used in other areas of the application. When the dataset size exceeds the capacity of RAM, FS900 would be a cost-effective alternative.

The flash memory in the IBM FS900 has higher performance due to hardware only data path, its distributed random-access memory and its allowance of massive parallelism in handling the data. The CAPI accelerator allows access to shared memory regions and cache areas as though they were a processor in the system. The CPU overhead in managing the IO request is now offloaded to the CAPI accelerator. The data transfer operation minimizes thousands of instructions and requires much fewer clock cycles in the processor. This improves the read/write performance of FS900 with CAPI unlike standard IO-attached flash storage. CAPI enables the class of IO-bound applications to perform better, where these advantages are a critical factor. Examples include weather prediction modeling and cybersecurity.

In future work, we plan to evaluate the FlashSystem 9150 utilizing the open-CAPI 3.1 on a Power 9+ architecture. We also hope to extend these studies to develop a real-time streaming grid application on the CAPI accelerator card using NASA's MODIS dataset.

Acknowledgement. We would like to thank Mike Vageline of IBM Cognitive Systems and Software Development for his support on the CAPIFlash - The IBM Data Engine for NoSQL library. We wish to acknowledge the NASA GSFC Distribution Active Archive Center (DAAC) for providing the MODIS Surface Reflectance (MOD09) data acquired from the Level-1 and Atmospheric Archive and Distribution System (LAADS) used for this study. We wish to thank Dale Pearson of IBM Yorktown Heights for providing this unique Power 8+ configuration with the FlashSystem 900. Finally, we wish to acknowledge the NSF Center for Accelerated Real-Time Analytics (NFS Award Number 1747724) and its industrial members for providing the resources to carry out this study.

References

1. Stuecheli, J., et al.: CAPI: a coherent accelerator processor interface. IBM J. Res. Dev. **59**(1), 1–7 (2015)
2. Adrian, M.: Big data. Teradata Magazine. http://www.teradatamagazine.com/v11n01/Features/Big-Data/
3. Jun, H., et al.: HBM (high bandwidth memory) DRAM technology and architecture. In: 2017 IEEE International Memory Workshop (IMW), pp. 1–4 (2017)
4. IBM Data Engine for NoSQL Software Libraries Source Code. https://github.com/open-power/capiflash
5. Solution Reference Guide to IBM Data Engine for NoSQL - Integrated Flsh Edition. http://ibm.biz/capiflash
6. Starke, W.J., et al.: The cache and memory subsystems of the IBM POWER8 processor. IBM J. Res. Dev. **59**(1), 1–3 (2015)
7. IBM Coherent Accelerator Processor Interface User's Manual. http://www.nallatech.com/wp-content/uploads/IBM_CAPI_Users_Guide.pdf
8. IBM CAPI Flash. https://developer.ibm.com/linuxonpower/capi/
9. Alexandre, et al.: IBM Power Systems S822LC Technical Overview and Introduction. IBM Red Books
10. Linux Coherent Accelerator driver cxlflash.txt manual. https://www.kernel.org/doc/Documentation/powerpc/cxlflash.txt

11. Gilge, M.: Redpaper Flash or SSD: Why and When to Use IBM FlashSystem Overview (2013)
12. IBM Power Systems Managing PCIe adapter for the S822LC and I/O expansion drawer Manual. ftp://ftp.software.ibm.com/systems/power/docs/hw/p8/p8hcd_85x.pdf
13. MODIS Surface Reflectance User Guide. http://modis-sr.ltdri.org/guide/MOD09_UserGuide_v1.4.pdf
14. Sendir, B., et al.: Optimized durable commitlog for Apache Cassandra using CAPI-Flash. In: 2016 IEEE 9th International Conference on Cloud Computing (CLOUD). IEEE (2016)

Porting Adaptive Ensemble Molecular Dynamics Workflows to the Summit Supercomputer

John Ossyra[1], Ada Sedova[2]([✉]) [iD], Arnold Tharrington[2] [iD], Frank Noé[3,4] [iD],
Cecilia Clementi[3,4] [iD], and Jeremy C. Smith[1,5] [iD]

[1] University of Tennessee, Knoxville, TN, USA
[2] Oak Ridge National Laboratory, Oak Ridge, TN, USA
sedovaaa@ornl.gov
[3] Freie Universität Berlin, Berlin, Germany
[4] Rice University, Houston, TX, USA
[5] Oak Ridge National Laboratory, University of Tennessee, Oak Ridge, TN, USA

Abstract. Molecular dynamics (MD) simulations must take very small (femtosecond) integration steps in simulation-time to avoid numerical errors. Efficient use of parallel programming models and accelerators in state-of-the art MD programs now is pushing Moore's limit for time-per-MD step. As a result, directly simulating timescales beyond milliseconds will not be attainable directly, even at exascale. However, concepts from statistical physics can be used to combine many parallel simulations to provide information about longer timescales and to adequately sample the simulation space, while preserving details about the dynamics of the system. Implementing such an approach requires a workflow program that allows adaptable steering of task assignments based on extensive statistical analysis of intermediate results. Here we report the implementation of such an adaptable workflow program to drive simulations on the Summit IBM Power System AC922, a pre-exascale supercomputer at the Oak Ridge Leadership Computing Facility (OLCF). We compare to experiences on Titan, Summit's predecessor, report the performance of the workflow and its components, and describe the porting process. We find that using a workflow program managed by a Mongo database can provide the fault tolerance, scalable performance, task dispatch rate, and reconfigurability required for robust and portable implementation of ensemble simulations such as are used in enhanced-sampling molecular dynamics. This type of workflow generator can also be used to provide

This manuscript has been authored by UT-Battelle, LLC under Contract No. DE-AC05-00OR22725 with the U.S. Department of Energy. The United States Government retains and the publisher, by accepting the article for publication, acknowledges that the United States Government retains a non-exclusive, paid-up, irrevocable, world-wide license to publish or reproduce the published form of this manuscript, or allow others to do so, for United States Government purposes. The Department of Energy will provide public access to these results of federally sponsored research in accordance with the DOE Public Access Plan (http://energy.gov/downloads/doe-public-access-plan.).

M. Weiland et al. (Eds.): ISC 2019 Workshops, LNCS 11887, pp. 397–417, 2019.
https://doi.org/10.1007/978-3-030-34356-9_30

adaptive steering of ensemble simulations for other applications in addition to MD.

Keywords: High Performance Computing · Molecular dynamics · Scientific workflows · Adaptive sampling

1 Introduction and Background

Molecular dynamics (MD) simulations of condensed-matter systems require small steps in simulation-time, due to the accumulation of numerical error caused by a discretized model of a continuous physical process; classical simulations are limited to a maximum simulation-step size of about 2–5 fs for all-atom models, otherwise unacceptable drifts in simulation energy occur. The best-performing MD programs used for computational biophysics on High Performance Computing (HPC) systems calculate an MD step in the range of 1 ms clock time, which is close to the performance roof-line set by the clock speed limit. This constrains the timescale that a simulation can model to a regime on the order of milliseconds. Obtaining simulation-times in the range of seconds or minutes, timescales relevant for comparison to many experimental measurements, is therefore not possible.

To overcome this Moore's-law limitation on our ability to sample configurational space with physical accuracy, ensemble methods using many parallel simulations are increasingly being used [4,25,47,57]. Using multiple parallel, short simulations throughout the simulation space to reconstruct sampling equivalent to much longer simulations with statistical methods is an approach frequently taken in MD simulations of condensed phases [11,18,22,27,53,55]. Here we refer to these methods as enhanced-sampling molecular dynamics (ESMD) [9]. For example, algorithms derived from the fluctuation-dissipation theory of near-equilibrium statistical mechanics [20,26] can be coupled with mathematical concepts from time-series and spectral analysis to determine rates and energetic barriers of physical processes [20,22,55]. The process of interacting with a ensemble simulation's progression to obtain optimal sampling of regions of interest is known as adaptive sampling [21,25]. Markov-state methods use the assumption that the dynamics trajectory can be approximated as a Markovian process on some timescale [40]. The appropriate timescale can be determined by a statistical analysis of correlations of features of the system, chosen to best describe the system's evolution in time [10,36]. Simulations can be launched from different points in the simulation space and new simulations can be started in regions that are under-sampled and important to the process of interest, based on additional statistical methods, in a progressively adaptive manner. If the final sampling performed by the simulations has been properly steered by this interactive analysis to cover the simulation space, a transition matrix can be assembled to report on transition rates between states. This Markov model can provide important long-timescale physical information such as kinetics, free energies, and dwell times of metastable states.

1.1   Scientific Workflow Platforms

Ensemble simulations require some type of workflow manager, or top-level program that manages parallel distributed tasks and then reduces the data into a final form. For simple ensembles home-made scripts can be used. However, as the workflow becomes more complex these scripts create impractical amounts of work and potentially can back-up shared launch-nodes and file systems.

For adaptive sampling MD implementations, the type of steering interaction used requires more complex solutions than simple checkpoint/restart management; new simulations must be initialized from correctly chosen conformations extracted from previous trajectories and the simulation program's starting files must be assembled in an automated manner. Additionally, records of the steering steps taken, analysis performed, and simulations launched throughout a complex ensemble workflow must be recorded as provenance metadata in a manageable format for later use, along with, potentially, more fine-grained logs of the compute components for benchmarking performance and debugging. Workflows should be able to support long-running heterogeneous applications such as multiple rounds of ensemble simulations combined with analysis tasks. State-of-the art molecular simulation requires that a workflow management program be able to integrate many separate jobs that each use, potentially, accelerators such as graphics processing units (GPUs), various levels of parallelism including threading and Message Passing Interface (MPI), along with multiple nodes per job. Managing ensemble-workflows of these types of programs quickly becomes a non-trivial task. Along with ensemble workflows to increase sampling of the conformational or energetic space, workflows to incorporate large datasets of either experimental data, or simulations at higher levels of theory, have recently become feasible.

Existing workflow programs have application programming interfaces (APIs) with different levels of complexity. General-use programs [2,13,14,16,24,54] and some programs specific for ESMD [7,41] have been developed. Radical Pilot (RP) [32,52] is written in Python, and has been used on a variety of compute resources, including some HPC systems for which it must be explicitly ported by the developers. Recently, some general-purpose [31,32] and some ESMD-based workflow programs [7,37] have been able to scale to tens of thousands of cores on HPC systems. The Ensemble toolkit [8] runs on top of Radical Pilot, has recently added adaptable workflow functionality, and has been used on the Extreme Science and Engineering Discovery Environment's (XSEDE) resources and on the Oak Ridge Leadership Computing Facility's (OLCF) Titan computer, a Cray XK7 [5,6]. However, none of these programs has been written specifically for pre-exascale and exascale use. As HPC systems approach exascale, we may find that some solutions may fail at this scale.

HPC-Specific Solutions. Groups in many areas of computational science are realizing that a need for HPC-specific workflow managers exists. There is a need for well-supported workflow programs that can handle account allocations, schedulers, and multiple levels of parallelism within each component, and can scale to thousands of nodes (hundreds of thousands of cores).

To address this need, the Swift/T dataflow parallel scripting language and run-time system was created to allow for the construction of large, scalable workflows on HPC systems [56]. The original Swift implementation was able to achieve a task-dispatch rate of 500 tasks launched per second, but these were dispatched from a single node, and thus the program was limited by the memory of that node. To overcome this limitation, inclusion of the Turbine engine allowed for the control of the program to be coordinated by several nodes, relieving these memory constraints and promoting scalability [56]. With this improvement the task dispatch rate exceeded 60 thousand tasks/sec and Swift/T was able to use 64 thousand cores at greater than 90% efficiency.

However, the Swift/T platform will not persist over multiple allocation resources, for example, over several different submitted jobs, each using the (often short, in MD terms) allowable job time-limits on many HPC systems such as at the OLCF. Furthermore, there is a limitation of fault tolerance handling, and hence the entire workflow may terminate when one task fails [15]. Other HPC-specific workflow efforts include those at the Livermore National Laboratory focusing on development of workflow managers that can provide experimental data analysis and visualization and incorporate some simulation as well [28], and initiatives within the Exascale Computing Project [33] such as the Advanced Technology, Development, and Mitigation (ATDM) software technology effort to develop a variety of solutions to support data management and workflows, primarily in nuclear science. However, these developments have not yet provided an HPC-based solution directly usable for adaptive enhanced-sampling workflows in MD.

Performance Portability over HPC Systems. Performance portability is essential for longevity of software products; with Department of Energy systems, architectures are cutting-edge and vary significantly between generations. Therefore, strict protocols for software design must be maintained to obtain robust, efficient and portable computational solutions [35,44,45,51]. Portable software design for HPC should include standard, well supported languages, modular, linear design, and simple construction [44,45]. Recent solutions for scientific workflow management systems have involved the use of a number of programming languages, and heavily nested programs, including extensive use of Python. Testing these solutions on the OLCF Summit IBM Power System AC922 computer will expose potential portability problems with programs that were deployed on previous HPC systems, thus facilitating a portable solution for adaptive MD workflows on future HPC systems.

Use of Database Management Programs. The use of database management systems within scientific workflow platforms is not a new concept; in 1998 Ailamaki and co-workers noted that a database management system (DBMS) has many essential properties of a workflow management system and with a data-object view of scientific workflows the DBMS could be effectively used to manage related parallel computational tasks [3]. The performance and variety of DBMS implementations have grown significantly in recent decades, and non-relational (NoSQL) databases have been found to perform better than relational (SQL) ones in a number of areas [29,34]. Recently several scientific workflow management solutions have incorporated both SQL and NoSQL DBMSs into their software design. For instance, Copernicus [41] uses the Python interface with sqlite, and Fireworks [24] and RP use MongoDB for task management. The use of DBMS in scientific workflow programs has been discussed in recent literature within the context of HPC and massively parallel distributed solutions [49].

Current Work. Here we test the performance and portability of a workflow management program driven by a DBMS on HPC systems. This was implemented first on the Titan supercomputer with the adaptive sampling method within ESMD as a use case. With this method we use inverse-count sampling [21] from a Markov model built with a TICA [43] and PCCA++ [23] analysis pipeline. The program, written in Python, has a database-centric architecture and uses the MongoDB NoSQL DBMS for status synchronization. The use of the DBMS allows for reliability and fault tolerance while the use of NoSQL provides a more flexible, distributed and scalable solution [46]. Here, we discuss the successive porting of components of this program to the Summit computer and testing for function and performance.

2   Building an Adaptive Ensemble-Simulation Program

We describe the implementation and performance testing of a Python program designed to create HPC-based scalable workflows for adaptive sampling of MD simulations. To run reliably and independently over possibly weeks to months, which can be typical of many use cases, the program was designed as a distributed application that can run from a laptop or directly on an HPC resource and can automate asynchronous workflow creation and execution. The program, available at https://github.com/markovmodel/adaptivemd, is an extension of a previous version of the code that was implemented [38] on smaller systems, and used programmatic elements from the "OpenPathSampling" program [39,50].

The program consists of a Python layer that interacts with a MongoDB database via the PyMongo interface [42]; worker units called executors use Python subprocesses to execute tasks. The database functions as a tool for a Python-based distributed task scheduler, as a peer-to-peer data sharing platform, and as a database for provenance information, task input data and reduced output data. The distributed task model could also allow for the use of different computer architectures for different computational tasks, where each may perform more optimally. Fields a user provides allow the program to bind resource-specific properties to the task descriptions at run-time. Several resources can be configured to be used simultaneously in this distributed computing model, and tasks can be targeted to any available resources.

While the program has an API that can be used to manage a number of different kinds of simulations and analysis or steering methods, our currently implemented use case seeks to improve the sampling of the slowest processes in a biomolecular simulation, using unbiased MD replicates and Markov-state modeling. The intent is to allow adaptive sampling procedures to either be fully automated or to proceed with varying amounts of user interaction at a number of levels, including, potentially, run-time steering. Run-time adaptions can be made to the (1) task properties such as analysis type or parameters, (2) workload properties such as task count, or (3) workflow properties such as convergence criteria. Using its native executor class, the program can address the entire chain from a workflow-generating instance down to task execution.

```python
def generate_workflow(length, loops):

    for _ in range(loops):
        restart_frames = sampling_function(project.models.last)

        trajs = project.new_trajectories(restart_frames)
        model = modeller.execute(*margs)
        tasks = [t.run() for t in [model]+trajs]

        project.queue(tasks)

        yield any([t.is_done for t in tasks])

    project.workers.command("shutdown")


project.add_event(
    generate_workflow(n_md_steps, n_workloads)
)
```

Listing 1.1. A simple workflow generating function that runs a fixed number of workloads with MD replicates of a fixed length. This generator can be written by a user (more sophisticated workflow generators are provided in the program) and given to the project event loop.

Listing 1.1 illustrates a simple workflow generating function that runs a fixed number of workloads with MD replicates of a fixed length. This generator can be written by a user (more sophisticated workflow generators are provided) and given to the project event loop, and must yield functions that return Boolean values. At run-time, the current Boolean function will be executed repeatedly in the event loop value until it evaluates to True, in this case when any task completes. On this event, the application will iterate the generator to yield a new function, executing a code block in which additional tasks are queued in the project and specified in the new progress function.

Our aim here is to test the scalability, robustness, and performance of our program on large HPC resources at the OLCF. To keep configuration and installation simple while providing reliable workflow execution on a wide range of computational resources, we have separated the workflow platform into hierarchical levels of complexity, and created removable interfacing with other Python-based workflow programs. The current implementation can function with or without an interface to RP.

Unlike a single large job that runs on an HPC system, workflows involve many initialization times over the course of the program. This initialization overhead may have a non-negligible impact on overall performance of the workflow and must be optimized. File accesses, such as accessing executables and task descriptions, must be handled efficiently when they occur repeatedly through the workflow. For example, launching many concurrent instances of an executable involves a decision about whether all executors access the same executable file, receive copies of the file, or access the file from the database. This decision may have to be made for many different executables and/or analysis tasks that may need to access the same copy of a Python library. The optimal decision will vary based on the task, the number of executors, and the size of files transferred, which may include larger data files and a library of dependencies. The optimal solution for a particular part of the workflow may vary by HPC system as well.

2.1 Using a Database Program to Support Interactive, Adaptable DAG-Based Task Scheduling, Analysis and Provenance

For adaptable and steered simulation workflows, we would like to allow as little or as much manipulation of the directed acyclic graph (DAG), which represents the workflow, as desired, including possibly an *in-situ* (run-time) interaction which would result in a constantly-adapting DAG. The database queuing functionality provides the potential for run-time steering of complex workflows: the database program facilitates multiple live connections which query a consistent state. This transfer of information allows for run-time processing of reduce operations, sampling from the database and the tasks in the workflow, and synchronization of new tasks to be executed by executors that are distributed on arbitrary resources.

An immediate, reliable and fault-tolerant utilization of tasks is therefore facilitated by the database program, as is the ability to increase file accessibility and redundancy. The DBMS provides the requirements to perform task-to-data targeting; code can be added that queries a task property and accepts or rejects a resource assignment.

Provenance data is an important consideration for workflows with many tasks [12,48]. The MongoDB dataflow collections provide a reliable mechanism for storing and managing our queues of tasks and their metadata. This metadata can facilitate the management of provenance information. In our usage, the database contains mainly the metadata about what happens, using a "pretask, main task, and posttask" abstraction.

2.2 Use of Radical Pilot

To test if incorporation of the RP intermediate job manager can provide more robust workflow management than with the base-level Python-MongoDB program, we created a version of the program on OLCF Titan which integrated with RP. This tool can enhance run-time error detection and correction functionality. However, it has a much higher installation and configuration overhead if not already available on a user's resource: it requires the RP developers to specifically configure the program for a particular HPC system. Results on Titan with and without the RP interface are reported below.

2.3 Experiences and Performance on OLCF Titan

A complete Markov-model ESMD workflow with TICA and PCCA++ analysis was deployed on the Titan Cray XK7 computer at OLCF, using the OpenMM simulation engine [17]. The program used the following versions of key programs: Mongo 3.3, PyMongo 3.6, Python 2.7.13, PyEmma 2.4, Numpy 1.15, OpenMM 7.0.1, and CUDA 7.5. Titan uses the Cray Linux Environment as its operating system. Titan nodes each contain a 16-core 2.2 GHz AMD Opteron 6274 (Interlagos) processor and NVIDIA Kepler K20X GPU.

Figure 1 illustrates performance of the workflow program with the RP interface, including the components of different parts of the workflow, and the latency (non-task time) divided by number of tasks. This normalized latency reports on the cost-per-task of the workflow program's overhead. The program was successfully implemented with and without the RP layer. Without RP, up to 5000 parallel, single node simulation tasks were executed with greater than 90% weak

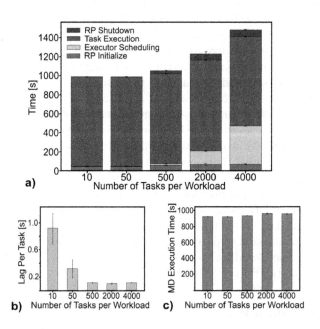

Fig. 1. Parallel performance of ensemble simulations on Titan, using the Radical Pilot (RP) interface. Data was gathered by running a single round of tasks, and the test was replicated 3 times. The workflow was configured using 1 task per node. Tasks were molecular dynamics simulations of small proteins using the OpenMM [17] MD program. (a) Time for each component of the workflow. (b) Total non-execution time (lag) divided by total tasks (c) Time for task execution only, for varying workload sizes.

scaling efficiency (data not shown), but we were unable to execute use case workflows including analysis tasks at this scale: our program deploys a number of executor units each with a connection to the database, and on Titan, network congestion and high hardware utilization made the database host unreliable in transferring the analysis output data with $O(10^3)$ tasks. To improve the network congestion of the stand-alone program, a splitting of traffic to the database server could be accomplished by the use of sharding. In addition, accessing the shared Python libraries with multiple tasks at start-up frequently resulted in a failure to find the file handles for the programs to be executed by the tasks. This seemed to be caused by conflicting file-reading attempts, and was mitigated by spacing out task launch times by small time increments.

A reduction in sensitivity to analysis-task synchronization was found when using RP. A single RP Agent replaces the program's executor reads from the database, reducing connection-associated network congestion and overhead on the host. The DBMS interactions are replaced by writing to local files. RP builds an execution script from each task's instructions, and replaces the spaced task-launch procedure with a uniform initialization time. We did not observe file system errors at high scale. However the scaling of the RP version of the program stopped at about 8000 nodes on Titan, at which point the RP program crashed with an out of memory error for the array used to keep track of the tasks. This limitation is currently being addressed by the RP developers. Figure 1a shows weak-scaling performance of the program using the Radical Pilot interface, for executing up to 4000 single-node tasks. The total workflow duration is shown partitioned to 4 duration intervals. The time to schedule then dispatch tasks, as well as latency between termination of the final task and workload termination, are seen to increase with scale. Figure 1b shows that these scheduling and shutdown latencies combine to a per-task cost that stabilizes to about 0.1 s per task with 500 or more tasks. Initial bootstrapping of the environment is seen to be independent of the number of tasks, and Figure 1c shows that the main simulation task duration is also largely independent of scale.

3   Experiences and Performance on OLCF Summit

We approached the transition from Titan to Summit by testing isolated components, and then testing several executables run by tasks within the program. OLCF Summit consist of 4608 IBM Power System AC922 nodes. Each node contains two IBM POWER9 processors and six NVIDIA Volta V100 accelerators. Summit uses Red Hat Enterprise Linux Server release 7.6 (Maipo) as an operating system. Currently RP is still being ported to Summit by the developers, so here we could only consider building and testing the program's stack without RP. We tested the performance of two MD programs to determine the optimal resource configurations for different sized biomolecular systems. Then after testing system functionality when scaling to thousands of simultaneous executables, we test the program itself. With the success of each component, we can interpret the contributions of each to the performance of the workflow program on Summit.

3.1 Python Packages on Summit: Scientific Libraries

Although Python is not traditionally used for parallel programming, HPC centers are increasingly seeing a large amount of Python usage as a wrapper-level "glue" for compiled libraries, especially for machine learning [30]. While Python is often referred to as a portable, ubiquitous language, on Summit we have noted several challenges in porting portions of our Titan workflow. Many Python packages contain inner regions of code written in C/C++ for performance, and also may require calls to additional libraries. On Summit, we found that the NumPy (https://www.numpy.org/) configuration interface does not support the native Summit Engineering and Scientific Subroutine Library for linear algebra. A version of OpenBLAS (http://www.openblas.net/) is available in a Power8 version and also in a PowerPC version, but there is no version of BLAS (http://www.netlib.org/blas/) optimized for Power9 that can be incorporated into NumPy easily. In addition, for future incorporation of RP, a Python virtual environment must be used, and we have found that a pip installation of NumPy using a `virtualenv` is not able to find the Power8 version of OpenBLAS. The analysis portion of our workflow uses the Python package PyEMMA for Markov modeling [43]. This package in turn uses the MDTraj Python package (http://mdtraj.org/1.9.0/). MDTraj contains several libraries written in C/C++ that contain hard-coded x86 single instruction, multiple data (SIMD) vector intrinsic functions, and therefore, the MDTraj package and PyEMMA cannot be built on Summit without manual removal of these SIMD-containing portions. Without MDTraj, streaming "load iterators," of large trajectory files cannot be utilized, and other essential processing tools for the OpenMM program become unavailable. Due to our distributed computing capabilities, we are able to run the analysis tasks on another computer, but this can become inconvenient when the MDTraj frame-finding tool cannot be used within a task running on Summit.

3.2 Single-Node Performance of Two State-of-the-Art Open-Source MD Programs

Measuring the single-node performance of the underlying MD programs used as the "engine" in the ensemble simulation is important for determining which program and configuration will be used in the workflow for a particular biomolecular system. These choices may vary with system size, and the requirements for individual simulation lengths which are ultimately dictated by the system kinetics and the resources available.

While the workflow program we are developing can use any executable, here we investigate single-node performance of two open source MD programs that are the best-performing for systems under 1 M atoms: OpenMM [17] and GROMACS [1]. We used OpenMM version 7.3, GROMACS 2018.3, CUDA 9.2, and gcc 6.4, with Spectrum MPI version 10.2. These programs both make heavy use of the GPUs, and GROMACS also uses several layers of parallelism on the CPU: MPI, OpenMP, and SIMD. GROMACS allows the user to specify if the Particle Mesh

Table 1. Single-node performance for OpenMM on Summit. Size of the simulation is determined by the number of atoms, listed in the first column. Sim-time: simulation time, perf: performance.

Size (no. atoms)	Sim-time (ns/day)	Time (ms/step)	Perf. (steps/sec)
29 K	292	0.6	1690
134 K	97	1.8	561
1 M	11	15.7	64

Ewald (PME) calculation should take place on the GPU or the CPU. Single-GPU GROMACS calculations used 1 MPI rank when PME was calculated on the CPU, and 2 ranks when PME was on the GPU. 6-GPU version used 6 MPI ranks. All simulations used 2 fs timesteps, and the NVT ensemble. OpenMM tasks used 1 GPU and 7 CPUs.

Table 2. Single-node performance for GROMACS on Summit, One GPU. First value: PME calculated on CPU, Second value: PME calculated on GPU. Size of the simulation is determined by the number of atoms, listed in the first column. Sim-time: simulation time, perf: performance.

Size (no. atoms)	Sim-time (ns/day)	Time (ms/step)	Perf. (steps/sec)
29 K	284/253	0.6/0.7	1644/1464
134 K	64/56	2.7/3.1	370/324
1 M	8/6	21.6/28.8	46/35

Tables 1, 2 and 3 display single-node performance of these two programs on Summit. We found that on Summit, these programs perform one MD step in sub-millisecond compute times on a single node, for systems with tens of thousands of atoms. GROMACS achieves under 2 ms per step for systems of around 100 K atoms on a single node, and close to 20 ns/day for a 1 M atom system on a single node, using 2 fs simulation-time integration steps. This is a result which previously was only attainable using hundreds of nodes on Titan. As a result, with adaptive sampling effective timescales of tens of milliseconds within a few weeks of simulation will be possible, increasing throughput by an order of magnitude compared to previous existing technology.

Thus it is possible to, for instance, run close to 24 thousand simultaneous MD tasks with a system of about 130 thousand atoms using OpenMM, with 6 tasks per node, and obtain close to 100 ns/day for each individual simulation, providing for excellent sampling within the MSM method. One could choose to use half of a Summit node, or an entire node, with GROMACS and obtain about twice the simulation time per day *versus* OpenMM, for a system of around 30 K atoms or 1 M atoms. The choice of whether to run six times more tasks, or aim for longer simulation times per day, per task, will depend on the biomolecular system and the dynamical relaxation times that must be sampled.

Table 3. Single-node performance for GROMACS on Summit, 6 GPUs. First value: PME calculated on CPU, Second value: PME calculated on GPU. Size of the simulation is determined by the number of atoms, listed in the first column. Sim-time: simulation time, perf: performance.

Size (no. atoms)	Sim-time (ns/day)	Time (ms/step)	Perf. (steps/sec)
29 K	231/423	0.8/0.4	1337/2448
134 K	66/110	2.6/1.6	382/637
1 M	11/18	15.7/9.6	64/104

Using Several Nodes per Job with GROMACS. Unlike OpenMM, GRO-MACS uses MPI. This implementation allows for linear scaling over tens of thousands of cores for larger systems. It is therefore possible to perform ESMD on systems containing several million atoms. On Summit, the simulation of 1 M atoms should be efficient on even a handful of nodes. We found the most efficient workflow configuration for running many parallel simulations of a 1 M atom system when using the GPU-offloaded PME calculation was three nodes per simulation instance. After this number, the GPU-based PME calculation suffers from high communication overhead, and performance is greatly improved by moving the PME calculation to the CPU.

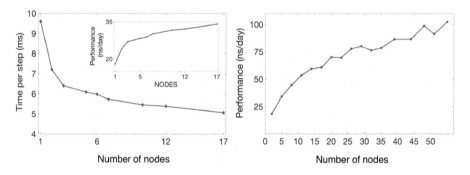

Fig. 2. Performance of GROMACS on Summit, 1 M atom system. Left panel: Using GPU offloading of the PME calculations as well as the non-bonded forces. Right panel: Without PME offloading. Configuration used 6 GPUs and 6 MPI ranks per node, with 7 OpenMP threads per MPI rank. PME offloading quickly becomes inefficient but can provide a good solution when using about 3 nodes per task. GROMACS scales linearly to much higher node counts when PME offloading is not used.

Figure 2 shows scaling of the 1 M atom system over 16 Summit nodes, using the GPU-based PME. Without GPU-PME, 100 ns/day can be achieved using 50 nodes. It should be noted that on Titan the same sized system achieved this performance using 1024 nodes. For ensemble MD, depending on available resources and timescales required, many tasks each using small numbers of nodes, or fewer tasks each using dozens of nodes could be performed.

3.3 Performance of Allocation Management Tools: Running Thousands of Small Concurrent Workflow Tasks

Here we describe tests of the allocation management system along with other aspects of system performance on Summit when running thousands of parallel tasks without an MPI programming model. This is relatively non-standard, historically, for HPC computing. However, the feasibility and appeal of ensemble simulations on these large systems is increasing, and therefore this model is becoming more popular.

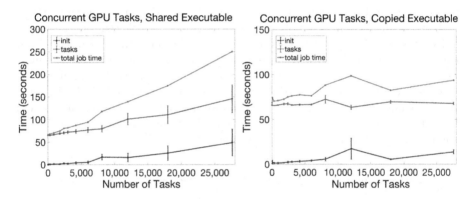

Fig. 3. Performance of concurrent tasks launched from a single `jsrun` on Summit, CUDA C executable. Left panel: a single executable was read by all processes. Right panel: executable was copied and each process read its own file. Copy time not included in total job time. Tasks were run 6 per node. Error bars show standard deviation of time over all tasks.

There are two configurations for launching multiple jobs within our workflow program. A single `jsrun` command (the IBM Job Step Manager tool for launching jobs) can launch thousands of instances of an executable using multiple resource sets, or thousands of tasks can each call a different instance of `jsrun`. Neither situation is commonly anticipated in the optimization of large HPC computers. In the following we describe the performance and stability of the Summit software stack under both configurations, without the workflow program.

Single jsrun Running Thousands of Tasks. Using a single instance of jsrun, up to 27600 simultaneous executions of simple programs were performed, using 6 instances per Summit node. This utilized up to 4600 of the 4608 nodes on Summit. Figures 3 and 4 show results from these tests, using a CUDA C executable or a C executable with OpenMP directives. For the latter, we used the HACCmk cosmology microkernel [19]. In contrast to Titan, we found that on Summit no errors were encountered while attempting to access the same executable by multiple processes. However, this procedure resulted in a large initialization overhead. In addition, in this situation the execution times of the tasks increased for high node counts (Fig. 3, left panel). Figure 4 shows performance of CPU executables, without threading (left panel) and with OpenMP threading (right panel). Total job latency was similar between the two versions: in both cases, for over 20,000 concurrent executions, job latency was appreciable, and less than for the GPU executable. However this difference may simply be a result of system fluctuations such as batch-node traffic. In all cases, the latency was significant and could cause job time to be more than double that of task time. With long running tasks, these effects become much less noticeable.

Thousands of Parallel jsrun Instances. We found that on Summit, thousands of concurrent instances of the jsrun tool were not allowed due to process limits set on the batch nodes. This behavior prevents more than 1000 tasks from being launched simultaneously from 1000 jsrun calls. Unfortunately this prevents the scaling of a workflow to all of Summit when using MPI-containing executables and single-node jobs, because they cannot be launched inside the same jsrun instance or they will couple. Therefore under the current circumstances the scaling to all of Summit of GROMACS inside of the workflow program would require the use of multiple nodes per simulation.

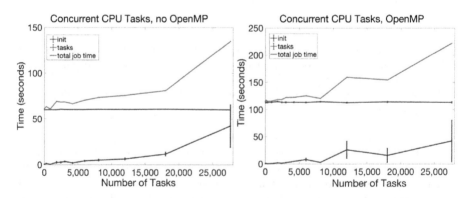

Fig. 4. Performance of concurrent tasks launched from a single jsrun command on Summit, CPU executable. Left panel: C executable, no OpenMP or other threading in executable. Right panel: OpenMP-containing executable run with 7 threads. Tasks were run 6 per node. Total task time for single executable is, left: 60 s, right: 113 s. Error bars show standard deviation of time over all tasks.

3.4 Testing the Adaptive Workflow with Executables Containing CUDA and OpenMP

Here the full workflow program was tested using executables containing CUDA, and C with OpenMP. MongoDB is a document database and thus each communication requires opening of a file. We used Mongo version 3.6.11 with the ppc64le build, PyMongo 3.7.2, Python 3.7.3, and NumPy 1.15.4.

We discovered a bug in the Summit IBM Spectrum Load Sharing Facility (LSF) batch scheduling system's configuration that propagates the wrong environment inside of a `jsrun` instance: while the hard maximum limit for number of file handles per process (`ulimit -n`) is set to around 65 K on the compute nodes, the `jsrun` environment incorrectly inherits the settings from nodes with a limit set to 4096. The database program requires two files opened to support a connection to each executor. Therefore, for concurrent launching of 6 tasks per node (run by 6 executors) using all of Summit, about 54 K files need to be opened by a single database process. Due to the current file limit problem, only about 2000 executors can be launched at a time if connecting to a single database host. Fault tolerance is provided by programmatic elements within the workflow and facilitated by the DBMS. As tasks are not bound to executors, the limited executors are able to execute well over 2048 tasks successfully: while some executor connections are rejected due to file limits, resulting in failure to initialize the executor process, remaining tasks are taken up by other executors after previous tasks are completed.

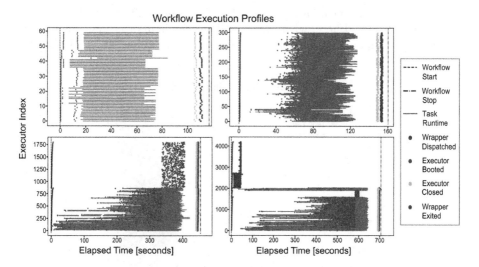

Fig. 5. Timelines of workflows for 60, 300, 1800, and 4200 tasks. Due to the short duration of tasks used here, under 1000 executors stay busy as previous executors pick up tasks after they finish. At around 2000 tasks, incorrectly inherited `ulimit` settings limit the number of file handles allowed and tasks are rejected, however, all required tasks are completed.

Figure 5 shows a breakdown of the timelines for components of single-workload jobs with 60, 300, 1800 and 4200 tasks. Each task contained an executable in CUDA/C and had a duration of about 60 s. Timestamps were taken at the start and end of each component of the workflow by each executor. Due to short duration of the tasks, executors were able to finish tasks before all executors were dispatched and start additional queued tasks. Under 1000 executors completed the 1800 task workflow, as all 1800 tasks were running or complete with 800 executors yet to dispatch. In the 4200 task workload, connections from executors numbered 2000 and above were rejected by the database host due to the above mentioned `ulimit` settings. All tasks finished successfully.

Figure 6 shows task completion timing profiles for workflows with 300, 900, 1800 and 6000 total tasks. These plots show that all tasks in each case were completed, and the rate at which this was accomplished for each workflow instance. 900 tasks are completed faster in the 900-task workflow job than are completed within the 1800 and 6000-task jobs: we found this was due to the `ulimit` settings that caused the database to close some existing executor connections as new connection requests were handled. This resulted in a latency as the running tasks had to start again in new executors due to this executor connection failure. Figure 7, left panel, shows the task dispatch rate for varying task numbers using the CUDA executable. This rate is calculated before any task rejections occur. The maximum task dispatch rate of 19.4 tasks/sec was achieved for 4200 tasks, and a rate of about 18 tasks/sec is maintained from 2400 to 6000 tasks. A similar rate is achieved by other ensemble simulation workflow platforms [24,37], however we have not seen rates for deployment of over 1000 tasks in most of these reports. This rate is much lower than that achieved by Swift/T, but for the type of workflows targeted here, where tasks will run for hours to days, this latency is negligible compared to the total run-time of the workflow. If rapid dispatch

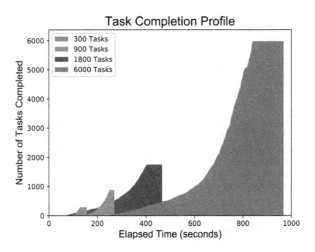

Fig. 6. Task completion profiles of workflows for 300, 900, 1800 and 6000 tasks.

and deployment of thousands of short simultaneous tasks is required as part of a workflow, it is possible that an instance of Swift/T can be executed inside of the workflow. Figure 7, right panel, shows the changes in the ratio of total workflow time to task number as it varies over job size. The ratio stays between 0.3 and 0.1 for all jobs with over 1000 tasks. This shows that the cost-per-task stabilizes for these large jobs. This overhead will be negligible for long jobs such as are common in MD simulation.

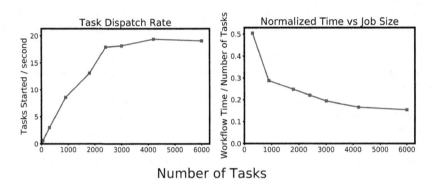

Fig. 7. Left panel: task dispatch rate over number of tasks. Right panel: change in workflow time to task ratio over number of tasks in worflow job.

4   Conclusions and Future Work

We have shown that the use of a DBMS can provide the infrastructure for a fault-tolerant, scalable, adaptable workflow-generation program that can be used to implement ESMD methods such as adaptive sampling with Markov models. Despite limitations imposed by system-level problems that must be corrected by the vendor and system administration personnel, on the Summit supercomputer preliminary tests of the components as well as initial tests of the complete program show that a workflow solution that uses Python and the MongoDB DBMS to create a dataflow-based platform for this type of workflow can be effective. Future work will involve implementation of the complete adaptive Markov-model workflow using several MD simulation programs, and investigation of possibilities for reducing database traffic using different database configurations.

Acknowledgements. The authors would like to acknowledge Nicholas Dean Smith for help with MD test systems preparation, and Shantenu Jha and lab for extensive help with incorporation of the Radical Cybertools software stack. An award of computer time was provided by the Innovative and Novel Computational Impact on Theory and Experiment (INCITE) program. This research used resources of the Oak Ridge Leadership Computing Facility, which is a DOE Office of Science User Facility supported under Contract DE-AC05-00OR227525. ORNL is managed by UT-Battelle, LLC for the US Department of Energy. FN acknowledges European Commission (ERC CoG 772230) and Deutsche Forschungsgemeinschaft (NO 825/3-1). JCS acknowledges DOE contract ERKP752. CC acknowledges support from the National Science Foundation (CHE-1265929, CHE-1740990, CHE-1900374, and PHY-1427654) and the Welch Foundation (C-1570).

References

1. Abraham, M.J., et al.: GROMACS: high performance molecular simulations through multi-level parallelism from laptops to supercomputers. SoftwareX **1**, 19–25 (2015)
2. Adorf, C.S., Dodd, P.M., Ramasubramani, V., Glotzer, S.C.: Simple data and workflow management with the signac framework. Comput. Mater. Sci. **146**, 220–229 (2018)
3. Ailamaki, A., Ioannidis, Y.E., Livny, M.: Scientific workflow management by database management. In: Proceedings of Tenth International Conference on Scientific and Statistical Database Management (Cat. No. 98TB100243), pp. 190–199. IEEE (1998)
4. Amaro, R.E., et al.: Ensemble docking in drug discovery. Biophys. J. **114**, 2271–2278 (2018)
5. Balasubramanian, V., Jensen, T., Turilli, M., Kasson, P., Shirts, M., Jha, S.: Implementing adaptive ensemble biomolecular applications at scale. arXiv preprint arXiv:1804.04736 (2018)
6. Balasubramanian, V., et al.: Harnessing the power of many: extensible toolkit for scalable ensemble applications. In: 2018 IEEE International Parallel and Distributed Processing Symposium (IPDPS), pp. 536–545. IEEE (2018)
7. Balasubramanian, V., et al.: Extasy: scalable and flexible coupling of MD simulations and advanced sampling techniques. In: 2016 IEEE 12th International Conference on e-Science, pp. 361–370. IEEE (2016)
8. Balasubramanian, V., Treikalis, A., Weidner, O., Jha, S.: Ensemble toolkit: scalable and flexible execution of ensembles of tasks. In: 2016 45th International Conference on Parallel Processing (ICPP), pp. 458–463. IEEE (2016)
9. Bernardi, R.C., Melo, M.C., Schulten, K.: Enhanced sampling techniques in molecular dynamics simulations of biological systems. Biochim. Biophys. Acta **1850**(5), 872–877 (2015)
10. Bowman, G.R., Pande, V.S., Noé, F. (eds.): An Introduction to Markov State Models and Their Application to Long Timescale Molecular Simulation. AEMB, vol. 797. Springer, Dordrecht (2014). https://doi.org/10.1007/978-94-007-7606-7
11. Buchete, N.V., Hummer, G.: Peptide folding kinetics from replica exchange molecular dynamics. Phys. Rev. E **77**(3), 030902 (2008)
12. Davidson, S.B., Freire, J.: Provenance and scientific workflows: challenges and opportunities. In: Proceedings of the 2008 ACM SIGMOD International Conference on Management of Data, pp. 1345–1350. ACM (2008)
13. Deelman, E., et al.: Pegasus, a workflow management system for science automation. Future Gener. Comput. Syst. **46**, 17–35 (2015)
14. Deelman, E., Vahi, K., Rynge, M., Juve, G., Mayani, R., da Silva, R.F.: Pegasus in the cloud: science automation through workflow technologies. IEEE Internet Comput. **20**(1), 70–76 (2016)

15. Dorier, M., Wozniak, J.M., Ross, R.: Supporting task-level fault-tolerance in HPC workflows by launching MPI jobs inside MPI jobs. In: Proceedings of the 12th Workshop on Workflows in Support of Large-Scale Science, p. 5. ACM (2017)

16. Dou, L., et al.: Scientific workflow design 2.0: demonstrating streaming data collections in Kepler. In: 2011 IEEE 27th International Conference on Data Engineering, pp. 1296–1299. IEEE (2011)

17. Eastman, P., et al.: OpenMM 7: rapid development of high performance algorithms for molecular dynamics. PLoS Comput. Biol. **13**(7), e1005659 (2017)

18. Garcia, A.E., Herce, H., Paschek, D.: Simulations of temperature and pressure unfolding of peptides and proteins with replica exchange molecular dynamics. Ann. Rep. Comput. Chem. **2**, 83–95 (2006)

19. HACCmk. https://asc.llnl.gov/CORAL-benchmarks/Summaries/HACCmk_Summary_v1.0.pdf

20. Hänggi, P., Talkner, P., Borkovec, M.: Reaction-rate theory: fifty years after Kramers. Rev. Mod. Phys. **62**(2), 251 (1990)

21. Hruska, E., Abella, J.R., Nüske, F., Kavraki, L.E., Clementi, C.: Quantitative comparison of adaptive sampling methods for protein dynamics. J. Chem. Phys. **149**(24), 244119 (2018)

22. Hummer, G.: Position-dependent diffusion coefficients and free energies from Bayesian analysis of equilibrium and replica molecular dynamics simulations. New J. Phys. **7**(1), 34 (2005)

23. Husic, B.E., McGibbon, R.T., Sultan, M.M., Pande, V.S.: Optimized parameter selection reveals trends in Markov state models for protein folding. J. Chem. Phys. **145**(19), 194103 (2016)

24. Jain, A., et al.: FireWorks: a dynamic workflow system designed for high-throughput applications. Concurr. Comput.: Pract. Exp. **27**(17), 5037–5059 (2015)

25. Kasson, P.M., Jha, S.: Adaptive ensemble simulations of biomolecules. Curr. Opin. Struct. Biol. **52**, 87–94 (2018)

26. Kubo, R.: The fluctuation-dissipation theorem. Rep. Prog. Phys. **29**(1), 255 (1966)

27. Kumar, S., Rosenberg, J.M., Bouzida, D., Swendsen, R.H., Kollman, P.A.: The weighted histogram analysis method for free-energy calculations on biomolecules. I. The method. J. Comput. Chem. **13**(8), 1011–1021 (1992)

28. Laney, D.: Workflow project overview. https://www.csm.ornl.gov/SOS20/documents/Laney-Workflow-Overview-SOS16.pdf

29. Li, Y., Manoharan, S.: A performance comparison of SQL and NoSQL databases. In: 2013 IEEE Pacific Rim Conference on Communications, Computers and Signal Processing (PACRIM), pp. 15–19. IEEE (2013)

30. MacLean, C.: Python usage metrics on Blue Waters. Cray User Group (2017)

31. Merzky, A., Santcroos, M., Turilli, M., Jha, S.: RADICAL-Pilot: Scalable execution of heterogeneous and dynamic workloads on supercomputers. Computer Research Repository (CoRR), abs/1512.08194 (2015)

32. Merzky, A., Turilli, M., Maldonado, M., Jha, S.: Design and performance characterization of radical-pilot on Titan. arXiv preprint arXiv:1801.01843 (2018)

33. Messina, P.: The exascale computing project. Comput. Sci. Eng. **19**(3), 63–67 (2017)

34. Parker, Z., Poe, S., Vrbsky, S.V.: Comparing NoSQL MongoDB to an SQL DB. In: Proceedings of the 51st ACM Southeast Conference, p. 5. ACM (2013)

35. Pennycook, S.J., Sewall, J.D., Lee, V.: A metric for performance portability. arXiv preprint arXiv:1611.07409 (2016)

36. Pérez-Hernández, G., Paul, F., Giorgino, T., De Fabritiis, G., Noé, F.: Identification of slow molecular order parameters for Markov model construction. J. Chem. Phys. **139**(1), 07B604_1 (2013)
37. Pouya, I., Pronk, S., Lundborg, M., Lindahl, E.: Copernicus, a hybrid dataflow and peer-to-peer scientific computing platform for efficient large-scale ensemble sampling. Future Gener. Comput. Syst. **71**, 18–31 (2017)
38. Prinz, J.H.: Git Commit. https://github.com/markovmodel/adaptivemd/commit/186ffa097059168cb6b17dfd2f0b01f83bc7b6e1
39. Prinz, J.H.: https://github.com/jhprinz
40. Prinz, J.H., et al.: Markov models of molecular kinetics: generation and validation. J. Chem. Phys. **134**(17), 174105 (2011)
41. Pronk, S., et al.: Molecular simulation workflows as parallel algorithms: the execution engine of Copernicus, a distributed high-performance computing platform. J. Chem. Theory Comput. **11**(6), 2600–2608 (2015)
42. PyMongo: https://github.com/mongodb/mongo-python-driver
43. Scherer, M.K., et al.: PyEMMA 2: a software package for estimation, validation, and analysis of Markov models. J. Chem. Theory Comput. **11**(11), 5525–5542 (2015)
44. Sedova, A., Eblen, J.D., Budiardja, R., Tharrington, A., Smith, J.C.: High-performance molecular dynamics simulation for biological and materials sciences: challenges of performance portability. In: 2018 IEEE/ACM International Workshop on Performance, Portability and Productivity in HPC (P3HPC), pp. 1–13. IEEE (2018)
45. Sedova, A., Tillack, A.F., Tharrington, A.: Using compiler directives for performance portability in scientific computing: kernels from molecular simulation. In: Chandrasekaran, S., Juckeland, G., Wienke, S. (eds.) WACCPD 2018. LNCS, vol. 11381, pp. 22–47. Springer, Cham (2019). https://doi.org/10.1007/978-3-030-12274-4_2
46. Venkatraman, S., Fahd, K., Kaspi, S., Venkatraman, R.: SQL versus NoSQL movement with big data analytics. IJ Inf. Technol. Comput. Sci. **8**, 59–66 (2016)
47. Sorin, E.J., Pande, V.S.: Exploring the helix-coil transition via all-atom equilibrium ensemble simulations. Biophys. J. **88**(4), 2472–2493 (2005)
48. Souza, R., Mattoso, M.: Provenance of dynamic adaptations in user-steered dataflows. In: Belhajjame, K., Gehani, A., Alper, P. (eds.) IPAW 2018. LNCS, vol. 11017, pp. 16–29. Springer, Cham (2018). https://doi.org/10.1007/978-3-319-98379-0_2
49. Souza, R., Silva, V., Oliveira, D., Valduriez, P., Lima, A.A., Mattoso, M.: Parallel execution of workflows driven by a distributed database management system. In: ACM/IEEE Conference on Supercomputing, Poster (2015)
50. Swenson, D.W., Prinz, J.H., Noe, F., Chodera, J.D., Bolhuis, P.G.: OpenPathSampling: a Python framework for path sampling simulations. 1. Basics. J. Chem. Theory Comput. **15**, 813–836 (2018)
51. Trott, C.R., Plimpton, S.J., Thompson, A.P.: Solving the performance portability issue with Kokkos (2017)
52. Turilli, M., Santcroos, M., Jha, S.: A comprehensive perspective on pilot-job systems. ACM Comput. Surv. (CSUR) **51**(2), 43 (2018)
53. Weinan, E., Ren, W., Vanden-Eijnden, E.: String method for the study of rare events. Phys. Rev. B **66**(5), 052301 (2002)
54. Wolstencroft, K., et al.: The Taverna workflow suite: designing and executing workflows of web services on the desktop, web or in the cloud. Nucleic Acids Res. **41**(W1), W557–W561 (2013)

55. Woolf, T.B., Roux, B.: Conformational flexibility of o-phosphorylcholine and o-phosphorylethanolamine: a molecular dynamics study of solvation effects. J. Am. Chem. Soc. **116**(13), 5916–5926 (1994)
56. Wozniak, J.M., Armstrong, T.G., Wilde, M., Katz, D.S., Lusk, E., Foster, I.T.: Swift/T: large-scale application composition via distributed-memory dataflow processing. In: 2013 13th IEEE/ACM International Symposium on Cluster, Cloud, and Grid Computing, pp. 95–102. IEEE (2013)
57. Wu, H., Paul, F., Wehmeyer, C., Noé, F.: Multiensemble Markov models of molecular thermodynamics and kinetics. In: Proceedings of the National Academy of Sciences, p. 201525092 (2016)

Performance Comparison for Neuroscience Application Benchmarks

Andreas Herten[(⊠)], Thorsten Hater, Wouter Klijn, and Dirk Pleiter

Forschungszentrum Jülich, JSC, 52425 Jülich, Germany
{a.herten,t.hater,w.klijn,d.pleiter}@fz-juelich.de

Abstract. Researchers within the Human Brain Project and related projects have in the last couple of years expanded their needs for high-performance computing infrastructures. The needs arise from a diverse set of science challenges that range from large-scale simulations of brain models to processing of extreme-scale experimental data sets. The ICEI project, which is in the process of creating a distributed infrastructure optimised for brain research, started to build-up a set of benchmarks that reflect the diversity of applications in this field. In this paper we analyse the performance of some selected benchmarks on IBM POWER8 and Intel Skylake based systems with and without GPUs.

Keywords: OpenPOWER · High-performance computing · Data analytics · GPU acceleration · Computational neuroscience

1 Introduction

As new computational and data science communities emerge, needs arise for having a benchmark suite reflecting the requirements of the respective communities, also for potential procurement of IT equipment. At the same time, experience needs to be collected regarding performance observations on different types of hardware architectures. In this contribution we address the latter by selecting a recently developed benchmark suite and comparing performance results obtained on servers based on different processor architectures, namely POWER8 and Skylake, with and without GPU acceleration.

The science community, on which we focus here, is the brain research community organised in the Human Brain Project (HBP).[1] HBP is a large-scale flagship project funded by the European Commission working towards the realisation of a cutting-edge research infrastructure that will allow researchers to advance knowledge in the fields of neuroscience, computing, and brain-related medicine. As part of HBP, the ICEI project (Interactive Computing e-infrastructure for the Human Brain Project) was started in early 2018. This project plans to deliver a set of e-infrastructure services that will be federated to form the Fenix Infrastructure.[2] The European ICEI project is funded by the European Commission

---

[1] https://www.humanbrainproject.eu/en/.
[2] https://fenix-ri.eu/.

© Springer Nature Switzerland AG 2019
M. Weiland et al. (Eds.): ISC 2019 Workshops, LNCS 11887, pp. 418–431, 2019.
https://doi.org/10.1007/978-3-030-34356-9_31

and is formed by the leading European Supercomputing Centres BSC in Spain, CEA in France, CINECA in Italy, CSCS in Switzerland and Jülich Supercomputing Centre (JSC) in Germany. To guide the creation of this infrastructure, the ICEI project started to build-up the "ICEI Application Benchmark Suite", which we use for this contribution.

This paper is organised as follows: We start with giving an overview of the ICEI benchmark suite as well as the systems used for collecting performance results in Sects. 2 and 3, respectively. The obtained results are documented in Sect. 4. We finally provide a summary and conclusions in Sect. 5.

2   ICEI Benchmark Suite

The components of the "ICEI Application Benchmark Suite" have been chosen such that it represents the breadth of research within HBP. The subset of benchmarks, which we consider in this paper, is directly based on real-life applications. *NEST* [8] is one of several simulators that became part of the benchmark suite. It is a simulator for spiking neural network models that focuses on the dynamics, size, and structure of neural systems rather than on the exact morphology of individual neurons. Recently, a significantly improved uptake of this simulators in different areas of brain research has been observed. NEST is a community code with an active user base. A key design goal is extreme (weak) scalability, which could be demonstrated different supercomputers (see, e.g., [5]). The program is written in C++ and Python, and uses MPI and OpenMP for parallelisation.

Unlike NEST, *Arbor* [2] is a simulation library for networks of morphologically detailed neurons. Simulations progress by taking half time steps for updating the states of the cells. This allows overlapping the exchange of the spikes generated by the cells. During the communication of spikes with other cells, similar operations need to be performed as in case of NEST. The performance in this step will mainly depend on memory and network performance. The step of updating the cells is, however, more compute intensive and can potentially benefit from compute acceleration through SIMD pipelines or GPUs. Cells are represented as trees of line segments, on which partial differential equations for potentials are solved using the finite-volume method. For complex cell models the second step will dominate application performance. Arbor is mainly written in C++ and employs MPI and OpenMP as well as CUDA for parallelisation.

The Virtual Brain (TVB) [3,4,11] is an application that aims at full brain network simulation. It uses mesoscopic models of neural dynamics, which model whole brain regions. For the interconnection of the different regions structural connectivity data sets are used. The application can generate outputs on different experimental modalities (for instance EEG or fMRI) and thus allows to compare simulated and experimental data. To enable exploitation of supercomputers, a new version of the application is being implemented, which is called *TVB-HPC*. TVB-HPC is written in Python and aims to automatically produce code for different targets, including processor architectures with SIMD pipelines or GPU accelerators. One of the targets is Numba [7], which is a tool that translates

Python functions to optimized machine code. TVB-HPC is using Numba for the benchmark at hand to just-in-time-compile Python code to CPU assembly. MPI is used to distribute tasks.

While the previous three applications enable different kind of brain simulations, the remaining applications, which have been used for the "ICEI Application Benchmark Suite" and are considered here, address data analysis tasks.

This includes *ASSET* [13], which is part of the Elephant (Electrophysiology Analysis Toolkit). Elephant is a library comprising a set of tools for analysing spike train data and other time series recordings obtained from experiments or simulations. Elephant is written in Python and relies on NumPy and SciPy for numerical tasks and MPI/mpi4py parallelisation. The tool ASSET (Analysis of Sequences of Synchronous EvenTs) was developed to automatise processing of spike data for sequences of synchronous spike events. In the ASSET benchmark at hand, one of the main compute kernels is compiled with Cython.

Another type of data processing challenge occurs in the context of analysis of high-resolution images of histological brain sections. To automatise the analysis of such images, applications based on deep learning techniques have been developed [12]. The *Neuroimaging Deep Learning* benchmark is derived from one such application. It is based on TensorFlow in combination with Horovod for parallelisation, using TensorFlow's GPU backend in the benchmark presented here.

3   Test Systems

The "ICEI Application Benchmark Suite" has been executed on a variety of systems to improve portability and collect performance results for different architectures. Here we focus on results obtained on two systems installed at Jülich Supercomputing Centre:

- JURON is a pilot system dedicated to users from HBP, which was delivered by IBM and NVIDIA in the context of a pre-commercial procurement that was executed during an the initial phase of the HBP.
- JUWELS is a flagship cluster system at JSC, which is one of the PRACE Tier-0 systems that are accessible for European researchers at large.

The 18 compute nodes of JURON are IBM S822LC servers (also known under the codename *Minsky*). Each node comprises two IBM POWER8 processors and four NVIDIA P100 GPUs. Each group of one processor and two GPUs is interconnected via NVLink links. The compute nodes are connected via Mellanox ConnectX-4 Infiniband EDR network adapters to a single switch. In the following we use the term "CPU-only nodes" when referring to JURON nodes where the GPUs are not used.

The JUWELS cluster comprises 2511 CPU-only and 48 GPU-accelerated compute nodes. Each comprises two Intel processors of the Skylake generation. The GPU-accelerated nodes are additionally equipped with four NVIDIA V100 GPUs. While the four GPUs are interconnected via NVLink in an all-to-all topology, each GPU is only connected via one PCIe Gen3 link to one of the CPUs. The compute nodes furthermore comprise a single Mellanox ConnectX-5 Infiniband EDR network adapter through which they are interconnected using a fat-tree topology.

A more detailed comparison of the hardware capabilities of the nodes used for either system are collected in Table 1. As the benchmarks considered here are compute-only (any time spent in I/O is not considered), we do not report on I/O capabilities of both systems.

Table 1. Comparison of node-level aggregated hardware parameters.

	JURON	JUWELS
Type of CPU	POWER8	Intel Xeon Platinum 8168 / Intel Xeon Gold 6148 (GPU-acc.)
Number of CPUs	2	2
Number of cores	20	48 / 40
Number of hardware threads	160	96 / 80
SIMD width / bit	128	512
Throughput / Flop/cycle	160	1536 / 1280
Memory capacity / GiB	256	$\geq$96
Memory bandwidth / GB/s	230	255
LLC capacity / MiB	160	66/27.5
Number of GPUs	4	$-$ / 4
Type of GPU	P100 SXM2	V100 SXM2
Throughput / Flop/cycle	14336	20480
Memory capacity / GiB	64	64
Memory bandwidth / GB/s	2880	3600

4   Results

In this section we document selected results for the benchmark derived from the applications introduced in Sect. 2, which have been obtained on the systems introduced in Sect. 3.

4.1   NEST

The benchmark is based on Version 2.14 of NEST [10].[3] Simulations are performed using a randomly connected network of 112 500 neurons with each neuron being connected to about 10% of the other neurons. While the problem size is kept fixed, the number of MPI tasks and OpenMP threads can be varied. Internally, NEST defines virtual processes (VP) and assigns one VP to each thread.

---

[3] https://github.com/nest/nest-simulator.git

The application first builds a network, i.e. creates all neurons and connects them. In a second step simulations are performed. Here, 1000 ms biological time are simulated. For this paper the GCC C++ compiler version 5.4.0 and 5.5.0 have been used on JURON and JUWELS, respectively. Since NEST does not support GPU acceleration, we use the CPU-only nodes on JUWELS.

In Figs. 1 and 2 we show how simulation time scales on a single node as a function of the number of VPs. The number of VPs is equal to the number of threads, which is the product of the number of nodes, tasks per node, and threads per task. The results for multi-node scaling are shown in Table 2.

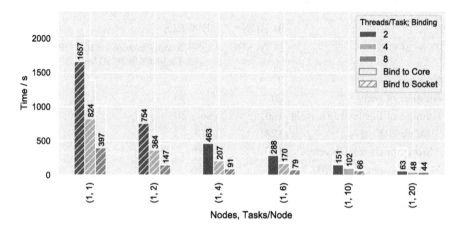

Fig. 1. NEST benchmark – JURON: Simulation time on a single JURON node for different numbers of virtual processes (VP, the product of the number of nodes, tasks per node, and threads per task). Different strategies of mapping and binding MPI tasks to the system have been tested and the best performing configuration selected; a shaded bar denotes *binding to socket*, a solid bar denotes *binding to core*.

NEST can efficiently exploit node- and thread-level parallelism and therefore exhibits a good scaling behaviour on both architectures. On POWER8 processors the application to some extent benefits from using up to 8 hardware threads per core. This trend can not compensate for the larger number of cores available on the Skylake processor. Since NEST is not capable of exploiting SIMD parallelism, the wider SIMD units of the Xeon processors do not add benefits for this application.

For NEST it is of special importance how the VPs are distributed to the available hardware resources. NEST uses OpenMP for shared-memory parallelism (*Threads/Task*) and MPI for task-based parallelism (*Tasks/Node*), potentially across node borders. The employed strategy to distribute OpenMP threads uses the `OMP_PLACES` environment variable to distribute along physical cores (`cores`); this variable might possibly interact with MPI binding options. To fix each OpenMP thread to a certain place, the affinity variable `OMP_PROC_BIND`

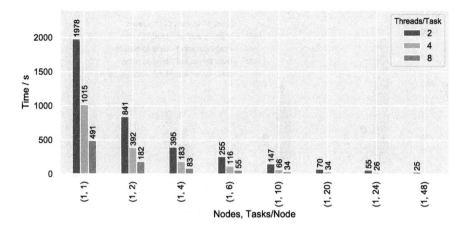

Fig. 2. NEST benchmark – JUWELS: Same as in Fig. 1 but for JUWELS.

Table 2. NEST benchmark: Build and simulation time for 1, 2 and 4 nodes and optimal number of tasks and threads per node.

Nodes	JURON		JUWELS	
	Build/s	Simulation/s	Build/s	Simulation/s
1	2.58	44.50	1.25	25.15
2	2.34	32.39	0.81	15.15
4	1.39	18.80	0.63	5.88

is set to TRUE. Of more importance for the two-socket system JURON is the employed distribution of MPI tasks. In Fig. 1, two binding schemes of Open-MPI were used. The hatched bars (usually for lower number of VPs) bind tasks to cores (--bind-to core) whereas the solid bars bind tasks to sockets (--bind-to socket); in both cases, a mapping along sockets is chosen (--map-by socket). Setting the *wrong* binding can entail serious performance penalties (see also the white-outlined bars in the background of Fig. 1). Figure 3 compares the two binding strategies for four selected distributions of 20 VPs along tasks and threads. It can clearly be seen that for few tasks and many threads in the left of the figure, --bind-to socket is the more beneficial binding option. For many tasks with each few threads (right of the figure), --bind-to core is the more sensible choice. While these results might be expected, they might not be the choice of distribution for the employed MPI. Figure 3 also shows two further optimized binding configurations: For the configuration of 1 Task and 20 Threads (the very left), disabling binding can improve performance further (--bind-to none) as now both sockets can be used by the 20 threads. Another way to bind can be seen for the case of 10 Tasks and 2 Threads per Task; by binding to cores but also mapping to the sockets such that

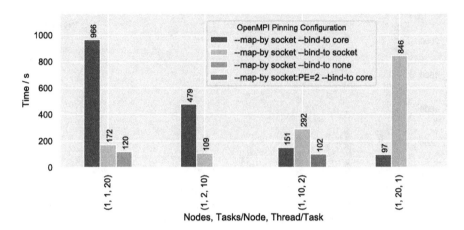

Fig. 3. NEST benchmark – JURON: Different binding strategies for different distributions of VPs.

exactly 2 cores (`PE=2`) are bound to each task, the MPI runtime has all information about tasks and threads to create a performance-beneficial task distribution (each task has two associated OpenMP places).

The mapping and binding options for JUWELS are more limited as the combination of job scheduler and MPI runtime currently don't offer similar high-level functionality as in the case for JURON. For JUWELS, the shown values are measured by using a pinning mask manually created by the tool `hwloc`, distributing tasks across the node architecture. In general, the default pinning of JUWELS is much better than the default pinning of JURON.

One of the main performance limiters for NEST on JURON are stalled processor cycles, as shown in Fig. 4. The figure shows measurements of a selection of hardware performance counters using the `perf` utility. Most of the stalls can be attributed to misses of the data cache, more specifically to cases were data was not in the L3 level cache.

4.2 Arbor

Arbor is a rather new simulator, which has been designed from scratch with the goal of supporting different HPC architectures in a performance portable manner. We use version 0.1 of Arbor [1].[4] The different simulation phases are similar as for NEST, but given that simulation of multi-compartment models of neurons are much more expensive, the benchmark focuses exclusively on the simulation phase. Simulation proceeds in a lock-step manner by first updating all cells half a time step and then overlapping the exchange of spikes with the further half time steps. Arbor allows to group cells in a flexible manner depending on the target architecture. For instance, large cell groups are used for GPUs that require

---

[4] https://github.com/arbor-sim/arbor.git.

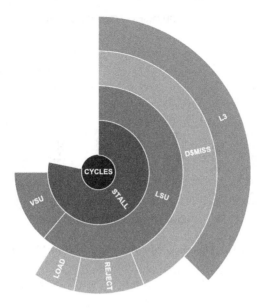

Fig. 4. NEST benchmark – JURON: Performance counters.

a very high level of parallelism. For this paper the GNU C++ compiler version 6.3.0 and 8.2.0 have been used on JURON and JUWELS, respectively, when running the CPU version of the benchmark, and 6.3.0 and 7.3.0, respectively, when running the GPU version of the benchmark. For the GPU benchmark CUDA 9.2.148 was used on JURON and CUDA 9.2.88 was used on JUWELS. We perform simulations involving 1000 cells covering a biological time of 1 s (GPU version) or 0.1 s (CPU version).

In Fig. 5 we show how performance scales on a single CPU-only node using 2 MPI tasks and a variable number of threads per MPI task. On POWER8 little benefit is observed from using multiple hardware threads per physical CPU core. The application is significantly faster on the Xeon nodes as it can efficiently exploit the wide SIMD units. The observed performance ratio roughly matches the ratio of throughput in floating-point operations (see Table 1). The higher clock frequency of the POWER8 processor does not seem to help improving performance significantly.

Next we compare performance using Arbor on GPU-accelerated nodes. The results are shown in Fig. 6. To highlight differences in scaling among different numbers of GPUs, the simulation time has been increased ten times compared to the CPU-only benchmark. Performance on JUWELS and JURON now is similar when taking into account that the V100 GPUs used in JUWELS have an about 40% higher throughput of double-precision floating-point operations compared to the P100 GPUs used in JURON.

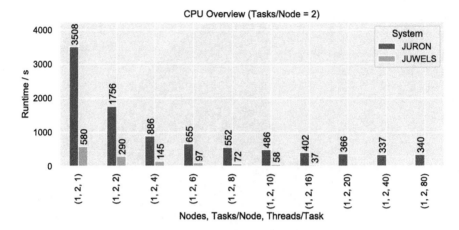

Fig. 5. Arbor benchmark: Time needed to simulate 100 ms biological time on a single CPU-only node.

4.3   TVB-HPC

The HPC version of TVB, which uses Numba for code generation, is still in development and we therefore use a pre-release version. The benchmark uses a simple mesoscopic model based on the Kuramoto model [6], which is used for the study of neuronal oscillations and synchronization. 1600 time steps are simulated. We use Python 3.6.1 (3.6.6) as well as version 0.39.0 (0.40.1) of Numba and version 1.14.2 (1.15.2) of Numpy on JURON (JUWELS).

In Fig. 7 we show the scaling of the benchmark on up to two nodes. The observed scaling behaviour is similar on both architectures with a parallel efficiency of about 80% when using 16 MPI tasks on a single node. On a single node the benchmark execution time on JURON is consistently about 35% slower compared to JUWELS when using the same number of MPI tasks. The difference drops to about 13% when using two nodes. This version of TVB-HPC is not able to exploit SIMD parallelism. This observation plus the limited scalability results in performance differences between JURON and JUWELS that are relatively small.

4.4   Elephant ASSET

The benchmark is based on version 1.0 of ASSET[5] as well as Python libraries neo (version 0.6.1), sklearn (version 0.19.1), and elephant (version 0.5.0), respectively. Most of the time is spent computing a set of survival functions, which requires computing of statistical distributions based on the input data. This makes speed of memory access in general a performance limiting factor, with efficiency of handling of Python arrays being an implementation specific aspect.

---

[5] https://github.com/INM-6/pcp_use_cases.git.

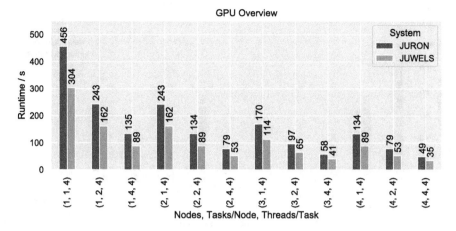

Fig. 6. Arbor benchmark: Time needed to simulate 1000 ms biological time on one or more GPU-accelerated nodes.

Parallelisation is realised by distributing the input data in an approximately fair manner to all available MPI tasks. While MPI parallelisation is done explicitly within the application, exploitation of any additional thread-level parallelism is left to Python.

In Fig. 8 we show benchmark run-time as well as the execution time of the main kernel, which computes the joint survival function, as a function of the number of tasks. While execution time on JUWELS is first lower than on JURON, the scaling behaviour on JUWELS is slightly worse, resulting in JURON having the lowest achieved benchmark time with a sufficient number of tasks (30).

4.5 Neuroimaging Deep Learning

The benchmark is a mini-application version of the real code. It is extracted such that input data is loaded first to main memory to separate performance impacts related to the capabilities of the storage system, in which the input data resides.[6] For the results shown below TensorFlow version 1.4.1 (1.8.0) and Horovod version 0.14.1 (both) was used on JURON (JUWELS).

A selection of benchmark results are listed in Fig. 9. The performance is measured in terms of time needed to process a single image. On both of considered architectures the intra-node scaling as well as the inter-node scaling behaviour is fair. The performance on JUWELS suffers efficiency losses of (max.) 30% and 23% for intra- and inter-node scaling, respectively; for JURON it is 10% and 6%. Absolute performance and scaling performance is significantly better on JURON despite an older generation of GPUs being used. This may be an indication of better data transport capabilities having an important performance impact in this application.

---

[6] I/O performance for this application is crucial and has been analysed in [9].

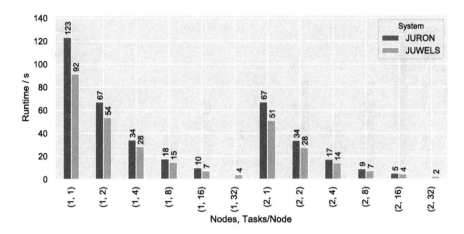

Fig. 7. TVB-HPC benchmark: Scaling of the benchmark on up to 2 CPU-only nodes as a function of the number of MPI tasks.

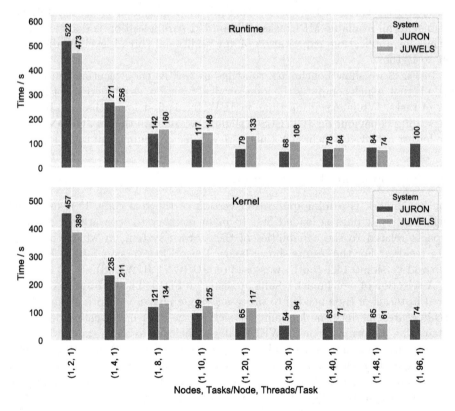

Fig. 8. Elephant-ASSET benchmark: Benchmark (top) and kernel (bottom) execution times as a function of tasks on one node for JURON and JUWELS.

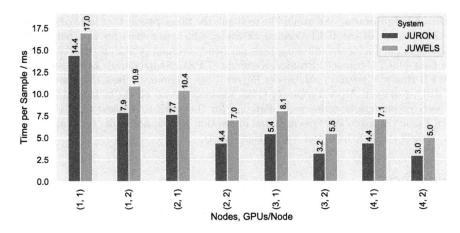

Fig. 9. Neuroimaging Deep Learning benchmark: Time per sample as a function of GPUs and tasks for JURON and JUWELS.

5 Summary and Conclusions

In this paper we presented selected performance results obtained for the "ICEI Application Benchmark Suite" using a slightly older system based on IBM POWER8 processors plus NVIDIA P100 GPUs (*JURON*) as well as a more recent system based on Intel Skylake processors plus NVIDIA V100 GPUs (*JUWELS*).

The example of Arbor indicates that for compute-limited applications, which can exploit wide SIMD pipelines without using GPUs as compute accelerators, the performance of CPU-only JUWELS nodes exceed those of JURON significantly. For processors based on the POWER architecture being competitive, higher throughput of floating-point operations would be desirable.

For applications, which cannot exploit SIMD parallelism, performance on JURON and JUWELS was found to be similar in case of TVB-HPC and ASSET. In case of NEST, which compared to the other applications is able to scale slightly better by making use of the larger number of available cores, JUWELS was found to perform better.

Finally, for the machine learning application the POWER-based system was found to be better.

The results provided in this paper give an overview over the performance trend for different applications from a benchmark suite that aims for reflecting the needs of the relatively diverse community of brain research. We plan for further efforts to analyse the causes for the different performance behaviour. This will help to guide designing future e-infrastructures optimised for this community. We believe that the increased choice of architectures and technologies, which can be used for this purpose, is helpful.

Acknowledgements. We would like to thank the many people that have contributed to the creation of the ICEI Benchmark Suite, which was used for this paper. This includes in particular the following persons: Ben Cumming (CSCS, Switzerland), Sandra Diaz (JSC, Germany), Pramod Kumbhar (EPFL, Switzerland), Lena Oden (JSC and FU Hagen, Germany), Alexander Peyser (JSC, Germany), Hans Ekkehard Plesser (NMBU, Norway), Alper Yegenoglu (FZJ, Germany), and all the collaborators of the respective community codes used. Funding for the work is received from the European Union's Horizon 2020 research and innovation programme under grant agreement No. 785907 (HBP SGA2) and No. 800858 (ICEI).

References

1. Akar, N.A., et al.: arbor-sim/arbor: Version 0.1: First release, October 2018. https://doi.org/10.5281/zenodo.1459679
2. Akar, N.A., et al.: Arbor - a morphologically-detailed neural network simulation library for contemporary high-performance computing architectures. In: 27th Euromicro International Conference on Parallel, Distributed and Network-Based Processing, PDP 2019, Pavia, Italy, 13–15 February 2019, pp. 274–282. IEEE (2019). https://doi.org/10.1109/EMPDP.2019.8671560
3. Jirsa, V., McIntosh, R., Ritter, P., Mersmann, J., et al.: http://www.thevirtual brain.org/
4. Jirsa, V.K., Sporns, O., Breakspear, M., Deco, G., McIntosh, A.R.: Towards The Virtual Brain: network modeling of the intact and the damaged brain. Arch. Ital. Biol. **148**(3), 189–205 (2010)
5. Jordan, J., et al.: Extremely scalable spiking neuronal network simulation code: from laptops to exascale computers. Front. Neuroinformatics **12**, 2 (2018)
6. Kuramoto, Y.: Self-entrainment of a population of coupled non-linear oscillators. In: Araki, H. (ed.) International Symposium on Mathematical Problems in Theoretical Physics. LNP, vol. 39, pp. 420–422. Springer, Heidelberg (1975). https://doi.org/10.1007/BFb0013365
7. Lam, S.K., Pitrou, A., Seibert, S.: Numba: a LLVM-based python JIT compiler. In: Proceedings of the Second Workshop on the LLVM Compiler Infrastructure in HPC, LLVM 2015, pp. 7:1–7:6. ACM, New York (2015). http://doi.acm.org/10.1145/2833157.2833162
8. Linssen, C., et al.: NEST 2.16.0, August 2018. https://zenodo.org/record/1400175
9. Oden, L., Schiffer, C., Spitzer, H., Dickscheid, T., Pleiter, D.: IO challenges for human brain atlasing using deep learning methods - an in-depth analysis. In: 27th Euromicro International Conference on Parallel, Distributed and Network-Based Processing, PDP 2019, Pavia, Italy, 13–15 February 2019, pp. 291–298. IEEE (2019). https://doi.org/10.1109/EMPDP.2019.8671630
10. Peyser, A., et al.: Nest 2.14.0, October 2017. https://doi.org/10.5281/zenodo.882971
11. Ritter, P., Schirner, M., McIntosh, A.R., Jirsa, V.K.: The Virtual Brain integrates computational modeling and multimodal neuroimaging. Brain Connect. **3**(2), 121–145 (2013)

12. Spitzer, H., Amunts, K., Harmeling, S., Dickscheid, T.: Parcellation of visual cortex on high-resolution histological brain sections using convolutional neural networks. In: 2017 IEEE 14th International Symposium on Biomedical Imaging (ISBI 2017), pp. 920–923, April 2017
13. Torre, E., Canova, C., Denker, M., Gerstein, G., Helias, M., Grün, S.: ASSET: analysis of sequences of synchronous events in massively parallel spike trains. PLoS Comput. Biol. **12**(7), 1–34 (2016)

Evaluating POWER Architecture for Distributed Training of Generative Adversarial Networks

Ahmad Hesam[1,2]([✉]), Sofia Vallecorsa[2], Gulrukh Khattak[2], and Federico Carminati[2]

[1] Delft University of Technology, Delft, Netherlands
a.s.hesam@tudelft.nl
[2] CERN, Geneva, Switzerland

Abstract. The increased availability of High-Performance Computing resources can enable data scientists to deploy and evaluate data-driven approaches, notably in the field of deep learning, at a rapid pace. As deep neural networks become more complex and are ingesting increasingly larger datasets, it becomes unpractical to perform the training phase on single machine instances due to memory constraints, and extremely long training time. Rather than scaling up, scaling out the computing resources is a productive approach to improve performance. The paradigm of data parallelism allows us to split the training dataset into manageable chunks that can be processed in parallel. In this work, we evaluate the scaling performance of training a 3D generative adversarial network (GAN) on an IBM POWER8 cluster, equipped with 12 NVIDIA P100 GPUs. The full training duration of the GAN, including evaluation, is reduced from 20 h and 16 min on a single GPU, to 2 h and 14 min on all 12 GPUs. We achieve a scaling efficiency of 98.9% when scaling from 1 to 12 GPUs, taking only the training process into consideration.

Keywords: Distributed training · Generative adversarial network · High Performance Computing · GPU · POWER8

1 Introduction

Deep Neural Networks (DNNs) are actively being used to solve complex problems by examining enormous amounts of data. The success of DNNs can be mainly attributed to advances in parallel computing. The introduction of the General Purpose Graphics Processing Unit (GPGPU) has allowed us to exploit the inherent parallelism of the computations that take place in deep learning applications. This development enabled data scientists to deploy deeper neural networks and handle larger datasets, in an effort to solve more complex problems. As a result, the training phase of DNNs may take days or weeks to come to completion. In order to meet the ever-increasing computational demand, distributed training is becoming very important, where the idea is to use computer clusters

© Springer Nature Switzerland AG 2019
M. Weiland et al. (Eds.): ISC 2019 Workshops, LNCS 11887, pp. 432–440, 2019.
https://doi.org/10.1007/978-3-030-34356-9_32

to train a neural network. Effectively utilizing state-of-the-art technologies in High-Performance Computing (HPC) for distributed learning will be integral in pushing the boundaries of the field of deep learning.

High Energy Physics (HEP) is a field that requires computationally demanding deep learning applications to solve complex scientific problems. The experiments at the Large Hadron Collider (LHC) at CERN are devoting more than 50% of their resources to Monte Carlo (MC) simulation tasks. The main reason for this, is because in HEP, particles are simulation in extreme detail as they traverse through matter. At the moment of writing, CERN has temporarily shut down the LHC experiments in preparation for their upgrade (High Luminosity LHC phase), after which the demand for simulated data is expected to increase by a factor of 100 [3]. Deep learning is a promising approach to replace traditional Monte Carlo simulations, and in particular generative models. Prior work have demonstrated that Generative Adversarial Networks (GANs) can partially replace MC task in HEP simulations with an acceptable accuracy [10]. The idea is for a GAN to generate a relatively large set of realistic simulation samples by training the model on a relatively small sample set of experimental or simulated data. The inference step of the GAN is orders of magnitude faster than the traditional Monte Carlo simulations, and could therefore meet the demands of the High Luminosity LHC phase. The training of the GAN is however very time consuming and its performance must be improved significantly in order to test and deploy this deep learning approach to various types of detectors and particles. This paper is an effort to assess the performance of IBM POWER architecture to fulfill this task.

The organization of the paper is as follows. Section 2 discusses related work. In Sect. 3 we define the problem in more detail. In Sect. 4 we describe the methodology of our approach. Section 5 describes the hardware and software setup. In Sect. 6 we present the results. And finally, in Sect. 7 we discuss the future works.

2   Related Work

The idea of adversarial training was originally introduced by Goodfellow in [7]. GANs generally consists of a generative network (generator) and a discriminative network (discriminator). The generator learns to map data from a random distribution to data that follows the distribution of interest. The discriminator learns how to distinguish between data produced by the generator from the true data distributions. Training a GAN involves presenting it with data samples from the training dataset until the generated candidates are indistinguishable from samples from the training dataset. The training is complete when the generator effectively managed to 'fool' the discriminator up to a desired accuracy.

The applications of GANs, and their variations, are being investigated in many fields [8,15,20]. In High-Energy Physics (HEP) we can consider particle detectors as cameras that capture the decay products of particle collisions in accelerators such as the Large Hadron Collider. Consequently, researchers have been exploring the applications of GANs in HEP, by generating images that mimic the complex distributions of these 'detector images' [16,17].

To reach convergence between the generator and discriminator, it can take quite a long time relative to other deep neural network architectures [14], and makes for an appealing use case for distributing the training process over many nodes. The distributed training of GANs is a relatively new research area, and there are only a few efforts made in that direction. We shall describe them in this section.

In [24], the authors investigate the performance of distributed training of GANs for fast detector simulations. The training is performed on an HPC cluster consisting of 256 CPUs, in a dual-socket configuration. The results show that the performance scales linearly, with a scaling efficiency of 94% when utilizing the entire cluster.

The authors in [23] performs a data-parallel training of GANs for high-energy physics simulations. For the distribution of the training workload, the authors rely on an MPI-based Cray Machine Learning Plugin to train the GAN over multiple nodes and GPGPUs. Preliminary results show that the training of 3 epochs on 16 NVIDIA P100 GPUs took 2 h.

The authors in [12] explore the scaling of a GAN to thousands of nodes on Cray XC supercomputing systems. The network that is used as a benchmark, CosmoGAN, is used to produce cosmology mass maps, which otherwise would be obtained through computationally expensive simulations. Several distribution frameworks were evaluated, on two HPC systems: one consisting of 9,688 CPUs, and one 5,320 hybrid CPU+GPU nodes. The work reports the strong and weak scaling behavior of both systems.

3   Problem Definition

Following up on related work, the main questions that this paper aims to answer is: *How does distributed training of adversarial generative networks performs on a POWER8 cluster, in terms of overall runtime, scalability, and power efficiency?*

We limit the scope of the question by focusing on a particular use case of generative adversarial networks (GANs) in high-energy physics simulations. The type of simulations that we are targeting are those of highly segmented calorimeters, as typically found in particle detectors, such as the LHC experiments at CERN. In this work we consider the use case of the Compact Linear Collider (CLIC), which is a conceptual linear accelerator study [2]. This use case is representative of the demand for simulated data as to be expect for the HL-LHC era. Moreover, the dataset is publicly available [4]. The dataset that we are considering consists of what is in high-energy physics referred to as electron showers. An electron shower is the result of a chain-reaction of electromagnetic collisions initiated by one electron penetrating a material (in this case a calorimeter). Electron showers are one of the main reasons why HEP simulations are very time-consuming, as all of the electrons that come forth from the shower need to be simulated through the matter in which they traverse. The High-Luminosity LHC upgrade will increase the energy level at which experiments are done significantly, and accordingly the simulations must be able to keep up. The trained

GAN will be able to replace the simulation of an electron shower with a single inference of the model. The neural architecture of the GAN we used is described in [22]. Based on the available dataset [4], we train a GAN to reproduce the energy distribution of the showers generated by electrons with energies ranging from 10 to 500 GeV.

4 Data-Parallel Distributed Training

Distributed training can generally be implemented according to two different paradigms: model parallelism, and data parallelism. As described in [11], data parallelism is more efficient when the number of computations per model weight is high, which is the case of the GAN we are considering, as it mostly consists of convolutional layers. For this reason, we decided to go for a data-parallel approach.

In data-parallel distributed training, we must run multiple instances of the stochastic gradient descent (SGD) algorithm (RMSProp in our use case). The gradients that are computed by each SGD instance must be propagated through the network to maintain a consistent model. Horovod [21] is a framework that works on top of well-known machine learning libraries (Tensorflow, Keras, PyTorch), and takes care of the model consistency. Under the hood, it uses the ring all-reduce [18] decentralized scheme to communicate the gradients across the network. The ring all-reduce scheme requires communication only between neighboring nodes in a ring-like network topology, effectively reducing the amount of cross-server communication.

5 Computing Configuration

The POWER8 cluster on which we performed the benchmarks consists of 3 IBM S822LC nodes, each consisting of 2 POWER8 sockets (8 cores per socket), 256 GB of DDR4 RAM, and 4 NVIDIA P100 GPUs (16 of RAM per GPU). Moreover, each node is provided with an 80 GB/s bidirectional NVLink interconnect between the POWER8 sockets and P100 GPUs, and also between the GPUs, as displayed in Fig. 1.

The GAN is implemented in Keras v1.2.2 [5], with Tensorflow 1.12.0 [1] as the backend execution framework, which is part of the IBM PowerAI DL stack. The distributed training is done through Horovod 0.15.1 [21], which makes use of the IBM Spectrum MPI [25] v10.2.0 with CUDA support, which is based on OpenMPI [6]. One MPI process was spawned for each instance of the GAN as part of the distributed stochastic gradient descent algorithm. In order to reduce the cross-talk between NUMA domains, and between servers, we pinned the fraction of the training data to the NUMA domain that corresponds to the GPU that ingests that fraction of the training data. This is achieved by enabling the `mpirun` option `--bind-to-socket`, and setting the `-rankfile` option to point to a rankfile that assigns one MPI process per GPU. The POWER8 system was configured with CUDA 10.0, which includes the CUDNN 7.5 library.

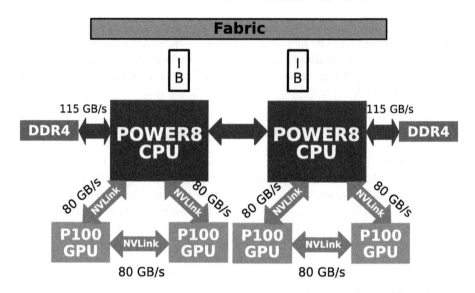

Fig. 1. An overview of the fabric of an IBM S822LC node. IB stands for InfiniBand.

The training data consist of 200,000 electron showers, spread over 80 files, which account for a total of 12 GB on disk. 90% of the dataset was used for training and the remainder for testing. Typically, within the training phase, one computes both the training loss (through backpropagation) and the test loss (through feed-forward propagation). To evaluate the overall runtime we take both computations into account, but for the scalability analysis, we take only training into account. A full training consists of 40 epochs, but for the scalability test, we timed only the training time per epoch, since each epoch is of the same duration[1]. In order to *warm up* the GPUs on the machine, we ran five warm-up epochs for every measurement. The choice of the mini-batch size for GANs is still an open research question, but empirically we observed that an increasingly larger mini-batch size reduced the overall training time, while resulting in the same convergence of the loss functions. Therefore, we fixed the mini-batch size to 512, which we found to be the largest batch size to perform training with, without facing out-of-memory issues.

6   Results

We performed a full training on the POWER8 cluster on a single GPU and measured the wall time to be 20 h and 16 min. On 12 GPUs the total training time is reduced to 2 h and 14 min, which is a speedup of approximately 9×. From the profiling results, it becomes clear that the main reason for the discrepancy

---

[1] Except for the first epoch, which includes the cuDNN configuration time. For this reason, we start timing from the second epoch.

with an ideal speedup is due to the single-GPU execution of the evaluation of the test losses. Unlike the training of the GAN, the evaluation is not executed in a distributed manner. Following Amdahl's law [9], the maximum theoretical speedup will be limited by the serial fraction of the code, which in this case is the code for computing the test losses. Compared to previous work on distributed training of the same neural architecture on 16 P100 GPUs (2 h for 3 epochs) [23], we have demonstrated a significant improvement.

For the scalability benchmark, we excluded the computation of the tests losses in the training phase. We performed the distributed training of the GAN for different numbers of GPUs and measured the time per epoch (averaged over five epochs). The results for speedup with respect to training on a single GPU are plotted in Fig. 3. We observe strong scaling performance as we increase the number of GPUs, with a scaling efficiency of 98.9% when utilizing the entire cluster. Profiling results from NVIDIA's GPU profiling tool nvprof show that the data transfer between neighboring nodes in the ring all-reduce scheme does not saturate the NVLink bandwidth (see Fig. 2), and therefore the scalability of the training depends on the computational throughput of the GPUs.

Power consumption is another metric we want to report in this benchmark. From the power consumption calculator that is referred to in [19] we calculated the estimated power consumption of an IBM S822LC node to be 1,800 W. The calculation includes the consumption of all electronic devices present in the node. For the entire POWER8 cluster this results in a total of 5,400 W. Since the computations of the GAN training are offloaded to the P100 GPUs, the CPUs do not contribute (significantly) to the computational throughput. According to the nvprof profiling results, the computational occupancy of the training phase was on average close to 85%. We experimentally measured the P100 GPU to have a throughput of 8.8 TFLOPs (single-precision floating points) with the matrix multiplication benchmark provided in the CUDA samples, since the GAN network consists primarily of convolutional layers. Therefore, we estimate the throughput of the GAN training to be 7.5 TFLOPs per GPU. Based off of this estimate, the cluster's overall power efficiency for training GANs is 16.6 GFLOPs/Watt.

7   Future Work

As part of the IBM PowerAI framework [25], the IBM DDL (Distributed Deep Learning) library offers, similarly to Horovod, an implementation of distributed deep learning. DDL offers multiple methods to perform the distributed stochastic gradient descent algorithm. It would be interesting to explore these options in an effort to improve the overall training time.

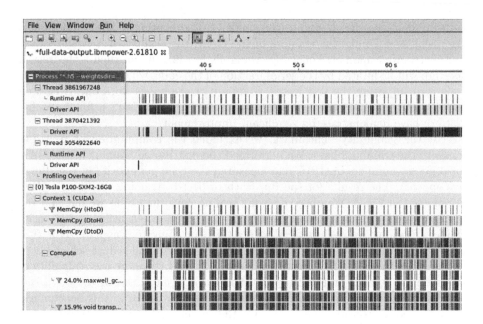

Fig. 2. Partial `nvprof` profiling output for one of the GPUs in a 12-GPU training, showing that training is compute-bound.

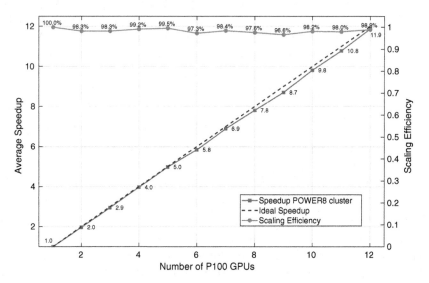

Fig. 3. Performance of scaling number of P100 GPUs and corresponding scaling efficiency.

Large Model Support (LMS) [13] is a feature of the IBM PowerAI framework, that enables the training of deep neural networks (DNNs) that would otherwise exceed the memory capacity of a GPU. LMS achieves this by swapping the feature maps of DNNs in and out of the GPU memory – keeping only the data in memory that is required at certain stages in the training pipeline. This approach puts a larger burden on the CPU-GPU interconnect, and could possibly saturate the bandwidth. The high-bandwidth NVLink interconnect between the CPU and the GPUs in modern POWER systems, however, makes LMS an appealing approach to scaling out the training of DNNs. We would be interested to find out how LMS performs against the data-parallel approach that is used in this work.

References

1. Abadi, M., et al.: TensorFlow: large-scale machine learning on heterogeneous systems (2015). https://www.tensorflow.org/
2. Aicheler, M., et al.: A multi-TeV linear collider based on CLIC technology: CLIC conceptual design report. CERN Yellow Reports: Monographs, CERN, Geneva (2012). https://doi.org/10.5170/CERN-2012-007. https://cds.cern.ch/record/1500095
3. Bird, I.: Workshop introduction, context of the workshop: half-way through run2; preparing for run3, run4. WLCG Workshop (2016)
4. Carminati, F., Khattak, G., Pierini, M., Vallecor-safa, S., Farbin, A.: Calorimetry with deep learning: particle classification, energy regression, and simulation for high-energy physics. In: NIPS (2017)
5. Chollet, F., et al.: Keras (2015). https://github.com/fchollet/keras
6. Gabriel, E., et al.: Open MPI: goals, concept, and design of a next generation MPI implementation. In: Kranzlmüller, D., Kacsuk, P., Dongarra, J. (eds.) EuroPVM/MPI 2004. LNCS, vol. 3241, pp. 97–104. Springer, Heidelberg (2004). https://doi.org/10.1007/978-3-540-30218-6_19
7. Goodfellow, I., et al.: Generative adversarial nets. In: Advances in Neural Information Processing Systems, pp. 2672–2680 (2014)
8. Goodfellow, I.J.: On distinguishability criteria for estimating generative models. arXiv preprint arXiv:1412.6515 (2014)
9. Hill, M.D., Marty, M.R.: Amdahl's law in the multicore era. Computer $41(7)$, 33–38 (2008)
10. Khattak, G., Vallecorsa, S., Carminati, F.: Three dimensional energy parametrized generative adversarial networks for electromagnetic shower simulation. In: 2018 25th IEEE International Conference on Image Processing (ICIP), pp. 3913–3917, October 2018
11. Krizhevsky, A.: One weird trick for parallelizing convolutional neural networks. arXiv preprint arXiv:1404.5997 (2014)
12. Kurth, T., Smorkalov, M., Mendygral, P., Sridharan, S., Mathuriya, A.: Tensorflow at scale: performance and productivity analysis of distributed training with Horovod, MLSL, and Cray PE ML. Concurr. Comput.: Pract. Exp. (2018). https://doi.org/10.1002/cpe.4989
13. Le, T.D., Imai, H., Negishi, Y., Kawachiya, K.: TFLMS: large model support in TensorFlow by graph rewriting. arXiv preprint arXiv:1807.02037 (2018)
14. Mescheder, L., Geiger, A., Nowozin, S.: Which training methods for GANs do actually converge? arXiv preprint arXiv:1801.04406 (2018)

15. Odena, A., Olah, C., Shlens, J.: Conditional image synthesis with auxiliary classifier GANs. In: Proceedings of the 34th International Conference on Machine Learning, vol. 70, pp. 2642–2651. JMLR.org (2017)
16. de Oliveira, L., Paganini, M., Nachman, B.: Learning particle physics by example: location-aware generative adversarial networks for physics synthesis. Comput. Softw. Big Sci. **1**(1), 4 (2017)
17. Paganini, M., de Oliveira, L., Nachman, B.: CaloGAN: simulating 3D high energy particle showers in multilayer electromagnetic calorimeters with generative adversarial networks. Phys. Rev. D **97**(1), 014021 (2018)
18. Patarasuk, P., Yuan, X.: Bandwidth optimal all-reduce algorithms for clusters of workstations. J. Parallel Distrib. Comput. **69**(2), 117–124 (2009)
19. Quintero, D.: IBM POWER8 high-performance computing guide: IBM power system S822LC (8335-GTB) edition. IBM Corporation, International Technical Support Organization, Poughkeepsie, NY (2017)
20. Radford, A., Metz, L., Chintala, S.: Unsupervised representation learning with deep convolutional generative adversarial networks. arXiv preprint arXiv:1511.06434 (2015)
21. Sergeev, A., Del Balso, M.: Horovod: fast and easy distributed deep learning in TensorFlow. arXiv preprint arXiv:1802.05799 (2018)
22. Vallecorsa, S.: Generative models for fast simulation. J. Phys.: Conf. Ser. **1085**, 022005 (2018). https://doi.org/10.1088/1742-6596/1085/2/022005
23. Vallecorsa, S., Moise, D., Carminati, F., Khattak, G.R.: Data-parallel training of generative adversarial networks on HPC systems for HEP simulations. In: 2018 IEEE 25th International Conference on High Performance Computing (HiPC), pp. 162–171, December 2018. https://doi.org/10.1109/HiPC.2018.00026
24. Vallecorsa, S., et al.: Distributed training of generative adversarial networks for fast detector simulation. In: Yokota, R., Weiland, M., Shalf, J., Alam, S. (eds.) ISC High Performance 2018. LNCS, vol. 11203, pp. 487–503. Springer, Cham (2018). https://doi.org/10.1007/978-3-030-02465-9_35
25. Wale, D.: IBM PowerAI : Deep Learning Unleashed on IBM Power Systems Servers. IBM Redbooks, S.l (2018)

A Study on the Performance of Reproducible Computations

Nico Bombace$^{(\boxtimes)}$ and Michèle Weiland

EPCC, Bayes Centre, The University of Edinburgh, Edinburgh, Scotland
{n.bombace,m.weiland}@epcc.ed.ac.uk

Abstract. Parallel computations are intrinsically non-reproducible, due to a combined effect of non-deterministic parallel reductions and non-associative floating point operations. Different strategies have been proposed in literature to alleviate this issue or eliminate it altogether, however at present there is no study on the performance impact of associative floating point operations on large scale applications. In this work, we implement associative operations using binned doubles in MiniFE, and perform various performance tests on Cirrus and Fulhame, two state-of-the-art HPC systems.

Keywords: Reproducibility · Binned doubles · Performance

1 Introduction

High performance parallel computers play an increasingly impactful role in everyday life, aiding and accelerating new discoveries in science by leveraging parallel programming idioms. However, parallel computing poses a strong challenge regarding the reproducibility of results, due to the non-deterministic behaviour of parallel operations together with the non-associativity of floating point operations.

One of the direct consequences of this phenomenon is the challenge of verification of parallel applications or libraries, where code is often tested against an "oracle" solution to detect and eliminate software bugs as early as possible. However, if the run-to-run behaviour of the code cannot be guaranteed in terms of reproducibility, bugs can potentially be hidden even in production code [6].

Different methodologies have been proposed to tackle this problem, where the easiest approach is to freeze the summands before the operation, generally via sorting. While effective, this method is computationally expensive and efforts have been devoted to designing less expensive methodologies. For instance, compensated sum techniques [4] introduce an error accumulator which alleviates the non-reproducibility issue. A bit-reproducible computation of the results can be guaranteed by designing new floating point operations that are associative by definition.

In particular, this work will focus on the technique proposed by Ahrens et al. in [2], in which the notion of *binned doubles* is introduced. Preliminary studies

© Springer Nature Switzerland AG 2019
M. Weiland et al. (Eds.): ISC 2019 Workshops, LNCS 11887, pp. 441–451, 2019.
https://doi.org/10.1007/978-3-030-34356-9_33

have shown that with respect to a standard double implementation, binned doubles introduce a slowdown of $4x$, however this is based only on the dot product operation. In our work, the proposed binned double is implemented in the Mantevo project [3], which is comprised of several mini-apps that represent different aspects of demanding computations. This study focuses on the MiniFE mini-app, an implicit finite element solver that supports the use of custom numerical types. With this set of operations we are able to perform an extensive study on the performance of reproducible operations. We show that:

1. Binned doubles ensure reproducibility of computations on different architectures,
2. It is possible to use the same code for both doubles and reproducible doubles using a non-invasive compile-time approach,
3. reproducibility requirements strongly affect performance.

2 Methodology

We provide a binned doubles implementation to use in the MiniFE application, which forms part of the Mantevo project [3], aimed at the analysis of HPC system performance. In particular, this mini-app provides a fully fledged implementation of unstructured finite elements, with support for multi-core operations.

2.1 MiniFE

MiniFE is written in C++ and relies heavily on the use of meta-programming techniques in the form of templates, which represent a compile-time mechanism to write generic code not coupled to a particular type [7]. As an example, let us consider the Vector declaration in MiniFE:

```
1  template<typename Scalar,
2          typename LocalOrdinal,
3          typename GlobalOrdinal>
4  struct
5  Vector{
6    ...
7    typedef Scalar        ScalarType;
8    typedef LocalOrdinal  LocalOrdinalType;
9    typedef GlobalOrdinal GlobalOrdinalType;
10   ...
11 };
```

Listing 1.1. Definition of MiniFE vector.

In Listing 1.1 the type of scalar and the variables used to store the local and global indexes defined respectively by the template parameters `Scalar`, `LocalOrdinal` and `GlobalOrdinal` can be swapped at compile time. Moreover, the types of the template parameters can be retrieved at compile time using the variables `ScalarType`, `LocalOrdinalType` and `GlobalOrdinalType`. This technique provides high design flexibility while avoiding performance issues of runtime techniques such as inheritance.

MiniFE supports scalar types which implement the standard $+, -, *, /$ operations as well as additional information required at compile-time: namely the **magnitude_type** required to compute the norm of the underlying numerical value, its **name** for report purposes and the **mpi_type()** used in MPI computations (not active in this work) . Such additional information can be provided through the specialization of ad-hoc template structures called traits. For example, the traits of a built-in C++ double type are defined as:

```
1  template<>
2  struct TypeTraits<double> {
3    typedef double magnitude_type;
4    static const char* name() {return "double";}
5  #ifdef HAVE_MPI
6    static MPI_Datatype mpi_type() {return MPI_DOUBLE;}
7  #endif
8  };
```

Listing 1.2. Double type traits specialization.

In Listing 1.2, it can be noted that the type traits also contain the corresponding MPI datatype. As an example we show the use of such type traits to resolve, at compile time, the name of the type used in a vector:

```
1  char* dataName = TypeTraits<
2              Vector<Scalar,
3                LocalOrdinal,
4                GlobalOrdinal>::ScalarType>::name();
```

Listing 1.3. Use of type traits specialization.

MiniFE provides type traits for all C++ built in types, while user defined types can specialise the **TypeTraits** structure, as well as overload the basic $+, -, */$ operations.

2.2 Implementation of Binned Doubles

The original C implementation of binned doubles provided in [2] is modified and encapsulated in a C++ class template, **reproducible::Double<K>**, which calls the original ReproBLAS [2] functions using overloaded operators. The K parameter is an integer that defines the number of bins available for a double. Each **reproducible::Double<K>** contains two private member variables: the original double, and a **std::array<double, 2*K>** that contains its binned representation. One of the tests used to verify the implementation checks that the sum of all the elements in a vector of **reproducible:Double<K>** always yields the same result, no matter how the vector is shuffled. A code snippet of such a test is shown in Listing 1.4.

```
1  std::vector<reproducible::Double<3> > reproX;
2  std::random_device rd;
3  std::mt19937 g(rd());
4  ...
5  auto reproSum1 = std::accumulate(reproX.begin(), reproX.end(), reproducible::
      Double<3>(0));
6  auto doubleReproSum1 = reproSum1.getDouble();
7  std::shuffle(std::begin(reproX), std::end(reproX), g);
8  auto reproSum2 = std::accumulate(reproX.begin(), reproX.end(), reproducible::
      Double<3>(0));
9  auto doubleReproSum2 = reproSum2.getDouble();
10 EXPECT_EQ(doubleReproSum1, doubleReproSum2);
```

Listing 1.4. Reproducible double Sum.

The `reproducible::Double<K>` and the associated `TypeTraits` cannot be readily used in the current OpenMP-parallel version of MiniFE, because it uses atomic and reduction clauses that do not support operator overloading [5]. To overcome this limitation we propose a modification of the MiniFE mini-app as follows:

– Substitution of atomic clauses with critical clauses;
– Substitution of reduction clauses, with a combination of a parallel private reduction and a critical accumulation section as shown in Listing 1.5.

```
1  #pragma omp parallel for          1  #pragma omp parallel
       reduction(+:result)           2  {
2  for(int i=0; i<n; ++i) {          3    MINIFE_SCALAR result_private = 0;
3    result += xcoefs[i] * ycoefs[i]; 4    #pragma omp for nowait
4  }                                  5    for(int i=0; i<n; ++i) {
                                      6      result_private += xcoefs[i] * ycoefs[i];
                                      7    }
                                      8    #pragma omp critical
                                      9    {
                                      10     result += result_private;
                                      11   }
                                      12 }
```

Listing 1.5. Original and modified MiniFE comparison. On the left side, parallel reductions are accomplished using a reduction clause. On the right side, the same result is achieved using a "parallel for", which accumulates in a private variable, and subsequently a critical section accumulates into a global variable.

In order to assess that such changes did not alter the performance of the code, we benchmarked the original and the modified version of MiniFE using standard doubles and 180 8-nodes 3D hexahedral elements in every direction. We used one node of the Cirrus UK National Tier-2 HPC Service at EPCC [1], which has a total of 280 compute nodes, each with 256 GB of memory and two

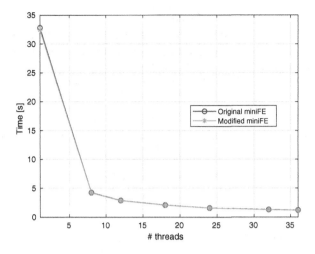

Fig. 1. Comparison of original and proposed modified version of MiniFE. The proposed modification do not alter the performance of the original code.

2.1 GHz, 18-core Intel Xeon (Broadwell) processors, connected using an Infiband FDR network using a hyper-cube topology. The compiler used is GCC 6.3.0. The results are reported in Figs. 1 and 2 for Cirrus and Fulhame respectively.

Figure 1 reports the runtime of the Conjugate Gradient solver in linear scale. It is clear that the modifications to the MiniFE mini-app do not change its performance. In the next section, the run times are compared against the same application using binned doubles.

3 Comparison of Doubles Against Binned Doubles

The modifications to MiniFE provided in the previous section allow the use different scalar types used by MiniFE at compile time, using the `TypeTraits` structure and the class template `reproducible::Double<K>`. We therefore compiled and ran MiniFE using `reproducible::Double<3>` and the inputs described in the previous section. Note that for the reproducible MiniFE, all the doubles in the application are substituted for binned doubles. To verify cross-platform reproducibility we compiled and ran MiniFe on one node of the Fulhame system at EPCC, a 64-node Arm-based HPE Apollo70 system, with two 32-core Marvell ThunderX2 processors and 256 GB memory per node. It uses an Infiniband EDR interconnect with a non-blocking fat tree topology.

3.1 Performance Comparison

The performance comparisons are reported in Figs. 2, 3, 4, and Tables 1, 2 for the Cirrus and Fulhame system respectively. There is an average slowdown of $36x$ in terms of runtime when using binned doubles, instead of built-in doubles on Intel architecture, while this gap is reduced to 26x on our Arm-based system. The log-log plot (Fig. 2 shows that the two versions (non-reproducible and reproducible) of MiniFE follow similar performance trends. The same information is reported in tabular form in Tables 1 and 2. In terms of speedup (Figs. 3 and 4), the reproducible MiniFE exhibits slight better scaling when increasing the number of cores.

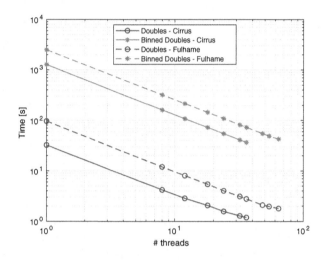

Fig. 2. Comparison of running time of Conjugate Gradient solver in log-log scale for built-in doubles and binned doubles with $K = 3$.

Table 1. Comparison between Non-reproducible and Reproducible Mini-FE on Cirrus using GCC and -O0 compiler flag. The residual is scaled by 1^{-15}.

Threads	non-reproducible MiniFE			reproducible MiniFE		
	Time [s]	Residual norm	N iterations	Time [s]	Residual norm	N iterations
1	63.3068	0.2115	391	4193.2	0.1984	350
8	7.5857	0.2089	365	533.7	0.1984	350
12	5.1138	0.2060	363	356.4	0.1984	350
18	3.6689	0.2028	361	238.3	0.1984	350
24	2.8148	0.1970	357	179.4	0.1984	350
32	2.2967	0.1963	359	134.9	0.1984	350
36	2.1214	0.1960	357	120.3	0.1984	350

3.2   Reproducibility

Figure 5 compares the final number of iterations necessary to achieve a prescribed residual norm obtained with doubles (non-reproducible MiniFE) and binned-doubles (reproducible MiniFE), using the aforementioned version of GCC

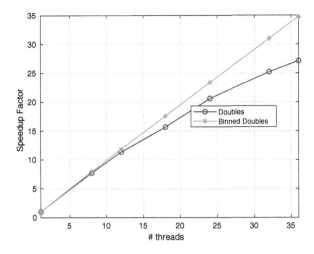

Fig. 3. Comparison of speedup factor of Conjugate Gradient solver for built-in doubles and binned doubles with $K = 3$ on Cirrus.

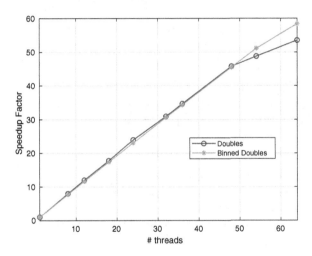

Fig. 4. Comparison of speedup factor of Conjugate Gradient solver for built-in doubles and binned doubles with $K = 3$ on Fulhame.

compiler, with -O0 compiler flag on Cirrus and Fulhame. The error-bars indicate a 95% confidence interval under the hypothesis of normal distribution, obtained processing five runs at each fixed number of processes. When using binned doubles, the final number of iterations of the finite element problem is constant and does not depend on the number of threads or architecture model. When using built-in doubles however, such values are not constant, and importantly their behaviour is also not predictable. The same information is reported in tabular form in Tables 1 and 2. An important detail is given by the serial run of

Table 2. Comparison between Non-reproducible and Reproducible MiniFE on Ful-hame using GCC and -O0 compiler flag. The residual is scaled by 1^{-15}.

Threads	non-reproducible MiniFE			reproducible MiniFE		
	Time [s]	Residual norm	N iterations	Time [s]	Residual norm	N iterations
1	186.6910	0.2115	391	4193.2	0.1984	350
8	22.7928	0.2067	365	533.7	0.1984	350
12	15.3523	0.2047	364	356.4	0.1984	350
18	10.4003	0.2165	361	238.3	0.1984	350
24	7.7301	0.1966	356	179.4	0.1984	350
32	5.9495	0.2015	358	134.9	0.1984	350
36	5.2481	0.1960	358	120.3	0.1984	350
48	3.9851	0.1962	356	90.7	0.1984	350
54	3.7412	0.1968	356	80.8	0.1984	350
64	3.3409	0.1960	356	71.7	0.1984	350

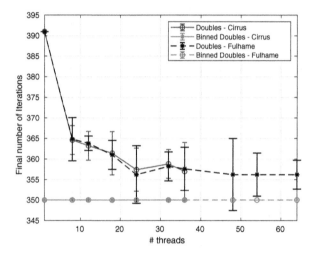

Fig. 5. Comparison of final number of iterations for built-in doubles and binned doubles with $K = 3$, on cirrus and fulhame with GCC and -O0 flag.

MiniFE using the standard doubles. In this case the final number of iterations is indeed reproducible due to the absence of the non deterministic effect of parallel reductions.

Figure 6 compares the final number of iterations on the same application but built supplying -O3 flag to the compiler. Differently from the previous case, there is an effect of the optimization on different platforms, even in the serial run for standard doubles. However, when using binned doubles, the results confirm that these yield reproducible results.

Finally, we investigated the reproducibility of binned doubles when using different compilers. In particular, we built MiniFE, using both GCC and Clang compilers on Fulhame. The results shown in Fig. 7 demonstrate that reproducibil-

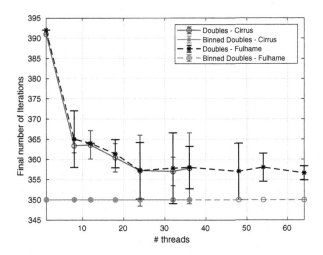

Fig. 6. Comparison of final number of iterations for built-in doubles and binned doubles with $K = 3$, on cirrus and fulhame with GCC and -O3 flag.

ity when using standard doubles, contrarily to binned doubles, is affected by the use of different compilers. These results confirm that binned doubles can be used to achieve reproducibility regardless of the degree of parallelism, architecture and compiler involved.

4   Discussion of Results

The performance results listed earlier show that using binned doubles results in is a significant performance hit. This is not unexpected of course as binned doubles are not a native type and crucial compiler optimisations will not be applied to them in the same way as built-in doubles. However, an important feature of the approach taken here is its flexibility. The choice of which numerical type to use is taken only at compile time, and it therefore does not impact the software development process. In this context therefore, binned doubles might be used in the development of new features and functionalities for existing software. In particular, we would propose the use of binned doubles as part of the feature testing and verification process of parallel software development, where performance is a secondary requirement with respect to correctness. Once a code's correctness has been verified, it can be used in production with the default built-in doubles compile flag enabled. The negative impact on performance is acceptable in that scenario.

As mentioned earlier, it is worth pointing out that the current version of MiniFe uses only one numerical type for all the computation phases, which means that using the compiler flags system the compiler will "blindly" substitute and swap the numerical types. This strategy is very aggressive, and we suggest the use of a multiple compile flags system, where binned doubles are used only in

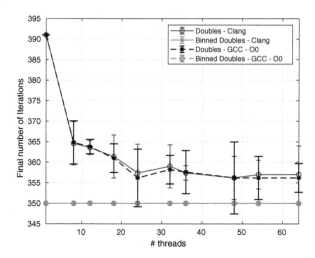

Fig. 7. Comparison of final number of iterations for built-in doubles and binned doubles with $K = 3$, on fulhame with GCC and Clang compilers.

critical parts of the code. This will decrease the performance penalty while still achieving reproducible results.

Finally, although a slowdown on the order on 30–40x is not acceptable for production runs, the use of binned doubles is nevertheless not prohibitively expensive for full application verification tests. In an environment where testing the correctness of a full application is critically important, using binned doubles remains an option.

5   Conclusions and Further Work

In this paper we have shown the use of binned doubles in a finite element application using the MiniFE proxy application. The proposed approach uses a compile type parameter to determine the use of built-in doubles or binned doubles. We have validated a modification to the original MiniFE application to make it compatible with types that overload the arithmetic operators $+, -, *, /$. Subsequently, we have created a new C++ class template in the reproducible namespace `reproducible::Double<K>`, which wraps the functionalities of the ReproBLAS library. The major advantage of this methodology is that the user of MiniFE can easily switch between customised and built-in types, through the change of a compile flag, effectively choosing between reproducible and non-reproducible computations.

While we have experienced a noticeable slowdown in terms of performance, the use of binned doubles has indeed achieved results which are reproducible (as evidenced by the final residuals) and independent of the number of parallel threads or architecture. This result establishes the use of binned doubles in the verification process of the development cycle, where reproducible results are a more stringent requirement than performance. Since the proposed methodology does not require alteration of the source code, but only affects the compilation flags, in other phases of the development cycle the numerical type used can be reverted to built-in doubles, which will deliver results in a fraction of the time (but non-reproducible).

To lower the impact on performance of the binned doubles, we are currently investigating a mixed double/binned doubles approach, in which binned doubles will only be used in parts of the code where reproducibility is lost, due to non-deterministic behaviour of reduction operations or vectorisation. Moreover, we are investigating the use and impact of reproducible doubles in distributed and heterogeneous parallel environments, using MPI and mixed-mode parallelism.

Acknowledgement. This research is supported by Rolls-Royce plc through the EPSRC ASiMoV Prosperity Partnership Project. The authors would like to thank Rolls-Royce plc for granting permission to publish this work. The experiments were undertaken on two different systems: the Cirrus UK National Tier-2 HPC Service at EPCC, funded by the University of Edinburgh and EPSRC (EP/P020267/1); and the Fulhame system, which is supplied to EPCC as part of the Catalyst UK program, a collaboration with Hewlett Packard Enterprise, Arm and SUSE to accelerate the adoption of Arm based supercomputer applications in the UK.

References

1. Cirrus UK National Tier-2 HPC service (2019) http://www.cirrus.ac.uk
2. Ahrens, P., Nguyen, H.D., Demmel, J.: Efficient reproducible floating point summation and BLAS. Technical report UCB/EECS-2015-229, EECS Department, University of California, Berkeley, December 2015
3. Heroux, M.A., et al.: Improving performance via mini-applications. Technical report SAND2009-5574, Sandia National Laboratories (2009)
4. Kahan, W.: Pracniques: further remarks on reducing truncation errors. Commun. ACM **8**(1), 40 (1965)
5. OpenMP Architecture Review Board: OpenMP application program interface version 3.1 (2001). https://www.openmp.org/wp-content/uploads/OpenMP3.1.pdf
6. Robey, R.W., Robey, J.M., Aulwes, R.: In search of numerical consistency in parallel programming. Parallel Comput. **37**(4–5), 217–229 (2011)
7. Vandevoorde, D., Josuttis, N.M.: C++ Templates. Addison-Wesley Longman Publishing Co., Inc., Boston (2002)

Three Numerical Reproducibility Issues That Can Be Explained as Round-Off Error

Michael Mascagni[1,2](✉) (iD)

[1] Florida State University, Tallahassee, FL, USA
mascagni@fsu.edu
[2] National Institute of Standards and Technology, Gaithersburg, MD, USA
mascagni@nist.gov
http://www.cs.fsu.edu/mascagni

Abstract. We explore an application from the author's work in neuroscience. A code used to investigate neural development modeled 100 neurons with all-to-all excitatory connectivity. We used a simple ordinary differential equation system to model each neuron, and this 100-neuron model was used to produce a paper published in the *Journal of Neurophysiology*. Later a colleague used our code to continue this work, and found he could not reproduce our results. This lead us to thoroughly investigate this code and we discovered that it offered many different ways to thwart reproducibility that could be explained by round-off error arising from floating-point arithmetic.

Numerical reproducibility is considered a task that directly follows from the determinism in computations. However, reproducibility has become an intense concern and issue for research. We will show how this particular code provides a lack of reproducibility from the following three mechanisms: (i) the introduction of floating-point errors in an inner product; (ii) introduction of floating-point errors at each an increasing number of time steps during temporal refinement (ii); and (iii) differences in the output of library mathematical functions at the level of round-off error. This code's sensitivity makes it a very powerful tool to explore many different manifestations of numerical reproducibility. However, this code is by no means exceptional, as in neuroscience these types of models are used extensively to gain insights on the functioning of the nervous system. In addition, these types of models are widely used in many other fields of study as they just nonlinear evolution equations.

Keywords: Numerical reproducibility · Round-off error · Computational neuroscience

I wish to thank Wilfredo Blanco Figuerola from the Universidade do Estado do Rio Grande do Norte, Brazil, who brought the behavior of this code to my attention.

M. Weiland et al. (Eds.): ISC 2019 Workshops, LNCS 11887, pp. 452–462, 2019.
https://doi.org/10.1007/978-3-030-34356-9_34

1 Introduction

1.1 Numerical Reproducibility

We assume that computations are completely deterministic and hence inherit certain characteristics. First, a computation is or can readily be made reproducible, i.e. another person can use the code and a written set of instructions to obtain the same computational results. We also expect that we can redo our own computations if necessary; this is reproducibility over time. Finally, we assume that computation used for publication can be documented sufficiently to be reproduced for the purposes of scientific rigor. We believe that the items needed to insure reproducibility include the code, compiler options/version, code input, and execution environment. In addition, a code correctly constructed is portable between architectures by virtue of the abstraction provided by the programming language and compilation process. Computations that are not reproducible are deficient in some way.

1.2 A Computation Used in Developmental Neurophysiology

We investigated a small network of excitable neurons, [6] to study neuronal development. The network consisted of 100 simple neurons with all-to-all connectivity, and each neuron is modeled as single compartment via an ordinary differential equation (ODE) system for the voltage. The ODE system is based on the Hodgkin-Huxley equations. At each time step, the input for each neuron was accumulated by summing up the output of each neuron times the synaptic strength, and the output we show was an average of the output of the 100 neurons. Note: in the research paper we also displayed a second variable, which is included in some of plots, but will not be discussed. The modeled neurons were all excitatory to simulate early neuronal development.

A colleague wanted to use our model, and so he decided to play around with code to see if he understood the model. He was confounded by behavior in the following two graphs. His understanding of the model was that both runs are on identical systems (Figs. 1 and 2).

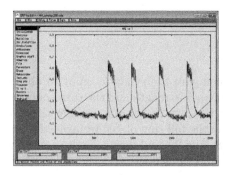
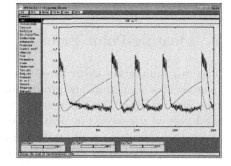

Fig. 1. Simulation of 100 excitatory neurons.

Fig. 2. Simulation of 80 "excitatory" neurons.

Fig. 3. A simulation of 100 excitatory neurons suing xpp that have the same properties but are labeled differently. Note the change in the final peak.

He ran the system using different invocations at the command line. The first figure is created with the following:

`a.out -case 21 -nBurst 50 -pExcN 1.0 -vInh 70`

The second with:

`a.out -case 21 -nBurst 50 -pExcN 0.8 -vInh 70`

The difference is that the second identifies the last 20 neurons as inhibitory, not excitatory. However, the properties of all the neurons in both cases are excitatory. Thus the system being studied in both cases is, in fact, the same. However, the identification of the last 20 (excitatory) neurons as inhibitory causes the summation at each time step to be done in a slightly different order. We can see this by examining the C++ code:

```
for (int i = 0; i < 10; i++)
// Total synaptic drive exc/inh for all cells atotExc = atotInh = 0.0;
// Synaptic drive from excitatory cells
// atotexc=sum(0,100)of(shift(s0,i')*shift(a0,i'))/100
// remembering the order: v, n, a, s -> 0, 1, 2, 3
    for ( n = 0; n < nExcNeurons; n++) {
    atotExc += network[n][3]*network[n][2];
        // Synaptic drive from inhibitory cells
    for ( n = nExcNeurons; n < nNeurons; n++) {
    atotInh += network[n][3]*network[n][2];
    }
    }
```

2   Floating-Point Errors

The two summation loops listed above compute the synaptic input to all the neurons by summing up the product of synaptic strength and the corresponding neuronal activity. The difference is that the last 20 neurons are identified as inhibitory in the second invocation, and so the full sum of 100 terms in the first invocation is broken up into two sums of 80 and 20, and then a single sum of the those two partial sums. Thus the inner product is done with the order of two sums changed between invocations.

This small difference in the order of summation results in different floating-point errors accumulating, and that manifests itself in the observed long-time differences.

We know that the summation of real numbers is associative (order can be permuted), but floating-point summation is not associative, and so differences can occur in sums where the order is changed. Summation is a classic example used to study problems in and the mitigation of floating-point errors, and inner products in particular are known to be particularly problematic.

The summation loops in question seemed intuitively to be the problem, but we wanted to confirm our suspicion. To do so, we modified to two summation loops to use the Boost library's extended precision capabilities to compute the inner products using an extended precision accumulator. The results are shown below, where the computations done in Fig. 3, are redone. We can see that in both cases the computation up to time $t = 8.0$ show no difference. However, if we take these computations farther, eventually the two figures diverge. So even with extended precision arithmetic, the same process that occurs in double precision is taking place, and we still will see $O(1)$ differences, only at later times. Extended precision does not mitigate the non-associativity of floating-point arithmetic (Fig. 4).

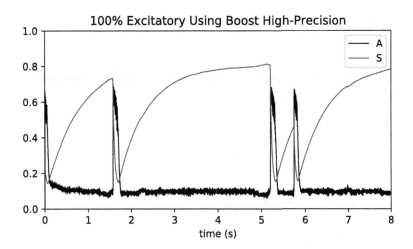

Fig. 4. Computation of All Excitatory Neurons Using Boost

Thus the use of extended precision is not a complete fix. However, it is one of many methods one can use to (partially) mitigate these problems. One is to use a more stable summation algorithm, such as those by Ogita and his colleagues, [4]. Another is to modify the computer arithmetic so that all arithmetic operations are computed to the correctly rounded floating-point value. One example of this is ACRITH, which was based on work by Kulisch and Miranker and was released by IBM Research, [3]. ACRITH was based on the so-called Kulisch accumulator, [2]. The idea of using long accumulators to mitigate floating-point loss of accuracy continue, as this was recently proposed for an ARM architecture to deal with loss of accuracy in GPS computations on cell phone processors.

Since the issue of floating-point arithmetic is inextricably entwined with modern computation, there have been other suggestions that are more far-reaching to mitigate the problem. A more conservative solution is to modify floating-point itself to modify the IEEE standard for floating-point arithmetic to minimize accuracy issued, [5]. A more radical proposal involves replacing floating-point with a totally different arithmetic, [1]. Unfortunately, is seems that both kinds of suggestions are unlike to see implementation as vendors are very reluctant to make such changes, as they will require complete redesigns of processor architecture down to a very fundamental level (Fig. 5).

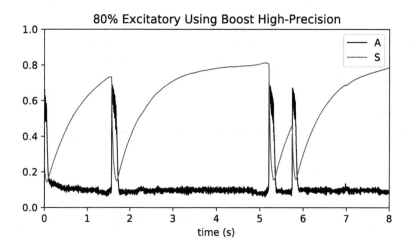

Fig. 5. Computation of Excitatory/Inhibitory Neurons Using Boost

3   Other Examples of Loss of Reproducibility

3.1   Temporal Refinement

The system under investigation is a very standard ODE model from computational neuroscience. The ODEs, which model neurons, exhibit the very nonlinear threshold phenomenon. By that we mean that small, $O(\epsilon)$, excitations in the neighborhood of the threshold can cause the system to respond with small, $O(\epsilon)$, or large, $O(1)$, behavior. It is this threshold behavior that leads to the accumulation of round-off errors to manifest itself in the manner discussed previously. In addition, the threshold phenomenon is also something that is indicative of systems that exhibit chaotic behavior.

One numerical study that is often applied to these types of systems is temporal refinement. In our code we use a standard fifth-order Runge-Kutta method as our integrator, and it seems reasonable to see how this system behaves as we refine the time step $\Delta t \to 0$. The numerical solution should converge. We have already seen that this system is extremely sensitive to accumulated round-off errors, and we expect that there is a trade off between numerical convergence and the effect of increasing the number of time steps ($N^{-1} \approx \Delta t \to 0$) in this computation. Thus, we will show some plots of our system integrated up to a fixed $t = 8.0$, using progressively smaller Δt's. We note that we now introduce a different plot to show the system activity, since it acts more like a fingerprint. Time is the independent variable, and we display a red or blank dot at each time step depending on whether a particular neuron is above a threshold. Thus, a vertical line denotes a time when all neurons are firing (a burst), and a horizontal line shows us a neuron that is always active (Figs. 6 and 7).

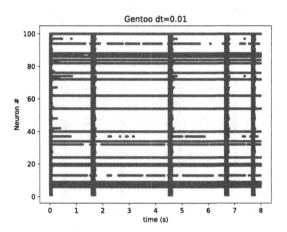

Fig. 6. A plot of system activity with $\Delta t = 0.01$

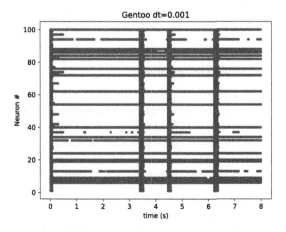

Fig. 7. A plot of system activity with $\Delta t = 0.001$

If we consider this as a convergence study then we see that as $\Delta t \to 0$ we do not get convergence. We only refined to $\Delta t = 0.0001$ as this non-convergence behavior continues as we use smaller Δt. We know that these systems are stiff, and we also suspect that these systems are inherently chaotic, and so this apparent lack of convergence is something that occurs even in well-posed systems.

We can explain this behavior with round-off. We know that the inner product sum introduces round-off error each time it is computed. If we integrate to a fixed time, T, then as Δt is decreased, the number of time steps is increased, and hence so is the number of times the summation round-off is introduced. In our three cases each has 10 times the number of sums computed that the previous case. Since some round-off occurs in each sum, we therefore expect this behavior.

We noted that these systems exhibit the threshold phenomenon. Thus this type of behavior is not unexpected, as these systems also exhibit chaotic behavior. And while these systems are very commonly used in computational neuroscience, their chaotic tendencies cause this behavior (Fig. 8).

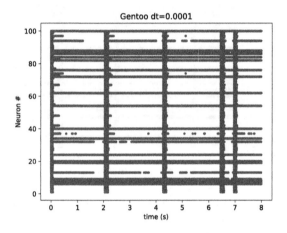

Fig. 8. A plot of system activity with $\Delta t = 0.0001$

3.2 Operating System Dependence

Are there other examples of the lack of numerical reproducibility with our ODE system? The answer is clearly, "yes." The code is written in very generic manner using C++. So we wondered if we could compile and execute the code on different environments and see the same behavior. This is asking whether our code was portable, which is related to the notion of reproducibility. Thus we took our code and complied and ran it on four different Unix systems:

- Windows/Cygwin: g++ (GCC) 5.4.0
- OS X: Apple LLVM version 6.0 (clang-600.0.56)
- Mint Linux: g++ (Ubuntu 5.4.0-6ubuntu1 16.04.4) 5.4.0 20160609
- Gentoo Linux g++ (Gentoo 5.4.0-r3 p1.3, pie-0.6.5) 5.4.0

We note the Cygwin and the two versions of Linux used "the same" version of g++. The outlier in this is the OS X implementation, which used the native Apple compiler, which is based on LLVM intermediate representation, which is fundamentally different than what is done with Gnu compilers. Below we show the results of four cases all using a $\Delta t = 0.01$.

The results show that the two Linux results were exactly the same while execution under Linux, Cygwin, and Mac OS all gave different results. As we mentioned above, the Mac OS C++ compiler is fundamentally different from the other three, and so while regrettable, the difference in behavior in Mac OS was somewhat expected. However, it was surprising to see the Windows/Cygwin did not produce the same results as the two pure Linux versions. We were quite

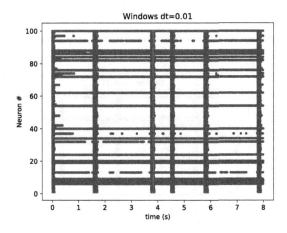

Fig. 9. A Computation with Code Showing Neuron Activity vs. Time in Windows/Cygwin

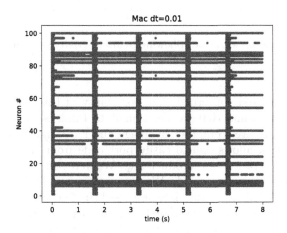

Fig. 10. A Computation with Code Showing Neuron Activity vs. Time in Mac OS

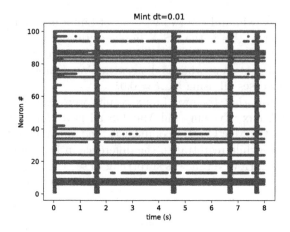

Fig. 11. A Computation with Code Showing Neuron Activity vs. Time in Mint Linux

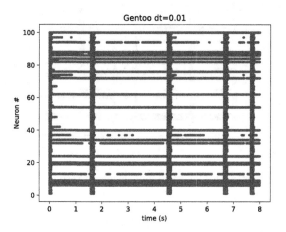

Fig. 12. A Computation with Code Showing Neuron Activity vs. Time in Gentoo Linux

perplexed by this, and concerned that portability of this code was somewhat compromised. One thing that we are taught to think is that the abstraction provided by a high-level computer language and its compiler, such as C++ and the Gnu compilers, allows one to easily port code from one place to another with the high expectation of reproducibility. We were fortunate that a graduate student working on this project, Mr. Woohyeong Kim, made the observation that the actual ODE definition in the code only used the C++ mathematical functions pow and exp. Thus we tried to see if replacing the Gentoo Linux versions of these functions with those from Gentoo Linux could cause the latter to produce the results we saw under Cygwin. The following figure shows that we can!! (Figs. 9, 10, 11 and 12).

It was quite shocking to realize that within different versions of the Linux libraries there are different implementations of the functions made available though `math.h`. This cries out to be fixed. However, if we agree that this is the case, then two different implementations of the same mathematical function may return slightly different values for the same input. These differences can be viewed as error that we expect will be on the order of floating-point error. Thus, we can think of these functional differences as again manifesting as errors that can be thought of as floating-point (Fig. 13).

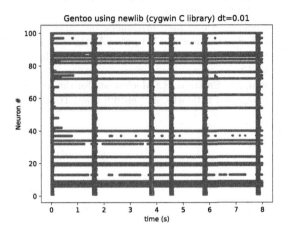

Fig. 13. A Computation with Linux Gentoo using the `pow` and `exp` functions from Cygwin

4   Conclusions and Further Work

We have a found a system of ODEs used in neuronal modeling that is extremely sensitive in at least three different ways that can be thought of as floating-point error. Specifically, errors in a summation, errors introduced in temporal refinement, and errors due to intrinsic mathematical function differences. This system is not unique, but these studies make it especially interesting for researchers working on numerical reproducibility. We hope that we will be able to use this system to answer some questions that are central in reproducibility. Given that reproducibility is not that easy to achieve in some cases:

1. Is there a way to determine if two computations are consistent to a model given the various causes of non-reproducibility?
2. Can we broaden the notion of reproducibility in a way that allows for scientific computational reproducibility validation?
3. What techniques or concepts do we need to explore to create the framework to answer these reproducibility questions?

References

1. Gustafson, J.L.: The End of Error: Unum Computing. Taylor & Francis, Abingdon (2015)
2. Kulisch, U.W.: Computer Arithmetic and Validity. Theory, Implementation, and Applications. De Gruyter, Berlin (2013)
3. Kulisch, U.W., Miranker, W.L.: Computer Arithmetic in Theory and Practice. Computer Science and Applied Mathematics. Academic Press, Cambridge (1981)
4. Ogita, T., Rump, S.M., Oishi, S.: Accurate sum and dot product. SIAM J. Sci. Comput. **26**(6), 1955–1988 (2005). https://doi.org/10.1137/030601818. http://dx.doi.org/10.1137/030601818
5. Riedy, E.J., Demmel, J.: Augmented arithmetic operations proposed for IEEE-754 2018. In: 25th IEEE Symposium on Computer Arithmetic, ARITH 2018, Amherst, MA, USA, 25–27 June 2018, pp. 45–52. IEEE (2018). https://doi.org/10.1109/ARITH.2018.8464813
6. Tabak, J., Mascagni, M., Bertram, R.: Mechanism for the universal pattern of activity in developing neuronal networks. J. Neurophysiol. **103**(4), 2208–2221 (2010)

Training Multiscale-CNN for Large Microscopy Image Classification in One Hour

Kushal Datta[1](✉) ⓘ, Imtiaz Hossain[2](✉) ⓘ, Sun Choi[1] ⓘ, Vikram Saletore[1] ⓘ, Kyle Ambert[1] ⓘ, William J. Godinez[3] ⓘ, and Xian Zhang[2] ⓘ

[1] Artificial Intelligence Products Group, Intel Corporation, Hillsboro, OR, USA
{kushal.datta,sun.choi,vikram.a.saletore,kyle.h.ambert}@intel.com
[2] Novartis Institutes for Biomedical Research, Basel, Switzerland
{imtiaz.hossain,xian-1.zhang}@novartis.com
[3] Novartis Institutes for Biomedical Research, Emeryville, CA, USA
william_jose.godinez_navarro@novartis.com

Abstract. Existing approaches to train neural networks that use large images require to either crop or down-sample data during pre-processing, use small batch sizes, or split the model across devices mainly due to the prohibitively limited memory capacity available on GPUs and emerging accelerators. These techniques often lead to longer time to convergence or time to train (TTT), and in some cases, lower model accuracy. CPUs, on the other hand, can leverage significant amounts of memory. While much work has been done on parallelizing neural network training on multiple CPUs, little attention has been given to tune neural network training with large images on CPUs. In this work, we train a multi-scale convolutional neural network (M-CNN) to classify large biomedical images for high content screening in one hour. The ability to leverage large memory capacity on CPUs enables us to scale to larger batch sizes without having to crop or down-sample the input images. In conjunction with large batch sizes, we find a generalized methodology of linearly scaling of learning rate and train M-CNN to state-of-the-art (SOTA) accuracy of 99% within one hour. We achieve fast time to convergence using 128 two socket Intel® Xeon® 6148 processor nodes with 192 GB DDR4 memory connected with 100 Gbps Intel® Omnipath architecture.

1 Introduction

Biomedical image analysis has been a natural area of application for deep convolutional neural networks (CNNs). Several uses of CNN-related topologies have been proposed in radiology [1,2], histopathology [3–5] and microscopy [6–8] (for a review, see [9]). High-content screening (HCS) [10–15], the use of microscopy at scale in cellular experiments, in particular, has seen progress in applying CNN-based analysis [6,7,16–18]. Instead of the conventional analysis approaches where

---

K. Datta and I. Hossain—These authors have made equal contributions to the paper.

© Springer Nature Switzerland AG 2019
M. Weiland et al. (Eds.): ISC 2019 Workshops, LNCS 11887, pp. 463–477, 2019.
https://doi.org/10.1007/978-3-030-34356-9_35

cellular objects are first segmented and then pre-defined features representing their phenotypes (characteristic image content corresponding to the underlying experimental conditions) are measured, deep learning approaches offer the promise to capture relevant features and phenotypes without *a priori* knowledge or significant manual parameter tuning. In deep CNNs, the deeper layers pick up high-levels of organization based on the input of many features captured in previous layers. Typically, a pooling operation (or a higher stride length in the convolution filter) is used to subsample interesting activations from one layer to the next, resulting in ever-coarser "higher-level" representations of the image content.

Despite the potential of deep learning in analyzing biomedical images, two outstanding challenges, namely the complexity of the biological imaging phenotypes and the difficulty in acquiring large biological sample sizes, have hindered broader adoption in this domain. To circumvent these challenges, architectural changes have been introduced into some models to make training easier without trading off model accuracy. One novel approach is to use wide networks, which explicitly model various levels of coarseness. In these topologies, several copies of the input image are downsampled and used to train separate, parallel convolutional layers, which are eventually concatenated together to form a single feature vector that is passed on to fully-connected layers (e.g., see Buyssens et al. [19]). A recent application of this idea to HCS is the Multiscale Convolutional Neural Network (M-CNN) architecture [16], which has been shown to be generally applicable to multiple microscopy datasets, in particular for identifying the effect of compound treatment.

The computational footprint of M-CNN, although relatively small as compared with other deep CNNs (e.g., Residual Neural Network 152), is still large when applied to high-content cellular imaging. Thus, it is important that model-related aspects of memory utilization and training performance are thoroughly understood, and that an end user knows *a priori* how to get maximum performance on their hardware. Commercial cloud service providers (CSPs) like Microsoft, Google, or Amazon–as well as on-premise HPC centers in academia and industry–are exploring custom hardware accelerator architectures, such as application-specific integrated circuits (ASICs) [20] or GPUs, to expedite training neural network models. In spite of the popularity of these technologies, several factors such as higher financial cost of ownership, lack of virtualization and lack of support for multi-tenancy, leading to poor hardware utilization, may be cited as reasons to consider CPU-centric performance optimizations in reducing the time-to-train for such models. Importantly, since almost all data centers, are already equipped with thousands of general-purpose CPUs, it makes a strong case for such an approach.

Existing approaches to improve the time to train convolutional image classification neural network model such as M-CNN designed to work with large high-content cellular images have needed to either crop or down-sample the images during pre-processing. Other ideas are to restrict to small batch sizes or split the model across multiple devices due to the limited memory capacity available on

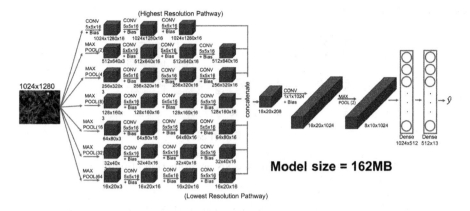

Fig. 1. Operations and kernels of the M-CNN model. Convolution is abbreviated *CONV*, and Max Pooling operations are abbreviated as *MAX POOL*

GPUs or accelerator cards. However, these techniques can lead to longer time to convergence or time to train (TTT), and in some cases, lower model accuracy. CPUs, on the other hand, can leverage large memory. Our primary contributions include,

1. Train M-CNN to achieve SOTA accuracy of 99% on multiple CPU servers without tiling or cropping of input images or splitting the model
2. Use large batch sizes per CPU exploiting large memory
3. Use multiple training instances/workers per CPU node to improve utilization
4. Use large batches and learning rate scaling to achieve fast convergence.

The ability to leverage large memory capacity on CPUs enables us to scale to larger batch sizes without having to crop or down-sample the input images. In conjunction with large batch sizes, we linearly scale learning rate with global batch size and train M-CNN to SOTA accuracy within one hour. We achieve this fast time to convergence using 128 two socket Intel® Xeon® 6148 processor nodes with 192 GB DDR4 memory connected with 100 Gbps Intel® Omnipath architecture.

2   Multi-scale Convolutional Neural Network

M-CNNs capture both fine-grained cell-level features and coarse-grained features observable at the population level by using seven parallel convolution pathways (Fig. 1). As in [16], image height and width are down-sampled by 64, 32, 16, 8, 4, and 2 times in the lower six pathways in ascending order, respectively, while images processed by the top-most path are operated on at the full resolution. The output of the last layers of convolution are down sampled to the lowest resolution and concatenated into a $16 \times 20 \times 208$ tensor. The concatenated

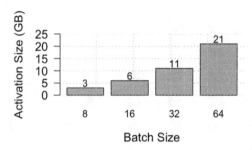

Fig. 2. Activation sizes in M-CNN as a function of batch size.

signals are passed through a convolution with rectified linear activation (ReLU) and two fully connected layers. A final softmax layer transforms probabilistic per-class predictions associated with each image into a hard class prediction. In Fig. 1, the size of convolution kernels are specified below the solid colored cubes, which represent the activations. The sum of the sizes of the convolution kernels and two dense layer, which are 1024 × 512 and 512 × 13, respectively, is 162.2 megabytes. Weights are represented as 32-bit floating point numbers.

The network's gradient and activation size determine the lower bound of its memory footprint. We plot the calculated activation size of the feed forward network as the global batch size is scaled from 8 to 64 by factors of two in Fig. 2. Note that the size of variables required for back propagation is identical to the size of the gradients and hence is determined by model size, not activation size.

3   Large Batch Training

Synchronous gradient descent and data-level parallelism are fundamental concepts to training a deep neural network. In this domain, the most common algorithm used for training is stochastic gradient descent (SGD), which exploits the fact that activation functions in a neural network are differentiable with respect to their weights. During training, batches of data are run through the network. This process is referred to as *forward propagation*. A loss function E is computed at each training iteration, which quantifies how accurately the network was able to classify the input. The SGD algorithm then computes the gradient $\nabla_W(E)$ of the loss function with respect to the current weights W. On the basis of the gradients, weights are updated according Eq. 1, where W_{t+1} are the updated weights, W_t are the weights prior to the adjustment (or previous iteration), and λ is a tunable parameter called the learning rate (LR).

$$W_{t+1} = W_t - \lambda \nabla_W E \tag{1}$$

Since each neural network layer is a differentiable function of the layer preceding it, gradients are computed layer-by-layer, moving from output to input in a process called backpropagation. Finally, the weights in the network are updated according to the computed gradient, and both forward and backpropagation are repeated with a new batch of data. We continue repeating these procedures until the network has reached a satisfactory degree of accuracy on a hold-out validation data set. Training can require running millions of iterations of this process on a given dataset. The most popular approach to speeding up network training makes use of a data-parallel algorithm called synchronous SGD [21]. Synchronous SGD works by replicating SGD across compute nodes, each working on different batches of training data simultaneously. We refer to these replicas as *workers*. A key requirement for synchronous SGD is for information to be synchronized and aggregated across all computing instances at each iteration. The update equation is show in Eq. 2, where B denotes the batch sampled from the training data, n is the size of the batch.

$$W_{t+1} = W_t - \lambda \frac{1}{n} \sum_{x \in B} \nabla_W E(x) \tag{2}$$

With k workers each training with B batches and learning rate λ', we updates the weights according to

$$W_{t+1} = W_t - \lambda' \frac{1}{kn} \sum_{j<k} \sum_{x \in B_j} \nabla_W E(x) \tag{3}$$

Thus, if we adjust the learning rate by k, the weight update equation stays consistent with the synchronous SGD update rule, helping the model to converge without changing the hyper-parameters. We refer to n or $|B|$ as the *local batch size*, and kn as the *global batch size*.

3.1 Learning Rate Schedule

In addition to scaling the model's learning rate parameter (LR) with respect to the batch size, others [22] have observed that gradually increasing it during initial epochs, and subsequently decaying it helps to the model to converge faster. This implies that LR is changed between training iterations, depending on the number of workers, the model, and dataset. We follow the same methodology. We start to train with LR initialized to a low value of $\lambda = 0.001$. In the first few epochs, it is gradually increased to the scaled value of $k\lambda$ and then adjusted following a polynomial decay, with momentum SGD (momentum = 0.9).

Reaching network convergence during training is not guaranteed–the process is sensitive to LR values and features in the data. Scaling this process out to large batch sizes on multiple workers concurrently has the same considerations. If the per-iteration batch size is too large, fewer updates per epoch are required (since an epoch is, by definition, a complete pass through the training data set), which can either result in the model diverging, or it requiring additional epochs to converge (relative to the non-distributed case), defeating the purpose of scaling to large batch sizes. Thus, demonstrating scaled-out performance with large batches without first demonstrating convergence is meaningless. Instead, we measure the time needed to reach state of the art accuracy or TTT. The ingestion method for each worker ensures that each minibatch contains randomly-shuffled data from the different classes.

4   Dataset

The Broad Bioimage Benchmark Collection BBBC021 image set [23] is a collection of 13,200 images from compound treatment on MCF-7 breast cancer cells. Each image consists of three channels: the cells are labeled for DNA, F-actin, and B-tubulin and imaged with fluorescence microscopy. Metadata on compound treatment and concentration is also available [24]. In all, 113 compounds have been used, each with varying concentrations and tested between 2 and 3 times each. Mechanism of action (MoA) labels are available for 103 compound-concentrations (38 compounds tested at between one and seven different concentrations each). In all, 13 MoAs (including the neutral control, DMSO) were available: 6 of the 12 MoAs were assigned visually. DMSO treatments were treated as neutral control and assigned a separate label. The others were defined based on information on the respective compounds in the available literature. We choose 1684 images from the BBBC021 dataset that are representative of all of the MoAs present. The distribution of the images according to MoA classes is shown in Fig. 4. The images are preprocessed and normalized as described in [16]. From the 1684 images, we create two datasets with different augmentation strategies:

- *Dataset A*: Images in this dataset are 1024 × 1280 pixesl wide with 3 channels. They are augmented to produce five copies as 1. 90° rotation, 2. a horizontal mirror, 3. vertical mirror, 4. 90° rotation of horizontal mirror and 5. 90° rotation of vertical mirror. Total number of images in the dataset is 1684 ∗ 6 (five rotations + original) = 10104. We take a 90-10 split and create a training set of 9093 images and validation set of 1011 images. The total size of the images on disk are 38 GB.
- *Dataset B*: This is a larger dataset. The dimensions of the images in this dataset are 724 × 724 pixesl with 3 channels. Similar to Dataset A, all images have 5 additional augmentations. Additionally, each image is rotated by 15° to create 23 more augmentations. The total size of the images on disk are 512 GB. Among them, 313282 images are used for training and 35306 are used for validation.

Ideally, we would have allocated a representative out-of-sample set of images as a validation set. However due to the paucity of MOA annotations in this dataset, and the fact that the main objective of this exercise is to reduce time

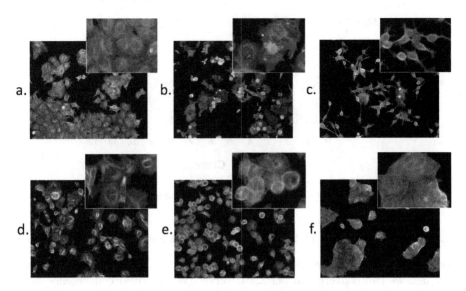

Fig. 3. Example images from the BBBC021 [23] dataset showing phenotypes from treatment with compound-concentration pairs with different mechanisms of action: (a) DSMO (neutral control), (b) Microtubule destabilizer, (c) Cholesterol lowering, (d) Microtubule stabilizer, (e) Actin disrupter, (f) Epithelial. DNA staining is shown in blue, the F-actin staining in red and the B-tubulin staining in green. The insets show a magnified view of the same phenotypes.

to convergence, we allow for the fact that the validation dataset may contain an augmented version of an image in the training data, although never a copy of the same image (Fig. 3).

5   Performance Results

5.1   Experimental Setup

All experiments are run on two socket (2S) 2.40 GHz Intel® Xeon® Gold 6148 processors. There are 20 cores per socket with 2-way hardware multi-threading. On-chip L1 data cache is 32 KB. L2 and L3 caches are 1 MB and 28 MB respectively. For multi-node experiments, we used up to 64 Intel® Xeon® Gold connected via 100 GB/s Intel® OP Fabric. Each server has 192 GB physical memory and a 1.6TB Intel SSD storage drive. The M-CNN topology was added to the standard benchmarking scripts [25] to leverage instantiation mechanisms of distributed workers. Gradient synchronization between the workers was done using Horovod, an MPI-based communication library for deep learning training [26]. In our experiments, we used TensorFlow 1.9.0, Horovod 0.13.4, Python 2.7.5 and OpenMPI 3.0.0.

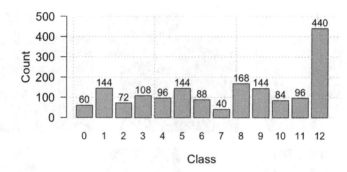

Fig. 4. Class distribution for the 1684 training images used in our experiment.

5.2   Scaling up TTT in One Node with Dataset A

We first performed a sweep of batch sizes from 4, 8, 16, 32 and 64 to check how fast we can converge on one CPU server. We acheived convergence in 5 h 31 min with batch size = 32. The resulting throughput and memory consumed are shown in Fig. 5(a) and (c), respectively. As shown in the latter figure, the memory footprint of M-CNN far exceeds the activation size of the model. For example, in case of batch size of 32, total memory used is 47.5 GB which is 4x larger than activation size of 11 GB as calculated in Fig. 2. The additional memory is allocated by TensorFlow to instantiate temporary variables used in both forward and backward propagation, buffers to read data and others operations. Due to these overheads, memory utilization of M-CNN is prohibitively high and it is difficult to scale to large batch sizes when memory in the system is limited.

Second, for all batch size configurations, CPU utilization was low meaning the cores were under-utilized. Upon further investigation with system profile, we found (1) there were lots of context switches and (2) processes or threads assigned to one CPU socket are accessing data from the other CPU socket including a long latency hop over the socket-to-socket interconnect. This led to the discovery that using multiple workers or instanes per socket can yield faster TTT. The essence of using multiple workers in a single CPU is to affinitize tasks to cores and bind their memory allocation to local non-uniform memory access (NUMA) banks as shown by the shaded rectangles in Fig. 6. Memory binding is key here as it avoids redundant fetches over the interconnect to the memory channels of the adjacent CPU socket. More detailed analysis of multiple workers or instances in training and inference are described in detail by Saletore and colleagues, in [27].

While the authors mention that instantiating multiple workers boosts performance, they do not specify the optimal number of workers, which can depend on a variety of factors, including the neural network topology being trained, CPU micro-architecture, and characteristics of the input data. To find the best combination of workers and local batch size per worker, we experimented with 1, 2, 4 and 8 workers per CPU. In this case, 4 workers with 8 local mini-batch size resulted in the highest throughput per node. A detailed analysis of throughput and memory utilization for 4 workers is shown in Fig. 5(b) and (d), respectively.

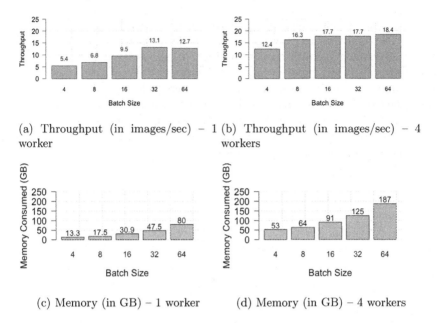

(a) Throughput (in images/sec) – 1 worker

(b) Throughput (in images/sec) – 4 workers

(c) Memory (in GB) – 1 worker

(d) Memory (in GB) – 4 workers

Fig. 5. Throughput (in images/second) and memory utilized (in GB) with batch sizes 4 to 64 for 1 and 4 training workers respectively (a and b) on a single 2S Intel® Xeon® Gold 6148 processor with Dataset A.

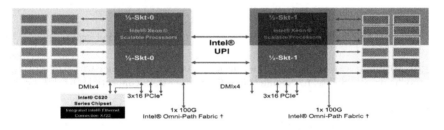

Fig. 6. Two socket Intel® Xeon® Gold 6148 processor NUMA configuration

Note that throughput with batch sizes of 64, 128, or 256 was higher than with a batch size of 32, but these configurations did not converge any faster.

5.3   Scaling Out TTT on 8 Servers with Dataset A

After determining the number of workers per node, we deployed the training on 8 nodes with 4 workers per node. We used the MPI Allreduce mechanism in Uber's Horovod library to synchronize the gradients. As indicated in Fig. 1, the model size is 162 MB which was the size of the gradients exchanged between the workers per iteration. Due to this high bandwidth requirement, we used a 100 Gbps Intel® Omni-Path Fabric (Intel® OP Fabric). Note here that each layer of M-CNN calls *Horovod_Allreduce*, resulting in a large variation in the

MPI negotaition calls. The MPI negotiation times range between 450ms and 858ms. The final time to convergence on 8 nodes is shown in Fig. 7. Figure 7(a) shows the training loss over epochs and Fig. 7(b) shows the time to achieve state of the art top-1 and top-5 accuracy on Dataset A. From the results, we see that using 8x more hardware resources we were able to scale TTT by 6.6X. With Dataset A, this means a TTT of 31 min which is well within our target of one hour. This also encouraged us to explore a larger dataset we would need more hardware resources. Hence, we chose Dataset B with 313,282 images. The experiment results follow in the next section.

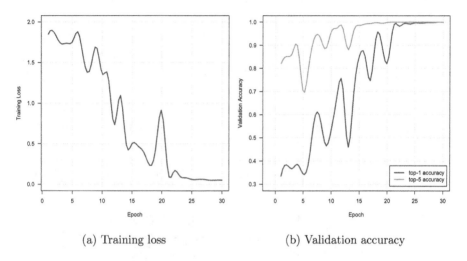

(a) Training loss   (b) Validation accuracy

Fig. 7. Training loss, top-1 and top-5 accuracy of M-CNN model with Dataset A in 30 epochs on 8x 2S Intel® Xeon® Gold 6148 processors connected with Intel® OP Fabric

5.4   Scaling Out TTT on 128 Servers with Dataset B

Table 1 summarizes the 19.2X performance improvement acheived by scaling from 1 to 128 Intel® Xeon® Gold 6148 processors with Dataset B bringing TTT to 50 min. The second column in the table shows number of epochs when training reach 99% top-1 accuracy and 100% top-5 accuracy. Subsequent columns show the global mini-batch size, time to train (in minutes) and effective throughput in images/second for each node configuration. 8 training workers per node were used in these experiments as the image dimensions in Dataset B are smaller than Dataset A.

The key takeaway here is that updates per epoch is critical to acheive convergence. Global mini batch size determines the number of updates per epoch and M-CNN did not converge beyond global batch sizes of 2048. Hence, we maintained the global batch size to 2048 while scaling from 16 to 128 nodes – the idea of strong scaling taken from HPC applications. As the same amount of work is

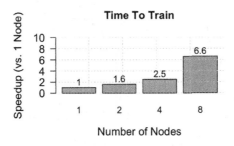

Fig. 8. Scaling M-CNN training with Dataset A from 1X to 8X 2S Intel® Xeon® Gold 6148 processors connected with 100 Gbps Intel® OP Fabric

increasingly divided across more CPU cores we observe diminishing returns in speedup albeit overall TTT improves. Note that our objective is to not show linear scaling here, but to see what resources will help us acheive a TTT less than one hour.

Anothe key takeaway is that large number of workers required larger number of epochs to converge. This also affects scaling. This is again an artifact of the dataset. Finally, in Fig. 9, we show the behavior of top-1 accuracy and learning rate per epoch for each of the configurations. Note here that use the linear learning rate scaling rule discussed in Subsect. 3.1. The learning rate is scaled according to the ratio of increase in global mini batch size. However, as shown in the Fig. 9 similar to global batch size, learning rate scaling has to capped to 2048 beyond 16 nodes for the model to converge.

Additionally, we show the scaling efficiency of M-CNN training from 1 to 64 nodes all running for 20 epochs. As shown in Fig. 10 time to train efficiently scales up to 16 nodes after which capping the global mini batch size shows diminishing returns.

Table 1. M-CNN training performance on 128 2S Intel® Xeon® Gold processors with Dataset B

# of nodes	# of epochs	Batch size	TTT (mins)	Images/sec
1	6.6	128	960	30
2	8	256	642	72
4	8.7	512	320	141
8	12	1024	240	262
16	15.9	2048	150	553
32	14.9	2048	85	893
64	15	2048	61	1284
128	15.2	2048	50	1587

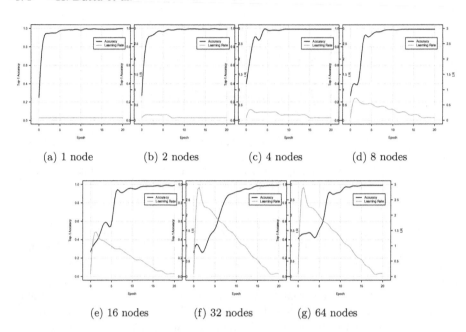

Fig. 9. Top-1 accuracy achieved in 20 epochs of M-CNN training and learning rate used on 1–64 2S Intel® Xeon® Gold processors. Dataset B is used for these experiments. Global minibatch size is capped at 2K from 16 to 64 nodes. The learning rate as shown in (f)–(h) is also scaled only to 0.032 to achieve convergence

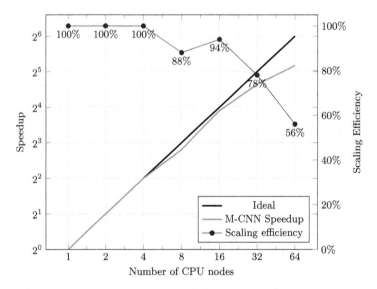

Fig. 10. Scalability of M-CNN training performance for 20 epochs on 64 2S Intel® Xeon® Gold 6148 processors. Note that global batch size is capped at 2K from 16 – 64 nodes. Intel® OP Fabric, TensorFlow-1.9.0+Horovod, OpenMPI v3.0.0, 8 workers/node

6   Discussion

In this work, we explored training a multi-scale convolutional neural network to classify large high content screening images within one hour by exploiting large memory in CPU systems. The cellular images used are over million pixels in resolution and are 26 times larger than those in the ImageNet dataset. We used two sets of cellular images with different resolutions to analyze the performance on multiple nodes of M-CNN training. The first set contains 10K full resolution cellular images ($1024 \times 1280 \times 3$) and the second dataset contains 313K images of smaller dimensions ($724 \times 724 \times 3$). With the first dataset, we were able to scale time to train linearly using 8X 2S Intel® Xeon® Gold processors. Large mini-batch sizes enabled by the large memory footprint in CPUs helped us achieve the speedup in training time. With the second data set, we were able to achieve TTT of 50 min, a 19.2X improvement in time to train using 128 Intel® Xeon® Gold processors. We learned that the updates per epoch is critical to achieve convergence and if the characteristics of the images in the dataset cannot tolerate scaling of updates per epoch beyond a certain threshold (2048 in our case), then adding more computational resources results in diminishing returns. In future work, we intend to explore larger datasets with more variation where images are chosen from different cohorts.

Acknowledgements. We would like to acknowledge Wolfgang Zipfel from the Novartis Institutes for Biomedical Research, Basel, Switzerland; Michael Derby, Michael Steeves and Steve Litster from the Novartis Institutes for Biomedical Research, Cambridge, MA, USA; Deepthi Karkada, Vivek Menon, Kristina Kermanshahche, Mike Demshki, Patrick Messmer, Andy Bartley, Bruno Riva and Hema Chamraj from Intel Corporation, USA, for their contributions to this work. The authors also acknowledge the Texas Advanced Computing Center (TACC) at The University of Texas at Austin for providing HPC resources that have contributed to the research results reported within this paper.

Conflicts of Interest. Intel® Xeon® Gold 6148 processor, Intel® OPA and Intel® SSD storage drive are registered products of Intel Corporation. The authors declare no other conflicts of interest.

References

1. Arbabshirani, M.R., et al.: Advanced machine learning in action: identification of intracranial hemorrhage on computed tomography scans of the head with clinical workflow integration. npj Digit. Med. **1**, 9 (2018)
2. Akkus, Z., Galimzianova, A., Hoogi, A., Rubin, D.L., Erickson, B.J.: Deep learning for brain MRI segmentation: state of the art and future directions. J. Digit. Imaging **30**, 449–459 (2017)
3. Cireşan, D.C., Giusti, A., Gambardella, L.M., Schmidhuber, J.: Mitosis detection in breast cancer histology images with deep neural networks. In: Mori, K., Sakuma, I., Sato, Y., Barillot, C., Navab, N. (eds.) MICCAI 2013. LNCS, vol. 8150, pp. 411–418. Springer, Heidelberg (2013). https://doi.org/10.1007/978-3-642-40763-5_51

4. Litjens, G., et al.: Deep learning as a tool for increased accuracy and efficiency of histopathological diagnosis. Sci. Rep. **6**, 26286 (2016)

5. Janowczyk, A., Madabhushi, A.: Deep learning for digital pathology image analysis: a comprehensive tutorial with selected use cases. J. Pathol. Inform. **7**, 29 (2016). https://doi.org/10.4103/2153-3539

6. Kraus, O.Z., et al.: Automated analysis of high-content microscopy data with deep learning. Mol. Syst. Biol. **13**(4), 924 (2017). https://doi.org/10.15252/msb. 20177551

7. Sommer, C., Hoefler, R., Samwer, M., Gerlich, D.W., Boone, C.: A deep learning and novelty detection framework for rapid phenotyping in high-content screening. Mol. Biol. Cell **28**(23), 3428–3436 (2017)

8. Ciresan, D.C., Giusti, A., Gambardella, L.M., Schmidhuber, J.: Deep neural networks segment neuronal membranes in electron microscopy images. In: Bartlett, P.L., Pereira, F.C.N., Burges, C.J.C., Bottou, L., Weinberger, K.Q. (eds.) NIPS, pp. 2852–2860 (2012)

9. Litjens, G., et al.: A survey on deep learning in medical image analysis. Med. Image Anal. **42**, 60–88 (2017)

10. Usaj, M.M., Styles, E.B., Verster, A.J., Friesen, H., Boone, C., Andrews, B.J.: High-content screening for quantitative cell biology. Trends Cell Biol. **26**(8), 598–611 (2016)

11. Boutros, M., Heigwer, F., Laufer, C.: Microscopy-based high-content screening. Cell **163**(6), 1314–1325 (2015)

12. Singh, S., Carpenter, A.E., Genovesio, A.: Increasing the content of high-content screening: an overview. J. Biomol. Screen. **19**, 640–650 (2014)

13. Scheeder, C., Heigwer, F., Boutros, M.: Machine learning and image-based profiling in drug discovery. Curr. Opin. Syst. Biol. **10**, 43–52 (2018). Pharmacology and drug discovery

14. Zock, J.M.: Applications of high content screening in life science research. Combin. Chem. High Throughput Screen. **12**(9), 870–876 (2009)

15. Buchser, W., et al.: Assay development guidelines for image-based high content screening, high content analysis and high content imaging. Eli Lilly & Company and the National Center for Advancing Translational Sciences (2014)

16. Godinez, W.J., Hossain, I., Lazic, S.E., Davies, J.W., Zhang, X.: A multi-scale convolutional neural network for phenotyping high-content cellular images. Bioinformatics **33**(13), 2010–2019 (2017)

17. Godinez, W.J., Hossain, I., Zhang, X.: Unsupervised phenotypic analysis of cellular images with multi-scale convolutional neural networks. bioRxiv (2018). https:// www.biorxiv.org/content/early/2018/07/03/361410

18. Ando, D.M., McLean, C., Berndl, M.: Improving phenotypic measurements in high-content imaging screens. bioRxiv (2017). https://www.biorxiv.org/content/early/2017/07/10/161422

19. Buyssens, P., Elmoataz, A., Lézoray, O.: Multiscale convolutional neural networks for vision–based classification of cells. In: Lee, K.M., Matsushita, Y., Rehg, J.M., Hu, Z. (eds.) ACCV 2012. LNCS, vol. 7725, pp. 342–352. Springer, Heidelberg (2013). https://doi.org/10.1007/978-3-642-37444-9_27

20. Jouppi, N.P., et al.: In-datacenter performance analysis of a tensor processing unit. In: 2017 ACM/IEEE 44th Annual International Symposium on Computer Architecture (ISCA), pp. 1–12. IEEE (2017)

21. Robbins, H., Monro, S.: A stochastic approximation method. Ann. Math. Stat. **22**, 400–407 (1951)

22. You, Y., Zhang, Z., Hsieh, C.-J., Demmel, J., Keutzer, K.: ImageNet training in minutes. In: Proceedings of the 47th International Conference on Parallel Processing, p. 1. ACM (2018)
23. Ljosa, V., Sokolnicki, K.L., Carpenter, A.E.: Annotated high-throughput microscopy image sets for validation. Nat. Methods **9**(7), 637 (2012)
24. Caie, P.D., et al.: High-content phenotypic profiling of drug response signatures across distinct cancer cells. Mol. Cancer Ther. **9**(6), 1913–1926 (2010)
25. Google. TPU benchmarks. https://github.com/tensorflow/tpu.git
26. Sergeev, A., Del Balso, M.: Horovod: fast and easy distributed deep learning in TensorFlow. arXiv preprint arXiv:1802.05799 (2018)
27. Saletore, V., Karkada, D., Sripathi, V., Sankaranarayanan, A., Datta, K.: Boosting deep learning training and inference performance on Intel Xeon and Intel Xeon Phi processors. https://software.intel.com/en-us/articles/boosting-deep-learning-training-inference-performance-on-xeon-and-xeon-phi

Benchmarking Deep Learning Infrastructures by Means of TensorFlow and Containers

Adrian Grupp[1], Valentin Kozlov[1(✉)] ⓘ, Isabel Campos[2] ⓘ, Mario David[3] ⓘ,
Jorge Gomes[3] ⓘ, and Álvaro López García[2] ⓘ

[1] Karlsruhe Institute of Technology (KIT), Karlsruhe, Germany
usmfz@student.kit.edu, valentin.kozlov@kit.edu
[2] Instituto de Fisica de Cantabria (IFCA - CSIC), Santander, Spain
[3] Laboratory of Instrumentation and Experimental Particle Physics (LIP),
Lisbon, Portugal

Abstract. Ever growing interest and usage of deep learning rises a question on the performance of various infrastructures suitable for training of neural networks. We present here our approach and first results of tests performed with TensorFlow Benchmarks which use best practices for multi-GPU and distributed training. We pack the Benchmarks in Docker containers and execute them by means of uDocker and Singularity container tools on a single machine and in the HPC environment. The Benchmarks comprise a number of convolutional neural network models run across synthetic data and e.g. the ImageNet dataset. For the same Nvidia K80 GPU card we achieve the same performance in terms of processed images per second and similar scalability between 1-2-4 GPUs as presented by the TensorFlow developers. We therefore do not obtain statistically significant overhead due to the usage of containers in the multi-GPU case, and the approach of using TF Benchmarks in a Docker container can be applied across various systems.

Keywords: Benchmarks · TensorFlow · ConvNet · Containers

1 Introduction

Growing interest and demand for deep learning applications and related intensive computing with large datasets poses a question on the efficiency of various hardware systems available for researchers in their institutions or from different cloud providers including commercial ones like Amazon Web Services (AWS) or Google Compute Engine (GCE). Many parameters can influence training efficiency among which are the performance of the GPU card, memory size and bandwidth, I/O or the network. Even on optimized hardware, a developer may suffer from the overhead of underlying libraries. Finally, a developer may want to compare the performance of his/her application to some best practices either within the same or between different deep learning frameworks. In the ideal case

M. Weiland et al. (Eds.): ISC 2019 Workshops, LNCS 11887, pp. 478–489, 2019.
https://doi.org/10.1007/978-3-030-34356-9_36

a tool for comparison should be optimized for the best performance at scale but not be affected by other pre-installed libraries or the operating system version and should be easily deployable in different environments.

In this paper we present our approach in using the optimized neural network code from the TensorFlow Benchmarks [9] (TF Benchmarks or Benchmarks in the following) packed into Docker containers. Using Docker containers allows to fix versions of all necessary Python packages and libraries and isolate the running environment. The Docker images with the TF Benchmarks are then executed by means of two container tools, *uDocker* [14] and *Singularity* [19], on two different multi-user multi-GPU systems.

In the following, we first describe the tools and related configurations, next the two hardware setups, then show our first results which are followed by the corresponding discussion.

2 Experimental Tools and Setups

2.1 TensorFlow Benchmarks

The TF Benchmarks [9] contain implementations of several popular convolutional models, e.g. AlexNet [18], ResNet [15], VGG [25] and InceptionV3 [26], and are designed for performance. The code supports both running on a single machine and in distributed mode across multiple hosts [9]. The TF Benchmarks can be executed on synthetic data (ImageNet emulation) and on real datasets, among which are CIFAR10 [17], ImageNet [24], COCO [20] and Librispeech [22]. The TensorFlow webpage [10] lists a few tests performed on Nvidia K80 and P100 GPU cards by means of these Benchmarks, mainly using synthetic data and the ImageNet dataset. In this work we also run tests with both synthetic and ImageNet data and use ResNet50 and AlexNet neural network architectures. The parameters used are the same as for the Google Compute Engine (GCE) in [10] and are listed in Table 1. For the performed experiments the TensorFlow version was fixed to 1.10.0, the git_hash is v1.10.0-0-g656e7a2b34.

Table 1. TF Benchmark parameters used in this work

Neural network	Batch size per GPU	Optimizer	variable_update	local_parameter_device
ResNet50	64	sgd	parameter_server	cpu
AlexNet	512	sgd	parameter_server	cpu

2.2 Datasets

In the context of this work we used synthetic data to remove disk I/O as an unknown parameter and two real datasets: CIFAR10 and ImageNet. In the following we compare the results for synthetic and ImageNet data. For the synthetic data the input is set to the same shape as the data expected by each model for ImageNet [10]. The ImageNet dataset amounting for ca. 150 GB of labeled images with one thousand object categories was downloaded from the Kaggle competition website [4] and pre-processed, i.e. converted into the TensorFlow `tfrecord` format, based on scripts available from [8].

2.3 Container Tools

Containers represent an operating-system level of virtualization, in comparison to *virtual machines* which express a hardware virtualization. This makes containers lightweight, smaller in size, and faster to deploy. They provide a way to pack and deploy software including all the dependencies in a way that can be seamlessly executed through the abstraction of the underlying Linux operating system and environment. The feature that all dependencies are packed together and transferable from one system to another makes containers ideally suitable for the purpose of benchmarking. This is also why containers attract an increasing attention in the scientific world in order to solve, for instance, the reproducibility crisis, see e.g. [13].

One of the most popular container virtualization tools is Docker [21] which also provides a public repository for Docker images, Docker Hub [3]. However, a serious limitation of Docker is the escalation of privileges, necessary to run containers. This basically forbids the usage of Docker tools in a multi-user environment. Nevertheless, there is a number of projects, e.g. *uDocker* [14], *Singularity* [19], *Shifter* [16] or *Charlie Cloud* [23], which allow in one or another way running Docker images on multi-user systems. One tool, *Singularity* , was already available in our both test systems (Sect. 2.4); another one, *uDocker* , is 100% a user tool and therefore could be installed and used by an ordinary user. Both *uDocker* and *Singularity* implement execution on GPU, which is very important for our benchmarks. In the following we give more details about the two container tools used.

uDocker combines pulling, extraction and execution of Docker containers without the necessity of root privileges. It is an integration tool that incorporates several methods to execute containers according to the target host capabilities [14] by providing a chroot-like environment over the extracted container. It supports several methods using tools and libraries such as: PRoot, Fakechroot, runC or *Singularity* . *uDocker* is written in Python and freely available on GitHub [12]. It has a command line interface similar to Docker and provides a subset of its commands aimed at searching, pulling and executing containers in a Docker-like manner. As it is entirely a user tool, it can be installed on any system running Linux operational system and having Python available. The version of *uDocker* used is 1.1.3 on both hardware setups, LSDF-GPU and ForHLR-II (see Sec. 2.4). It was executed in the default 'P1' mode (PTRACE) with `--nvidia` flag.

Singularity is another container solution created by necessity for scientific application driven workloads [19]. *Singularity* offers mobility of compute by enabling environments to be portable via a single custom image file that encapsulates the entire container and stack. It also supports other container formats, e.g. Docker images. It makes use of kernel features such as e.g. chroot, bind mounts, Linux namespaces and cgroups. While it has to be installed by a system administrator, *Singularity* was designed with the usage in a multi-user environment in mind and therefore does not generally allow escalation of privileges when executed by a user. The *Singularity* versions available for our benchmarks were 2.6.0-dist at LSDF-GPU and 2.5.2-dist at ForHLR-II. Default settings and the --nv flag were used.

2.4 Experimental Setups

The main parameters of the two hardware setups used are listed in Table 2. The operating system in both cases is RedHat Enterprise Linux 7.5. The LSDF-GPU setup has two Nvidia Tesla K80 modules installed where each module consists of two GPU cards that can be used separately. Two K80 modules are seen as four GPU cards by the Linux system and therefore listed as four GPU cards in the table. Both experimental setups are multi-user environments with LSDF-GPU being a single machine, while ForHLR-II [1] is an HPC system with computing nodes connected via EDR Infiniband.

Table 2. Experimental setups used in the experiments.

Setup	CPU	RAM	Nvidia GPU (driver version)	Storage	Batch system
LSDF-GPU	2 × Intel Xeon E5-2630 v3	128 GB	4 × Tesla K80, 12 GB (410.72)	NFS mount via 10 Gb/s Ethernet	None
ForHLR-II	4 × Intel Xeon E7-4830 v3	1 TB	4 × GTX980 Ti, 6 GB (418.56)	Lustre with 2 GB/s r/w per node	SLURM

3 Evaluation

The TF Benchmarks code provides a way to store parameters of each run, e.g. CPU-, GPU-type, amount of memory, amount of GPUs, neural network model, type of dataset, batch size per device, etc. in the benchmark_run.log file. We rename this file into benchmark.log in the case of training, and into eval.log if we run an evaluation of the trained model. The results of the training and evaluation processes are stored in the metric.log file. The log files of all our benchmark runs can be found in [7]. In order to automatize the submission of jobs for various configurations, a number of bash scripts was written and is available in [11]. Finally, the results of our benchmarks were analyzed and plotted with the Python script found in [7].

All the results described below, unless stated otherwise, are relatively short runs of 500 batches (--num_batches=500). At the end, in order to test if an achieved accuracy of training varies with the number of GPUs used, we perform training with the real ImageNet dataset on LSDF-GPU and ForHLR-II setups for 5 and 10 epochs respectively (--num_epochs={5,10}).

3.1 Using Synthetic Data

First, TF Benchmarks are run with synthetic data by means of *uDocker* on the LSDF-GPU system which has the same Nvidia Tesla K80 GPU card as listed in [10]. Our results for all cases: one, two and four GPUs and both ResNet50 and AlexNet neural networks, are in good agreement with the official TF Benchmarks results for synthetic data [10], as shown in parentheses on Fig. 1. Figure 2 shows the corresponding speedup for two and four GPU cards compared to ideal linear scaling. As our numbers are either close to or slightly better than those reported in [10], we conclude that there is no any significant overhead due to the usage of containers and the *uDocker* tool.

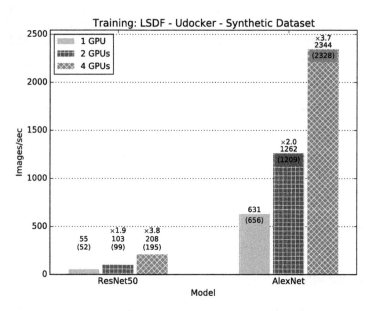

Fig. 1. TF Benchmarks run on the system with Nvidia K80 GPU cards by means of *uDocker* . ResNet50 and AlexNet architectures are used with the synthetic dataset. In parentheses are the corresponding results from [10].

3.2 Comparing Synthetic vs. Real ImageNet Data

The next step is to compare training performance with synthetic and ImageNet data which allows checking the training pipeline on the large dataset as a whole. Figures 3 and 4 show results for two neural networks under study: ResNet50 and AlexNet correspondingly. While there is no penalty for ResNet50 and our numbers are even slightly better than in [10] for this case, AlexNet training

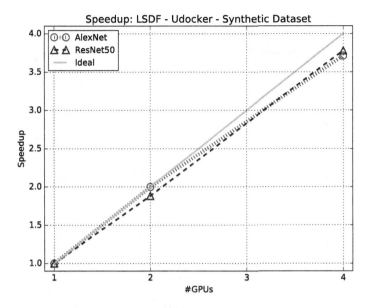

Fig. 2. Speedup plots for the runs presented in Fig. 1 showing scaling between 1-2-4 GPU cards. Also ideal linear expectation is drawn.

with ImageNet shows clear degradation by about 14–15% for two and four GPU cases in comparison with the synthetic data. The official TF Benchmarks results in [10] also indicate degradation in performance for AlexNet but only by about 6–11%. We attribute this degradation to the throughput of our network storage. In any case, our results are in agreement within just a few percent with those reported in [10], showing applicability of our container-based approach.

3.3 Comparing Two Container Tools

There exist various container tools (see Sect. 2.3) which may use different methods to execute the very same Docker image. In addition to *uDocker* we could also assess *Singularity* and compare training performance between the two container tools. The results presented in Figs. 5 and 6 do not indicate any valuable difference between both.

3.4 Three Systems Comparison Using Real ImageNet Data

Once the approach of using TF Benchmarks in a Docker container executed by means of *uDocker* was verified on the setup similar to the one tested in [10], it was applied on a different system. This system is the ForHLR-II High Performance Computing cluster at Karlsruhe Institute of Technology [1]. Table 3 summarizes the TF Benchmarks runs performed on both LSDF-GPU and ForHLR-II using the ImageNet dataset and two neural network architectures, ResNet50

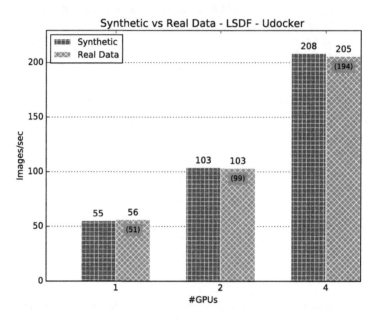

Fig. 3. Comparison between runs with synthetic data and using the ImageNet dataset. ResNet50 architecture is used. In parentheses are the corresponding results from [10].

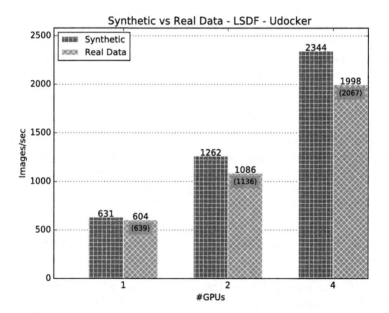

Fig. 4. Comparison between runs with synthetic data and using the ImageNet dataset. AlexNet architecture is used. In parentheses are the corresponding results from [10].

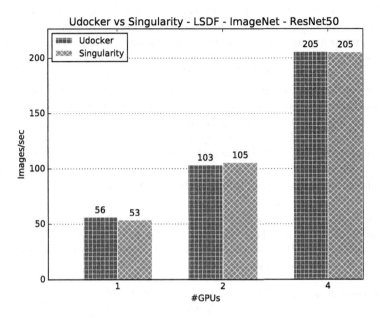

Fig. 5. Comparison of two container tools, *uDocker* and *Singularity* . ResNet50 architecture run on the ImageNet dataset.

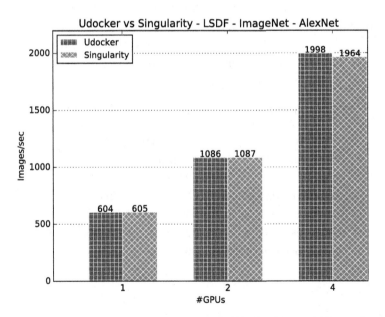

Fig. 6. Comparison of two container tools, *uDocker* and *Singularity* . AlexNet architecture run on the ImageNet dataset.

and AlexNet, and compares them with the corresponding official TF Benchmarks results from [10]. One can see that the two systems featuring Tesla K80 GPU cards are very similar in performance namely in the absolute number of images processed per second. This as well applies to the scaling between one, two, and four GPUs. ForHLR-II profits from its GTX980 Ti GPU card and outperforms both K80-based setups by slightly more than factor of two. The results, however, indicate a stronger deviation from the linear scaling in the case of four GPU cards, which we at first relate to the network storage. The performance of the GTX980-based system being twice as good as the K80-based setup can be attributed to the faster base core clock, memory clock, and larger memory bandwidth, see Table 4. However, we do not assess what exactly leads to the measured performance difference but rather emphasize the practical applicability of the used tools.

Table 3. Results of the runs for two neural network architectures executed on two platforms: LSDF-GPU and ForHLR-II, and comparison with the Official TF Benchmarks results for GCE [10]. Shown are the number of processed images per second and the scaling factor in relation to one GPU.

Neural network	#GPUs	LSDF-GPU (Tesla K80)		Official TF Benchmarks (Tesla K80)		ForHLR-II (GTX980 Ti)	
ResNet50	1	56		51		118	
	2	103	×1.8	99	×1.9	225	×1.9
	4	205	×3.7	194	×3.8	426	×3.6
AlexNet	1	604		639		1314	
	2	1086	×1.8	1136	×1.8	2320	×1.8
	4	1998	×3.3	2067	×3.2	4006	×3.0

Table 4. Key features of Nvidia Tesla K80 and GTX980 Ti

Parameter	Tesla K80 [6]	GTX980 Ti [5]
Architecture	Kepler™	Maxwell™
N Cores	2496	2816
Base core clock, MHz	560	1000
Boost clocks, MHz	562 to 875	1075
Memory clock, GHz	2.5	7.0 (effective)
Memory bandwidth, GB/sec	240	336.5

3.5 Long-Term Training Tests

TF Benchmarks allow to evaluate fast the number of processed images per second. It is, of course, also important to test a system of interest under high load for an extended period of time. Taking into account the time and availability of resources, we executed training of the ResNet50 neural network on the ImageNet dataset on LSDF-GPU and ForHLR-II setups for 5 and 10 epochs correspondingly. It was important to verify that the achieved accuracy does not degrade with an increased number of GPUs. Table 5 summarizes the results and shows no difference between the runs with one, two, or four cards for either top_1 or top_5 accuracy. The total training time was recorded and demonstrates very good linear scaling between the number of GPU cards and the speedup for the LSDF-GPU setup. ForHLR-II scaling is very similar to the results achieved with shorter runs, see Table 3. The training loss was also monitored, and as presented in Fig. 7, the learning curves show very similar behaviour in all three cases.

Table 5. Results of TF Benchmarks using the ImageNet dataset and the ResNet50 network trained on two platforms, LSDF-GPU and ForHLR-II, for 5 and 10 epochs respectively. Docker containers are executed by means of *uDocker* . Shown are top_1 and top_5 accuracy, total training time in hours:minutes and the speedup in relation to one GPU.

#GPUs	LSDF-GPU 5 epochs			ForHLR-II 10 epochs		
	Accuracy		Training time	Accuracy		Training time
	top_1	top_5	hh:mm	top_1	top_5	hh:mm
1	0.36	0.63	33:45	0.53	0.78	30:23
2	0.37	0.64	16:46 ×2.0	0.53	0.79	15:50 ×1.9
4	0.35	0.62	8:34 ×3.9	0.51	0.76	8:16 ×3.7

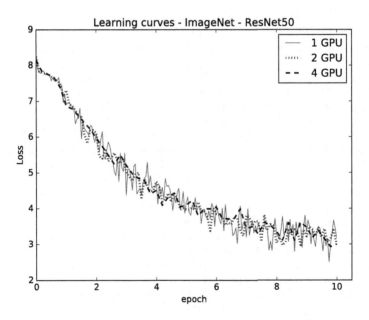

Fig. 7. Learning curves for training on 1-2-4 GPUs. ResNet50 neural network architecture run on the ImageNet dataset via *uDocker* on ForHLR-II.

4   Conclusion and Outlook

This work suggests a usage of TF Benchmarks packed in a Docker image and executed by means of the *uDocker* container tool as means to evaluate deep learning infrastructures. Thanks to the optimized TF Benchmarks code, the good speedup is demonstrated between one, two, and four GPU cards for two different setups: LSDF-GPU and ForHLR-II. Usage of containers ensures isolation of the running environment and easiness in transferring it to various systems. The *uDocker* user tool allows deployment of containers in a multi-user system without the need for administrator privileges. All performed tests do not indicate an overhead due to usage of containers and support our approach.

As next steps we are going to evaluate more datasets and neural network architectures, integrate DEEPaaS API [2] for more user-friendly access to TF Benchmarks via the REST API and perform distributed training across different computing nodes.

Acknowledgments. *uDocker* is being developed within the DEEP HybridDataCloud project, which receives funding from the European Union's Horizon 2020 research and innovation program under agreement RIA 777435.

A part of this work was performed on the computational resource ForHLR-II funded by the Ministry of Science, Research and the Arts Baden-Wuerttemberg and DFG ("Deutsche Forschungsgemeinschaft").

References

1. Computational resource ForHLR-II available at Karlsruhe Institute of Technology. https://wiki.scc.kit.edu/hpc/index.php/Category:ForHLR. Accessed 12 Apr 2019
2. DEEP as a Service (DEEPaaS) API. https://deepaas.readthedocs.io. Accessed 12 Apr 2019
3. Docker Hub website. https://hub.docker.com. Accessed 12 Apr 2019
4. ImageNet Object Localization Challenge at Kaggle. https://www.kaggle.com/c/imagenet-object-localization-challenge. Accessed 12 Apr 2019
5. Nvidia Geforce GTX980 Ti specifications. https://www.geforce.com/hardware/desktop-gpus/geforce-gtx-980-ti/specifications. Accessed 12 Apr 2019
6. Nvidia Tesla K80 GPU Accelerator, Board Specification (2015). https://www.nvidia.com/content/dam/en-zz/Solutions/Data-Center/tesla-product-literature/Tesla-K80-BoardSpec-07317-001-v05.pdf. Accessed 12 Apr 2019
7. Results of TF Benchmarks runs, GitHub repository. https://github.com/adriangrupp/tf_cnn_benchmarks_evaluation. Accessed 12 Apr 2019
8. Scripts for downloading and converting ImageNet data to TFRecord format. https://github.com/tensorflow/models/tree/master/research/inception/inception/data. Accessed 12 Apr 2019
9. TensorFlow Benchmarks, GitHub repository. https://github.com/tensorflow/benchmarks/. Accessed 8 Apr 2019
10. TensorFlow Benchmarks webpage. https://www.tensorflow.org/guide/performance/benchmarks. Accessed 8 Apr 2019
11. TF Benchmarks fork for TF 1.10.0, KIT Gitlab. https://git.scc.kit.edu/tf-benchmarks/tf_cnn_tf_benchmarks. Accessed 12 Apr 2019

12. udocker: A basic user tool to execute simple docker containers in batch or interactive systems without root privileges. GiHub repository. https://github.com/indigo-dc/udocker. Accessed 8 Apr 2019
13. Baker, M.: Is there a reproducibility crisis? Nature **533**, 452–454 (2016)
14. Gomes, J., et al.: Enabling rootless linux containers in multi-user environments: the udocker tool. Comput. Phys. Commun. **232**, 84–97 (2018). https://doi.org/10.1016/j.cpc.2018.05.021
15. He, K., Zhang, X., Ren, S., Sun, J.: Deep residual learning for image recognition. In: 2016 IEEE Conference on Computer Vision and Pattern Recognition (CVPR), pp. 770–778 (2015)
16. Jacobsen, D.M., Canon, R.S.: Contain this, unleashing Docker for HPC. Cray User Group 2015 (2015)
17. Krizhevsky, A.: Learning multiple layers of features from tiny images. Technical report (2009). https://www.cs.toronto.edu/~kriz/learning-features-2009-TR.pdf
18. Krizhevsky, A., Sutskever, I., Hinton, G.E.: ImageNet classification with deep convolutional neural networks. In: Pereira, F., Burges, C.J.C., Bottou, L., Weinberger, K.Q. (eds.) Advances in Neural Information Processing Systems, vol. 25, pp. 1097–1105. Curran Associates, Inc. (2012). http://papers.nips.cc/paper/4824-imagenet-classification-with-deep-convolutional-neural-networks.pdf
19. Kurtzer, G.M., Sochat, V., Bauer, M.W.: Singularity: scientific containers for mobility of compute. PLoS One (2017). https://doi.org/10.1371/journal.pone.0177459
20. Lin, T., et al.: Microsoft COCO: common objects in context. CoRR abs/1405.0312 (2014). http://arxiv.org/abs/1405.0312
21. Merkel, D.: Docker: lightweight Linux containers for consistent development and deployment (2014). https://doi.org/10.1097/01.NND.0000320699.47006.a3
22. Panayotov, V., Chen, G., Povey, D., Khudanpur, S.: Librispeech: an ASR corpus based on public domain audio books, pp. 5206–5210, April 2015. https://doi.org/10.1109/ICASSP.2015.7178964
23. Priedhorsky, R., Randles, T.C., Randles, T.: Charliecloud: unprivileged containers for user-defined software stacks in HPC. In: SC17: International Conference for High Performance Computing, Networking, Storage and Analysis (2017). https://doi.org/10.1145/3126908.3126925
24. Russakovsky, O., et al.: ImageNet large scale visual recognition challenge. Int. J. Comput. Vis. (IJCV) **115**(3), 211–252 (2015). https://doi.org/10.1007/s11263-015-0816-y
25. Simonyan, K., Zisserman, A.: Very deep convolutional networks for large-scale image recognition. CoRR abs/1409.1556 (2014)
26. Szegedy, C., Vanhoucke, V., Ioffe, S., Shlens, J., Wojna, Z.: InceptionV3. In: 2016 IEEE Conference on Computer Vision and Pattern Recognition (CVPR), pp. 2818–2826 (2016)

MagmaDNN: Towards High-Performance Data Analytics and Machine Learning for Data-Driven Scientific Computing

Daniel Nichols[1], Nathalie-Sofia Tomov[1], Frank Betancourt[1], Stanimire Tomov[1(✉)], Kwai Wong[1], and Jack Dongarra[1,2]

[1] University of Tennessee, Knoxville, TN 37996, USA
{dnicho22,ntomov,fbetanco}@vols.utk.edu,
{tomov,dongarra}@icl.utk.edu, kwong@utk.edu
[2] Oak Ridge National Laboratory, Oak Ridge, TN 37831, USA

Abstract. In this paper, we present work towards the development of a new data analytics and machine learning (ML) framework, called MagmaDNN. Our main goal is to provide scalable, high-performance data analytics and ML solutions for scientific applications running on current and upcoming heterogeneous many-core GPU-accelerated architectures. To this end, since many of the functionalities needed are based on standard linear algebra (LA) routines, we designed MagmaDNN to derive its performance power from the MAGMA library. The close integration provides the fundamental (scalable high-performance) LA routines available in MAGMA as a backend to MagmaDNN. We present some design issues for performance and scalability that are specific to ML using Deep Neural Networks (DNN), as well as the MagmaDNN designs towards overcoming them. In particular, MagmaDNN uses well established HPC techniques from the area of dense LA, including task-based parallelization, DAG representations, scheduling, mixed-precision algorithms, asynchronous solvers, and autotuned hyperparameter optimization. We illustrate these techniques and their incorporation and use to outperform other frameworks, currently available.

Keywords: Machine learning · High-performance DNN · Data-driven scientific computing

1 Introduction

Powered by hardware advances and availability of massive training data, data analytics and machine learning (ML) research, e.g., using Deep Neural Networks (DNN), have exploded in recent years, making major contributions in applications of computer vision, speech recognition, robotics, natural language processing, and many others. Many of these are scientific applications, where accelerating the DNN training is a major challenge and a current main bottleneck to scale the computation on current and up-coming architectures. In

M. Weiland et al. (Eds.): ISC 2019 Workshops, LNCS 11887, pp. 490–503, 2019.
https://doi.org/10.1007/978-3-030-34356-9_37

this paper, we present a new data analytics and machine learning framework, called MagmaDNN. Our main goal is to provide scalable, high-performance data analytics and ML solutions for scientific applications running on current, as well as upcoming heterogeneous many-core GPU-accelerated architectures. To this end, as much of the functionalities needed are based on standard linear algebra routines, we designed MagmaDNN to derive its power from the MAGMA library [15]. The close integration provides the fundamental (scalable high-performance) linear algebra routines available in MAGMA as a backend to MagmaDNN. We present some design issues for performance and scalability that are specific to machine learning (ML) using Deep Neural Networks (DNN), as well as the MagmaDNN designs towards overcoming them. In particular, MagmaDNN uses well established HPC techniques from the area of dense linear algebra, including task-based parallelization, DAG representations, scheduling, mixed-precision algorithms, asynchronous solvers, and autotuning. We illustrate these techniques and their incorporation and use to outperform other frameworks, currently available.

2 MagmaDNN Design

Many ML and data analytics problems can be cast as linear algebra (LA) problems, and therefore can be accelerated with familiar algorithms, e.g., BLAS, linear solvers, eigensolvers, or singular value decomposition (SVD), that are routinely used in HPC. These LA algorithms are readily available in highly optimized numerical LA libraries on new architectures, like MAGMA, which is used by MagmaDNN (see the MagmaDNN software stack illustrated on Fig. 1, Left). Figure 1, Right shows that significant acceleration can be achieved by using HPC library like MAGMA, e.g., in this case on SVD for square matrices in double

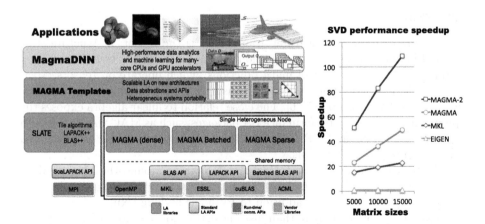

Fig. 1. Left: MagmaDNN software stack. Right: MAGMA backend speedup in accelerating fundamental data analytics kernels, e.g., SVD.

precision on two 10 core Intel Haswell E5-2650 v3 CPUs with an NVIDIA V100 GPU accelerator [7].

Related to DNNs, MagmaDNN's design is modular with each component built on top of each other in increasing levels of abstraction. The core component is the **MemoryManager** (Sect. 2.1), which handles the underlying memory operations. On top of the MemoryManager, sits 3 other components: **Tensor** (Sect. 2.2), **Layer** (Sect. 2.3), and **Model** (Sect. 2.4). All of these compose the typical MagmaDNN program workflow (Sect. 2.5).

2.1   MemoryManager

Typical deep learning frameworks hide memory from the user in a Python interface. MagmaDNN accomplishes similar abstraction through its MemoryManager class, which defines and controls memory movement in the framework. Memory is broken into four types: *HOST*, *DEVICE*, *MANAGED*, and *CUDA_MANAGED*. The latter two are both managed style memory, which keep track of data on both the CPU and GPU. *CUDA_MANAGED* uses CUDA's unified memory. Similar to unified memory *MANAGED* keeps track of CPU and GPU data, however it must be explicitly synchronized.

Memory bugs are common in GPU and especially C/C++ code. The MemoryManager solves this development hurdle for the library user, while still giving explicit control over memory transactions.

In addition to providing a simple modular interface the MemoryManager provides a flexible platform for MagmaDNN to optimize memory tasks in training. In deep learning data sets are typically large and create a memory bandwidth bottleneck. Several tricks are employed in MagmaDNN such as asynchronous data prefetching and custom synchronization scheduling. Additionally, the customizable nature of the class allows for future work in memory optimization.

2.2   Tensor

At the core of most deep learning frameworks is the tensor: a structure storing multi-dimensional data. In addition to the tensor itself, essential to deep learning is also a collection of math functions, which operate on tensors. MagmaDNN defines many tensor operations using a combination of its own definitions, MAGMA, and CuDNN [6]. The close relation to linear algebra exposes the opportunity to use high performance LA packages, such as MAGMA, to use both the multi-core CPU and GPU devices [15]. Other operations are implemented using optimized CUDA kernels.

The tensor implementation in MagmaDNN wraps around the MemoryManager and gives structure to the linear memory. It aims to provide a simple interface for tensor interaction in addition to Pythonic style indexing.

Modern networks are more than just linear transformations and are typically composed of convolutional and recurrent layers. MagmaDNN provides convolutional support through Batched GEMMs [2], the Winograd algorithm [5], and FFTs [13,16], but for current performance defaults to CuDNN [6].

2.3 Layer

MagmaDNN provides a simple Layer interface for creating network layers. Each layer keeps track of its own forward/backward pass function, weight tensor and bias tensor. Currently MagmaDNN provides seven layer types: *Input*, *Fully Connected*, *Activation*, *Conv2D*, *Pooling2D*, *Dropout*, and *Output*.

Despite all layers inheriting from a base Layer class they each define their own set of parameters. The activation layer accepts `tanh`, `sigmoid`, and `relu` as activation functions and it is simple to define new ones. By all inheriting from the same Layer superclass it is possible to define custom layers for use in training.

2.4 Model

MagmaDNN's Model class defines a typical training routine. This routine will load new data, forward propagate, backward propagate, and update the network. It calculates and stores simple training metrics such as loss, accuracy, and training time.

Typical DNN framework users are not concerned with the specifics of network training routines. Models removes the necessity for end-users to implement their own training loop.

2.5 Workflow

Figure 2 illustrates the typical kernels that are needed in a DNN. As shown, the neural network can be organized into L fully-connected 'layers' ($i = 1, ..., L$) with n_i nodes (or *artificial neurons*) per layer that function together to make a prediction. The connections between layers $i - 1$ and i are represented by numerical weights, stored in matrix W_i of size $n_i \times n_{i-1}$, and vector b_i of length n_i. Thus, if the input values for layer i, given by the values at the n_{i-1} nodes of layer $i - 1$, are represented as a vector a_{i-1} of size n_{i-1}, the output of layer i will be a vector of size n_i, given by the matrix-vector product $W_i a_{i-1} + b_i$. As training will be done in parallel for a batch of nb vectors, the input matrices A_{i-1} are of size $n_{i-1} \times nb$ and the outputs are given by the matrix-matrix products $Z_i = W_i A_{i-1} + b_i$, where "+" adds b_i to each of the nb columns of the resulting matrix. The *Forward propagation* process, given by steps $0, ..., L$, represents a non-linear hypothesis/prediction function $H_{W,b}(X) \equiv A_L$ for given inputs of X and fixed weights W, b. The weights must be modified so that the predictions $H_{W,b}(X)$ become close to given/known outcomes stored in Y. This is known as a *classification* problem and is a case of so called *supervised learning*. The modification of the weights is defined as a minimization problem on a cost function J, e.g.,

$$\min_{W,b} J(W,b), \text{ where } J(W,b) = -\frac{1}{N} \sum_{i=1}^{N} y_i \log H_{W,b}(x_i) + (1 - y_i) \log(1 - H_{W,b}(x_i)).$$

This is solved by a batch SGD that uses a batch of nb training examples at a time. The derivatives of J with respect to the weights (W and b) are derived over the layers using the chain rule for differentiating compositions of functions. They are computed then by the *backward propagation* steps $L+1$, ..., $2L$, and used to modify their respective weights W_i, b_i during the iterative training process for each layer i as:

$$W_i = W_i - \lambda dW_i, \quad b_i = b_i - \lambda db_i,$$

where λ is a hyperparameter referred to as *learning rate*. The $\sigma_1, ..., \sigma_L$ functions are the activation functions for the different layers of the network, and σ' are their derivatives. The ".*" notation is for point-wise multiplication. The case of $nb = 1$ is the standard (synchronous) SGD. As illustrated, the main kernels are GEMMs, other BLAS, simple auxiliary LA kernels, and various activation functions, which are accelerated using the MAGMA backend.

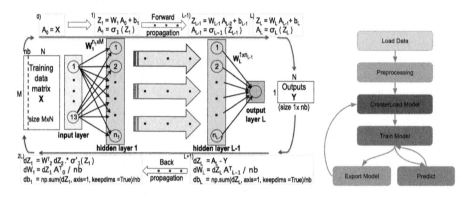

Fig. 2. Typical DNN computational kernels (Left) and MagmaDNN workflow (Right).

MagmaDNN is capable of many different workflows, however it is designed towards the linear one depicted in Fig. 2, Right. Each level of the workflow is supported by some functionality in MagmaDNN, however, currently the *Train Model* step is the focus of development.

3   Hyperparameter Optimization

MagmaDNN uses a Random and/or Exhaustive Grid Search technique to optimize hyperparameters. The routine is modular and able to add new dimensions to the search space. In grid search, a parameter server sends a parameter set to each node, where the model is trained according to its received parameters. The parameter server, or master, in turn receives the training time, accuracy, and loss associate with each parameter set. Using some objective function, typically a combination of training duration and accuracy, the optimization routine gives the optimal training parameters. Grid search can be run to exhaustively search a range of parameters (with a given step size). MagmaDNN provides the full search capability as one option. However, this is often too large to be feasible. For these reasons grid search can be ran using random sampling until some accuracy threshold is met. We use the openDIEL framework [17], described next, to run the hyperparameter search in parallel.

3.1   openDIEL Framework Design Overview

The openDIEL system consists of a library that contains all of the function needed to manage modules. Typically, a main driver file is created which contains all of the needed function calls to set up the main MPI communicator that the IEL library uses, set up necessary modules for tuple space communication, and calling the user defined modules.

The main way that users interact with the system is through a configuration file. There are two major components of the openDIEL system: the executive library, and the communication library (see Fig. 3).

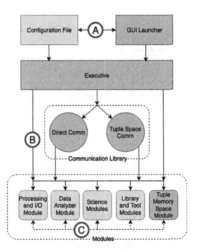

Fig. 3. openDIEL architecture: (A) GUI launcher creates a configuration file for the workflow, and **executive** will read this file to set up workflows; (B) After initial configuration, **executive** starts all modules; (C) The modules have access to the communication library, and directly communicate or utilize tuple space communication.

Configuration File. Information about how modules communicate and rely on one another is contained in a configuration file. The configuration file defines what resources the modules requires, such as the number of cores, and number of GPUs required by the module. After defining the modules themselves, a section of the file subsequently defines the manner in which groups of modules depend on one another, how many iterations need to run, amongst other characteristics.

Communication Library. The communication library is essentially a wrapper around various MPI calls, and is responsible for managing both tuple space and direct communication between modules. This is done by creating a main MPI_COMM_WORLD communicator in which all of the modules run, and then subdividing this main communicator at the level of single modules. If there are multiple concurrent copies of the same module running at the same time, the module sub-communicator is further subdivided between the copies [17].

Two different methods of communication are provided by an API: tuple space communication, and direct module-to-module communication. With tuple space communication, a tuple server module is used that allows modules to concurrently send data to and receive data from a shared associative array. Modules can use this form of communication to send and receive data from the tuple space respectively. Each module that puts data into the tuple space can issue a non-blocking (IEL_tput) function call, and provide a tag for the data placed in the tuple space. The receiving module can use a blocking (IEL_tget) function call to retrieve the data with the specified tag (Fig. 4).

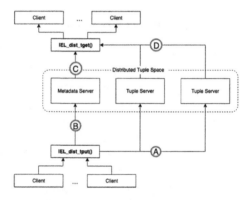

Fig. 4. Distributed tuple server model: (A) Client data is distributed across an array of tuple servers; (B) Metadata for the distributed data is stored in a metadata server; (C) When data is to be retrieved, first the metadata is retrieved, and (D) the data itself is retrieved from the distributed array of tuple servers. The received data is then reconstructed and returned to the requesting client.

The tuple space can also be distributed across a number of different modules, essentially providing a way to store and retrieve data in a distributed manner. The functions IEL_dist_tget and IEL_dist_tget utilize this multiple tuple server model. The IEL_dist_tget function will take a pointer to data and a string to tag the data, and distribute it amongst an array of tuple servers. Information about the distribution of the data is stored on a meta-data server. The IEL_dist_tget function will retrieve the data by querying the meta-data server, which returns the locations of the servers holding the data, the data servers are queried, and the stored data is reconstructed.

Executive Library. The executive library is the other major part of the library responsible for starting job and managing dependencies. When a job starts, the executive will read in a workflow configuration file, and then based on this file, the executive will create a dependency graph of the specified workflow, and then start modules based on the graph. Typically, a module is included in openDIEL by linking a library against a driver file, and function pointers are provided to the executive so that they can be called with the appropriate arguments [17]. Executables can also be run by calling fork() and exec() in an MPI process, but limits the ability of the module to use the inter-modular communication provided by openDIEL.

Typical Usage. Typically, all of the needed functions are called in a main driver file. This driver file will call MPI_init, and then it will call openDIEL member function IELAddModule, which will take a pointer to the function in the linked library for the module. This will be used later to start the module in the workflow. For modules that are executables, a model that calls fork() and exec() on the proper arguments is started for each serial module. After this setup, the main IELExecutive() member function is called. This function will split up the MPI_COMM_WORLD communicator into the appropriate subcommunicators, resolve dependencies from the configuration file, and then start modules.

3.2   Grid Engine

One of the goals of the framework is to not only provide facilities for hyperparameter optimization and search, but also to allow for users to readily use existing libraries to perform these tasks. One such implementation is a grid search engine that uses the openDIEL tuple space communication to distribute parameters to worker processes in an exhaustive search of a specified parameter space, collect the results, and report the best parameters found.

The module consists of a master process that chooses hyperparameters, and a set of processes that receive the hyperparameters. The master process first selects a set of parameters, distributes them to the workers via the tuple space, and waits for the group to finish. The group of worker processes receive the parameters, train, and report their results to the trainer via tuple space communication. These results are then gathered by the master process, and then the next group of processes is started on the next batch of parameters.

4   Performance Results

4.1   MNIST Test

Since its introduction by Lecun et al. [11] the MNIST data set has become a standard for learning and training neural networks. The data set consists of 60000 images of handwritten digits that are 28×28 pixels in size.

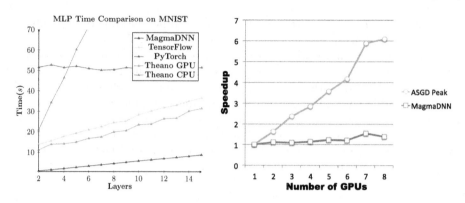

Fig. 5. Left: time comparisons of MagmaDNN training to other popular frameworks on a single GPU. Right: scalability and MagmaDNN SGD speedup and peak asynchronous SGD (ASGD) speedup vs. TensorFlow SGD training.

As a baseline test MagmaDNN was compared to Tensorflow, PyTorch, and Theano (see Fig. 5, Left) on a dense network using the MNIST data set. The layers were increased with each test to show how each framework scaled in training time. A learning rate of $\eta = 0.05$, a weight decay of $\alpha = 0.001$ and activation function `sigmoid` were used in training the network. Data was loaded into the network with a batch size of 100 samples and ran for 5 epochs. The tests were conducted on an Intel Xeon X560 processor alongside an Nvidia 1050 Ti GPU card. Theano was also run on CPU only to give reference to the speedups gained by using GPUs.

From the above test MagmaDNN was the fastest at each data point. It ran approximately 6.8× faster than TensorFlow, and 17.8× faster than Theano-CPU. The performance results shown are averaged over five runs.

4.2   Scaling

Despite being the fastest MagmaDNN scaled the second fastest in terms of training time. PyTorch, being the fastest scaling, performed poorly on the small data set, but did not gain much training time as the network size increased (Table 1).

Table 1. Change in training time with number of layers

Framework	Δ time/Δ layer
MagmaDNN	0.6197
TensorFlow	1.7524
Theano (GPU)	1.5271
Theano (CPU)	12.5071
PyTorch	−0.08

Due to the computational size of deep networks much effort has been put into distribution strategies. Parallelization introduces speed increases, but can also hurt convergence.

As evinced by Fig. 5, GPUs provide a significant performance boost in training deep networks. Thus making full use of the GPU is vital for a new deep learning framework.

Even with the advent of GPUs in training, they are still insufficient for training larger networks (such as ResNet-50 or DenseNet) in a reasonable amount of time. These large networks typically train on vast data sets causing memory transferring to bottle neck the training. One solution to this problem is to use minibatches. Batches reduce the total number `cudaMemcpy` calls. Using batches also introduces additional optimization complexity by creating a new hyperparameter *batch size*.

In addition to adding new hyperparameters, using large batch sizes can also hinder the convergence of the network. In order to combat the poor convergence, tricks such as growing batch sizes [12], warm-up [8], or layer-wise adaptive rate scaling (LARS) [18] must be used. In practice these tricks are often successful, but only raise the batch size barrier [3]. Using these techniques and various others You et al. were able to train AlexNet in 11 min on the ImageNet-1k data set [19].

All of the above techniques are typical to modern deep learning approaches, however, they do not address multi-node training. DNN parallelization can also be implemented to accelerate training, while retaining convergence.

The most common of these techniques is *Data-Parallelism* (see Fig. 6). Older implementations of data parallelism use a master-worker model (see Fig. 6, Left) for averaging weights. In this model weights are sent from a master node to N worker nodes. Let w^j be the weights of the j-th worker node. Each node computes the gradient ∇w^j and sends it back to the master node. Once the master node has received the gradients from each worker it calculates $\overline{w} \leftarrow \overline{w} - \eta/N \sum_{j=1}^{N} \nabla w^j$, the average weight, and broadcasts $\overline{w}$ back to each worker. Modern implementations, as well as MagmaDNN's implementation, remove the Master node and average the gradients using `AllReduce`. Any CUDA-aware MPI implementation can perform this operation, however, Nvidia's NCCL has in general a much faster `ncclAllReduce` between GPU nodes. Data parallelism is a typical method used in scaling deep learning and it has shown promising results [4,9].

While providing significant speed ups, data parallelism also provides some drawbacks. In the `Allreduce` approach nodes that finish training early sit idle while waiting on others. This creates "lulls" where more work could be done. To address this issue some parallel trainers utilize *Model-Parallelism*. Here models are partitioned across nodes and trained in parallel. This approach can quickly fill up device memory, thus restricting itself to smaller models and/or batch sizes.

Layer-Parallelism aims to solve the idle processor issue by pipelining network layers, computing layers in parallel as soon as possible. Layer parallelism offers

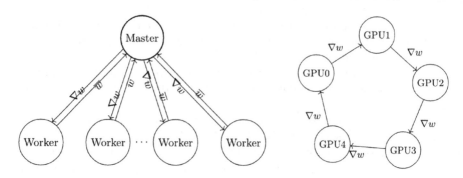

Fig. 6. Master-worker reduce (Left) and ring AllReduce (Right).

some performance benefits and is used in practice [1,10], but creates irregular transfer rates between processors [3].

As each distribution strategy offers unique solutions and drawbacks the best strategy is *Hybrid-Parallelism*, which combines each of the previous in some custom manner to exploit the parallel nature of a specific model. However, this makes hybrid parallelism model specific and non generalizable.

MagmaDNN makes use of MAGMA to exploit best fine-grained parallel practices. CUDA and CuDNN are additionally utilized to exploit the highly parallel GPU architectures. Other fine-grained acceleration is currently not within the projects scope.

Techniques such as data parallelism and distributed training with CUDA-aware MPI are included in MagmaDNN to employ course-grained parallelism.

MPI is utilized to distribute networks across nodes in MagmaDNN using `Allreduce` to implement data parallelism. Despite MPI not being fault-tolerant training is typically not hindered due to the large number of samples trained on and the resilience of deep networks.

Figure 5, Right shows the speedup of MagmaDNN's SGD training vs. Tensor-Flow train- ing on a system with up to 8 V100 GPUs. In this case MagmaDNN outperforms TensorFlow by about 50%. Shown also is a comparison to a peak performance of an asynchronous SGD. The large speedups illustrate the high potential that asynchronous methods have for accelerating the computation.

4.3 Hyperparameter Optimizations

We tested the hyperparameter optimization framework on a number of applications. Most notably, we used it as a proof of concept in the design, evaluation, and optimization of DNN architectures of increasing depth. For example, when applied to heart disease diagnosis [14], the hyperparameter optimization led to the discovery of a novel five layer DNN architecture that yields best prediction accuracy (using the publicly available Cleveland data set of medical information and a predefined search space), e.g., yielding 99% accuracy and 0.98 Matthews correlation coefficient (MCC), significantly outperforming currently published research in the area [14].

5 Conclusions and Future Directions

As the availability of exaflop computing capabilities approaches, deep learning continues to be far from utilizing the entirety of available computing power. Thus, it is crucial to continue and pursue distribution strategies and techniques for training deep networks on clusters and supercomputers.

MagmaDNN, due to its HPC MAGMA backend and initial speed, shows potential in becoming a tool for future deep learning applications. Its native C++ interface allows easier integration with existing C and fortran scientific codes. However, MagmaDNN currently lacks the arsenal of features present in other popular frameworks due to its infancy.

MagmaDNN aims to continue to add the necessary features for a full deep learning suite, while maintaining a fast scalable interface. Future development will focus on performance enhancements in distributed training, while providing a modular framework that allows for customization and tuning. Interfaces and ease of use are also very important, and to be able to compete with other frameworks, we are considering adding Python APIs to MagmaDNN.

6 Availability

MagmaDNN is currently developed and supported by the Innovative Computing Laboratory (ICL) and Joint Institute for Computer Science (JICS) at the University of Tennessee, Knoxville and Oak Ridge National Laboratory. Source code, documentation, tutorials, and licensing can all be found on the project's homepage[1].

Acknowledgments. This work was conducted at the Joint Institute for Computational Sciences (JICS) and the Innovative Computing Laboratory (ICL). This work is sponsored by the National Science Foundation (NSF), through NSF REU Award #1659502, with additional Support from the University of Tennessee, Knoxville (UTK), the National Institute for Computational Sciences (NICS), and NSF Awards #1740250 and #1709069. This work used the Extreme Science and Engineering Discovery Environment (XSEDE), which is supported by NSF grant #ACI-1548562. Computational Resources are available through a XSEDE education allocation awards TG-ASC170031 and TG-ASC190013. In addition, the computing work was also performed on technical workstations donated by the BP High Performance Computing Team, as well as on GPUs donated by NVIDIA.

---

[1] https://bitbucket.org/icl/magmadnn/.

References

1. Abadi, M., et al.: TensorFlow: large-scale machine learning on heterogeneous distributed systems. CoRR abs/1603.04467 (2016). http://arxiv.org/abs/1603.04467
2. Abdelfattah, A., Haidar, A., Tomov, S., Dongarra, J.: Performance, design, and autotuning of batched GEMM for GPUs. In: Kunkel, J.M., Balaji, P., Dongarra, J. (eds.) ISC High Performance 2016. LNCS, vol. 9697, pp. 21–38. Springer, Cham (2016). https://doi.org/10.1007/978-3-319-41321-1_2
3. Ben-Nun, T., Hoefler, T.: Demystifying parallel and distributed deep learning: an in-depth concurrency analysis. CoRR abs/1802.09941 (2018). http://arxiv.org/abs/1802.09941
4. Chen, J., Monga, R., Bengio, S., Józefowicz, R.: Revisiting distributed synchronous SGD. CoRR abs/1604.00981 (2016). http://arxiv.org/abs/1604.00981
5. Chen, S., Gessinger, A., Tomov, S.: Design and acceleration of convolutional neural networks on modern architectures. Technical report, Joint Institute for Computational Sciences (JICS), UTK (2018). 2018 Summer Research Experiences for Undergraduate (REU), Knoxville, TN 2018
6. Chetlur, S., et al.: cuDNN: efficient primitives for deep learning. CoRR abs/1410.0759 (2014). http://arxiv.org/abs/1410.0759
7. Gates, M., Tomov, S., Dongarra, J.: Accelerating the SVD two stage bidiagonal reduction and divide and conquer using GPUs. Parallel Comput. 74, 3–18 (2018). https://doi.org/10.1016/j.parco.2017.10.004. http://www.sciencedirect.com/scien ce/article/pii/S0167819117301758. Parallel Matrix Algorithms and Applications (PMAA'16)
8. Goyal, P., et al.: Accurate, large minibatch SGD: training imagenet in 1 hour. CoRR abs/1706.02677 (2017). http://arxiv.org/abs/1706.02677
9. Iandola, F.N., Ashraf, K., Moskewicz, M.W., Keutzer, K.: FireCaffe: near-linear acceleration of deep neural network training on compute clusters. CoRR abs/1511.00175 (2015). http://arxiv.org/abs/1511.00175
10. Jia, Y., et al.: Caffe: convolutional architecture for fast feature embedding. CoRR abs/1408.5093 (2014). http://arxiv.org/abs/1408.5093
11. Lecun, Y., Bottou, L., Bengio, Y., Haffner, P.: Gradient-based learning applied to document recognition. Proc. IEEE 86(11), 2278–2324 (1998). https://doi.org/10.1109/5.726791
12. Smith, S.L., Kindermans, P., Le, Q.V.: Don't decay the learning rate, increase the batch size. CoRR abs/1711.00489 (2017). http://arxiv.org/abs/1711.00489
13. Sorna, A., Cheng, X., D'Azevedo, E., Wong, K., Tomov, S.: Optimizing the fast fourier transform using mixed precision on tensor core hardware. In: 2018 IEEE 25th International Conference on High Performance Computing Workshops (HiPCW). pp. 3–7, December 2018. https://doi.org/10.1109/HiPCW.2018.8634417
14. Tomov, N., Tomov, S.: On deep neural networks for detecting heart disease. CoRR abs/1808.07168 (2018). http://arxiv.org/abs/1808.07168
15. Tomov, S., Dongarra, J., Baboulin, M.: Towards dense linear algebra for hybrid GPU accelerated manycore systems. Parallel Comput. 36(5), 232–240 (2010). https://doi.org/10.1016/j.parco.2009.12.005. http://www.sciencedirect.com/scien ce/article/pii/S0167819109001276. Parallel Matrix Algorithms and Applications

16. Tomov, S., Haidar, A., Ayala, A., Schultz, D., Dongarra, J.: Design and implementation for FFT-ECP on distributed accelerated systems. ECP WBS 2.3.3.09 Milestone Report FFT-ECP ST-MS-10-1410, Innovative Computing Laboratory, University of Tennessee, April 2019. 04–2019 revision

17. Wong, K., Brown, L., Coan, J., White, D.: Distributive interoperable executive library (DIEL) for systems of multiphysics simulation. In: 2014 15th International Conference on Parallel and Distributed Computing, Applications and Technologies, pp. 49–55. IEEE (2014)

18. You, Y., Gitman, I., Ginsburg, B.: Scaling SGD batch size to 32k for imagenet training. CoRR abs/1708.03888 (2017). http://arxiv.org/abs/1708.03888

19. You, Y., Zhang, Z., Hsieh, C., Demmel, J.: 100-epoch imagenet training with AlexNet in 24 minutes. CoRR abs/1709.05011 (2017). http://arxiv.org/abs/1709.05011

Open OnDemand: HPC for Everyone

Robert Settlage[1]([⊠]) [iD], Alan Chalker[2] [iD], Eric Franz[2] [iD], Doug Johnson[2] [iD],
Steve Gallo[3] [iD], Edgar Moore[1] [iD], and David Hudak[2] [iD]

[1] Advanced Research Computing, Virginia Tech, Blacksburg, VA 24060, USA
rsettlag@vt.edu
[2] Ohio Supercomputer Center, Columbus, OH 43212, USA
[3] Center for Computational Research, University of Buffalo, Buffalo, NY 14203, USA

Abstract. Open OnDemand is an open source project designed to lower the barrier to HPC use across many diverse disciplines. Here we describe the main features of the platform, give several use cases of Open OnDemand and discuss how we measure success. We end the paper with a discussion of the future project roadmap.

Keywords: Open OnDemand · Science gateways · High performance computing · Interactive · HPC

1 Introduction

In today's world, where we are producing, monitoring and making decisions based on many zettabytes of data daily, access to computing is of paramount importance [1]. To make sense of all of this data, many scientists rely on high performance computing (HPC) clusters. These clusters have been the workhorse in many domains such as engineering, physics, computational chemistry, and geosciences. Unfortunately, access to these computational tools is generally not through familiar web-based tools, but instead most frequently access is through a Secure Shell (SSH), requires familiarity with Linux and command-line, and file transfer tools (FTP) etc which, when taken in aggregate, has introduced a barrier to access of the computational power available in these HPC clusters. This accessibility gap is a long standing and recognized issue in HPC. Reducing, or ideally removing, this barrier will lead to immediate improvements in cluster accessibility and productivity across a wide range of data intensive disciplines.

Open OnDemand [2] is an innovative, open-source, web-based portal for accessing HPC services that removes these intricacies. By providing more familiar web-based access to the HPC clusters, not only does Open OnDemand reduce the barrier to use, it has also been shown to reduce the time to science. In fact, the median time from initial login to first job submission for all new OSC clients in 2017 using OnDemand was 10 times faster than those using traditional access methods. Through OnDemand, HPC users can upload and download files, create, edit, submit and monitor jobs, create and share apps, run GUI applications and

Supported by National Science Foundation grant 1835725.

M. Weiland et al. (Eds.): ISC 2019 Workshops, LNCS 11887, pp. 504–513, 2019.
https://doi.org/10.1007/978-3-030-34356-9_38

connect to a terminal, all via a web browser, with no client software to install and configure. OnDemand greatly simplifies access to HPC resources, freeing disciplinary scientists from having to worry about the operating environment and instead focus on their research. In this paper, we will focus on:

1. Open OnDemand features highlighting ease-of-use,
2. Examples and use cases,
3. Success stories,
4. Future work, i.e. the roadmap.

2 Features – Ease of Use

Open OnDemand is a web-based portal of entry to HPC clusters with a primary goal of lowering the barrier to use of the computational power and tools within the cluster. Open OnDemand provides a rich set of core web applications which leverage HTML5 standards and are securely hosted behind a web proxy providing federated authentication. All the user needs to access OnDemand is a modern web browser and their HPC credentials. OnDemand provides HPC centers a "zero-install" (i.e. no native SSH, SFTP, or VNC client necessary) and single sign-on (SSO) solution for their users.

In an Open OnDemand enabled HPC center, a user can access the clusters by using command line SSH or by browsing to the OnDemand URL hosted by the HPC center and authenticating with their HPC credentials. Thus, Open OnDemand does not replace traditional access but rather provides another avenue to gain access. Upon authentication, the user is presented with the Dashboard App which serves as the landing page for OnDemand and enables discovery of the various OnDemand apps, Fig. 1. Note the Dashboard App allows for HPC center branding and news/message of day display (left Fig. 1). A default installation of OnDemand includes the following core apps: File Explorer and File Editor for file management, Active Jobs and Job Composer for job management and monitoring, as well as a Shell App for command line access. Note that OnDemand allows a single portal to several clusters within the HPC center. For instance, at Virginia Tech, we currently have an IBM Power8 and two X86 clusters served by a single OnDemand portal.

In this basic installation, Open OnDemand has simplified the user experience by giving users a more familiar web portal to the HPC systems and simple tools to transfer files to/from the system and finally both a text editor and job composer. These basic tools are all web based and allow users to skip the command line to move files, edit scripts and submit job requests all via the web portal.

The basic functionality described above is really the launching point for center and user customization. HPC Centers can tailor the application set to those found most used or that cause the most tickets to create a highly customized installation. Open OnDemand supports web applications written in a variety of languages including Ruby, Python and Node.js and allows for creating custom user applications. These can, for instance, be used to make portals for interactive apps such as Jupyter Notebooks, Rstudio, Matlab, ParaView, Comsol, etc

Fig. 1. On the left, the Dashboard app landing page showing branding and message of day. On the right, an example of the app landing page showing users the current apps installed at VT.

(see Fig. 1 right for example). Similarly, users can create modifications to the standard (or Center) installed set of applications to create tools more suitable to their individual workflows. To further enable this, the Dashboard comes with a plug-in style wrapper to stream-line the App development process. Not only can users edit and create custom apps, they can share these new apps with other users. Through this extensibility mechanism, we envision OnDemand capable of remaining a relevant tool to enabling use of HPC resources across many disciplines today and in the future.

3   Example Apps and Use Cases

At this point, Open OnDemand has a diverse user base and has seen many successes. Below we highlight three important applications, two are standard upon installation of Open OnDemand while the third is an Interactive App showing the extensibility of the platform.

3.1   Files App

The Files App is perhaps the most important example of how presenting users with familiar tools can lower the barrier to use of HPC clusters. Traditional command line access via SSH requires file management from a terminal. While users familiar with Linux are used to the raw and powerful file editing and transfer tools such as vim, ftp, scp and rsync, for new users, this is often a formidable barrier. The Files App (Fig. 2) provides another avenue to create files and folders, view files,

Fig. 2. The Files App gives users a web-based look at HPC storage allowing them to manage files in a familiar environment.

manipulate file locations, upload and download files all in the familiar tree view users are accustomed to using on their local system. Providing this file management interface both reduces the anxiety of new users and reduces inadvertent learning errors (e.g. *rm -rf*).

3.2   Job Composer

The most important aspect of working in an HPC environment is navigating the complexities of submitting compute tasks as a job to a resource scheduler such as PBS, LSF or Slurm. Indeed, interacting with resource schedulers is an often daunting, confusing and yet necessary component of working on shared HPC systems. To facilitate the use of schedulers, Open OnDemand has an application, the Job Composer, which provides a web-based utility for creating and managing batch jobs from template directories (Fig. 3). The Job Composer App attempts to model a simple but common workflow typical of users in HPC centers. When users create new batch jobs they often:

1. Copy a directory of a previous job, either one of their previous jobs or a job from a group member
2. Make minor modifications to the input files
3. Submit this new job.

Through the Job Composer, users can create new jobs based on previous jobs (templates), create new job templates, view status of jobs, view results and more. By abstracting away the command line to facilitate this workflow, the Job Composer again allows use of familiar tools to accomplish HPC tasks such as job creation, scheduling and deletion.

Fig. 3. The Job Composer App provides a template based abstraction to submit jobs to HPC schedulers.

3.3   Jupyter Notebooks

Much of science is accomplished through interactive GUI based applications, if not for the full compute, for prototyping, troubleshooting, experimenting and creating figures. A hallmark of Open OnDemand is that not only does it *allow* interactive applications, it *facilitates* their use through providing a mechanism to abstract the environment setup and gives users a mechanism to connect to the running application (often a weblink). In the case of Jupyter Notebooks, OnDemand creates a batch job, configures the environment and gives the user a clickable weblink to the running Jupyter Notebook (Fig. 4). Due to the demand for interactive GUI applications such as Jupyter Notebooks, Matlab, Rstudio, Comsol etc, the Dashboard comes with a plug-in style wrapper designed to streamline App development. Importantly, sites can develop site specific apps for distribution to their users.

Fig. 4. Interactive App page showing status of a Jupyter Notebook job (left). The link sends the user to the running Jupyter Notebook (right).

4   Successes

4.1   VT OpenPOWER Hackathon

In Spring 2019, VT hosted an OpenPOWER Hackathon. The goal of the hackathon was to expose users to the acceleration possible when using the PowerAI framework on an IBM Power8 cluster. Many of the participants were new HPC users but had significant experience with creating Deep Learning applications on local hardware. Often, new HPC cluster users, even those familiar with Linux, experience some amount of time lag between account creation and first successful job. In a limited time hackathon, this added overhead distracts from the goal of the hackathon by shifting the focus from the hackathon topic to learning HPC idiosyncrasies. By utilizing the Open OnDemand web portal, we were able to successfully launch the hackathon with no user setup and had users computing in Jupyter Notebooks as soon as they typed in the web address. Further, we were able to create an OnDemand App with the PowerAI environment preloaded as a conda environment. The conda environment included all the PowerAI optimized tools including TensorFlow, mpi, ddlrun etc. For those users that took advantage of the Open OnDemand interface, we had zero issues and very little time was required to get these users into a computing environment such that we had more time to discuss the hackathon topics and less time was devoted to troubleshooting user environment issues. As an added benefit, some users were interested in using TensorBoard to view the neural networks they were creating to troubleshoot, monitor performance, etc. Typically, this is an added complexity many users struggle with. Of course, users familiar with creating SSH tunnels and using port forwarding are fully capable of setting up the environment and starting a TensorBoard. However, our observation is even more sophisticated users choose to use the OnDemand app when available so that they can focus on the compute task rather than environment setup.

4.2 Using HPC in the Classroom

Similar to the issues faced in a limited duration hackathon, introducing students to HPC in a classroom setting can be daunting if the students are new to the command line, unfamiliar with SSH, and likely new to Linux. OnDemand simplifies this introduction by abstracting away the initial SSH via the Shell App and unifies the user experience by providing a single portal to gain access to the HPC compute. At VT, we have seen a dramatic decrease in the initial time to get students on our local HPC clusters. What was taking 45 min of an hour lecture, making sure all the students had the proper tools installed (Putty, Terminal, etc) and logged in via 2-factor authentication, now takes less than 15 min and frees the instructor from troubleshooting local student platform issues allowing the focus to quickly return to the domain topic the instructor had planned. Improving this initial experience is often critical in keeping the attention and participation within a classroom setting. Even if the instructor simply uses OnDemand as the portal to the Shell App, we see an improved experience from two features: (1) all clusters enabled in the OnDemand installation are available in a pull-down menu (Fig. 5) and (2) in our 2-factor environment, users are fully authenticated in the browser such that the Shell App is running as user. It is our observation that this simple change, moving from multiple platform based shell access tools, to a single web-based shell tool is the single largest momentum changer when instructors are choosing local vs cloud resources for compute intensive courses.

 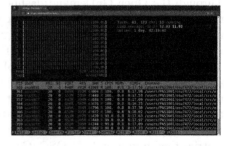

Fig. 5. Left: The Dashboard app landing page showing the shell app pulldown allowing users to select target cluster. Right: A running shell.

5   Future Work

In 2018, OSC with partners from Virginia Tech and SUNY Buffalo were awarded an NSF grant under the CSSI program managed by the Office of Advanced Cyber-infrastructure This $3.3M award (#1835725) provides funding through the end of 2023 and is formally titled "Frameworks: Software NSCI-Open OnDemand 2.0: Advancing Accessibility and Scalability for Computational Science through Leveraged Software Cyberinfrastructure" This new project combines two widely used HPC resources:

- Open OnDemand 1.0 - an existing open-source, web-based project for accessing HPC services; and
- Open XDMoD - an open-source tool that facilitates the management of HPC resources.

with the following objectives:

1. Visibility: Leverage XDMoD seamlessly from OnDemand, creating a unified platform for scientists to work with and optimize their HPC work.
2. Accessibility: Improve the OnDemand interface for more scientists & fields of science.
3. Scalability: Extend the scalability of OnDemand for more platforms and applications.
4. Engagement: Conduct a program to engage departmental, campus and national HPC users along with the Science Gateway community to drive adoption and follow-on development.

Here we highlight three aspects of the current efforts.

5.1   Visibility

Monitoring system health and job performance is an important aspect of operating and using high performance computing clusters. The overall system health and status of a cluster is useful on many levels but from a users perspective is often an indicator of where (what queue or cluster) they should submit new jobs. Through the Open OnDemand dashboard, HPC administrators currently have the ability to give system status messages (Message of Day). While this can alert users to quality of service issues, more granular and informative statistics as provided by XDMoD are often desirable. Efforts are currently underway to provide a mechanism for integration of XDMoD into Open OnDemand. A prototype is shown in Fig. 6. Through this integration project, OnDemand users will be able to explore HPC resource availability at their local center. By exposing this data to the users, they will have the information available to choose systems based on shorter queue time, higher availability of resources, quality of service, or other metrics they find useful. At OSC, Ganglia graphs providing static views of high level compute job resource utilization statistics have been integrated into job summaries. Through this integration project, we will expose users to the additional functionality offered by XDMoD. XDMoD allows users to view detailed performance information on their individual jobs and drill down to gain additional insights into how a job has performed including utilization of individual cores, filesystem throughput, and network activity over the course of the job. By providing this easily accessible and usable view into job performance, we anticipate both experienced and novice users alike will identify aspects of their computations to optimize and improve.

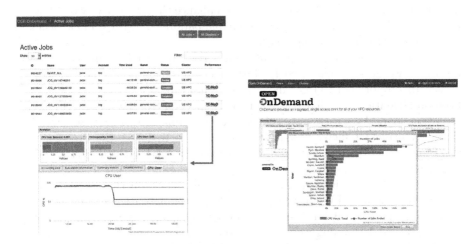

Fig. 6. On the left, completed jobs showing XDMoD links for exploration of job performance. On the right, the prototype XDMoD dashboard in Open OnDemand. Clicking on any chart displays an expanded view and allows the user to also view the chart directly in XDMoD for additional functionality.

5.2 Accessibility and Scalability

Open OnDemand has an overarching goal of presenting HPC in a way that makes the computing resources more accessible to more users. We see this as a challenge to both enable less sophisticated users and enhance the veteran power user. For the less sophisticated user, as discussed above, the first step in accessibility is providing the user with more familiar tools to access the resources, i.e. web-based file management, job management and file editors. As we move forward with these users, we envision we will need to further simplify the job execution phases of HPC use. This could come in the form of (a) tailoring some functionality towards a specific user base and (b) providing more available apps spanning more fields of science. In many cases, job execution could be completely automated and the functionality pushed from the users local desktop. For these situations, we envision creation of a "desktop metaphore". In our vision, a user could have an icon on their local computing device with the built in functionality to transfer data, submit a job to computing queue, and notify the user of successful completion of the compute job. In a simple example, a user may drag and drop a Matlab file on a Matlab icon preconfigured to send the file and start the simulation on the local cluster.

Many data science and computing fields have been emphasizing repeatability and reproducibility. To facilitate this, we will enable git functionality within the Job Composer to allow users to automatically commit job scripts into a code repository. This will serve two purposes. First, users will have an offline copy of their working scripts. Second, in team settings, code repositories are an oft used method of collaboration. While much of our effort has been lowering the barrier for novice users, we are looking for ways to enhance the productivity of all users. For advanced users, we are working to enable parameter sweeps, job arrays and more advanced multi-step pipelines.

While the Files App in it current form is transformative for many users and use cases, we do see some need for further enhancements. Specifically, there is a need to support both larger file transfers and directory transfers. Both have been problematic for similar reasons, namely speed of transfer and length of user attention span. As a user moves their attention from the current task which is queued waiting for file(s) upload, the tendency is to forget the process is in-flight and inadvertently the system is shutdown, laptop lid closed, etc. These are solvable issues and simply need some development time.

Cloud computing is an important computing platform that is complementary to traditional HPC clusters. Some compute jobs/duties are better suited to a cloud environment but are still an important part of computing workloads. Examples include running webservers as data collection devices, web based portals to submit data queries that may spawn HPC jobs, support of multiple operating systems for specialty software, etc. In our view, cloud is simply another tool in a computing environment that enables our researchers. As such, supporting spawning of virtual machines (VMs) in a cloud system should be another app in Open OnDemand. Work is currently underway to extend the OnDemand apps to include native spawning of VMs though calls to an on-prem OpenStack installation at Virginia Tech. This work will also be extended to provisioning VMs on public cloud systems as well.

5.3 Engagement

As with any software development project, success is an iterative milestone. As this is community software, our users need to specify the milestones and give the measure of success. Key to any community project is engagement and outreach to keep the project focused on user needs. To keep Open OnDemand relevant to the community, we need to engage the community of users continuously to stay abreast of the state of the art codes and processing methods. As the community develops, OnDemand must follow. Today, web-based portals are the familiar interface users are looking for. Perhaps the next wave will be towards mobile device applets. To ensure we are connected to the community, we have formed an Advisory Group with representatives from many institutions spanning academia and industry. This group meets at least Quarterly and discusses topics relevant to Open OnDemand usefulness, adoption, design, code sharing etc. Our current schedule has us meeting at PEARC and Supercomputing with more frequent user meetings.

References

1. Reinsel, D., Grantz, J., Rydning, J.: The Digitization of the World - From Edge to Core. IDC White Paper - #US44413318 (2018)
2. Hudak, D., et al.: Open OnDemand a web-based client portal for HPC centers. J. Open Sour. Softw. **3**(25), 622 (2018). https://doi.org/10.21105/joss.00622

Highly Interactive, Steered Scientific Workflows on HPC Systems: Optimizing Design Solutions

John R. Ossyra[1], Ada Sedova[2]([✉]) [ID], Matthew B. Baker[2] [ID], and Jeremy C. Smith[1,2] [ID]

[1] University of Tennessee, Knoxville, TN, USA
[2] Oak Ridge National Laboratory, Oak Ridge, TN, USA
sedovaaa@ornl.gov

Abstract. Scientific workflows are becoming increasingly important in high performance computing (HPC) settings, as the feasibility and appeal of many simultaneous heterogeneous tasks increases with increasing hardware capabilities. Currently no HPC-based workflow platform supports a dynamically adaptable workflow with interactive steering and analysis at run-time. Furthermore, for most workflow programs, compute resources are fixed for a given instance, resulting in a possible waste of expensive allocation resources when tasks are spawned and killed. Here we describe the design and testing of a run-time-interactive, adaptable, steered workflow tool capable of executing thousands of parallel tasks without an MPI programming model, using a database management system to facilitate task management through multiple live connections. We find that on the Oak Ridge Leadership Computing Facility pre-exascale Summit supercomputer it is possible to launch and interactively steer workflows with thousands of simultaneous tasks with negligible latency. For the case of particle simulation and analysis tasks that run for minutes to hours, this paradigm offers the prospect of a robust and efficient means to perform simulation-space exploration with on-the-fly analysis and adaptation.

Keywords: High performance computing · Scientific workflows · External steering · Adaptable workflows

This manuscript has been authored by UT-Battelle, LLC under Contract No. DE-AC05-00OR22725 with the U.S. Department of Energy. The United States Government retains and the publisher, by accepting the article for publication, acknowledges that the United States Government retains a non-exclusive, paid-up, irrevocable, world-wide license to publish or reproduce the published form of this manuscript, or allow others to do so, for United States Government purposes. The Department of Energy will provide public access to these results of federally sponsored research in accordance with the DOE Public Access Plan (http://energy.gov/downloads/doe-public-access-plan).

© Springer Nature Switzerland AG 2019
M. Weiland et al. (Eds.): ISC 2019 Workshops, LNCS 11887, pp. 514–527, 2019.
https://doi.org/10.1007/978-3-030-34356-9_39

1 Introduction and Background

Scientific workflows are an increasingly common tool for high performance computing (HPC) based scientific efforts. As performance and system size increase in HPC systems, the numbers of single, static computing problems that can utilize the entire machine efficiently are decreasing. Meanwhile, the feasibility, efficiency, and appeal of multiple simultaneous but heterogeneous calculations, including simulations, data analysis, model re-parameterization, and incorporation of machine learning on leadership resources, is increasing. In the HPC environment there is a need for workflow software that can handle account allocations, schedulers, and multiple levels of parallelism within each component, and can scale to thousands of nodes.

Recently, groups in many areas of computational science have realized that a need for HPC-specific workflow managers exists [28]. However, currently no such platform supports a dynamically adaptable workflow with interactive steering at run-time. In fact, in a recent overview of existing workflow management systems, the ability to externally steer the workflow was not a supported feature in any of the commonly used programs studied [23]. With designs that use the Message Passing Interface (MPI), the directed acyclic graph (DAG) that represents the workflow is relatively rigid, as the allocated hardware resources are fixed for a given instance. In addition, there may be limitations of fault tolerance handling: the entire workflow may terminate when one task fails [6].

A family of relevant use cases is based in condensed matter particle simulations, which increasingly utilize ensemble calculations (many parallel compute jobs) to enhance sampling of simulation phase space [2,3,14,24,29]. It is possible to reconstruct physical processes on timescales much longer than those directly sampled by simulations with statistical methods [5,8,11,16,26,27]. For example, algorithms derived from statistical mechanics [9,15] can be coupled with time-series and spectral analysis to determine rates and energetic barriers of physical processes [9,11,27].

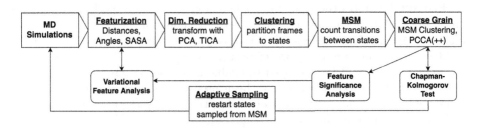

Fig. 1. Flowchart of the iterative analyses used to determine the degree of sampling of an Markov-state model (MSM)-based ensemble MD simulation, leading to adaptive selection of restart states targeted to simulate poorly sampled regions.

Adaptive sampling from Markov-state models (MSM) is one such technique. MSMs describe a dynamical phenomenon as a Markovian process on some timescale [17,21]. The appropriate timescale can be determined by a statistical analysis of time-correlations of features of the system, chosen to best describe the temporal evolution of the process of interest [4,19].

An extensive analysis pipeline has been developed to build a Markov model from ensembles of molecular dynamics (MD) simulations using TICA (Time-lagged Independent Component Analysis), various clustering techniques, PCCA+ (Perron Cluster Cluster Analysis), and validated by Chapman-Kolmogorov tests [10,12,22]. This analysis has been implemented using the Python package PyEmma [22]. Figure 1 illustrates the steps involved in building an MSM and sampling restart states from it.

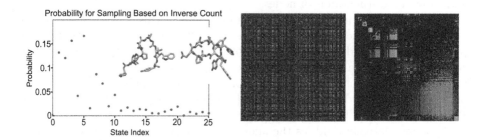

Fig. 2. Left panel: Discrete probability distribution for sampling of starting positions for second round of ensemble simulations in an MSM-driven adaptive sampling workflow; Inset: Two macrostates of chignolin protein determined by an adaptive sampling workflow, the stable and the metastable state. Right panel: Markov matrix of preliminary transition probabilities for microstates before (left side) and after (right side) grouping into macrostates using PCCA+, during a particular iteration of the workflow cycle. Heat map goes from low probability, dark blue, to high probability, light green. Light-colored blocks in the sorted matrix correspond to transition probabilities between distinct macrostates determined at that analysis step.

Figure 2 illustrates the results of some analyses that were performed within an MSM simulation workflow on a small protein, chignolin, using the Titan computer, a Cray XK7 machine at the Oak Ridge Leadership Computing Facility (OLCF). With an interactive workflow this analysis would be performed *in situ* and output could be displayed to enable user interactions that ultimately steer the DAG. Workflow tools have been used by our team to run ensemble MSM molecular dynamics simulations using the OpenMM program [7] as the MD simulation engine, and statistical analysis done with the PyEMMA library [22]. Workflows were executed over multiple instances of resource allocation, for example, over several HPC jobs that use the (often short) allowable job time limits on many HPC systems, using a Python-based workflow tool with the MongoDB NoSQL database management system (DBMS) providing a database-centric architecture [18] for synchronization of analysis data and workflow state. While not a new concept [1], use of DBMS programs within scientific workflow platforms has recently increased: several scientific workflow management solutions have incorporated both SQL and NoSQL DBMSs into their software design. For instance, Copernicus uses a Python interface with sqlite [20], and the Fireworks workflow program uses MongoDB [13].

Remarkably, none of these programs, including those we have developed, has to our knowledge used the functionality of the DBMS to provide interactive and externally steered workflow solutions. In the context of adaptive sampling workflows, the ability to analyze at run-time a set of simulations in order to determine the amount of sampling and degree of Markovianity of the modeled stochastic process at a given point, and to steer the DAG to better sample the space by starting new tasks, killing tasks, and modifying existing tasks, provides a means to maximize the efficiency of the process and the usage of allocation time.

Figure 3 illustrates run-time steering, with a DAG adaptation that can be employed for resource-use optimization in particle-simulation workflows. In this case, a user would like to maximize the efficient use of a limited allocation on a supercomputer, by determining the best compute task configuration for ensemble simulations of protein folding using the same total node hours: many short simulations, or fewer, longer simulations. The example shows how a measurement can be made on the dataset, in this case, each simulation frame's "distance" from the starting state measured by the root-mean-square deviation (RMSD) of atomic positions. We see in Fig. 3 that an increased RMSD distance between the unfolded starting structure and the structures sampled over the longer simulations corresponds with a decrease in RMSD to the final folded state. While the final state may not be known, the increased RMSD from starting state may provide one of many heuristics that can be used to steer the initial phases to

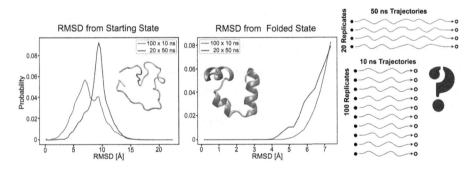

Fig. 3. Example of an interactive steering action. Given a limited HPC allocation, a researcher would like to find regions of conformation space of a protein closest to a folded state. Left panel: RMSD from unfolded starting state. Middle panel: RMSD from folded crystal structure. This folded structure may not be available. However, the increased RMSD away from the starting state is seen to correspond to smaller RMSD distance from folded state in this dataset. Right panel: A choice can be made during run-time to launch fewer, longer trajectories vs. more numerous, shorter trajectories to use a fixed HPC allocation in the next round of simulations.

more efficient exploration. This RMSD analysis informs the choice of trajectory layout for the next round of simulations (indicated by the right panel).

2 Design of an Interactive, Externally-Steered DBMS-Based Workflow Tool

Here we describe the design of a run-time-interactive, adaptable, steered workflow tool capable of executing thousands of parallel tasks without an MPI programming model. A limited implementation of the lower-level components can be found at https://github.com/pawtools/nopaw. In creating such an externally-steered simulation workflow, we would like to allow as much interactive manipulation of the directed acyclic graph DAG and the underlying tasks as desired. The use of DBMS software in scientific workflow programs has been discussed in recent literature within the context of HPC and massively parallel distributed solutions [25], but has not been extensively studied for performance, scalability, and reliability on leadership systems. However, we hypothesize that the DBMS can allow highly-interactive run-time steering of complex workflows even on pre-exascale systems. In this design, the database program facilitates multiple live connections which rapidly query a consistent universal state. This transfer of information allows for on-the-fly receipt of workflow component operations, sampling from the database and the tasks in the workflow, and synchronization of new tasks to be executed, potentially immediately, by executors who are distributed on arbitrary resources. Here we show results of tests of these capabilities on the Summit supercomputer (https://www.olcf.ornl.gov/olcf-resources/compute-systems/summit), an IBM Power System AC922, and discuss how these results inform design requirements for successful implementation of an interactively-steerable workflow tool.

2.1 Requirements for Workflow Interactivity

In order to determine design requirements for an interactive DBMS-based workflow tool, we created a modular, minimal working example of a steerable and run-time interactive scientific workflow platform. This allows us to test the performance and scaling in a systematic, building-block manner.

Table 1. Requirements for externally steered interactive workflow program using a DBMS

Requirement	Function
Multiple live connections	Direct signaling activity
Mirrored objects	Continual state synchronization
Controller object	Signal propagation, resource management
Heartbeat signal	Robust resource control
Locales	Resolved everywhere in distributed application

Table 1 displays the components we found were essential to an interactive and externally-steered workflow. For an interactive, asynchronous, distributed, workload-execution application we noted the need for easy and direct access to the working directory of task instances from the task and executor APIs. This functionality was not included in a non-interactive version of the workflow tool, and presented a challenge to resolve and add to the API *ex post facto*. This and similar experiences led us to conclude that design choices for a steerable application must be included in the preliminary program design, as first-class programmatic elements and architectural features.

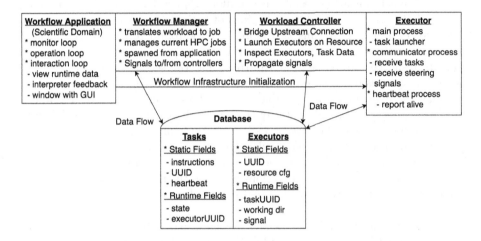

Fig. 4. Design of a complete, interactive workflow application, with top panel showing programmatic infrastructure, and bottom panel indicating essential data fields for information flow resulting in steering. Requirements include live mapping of output data to the application for interactive visualization (GUI or text), a connection for input to and feedback from the task-management (workflow) infrastructure, and universal locale fields for targeting specific components and/or their data.

Figure 4 illustrates the complete design that we have arrived at for an interactively steered workflow program. Six major hierarchical components constitute this steerable, distributed, and asynchronous application design:

- a **scientific workflow application** generates the workflow instructions (i.e. tasks and the DAG),
- a **workflow manager** submits workloads, i.e. batches of tasks, to possibly multiple HPC Local Resource Management Systems (LRMS),
- a **workload controller** propagates instructions and manages workload execution in an HPC job at run-time,
- **executors**, distributed on the compute resource, acquire task instructions and execute them,
- a **DBMS** stores fields used to compose workflow object instances, including static object data and stateful run-time data, and

– **tasks**, each consisting of a set of instructions, are executed using a share-nothing dataflow programming model.

The steering capability itself originates from two related design choices. One of these is a **multiconnection model**, wherein multiple components (executors and controller in the test cases) are provided live connections to the database. These multiple live connections are required for immediate querying of task states, task locations, and the ability to change a task. The second design choice requires each connected component run a **synchronization loop** in a background process that continually synchronizes instances with the database. This continual synchronization results in workflow application instances containing *mirrored objects*, i.e. up-to-date reflections of their state in the database.

A steerable executor runs two loops in background processes. A repeated regular "heartbeat" signal is broadcast from one loop so the controller can easily validate resource use on tasks at run-time, and the second loop iterates state and signal queries to synchronize with the database and controller. To facilitate steering, the controller must be able to close down components and relinquish resources quickly but reliably at any time. One challenging scenario to manage without a heartbeat is the case of a silent executor failure; without a continual communication channel, the controller does not register that the resource has failed. To efficiently utilize an allocation in the case of failures, the controller can checkpoint job shutdown operations based on the time since a heartbeat was detected, or try to restart failed executors based on their individual heartbeat signals.

Tasks run inside executors, which are launched onto a compute resource using command-line tools provided by the system job launcher, such as `mpirun`. Executors are not explicitly bound to tasks until they poll the database for new tasks that match the compute resource they provide. This design offers a layer for control of operations such as stopping or releasing tasks, unexpected shutdown, or starting a new task. An individual task can itself be a parallel executable that uses a threaded or Message Passing Interface (MPI) based programming model. Executors for batches of homogeneous, non-MPI tasks can be launched using a single launch call, whereas N inhomogeneous or MPI-containing tasks require N individual calls to the task launcher.

Executors each connect to the database, thus communication to the database host(s) increases with growth in workload scale. The ability of the host hardware and the network to support the growing number of connections is the limitation on the performance of workflow activity associated with run-time interaction and steering. The controller is supported by a single connection. The controller reads and writes more data than the executors by a factor on the order of the number of live executors it controls. Performance and scaling of these communication operations for each software component on Summit is discussed below.

In a distributed workflow system, the network address, data file locations, and workflow component identities must be accessible to be utilized at run-time by controlling components and the application instance to enable the steering capability. Uniform Resource Locators (URLs) were used in the test application to navigate within local workloads. A data structure may be required for expanding the capacities of the program. Interactive requests can be made by the application, and propagated by messages to the controller/executors to alter their behavior or inspect run-time data. To accurately target these requests to the correct location within distributed resource network, locale information must be registered in the database system as each component is initialized. We assigned a universal unique identifier (uuid) to all workflow components, including output-file representations in the database, to ensure that every component can be easily and uniquely targeted with instructions, signals, and data-specific future tasks, and located by controllers for inspection.

In the general case, signalled activity may include pre-programmed workflow operations such as starting, pausing, or restarting tasks, or other functionality defined by the user. In many use-cases, these steering signals will result from user inspection of workflow/task output data synchronized at run-time by a controller with the upstream domain application. This ability to propagate both a signal and associated action defined by the user at run-time is an essential capability for a steered scientific workflow.

2.2   Implementation for Performance Testing

The minimal workflow tool used for testing the performance of workflow steering operations includes controller, executor, and task objects. The DBMS-based communication was implemented using minimal task and executor documents similar to that shown in Fig. 4. Run-time data included executor/task states and steering messages incumbent from the interaction.

Signaling messages propagate from an off-resource interaction by first assigning a value (e.g. the message) to the signal attribute of the executors. The synchronization loop then inserts the message into the database so the DMBS state reflects the updated instance. The resource-bound, live executor then synchronizes the new value to its instance to reflect the changed database state. These signals trigger a corresponding activity in the live executor and then are cleared by that executor. Synchronization loops can inspect heartbeat time-stamps when a discrepancy is encountered between an instance and the database, indicating an updated value, to accurately determine the old and updated states. Another approach would be to reserve special attributes that lists changes and their originating instances (i.e. object or database), so that the update can be correctly targeted to either the instance or database. The continual synchronization of changed values, so that the instances and corresponding database documents are mirrored, is the basis of the steering functionality.

3   Testing the Components of the Program

Interactively-steered workflows using a DBMS and designed with many live connections increase the network traffic to and from the database server, compared to non-interactive models. Therefore the ability of a server that is launched on a single compute node to simultaneously perform many thousands of communications must be tested. In addition, it is necessary to test whether the interaction with the workflow, as well as the steering actions, affect workflow performance.

We tested the workflow components on the Oak Ridge Leadership Computing Facility (OLCF) Summit computer, an IBM Power System AC922. OLCF Summit consist of 4608 IBM Power System AC922 nodes. Each node contains two IBM POWER9 processors and six NVIDIA Volta V100 accelerators. Summit uses Red Hat Enterprise Linux Server release 7.6 (Maipo) as an operating system. We used the MongoDB DBMS, version 3.6.11 with the ppc64le build, PyMongo 3.7.2, Python 3.7.3, and NumPy 1.15.4. Figure 5 displays the components of the workflow which were timed with internal timers to provide performance data.

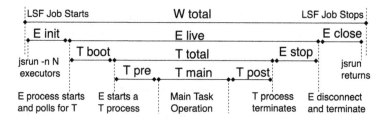

Fig. 5. Diagram of the components of the interaction tests that were timed.

3.1 Testing the Database Program

To characterize the baseline performance of a workflow application that relies on small document transactions to propagate information flow between execution and application layers, we measured the performance of read and write operations on Summit using the Mongo database program. Communication by these document transactions constitutes the information flow resulting in interaction and steering. The majority of these documents in typical use cases will contain only small fields describing task operations, metadata, state updates, and signals to the executors. A weak-scaling experiment was used to test the performance of single instances of mass workflow communication for both reads and writes between executors and a database instance, corresponding to the cases of task initialization by the executor and feedback by executors to the application or a controller.

To perform the experiment, single LSF jobs were used to run workloads consisting of a batch of tasks. The number of concurrent tasks was varied from 250 to 16,000, and message size from 3.2 kB to 1.6 MB. Executors on single CPUs (42 per node on Summit) ran tasks consisting of the given read or write operation, followed by a 60 s sleep. Figure 6 displays the results of these scaling tests. We also tested a 13 MB file size, which is near the MongoDB per-document size limit of 16 MB and is not included in the figures, but was run to test for

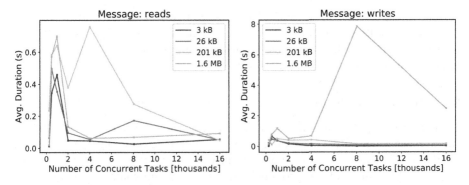

Fig. 6. Scaling of MongoDB database communication tasks on Summit, using variable file sizes. Left panel: reads. Right panel: writes. Standard deviation for all read and most write tests was below 0.7 s. Standard deviation for writing 1.6 MB documents was approximately 2 s for 4000 and 16000 tasks, and 15 s for 8000 tasks. This variability may be a reflection of system fluctuations at the time the tests were executed.

general points of failure. The expected use cases are not likely to require MBs of task-associated instructions and documents, and so are bounded by the 1.6 MB case of this test.

The average duration of the majority of these communication tests is on the order of one second or less, with the exception of instances executing many thousands of simultaneous large-size write operations (Fig. 6, right panel). Write operations of this size and concurrency would only occur when updating raw output data from highly synchronized executors. These tests showed a total latency of 5–10 s, thus it is likely that synchronizing data output from all tasks might take seconds to propagate to the controller and application components. Notably this delay is only in the case of the DMBS receiving data from completely synchronized tasks, which is not an activity expected at high scales. As tested and discussed below, controllers local to executors at run-time can inspect on-disk task data with no such penalty.

Read and write tests with smaller documents correspond to the majority of communication activity expected in a workflow, such as repeated status and heartbeat updates from each executor. These data indicate that no appreciable latency occurred as a controller queries the moment-to-moment state of its executors at any tested scale. The low latency observed for reads of any document size and tested scale indicates that the ability to expediently poll the database is not affected by the number of simultaneous requests from other components or the size of the requested document. All connections supported successful transactions for the scales and data sizes shown in Fig. 6, indicating the resiliency of a DBMS-based workflow program. When transacting 13 MB, read operations succeeded with negligible latency at all scales, however write operations failed for 3.0% (241) of 8,000 tasks, and 33.7% (5394) of 16,000 tasks.

The total time required for up to 16,000 read or write communications, for any of the data sizes shown, is much less than the typical simulation workflow length, which can last for dozens of minutes to hours. Thus we find this design of using a DBMS to synchronize workflow components, propagate signals, and transfer workflow/task output data, provides a suitable basis for creating a low-latency run-time-interactive and steerable workflow program.

3.2   Testing the Performance of Steering Interactions

There are two modes of steering activity that we consider: interactions that change the number of executors, and interactions that steer the executors themselves. Assuming efficient use of the allocation in which resources are not left to idle, changing the number of executors results from some combination of acquiring of new compute resources to spawn new executors, and remapping existing executors to provide a different hardware configuration. This remapping capability is implemented in some programs for non-steered workflows: in a single HPC job executors can be launched multiple times and with different resource configurations, from a previously characterized DAG. The second mode of steering activity requires an executor to start a new task after stopping its current task, or modifying its current task in some way. Each case requires a component that continually interacts with the database to receive messages, achieved with background synchronization loops. This functionality may be restricted to the controller in the first mode of steering, but the second mode requires executor synchronization to change tasks that are currently running, and update state and task data for inspection and further interaction by upstream workflow components.

Executor Spawn: Acquisition of New Resources. To spawn new executors and increase the number of running tasks, a new workload is queued to acquire additional compute resources from the Local Resource Management System (LRMS). This was successfully tested on OLCF Titan and Summit by making a submission to the LRMS by the controller component (from inside an HPC job). In the case of HPC systems that do not allow job submission from within a running job, the submission would be made from a login node by the workflow manager.

Executor Steering: Check, Pause, and Restart. Results of three executor steering tests, displayed in Fig. 7, show the effect on task-execution time from: a run-time inspection of output data, a pause in the task, and a task restart. A control test used executors and a controller with no synchronization loops, and thus no interaction that might affect task execution. For each case the main task was delegated to a subprocess, and consisted of an executable repeatedly writing a string to a task data output file for 60 s. In the three steering cases, non-blocking synchronization loops were run by the executors in background processes to mitigate or eliminate any effect on the main process execution. The controller similarly ran synchronization and interaction loops in the background, which repeatedly queried the state and task properties of all executors. The output data file locations were determined by the controller from task and executor properties.

These tests emulated steering operations propagated from a domain application or user triggering the controller to inspect all task data in a synchronization loop at some time after all executors have started their tasks. After inspection, the controller either did not issue a signal, signalled a 15 s pause, or signalled a task restart to all executors. The effect of including the synchronization loops in the design without performing steering is shown by the inspection-only case (Fig. 7, orange vs. blue bars, left panel). Task execution is seen to be unaffected by both the presence of the background synchronization operations in the executor component and data inspection operations done by the controller.

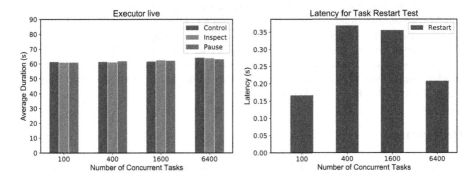

Fig. 7. Performance testing of three steering interactions. Left: total live executor time for the inspect and pause tests, versus a control with no interaction. The total duration for pause tests excludes the 15 s pause. Right: latency incurred for task restarts. This test involves stopping running executables at unpredictable times, so latency was calculated by subtracting the total task time for the incomplete and complete tasks from the executor live time.

Pause and restart signals were propagated by the controller first modifying all executors simultaneously, and the live executors subsequently reading the signal via the synchronization loop. The executors were thus directed to execute an action by the controller's signal. Full-scale steering of every executor was conducted here to test the limit of performance. Figure 7 shows that the total run-time (excluding time in paused state) for tasks was not affected by signal processing activity in the executor. The case of directing executors to restart a task introduces latency inherent from terminating the task process, and restarting the task in a new process. This latency was observed to be independent of the tested scales for the relatively lightweight Python scripts and C executable tested (Fig. 7, right panel).

4   Conclusions

In this paper we have shared lessons learned when designing an externally-steered, interactive scientific workflow program. We showed by testing components with a ground-up design for steered applications, that a DBMS-based scientific workflow tool can provide a highly-interactive, externally steered solution at the pre-exascale HPC level. On the Summit supercomputer it is possible to launch and manage of tens thousands of tasks with negligible latency, each supported by a live connection, from a single MongoDB server on a compute node. This can serve as a basis to create a workflow tool capable of run-time interaction, analysis, and modification of the workflow, both in terms of task details and number of tasks. In addition, the design provides location information for tasks to facilitate the movement of tasks and other workflow operations to data, and the strategic arrangement of tasks on particular resources.

Acknowledgements. An award of computer time was provided by the Innovative and Novel Computational Impact on Theory and Experiment (INCITE) program. This research used resources of the Oak Ridge Leadership Computing Facility, which is a DOE Office of Science User Facility supported under Contract DE-AC05-00OR227525. JCS acknowledges ORNL LDRD funds. The authors would like to thank Oscar Hernandez, Frank Noé and group, Cecilia Clementi and group, and Shantenu Jha and group, for valuable insight and discussions.

References

1. Ailamaki, A., Ioannidis, Y.E., Livny, M.: Scientific workflow management by database management. In: Proceedings of the Tenth International Conference on Scientific and Statistical Database Management (Cat. No. 98TB100243), pp. 190–199. IEEE (1998)
2. Amaro, R.E., et al.: Ensemble docking in drug discovery. Biophys. J. **114**, 2271–2278 (2018)
3. Bernardi, R.C., Melo, M.C., Schulten, K.: Enhanced sampling techniques in molecular dynamics simulations of biological systems. Biochim. Biophys. Acta **1850**(5), 872–877 (2015)
4. Bowman, G.R., Pande, V.S., Noé, F. (eds.): An Introduction to Markov State Models and Their Application to Long Timescale Molecular Simulation. AEMB, vol. 797. Springer, Dordrecht (2014). https://doi.org/10.1007/978-94-007-7606-7
5. Buchete, N.V., Hummer, G.: Peptide folding kinetics from replica exchange molecular dynamics. Phys. Rev. E **77**(3), 030902 (2008)
6. Dorier, M., Wozniak, J.M., Ross, R.: Supporting task-level fault-tolerance in HPC workflows by launching MPI jobs inside MPI jobs. In: Proceedings of the 12th Workshop on Workflows in Support of Large-Scale Science, p. 5. ACM (2017)
7. Eastman, P., et al.: OpenMM 7: rapid development of high performance algorithms for molecular dynamics. PLoS Comput. Biol. **13**(7), e1005659 (2017)
8. Garcia, A.E., Herce, H., Paschek, D.: Simulations of temperature and pressure unfolding of peptides and proteins with replica exchange molecular dynamics. Annu. Rep. Comput. Chem. **2**, 83–95 (2006)
9. Hänggi, P., Talkner, P., Borkovec, M.: Reaction-rate theory: fifty years after Kramers. Rev. Mod. Phys. **62**(2), 251 (1990)
10. Hruska, E., Abella, J.R., Nüske, F., Kavraki, L.E., Clementi, C.: Quantitative comparison of adaptive sampling methods for protein dynamics. J. Chem. Phys. **149**(24), 244119 (2018)

11. Hummer, G.: Position-dependent diffusion coefficients and free energies from Bayesian analysis of equilibrium and replica molecular dynamics simulations. New J. Phys. **7**(1), 34 (2005)
12. Husic, B.E., McGibbon, R.T., Sultan, M.M., Pande, V.S.: Optimized parameter selection reveals trends in Markov state models for protein folding. J. Chem. Phys. **145**(19), 194103 (2016)
13. Jain, A., et al.: FireWorks: a dynamic workflow system designed for high-throughput applications. Concurr. Comput.: Pract. Exp. **27**(17), 5037–5059 (2015)
14. Kasson, P.M., Jha, S.: Adaptive ensemble simulations of biomolecules. Curr. Opin. Struct. Biol. **52**, 87–94 (2018)
15. Kubo, R.: The fluctuation-dissipation theorem. Rep. Prog. Phys. **29**(1), 255 (1966)
16. Kumar, S., Rosenberg, J.M., Bouzida, D., Swendsen, R.H., Kollman, P.A.: The weighted histogram analysis method for free-energy calculations on biomolecules. I. The method. J. Comput. Chem. **13**(8), 1011–1021 (1992)
17. Noé, F., Horenko, I., Schütte, C., Smith, J.C.: Hierarchical analysis of conformational dynamics in biomolecules: transition networks of metastable states. J. Chem. Phys. **126**(15), 04B617 (2007)
18. Ossyra, J.R., Sedova, A., Tharrington, A., Noé, F., Clementi, C., Smith, J.C.: Porting adaptive ensemble molecular dynamics workflows to the summit supercomputer. In: Proceedings of ISC 19; IWOPH. SLNCS (2019, in press)
19. Pérez-Hernández, G., Paul, F., Giorgino, T., De Fabritiis, G., Noé, F.: Identification of slow molecular order parameters for Markov model construction. J. Chem. Phys. **139**(1), 07B604_1 (2013)
20. Pouya, I., Pronk, S., Lundborg, M., Lindahl, E.: Copernicus, a hybrid dataflow and peer-to-peer scientific computing platform for efficient large-scale ensemble sampling. Future Gener. Comput. Syst. **71**, 18–31 (2017)
21. Prinz, J.H., et al.: Markov models of molecular Kinetics: generation and validation. J. Chem. Phys. **134**(17), 174105 (2011)
22. Scherer, M.K., et al.: PyEMMA 2: a software package for estimation, validation, and analysis of Markov models. J. Chem. Theory Comput. **11**(11), 5525–5542 (2015)
23. da Silva, R.F., Filgueira, R., Pietri, I., Jiang, M., Sakellariou, R., Deelman, E.: A characterization of workflow management systems for extreme-scale applications. Future Gener. Comput. Syst. **75**, 228–238 (2017)
24. Sorin, E.J., Pande, V.S.: Exploring the helix-coil transition via all-atom equilibrium ensemble simulations. Biophys. J. **88**(4), 2472–2493 (2005)
25. Souza, R., Silva, V., Oliveira, D., Valduriez, P., Lima, A.A., Mattoso, M.: Parallel execution of workflows driven by a distributed database management system. In: ACM/IEEE Conference on Supercomputing, Poster (2015)
26. Weinan, E., Ren, W., Vanden-Eijnden, E.: String method for the study of rare events. Phys. Rev. B **66**(5), 052301 (2002)
27. Woolf, T.B., Roux, B.: Conformational flexibility of o-phosphorylcholine and o-phosphorylethanolamine: a molecular dynamics study of solvation effects. J. Am. Chem. Soc. **116**(13), 5916–5926 (1994)
28. Wozniak, J.M., Armstrong, T.G., Wilde, M., Katz, D.S., Lusk, E., Foster, I.T.: Swift/T: large-scale application composition via distributed-memory dataflow processing. In: 2013 13th IEEE/ACM International Symposium on Cluster, Cloud, and Grid Computing, pp. 95–102. IEEE (2013)
29. Wu, H., Paul, F., Wehmeyer, C., Noé, F.: Multiensemble Markov models of molecular thermodynamics and Kinetics. Proc. Natl. Acad. Sci. **113**, E3221–E3230 (2016). https://doi.org/10.1073/pnas.1525092113

The Role of Interactive Super-Computing in Using HPC for Urgent Decision Making

Nick Brown[1][✉], Rupert Nash[1], Gordon Gibb[1], Bianca Prodan[1], Max Kontak[2], Vyacheslav Olshevsky[3], and Wei Der Chien[3]

[1] EPCC, The University of Edinburgh, Bayes Centre, Edinburgh, UK
n.brown@epcc.ed.ac.uk
[2] German Aerospace Center, High-Performance Computing Group, Cologne, Germany
[3] KTH Royal Institute of Technology, Stockholm, Sweden

Abstract. Technological advances are creating exciting new opportunities that have the potential to move HPC well beyond traditional computational workloads. In this paper we focus on the potential for HPC to be instrumental in responding to disasters such as wildfires, hurricanes, extreme flooding, earthquakes, tsunamis, winter weather conditions, and accidents. Driven by the VESTEC EU funded H2020 project, our research looks to prove HPC as a tool not only capable of simulating disasters once they have happened, but also one which is able to operate in a responsive mode, supporting disaster response teams making urgent decisions in real-time. Whilst this has the potential to revolutionise disaster response, it requires the ability to drive HPC interactively, both from the user's perspective and also based upon the arrival of data. As such interactivity is a critical component in enabling HPC to be exploited in the role of supporting disaster response teams so that urgent decision makers can make the correct decision first time, every time.

Keywords: Urgent decision making · Disaster response · Interactive HPC · VESTEC

1 Introduction

The ability to perform faster than real-time simulations of large-scale situations is becoming a reality due to the technological advances that computing, and specifically HPC, has enjoyed over the past decade. This opens up a host of opportunities including the ability to leverage HPC in the role of time-critical decision support for unfolding emergency scenarios. However to do this one must extend the state of the art in numerous fields such as in-situ HPC data analytics, the assimilation and ingestion of data sources (e.g. from sensors measuring actual situational conditions), data reduction and statistical sampling for real-time visualization.

© Springer Nature Switzerland AG 2019
M. Weiland et al. (Eds.): ISC 2019 Workshops, LNCS 11887, pp. 528–540, 2019.
https://doi.org/10.1007/978-3-030-34356-9_40

The Visual Exploration and Sampling Toolkit for Extreme Computing (VESTEC) project is exploring the fusion of HPC with real-time data for supporting urgent decision makers in the role of disaster response. In this project we are concerned with three use-cases that drive our research in this area. The first one is the spread of mosquito borne diseases, which is a major health challenge around many parts of the world. This spread is heavily influenced by weather and current mosquito conditions, so being able to combine real world mosquito reports, accurate temperature values and short range weather forecasts is critical when simulating how the spread will progress in the short to medium term.

The second VESTEC use-case is the progression of forest fires and the ability to explore the impact of different response scenarios. Based on the successful Wildfire Analyst application, this code is currently fed manually with data from the field, but this is a labour intensive process generating extra work for the disaster response teams and inducing a time lag on information, limiting the real-time use of this tool. By automating the process it will make this things far more dynamic, reduce the load on the operators and enable a much greater quantity of data to be exploited in the simulation of wildfires. The third use-case is that of space weather, for instance solar storms, which is very costly because of the damage done to satellites. Whilst it is possible for satellites to be switched off, thus protecting them, one needs prior warning and-so being able to ingest the current space weather conditions and run this through simulation tools is a very valuable proposition as it enables the estimation of risk to assets.

Whilst these three use-cases represent very different areas, all with novel challenges, there are a number of general similarities. All three involve the ingestion of large volumes of data and, as it currently stands, all generate large volumes of output data which is then processed offline by downstream tools. All use-cases involve coupled simulations where a number of distinct codes must be executed in a specific order, for example the execution of a high resolution weather model before feeding the results into the mosquito borne diseases simulation. Lastly, all models involve, to some extent, ensembles which need to be rapidly started and stopped based on new data arriving unpredictably, and also steered by the urgent decision maker.

In order to fully leverage HPC for disaster response, one must embrace the interactive nature of these workflows, selecting the appropriate tools and techniques to support how these technologies can support emergency decision makers in their work. The rest of this paper is organised as follows, after briefly considering related work and background in Sect. 2, we then explore the role of interactivity in Sect. 3 by considering the three main interactivity challenges one faces when using HPC for urgent decision making. In Sect. 4 we explore the role of cloud computing in urgent decision making before drawing conclusions in Sect. 5.

2   Background and Related Work

In Sect. 1 we highlighted the fact that the three VESTEC use-cases currently write their data to disk for offline processing at some later point. When moving to exploiting HPC in a more real-time urgent decision responsive mode, where operators need the results ASAP, then the overhead of IO makes this offline analytics approach prohibitive. Therefore a logical starting point is to consider the current state of the art in processing data from simulations in-situ. This is illustrated in Fig. 1, where cores of a processor are shared between compute (C) and data analytics (D). The general idea is that a number of compute cores are serviced by a data analytics core, and these compute cores *fire and forget* their raw data over to the corresponding data core for analytics whilst the computation proceeds. The major benefit of this is that the raw data is never written to disk, thus avoiding the overhead of IO and the compute cores can continue to work with data analytics proceeding concurrently. Typically this data analytics involves some form of data reduction, or live visualisation.

Existing frameworks such as XIOS [3], Damaris [6], ADIOS [5], and MONC [4] are examples of in-situ data analytics commonly used by HPC simulation codes. While these approaches have proven effective and efficient at interleaving data analytics with running simulations none of them do so in real-time, address the issues of ensemble simulation or, most importantly, support the assimilation and incorporation of new data into running simulations. These limitations are key requirements for a system that is required to support urgent decision making and, as such, one needs to go further than the current state of the art in in-situ data analytics.

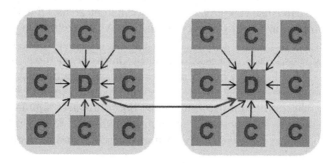

Fig. 1. In-situ data analytics, where cores are shared between computation and data handling

More generally there have been previous attempts at using HPC for urgent decision making. One such example was the SPRUCE project [1], which agreed with machine owners a priori that their resource could be used to run urgent workloads. Responders were given tokens which represented the amount of time they had available on the specific machine for their workload. The solution was somewhat more nuanced than this because a number of modes of access were supported. These ranged from jobs submitted with some sort of priority in the batch queue, all the way to forcibly terminating already running jobs and replacing them for with the urgent job. The more severe the mode, the more user tokens were used up.

However these previous uses of HPC for urgent decision making still involved a batch processing model, where operators submit jobs, commonly with some priority in the queue, and once these have completed the results are used to inform response decisions. However this is not sufficient for our approach because, to take advantage of the high velocity data and live data analytics methods which are becoming commonplace, a much more interactive pattern must be embraced. The traditional batch processing organisation, which has served classic HPC workloads so well over many decades, is simply not appropriate here as we require the execution of ensemble models driven by the unpredictable arrival of data and chaining of HPC codes. This is further complicated by the fact that, in order for the results to be of use to the disaster response team, these urgent jobs must run within a specific bounded time. Furthermore, as simulations are then progressing it is crucially important for a user to be able to interacting with them and exploring numerous options and response techniques.

3   The Role of Interactivity

We believe that using HPC for urgent decision making requires interactivity in three main areas:

1. **User interaction with running simulations:** gaining feedback as the code is running and the ability to modify the simulation state and parameters as it is executing
2. **Dynamic ensemble simulations:** where jobs can be started and stopped on the fly. This is either driven directly by the user, or automatically based on the arrival of sensor data
3. **Supporting an interactive workload:** where the arrival of new data, or completion of another code, such as a weather model, automatically starts new jobs.

These three points are illustrated in Fig. 2, where a central VESTEC system connects data sources and disaster response teams, to HPC machines. Taking the Wildfire Analyst use-case as an example, it was highlighted in Sect. 2 that until now interaction with this code is manual, where first line responders have to explicitly start new simulations based upon updated information they have received and entered. Instead, as per Fig. 2, the ability to drive the code dynamically, so that data is automatically picked up as it streams in and leveraged according to some predefined rules, relieves considerable pressure from the disaster response team and potentially results in much more accurate, up to date, perspective of the situation.

In this section We explore the challenges and solutions associated with each of these three components of interactivity in using HPC for urgent decision making.

3.1   Interacting with Running Simulations

At many GBs in size, the data generated by the codes involved in our three use-cases is substantial and, as discussed in Sect. 2, it is already understood that,

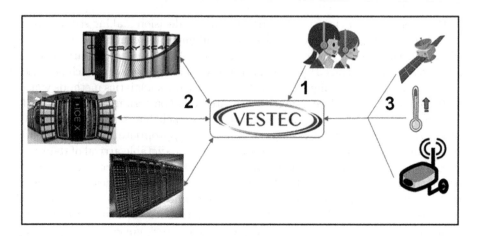

Fig. 2. Overview of interactivity involved in using HPC for urgent decision making

to enable efficient data processing, then an in-situ method, where the data is handled as it is generated rather than written out to disk first, is crucial. Furthermore, there is a requirement for feeding back from the user to the simulation in order to modify the state *on the fly* as the code is running. The unique requirements of urgent decision making means that driving this analysis and interaction via a visual program is highly desirable and ParaView [7] is being used for this in the VESTEC project.

ParaView [7] is an open source data analysis and visualisation application used in many different application areas to analyze and visualize scientific data sets. Designed as a framework, tools are provided to build visualisations appropriate to specific application data analytics and then exploration can be performed interactively in 3D or via ParaView's batch processing capabilities. ParaView supports execution over distributed memory and, as such, can handle very large datasets, which is important in the context of disaster response. Under the hood, ParaView uses the highly popular Visualization ToolKit (VTK) for graphics rendering and Qt for windowing support. In this project we are combining ParaView with Catalyst [8], an in-situ library which orchestrates the simulation with analysis and/or visualization and connects to ParaView. A major benefit of these tools is that the analysis and visualization tasks can be implemented in a high level language such as Python or C++, or via the ParaView GUI.

The role of ParaView and Catalyst is illustrated in Fig. 3, servicing a number of ensemble simulations that are running on an HPC machine. These ensembles are integrated with Catalyst and raw timestep data from each job is passed to a user provided pipeline of analysis scripts which reduce it, for instance via sampling. This reduced data is then transmitted to the ParaView GUI, typically running on a client machine and connected by TCP/IP, but it can also pick up files using the file system or run directly on the HPC machine and be forwarded via X11. Depending on how the ParaView GUI has been set up for the specific

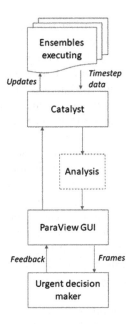

Fig. 3. Example of the interaction with running ensembles

disaster response job, the user is able to provide feedback which, via the Catalyst tool, is delivered to the appropriate ensemble job(s). Whilst the simulation itself still needs to implement the specific details of how to process the user's feedback, using the Catalyst tool means that they do not need to be concerned with the mechanism of how the feedback is delivered.

However, it is not just HPC technology that needs to be considered here, as the data sizes involved mean that underlying data science and visualisation techniques must also be addressed. For instance, the VESTEC project is also researching novel data reduction techniques that support the identification of topologically relevant features from individual simulation step data. This relies on sampling raw data from topological proxies and then isolating the most representative members from the ensembles and estimating the probabilities of the appearance of specific features from this. Furthermore, graphical techniques such as in-situ ray tracing, must also be further developed to support scalable image generation and fast access to full-resolution simulation state.

3.2 Dynamic Ensemble Simulations

Previous research around using HPC for urgent decision making has identified how important it is for simulations to be started quickly, rather than languishing in the batch queue system [2]. Whilst using a dedicated machine for urgent decision making might seem like an obvious choice, the relative rarity of these disasters means that such a machine could be lightly used. Furthermore, the ability to run very large, high resolution jobs, is often desirable when it comes to urgent decision workloads, and as such the use of existing HPC resources is attractive. A common approach is to leverage queue priorities, such that jobs submitted to specific queues will run first or even terminate currently running jobs. However, this approach requires significant policy agreement with the individual HPC machine operators, and the execution of urgent jobs will inevitably cause disruption. This might not matter too much with previous urgent decision approaches, which involved running a small number of jobs, but our approach involves running ensemble simulations which can be started unpredictably based on sensor data streaming in over time, meaning that many runs over a not insignificant time period is likely.

In VESTEC we have adopted the idea of a central VESTEC server federating over many HPC machines as per Fig. 2. This system periodically tracks the utilisation of each HPC machine and, based upon this knowledge and the specifics of the job, will submit to which ever machine is deemed most appropriate. Federation is entirely hidden from the end-user and, whilst specific HPC machines might still employ further measures such as high priority queue which the VESTEC system can be aware of, the load will be spread out across multiple supercomputers if a significant number of jobs need to be executed. Being a European project, it is our vision that all the major supercomputers of Europe would eventually sign up to such a scheme, although for the purposes of the VESTEC research project we are federating over a smaller number of HPC machines to develop and prove the underlying concepts.

This approach solves another challenge in using HPC machines for urgent decision making, which is that of resilience. Most general purpose HPC machines simply do not operate with the guaranteed level of service availability required for life saving workloads. Even those that currently do, such as the Met Office, are fairly crude in their approach of relying on a hot backup machine which will clear itself of jobs and run the main workload if a failure is detected in the other machine. By contrast, in our approach the federator tracks which jobs are submitted to which machine, and if a supercomputer fails then not only will no more jobs be submitted to it, but also any queued or running jobs will be automatically resubmitted elsewhere. All of this is transparent to the user and more generally a single job might also be submitted to more than one machine speculatively, either to guard against machine failure or to simply hedge bets about which system will run the job first.

Of course there are still challenges involved and an open question is whether this approach of polling machine status provides a level of control is fine grained enough to fully support the execution of codes within a bounded time frame. For instance, a major question which we are looking to answer in this project is whether it will be possible to collect enough data and make accurate enough predictions around machine state and queue times to provide this bounded execution time, or will some combination of special priority queues still be required in the most critical of situations?

Our federation approach does not get us entirely round the challenges of machine policy either. For instance, many operators of supercomputers have fairly strict policies around accounts and who may execute what. In some cases it might not be possible to have a single VESTEC user per system as this could be seen as account sharing which many systems disallow. Instead, individual users might still need their own accounts on the machines and their credentials then provided to VESTEC system for accessing the HPC machines on their behalf. Whilst this is not a major blocker in the context of a research project, in order to roll this approach out across very many machines, such as all supercomputers in Europe which is our vision, then such challenges must be considered and solved.

3.3   Supporting an Interactive Workload

When it comes to an interactive workload there are two concerns to bear in mind. Firstly, new data arriving from sensors must be processed in some manner, either by performing preliminary analysis or feeding it directly into simulation runs. Secondly, it is desirable to chain the running of simulation codes together, for instance, the execution of a weather model first generates a forecast which is then used by a simulation codes such as Wildfire Analyst, as details of the wind significantly impact how forest fires progress. Both of these requirements need to be handled in a way that requires minimal intervention from the already busy front line responders.

We have identified that a workflow approach is appropriate here, where specific activities are performed and their status tracked. Once activities have completed then their results can be used to drive further activities as per a set of predefined rules. Figure 4 illustrates an example workflow for the forest fire use-case, where the arrival of new data will either update already running ensemble simulations, or start new ones. This is further complicated by the fact that the data might require pre-processing and new instances of the high resolution weather model might need to be executed too, and the weather forecast results provided to new instances of Wildfire Analyst.

Whilst there are very many workflow technologies available, arguably the two most mature and ubiquitous are the Common Workflow Language (CWL) [10] and Apache Taverna [11]. In fact CWL is not a specific technology per-se, but instead a standard for describing workflows which numerous projects have implemented. By contrast, Apache Taverna provides its own workflow description language and ecosystem of tools such as GUIs for designing workflows. These technologies have not grown from an HPC perspective and as such neither is perfectly suited to our needs. When one considers the workflow in Fig. 4, they can observe a number of conditionals based on the state of the system or data. However, CWL does not support conditional branching in the workflows directly, so its ability to fully describe the workflows of our use-cases is limited. Apache Taverna by contrast does have some support for conditionals in the workflow, although this is not a commonly used feature, but Taverna is very heavy weight and at the current time of writing uses a description interface which is

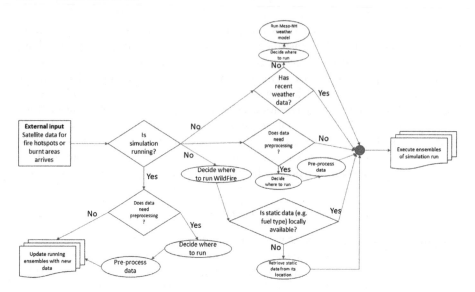

Fig. 4. Example workflow for executing or updating Wildfire Analyst in response to the arrival of new data

currently non-standard and in flux as the technology matures and moves towards full acceptance as an Apache project.

Therefore the approach we have adopted in the VESTEC project is to use CWL, due to its standardised nature, but only use this to describe each individual activity of the workflow and connect these using our own bespoke implementation in the VESTEC system. Whilst this isn't ideal, given the current state of these technologies we believe it is the best work around and potentially as these become more mature for HPC then we can move to standardising the links between activities.

4   The Role of the Cloud

From the discussions in Sect. 3 it might seem to the reader that many of the requirements for fusing real-time data with HPC for urgent decision making overlap with those of cloud computing. Hence a natural question is whether the adoption of some public cloud, such as Azure or AWS, could be appropriate here. One could go even further and argue that much of the work we are doing on the VESTEC system duplicates functionality already provided by the cloud, for instance supporting elastic compute, and as such a cloud-first solution could be more appropriate.

However, the cloud is not a silver bullet and there are specific limitations that impact its overall suitability for this kind of high performance work load. One such limitation is the fact that the user must set up the entirely of the infrastructure themselves and it is very easy to make decisions that, later down the line, significantly limit performance. Whilst the compute power of the cloud hardware and the interconnect is of high performance, selecting and configuring an appropriate file system can be a major issue. As such, it can be challenging to obtain high performance from codes that require significant IO, which is common place in HPC and involves all three of our VESTEC use-cases. Whilst high performance file-systems are often available on the cloud, these must be setup and configured by the user which is complex and beyond the capabilities of many users and developers. The common choice is to select a more common parallel file-system technology, such as NFS, and whilst this is still a non-trivial task to set up and configure, it is at-least doable in a realistic time frame.

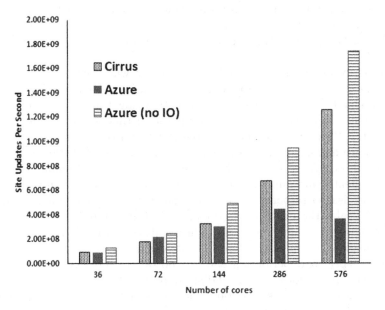

Fig. 5. Performance comparison, in Site Updates Per Second (higher is better) of HemeLB running on Cirrus, Azure and Azure with no IO

Figure 5 illustrates a performance comparison for HemeLB [9], a CFD code based on the lattice Boltzmann method, on Cirrus which is a HPE/SGI 8600 HPC system (36 Broadwell cores per node, connected via InfiniBand), and Azure (16 Haswell cores per node, connected via InfiniBand). In this experiment we have picked a domain based on a 3d rotational angiography scan of an anonymous patient with a cerebral aneurysm being treated at the National Hospital for Neurology and Neurosurgery in London, UK. The simulations are concerned with modelling the region around the bifurcation of the internal carotid artery's bifurcation into the anterior cerebral artery and the middle cerebral artery and the code is configured to use a block size of 8, block counts of 13, 26, and 27, and 650492 total fluid sites. This code is not specifically part of one of the VESTEC use-cases, but we believe that this application area would be applicable to using HPC for urgent decision making in the future.

Whilst the processor technologies between Cirrus and Azure are different, we can still observe patterns here and draw some conclusions. The *Cirrus* and *Azure* runs are executing with IO in HemeLB enabled, whereas the *Azure (no IO)* runs have had IO disabled at the application level. This last configuration, over Azure with no IO, is the fastest and this is because of the absence of IO, which adds some overhead to the code regardless. However it can be seen that when enabling IO on Azure the performance very significantly decreases, 4.7 times slower at 576 cores. The performance on Cirrus with IO enabled is 3.4 times faster than that of Azure with IO enabled. Whilst the Xeon processors are the next generation on Cirrus (Broadwell vs Haswell), we are still using the exact same number of cores and when profiling the code in more detail we found that the vast majority of this time difference was due to the overhead of IO on the cloud.

Another benefit of the cloud is that of elasticity, where new VMs can be spun up quickly rather than having to wait in a batch queue as per HPC machines. However, clouds are not always as elastic as they might initially seem and prior resource requests often have to be made ahead of time for significant amounts of compute. When one considers that the cloud companies must still provision the hardware and ensure that there is enough resource, then this isn't hugely surprising. It does however mean that requesting a very large amount of compute, very infrequently and unpredictably, as would be the case with urgent decision making for disaster response, is not what the cloud has been designed for.

There is also the question of cost and Fig. 6 illustrates a cost comparison between HemeLB running on Cirrus, Azure and Azure with no IO. The cost has been normalised, so we can explore the different configurations from a cost perspective irrespective of performance. It is important to note that the costs quoted here are the *full* cost for Cirrus, including support, but Azure configurations only depict the cost of the VMs. Additional activities on the cloud after the job has finished, such as data storage, ingress and egress will incur additional charges. It can be seen that, running on Cirrus is consistently the cheapest option, being 2.7 times cheaper than Azure without any IO and over 12 times cheaper than Azure with IO at 576 cores. The most costly configuration is that of Azure with IO enabled and this is because of the additional file server support VMs that must be stood up.

Whilst the numbers in Figs. 5 and 6 illustrate the limitations of the cloud for HPC workloads, the cloud does have a number of features which could be of benefit in the use of computing for disaster response. Firstly, a cloud system could be one of our target machines, with the VESTEC system then federating over this exactly like the HPC machines. Secondly, we believe that some technologies which are closely tied with the cloud, such as object stores, will be very applicable to the technology solution employed by VESTEC.

In fact, in a way, the VESTEC system can be thought of a private cloud, with machines that subscribe to this then providing the compute resource and our

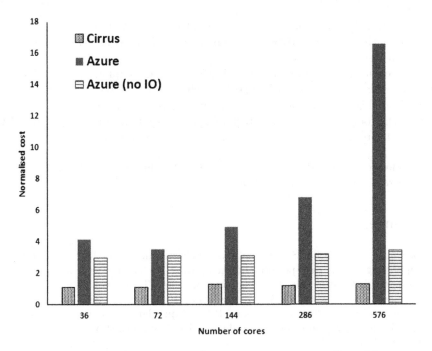

Fig. 6. Normalised cost (lower is better) comparison of running HemeLB running on Cirrus, Azure and Azure with no IO

VESTEC control system the overall marshaller. Whilst this does look different to public clouds such as Azure and AWS, there is an overlap of requirements and features, and whilst the implementation of these will by necessity be different, it could be said that the ability to provide the flexibility of the cloud but within the HPC space, is highly desirable for disaster response.

5   Conclusions

The use of HPC for urgent decision making is an exciting new domain for the super-computing community. However there are numerous challenges and barriers that need to be overcome in order for this to be a success, not least because HPC machines, which traditionally favour throughput over individual job latency, are not set up for this sort of workload. In this paper we have identified three major challenges around interactivity that need to be addressed in order to successfully use HPC for disaster response; interacting with running simulations, dynamic ensemble control, and supporting an interactive workload.

The role of interactivity is crucial here and, whilst no existing technologies are absolutely perfect, with further enhancements they can be made to work together but the devil is in the detail in terms of how one actually achieves this. It is clear that this effort requires expertise from across numerous domains, from traditional simulation, to data analysis, to visualisation techniques, to real-time computing, all these different components must be considered if we are to transform disaster response.

We are currently building the VESTEC system and exploring the hypothesis that by federating across multiple HPC machines, one addresses the limitations of HPC for this type of workload. Whilst it involves significant effort to further develop the tools, techniques and technologies, the potential payoff for the HPC and disaster response communities is significant if we are successful.

Acknowledgements. This work was funded under the EU FET VESTEC H2020 project, grant agreement number 800904.

References

1. Beckman, P., Nadella, S., Trebon, N., Beschastnikh, I.: SPRUCE: a system for supporting urgent high-performance computing. In: Gaffney, P.W., Pool, J.C.T. (eds.) Grid-Based Problem Solving Environments. ITIFIP, vol. 239, pp. 295–311. Springer, Boston, MA (2007). https://doi.org/10.1007/978-0-387-73659-4_16
2. Yoshimoto, K.K., Choi, D.J., Moore, R.L., Majumdar, A., Hocks, E.: Implementations of urgent computing on production HPC systems. Procedia Comput. Sci. **9**, 1687–1693 (2012)
3. Meurdesoif, Y.: XIOS: an efficient and highly configurable parallel output library for climate modelling. In: The Second Workshop on Coupling Technologies for Earth System Models (2013)
4. Brown, N., Weiland, M., Hill, A., Shipway, B.: In situ data analytics for highly scalable cloud modelling on Cray machines. Concurr. Comput.: Pract. Exp. **30**(1), e4331 (2018)
5. Liu, Q., et al.: Hello ADIOS: the challenges and lessons of developing leadership class I/O frameworks. Concurr. Comput.: Pract. Exp. **26**(7), 1453–1473 (2014)
6. Dorier, M., Antoniu, G., Cappello, F., Snir, M., Orf, L.: Damaris: how to efficiently leverage multicore parallelism to achieve scalable, Jitter-free I/O. In: CLUSTER - IEEE International Conference on Cluster Computing, Beijing, China, pp. 155–163 (2012)
7. Ayachit, U.: The Paraview Guide: a Parallel Visualization Application. Kitware Inc., Clifton Park (2015)
8. Ayachit, U., et al.: Paraview catalyst: enabling in situ data analysis and visualization. In: Proceedings of the First Workshop on In Situ Infrastructures for Enabling Extreme-Scale Analysis and Visualization, pp. 25–29. ACM, November 2015
9. Mazzeo, M.D., Coveney, P.V.: HemeLB: a high performance parallel lattice-Boltzmann code for large scale fluid flow in complex geometries. Comput. Phys. Commun. **178**(12), 894–914 (2008)
10. Amstutz, P., et al.: Common workflow language, v1. 0 (2016)
11. Hull, D., et al.: Taverna: a tool for building and running workflows of services. Nucleic Acids Res. **34**(suppl_2), W729–W732 (2006)

Deep Learning at Scale for Subgrid Modeling in Turbulent Flows: Regression and Reconstruction

Mathis Bode[1]([✉]) [ID], Michael Gauding[2] [ID], Konstantin Kleinheinz[1] [ID], and Heinz Pitsch[1] [ID]

[1] Institute for Combustion Technology, RWTH Aachen University, Templergraben 64, 52062 Aachen, Germany
{m.bode,k.kleinheinz,h.pitsch}@itv.rwth-aachen.de
[2] CORIA – CNRS UMR 6614, Saint Etienne du Rouvray, France
michael.gauding@coria.fr

Abstract. Modeling of turbulent flows is still challenging. One way to deal with the large scale separation due to turbulence is to simulate only the large scales and model the unresolved contributions as done in large-eddy simulation (LES). This paper focuses on two deep learning (DL) strategies, regression and reconstruction, which are data-driven and promising alternatives to classical modeling concepts. Using three-dimensional (3-D) forced turbulence direct numerical simulation (DNS) data, subgrid models are evaluated, which predict the unresolved part of quantities based on the resolved solution. For regression, it is shown that feedforward artificial neural networks (ANNs) are able to predict the fully-resolved scalar dissipation rate using filtered input data. It was found that a combination of a large-scale quantity, such as the filtered passive scalar itself, and a small-scale quantity, such as the filtered energy dissipation rate, gives the best agreement with the actual DNS data. Furthermore, a DL network motivated by enhanced super-resolution generative adversarial networks (ESRGANs) was used to reconstruct fully-resolved 3-D velocity fields from filtered velocity fields. The energy spectrum shows very good agreement. As size of scientific data is often in the order of terabytes or more, DL needs to be combined with high performance computing (HPC). Necessary code improvements for HPC-DL are discussed with respect to the supercomputer JURECA. After optimizing the training code, 396.2 TFLOPS were achieved.

Keywords: Turbulence · Large-eddy simulation · Deep learning · Direct numerical simulation · High performance computing

1 Introduction

The turbulent motion of fluid flows poses some of the most difficult and fundamental problems in classical physics as it is a complex, strongly non-linear, multi-

---

The original version of this chapter was revised: It has been changed to non-open access and the copyright holder is now "Springer Nature Switzerland AG". The correction to this chapter is available at https://doi.org/10.1007/978-3-030-34356-9_50

M. Weiland et al. (Eds.): ISC 2019 Workshops, LNCS 11887, pp. 541–560, 2019.
https://doi.org/10.1007/978-3-030-34356-9_41

scale phenomenon [36]. A general challenge in turbulence research is to predict the statistics of fluctuating velocity and scalar fields and develop models for a precise statistical prediction of these fields even in scale-resolved simulations [21,34].

Large-eddy simulation (LES) is known to be a suitable modeling approach for turbulent flows and solves for the larger, flow-dependent scales of the flow by modeling all scales below a particular filter width [15,28]. It is assumed that the smaller, unresolved scales reveal certain universal features and decouple from the larger non-universal scales. As a consequence, models for LES can be built from relatively simple, semi-empirical algebraic relations that are oftentimes based solely on dimensional arguments [40]. One approach to develop and test such models is to perform fully resolved direct numerical simulations (DNSs), filter the resulting data with a given filter kernel, and find functional relations between the DNS results and the filtered data. The objective of the present work is to move beyond simple algebraic models for LES and use a data-driven approach with deep learning (DL) for modeling and reconstructing subfilter statistics for turbulent flows.

DL has gained immense interests from various industries and research groups in the age of big data. Prominent applications of DL include image processing [8,17,42,43], voice recognition [18], or website customization [24]. Reasons for that are the continued growth of computational power (especially GPUs) and the availability of exceptionally large labeled experimental data sets. Also in the field of fluid mechanics and especially turbulence research, data-driven methods and DL have become more popular over the last years. However, often the applications are limited by either using only simple networks or small, artificial datasets.

Parish and Duraisamy [33] used an approach called field inversion and machine learning (FIML), which moves beyond parameter calibration and uses data to directly infer information about the functional form of model discrepancies. They applied their approach to turbulent channel flows. Srinivasan et al. [41] assessed the capabilities of neural networks to predict temporally evolving turbulent flows and concluded that long short-term memory (LSTM) networks perform better than multi-layer perceptron (MLP) approaches. Ling et al. [29] also presented a method using deep neural networks to learn a model for the Reynolds stress anisotropy tensor from high-fidelity simulations and experimental data. The Reynolds stress anisotropy predictions were found to be more accurate than conventional Reynolds-averaged Navier-Stokes (RANS) models, however the network could not perfectly reproduce the DNS results. Milano and Koumoutsakos [31] modeled the near-wall region of turbulent flows. Lapeyre et al. [25] and Beck et al. [4] have documented the possibility of using ML in designing subgrid-scale models for LES. Maulik and San [30] presented their use of a single-layer feedforward artificial neural network (ANN) architecture trained through a supervised learning approach for the deconvolution of flow variables from their coarse-grained computations such as those encountered in LES. The subfilter-scale content recovery was benchmarked against several popular structural closure modeling strategies. Bode et al. [5] studied the accuracy of various network architectures for predicting statistics of turbulent flows. Machine learning (ML) and DL have also been applied to flow control [14,27], development of low-dimensional models [38], generation of inflow conditions [11], or structure identification in two-dimensional (2-D) decaying turbulence [19]. Kutz [23] summarized more applications of DL in the field of fluid dynamics.

This work focuses on two different approaches in the context of data-driven turbulence modeling with DL: regression and reconstruction. In the regression part, a supervised learning method is used to predict closure terms in the context of LES modeling based on filtered quantities. Simple ANNs are employed to predict, for example, the turbulent viscosity or the scalar dissipation rate. In the reconstruction part, a generative adversarial network (GAN) approach is followed to reconstruct fully-resolved turbulence fields from filtered data. Results with respect to different network architectures and different quantities are discussed here. Furthermore, DL based on 3-D scientific data differs from DL on images not only in terms of the size of total data but also in the size of a single realization used for training. The size of scientific data can easily be in the order of hundreds of terabytes while training is traditionally performed with much smaller data. Therefore, DL on scientific data is often not possible without the usage of supercomputers and corresponding high performance computing (HPC) approaches. These computing aspects are also discussed in this work.

The remainder of this article is organized as follows. Section 2 describes the used datasets. In Sect. 3, details about the regression and reconstruction methodologies are given, and results are discussed. Challenges with respect to computational aspects are addressed in Sect. 4. The paper finishes with conclusions.

2 Dataset Description

The training and reconstruction is based on data obtained from high-fidelity homogeneous isotropic forced turbulence simulations [12,13] in this work. The data was generated by DNSs of the incompressible Navier-Stokes equations (NSEs) in a triply periodic cube with size 2π and 256^3 collocation points. Moreover, advection-diffusion equations of passive scalars were solved, which were used for tracking species or mixture factions. Turbulence was kept in a statistically steady state by a large-scale stochastic forcing scheme [10], whereas the passive scalars were forced by an imposed uniform mean gradient. The governing equations were solved by an accurate pseudo-spectral approach with integrating factor technique. A pseudo-spectral approach with integrating factor technique was used for accuracy. For efficiency, the non-linear transport term of the NSEs was computed in physical space, and a truncation technique with a smooth spectral filter was applied to reduce aliasing errors. The library P3DFFT was used for the spatial decomposition and to perform the fast Fourier transform. The code employs a hybrid MPI/OpenMP parallelization and reveals a nearly linear scaling up to two million threads.

Turbulence in simple incompressible flows can be characterized by a single characteristic number, the Reynolds number Re, for example defined based on the Taylor length scale λ as

$$\text{Re}_\lambda = \frac{u'\lambda}{\nu}, \tag{1}$$

where ν is the kinematic viscosity and u' is the root-mean-square deviation of the velocity vector $\mathbf{u}$. u' is defined as

$$u' = \sqrt{\left\langle \frac{(\mathbf{u} - \langle \mathbf{u} \rangle) \cdot (\mathbf{u} - \langle \mathbf{u} \rangle)}{3} \right\rangle} \tag{2}$$

with bold indicating tensors including vectors. Ensemble-averages are denoted by angular brackets and computed over the full computational domain due to statistical homogeneity of the DNS setup. All velocity component fields are shifted to zero mean in this work as typically done for homogeneous isotropic turbulence. The Taylor-based Reynolds numbers of the used DNSs equals approximately 43, which is large enough to ensure a non-linear transfer of turbulent energy from the large, energy-containing scales toward the small, dissipative scales.

The coarse-grained data was generated by applying a filter-kernel $G(\mathbf{r})$ to the DNS data, i.e.

$$\bar{\{\cdot\}}(\mathbf{x}) = \iiint \{\cdot\}(\mathbf{r}) G(\mathbf{x} - \mathbf{r}) \, d\mathbf{r}, \tag{3}$$

where an overbar denotes filtered quantities. For efficiency, the filtering procedure is applied in spectral space, where a rotationally symmetric Gaussian filter kernel, defined as

$$\hat{G}(\kappa) = \exp\left(-\frac{\kappa^2 \Delta^2}{24}\right) \tag{4}$$

with κ as the magnitude of the wavenumber vector $\boldsymbol{\kappa}$, is used. The Gaussian filter kernel is local in both spectral and real space and avoids erroneous fluctuations in the filtered fields. The cut-off wavenumber κ_c is related to the filter-width Δ by

$$\kappa_c = \frac{\pi}{\Delta}. \tag{5}$$

In this paper, two statistically independent flow time-steps (denoted by case A and case B) with about two integral times in between are studied. The filter width was chosen as $\kappa_c = 16$, which corresponds to a length scale at the end of the restricted scaling range. Characteristic quantities of the DNSs and the filtered data are given in Table 1. Here, $\langle k \rangle$ denotes the ensemble-averaged turbulent kinetic energy, $\langle \varepsilon \rangle$ the ensemble-averaged dissipation rate of turbulent kinetic energy, and $\langle \chi \rangle$ the ensemble-averaged dissipation rate of scalar variance. All quantities in this work are arbitrarily normalized without loss of generality.

Table 1. Characteristic properties of the DNSs and the filtered velocity and scalar field.

	Case A	Case B
$\langle k \rangle$	9.67	10.93
$\langle \bar{k} \rangle$	9.19	10.36
$\langle \varepsilon \rangle$	10.69	13.06
$\langle \bar{\varepsilon} \rangle$	8.62	10.11
$\langle \chi \rangle$	3.30	6.59
$\langle \bar{\chi} \rangle$	2.16	4.11
Re_λ	42.7	43.7

3   Modeling

This section describes the regression and reconstruction approaches by showing results for two network architectures. All networks were implemented using the Keras API [1] built on the TensorFlow [2] backend.

3.1   Regression

The filtered NSEs contain unclosed terms which need to be modeled [6]. An often used closure for the filtered momentum equation relies on the eddy-viscosity ν_T modeled as

$$\nu_T = (C_s \Delta)^2 \sqrt{\bar{\mathbf{S}} : \bar{\mathbf{S}}}, \tag{6}$$

where C_s is a model constant, Δ is the filter width, and $\bar{\mathbf{S}}$ is the filtered rate of strain tensor defined as

$$\bar{\mathbf{S}} = \frac{1}{2} \left(\nabla \bar{u} + (\nabla \bar{u})^\mathsf{T} \right) \tag{7}$$

with ∇ being the del operator. Furthermore, the prediction of turbulent mixing requires an accurate prediction of the mean scalar dissipation rate $\langle \chi \rangle$, which is the sink term in the transport equation of the mean scalar variance $\langle (\phi - \langle \phi \rangle)^2 \rangle$. Here, the local instantaneous scalar dissipation rate is defined as

$$\chi = 2D \nabla (\phi - \langle \phi \rangle) \cdot \nabla (\phi - \langle \phi \rangle), \tag{8}$$

where ϕ denotes the transported scalar quantity, and D is the molecular diffusivity. All scalars were shifted to zero mean in this work. The mean scalar dissipation rate is related to the scalar variance spectrum E_ϕ by

$$\langle \chi \rangle = 2D \int_0^\infty \kappa^2 E_\phi(\kappa) \, d\kappa, \tag{9}$$

which signifies that mainly the smaller scales contribute to the mean scalar dissipation rate $\langle \chi \rangle$. As these scales are not available in coarse-grained fields or LES, an accurate modeling of χ is necessary.

In the context of LES modeling, regression evaluated with neural network architectures can be used to obtain optimal predictions of subgrid quantities or contributions based on the incomplete information resolved in the LES. One example is to train a DL network with filtered DNS quantities as input and the corresponding DNS quantities as 'label' to learn the relation between the quantities resolved in LESs and their subgrid contributions. In the following subsections, this will be shown with simple feedforward ANNs. Unlike classical linear or logistic regression models, regression through neural networks can represent more complex functions by data manipulations through dense layers. The number of layers and the number of nodes in each layer can be varied to obtain optimal networks and results [29]. Activation functions in each layer can be used to add non-linearity to the regression model, and a dropout layer can be added for regularization, so that certain nodes are ignored during training to reduce overfitting or high variance. In the next subsection, regression is used to reproduce the turbulent viscosity model introduced in Eq. (6), which will show that simple DL networks are able to learn from the considered DNS data. Afterwards, several regression models for the scalar dissipation rate are evaluated. All cases were run for 7000 epochs, and the evolutions of the loss functions are shown to evaluate the convergence of the training.

ν_T **Prediction Using** $\bar{S}$: As network validation, a single input value, single output value mapping was implemented relating $\bar{S} : \bar{S}$ and ν_T by means of a 3-layer neural network as shown in Fig. 1. Figure 2 compares the modeled ν_T, obtained from Eq. (6), with the prediction from the network. The good collapse of both curves for all values of $\bar{S} : \bar{S}$ validates that the network is able to learn simple relations as given by Eq. (6).

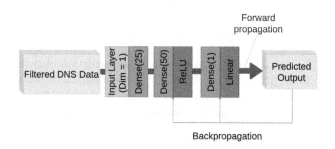

Fig. 1. Sketch of the network for ν_T prediction.

χ **Prediction Using** $\bar{\phi}$: After validating the network with predicting ν_T, feedforward networks are used to predict the resolved scalar dissipation rate χ. The accuracy of the prediction is strongly affected by the considered input variables and the network architecture and parameters. It was found that the 3-layer network shown in Fig. 1, which works well for predicting ν_T, leads to inaccuracies for predictions of the resolved scalar dissipation rate. The accuracy could be

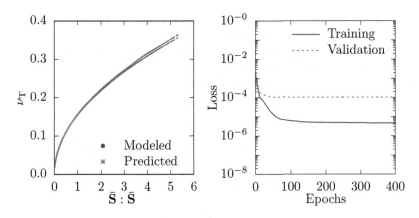

Fig. 2. Visualization of the modeled and DL-predicted turbulent viscosity ν_T using the double inner product of two filtered rate of strain tensors $\bar{S} : \bar{S}$ as input (left) and the corresponding loss as function of number of epochs (right).

improved by switching to a 5-layer network architecture as visualized in Fig. 3. Even more layers did not improve the prediction accuracy further, and therefore, the following plots are based on training with the 5-layer network.

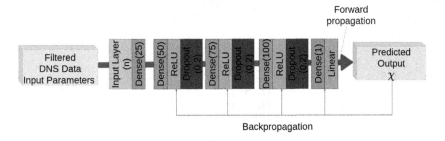

Fig. 3. Sketch of the network for χ prediction.

The simplest approach is to use the filtered scalar $\bar{\phi}$ as only input to the network, which is equal to the filtered scalar fluctuations $\overline{\phi - \langle \phi \rangle}$ here. The obtained results are shown in Fig. 4, and good correlation between the DNS and the DL-predicted values of χ can be seen. Note that the negative values of the scalar dissipation rate result from a centering and rescaling of the scalar dissipation rate fields indicated by the tilde symbol. The good correlation implies that the network is able to learn the derivatives of $(\phi - \langle \phi \rangle)$ (cf. Eq. (8)), even though no convolutional layer was used here. Moreover, the probability density function (PDF) of χ is plotted in Fig. 5 to further assess the accuracy of the prediction. The scalar dissipation rate is a very intermittent quantity, which implies the presence of very strong but very rare events. These strong events are characteristic features of turbulence and play an important role for small-scale mixing or turbulent combustion. Comparing the PDFs of the DNS and DL-predicted scalar dissipation rates indicates that the dense fully connected neural network is able to reproduce the PDF of χ with moderate accuracy as clear deviations are seen in the logarithmic plot.

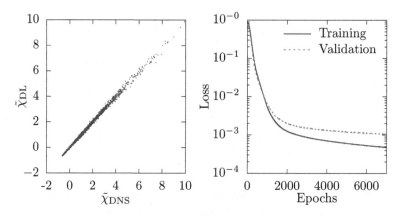

Fig. 4. Visualization of the correlation between DNS and DL-predicted rescaled scalar dissipation rate $\tilde{\chi}$ using the filtered passive scalar $\bar{\phi}$ as input (left) and the corresponding loss as function of number of epochs (right).

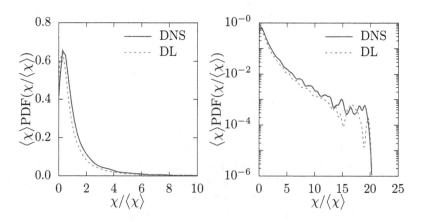

Fig. 5. Visualization of the normalized PDF of the DNS and DL-predicted scalar dissipation rate χ with linear (left) and logarithmic (right) ordinate for the network with filtered passive scalar $\bar{\phi}$ as input.

χ **Prediction Using** $\bar{\phi}$ **and** $\bar{\varepsilon}$: Classical models in turbulence propose that the mean scalar dissipation rate $\langle\chi\rangle$ depends on the scalar variance $\langle(\phi - \langle\phi\rangle)^2\rangle$ and a characteristic time-scale τ, i.e.

$$\langle\chi\rangle = c_\chi \frac{\langle(\phi - \langle\phi\rangle)^2\rangle}{\tau}, \tag{10}$$

where c_χ is a constant. τ is usually chosen as an integral time-scale and can be defined as

$$\tau = \frac{\langle k\rangle}{\langle\varepsilon\rangle}. \tag{11}$$

The integral time-scale is a characteristic time-scale of the larger eddies in a turbulent flow, which determine the rate of turbulent mixing.

Inspecting the relation given by Eq. (10) insinuates that the mapping shown in Figs. 4 and 5 may be incomplete, since it neglects the dependence of χ on the characteristic time-scale τ, which leads to the observed deviations. Following Overholt and Pope [32] and motivated by Eq. (10), the input for the network predicting the scalar dissipation rate χ is extended by the resolved energy dissipation rate $\bar{\varepsilon}$, defined as

$$\bar{\varepsilon} = \frac{1}{2}\nu\left(\nabla\overline{(\mathbf{u} - \langle\mathbf{u}\rangle)} + (\nabla\overline{(\mathbf{u} - \langle\mathbf{u}\rangle)})^\mathsf{T}\right) : \left(\nabla\overline{(\mathbf{u} - \langle\mathbf{u}\rangle)} + (\nabla\overline{(\mathbf{u} - \langle\mathbf{u}\rangle)})^\mathsf{T}\right), \tag{12}$$

which simplifies to

$$\bar{\varepsilon} = 2\nu\bar{\mathbf{S}} : \bar{\mathbf{S}} \tag{13}$$

for the data considered in this work. As can be seen in Figs. 6 and 7, the prediction quality improves, probably because $\bar{\varepsilon}$ provides additional information about the local time scales of turbulence to the network.

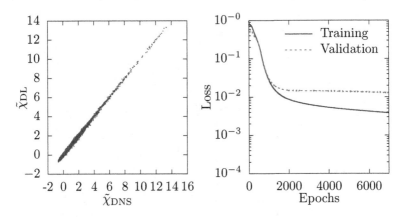

Fig. 6. Visualization of the correlation between DNS and DL-predicted rescaled scalar dissipation rate $\tilde{\chi}$ using the filtered passive scalar $\bar{\phi}$ and filtered energy dissipation rate $\bar{\varepsilon}$ as inputs (left) and the corresponding loss as function of number of epochs (right).

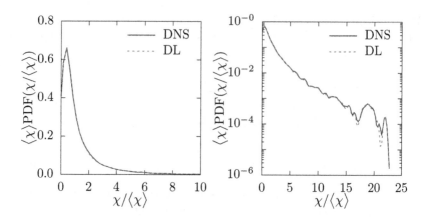

Fig. 7. Visualization of the normalized PDF of the DNS and DL-predicted scalar dissipation rate χ with linear (left) and logarithmic (right) ordinate for the network with filtered passive scalar $\bar{\phi}$ and filtered energy dissipation rate $\bar{\varepsilon}$ as inputs.

χ **Prediction Using $\bar{\phi}$ and $\bar{u}$:** After successfully predicting the scalar dissipation rate with good accuracy, it is tested whether the network is also able to extract the time scale information contained in the filtered energy dissipation rate from the filtered velocity $\bar{u}$, which is used to compute the filtered energy dissipation rate (cf. Eqs. (7) and (13)). Therefore, the network inputs are changed to $\bar{\phi}$ and $\bar{u}$, and the results are shown in Figs. 8 and 9. It can be seen that the prediction quality is worse compared to Figs. 6 and 7, which indicates that the network is not fully able to learn the tensor operations performed in Eqs. (7) and (13). Interestingly, the result is also worse than the results shown in Figs. 4 and 5, which might be due to overfitting.

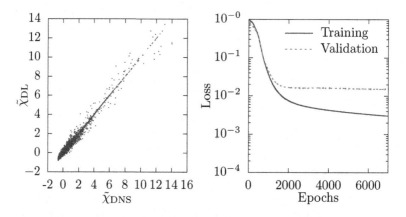

Fig. 8. Visualization of the correlation between DNS and DL-predicted rescaled scalar dissipation rate $\tilde{\chi}$ using the filtered passive scalar $\bar{\phi}$ and filtered velocity $\bar{u}$ as inputs (left) and the corresponding loss as function of number of epochs (right).

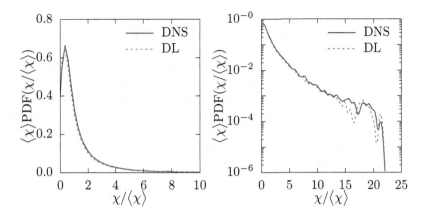

Fig. 9. Visualization of the normalized PDF of the DNS and DL-predicted scalar dissipation rate χ with linear (left) and logarithmic (right) ordinate for the network with filtered passive scalar $\bar{\phi}$ and filtered velocity $\bar{\mathbf{u}}$ as inputs.

3.2 Reconstruction

Reconstructing the fully-resolved flow from large-scale or coarse-grained data has significant applications in various domains. For example, particle image velocimetry (PIV) measurements can only resolve information on large scales due to limited spatial resolution [7]. Similarly, LES is widely used for weather predictions [35], where resolving the small-scale information is prohibitively expensive. The reconstruction of subgrid information with deep learning networks is a promising approach to link the large-scale results obtained from experiments or filtered equations to the actual flow fields.

In this subsection, a GAN-approach is used to reconstruct fully-resolved 3-D velocity fields from filtered data. With these fields, the filtered NSEs can be closed.

Network Motivation: The DL network used for reconstruction in this work is inspired by the enhanced super-resolution GAN (ESRGAN) introduced by Wang et al. [43] for reconstructing filtered features in 2-D images, which is a leading DL-approach in the field of single image super-resolution (SISR). A pioneering work in the field of SISR was the SRCNN proposed by Dong et al. [8]. The general concept of GANs was presented by Goodfellow et al. [16]. A GAN is composed of two models, a generator that captures the data distribution and generates new data, and a discriminator that learns to distinguish whether a sample stems from the original data distribution (genuine) or the generator (fake). During training, the generator learns to produce samples that are indistinguishable for the discriminator, while the discriminator learns to more accurately judge the genuineness. For better perceptual similarities, Ledig et al. [26] introduced the

SRGAN, which takes the perceptual loss into consideration while evaluating the cost function. Instead of calculating the root-mean-square error (RMSE) in pixel space, the content loss is implied by calculating the RMSE in VGG19 [39] feature space, i.e. the VGG loss. This grants the SR-images produced by a SRGAN generator satisfying perceptual similarity to the original image as well as optimized recovery of the high frequency details. However, SRGAN produced hallucinated details accompanied with unpleasant artifacts in the images [43]. Hence, Wang et al. proposed the Enhanced SRGAN (ESRGAN) to alleviate such problems by building a residual-in-residual dense block (RRDB) into the SRGAN generator and adopting the idea of relativistic GAN [20].

The ESRGAN has been extended to a turbulence super-resolution GAN (TSRGAN) for this work, as shown in Fig. 10. The TSRGAN is able to deal with 3-D subboxes of the filtered DNS data (scalar and vector fields) as input and employs physics-based loss functions for training of the network. Validation results of the TSRGAN trained with 800 images from the DIV2K archive [3] over 50000 epochs are presented in Fig. 11. Besides the good quality of 2-D reconstruction on images, also the similarity in terms of tensor operations seems to make the TSRGAN a promising candidate for reconstruction of filtered flow data. A filter operation can be seen as convolution, and the network architecture of the TSRGAN heavily relies on convolutional layers.

Loss Function: The perceptual loss proposed for the ESRGAN based on VGG-feature space is apparently not as suitable for the turbulence data, as the geometrical features from VGG19 are not representative for turbulent flows. Hence, a new formulation for the cost function was developed inspired by physical flow constraints.

Before training the TSRGAN as a combined model, the generator is pre-trained with RMSE due to the complexity of the RRDB. For the combined model, the loss function for reconstructing velocity fields is proposed as

$$l = \beta_1 l_{\text{RADG}} + \beta_2 l_{\text{pixel}} + \beta_3 l_{\text{gradient}} + \beta_4 l_{\text{continuity}} \tag{14}$$

with $\beta_1, \beta_2, \beta_3$, and β_4 being coefficients weighting the different loss term contributions. l_{RADG} is the 'realistic average' discriminator/generator loss, which is the accuracy feedback between discriminator and generator as given by Wang et al. [43]. The pixel loss l_{pixel} is defined as

$$l_{\text{pixel}} = \text{MSE}(\mathbf{u}^{\text{predicted}}, \mathbf{u}^{\text{DNS}}). \tag{15}$$

The mean-scare error (MSE) operator is given by

$$\text{MSE}(\{\cdot\}_1, \{\cdot\}_2) = \frac{1}{N_{\text{samples}}} \sum_{i=1}^{N_{\text{samples}}} (\{\cdot\}_1^i - \{\cdot\}_2^i)^2 \tag{16}$$

with N_{samples} as number of all samples, i.e. the total number of grid points of the reconstructed field. If the MSE operator is applied on tensors including vectors,

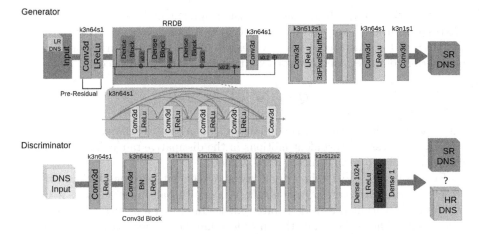

Fig. 10. Sketch of the network used for the reconstruction.

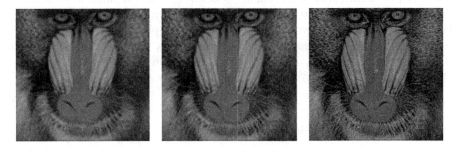

Fig. 11. Comparison of an original (left), bicubic interpolated (center), and TSRGAN-reconstructed image. The original image is taken from the DIV2K archive [3].

it is applied to all elements separately. Afterwards the resulting tensor is mapped into a scalar using the 1-norm. The gradient loss l_{gradient} is defined as

$$l_{\text{gradient}} = \text{MSE}(\nabla \mathbf{u}^{\text{predicted}}, \nabla \mathbf{u}^{\text{DNS}}). \tag{17}$$

$l_{\text{continuity}}$ is the continuity loss, which enforces the continuity equation in the reconstructed field and reads

$$l_{\text{continuity}} = \text{MSE}(\nabla \cdot \mathbf{u}^{\text{predicted}}, \mathbf{0}). \tag{18}$$

Results: To assess the performance of the TSRGAN, the network is trained with Case A and evaluated on Case B. Figure 12 shows 2-D slices of the original DNS velocity fields, the filtered velocity fields, and reconstructed velocity fields. Additionally, Fig. 13 shows 2-D slices of turbulent kinetic energy snapshots. It is clearly visible that small-scale structures are missing in the filtered data. The TSRGAN predicts these structures based on the large-scale features that are present in the filtered field, and the visual agreement between DNS and the predicted solution is very good. Moreover, Fig. 14 shows the vortex structure of the DNS and reconstructed velocity fields, defined by the Q-criterion [9]. The Q-criterion identifies coherent vortex structures by an iso-surface of

$$Q = \frac{1}{4} \left(\boldsymbol{\omega} \cdot \boldsymbol{\omega} - 2\mathbf{S} : \mathbf{S} \right), \tag{19}$$

where $\boldsymbol{\omega} \cdot \boldsymbol{\omega}$ is the enstrophy. By definition, Q is a small-scale quantity, which is suitable to assess the turbulent motions in the dissipative range. The agreement between DNS and reconstructed data is good.

Figures 12, 13, and 14 show good visual agreement between DNS and reconstructed data. However, as turbulence is a multi-scale phenomenon, a visual evaluation of turbulence fields is often misleading, and a statistical assessment is necessary. The spectrum of the turbulent kinetic energy $E(\kappa)$ is a statistical representation of the turbulent kinetic energy in wavenumber space. Different scales can be distinguished: the energy-containing range at small wavenumbers, the inertial subrange at intermediate wavenumbers, and the dissipative range at large wavenumbers. However, it is important to emphasize that a well defined scale-separation between small and large scales only exists at sufficiently high Reynolds numbers. When $E(\kappa)$ is known, the mean turbulent energy can be obtained by

$$\langle k \rangle = \int_0^\infty E(\kappa) \, d\kappa, \tag{20}$$

whereas the mean energy dissipation rate equals

$$\langle \varepsilon \rangle = 2\nu \int_0^\infty \kappa^2 E(\kappa) \, d\kappa. \tag{21}$$

In the context of LES, the filtering operation acts like a low-pass filter and mainly affects the dissipative range, which in turn has a stronger impact on the filtered mean dissipation rate $\langle \bar{\varepsilon} \rangle$ than on the filtered mean turbulent energy $\langle \bar{k} \rangle$.

Figure 15 compares the energy spectrum evaluated on the DNS, reconstructed, and filtered data. It can be observed that the filtering operation is limited to the large wavenumbers and that it removes most energy from the dissipative range. The TSRGAN is able to predict these scales resulting in good agreement between DL-predicted and DNS spectra, except for very large wave numbers in the far dissipative range, where the TSRGAN slightly over-predicts the turbulent energy. These findings support the hypothesis that the TSRGAN is able to learn and reproduce features of small-scale turbulence and can be used to close the LES equations.

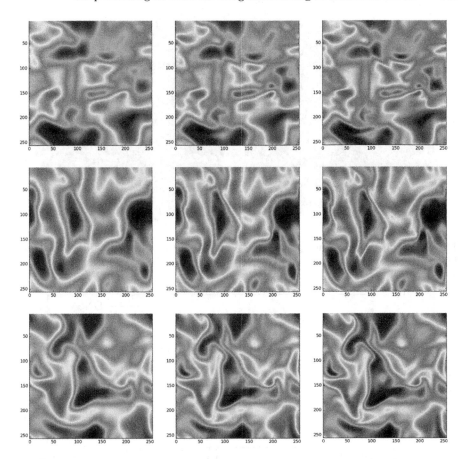

Fig. 12. Comparison of 2-D slices of the filtered (left), DL-reconstructed (center), and DNS (right) data. Snapshots of the three elements of the velocity vector **u** are shown row-by-row.

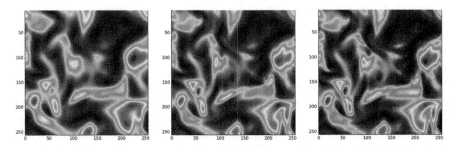

Fig. 13. Comparison of 2-D slices of turbulent kinetic energy k snapshots for filtered (left), DL-reconstructed (center), and DNS (right) data.

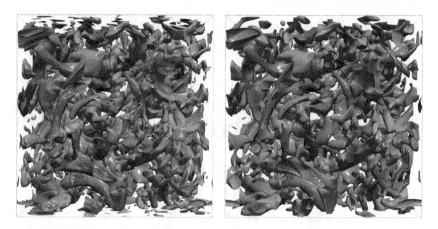

Fig. 14. Comparison of the Q-criterion evaluated on the DL-reconstructed (left) and DNS (right) data.

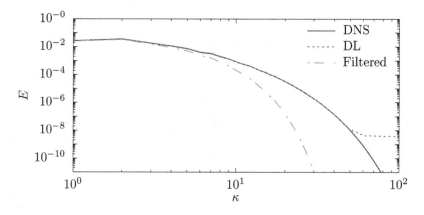

Fig. 15. Comparison of the energy spectra $E(\kappa)$ evaluated on the DNS, DL-reconstructed, and filtered data.

4 Computing

Typically, the single node performance of DL training is very good due to the heavy use of linear algebra-based primitives and the optimization of current GPUs for tensor operations. This is especially true if state-of-the-art libraries, such as TensorFlow, which are highly optimized for GPU usage, are used, as in this work. However, HPC-DL is still challenging. A common way for parallelizing the training of DL networks is to replicate the network across ranks. Thus, each rank processes a different local batch of DNS data, and updates to the network are aggregated among ranks during each training step.

For transforming single-process TensorFlow entities into a data-parallel implementation, Horovod [37] was used, which adds allreduce operations into the back-propagation computation to average the computed gradients from each rank's network. The local networks are updated by the ranks independently, which results in synchronous distributed training due to the use of gradients averaged across all ranks. Obviously, two main challenges are the communication of the information and I/O of data for this procedure. They are addressed separately in the next two subsections. All highly-parallel training for this work was performed on the Supercomputer JURECA at Jülich Supercomputing Centre (JSC), which features nodes equipped with two NVIDIA K80 GPUs (four visible devices per node). Finally, it was possible to train networks with up to 396.2 TFLOPS on JURECA.

4.1 Communication

Horovod uses the first rank as central scheduler for all Horovod operations, employing a dynamical reordering of allreduce operations in order to achieve consistency among all ranks and avoid deadlock due to the independent scheduling of all TensorFlow entities. With an increasing number of ranks, the central scheduler becomes more and more a communication bottleneck as it needs to handle all readiness messages of all other ranks. As a distribution of this scheduling load is not possible due to the required total order of the collective operations, a communication tree was employed in this work. It allows to use Horovod's original scheduler but limits the message load due to the recursive broadcast.

4.2 I/O

As a large amount of DNS data is required for the training of the network, the data transfer to the GPUs is often a bottleneck as the file system - on JURECA GPFS is used - is not fast enough to feed the GPUs in a timely fashion. For this work, a similar strategy as suggested by Kurth et al. [22] was employed. Only a significant fraction of the overall data set was made accessible to each node for the distributed training setting. The locally available data were combined to a local batch in such a way that the set of samples for each rank was statistically similar to a batch selected from the entire data set. Technically, a distributed data staging system was used that first divided the data set into disjoint pieces to be read by each rank, before distributing copies of each file to other nodes by point-to-point MPI messages. This approach takes advantage of the high bandwidth of the InfiniBand network without increasing the load on the file system.

5   Conclusion

Two DL approaches for modeling of subgrid statistics are presented in this paper. It is shown that simple feedforward ANNs are able to learn subgrid statistics with good accuracy if appropriate inputs are chosen. Furthermore, ESRGAN is extended to TSRGAN and used to reconstruct fully-resolved 3-D velocity fields.

Both the visual agreement and the statistical agreement are very good, which indicates that the TSRGAN is able to predict small-scale turbulence. Finally, the code framework used for learning was optimized to achieve 396.2 TFLOPS on the supercomputer JURECA.

Acknowledgment. The authors gratefully acknowledge the computing time granted for the project JHPC55 by the JARA-HPC Vergabegremium and provided on the JARA-HPC Partition part of the supercomputer JURECA at Forschungszentrum Jülich. Also financial support by the Cluster of Excellence "The Fuel Science Center", which is funded by the Deutsche Forschungsgemeinschaft (DFG, German Research Foundation) under Germany's Excellence Strategy – Exzellenzcluster 2186 "The Fuel Science Center" ID: 390919832, and from of the European Research Council (ERC) under the European Union's Horizon 2020 research and innovation program under grant agreement No. 695747 is acknowledged. MG acknowledges financial support provided under the grant EMCO2RE. Furthermore, the authors want to thank Jenia Jitsev, Zeyu Lian, and Mayur Vikas Joshi for their help.

References

1. Keras. https://keras.rstudio.com/index.html
2. Abadi, M., et al.: TensorFlow: large-scale machine learning on heterogeneous systems. https://tensorflow.org
3. Agustsson, E., Timofte, R.: NTIRE 2017 challenge on single image super-resolution: dataset and study. In: The IEEE Conference on Computer Vision and Pattern Recognition (CVPR) Workshops, July 2017
4. Beck, A.D., Flad, D.G., Munz, C.D.: Neural networks for data-based turbulence models. arXiv preprint arXiv:1806.04482 (2018)
5. Bode, M., Gauding, M., Göbbert, J.H., Liao, B., Jitsev, J., Pitsch, H.: Towards prediction of turbulent flows at high reynolds numbers using high performance computing data and deep learning. In: Yokota, R., Weiland, M., Shalf, J., Alam, S. (eds.) ISC High Performance 2018. LNCS, vol. 11203, pp. 614–623. Springer, Cham (2018). https://doi.org/10.1007/978-3-030-02465-9_44
6. Bode, M., Collier, N., Bisetti, F., Pitsch, H.: Adaptive chemistry lookup tables for combustion simulations using optimal B-spline interpolants. Combust. Theor. Model. **23**(4), 674–699 (2019)
7. Cao, Z.M., Nishino, K., Mizuno, S., Torii, K.: PIV measurement of internal structure of diesel fuel spray. Exp. Fluids **29**(1), S211–S219 (2000)
8. Dong, C., Loy, C.C., He, K., Tang, X.: Learning a deep convolutional network for image super-resolution. In: Fleet, D., Pajdla, T., Schiele, B., Tuytelaars, T. (eds.) ECCV 2014. LNCS, vol. 8692, pp. 184–199. Springer, Cham (2014). https://doi.org/10.1007/978-3-319-10593-2_13
9. Dubief, Y., Delcayre, F.: On coherent-vortex identification in turbulence. J. Turbul. **1**(1), 011 (2000)
10. Eswaran, V., Pope, S.: An examination of forcing in direct numerical simulations of turbulence. Comput. Fluids **16**(3), 257–278 (1988)
11. Fukami, K., Nabae, Y., Kawai, K., Fukagata, K.: Synthetic turbulent inflow generator using machine learning. Phys. Rev. Fluids **4**(6), 064603 (2019)
12. Gauding, M., Danaila, L., Varea, E.: High-order structure functions for passive scalar fed by a mean gradient. Int. J. Heat Fluid Flow **67**, 86–93 (2017)

13. Gauding, M., Wang, L., Goebbert, J.H., Bode, M., Danaila, L., Varea, E.: On the self-similarity of line segments in decaying homogeneous isotropic turbulence. Comput. Fluids **180**, 206–217 (2019)
14. Gautier, N., Aider, J.L., Duriez, T., Noack, B., Segond, M., Abel, M.: Closed-loop separation control using machine learning. J. Fluid Mech. **770**, 442–457 (2015)
15. Germano, M., Piomelli, U., Moin, P., Cabot, W.H.: A dynamic subgrid-scale eddy viscosity model. Phys. Fluids A **3**(7), 1760–1765 (1991)
16. Goodfellow, I., et al.: Generative adversarial nets. In: Advances in Neural Information Processing Systems, pp. 2672–2680 (2014)
17. Greenspan, H., Van Ginneken, B., Summers, R.M.: Guest editorial deep learning in medical imaging: overview and future promise of an exciting new technique. IEEE Trans. Med. Imaging **35**(5), 1153–1159 (2016)
18. Hinton, G., et al.: Deep neural networks for acoustic modeling in speech recognition. IEEE Signal Process. Mag. **29**, 82–97 (2012)
19. Jiménez, J.: Machine-aided turbulence theory. J. Fluid Mech. **854**, R1 (2018). https://doi.org/10.1017/jfm.2018.660
20. Jolicoeur-Martineau, A.: The relativistic discriminator: a key element missing from standard GAN. arXiv preprint arXiv:1807.00734 (2018)
21. Kerstein, A.R.: Turbulence in combustion processes: modeling challenges. Proc. Combust. Inst. **29**(2), 1763–1773 (2002)
22. Kurth, T., et al.: Exascale deep learning for climate analysis. In: Proceedings of the International Conference for High Performance Computing, Networking, Storage, and Analysis (2018)
23. Kutz, J.: Deep learning in fluid dynamics. J. Fluid Mech. **814**, 1–4 (2017)
24. Langheinrich, M., Nakamura, A., Abe, N., Kamba, T., Koseki, Y.: Unintrusive customization techniques for web advertising. Comput. Netw. **31**(11–16), 1259–1272 (1999)
25. Lapeyre, C.J., Misdariis, A., Cazard, N., Veynante, D., Poinsot, T.: Training convolutional neural networks to estimate turbulent sub-grid scale reaction rates. Combust. Flame **203**, 255–264 (2019)
26. Ledig, C., et al.: Photo-realistic single image super-resolution using a generative adversarial network. In: Proceedings of the IEEE Conference on Computer Vision and Pattern Recognition, pp. 4681–4690 (2017)
27. Lee, C., Kim, J., Babcock, D., Goodman, R.: Application of neural networks to turbulence control for drag reduction. Phys. Fluids **9**(6), 1740–1747 (1997)
28. Leonard, A.: Energy cascade in large-eddy simulations of turbulent fluid flows. Adv. Geophys. **18**, 237–248 (1975)
29. Ling, J., Kurzawski, A., Templeton, J.: Reynolds averaged turbulence modelling using deep neural networks with embedded invariance. J. Fluid Mech. **807**, 155–166 (2016)
30. Maulik, R., San, O.: A neural network approach for the blind deconvolution of turbulent flows. J. Fluid Mech. **831**, 151–181 (2017)
31. Milano, M., Koumoutsakos, P.: Neural network modeling for near wall turbulent flow. J. Comput. Phys. **182**(1), 1–26 (2002)
32. Overholt, M., Pope, S.: Direct numerical simulation of a passive scalar with imposed mean gradient in isotropic turbulence. Phys. Fluids **8**, 3128–3148 (1996)
33. Parish, E.J., Duraisamy, K.: A paradigm for data-driven predictive modeling using field inversion and machine learning. J. Comput. Phys. **305**, 758–774 (2016)
34. Piomelli, U.: Large-eddy simulation: achievements and challenges. Prog. Aerosp. Sci. **35**(4), 335–362 (1999)

35. Rotunno, R., Chen, Y., Wang, W., Davis, C., Dudhia, J., Holland, G.: Large-eddy simulation of an idealized tropical cyclone. Bull. Am. Meteorol. Soc. **90**(12), 1783–1788 (2009)
36. Ruelle, D., Takens, F.: On the nature of turbulence. Les rencontres physiciens-mathématiciens de Strasbourg-RCP25 **12**, 1–44 (1971)
37. Sergeev, A., Balso, M.: Horovod: fast and easy distributed deep learning in TensorFlow. arXiv:1802.05799 (2018)
38. Shimizu, M., Kawahara, G.: Construction of low-dimensional system reproducing low-Reynolds-number turbulence by machine learning. arXiv preprint arXiv:1803.08206 (2018)
39. Simonyan, K., Zisserman, A.: Very deep convolutional networks for large-scale image recognition. arXiv preprint arXiv:1409.1556 (2014)
40. Smagorinsky, J.: General circulation experiments with the primitive equations: I. The basic experiment. Mon. Weather Rev. **91**(3), 99–164 (1963)
41. Srinivasan, P., Guastoni, L., Azizpour, H., Schlatter, P., Vinuesa, R.: Predictions of turbulent shear flows using deep neural networks. Phys. Rev. Fluids **4**(5), 054603 (2019)
42. Wang, N., Yeung, D.Y.: Learning a deep compact image representation for visual tracking. In: Advances in Neural Information Processing Systems, pp. 809–817 (2013)
43. Wang, X., et al.: ESRGAN: enhanced super-resolution generative adversarial networks. In: Leal-Taixé, L., Roth, S. (eds.) ECCV 2018. LNCS, vol. 11133, pp. 63–79. Springer, Cham (2019). https://doi.org/10.1007/978-3-030-11021-5_5

Using FPGAs to Accelerate HPC and Data Analytics on Intel-Based Systems

Thomas Steinke$^{1(\boxtimes)}$ (ID), Estela Suarez^2, Taisuke Boku^3, Nalini Kumar^4, and David E. Martin^5 (ID)

^{1} Zuse Institute Berlin (ZIB), Takustr. 7, 14195 Berlin, Germany
steinke@zib.de
^{2} Jülich Supercomputing Centre (JSC) - Forschungszentrum Jülich GmbH, Jülich, Germany
^{3} University of Tsukuba, Tsukuba, Ibaraki 305-8577, Japan
^{4} Intel Corporation, Santa Clara, CA 95054, USA
^{5} Argonne National Laboratory, Argonne, IL 60657, USA

Abstract. FPGAs can improve performance, energy efficiency and throughput by boosting computation, I/O and communication operations in HPC, data analytics (DA), and machine learning (ML) workloads and thus complement general-purpose CPUs and GPUs. Recent innovations in hardware and software technologies make FPGAs increasingly attractive for HPC and DA workloads. This first FPGA-focused workshop organized by the IXPUG community gathered experts in the design, programming and usage of reconfigurable systems for HPC and DA workloads to share there experiences with the community.

Keywords: FPGA · Reconfigurable computing · High-performance computing · Data analytics · Machine learning · Intel FPGA ecosystem

1 Field-Programmable Gate Arrays in the Intel Ecosystem

In support of the **Intel eXtreme Performance User's Group** (IXPUG) [1] mission to build a community around Intel HPC technology, members organized a workshop at ISC'19 dedicated to field-programmable gate arrays (FPGA) in Intel-based systems. FPGAs provide the flexibility of configuring hardware building-blocks according to algorithmic descriptions. This flexibility can enable improved performance, energy efficiency and throughput by boosting computation, I/O and communication operations in HPC, data analytics (DA), and machine learning (ML) workloads and thus complement general-purpose CPUs and GPUs.

Recent innovations in hardware and software technologies make FPGAs increasingly attractive for HPC, DA and ML workloads. The technological

M. Weiland et al. (Eds.): ISC 2019 Workshops, LNCS 11887, pp. 561–566, 2019.
https://doi.org/10.1007/978-3-030-34356-9_42

progress includes new FPGA system-on-a-chip (SoC)s featuring multi-core CPUs, an increasingly massive number of reconfigurable logic elements and many hardened floating-point DSP blocks. Improved compiler technologies capable of targeting heterogeneous systems and better tools for transforming intermediate representation objects into a hardware description language enable broader use of FPGAs. Parallel programming models and standard APIs (OpenCL, OpenMP) are evolving to better expressing data parallelism and data dependencies.

With its FPGA flagship products Stratix 10 and Arria 10, Intel is well positioned in the FPGA landscape. Moreover, for over eight years the high-level OpenCL programming model has been supported on Altera/Intel FPGA platforms to lower the barrier for programming for FPGAs.

This workshop provided a unique opportunity to present the status and success stories of using FPGA platforms for HPC, DA and ML workloads, as well as the challenges associated with the migration and optimization of codes for FPGA systems.

2   Workshop Overview

The half day workshop

Using FPGAs to Accelerate HPC & Data Analytics on Intel-Based Systems

brought together over 30 software developers and technology experts from a world-wide community to share challenges, experiences and best-practice methods for using and optimizing HPC and Data Analytics workloads on FPGAs.

The workshop started with a keynote presentation from Christian Plessl (University Paderborn). He provided a introduction into the specific hardware features of FPGAs, and then detailed the performance results and challenges his team faced with during the migration of a Discontinuous Galerkin PDE solver for Maxwell's equations to a Cray CS FPGA cluster with 16 state-of-the-art FPGA nodes containing dual Intel Stratix 10 FPGA cards.

Herman Lam (University of Florida) presented a joint research paper with colleagues from SHREC, CERN, NERSC and Dell that showed the results of accelerating deep learning models by using Intel FPGAs. Nick Brown (EPCC UK) gave a vivid talk about exploring the acceleration of the UK Met Office NERC cloud model using FPGAs in which he guided the audience through various optimization steps, from initial frustration up to shining opportunities to increase far beyond CPU-based approaches. Examples of larger FPGA cluster installations and the associated research on system-middleware in Japan where presented next. Kentaro Sano (RIKEN Center for Computation Science) discussed aspects of using a Stratix 10 FPGA cluster as custom compute engine for supercomputers. Taisuke Boku (University of Tsukuba) presented aspects of heterogeneous computing and low-latency communication between FPGAs and GPUs within the Cygnus cluster at the University of Tsukuba. Staff from ZIB, NESRC and ALCF gave updates of their recent system installations or future plans in short presentations.

Finally, in an invited talk, José Roberto Alvarez (Intel) addressed heterogeneous solutions for artificial intelligence and data analytics using Intel FPGA and CPU platforms.

3 Call for Papers

The call for papers to the ISC'19 IXPUG Workshop opened on January 8, 2019.

IXPUG welcomed paper submissions on innovative work from users of Intel FPGA and Intel processor technologies in academia, industry and government labs, describing original discoveries and experiences that will promote and prescribe efficient use of FPGA systems. Authors were requested to submit papers not published in or being in preparation for other conferences, workshops or journals.

Topics of interest are (but not limited to):

- FPGA programming environments and abstraction tools,
- FPGA programming models,
- comparison of FPGA performance vs. traditional or GPU hardware,
- embedded memory architectures,
- algorithmic techniques and mapping to FPGAs,
- machine learning algorithms on FPGAs,
- FPGA offload techniques,
- FPGA interfaces to traditional hardware,
- integrating FPGAs into an existing HPC environment.

4 Workshop Agenda

Time	Title	Authors (Speaker*)
14:00	IXPUG Welcome	Thomas Steinke (ZIB)
14:05	KEYNOTE: High-Performance Computing with FPGAs	Christian Plessl (Universität Paderborn)
14:45	Acceleration of Scientific Deep Learning Models on Heterogeneous Computing Platform with Intel® FPGAs	Chao Jing, David Ojika, Thorsten Kurth, Prabhat, Sofia Vallecorsa, Bhavesh Patel, and Herman Lam*
15:15	Accelerating the MET Office NERC Cloud Model Using FPGAs	Nick Brown (EPCC UK)
15:45	Cygnus FPGA+GPU Accelerated Cluster at University of Tsukuba	Taisuke Boku (University of Tskuba)
16:00	Break	
16:30	INVITED TALK: Stratix 10 FPGA Cluster as Off-Loaded Custom Computing Engine for Supercomputers	Kentaro Sano (RIKEN Center for Computational Science)
17:05	Research and Development Activities in SHREC@UF* using Intel FPGAs	Herman Lam (University Florida)
17:20	Site Updates: Argonne Nat. Lab, NERSC, ZIB/HLRN	David Martin (ANL), Brandon Cook (NERSC), Thomas Steinke (ZIB)
17:30	INVITED TALK: An Overview of Heterogeneous Solutions for Artificial Intelligence and Data Analytics	José Roberto Alvarez (Sr. Director, PSG CTO Office, Intel Corporation)
18:00	Closing	Thomas Steinke (ZIB)

5   Program Committee

Fabio Affinito	CINECA
R. Glenn Brook	University of Tennessee, Knoxville
Richard Gerber	NERSC/LBNL
Clay Hughes	Sandia National Laboratories
David Keyes	KAUST
James Lin	Shanghai Jiao Tong University
Kent Milfeld	Texas Advanced Computing Center, University of Texas at Austin
Vladimir Mironov	Lomonosov Moscow State University
John Pennycook	Intel Corporation
Sergi Siso	UK Science & Technology Facilities Council
Vit Vondrak	VSB-Technical University of Ostrava

6   Workshop Organizers

Taisuke Boku	University of Tsukuba
David E. Martin	Argonne National Laboratory
Nalini Kumar	Intel Corporation
Thomas Steinke	Zuse Institute Berlin (ZIB)
Estela Suarez	Jülich Supercomputing Centre

7   What You Should Know About IXPUG

The **Intel eXtreme Performance User's Group** (IXPUG) is an independent users group whose mission is to provide a forum for the free exchange of information that enhances the usability and efficiency of scientific and technical applications running on large high performance computing (HPC) systems using data processing devices, network, or storage and other system-critical technologies developed by Intel. IXPUG is administered by representatives of member sites that operate large Intel-based HPC systems.

IXPUG holds meetings and other activities as determined by its members to further its mission. Participation in IXPUG meetings and other activities is open to anyone interested in using Intel technology for HPC systems - today Xeon processors, the Omni-Path interconnect, heterogeneous configurations including FPGAs - for large-scale scientific or technical computing. Current participants include staff from member sites, users of member sites' facilities, Intel staff, and others with an interest in using the Intel technology offerings for scientific computing and data analytics/artificial intelligence on large HPC systems.

A Steering Committee (see Sect. 7.2) manages the overall direction of IXPUG, planning meetings and activities and working with members and sponsors to determine the most effective way to serve the HPC community.

IXPUG provides an effective conduit for application developers to interact directly with Intel engineers and other experts. As part of its community activities, IXPUG regularly organizes workshops and BoFs at the major supercomputing conferences, plus longer self-hosted user meetings distributed througout the year and over a world-wide geography.

The IXPUG Workshop at ISC'19 is the fifth of a workshop series initiated at ISC 2015, which have received active participation and very positively responses by the community. Slides and training materials presented at IXPUG events are accessible through http://www.ixpug.org.

IXPUG workshops cover topics related to application performance and scalability challenges at all levels - from single processors devices to moderately-scaled clusters, up to large HPC systems with complex configurations, e.g. Intel Xeon and Xeon Phi CPUs and heterogeneous data processing devices, and high-performance interconnects (Intel Omni-Path). These hardware related topics are complemented by software aspects, e.g. programming models, languages, communication libraries, high-level frameworks for machine learning, and scalable data management frameworks.

Further information can be found at http://www.ixpug.org/events.

7.1 IXPUG Webinar Series

The IXPUG Webinar Series provides up-to-date insights into a specific topic ranging from new OpenMP extensions, high-performance languages, advanced performance analysis over recent memory technologies up to machine learning with FPGAs and DNN training with Intel optimized software stacks. Registration for future webinars as well as the recorded previous events are public accessible at https://www.ixpug.org/webinar-series.

7.2 The IXPUG Steering Committee

The IXPUG Steering Committee oversees the development of IXPUG and guides the organization of IXPUG events, workshops, and the webinar series. The following list covers a wide range of Intel-based supercomputing institutions and geographic areas:

- Fabio Affinito, CINECA (Italy)
- Taisuke Boku, University of Tsukuba (Japan)
- Richard Gerber, NERSC - National Energy Research Scientific Computing Center/LBL - Lawrence Berkeley National Laboratory (USA)
- Clay Hughes, Sandia National Laboratory (USA)
- David Keyes, KAUST - King Abdullah University of Science & Technology (Saudi Arabia)
- James Lin, Shanghai Jiao Tong University (China)
- David Martin, Argonne National Laboratory (USA)
- Sergi Siso, UK Science & Technology Facilities Council (UK)

- Estela Suarez, Jülich Supercomputing Center, Forschungszentrum Jülich GmbH (Germany)

The steering board is chaired by a leadership board. Its current members are:

- **President:** Thomas Steinke, Zuse Institute Berlin (Germany)
- **Vice-President:** R. Glenn Brook, University of Tennessee Knoxville (USA)
- **Secretary:** Melyssa Fratkin, Texas Advanced Computing Center, The University of Texas at Austin (USA)

References

1. IXPUG: The Intel eXtreme Performance User's Group. http://www.ixpug.org

Exploring the Acceleration of the Met Office NERC Cloud Model Using FPGAs

Nick Brown[(✉)]

EPCC, The University of Edinburgh, Bayes Centre, Edinburgh, UK
n.brown@epcc.ed.ac.uk

Abstract. The use of Field Programmable Gate Arrays (FPGAs) to accelerate computational kernels has the potential to be of great benefit to scientific codes and the HPC community in general. With the recent developments in FPGA programming technology, the ability to port kernels is becoming far more accessible. However, to gain reasonable performance from this technology it is not enough to simple transfer a code onto the FPGA, instead the algorithm must be rethought and recast in a data-flow style to suit the target architecture. In this paper we describe the porting, via HLS, of one of the most computationally intensive kernels of the Met Office NERC Cloud model (MONC), an atmospheric model used by climate and weather researchers, onto an FPGA. We describe in detail the steps taken to adapt the algorithm to make it suitable for the architecture and the impact this has on kernel performance. Using a PCIe mounted FPGA with on-board DRAM, we consider the integration on this kernel within a larger infrastructure and explore the performance characteristics of our approach in contrast to Intel CPUs that are popular in modern HPC machines, over problem sizes involving very large grids. The result of this work is an experience report detailing the challenges faced and lessons learnt in porting this complex computational kernel to FPGAs, as well as exploring the role that FPGAs can play and their fundamental limits in accelerating traditional HPC workloads.

Keywords: FPGAs · High Level Synthesis · MONC · HPC acceleration

1 Introduction

The Met Office NERC Cloud model (MONC) [1] is an open source high resolution modelling framework that employs Large Eddy Simulation (LES) to study the physics of turbulent flows and further develop and test physical parametrisations and assumptions used in numerical weather and climate prediction. As a major atmospheric model used by UK weather and climate communities, MONC replaces an existing model called the Large Eddy Model (LEM) [2] which was an instrumental tool, used by scientists, since the 1980s for activities such as development and testing of the Met Office Unified Model (UM) boundary layer

© Springer Nature Switzerland AG 2019
M. Weiland et al. (Eds.): ISC 2019 Workshops, LNCS 11887, pp. 567–586, 2019.
https://doi.org/10.1007/978-3-030-34356-9_43

scheme [3], convection scheme [4] and cloud microphysics [5]. In order to further the state of the art, scientists wish to model at a greater resolution and/or near real time which requires large amounts of computational resources. The use of modern HPC machines is crucial, however the problems are so challenging that any opportunity to accelerate the model is important. Whilst MONC has traditionally been run across thousands of Intel CPU cores in modern supercomputers [1], a key question is what sort of architecture is optimal going forwards, and what changes are required to the code?

The idea of converting an algorithm into a form that can program a chip directly, and then executing this at the electronics level, has the potential for significant performance and energy efficiency advantages in contrast to execution on general purpose CPUs. However, the production of Application Specific Integrated Circuits (ASICs) is hugely expensive, and so a middle ground of Field Programmable Gate Arrays (FPGAs) tends to be a good choice. This technology provides a large number of configurable logic blocks sitting in a sea of configurable interconnect, and the tooling developed by vendors supports programmers converting their algorithms down to a level which can configure these fundamental components. With the addition of other facets on the chip, such as fast block RAM (BRAM), Digital Signal Processing (DSP) slices, and high bandwidth connections off-chip, FPGAs are hugely versatile. It's a very exciting time for this technology because, whilst they have a long heritage in embedded systems and signal processing, more recently there has been significant interest in using them more widely, such as the deployment of FPGAs in Amazon's F1 cloud computing environment.

However, the use of FPGAs in scientific computing has, until now, been more limited. There are a number of reasons for this, not least the significant difficulty in programming them. But recent advances in high level programming tools means that this technology is now more accessible for HPC application developers. However it isn't enough to simply copy some code over to the FPGA tooling and synthesise it, a programmer must also change the entire way in which they approach their algorithms, moving to a data-flow style [6], in order to achieve anywhere near good performance.

In this paper we describe the work done porting the computationally intensive advection kernel of the MONC atmospheric model to FPGAs. We compare this against the performance one can expect from more traditional Intel based CPU systems, and explore the many options and pitfalls one must traverse in order to obtain good performance of codes on FPGAs. In short, the contributions of this paper are

- Exploration of the steps required to port a computationally intensive kernel onto FPGAs using HLS. We will show that it is not enough to simply copy the code over, but instead the whole approach needs to be rethought and recast.
- An experience report of using FPGAs to solve a computationally intensive kernel on large grids. We run experiments up to grid cells of 257 million grid points, each point requiring over fifty double precision operations.

– A detailed performance comparison, for this application, of the performance characteristics of our FPGA accelerated kernel in comparison to running on Intel CPUs commonly found in HPC machines. We are looking to answer the question, is it worth fitting Intel based systems with FPGAs?

This paper is structured as follows, in Sect. 2 we describe the general background, introducing the MONC model in more detail, the FPGA hardware we are using in this work and describe the approach we have adopted in terms of programming the FPGA. In Sect. 3 we describe the development of our FPGA kernel, in HLS, and explore the different steps that were required to obtain reasonable performance from this code. In Sect. 4 we explore the block design adopted to integrate our kernel with the wider infrastructure supporting it. A performance comparison of our FPGA solution against Intel CPU products commonly found in HPC machines is explored in Sect. 5, before we draw conclusions and discuss further work in Sect. 6.

2 Background

2.1 Met Office NERC Atmospheric Model

The Met Office NERC Cloud model (MONC) has been developed in Fortran 2003 and, like many LES models, proceeds in timesteps, gradually increasing the simulation time on each iteration until reaching a predefined termination time. The model works on prognostic fields, u, v and w for wind in the X, Y and Z dimensions, and a number of other fields which we do not considered in this paper. Figure 1 illustrates the high level structure of a timestep, where each piece of functionality executes sequentially, one after another. Initially, all prognostic fields are halo swapped between neighbouring processes and then the sub-grid functionality determines model parameterisations. Next, the dynamics group, often referred to as the dynamical core, performs Computational Fluid Dynamics (CFD) in order to solve modified Navier-Stokes equations, which is followed by the pressure solver, solving the Poisson equation. The timestep then concludes with some miscellaneous functionality such as checking for model termination. Over 70% of the runtime is spent in the dynamical core and, in particular, the advection scheme. Advection calculates movement of values through the atmosphere due to wind, and at around 50% of the overall runtime, is the single longest running piece of functionality. A number of different advection schemes are provided, and these require all the model's prognostic fields in order to complete their computation.

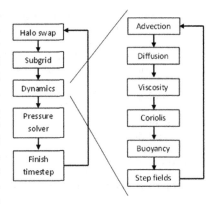

Fig. 1. High level structure of a single MONC timestep

In this work we concentrate on the Piacsek and Williams [7] advection scheme which accounts for around 40% of the model runtime. Listing 1.1 illustrates the MONC Fortran PW advection for advecting the u variable with this scheme. Although this kernel also advects the v and w fields inside the same loop, details for those fields are omitted from Listing 1.1 for brevity as the calculations involved are very similar to those for advecting u. It can be seen that the kernel is composed of three loops, each representing a dimension of our 3D space, and the inner loop, k, in dimension Z loops up a single column. Starting at the second element of the column, this calculates contributions to the *source term* of the flow field, su, based upon values held in u, v and w. Later on in the timestep, after the dynamical core has run, the source terms are then integrated into the flow fields. This advection kernel is a stencil based code, of depth one, accessing values of the three flow fields across all the three dimensions. All calculations are performed in double precision.

```
1   do i=1, x_size
2     do j=1, y_size
3       do k=2, z_size
4         su(k, j, i) = tcx * (u(k,j,i−1) * (u(k,j,i) + u(k,j,i−1)) − u(k,j,i+1) * (u(k,j,i) +
              u(k,j,i+1)))
5
6         su(k, j, i) = su(k, j, i) + tcy * (u(k,j−1,i) * (v(k,j−1,i) + v(k,j−1,i+1)) − u(k,
              j+1,i) * (v(k,j,i) + v(k,j,i+1)))
7
8         if (k .lt. z_size) then
9           su(k, j, i) = su(k, j, i) + tzc1(k) * u(k−1,j,i) * (w(k−1,j,i) + w(k−1,j,i+1))
                − tzc2(k) * u(k+1,j,i) * (w(k,j,i) + w(k,j,i+1))
10        else
11          su(k, j, i) = su(k, j, i) + tzc1(k) * u(k−1,j,i) * (w(k−1,j,i) + w(k−1,j,i+1))
12        end if
13      end do
14    end do
15  end do
```

Listing 1.1. Illustration of the PW advection scheme for the u field only

2.2   Hardware Setup

For the work described in this paper we are using an ADM8K5 PCI Express card, manufactured by Alpha Data, which mounts a Xilinx Kintex Ultrascale KU115-2 FPGA. This FPGA contains 663,360 LUTs, 5520 DSP48E slices and 4320 BRAM 18K blocks. The card also contains two banks of 8 GB DDR4-2400 SDRAM, external to the FPGA, and a number of other interfaces which are not relevant to this work. Because the FPGA used for this work is part of the Xilinx product family, it is their general ecosystem, including tooling, that we use in this work. However, we believe that the lessons learnt apply more generally to product families of FPGAs from other vendors too.

This PCIe card is plugged into an Intel Xeon system, which contains two Sandybridge CPUs, each with four physical cores running at 2.40 GHz, and

32 GB RAM (16 GB per NUMA region). Our approach is to run MONC on the CPU and study the benefit of offloading the PW advection scheme onto the PCIe mounted FPGA. Not only does this involve performing the double precision calculations for all three fields illustrated in Listing 1.1, but also transferring the necessary flow field data onto, and resulting source terms back from, the card. Whilst some FPGAs such as the Zynq use a more embedded style, where typically ARM cores are combined with FPGA fabric on the same chip, we believe this PCIe setup is more interesting in the field of HPC. There are a number of reasons for this, firstly because a powerful Xeon CPU can be used on the host side, secondly because a large amount of memory can be placed close to the FPGA on the PCIe card to handle the processing of large problems, and thirdly because this is a very common accelerator architecture already adopted in HPC GPU systems.

2.3   FPGA Programming Techniques and Our Approach

The traditional approach to programming FPGAs has been to develop codes in a Hardware Description Language (HDL) such as VHDL or Verilog. However, this is a very time consuming process [8] which requires significant expertise and experience. As such, higher level programming tools have been developed to assist in programming, and High Level Synthesis (HLS) is amongst the most prevalent of these. A kernel, written in C, C++ or System C, is automatically translated, via HLS, into the underlying HDL. Driven by pragma style hints provided by the programmer, this substantially speeds up development time and allows for application developers to take advantage of the knowledge and experience of the FPGA vendor. An example of this is in floating point operations, where HLS will automatically include pre-built floating point cores to perform operations, instead of the HDL developer having to develop their own solution.

HLS can be used as a building block of further programming abstractions, and recently the use of OpenCL for programming FPGAs has become popular [9]. Decorating their code via OpenCL abstractions, a tool-chain such as Xilinx's SDAccel converts this into a form understandable by HLS, then uses HLS to generate the appropriate HDL and integrates this into a wider design based upon a board specific support package. An alternative approach which, in contrast to OpenCL, requires a bit more work on behalf of the programmer, is the use of the high-level productivity design methodology [10]. In this technique, the FPGA is configured using a block design approach, where existing IP blocks are imported and connected together by the programmer. This emphasises the reuse of existing IP and the idea of a *shell*, providing general foundational functionality that the programmer's kernel, via an IP block generated by HLS, can be dropped into and easily integrated. By separating the shell from the kernel, the general shell infrastructure can be reused for many different applications, and updating the functionality of the kernel, which is quite common during development, often just requires re-importing the IP block into the board design. This approach also eases testing, as the kernel and shell can be validated separately.

In this work we followed the high-level productivity design methodology, where one explicitly writes a C kernel for HLS, generates the HDL and export this as an IP block. This block is then integrated with a shell, providing the general infrastructure. There were two reasons for adopting this approach, firstly because it gave us more control over the configuration of our design, and we think that some of the lessons learnt for HPC codes could then potentially feed into higher level abstractions, such as those provided by OpenCL. Secondly, we chose this approach because SDAccel, the implementation of OpenCL for Xilinx FPGAs, is an extra commercial product that requires further licencing.

There have been a number of previous activities investigating the role that FPGAs can play in accelerating HPC codes. One such example is [11], where the authors investigated using the high-level productivity design methodology to accelerate solving of the Helmholtz equation. They offloaded the matrix-vector updates requires as part of this solver onto a Zynq Ultrascale, however the performance they observed was around half of that when the code was run on a twelve core Broadwell CPU. Crucially, in our work, we are focused on accelerating a much more complicated kernel. In [11] the author's matrix-vector kernel involved looping over two double precision floating point operations, whereas in comparison the kernel we are offloading to the FPGA comprises of fifty three double precision floating point operations, twenty one double precision additions or subtractions, and thirty two double precision multiplications. We are also running on much larger grid sizes, and whereas in [11] the authors were limited to a maximum data size of 17 MB due to keeping within the BRAM on the Zynq, in the work detailed in this paper we consider grid sizes resulting in 6.44 GB of prognostic field data (and a further 6.44 GB for the field source terms), necessitating the use of external SDRAM on the PCIe card.

3   Developing the PW Advection HLS Kernel

Figure 2 illustrates the performance of our HLS PW advection kernel over numerous steps that we applied one after another, for an experiment of x = 512, y = 512,

Kernel description	Runtime (ms)	LUT usage	DSP48E usage	BRAM-18K usage
Reference on CPU	676.4	NA	NA	NA
Initial port	51498	9743	85	0
Pipeline directive on inner loop	14130	11356	58	64
Local BRAM for column data	3213.2	27598	267	130
Local BRAM batches columns in Y	1513.2	37474	393	453
Extract all variables	1301.6	38393	469	312
Burst mode on port	1097.2	40913	469	324
Re-order X and Y loops	621.3	41151	469	324
Replace memcpy with explicit loops	568.1	40638	466	324
Tune double precision cores and clock to 310Mhz	514.9	27601	406	324

Fig. 2. Runtime of the PW advection kernel alone for different steps taken when porting it to HLS for a problem size of x = 512, y = 512, z = 64 (16.7 million grid cells)

$z = 64$ (16.7 million grid cells). We use this table to drive our discussions in this section about the different steps required to optimise an HLS kernel and, for reference, the top entry of Fig. 2, *Reference on CPU*, illustrates the kernel's runtime over a single Sandybridge CPU core on the host. Our focus in this section is the HLS kernel alone, and as such we ignore the transferring of data which must occur to the PCIe before the kernel runs and the copying back of data once the kernel has completed. This transferring is considered in more detail in the next section.

As a first step we ported the Fortran PW advection kernel for advecting the u, v and w flow fields, (see Listing 1.1) into C and the initial port of this onto the FPGA involved little more than just copying the C into the HLS tool and applying the correct directives to determine the type of external port interfaces. This is illustrated in Listing 1.2, for the double precision array u, representing wind in the X dimension, and source term su which containing advected values calculated by this kernel for the X dimension. There are also arrays for v, sv, w and sw which are omitted from Listing 1.2 due to brevity. In this section we refer to these six arrays as the *kernel's external data arrays*, and these use the AXI4 protocol. The *offset=slave* specifier bundles them into a single port and instructs HLS that these point to different addresses in the control bus port. Other scalar variables such as the size of the data in each dimension, $size\_x$ and $size\_y$ in Listing 1.2, are also provided via the AXI4-Lite control bus port. This control bus port is exposed to the host as a memory block, which the host can then write to, and HLS provides the explicit location in this block of the different variables. This initial version was trivial, both from a code and FPGA utilisation perspective, requiring less than 10,000 LUTs, a handful of DSP48E slices and no BRAM, however at 51498 milliseconds (51 s) it was very slow.

```
1    int pw_advection(double * u, double * su, ..., int size_x, int size_y, ...) {
2        #pragma HLS INTERFACE m_axi port=u offset=slave
3        #pragma HLS INTERFACE m_axi port=su offset=slave
4
5        #pragma HLS INTERFACE s_axilite port=size_x bundle=CTRL_BUS
6        #pragma HLS INTERFACE s_axilite port=size_y bundle=CTRL_BUS
7        #pragma HLS INTERFACE s_axilite port=return bundle=CTRL_BUS
8        .....
9    }
```

Listing 1.2. Skeleton of HLS main function, illustrating external data interfaces

We next added the HLS pipeline directive, *#pragma HLS PIPELINE II=1*, to our inner loop, working up a single column. This instructs HLS to pipeline the processing of the inner loop and *II* is the initiation interval latency, which instructs HLS how often to add a new element of data to the pipeline, in this case every cycle if possible. HLS takes the inner loop, containing our 53 double precision operations, and breaks this up into individual pipeline stages which can run concurrently. These are then fed with data from the outer loops and, once the pipeline is filled, each stage is running, at the same time, on a different element of data before passing the result to the next stage. From Fig. 2 it can be seen that this significantly decreased the runtime of the kernel, by around five times, but this was still around twenty time slower than running on the CPU.

The bottleneck at this stage was that the data port, used to implement the kernel's external data arrays, that we read from extensively in the calculation of a single column, does not support more than one access per clock cycle. Hence we were instructing HLS to pipeline the inner loop, so that functionality within it runs concurrently on different elements of data. But crucially HLS realised that there would be numerous conflicts on the data port if it fully pipelined the calculations, and as such very severely limited the design of the pipeline. To address this, we created a number of local arrays to hold all the data required for working with a single column, and this is illustrated in Listing 1.3. We actually created twenty two arrays, for the six kernel external data arrays, three input flow field and three output source term arrays, which included columns in other X and Y dimension indexes. Threes of these local arrays, *u_vals*, *u_xp1_vals* (holding a column of data of the X+1 column) and *u_vals2* are illustrated in Listing 1.3 and these are set to a static size (*MAX_VERTICAL_SIZE*) as array sizes can not be dynamically sized in HLS. The arrays are filled with the data required for a column via the memory copies at lines 5 to 7 (note *u(i,j,0)* is a preprocessor directive that expands out to index the appropriate 3D location in the array), before executing the calculations needed on that column. The idea was that all accesses on the port are before the calculations start and therefore there are no conflicts during the pipelined inner loop. We use on-chip BRAM to store these array, and HLS can make these either single ported or dual ported, meaning that it can either be accessed once or twice independently in a clock cycle. The challenge here is that, for a specific column, there are a large number of accesses to each array within the inner loop, for instance there are nine accesses to the *u_vals* array which holds the current column's data for the *u* external data array.

```
1   double u_vals[MAX_VERTICAL_SIZE], u_xp1_vals[MAX_VERTICAL_SIZE], u_vals2
        [MAX_VERTICAL_SIZE], ....;

2
3   for (unsigned int i=start_x;i<end_x;i++) {
4       for (unsigned int j=start_y;j<end_y;j++) {
5           memcpy(u_vals, &u(i,j,0), sizeof(double) * size_z);
6           memcpy(u_xp1_vals, &u(i+1,j,0), sizeof(double) * size_z);
7           memcpy(u_vals2, &u(i,j,0), sizeof(double) * size_z);
8           ....
9           for (unsigned int k=1;k<size_z;k++) {
10              #pragma HLS PIPELINE II=1
11              .....
12          }
13      }
14  }
```

Listing 1.3. Using local BRAM to store data for a single column data

To address this we duplicated these same arrays, for instance *u_vals2* which holds the same data as *u_vals*. Whilst another way around this in HLS is to use partitioning, effectively splitting the array up across multiple BRAM controllers, due to the dynamic size of the inner loop, we would have been forced to partition the arrays into single elements, and this resulted in worse utilisation and performance. In comparison, duplicating the BRAM array worked well.

It can be seen from Fig. 2 that this local copying of data decreased the runtime by over four times. However, the major disadvantage of the approach in Listing 1.3 is that the outer loops of j in the Y dimension and i in the X dimension are no longer continually feeding data into the pipelined inner loop. Instead, the inner loop runs in a pipelined fashion just for a single column, in this case of maximum 64 data elements, and then must drain and stop, before memory copies into local arrays are performed for the next column. Bearing in mind the pipeline of this inner loop is, as reported by HLS, 71 cycles deep, with an initiation interval, the best HLS can provide, of 2 cycles and assuming a column size of 64 elements, for each column the pipeline will run for 199 cycles but for only 57 of these cycles (28%) is the pipeline full utilised, the rest of the time it is either filling or draining.

To address this we extended our local BRAM arrays to hold data for multiple columns in the Y dimension, extending each array from $MAX\_VERTICAL\_SIZE$ to $MAX\_VERTICAL\_SIZE * Y\_BATCH\_SIZE$. In this situation the middle loop, j, working in the Y dimension runs in batches, of size Y_BATCH_SIZE. For each batch it will copy the data for Y_BATCH_SIZE columns, and then process each of these columns. The major benefit of this approach is that our pipeline, working up the column in the inner loop, is now fed by Y_BATCH_SIZE columns rather than one single column. Additionally, at this point, HLS reported that it had been able to reduce the initiation interval down from two to one, effectively doubling the performance of the inner loop pipeline. Assuming a Y_BATCH_SIZE of 64 and that the column size is still 64, the pipeline now runs for 4167 cycles, 97% of which the pipeline is fully filled. This represents a significant increase in utilisation, and ultimately performance, because the pipeline is able to process, and hence generate a result, every clock cycle for 97% of the time it is running. As per Fig. 2, this over halved the kernel execution time at the cost of increasing the BRAM usage by over three times.

At this point the individual lines of code for our inner loop kernel, containing the fifty three double precision floating point operations, were still laid out similarly to Listing 1.1, where the calculations for a specific value of the source term were in one line. We had trusted HLS to extract out the individual variable accesses, and structure these appropriately, but we found that actually HLS does a fairly poor job of identifying which variables are shared and hence can be reused between calculations. As such, we significantly restructured the code, splitting up calculations into their individual components of reading data into temporary variables and then using that single variable whenever the value is required in the inner loop. This is the *Extract all variables* entry of Fig. 2 and had two impacts. Firstly, it reduced the pipeline depth from 71 cycles deep to 65, and hence provided a modest increase in performance, but also it reduced the number of reads on our local arrays and so we were able to remove a number of duplicate local arrays which reduced the overall BRAM usage by around 30%.

When issuing memory copies, for instance in lines 5 to 7 of Listing 1.3, the port must be read which accesses data from external SDRAM, and the same is true in the other direction when writing data. In the default mode, ports will tend to issue an access for every individual element, but instead it is possible to decorate the kernel's external data array variable definitions (e.g. u and su) with pragmas to instruct HLS to issue bursts of data, retrieving n elements in one go. This is important in our situation because we are never just reading one element at a time, but instead the data for Y_BATCH_SIZE columns. The $HLS\ INTERFACE$ pragma, as illustrated in Listing 1.2, was modified for our kernel's external data arrays (e.g. u and su) with the addition of $num\_read\_outstanding=8$ $num\_write\_outstanding=8$ $max\_read\_burst\_length=256$ $max\_write\_burst\_length=256$. This directs HLS to read and write in bursts of size 256, the maximum size, and supports holding up to eight of these bursts at any one time. The $latency$ modifier advises HLS to issue the access before it is needed, in this example around 60 cycles beforehand. HLS uses BRAM to store these bursts and, as can be seen in Fig. 2, resulted in a modest increase in BRAM usage but also a reasonable decrease in execution time.

At this point we are working in batches of columns and as our middle, i, loop running over the Y dimension, reaches the limit of one batch it stops and retrieves data from memory for the next batch. Crucially, this happens for every iteration in the outer loop, i, over the X dimension and as the code progresses from one level in X to the next, then all batches in Y are run again. The problem with this is that there are fifteen memory copies required for every batch and this involves significant amounts of time accessing the DRAM. It is possible to address this by moving the outer loop, i, over the X dimension, inside the j middle loop which is running over a single batch of columns. This means that memory accesses themselves in the X dimension are effectively pipelined too, and is illustrated by Listing 1.4. For brevity we just show a subset of the variables and local arrays, but it is enough to demonstrate the approach. It can be seen that the loop ordering has changed, such that the outer loop is now looping m times, once per batch of MAX_Y_SIZE columns at line 1. The start of a batch requires data to be copied into the $up1\_vals$ variable, representing the column plus one in the X dimension. Then, as the loop progresses through levels in the X dimension, for each next level, u_vals is populated with data from $up1\_vals$ and only the plus one level in the X dimension, i.e. $up1\_vals$ needs to go to SDRAM memory to retrieve the $i+1$ column in X. All other copies, for instance u_vals at line 5, are accessing chip local BRAM which is much faster than going off chip to the SDRAM. This significantly reduces the number of off chip data accesses to DRAM that need to be performed and almost halves the runtime of the kernel.

```
1   for (unsigned int m=start_y;m<end_y;m+=MAX_Y_SIZE) {
2       memcpy(up1_vals, &u(start_x,m,0), sizeof(double) * MAX_VERTICAL_SIZE*
        MAX_Y_SIZE);
3       ....
4       for (unsigned int i=start_x;i<end_x;i++) {
5           memcpy(u_vals, up1_vals, sizeof(double) * MAX_VERTICAL_SIZE*
            MAX_Y_SIZE);
```

```
6          memcpy(up1_vals, &u(i+1,m,0), sizeof(double) * MAX_VERTICAL_SIZE*
               MAX_Y_SIZE);
7          ....
8          for (unsigned int j=0;j<MAX_Y_SIZE;j++) {
9              ....
10         }
11     }
12 }
```

Listing 1.4. Reordering the X and Y loops to pipeline memory access in the X dimension

Until this point we have relied on the use of the *memcpy* function to copy data from one location to another. However bearing in mind there are multiple copies of local column data arrays due to BRAM port limits, e.g. *u_vals* and *u_vals2*, issuing a separate memcpy for each of these when we loop into the next X dimension is quite slow because HLS will not execute these memory copies concurrently. Instead, replacing the *memcpy* calls with explicit loops, where each index location is read from the source array and then written to each of the target arrays was faster. In fact, more generally we found that replacing all the *memcpy* calls with an explicitly pipelined loop that performed the copying in user code, was beneficial. This is represented as the *Replace memcpy with explicit loops* entry of Fig. 2 and it can be seen that not only did we obtain a modest increase in performance, but it also decreased our LUT utilisation slightly.

The default clock on the ADM8K5 board is 250 Mhz, and so a period of 4ns was used initially, with HLS estimating a clock period of 3.75 ns due to limits in double precision multiplication. However, via configuring the HLS floating point kernels it was possible to tune them. Using *#pragma HLS RESOURCE variable=a core=DMul_maxdsp latency=14*, HLS was instructed to use the *DMul_maxdsp* double precision floating point core (leveraging DSP slices as much as possible for the double precision multiplication) with a latency of 14 cycles for all multiplications involving the variable *a*. This latency is the core's pipeline depth and, by increasing it, it is possible to reduce the minimum clock period. We applied this directive to all variables that are involved in double precision multiplication, and found that the best clock period we could get from the double precision multiplication core was 2.75 ns. Whilst the latency value can go all the way up to twenty, above fourteen made no difference to the period. As such we were able to reduce our clock period to 3.2 (there is a 12.5% clock uncertainty), meaning we could run our kernel at 310Mhz instead of 250Mhz. The pipeline depth has increased from 65 to 72, but due to the increase in clock frequency, the overall latency for data to progress through the pipeline has gone from $2.6e-7$ s to $2.3e-7$ s, so there is an increase in overall performance.

From Fig. 2 it can be seen that the LUT and DSP48E utilisation dropped very significantly with this last configuration. This was because we also instructed HLS to use the full DSP core when it came to double precision addition and subtraction. It is the use of this core that reduced the LUT usage by around a quarter, and also, ironically, slightly reduced the number of DSP48E slices too.

As a result of the steps applied in this section, we have reduced the runtime of our HLS kernel by over 100 times, from being 75 times slower than running over a single Sandybridge CPU core on the host, to being around a quarter faster, however as noted at the start of the section this is just the kernel execution time and ignores the DMA transfer time needed to get data on and off the board before and after the kernel runs.

4   Putting It All Together, the Block Design

Once developed, we then need to integrate our PW advection kernel with general infrastructure to connect our kernel to the PCIe interface and on card SDRAM. The general workflow is that field data is transferred from the host to the on card SDRAM via DMA and kernels are then run, reading data from the SDRAM and writing source term results to SDRAM, and once complete results are transferred back from the SDRAM to the host via DMA. Figure 3 illustrates the block design of our system, and in this design we are using four PW advection kernels, towards the top centre of Fig. 3 with the HLS logos. The IP block on the bottom left is the PCIe interface, providing four independent DMA channels that can be used for communication and a direct slave interface that can also be used for communication. The two big blocks on the far right are memory controllers for the on card SDRAM, each controller responsible for one of the two banks of on card 8GB memory. We connect the first two PCIe interface DMA channels to the first memory controller, and the other two DMA channels to the second memory controller. In between the PCIe interface and their corresponding SDRAM memory controller, these connections pass through infrastructure which, for instance, converts the clock from the PCIe clock domain to the SDRAM memory controller clock domain. In this design, to avoid bottlenecks, the two banks of 8GB memory are entirely separate and it is not possible for an IP block connected to one bank to access memory of the other bank.

Figure 4 provides a more detailed view of the integration of our PW advection kernel IP blocks. For purposes of illustration, we have slightly moved the appropriate IP blocks around, when compared to Fig. 3, so the topical ones are in the same image. On the bottom left of Fig. 4, the *ADM PCIe* block is the PCIe interface and the four DMA channel ports on the right of this IP block, along with the direct slave port can be clearly seen. The clocking wizard, top left, converts the 250 Mhz reference clock up to 310 Mhz for the PW advection IP blocks as described in Sect. 3. The direct slave interface is connected to the kernel's control port, and by writing or reading the appropriate bit we can manage the kernels such as starting or tracking progress. This connection goes, via an AXI4 clock converter IP block, to the slave interface of the left most AXI interconnect. This interconnect splits the direct slave data according to its address, the appropriate data then routed to its corresponding PW advection kernel. These addresses are defined in the block design address editor.

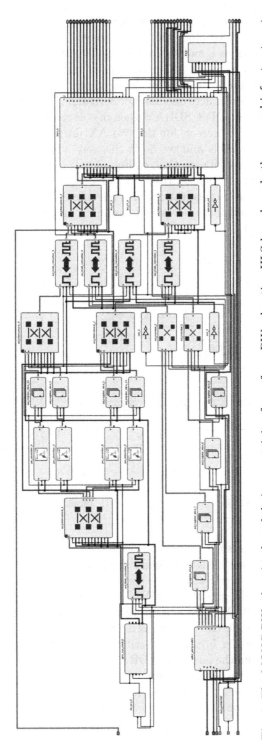

Fig. 3. The MONC PW advection board design, containing four of our PW advection HLS kernels and other general infrastructure to support this

The main data port, m_axi_gmem, of the PW advection kernel is on the right of the PW advection IP block and it is through this port that the kernel's external data arrays such as u and su are routed. This AXI4 data port connects, via an AXI register slice, to an AXI interconnect on the right of Fig. 4. Our PW advection kernels are split into two groups, one group connecting to the first SDRAM memory controller (one bank of 8GB RAM) and the second group connecting to the second DDR SDRAM memory controller (the second bank of 8GB RAM). This is the reason for the two AXI interconnects on the right, one for each group of kernels and we do it this way with the aim of reducing congestion. For purposes of illustration, in Figs. 3 and 4 we limited ourselves to just four PW advection IP blocks. However our design is scalable and adding additional PW advection kernels just requires reconfiguration of the appropriate AXI interconnects to add more ports and assigning an address to the new IP block's control bus port.

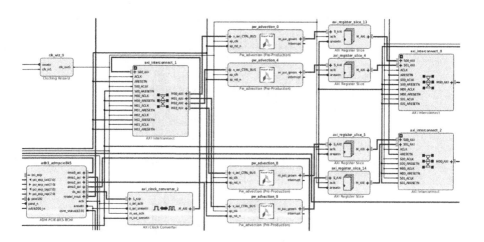

Fig. 4. Integration of the PW advection HLS IP blocks in our board design

When it came to the shell and overall kernel integration, we experimented with a number of different designs to understand which would provide the best performance. The main driver here is the speed to access the SDRAM and avoid memory accesses becoming a bottleneck. We found this design, where we keep the two banks of 8GB SDRAM entirely separate and connect each to two different DMA channels, to provide the best performance. A summary of these investigations is illustrated in Fig. 5, which describes the transfer time, via DMA, to copy 1.6 GB of data from the host to the DRAM on the PCIe card. The first row of Fig. 5 is the design that we have described in this section. The second row, *one memory controller only*, is when all four DMA channels are used but we only copy the data into one of the memory controllers, and it can be seen that this increases the transfer time by around a fifth. The third entry is where there are two memory controllers, each serviced by two DMA channels, but these are connected together in one large memory space so any memory access can see all the 16 GB SDRAM. This is slightly slower than our split approach, because all memory accesses go through a single AXI interconnect, but there isn't much in it. The last entry of the table, is where the two banks of memory is kept separate, but we only drive these via one single DMA channel. This adds around a third to the overall DMA transfer time because transfers on the same channel need to queue up and so being able to spread them out across multiple channels and transfer concurrently is optimal.

Description	DMA transfer time (milliseconds)
Design described here	232
One memory controller only	280
Two memory controllers connected	239
One DMA channel per memory controller	342

Fig. 5. DMA transfer time for different configurations with a data size of 1.6 GB

5   Performance Comparison

We built the block design described in Sect. 4 with twelve PW advection kernels as described in Sect. 3. In order to fit within the limits of the Kintex FPGA we instructed HLS to use the medium DSP core for double precision multiplication. This resulted in an overall design utilisation of 78.5% of the Kintex's LUTs, 84.2% BRAM-18k blocks and 89% of the chip's DSP48E slices. It took around fifteen hours of CPU time to build the entire design, most of which was spent in the place and route phases.

Once built, we compared the performance of our PW advection FPGA design against a C version of the same PW advection algorithm, threaded via OpenMP across the cores of the CPU. For all runs the host code was compiled with GCC version 4.8 at optimisation level 3 and the results reported are averaged across fifty timesteps. Figure 6 illustrates a performance comparison of our FPGA kernel against the CPU only code running on Sandybridge, Ivybridge and Broadwell CPUs for a standard MONC stratus cloud test case of size $x = 1012$, $y = 1024$, $z = 64$ (67 million grid cells). For each technology there are two runtime numbers, in milliseconds. The first, *optimal performance*, illustrates the best performance we can get on the CPU by threading over all the physical cores (4 in the case of Sandybridge, 12 in the case of Ivybridge, 18 in the case of Broadwell, and 12 in the case of our FPGA design.) We also report a four core number, which includes only running over four physical cores, or PW advection kernels in the case of our FPGA design, as this is the limit of the Sandybridge CPU and it allows more direct comparison.

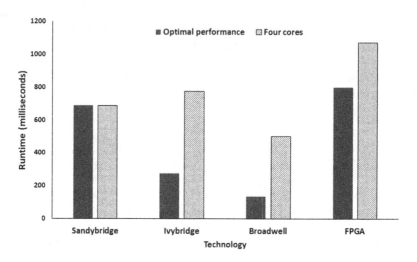

Fig. 6. Performance comparison of $x = 1012$, $y = 1024$, $z = 64$ (67 million grid points) with a standard status cloud test-case

It can be seen from Fig. 6 that our optimal FPGA version performs slower in comparison to all CPU products tested and this trend continues when we consider four core performance. This might seem strange seeing that, in Sect. 3, our HLS kernel is faster than running on a single core of Sandybridge and actually is comparable to running on a single core of Broadwell. However, crucially there we were just concerned with the kernel execution time and ignored the DMA transfer time and the results reported in Fig. 6 contain both these aspects.

To understand this further, Fig. 7 illustrates the same experiment setup as we scale the number of PW advection kernels from one to twelve. For each configuration we report the total runtime and then break it down to the total time required for DMA transfer of data both to and from the card, and the kernel execution time. In all cases we distribute the cores as evenly as possible across groups, for instance two cores uses 1 core from each group, four cores uses two cores from each group. This experiment represents a grid size of 67 million points, and three fields, each point of which is double precision, hence a total of 3.32 GB is being transferred. It can be seen that, for small numbers of advection kernels, the kernel runtime is by far the most significant. However this scales well and as we reach four kernels and beyond the DMA transfer time becomes dominant and 70% of the total time with twelve kernels is in DMA transfer.

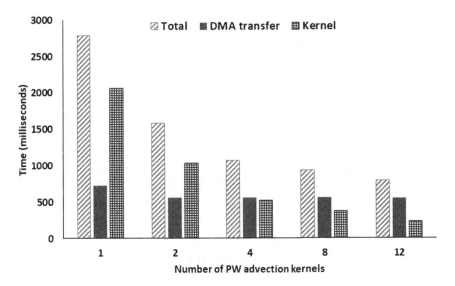

Fig. 7. Runtime of different numbers of PW advection kernel broken down into constituent parts when scaling number of kernels, x = 1012, y = 1024, z = 64 (67 million grid cells) with a standard status cloud test-case

Figure 8 illustrates how the time, in milliseconds, changes as we scale the number of grid cells, note that this is a log scale. We report three numbers for our FPGA approach (12 PW advection kernels), the total time, the execution time of the kernel and the total DMA transfer time. For comparison we also illustrate the runtime of the code on 18 physical cores of Broadwell and 12 physical cores of Broadwell (as we have 12 PW advection kernels). Whilst our PW advection FPGA version is slower than both Broadwell configurations, the FPGA HLS kernel itself is faster at 1 million grid cells, competitive with both at 4 million grid cells and competitive with the 12 Broadwell cores until 16 million grid cells. In terms of FLOPs, at 268 million grid cells our HLS kernel is providing 14.36 GFLOP/s (in comparison to 12 cores of Broadwell at 17.75 GFLOPs/), however when one includes the DMA transfer time this drops down to 4.2 GFLOP/s and so illustrates the very significant impact that DMA transfer time has on our results. The limit with some other investigations such as [11], is that they focus on the embedded CPU-FPGA Zynq chip, and limit their system size very severely to the BRAM on that chip. As such they don't encounter this transfer time overhead, but this is crucially important to bear in mind for processing realistic problems that are of interest to scientists.

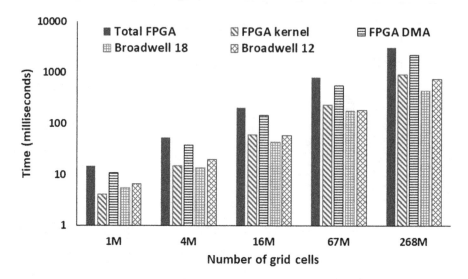

Fig. 8. Runtime of our FPGA PW advection code (12 kernels) vs Broadwell as we scale the grid size with a standard stratus cloud test-case

6   Conclusions and Further Work

In this paper we have described our approach in porting the PW advection kernel of the MONC atmospheric model onto FPGAs. Using HLS, we explored in detail the different steps required in porting the kernel and how best to structure the board design. We have shown that it is crucial that HPC application developers rethink and recast their code to suit the data-flow pattern, and have demonstrated a 100 times performance difference between code that does not do this and the same functionality, albeit where the code looks very different, tuned for the FPGA. This re-enforces the point that, whilst it is fairly simple for an HPC applications developer to import some C code into HLS and synthesis this, significant work and experimentation is required to get reasonable performance.

When considering only the kernel execution time, our HLS kernel outperformed a single core of Sandbridge and performs comparable with a single Broadwell core. But when including the DMA transfer time we found that this is a very severe limitation of our FPGA design in contrast to the performance one can gain from the same advection kernel threaded over the cores of Intel CPUs commonly found in HPC machines.

When it comes to further work, it is this DMA transfer time that needs to be tackled. At the largest problem size of 268 million grid cells explored in this paper, a total of 12.88 GB needs to be transferred which takes 2.2 s and represents a transfer rate of 5.85 GB/s, which is reasonable based on the specifications of this PCIe card. One idea is to use single rather than double precision, which would effectively halve the amount of data that needs to be transferred, although the DMA transfer time at 134 million grid points is still substantially slower than

Broadwell execution time at 268 million grid points. Another idea is to chunk up the DMA transfer, starting the appropriate PW advection kernel as soon as the applicable chunk has arrived rather than all the data, this could be driven by a host thread or extra logic in the block design.

There is also further exploration that can be done based on our HLS kernel and one aspect would be to look at how best to further increase the clock speed. The 2.8 ns period of the double precision multiply currently limits us to 310 Mhz, but replacing double precision with single or fixed point could enable higher clock frequencies and single precision would also halve the amount of data transferred from SDRAM to the kernels. This last point is important, because we believe that SDRAM access time is now the major source of overhead in our HLS kernel.

Therefore, we conclude that, whilst FPGAs are an interesting and generally speaking viable technology for accelerating HPC kernels, there is still work to be done to obtain performance competitive to modern day Intel CPUs. When running large system sizes on PCIe mounted FPGAs, the cost of transferring data to and from the card can be very significant and severely limits performance. This is important to bear in mind and, going forwards, if we can address these limits then we feel that FPGAs will become a much more competitive approach.

Acknowledgements. The authors would like to thank Alpha Data for the donation of the ADM8K5 PCIe card used throughout the experiments of work. This work was funded under the EU FET EXCELLERAT CoE, grant agreement number 823691.

References

1. Brown, N., et al.: A highly scalable Met Office NERC Cloud model. In: Proceedings of the 3rd International Conference on Exascale Applications and Software, pp. 132–137. University of Edinburgh, April 2015
2. Brown, A.R., et al.: Large-eddy simulation on a parallel computer. In: Proceedings Turbulence and Diffusion, no. 240 (1997)
3. Lock, A.P.: The parametrization of entrainment in cloudy boundary layers. Q. J. R. Meteorol. Soc. **124**(552), 2729–2753 (1998)
4. Petch, J.C., Gray, M.E.B.: Sensitivity studies using a cloud-resolving model simulation of the tropical west Pacific. Q. J. R. Meteorol. Soc. **127**(577), 2287–2306 (2001)
5. Hill, A.A., et al.: Mixed-phase clouds in a turbulent environment. Part 1: large-eddy simulation experiments. Q. J. R. Meteorol. Soc. **140**(680), 855–869 (2014)
6. Ma, Y., et al.: Optimizing loop operation and dataflow in FPGA acceleration of deep convolutional neural networks. In: Proceedings of the 2017 ACM/SIGDA International Symposium on Field-Programmable Gate Arrays, pp. 45–54. ACM, February 2017
7. Piacsek, S.A., Williams, G.P.: Conservation properties of convection difference schemes. J. Comput. Phys. **6**(3), 392–405 (1970)
8. Maxfield, C.: The Design Warrior's Guide to FPGAs: Devices, Tools and Flows. Elsevier, Amsterdam (2004)
9. Muslim, F.B., et al.: Efficient FPGA implementation of OpenCL high-performance computing applications via HLS. IEEE Access **5**, 2747–2762 (2017)

10. Xilinx: High-Level Productivity Design Methodology Guide (2018). https://www.xilinx.com/support/documentation/sw_manuals/ug1197-vivado-high-level-productivity.pdf. Accessed 11 Apr 2019
11. Ashworth, et al.: First steps in porting the LFRic weather and climate model to the FPGAs of the EuroExa architecture (2018)

Acceleration of Scientific Deep Learning Models on Heterogeneous Computing Platform with Intel® FPGAs

Chao Jiang[1]([⊠]) , Dave Ojika[1] , Thorsten Kurth[2] , Prabhat[2],
Sofia Vallecorsa[3], Bhavesh Patel[4], and Herman Lam[1]

[1] SHREC: NSF Center for Space, High-Performance and Resilient Computing,
Gainesville, USA
{jc19chaoj,davido,hlam}@ufl.edu
[2] National Energy Research Scientific Computing Center (NERSC), Berkeley, USA
{tkurth,prabhat}@lbl.gov
[3] CERN openlab, Geneva, Switzerland
sofia.vallecorsa@cern.ch
[4] Dell EMC, Hopkinton, USA
bhavesh.a.patel@dell.com

Abstract. AI and deep learning are experiencing explosive growth in almost every domain involving analysis of big data. Deep learning using Deep Neural Networks (DNNs) has shown great promise for such scientific data analysis applications. However, traditional CPU-based sequential computing can no longer meet the requirements of mission-critical applications, which are compute-intensive and require low latency and high throughput. Heterogeneous computing (HGC), with CPUs integrated with accelerators such as GPUs and FPGAs, offers unique capabilities to accelerate DNNs. Collaborating researchers at SHREC[1] at the University of Florida, NERSC[2] at Lawrence Berkeley National Lab, CERN Openlab, Dell EMC, and Intel are studying the application of heterogeneous computing (HGC) to scientific problems using DNN models. This paper focuses on the use of FPGAs to accelerate the inferencing stage of the HGC workflow. We present case studies and results in inferencing state-of-the-art DNN models for scientific data analysis, using Intel distribution of OpenVINO, running on an Intel Programmable Acceleration Card (PAC) equipped with an Arria 10 GX FPGA. Using the Intel Deep Learning Acceleration (DLA) development suite to optimize existing FPGA primitives and develop new ones, we were able accelerate the scientific DNN models under study with a speedup from 3× to 6× for a single Arria 10 FPGA against a single core (single thread) of a server-class Skylake CPU.

1   Introduction

AI and deep learning are experiencing explosive growth in almost every domain involving analysis of big data. Deep learning(DL) using Deep Neural Networks

© Springer Nature Switzerland AG 2019
M. Weiland et al. (Eds.): ISC 2019 Workshops, LNCS 11887, pp. 587–600, 2019.
https://doi.org/10.1007/978-3-030-34356-9_44

(DNNs) has shown great promise for such scientific data analysis applications. However, traditional CPU-based sequential computing without special instructions can no longer meet the requirements of mission-critical applications, which are compute-intensive and require low latency and high throughput. Heterogeneous computing (HGC), using CPUs integrated with accelerators such as GPUs and FPGAs, offers unique capabilities to accelerate DNNs. At the University of Florida site of the NSF Center for Space, High-Performance, and Resilient Computing (SHREC: www.nsf-shrec.org), we are developing such an HGC system to support a complete HGC workflow for deep learning. This project is a collaborative effort between SHREC and NERSC at Berkeley National Lab, CERN openlab, Dell EMC, and Intel.

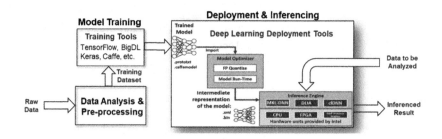

Fig. 1. Heterogeneous computing workflow for machine learning

The concept diagram for the HGC workflow for deep learning is shown in Fig. 1. The HGC workflow consists of three stages:

1. Data Analysis and Pre-processing
2. Model Training
3. Deployment and Inferencing

The Data Analysis and Pre-processing stage converts raw data from an application of interest into a form that is suitable for model training using any of the training frameworks. Current pre-processing methods include data cleaning, data normalization, and data augmentation [13]. In the HGC workflow, the pre-processed data is used as inputs to the training tools in the Model Training stage. Currently, popular open-source frameworks for training these models include TensorFlow [2], Keras [5], Caffe [17], and BigDL [6]. The output of the Training stage is trained models which are used in inference engines in the Deployment and Inferencing stage. Some of the common approaches for running inferencing primarily use Xeon CPU; but recently there has been much interest in using FPGAs (field programmable gate arrays) for inferencing. This paper will focus on how we can use Intel Arria 10 FPGAs for inferencing and what is the work flow behind it.

The remainder of this paper is organized as follows. Section 2 provides a survey of the recent and the state-of-the-art FPGA deep-learning acceleration tools that are available in research and commercially. In Sect. 3, the experimental setup is described, including the case-study models used for our study, and how they are pre-processed and trained in preparation for the Deployment and Inferencing stage. The three state-of-the-art DNN models used are HEP-CNN, CosmoGAN, and 3DGAN. HEP-CNN [19,20] is a deep-learning model used by NERSC to identify new particles produced during collision events at particle accelerators such as the Large Hadron Collider (LHC). CosmoGAN [22], also under study by NERSC, is used to generate cosmology weak lensing convergence maps to study GAN model for science applications. The 3DGAN model [11] is a generative model under study by CERN openlab to replace the Monte Carlo method for particle collision simulations. Also in Sect. 3 is the description of the platform setup for FPGA-based inferencing. The hardware platform for the inference engine is the Intel Programmable Acceleration Card (PAC), equipped with an Arria 10 GX FPGA. The PAC card is installed in a Dell server equipped with an Intel gold-level Skylake CPU. Intel distribution of OpenVINO toolkit is used to optimize and deploy the trained models onto the FPGA.

In Sect. 4, we present and discuss the inference results in our study. First, the initial findings using the native DLA runtime are described. Next, we described how we used the Intel Deep Learning Accelerator (DLA) development suite to optimize existing FPGA primitives in OpenVINO to improve performance and develop new primitives to enable new capabilities for FPGA inferencing. For the scientific DNN models under study, we were able to demonstrate a speedup from 3x to 6x for a single Arria 10 FPGA against a single core (single thread) of a server-class Skylake CPU. The studies described in this section and a demonstration of the HGC workflow were submitted to and declared the winner of the first-ever Dell EMC AI Challenge in 2018 [1]. Finally Sect. 5 will provide the conclusions of the paper and a discussion of future work.

2   Related Works

Although CPUs and GPUs have been widely used for DNN inferencing, inference engines accelerated with FPGAs have recently emerged. Recent improvements in FPGA technologies greatly increased the performance for DNN applications, e.g., with a reported performance of 9.2 TFLOPS for Intel Stratix 10 FPGA [23]. Furthermore, FPGAs have other advantages important to many mission-critical applications such as low latency and energy efficiency. As a result, the amount of research and development on deploying and accelerating DNN models on FPGAs in recent years has grown, demonstrating great interest in both academia and industry. While some of the works focused on optimizing datapaths or computation algorithms for FPGA devices, many also involve developing tools for DNN model inferencing on FPGA platforms to provide a generalized framework for developers to build their customized applications.

One notable tool developed in the research community is PipeCNN [25], an OpenCL-based FPGA accelerator designed for large-scale convolutional neural networks (CNNs). The main goal of PipeCNN is to provide an FPGA accelerator architecture of deeply pipelined CNN kernels to achieve improved throughput in the inference stage. Unlike previous OpenCL design, memory bandwidth is minimized by pipelining CNN kernels. Efficiency is enhanced by using task-mapping techniques and data reuse. The PipeCNN architecture was verified by implementing two CNNs, AlexNet and VGG, on an Altera Stratix-V A7 FPGA, achieving a peak performance of 33.9 GOPS with a 34% resource reduction on DSP blocks.

Another notable FPGA-based inference tool is hls4ml from Fermilab [9], which is a deep neural network compiler based on HLS (High-level Synthesis language). The input to hls4ml is a fully connected neural network trained from conventional training frameworks such as Keras and PyTorch. The network is translated to Vivado HLS (from Xilinx) and then compiled for the target FPGA. For the first result in using this framework, the researchers focused on using FPGA for machine learning in an application of real-time event reconstruction and filtering in the Large Hadron Collider at CERN. The accessibility and ease of configurability in HLS allows for physicists to quickly develop and optimize machine learning algorithms targeting FPGA hardware.

The success of deploying and accelerating DNN models on FPGAs resulted in commercial offerings of these tools from both major FPGA vendors. OpenVINO, from Intel/Altera [15], is a comprehensive toolkit designed to support deep learning, computer vision, and hardware acceleration using heterogeneous (CPU, GPU, FPGA) platforms. The OpenVINO toolkit comprises of a Model Optimizer and an Inference Engine. The Model Optimizer takes, as input, a trained deep-learning model outputted from one of the supported frameworks (e.g., TensorFlow, Keras). It performs static model analysis and adjusts the deep learning model for optimal execution on end-point target devices, CPU, GPU, FPGA, or HETERO (CPU+GPU or CPU+FPGA). In this project, our focus is on the use of OpenVINO in the FPGA mode to accelerate the inferencing of state-of-the-art, scientific DNNs. OpenVINO and its components will be described in more details in Sects. 3 and 4.

With the recent acquisition of DeePhi, Xilinx provides the Deep Neural Network Development Kit (DNNDK)[8] to enable the acceleration of the deep learning algorithms in FPGAs and SoCs. At the heart of the DNNDK is the deep learning processor unit (DPU). The basic stages of deploying a deep learning application into a DPU are:

1. Compress the DNN model (using the Deep Compression Tool) to reduce the model size without loss of accuracy.
2. Compile the DNN model (using the Deep Neural Network Compiler) into DPU instruction code.
3. Create an application using DNNDK (C/C++) APIs.
4. Use the hybrid compiler to compile the hybrid DPU application.
5. Deploy and run the hybrid DPU executable on the target DPU platform.

The DNNDK deep learning SDK is designed as an integrated framework which aims to simplify and accelerate deep learning applications development and deployment for Xilinx DPU platforms.

3   Experimental Setup

As illustrated in Fig. 1, the heterogeneous computing workflow for DNN consists of three stages: (1) Data Analysis and Pre-processing, (2) Model Training, and (3) Deployment and Inferencing. In Sect. 3.1, we describe the three case-study models used for this project, and how they are pre-processed and trained in preparation for the Deployment and Inferencing stage. In Sect. 3.2, the platform setup for FPGA-based inferencing is described: hardware platform and the OpenVINO deployment tool. Inference results using OpenVINO are presented in Sect. 4.

3.1   Overview of Case Studies

HEP-CNN. HEP-CNN [19,20] was developed as a proof-of-concept study for improved event selection at particle collider experiments. For example, at the Large Hadron Collider experiment (LHC) at CERN, protons are collided at almost the speed of light and disintegrated in the process, forming showers of particles which are detected by experiments such as ATLAS or CMS. These experiments generate large amounts of data in units of *events*, which correspond to a detector snapshot after a number of particle collisions. Most of the events can be explained by the well understood Standard Model of Particle Physics, also referred to as *background*. The challenge is to find and select events which potentially contain candidates for new physics. More specifically, HEP-CNN was designed to distinguish events containing r-parity violating supersymmetric particle signatures from background. It is comprised of 5 convolution and max-pooling layers with Leaky ReLU activations [12,14]. The kernel and stride sizes are 3×3 and 1×1 respectively and it employs 128 filters per layer. The final set of layers consists of an average pooling across the dimensions output image followed by a fully connected layer with softmax activation which performs the binary classification. The training data was obtained by coupling the Pythia [24] event generator to the Delphes [7] fast detector simulator. The cylindrical data is represented as a 2D image of size 224×224, where the two dimensions represent the binned azimuth angle and pseudorapidity [26] coordinates. The three input channels are given by the hadron and electromagnetic calorimeter energy deposits as well as the multiplicity of reconstructed tracks from the pixel detector. Trained using the ADAM optimizer [18], the model outperforms its benchmark, i.e. a hand crafted decision tree, by more than 2x in true positive rate at the same false negative rate.

Because of the lightweight and simplistic nature of the model as well as the importance of real-time event selection in particle detectors, we consider HEP-CNN a suitable prototype for inference performance exploration on embedded systems or deep learning accelerators.

CosmoGAN. Cosmological simulations of the ΛCDM model are traditionally very expensive: they consist of three dimensional n-body simulations followed by raytracing steps in order to obtain two dimensional weak gravitational lensing maps which are observed in large angle sky surveys. CosmoGAN [22] is a deep convolutional generative adversarial network (DC-GAN) which was designed to serve as a cheap emulator for these simulations. It is an unconstrained GAN which is able to reproduce these mass maps to very high statistical accuracy (cf. [22]) for a fixed set of cosmological parameters. The network input is a 64-dimensional vector of uncorrelated gaussian noise, followed by a fully connected layer to cross-correlate all inputs, followed by a series of four transpose convolutions, leading to a single 256×256 output image. Each inner layer is batch-normalized [16] and uses Leaky ReLU activation, while the output layer uses a tanh activation. For more details on the network parameters cf. [22]. We decided to include this model into this paper because it is a scientific example of an important new class of generative deep neural network architectures. Another important aspect is that it does not require a data input pipeline, as the random numbers can be easily generated on the devices considered in this study. Therefore, it allows us to more precisely measure the compute and latency capabilities because the model is not limited by DRAM or PCIe bus bandwidth and latency.

3DGAN. 3DGAN represents the first application of three-dimensional convolutional Generative Adversarial Networks to the simulation of high granularity electromagnetic calorimeters. The aim of the study is to produce a network which can be passed as input a particle type, energy and trajectory, and which will produce an accurate simulation of the corresponding particle detector output. Our study is based on pseudo-data simulated with GEANT4 [4] in the proposed Linear Collider Detector (LCD) for the CLIC accelerator [21]. The LCD consists of a regular grid of 3D cells with cell sizes of $5.1\,\mathrm{mm}^3$ and an inner calorimeter radius of 1.5 m. Individual electron, photon, charged pion, and neutral pion particles are shot into the calorimeter at various energies and at various angles to the calorimeter surface. For each event we take a $25 \times 25 \times 25$ cell slice of the electromagnetic calorimeter (ECAL) and store them as two 3D arrays containing information about the energy deposited in each cell. The 3DGAN generator and discriminator models consist of four 3D convolution layers. Leaky ReLU activation functions are used for the discriminator network layers. A batch normalization layer is added after all activations except the first layer. The output of the final convolution layer is flattened and connected to a sigmoid neuron corresponding to real/fake output of GAN as well as a linear unit for energy regression. The generator has a latent vector of size 128 and a similar architecture with leaky ReLU (ReLU for the last layer) activation functions. Batch normalization layers were added after the first and second layers. The GAN cost function was modified to include an auxiliary energy regression task as well as checks on total energy deposited in order to constrain the distribution of individual cell energies. The model is implemented using Keras and Tensorflow. The network is trained for 30 epochs using the RMSprop optimiser. Results show a remarkable agreement to standard Monte Carlo output (within a few percents) [11].

3.2 Platform Setup

As shown in Fig. 1, OpenVINO consists of two parts: Model Optimizer and Inference Engine. The OpenVINO software is built to emulate the Open Visual inference and neural network optimization. The OpenVINO toolkit extends the workload across Intel hardware and maximizes performance. The Model Optimizer is a cross-platform, command-line tool that facilitates the transition between the training and deployment environment on a target inference engine. The input to the Model Optimizer is a network model trained using one of the supported frameworks. It performs static model analysis and adjusts the input deep learning models for optimal execution on end point target devices, which can be a CPU, GPU, FPGA, or a combination (HETERO). The output of the Model Optimizer is an Intermediate Representation (IR) suitable as input to the selected target inference engine. In our study, our goal in the Deployment and Inferencing stage is to deploy the trained model on an FPGA to accelerate the classification process.

In addition to the trained model from the Model Optimizer, the other input to the OpenVINO Inference Engine is the data to be analyzed. The output is a probability-based classification. The Inference Engine is a C++ library with a set of C++ classes to infer data (images) to obtain a result. The C++ library provides an API to read the Intermediate Representation (IR), set the input and output formats, and execute the model on devices.

The hardware platform used in this study for the FPGA-accelerated inference engine is the Intel Programmable Acceleration Card (PAC). The PAC card contains an Arria 10 GX, a moderate-sized FPGA fabricated using 20 nm process technology. The PAC card is installed in a Dell server equipped with an Intel Gold 6130 Skylake CPU (14 nm process technology), running at a clock speed of 2.1 GHz. The Skylake is a dual-socket CPU, with 16 cores per socket, and 2 threads per core. Performance comparisons to be presented in Sect. 4 will be with a single Arria 10 FPGA versus different numbers of Skylake cores (threads).

4 Experimental Results

In this section, we present and discuss the inference results in our study. Section 4.1 discusses the initial findings using the native DLA runtime which was delivered with OpenVINO. In Sect. 4.2, we described how we used the DLA development suite (obtained from Intel via NDA) to optimize existing FPGA primitives in OpenVINO to improve performance and develop new ones to enable new capabilities for FPGA inferencing. The optimized results are presented in Sect. 4.3.

4.1 Native OpenVINO Results

Table 1 summarizes our initial inferencing performance results of two of the above scientific DNN models (HEP-CNN and CosmoGAN) using the OpenVINO toolkit with native Deep Learning Accelerator runtime.

Table 1. Inferencing performance of HEP-CNN and CosmoGAN with native Open-VINO. (*HETERO: OpenVINO heterogeneous inferencing mode with FPGA + CPU)

DNN model	HETERO* throughput (images/s)	Speedup vs. CPU		
		1 core/1 thread	1 core/2 threads	32 cores/64 threads
HEP-CNN	66.3	2.52	1.32	0.25
CosmoGAN	4.7	0.21	0.11	0.03

Using the native DLA runtime, we cannot perform inferencing on either model *completely* on the FPGA. OpenVINO automatically use the HETERO (heterogeneous) mode with CPU as a fallback device on parts of the DNN which cannot be run on the FPGA. Still HEP-CNN achieved 2.52× speedup vesus the Skylake CPU (1 core/1 thread). Although having a regular AlexNet-like CNN topology, HEP-CNN could not be completely inferenced on the FPGA because of its unsupported (by OpenVINO) "average pooling" layer between the last convolutional and the fully-connected layer. Thus, during inferencing, Open-VINO automatically maps the average pooling layer onto the CPU and transfers outputs of the last convolutional layer to the main memory. It then transfers results back to the FPGA to complete its operation. This back-and-forth transfer between CPU and FPGA introduces a large overhead that negatively impacts the inferencing performance of the HEP-CNN model. An optimized result will be shown in Sect. 4.3.

The CosmoGAN model also cannot be completely inferenced on the FPGA due to the unsupported "deconvolutional" layers. As a result, the HETERO mode causes multiple data transferring between the FPGA and CPU (2N times), where N equals the number of deconvolutional layers in the model. This overhead is reflected in the extremely poor performance of CosmoGAN shown in Table 1.

In order to improve the performance, we optimized the inferencing of HEP-CNN and CosmoGAN by enabling the FPGA primitives (using the DLA developer suite - Sect. 4.2) for the "average pooling" layer and "deconvolution" layer, respectively. This optimization eliminates the back-and-forth, data-transfer overhead and greatly improve the inference performance. Design space exploration of the FPGA architecture was also performed to further improve the result (Sect. 4.3).

4.2 Deep Learning Accelerator Suite

In order to customize the FPGA architecture for our needs, we acquired the Intel Deep Learning Accelerator (DLA) developer suite, which is the underlying tool that enables inferencing of DNN models on FPGA devices with OpenVINO. DLA consists of a high-level API (DLIA plugin) that interacts with OpenVINO's inference engine and an FPGA bitstream that creates the architecture shown in Fig. 2.

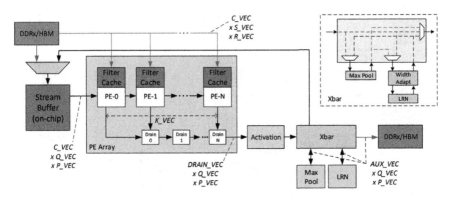

Fig. 2. DLA architecture [3]

The architecture contains a stream buffer, a PE (Processing Element) array, and various other modules that compute activation function, max-pooling, and normalization (LRN). The stream buffer takes advantage of the high bandwidth internal RAM of the FPGA, preparing the input data for the PE array. The PE array performs matrix multiplications and accumulations by utilizing DSP resource of the FPGA. DLA inferences a DNN model by first separating it into multiple sub-graphs, which typically consist of a convolutional layer, an activation layer, a max-pooling layer, and a normalization layer. The sub-graphs are then iteratively processed.

The DLA FPGA architecture (Fig. 2) can be customized for inferencing different DNN models. For example, DLA connects the max-pooling and the normalization modules to an "Xbar" module which can be configured to bypass or determine the execution order of pooling and normalization layers. It also allows the developer to create new primitives and connecting them to the "Xbar". Moreover, the stream buffer size can be configured to reduce the number of memory requests to the main memory. The PE array can also be configured by changing "C_VEC" and "K_VEC" in Fig. 2. C_VEC defines the channel depth of the input data and convolution kernels streaming out from the stream buffer; while K_VEC defines the number of PEs in the PE array, which is also equivalent to the channel depth of the output data. Due to the resource constraint of the Arria 10 FPGA, DLA slices the input data along the channel dimension to complete the inferencing of a convolutional layer in multiple iterations. We will see in Sect. 4.3 how various configurations can affect performance.

4.3 Optimized Results

HEP-CNN. As mentioned in Sect. 4.1, the inference performance of HEP-CNN can be greatly improved by implementing the "average pooling" computation primitive on FPGA. By modifying DLA's architecture configuration, we are able to enable the "average pooling" computation inside the "Pooling" module, as shown in Fig. 3.

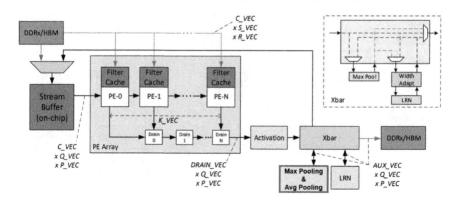

Fig. 3. Customized DLA architecture with average pooling enabled

The implementation of "average pooling" function eliminates the need of using OpenVINO's HETERO mode and thus the overhead of data transfer between CPU and FPGA, improving the performance over that of the native architecture. We also performed design space exploration (size of the stream buffer, size (C_VEC) and number of PEs (K_VEC)) to further investigate the tradeoffs for HEP-CNN. Table 2 shows the comparison of the inferencing performance with different configurations for C_VEC and K_VEC. Also shown in Table 2 is the performance comparison for different configurations of the CPU:

- 1 core, 1 thread: representing mission-critical applications with SWaP (space, weight, and power) constraints
- 1 core, 2 threads (both threads in the core): represents applications in between
- 32 cores, 64 threads: represents data-center applications

Table 2. Comparison of inferencing performance of HEP-CNN with different configurations (batch size = 16)

PE array size (C_vec × K_vec)	FPGA throughput (images/s)	Speedup vs. CPU		
		1 core/1 thread	1 core/2 threads	32 cores/ 64 threads
8 × 48 (default)	138.4	5.26	2.76	0.55
8 × 64	**164.9**	**6.27**	**3.3**	**0.66**
16 × 64	148.2	5.63	2.96	0.59

Since all convolutional layers of HEP-CNN have an output channel depth of 128, as mentioned in Sect. 4.2, the default K_VEC value of 48 will cause DLA slicing the input data three times along the channel depth, resulting in $\frac{48 \times 3 - 128}{48 \times 3} = 11.1\%$ wasting of computational resources. Thus, an optimal K_VEC should be one of the factors of 128 (e.g., 16, 32, or 64). It is also important to consider the balance of the resource consumption of the stream buffer and the PE array. Moreover, larger computing logic in the PE array could also results in a lower clock frequency in the FPGA as shown in Table 3.

Table 3. Effect of PE array configuration on stream buffer size and clock frequency

PE array size (C_vec × K_vec)	Stream buffer depth	FPGA clock frequency
8 × 48 (default)	12768	252 MHz
8 × 64	11480	235 MHz
16 × 64	5040	190 MHz

CosmoGAN. For inferencing CosmoGAN on an FPGA, the deconvolutional layers need to be computed in the PE array. The term "deconvolutional" here does not refer to its mathematical definition, which defines the inverse of the convolutional operation. Instead, "deconvolution" often refers to the "transposed convolution" in deep learning literature and programming frameworks. Computation for DNN deconvolution is roughly equivalent to convolving an input signal with a transposed kernel [10]. Depending on its padding type and the number of strides, the input of a deconvolutional layer may also need to be zero padded and/or be dilated. Computing deconvolution for DNN by using convolution is illustrated in Fig. 4, which shows the deconvolution of a stride of 2 (Fig. 4(a)) is equivalent to the convolution of a stride of 1 with the transposed kernel and the dilated input.

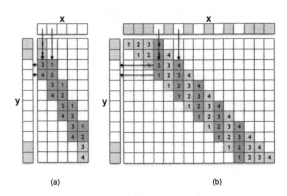

(a)   (b)

Fig. 4. (a) Deconvolution of stride 2 is equivalent to (b) Convolution of stride 1 with transposed kernel and dilated input

The DLA contains the primitive utilizing the PE array to compute deconvolution in the same way as computing regular convolution without changing its original logic and behavior. It also adds additional logic that transposes the weights matrix, and if needed, adds zero padding and dilates the input before streaming them into the PE array. Table 4 shows the inferencing performance of CosmoGAN model after we have made the enhancements to enable the deconvolution primitives in the DLA architecture configuration.

Table 4. Comparison of inference performance of CosmoGAN.

PE array size (C_vec × K_vec)	FPGA throughput (images/s)	Speedup vs. CPU		
		1 core/1 thread	1 core/2 threads	32 cores/64 threads
8 × 48 (default)	22.2	0.98	0.52	0.14
8 × 64	**24.2**	**1.07**	**0.57**	**0.16**
16 × 64	19.9	0.88	0.47	0.13

As you can see, the performance on FPGA for CosmoGAN is very poor. Upon further investigation, we determined the DLA architecture has a limitation that the "activation" layer is hardwired to the PE array so it has to be executed before the "pooling" or "normalization" layer within one sub-graph (see Fig. 2). This architecture makes sense for many mainstream CNN model, but not for models such as CosmoGAN which implements the normalization layer before ReLU activation. As a result, using the current DLA architecture, the CosmoGAN DNN has to be inferenced in two separated iterations. We hypothesize that this limitation caused the FPGA performance to be reduced by half. To confirm this hypothesis, we manually switched the execution order of normalization and activation layers in the CosmoGAN model, simply for the purpose of exploring the theoretically best inferencing performance of CosmoGAN on the FPGA. Of course, the actual classification will not be correct, but the inferencing process should require the same amount of computation. The corresponding performance results are shown in Table 5, which are consistent with our expectation. The new speedup against 1 Skylake CPU core (1 thread) is approximately 3×. Note the speedup against the HETERO mode (FPGA + CPU in Table 1) is 14×.

Table 5. Comparison of inferencing performance of CosmoGAN after switching the execution order of activation layer and normalization layer

PE array size (C_vec × K_vec)	FPGA throughput (images/s)	Speedup vs. CPU		
		1 core/1 thread	1 core/2 threads	32 cores/64 threads
8 × 48 (default)	39.4	1.74	0.92	0.25
8 × 64	**67.5**	**2.97**	**1.58**	**0.43**
16 × 64	39.9	1.76	0.93	0.26

5   Conclusions and Future Directions

Heterogeneous computing (HGC), using CPUs integrated with accelerators such as GPUs and FPGAs, offers unique capabilities to accelerate DNNs. In this paper, we presented an HGC workflow in performing deep learning studies on scientific DNN models. In particular, we focused on the use of Intel's OpenVINO to facilitate the use of FPGA-accelerated inferencing on the HEP-CNN and CosmoGAN models from NERSC (Lawrence Berkeley Lab) and the 3DGAN model from CERN openlab.

From the results presented in Sect. 4, we demonstrated that, for scientifically relevant DNN models such as HEP-CNN and CosmoGAN, a single Arria 10 FPGA (20 nm technology) can produce speedups of 6× and 3×, respectively, against a single core (single thread) of a server-class CPU (Skylake CPU, 14 nm technology). Going forward, from a FPGA device point of view, we are looking forward to working with the PAC card equipped with an Intel Stratix 10 (14 nm technology).

From a framework and tools point of view, the lessons learned thus far in using OpenVINO and the DLA development suite will be invaluable in our effort to enhance the DLA primitives and architecture to support existing and emerging scientific DNN models and applications. In particular, we have been developing the necessary primitives to support the 3DGAN model from CERN openlab.

Finally, the results from this study, as exemplified by the results presented in Sect. 4, provide an excellent foundation for more extensive data space exploration going forward to investigate various architectural, model, and tool tradeoffs on performance and other important metrics such as power and cost.

Acknowledgement. This research is funded in part by the NSF SHREC Center and the National Science Foundation (NSF) through its IUCRC Program under Grant No. CNS-1738420; and by NSF CISE Research Infrastructure (CRI) Program Grant No. 1405790.

References

1. Dell EMC AI challenge. https://insidehpc.com/aichallenge
2. Abadi, M., et al.: TensorFlow: large-scale machine learning on heterogeneous systems (2015). http://tensorflow.org/. Software available from tensorflow.org
3. Abdelfattah, M.S., et al.: DLA: compiler and FPGA overlay for neural network inference acceleration. arXiv e-prints arXiv:1807.06434, July 2018
4. Agostinelli, S., et al.: GEANT4: a simulation toolkit. Nucl. Instrum. Meth. **A506**, 250–303 (2003). https://doi.org/10.1016/S0168-9002(03)01368-8
5. Chollet, F., et al.: Keras (2015). https://github.com/fchollet/keras
6. Dai, J., et al.: BigDL: a distributed deep learning framework for big data. arXiv e-prints arXiv:1804.05839, April 2018
7. de Favereau, J., et al.: DELPHES 3: a modular framework for fast simulation of a generic collider experiment. J. High Energy Phys. **2014**, 57 (2014). https://doi.org/10.1007/JHEP02(2014)057
8. DeePhi: Deephi dnndk. http://www.deephi.com/technology/dnndk

9. Duarte, J., et al.: Fast inference of deep neural networks in FPGAs for particle physics. J. Instrum. **13**(7), P07027 (2018). https://doi.org/10.1088/1748-0221/13/07/P07027

10. Dumoulin, V., Visin, F.: A guide to convolution arithmetic for deep learning. ArXiv e-prints, March 2016

11. Carminati, F., Khattak, G., Vallecorsa, S.: 3D convolutional GAN for fast simulation. Presented at the 23rd International Conference on Computing in High Energy and Nuclear Physics (CHEP 2018). Proceedings in publication

12. Hahnloser, R.H.R., Sarpeshkar, R., Mahowald, M.A., Douglas, R.J., Seung, H.S.: Digital selection and analogue amplification coexist in a cortex-inspired silicon circuit. Nature **405**, 947–951 (2000). https://doi.org/10.1038/35016072

13. Han, J., Pei, J., Kamber, M.: Data Mining: Concepts and Techniques. Elsevier, Amsterdam (2011)

14. He, K., Zhang, X., Ren, S., Sun, J.: Delving deep into rectifiers: surpassing human-level performance on imagenet classification. arXiv e-prints arXiv:1502.01852, February 2015

15. Intel: Openvino toolkit. https://software.intel.com/en-us/openvino-toolkit

16. Ioffe, S., Szegedy, C.: Batch normalization: accelerating deep network training by reducing internal covariate shift. arXiv e-prints arXiv:1502.03167, February 2015

17. Jia, Y., et al.: Caffe: convolutional architecture for fast feature embedding. arXiv preprint arXiv:1408.5093 (2014)

18. Kingma, D.P., Ba, J.: Adam: a method for stochastic optimization. arXiv e-prints arXiv:1412.6980, December 2014

19. Kurth, T., et al.: Deep learning at 15PF: supervised and semi-supervised classification for scientific data. arXiv e-prints arXiv:1708.05256, August 2017

20. Kurth, T.: Hep-cnn github repository. https://github.com/NERSC/hep_cnn_benchmark.git

21. Lebrun, P., et al.: The CLIC programme: towards a staged e+e− linear collider exploring the terascale : CLIC conceptual design report (2012). https://doi.org/10.5170/CERN-2012-005

22. Mustafa, M., Bard, D., Bhimji, W., Lukić, Z., Al-Rfou, R., Kratochvil, J.: CosmoGAN: creating high-fidelity weak lensing convergence maps using generative adversarial networks. arXiv e-prints arXiv:1706.02390, June 2017

23. Nurvitadhi, E., et al.: Can FPGAs beat GPUs in accelerating next-generation deep neural networks? In: Proceedings of the 2017 ACM/SIGDA International Symposium on Field-Programmable Gate Arrays - FPGA 17 (2017). https://doi.org/10.1145/3020078.3021740

24. Sjöstrand, T., Mrenna, S., Skands, P.: A brief introduction to PYTHIA 8.1. Comput. Phys. Commun. **178**(11), 852–867 (2008). https://doi.org/10.1016/j.cpc.2008.01.036. http://www.sciencedirect.com/science/article/pii/S0010465508000441

25. Wang, D., An, J., Xu, K.: PipeCNN: an OpenCL-based FPGA accelerator for large-scale convolution neuron networks. arXiv e-prints arXiv:1611.02450, November 2016

26. Wikipedia: Wikipedia pseudorapidity. https://en.wikipedia.org/wiki/Pseudorapidity

In-Situ Data Reduction via Incoherent Sensing

Kai Zhang[✉] and Alireza Entezari

University of Florida, Gainesville, FL 32608, USA
{zhangkai6,entezari}@ufl.edu

Abstract. We present a framework for in-situ processing of large-scale simulation data that performs a universal data reduction. Instead of direct compression of the data, we propose a different approach that can be benefit from compressed sensing (CS) theory. Unlike the direct data compression techniques where the accuracy of recovery is fixed, the proposed framework enables more accurate recovery (after in situ data reduction), with using better sparse representations, that can be learned from and optimized for the simulation data. Moreover, we discuss the practical case when the assumption of sparsity doesn't hold, the optimization-based recovery algorithm is able to recover the most important elements in the data (characterized by the best k-term approximation), despite significant reduction in the data. We provide theoretical arguments from CS theory and demonstrate experimentally the error behavior exhibited by the proposed approach compared by the best k-term approximation. These arguments, together with our experiments, support the unique feature of the proposed in-situ data reduction: the accuracy of the recovery algorithm can be improved after data reduction by learning better representations for simulation data. The proposed approach provides opportunities for developing new data reduction mechanisms in high performance computing and simulation environments.

Keywords: In-situ data reduction · Compressed sensing · Volume rendering

1 Introduction

With the ever increasing computing power available for extreme-scale simulations, processing, storage and visualization of such large-scale data has been and continues to be an important problem hindering our ability to harness the power of extreme-scale computing ecosystems. Data reduction has become inevitable in such environments as the performance of I/O modules, constrained by physical limits, has not kept pace with the growth in computational power. Often, simulation results are discarded for a range of time-steps and compression algorithms

This project was funded in part by NSF grant IIS-1617101.

are used for data reduction for managing the volume of the data to be stored and further processed [17, 18].

A fundamental principle leveraged in data reduction algorithms is that despite the high dimensional representation of the datasets, natural phenomena are often governed by few degrees of freedom compared to the dimension (resolution) of the ambient space they reside. This principle justifies modeling high dimensional data in low dimensional linear subspaces and nonlinear manifolds – the common theme in dimensionality reduction. Similarly the assumption that most datasets can be sparsely represented in a feature domain, is key for compression algorithms. For example, natural images, when represented in wavelet domains, exhibit very few degrees of freedom observable by the sparsity of coefficients. Compression algorithms exploit such dimensionality reduction algorithms to efficiently encode transform coefficients with low entropy. Significant compression of the data necessitates a lossy process that often involves truncation in a transform domain. Compression techniques have been explored for in-situ data processing as well as for large-scale visualization problems. Several compression - domain volume rendering techniques have been proposed in the visualization community [12, 13, 23, 24], where the decoding is combined with rendering such that data transfer rate to the GPU is minimizes. In these approaches, the data is efficiently represented, for example, by vector quantization [23], transform coding [12], dictionary learning [13], or tensor approximation [24]. During the rendering stage, only the features are transferred to the GPU and decoded on-the-fly. We discuss the merits for a different strategy than the direct compression of the data. Based on results from stable embedding and compressed sensing theory, we present arguments for using *incoherent sensing*, instead of compression, for in-situ data reduction. The key motivation behind the proposed approach is its ability to learn from data to improve the quality of recovery after the data reduction has been performed. Unlike the compression paradigm that the quality of recovery (decompression) is fixed, the proposed approach is able to improve the accuracy of recovery with learning better sparse representations from more and more data [25]. In this paper we show that even with sub-optimal sparse representations (e.g., when the assumption of sparsity fails), the recovery algorithm is able to preserve the most important elements, while significantly reducing the data size. This notion of most important elements is formally characterized by the best k-term approximation. As we demonstrate in the following section, the error in the recovery algorithm is bounded by the error committed by the best k-term approximation – that we could only have obtained if we knew exactly the location and value of the most important elements. With learning better sparse representations (e.g., from wavelets to ridgelets to surfacelets or dictionary learning) more and more of the most important elements in the data are recovered from the same reduced-scale data (incoherently sensed). We also discuss practical considerations for applying incoherent sensing for large-scale data reduction, where sensing matrices can not be stored, but efficiently computed and implemented as operators.

2   Compressed Sensing Framework

The Compressed Sensing (CS) theory, was developed by Donoho [11] and Candés [8], and has transformed many data acquisition systems, including Fourier imaging (e.g., MRI, RADAR) and computed tomography (e.g., coded aperture X-ray).

Formally, let $\mathbf{x} \in \mathbb{R}^N$ be the vectorized dataset comprising N voxels, matrix $\mathbf{A} \in \mathbb{R}^{m \times N}$ ($m \ll N$) (with special properties as described in the next subsection) be the sensing matrix, and $\mathbf{y} \in \mathbb{R}^m$ the *incoherently sensed* measurements are obtained from a linear projection:

$$\mathbf{y} = \mathbf{Ax}. \tag{1}$$

Given the incoherently sensed data, $\mathbf{y}$, the recovery algorithm involves an optimization procedure that solves the above underdetermined linear system for $\mathbf{x}$. For simplicity of presentation, we first assume that the original dataset $\mathbf{x}$ is sparse itself (it has relatively small number of non-zero voxels). We then discuss the more realistic case in which the data is sparsified only after a transformation to a different (e.g., wavelet, Fourier) domain.

2.1   Restricted Isometry Property (RIP)

The underdetermined linear system (1) has infinite many solutions and without further knowledge it is impossible to recover the original data $\mathbf{x}$. To be able to recover $\mathbf{x}$ (or a good approximation to it) from this underdetermined system, the sensing matrix has to satisfy a condition known as Restricted Isometry Property (RIP) [8]: A matrix satisfies RIP of order k if there exists a constant δ_k (the smallest possible one) such that matrix $\mathbf{A}$ obeys

$$(1 - \delta_k)\|\mathbf{x}\|_2^2 \leq \|\mathbf{Ax}\|_2^2 \leq (1 + \delta_k)\|\mathbf{x}\|_2^2 \tag{2}$$

for any k-sparse (at most k components are non-zero) vector $\mathbf{x}$.

Intuitively, inequality (2) states the energy of $\mathbf{x}$ in projection from high dimension to low dimension is mostly preserved and is distorted at most by δ_k. Hence δ_k represents the almost orthogonality of the collection of every k columns of $\mathbf{A}$. For the extreme case, if the support of vector $\mathbf{x}$ corresponds to the k columns of $\mathbf{A}$ that are orthogonal, then the distortion of $\mathbf{x}$ will be 0 which indicates that $\delta_k = 0$.

2.2   Best k-term Approximation

It is demonstrated that if $\delta_{2k} < 1$, the Eq. (1) has a unique k-sparse solution, therefore, in this situation, only the k-sparse vector can be recovered. This also means that, in theory, by promoting the sparsity of vector $\mathbf{x}$, it's possible to solve the underdetermined linear system (1). Then we can change the problem (1) as an optimization problem (P_0):

$$\min_{\mathbf{u}} \|\mathbf{u}\|_0,$$
$$\text{subject to } \mathbf{Au} = \mathbf{y}, \tag{3}$$

where the ℓ_0 pseudo-norm of $\mathbf{x}$, $\|\mathbf{x}\|_0$, represents the number of non-zero elements (sparsity) in vector $\mathbf{x}$. However, because ℓ_0 norm is non-convex, the problem (3) is turned out to be NP-hard. It implies that we can not use standard optimization algorithm to solve this. Although there are several iteration-based greedy algorithm [20,22] can be used to solve this problem and the compute time is always linear with the number of non-zeros in $\mathbf{x}$, the performance is not robust in general, especially when noise presents in the measurements. Therefore, there has to be some relaxation on this problem. Candés and Tao [5,8] show that instead of using ℓ_0 norm, but using ℓ_1 norm (that is convex) can achieve the same result when $\delta_{2k} < \sqrt{2} - 1$. Hence, we can relax the $P0$ problem (3) to $P1$ problem:

$$\min_{\mathbf{u}} \|\mathbf{u}\|_1,$$
$$\text{subject to } \mathbf{Au} = \mathbf{y}, \tag{4}$$

and this is as easy as a linear programming problem which can be solved in polynomial-time. In [7], it is also proved that if the RIP condition is satisfied, the solution $\mathbf{x}^*$ of (4) obeys:

$$\|\mathbf{x} - \mathbf{x}^*\|_2 \leq C_0 \frac{\|\mathbf{x} - \mathbf{x}_k\|_1}{\sqrt{k}}, \tag{5}$$

where C_0 is some well-behaved constant and $\mathbf{x}_k$ as the best k-terms approximation of $\mathbf{x}$. This indicates that the error of the recovered data is bounded by the error of the best $k-$term approximation of the ground truth. Therefore, this theory shows robust performance when the signal is sparse or has sparse representation.

2.3   Sparsifying Transformations

Most of the natural signals are not necessarily sparse in canonical space domain, however, lots of transform bases can sparsely represent signals. For example, DCT, wavelet, curvelet, surfacelet, dictionary learning and deep learning based non-linear transform can lead many kinds of signals to sparse or compressible representations, that is to say most of the transform coefficients are zero or very close to zero.

Let denote $\boldsymbol{\Psi} \in \mathbb{R}^{N \times N}$ as the transform basis, and $\mathbf{z} = \boldsymbol{\Psi}\mathbf{u}$ denote the sparse representation of variable $\mathbf{u}$. Then the optimization problem (4) can be reformulated as:

$$\min_{\mathbf{u}} \|\mathbf{z}\|_1,$$
$$\text{subject to } \mathbf{Au} = \mathbf{y}, \tag{6}$$

this provides us a convenience that instead of regularizing the sparsity of signal itself, the signal can be recovered by promoting the sparsity in any "well-chosen" sparsifying domain. Since the measurement vector **y** here is obtained only via the sensing matrix **A** without any priori knowledge of **x** and transform basis **Ψ**. This implies that we can choose any superior basis or dictionary learned by some learning algorithms as **Ψ** *after in-situ data reduction* producing **y**.

2.4 Practical RIP Matrices

Because the sensing matrix has to satisfy the RIP, randomly sensing is naturally suitable in such case. In this section, we will introduce three deeply analyzed random matrices.

Gaussian Matrix [10]. Assume that the sensing matrix $\mathbf{A} \in \mathbb{R}^{m \times N}$ satisfies that the entries are i.i.d.(independently and identically distributed) and drawn from the normal distribution with mean 0 and variance $1/m$, then if

$$k = \mathcal{O}(\frac{m}{\log \frac{N}{m}}), \tag{7}$$

then with high probability $(1 - O(e^{-\gamma N}))$ with some $\gamma > 0$, the signal can be recovered by solving P_1 problem.

Bernoulli Matrix [9]. If entries of **A** are i.i.d. and drawn from symmetric Bernoulli distribution $(P(A_{i,j} = \pm 1/\sqrt{m}) = 1/2)$, then if k obeys condition (7), the same result as Gaussian Matrix can be achieved.

Partial Fourier Matrix [21]. Suppose **A** is a partial Fourier matrix by uniformly randomly selecting m rows from an N by N Fourier matrix, then if

$$k = \mathcal{O}((\frac{m}{\log N})^4), \tag{8}$$

with overwhelming probability (the probability decays exponentially in m), we can get same result as Gaussian matrix.

3   Data Reduction Via CS

For in-situ processing of large scale data by the incoherent sensing framework, the extremely large size of the sensing matrix **A** is impractical to be stored into system memory, and the performance of the I/O module limiting the bandwidth also becomes the bottleneck for the data reduction process. Fortunately, all of the "good" sensing matrices discussed in Sect. 2.4 have the superiority that is able to be computed parallelly on-the-fly. This results in the incoherent sensing naturally fit for large scale in-situ processing.

For aspect of implementation, the matrix **A** can be represented by the indices of the frequencies when the random DFT or DCT are selected as sensing matrix and just requires as few as $\mathcal{O}(m)$ bytes storage space. If Gaussian or Bernoulli measurements are used in the application, only seeds need to be loaded into memory to generate sensing matrix. For the sparse presentation, when the transform basis **Ψ** is determined, the there are also fast and patented parallel algorithms to perform the domain transformations on-the-fly (e.g. FFT [14], FWT [3], FCT [4,19]), therefore, only small bandwidth is needed in domain transform as well. At last, the only relatively large scale data has to be transferred is the measurements vector **y**. However, as described above, in the CS framework, only m measurements, which is much less than dimensionality of **x**, needed to recover the original data **x**.

4   Experiments

In this section, we show the accuracy of incoherent sensing framework for in-situ data reduction. Theoretically, we present the error bound as statement in (5) to show the robustness of incoherent sensing methods. Piratically, we visualize the reconstruction of the large scale volumetric dataset. In addition, we compare our volumetric data reduction by using our incoherent sensing with commonly used data reduction algorithms including run-length encoding and downsampling. We exhibit that our incoherent sensing method is comparable or superior to those methods. At last, We argue that the random behavior of the incoherent sensing that requires no priori knowledge in terms of the data can be regarded as a universal encoder. By only using the small mount of reusable "code" (sensing data) and a sparse transform basis, this alternative data reduction method can flexibly refine the reconstruction and, in turn, improve the quality of the visualization.

4.1 ℓ_2 Norm Bound

In this section, we present the experiment showing that the error of the recovered data is bounded by the best $k-$term approximation. We demonstrate that with small set of random Gaussian measurements, the recovered data achieved by solving Eq. (4) will always obey the bound (5).

We randomly generate the data vector **x** with dimension $N = 200$ and fix the sparse level (the number of non-zeros) as $k = 30$. Then we generate the Gaussian sensing matrix $\mathbf{A} \in \mathbb{R}^{m \times 200}$ with mean 0 and variance $1/m$, and vary the number of samples, m, from 30 to 100. For the optimization, we choose the FISTA [1] algorithm which is fastest algorithm compare to other iterative algorithms in this case. In order to get the average performance, for each m, we reconstruct the signal 100 times and regenerate the sensing matrix for each reconstruction. Figure 1 shows the results of our experiments. Obviously, the ℓ_2 norm of the recovered error is bounded by the error introduced by best $k-$term approximation and also it should be noticed that with increasing the number of measurements, the error keeps decreasing, which is reasonable because the larger number of measurements guarantees the accuracy of reconstruction.

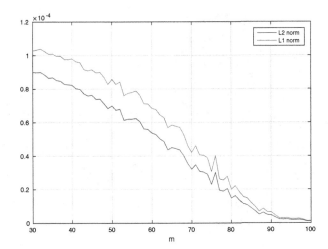

Fig. 1. The blue line represents the reconstruction error, which is $\|\mathbf{x} - \mathbf{x}^*\|_2$ where $\mathbf{x}^*$ is the solution for Eq. (4), the red line shows the error of best k-term approximation which is $\|\mathbf{x} - \mathbf{x}_k\|_1/\sqrt{k}$. (Color figure online)

4.2   Volumetric Dataset

As stated in Sect. 2.3, due to the fact that most of nature signals or data are not necessarily sparse in canonical space domain, in order to increase the accuracy of the reconstruction, seeking the transform for sparse representation of the data is important. The common choice of the transform basis is wavelet (JPEG2000 image format) or discrete cosine transform (DCT) (JPG image format), however, DCT provides worse compression performance and wavelet is unable to efficiently approximate curve or surface which are usually presented in volumetric dataset. In this experiment, we will choose several geometric extensions of wavelet comprised of curvelets [6], shearlets [15] and surfacelets [16] as the transform bases and compare their performance with other data reduction methods (e.g. run-length encoding and downsampling). For the evaluation of reconstruction accuracy, we use the signal to noise ratio (SNR) which is measured logarithmic scale (dB) over the entire volumetric data as the metric.

Hydrogen. The ground truth of Hydrogen dataset is a volumetric dataset with resolution $128 \times 128 \times 128$. Our experiment (from [25]) compares the volumetric incoherent sensing framework with dataset reconstructed from interpolation of downsampled dataset. For the interpolation, we use both linear and cubic spline as the filters. The NESTA [2] algorithm is used to solve the P_1 problem (6). For the measurements, it randomly chooses $m = 12.5\%N$ columns of discrete cosine transform (DCT) measurements. For downsampling case, the sampling rate is set to a factor of two for each dimension, resulting in rate $\rho = 12.5\%$.

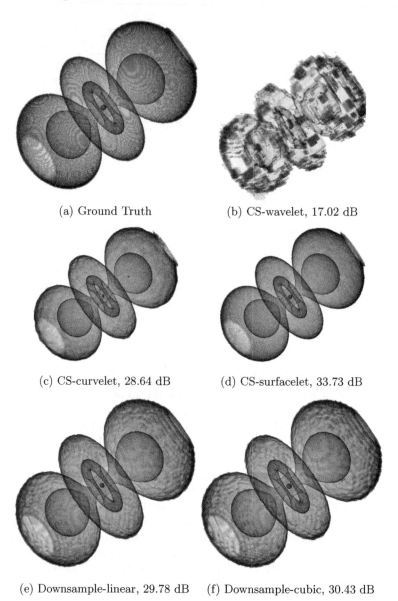

(a) Ground Truth

(b) CS-wavelet, 17.02 dB

(c) CS-curvelet, 28.64 dB

(d) CS-surfacelet, 33.73 dB

(e) Downsample-linear, 29.78 dB

(f) Downsample-cubic, 30.43 dB

Fig. 2. Hydrogen dataset: Sparse approximation and Downsample with sample rate $\rho = 12.5\%$.

Both of these two techniques stores the same size of data (Measurements size in incoherence sensing is 12.5% of dataset size, and sampling rate in downsampling is also 12.5%). Figure 2 shows the volume rendering images of the CS reconstruction as well as interpolation from downsampling dataset. It's obvious

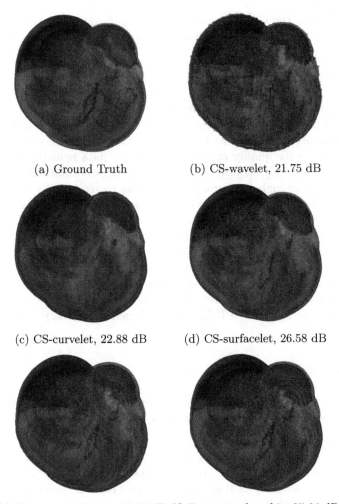

(a) Ground Truth   (b) CS-wavelet, 21.75 dB

(c) CS-curvelet, 22.88 dB   (d) CS-surfacelet, 26.58 dB

(e) Downsample-linear, 25.07 dB (f) Downsample-cubic, 25.64 dB

Fig. 3. Supernova dataset: Sparse approximation and Downsample with sample rate $\rho = 12.5\%$.

that CS reconstruction can achieve higher SNR than downsampling method. We can also observe that changing sparsifying domain can improve the CS recon- struct performance, and surfacelets yield the best result. It verifies that better sparse representations is able to improve the accuracy of recovery.

Supernova. The supernova datasets is a volumetric dataset with resolution of $432 \times 432 \times 432$. Still we use the 12.5% measurements and downsampling rate is set to $\rho = 12.5\%$. The visualizations are shown in Fig. 3. The result is similar to Hydrogen dataset. We also observe that CS reconstruction tends to smooth the dataset, because the CS recovers the most significant coefficients (usually low frequency) while keeps other coefficients (usually high frequency) as zeros.

5 Conclusion

We present the merits of using incoherent sensing, originally introduced in compressed sensing, for in-situ processing and reduction of large-scale simulation data from theoretical and practical aspects. This approach is able to learn from data to improve the quality of recovery after the data reduction has been performed. With carefully choosing better sparse representations the recovery algorithm can achieve higher accuracy as it is able to recover the most important elements in the data. Only a little measurements needed in the process leads to significant decrease in the data storage and saves the bandwidth. The universality of random measurements requiring no priori knowledge in terms of signal also shows the attractive utility of incoherent sensing. In the future work, we will study on the learning-based or customer-designed sparse representations of volumetric data. Additionally, since the reconstruction algorithm current is implemented in CPU that heavily limits the speed of the framework, we will migrate the algorithm to GPU in order to benefit from the parallel computing resources.

References

1. Beck, A., Teboulle, M.: A fast iterative shrinkage-thresholding algorithm for linear inverse problems. SIAM J. Imaging Sci. **2**(1), 183–202 (2009)
2. Becker, S., Bobin, J., Candès, E.J.: NESTA: a fast and accurate first-order method for sparse recovery. SIAM J. Imaging Sci. **4**(1), 1–39 (2011)
3. Beylkin, G., Coifman, R., Rokhlin, V.: Fast wavelet transforms and numerical algorithms I. Commun. Pure Appl. Math. **44**(2), 141–183 (1991)
4. Candés, E., Demanet, L., Donoho, D., Ying, L.: Fast discrete curvelet transforms. Multiscale Model. Simul. **5**(3), 861–899 (2006)
5. Candés, E.J.: The restricted isometry property and its implications for compressed sensing. C. R. Math. **346**(9–10), 589–592 (2008)
6. Candés, E.J., Donoho, D.L.: Curvelets: a surprisingly effective nonadaptive representation for objects with edges. Stanford University, CA, Department of Statistics, Technical report (2000)
7. Candés, E.J., Romberg, J.K., Tao, T.: Stable signal recovery from incomplete and inaccurate measurements. Commun. Pure Appl. Math. **59**(8), 1207–1223 (2006)
8. Candés, E.J., Tao, T.: Decoding by linear programming. IEEE Trans. Inf. Theory **51**(12), 4203–4215 (2005)
9. Davidson, K.R., Szarek, S.J.: Local operator theory, random matrices and banach spaces. In: Handbook of the Geometry of Banach Spaces, vol. 1, no. 317–366, p. 131 (2001)
10. Donoho, D., Tanner, J.: Counting faces of randomly projected polytopes when the projection radically lowers dimension. J. Am. Math. Soc. **22**(1), 1–53 (2009)
11. Donoho, D.L.: Compressed sensing. IEEE Trans. Inf. Theory **52**(4), 1289–1306 (2006)

12. Fout, N., Ma, K.L.: Transform coding for hardware-accelerated volume rendering. IEEE Trans. Visual Comput. Graphics **13**(6), 1600–1607 (2007)
13. Gobbetti, E., Iglesias Guitián, J.A., Marton, F.: COVRA: a compression-domain output-sensitive volume rendering architecture based on a sparse representation of voxel blocks. In: Computer Graphics Forum, vol. 31, pp. 1315–1324. Wiley Online Library (2012)
14. Govindaraju, N.K., Lloyd, B., Dotsenko, Y., Smith, B., Manferdelli, J.: High performance discrete Fourier transforms on graphics processors. In: Proceedings of the 2008 ACM/IEEE Conference on Supercomputing, p. 2. IEEE Press (2008)
15. Kutyniok, G., Labate, D.: Shearlets: Multiscale Analysis for Multivariate Data. Springer, Heidelberg (2012). https://doi.org/10.1007/978-0-8176-8316-0
16. Lu, Y.M., Do, M.N.: Multidimensional directional filter banks and surfacelets. IEEE Trans. Image Process. **16**(4), 918–931 (2007)
17. Ma, K.L.: In situ visualization at extreme scale: challenges and opportunities. IEEE Comput. Graphics Appl. **29**(6), 14–19 (2009)
18. Ma, K.L., Wang, C., Yu, H., Tikhonova, A.: In-situ processing and visualization for ultrascale simulations. J. Phys.: Conf. Ser. **78**, 012043 (2007)
19. Motamedi, M., Sobhieh, S., Motamedi, S.A., Rezaie, A.H.: An ultra-fast, optimized and massively-parallelized curvelet transform algorithm on GP-GPUs. In: 2013 21st Iranian Conference on Electrical Engineering (ICEE), pp. 1–6. IEEE (2013)
20. Needell, D., Tropp, J.A.: CoSaMP: iterative signal recovery from incomplete and inaccurate samples. Appl. Comput. Harmonic Anal. **26**(3), 301–321 (2009)
21. Rudelson, M., Vershynin, R.: Sparse reconstruction by convex relaxation: Fourier and Gaussian measurements. In: 2006 40th Annual Conference on Information Sciences and Systems, pp. 207–212. IEEE (2006)
22. Sahoo, S.K., Makur, A.: Signal recovery from random measurements via extended orthogonal matching pursuit. IEEE Trans. Signal Process. **63**(10), 2572–2581 (2015)
23. Schneider, J., Westermann, R.: Compression domain volume rendering. In: 2003 IEEE Visualization, VIS 2003, pp. 293–300. IEEE (2003)
24. Suter, S.K., et al.: Interactive multiscale tensor reconstruction for multiresolution volume visualization. IEEE Trans. Visual Comput. Graphics **17**(12), 2135–2143 (2011)
25. Xu, X., Sakhaee, E., Entezari, A.: Volumetric data reduction in a compressed sensing framework. In: Computer Graphics Forum, vol. 33, pp. 111–120. Wiley Online Library (2014)

In-Situ Processing in Climate Science

Niklas Röber[✉] and Jan Frederik Engels

German Climate Computing Center, Hamburg, Germany
{roeber,engels}@dkrz.de

Abstract. With climate simulations and earth observations, earth system sciences belong to the most data intensive scientific disciplines, and the rate at which the data is produced increases continuously. Current models supporting a higher complexity paired with an increased resolution produce more and more data that needs to be analyzed and understood. The development of alternatives to the classic post processing/visualization pipeline are therefore mandatory and discussed within this paper, with a strong focus on in-situ visualization and in-situ data processing. Although the work described here is work in progress, large parts are already implemented and tested and on the verge to be deployed in production mode.

1 Visualization in Climate Science

The output generated by current climate simulations is increasing both in size, as well as in complexity. Both aspects pose equal challenges for the visualization and an ideally interactive visual analysis of the simulated data. The increase in complexity is due to a maturing of models that are able to better describe the intricacies of the climate system, while the gain in size is a direct result of finer spatial and temporal resolutions.

ICON, the **ICO**sahedral **N**on-hydrostatic model, that is jointly developed by the Max Planck Institute for Meteorology (MPI-M) and the German Weather Service (DWD), is a framework based on an icosahedral grid with an equal area projection, on which data sets are sampled via primal triangular cells, dual hexagonal cells and hybrid quadrilateral cells [1]. Figure 1 shows the horizontal layout of the ICON grid, visualizing the relationship between cell (triangle) and point (hexagon) data. The vertical layout is a rectilinear grid, that is sampled more densely close to the Earth's/Ocean's surface. ICON – though unstructured – has several advantages over other grids that are regularly used in climate science: is has no computational poles, it allows for an easy refinement in local areas and it provides a simplified coupling between its oceanic, atmospheric and land components. Over the last years, ICON was extended to permit large eddy simulations at cloud resolving resolutions in a regional setup as part of the HD(CP)^2 project[1] [2] to advance the understanding of clouds, cloud building and precipitation processes. Although the data produced was quite large (22 million/3.5 billion

---

[1] HD(CP)^2 – **HighH**igh-**D**efinition **C**louds and **P**recipitation to advance **C**limate **P**rediction.

© Springer Nature Switzerland AG 2019
M. Weiland et al. (Eds.): ISC 2019 Workshops, LNCS 11887, pp. 612–622, 2019.
https://doi.org/10.1007/978-3-030-34356-9_46

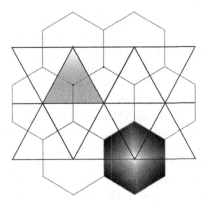

Fig. 1. Horizontal ICON grid layout showing triangles (cell data) and hexagons (point data).

cells 2D/3D), a classic post visualization approach using ParaView employing a parallel processing/visualization setup on several fat nodes was still possible.

Within the recently started EU funded project of ESiWACE2[2], the spatial – and the temporal – resolution will be further refined down to 1.25 km globally, resulting in approximately 360 million cells per level, and – depending on the number of levels – around 30 to 60 billion cells in 3D, per variable and time step. In order to explore, and actually be able to access such data, let alone writing the data to disk, other workflows than the currently employed post visualization are necessary. Examples include in-situ visualization in its many forms and in-situ compression/transformation, which reorders and possibly also compresses the data to make it accessible within a modified post visualization pipeline. This paper illuminates these approaches from a climate science perspective, thereby focusing explicitly on climate science visualization needs. It also discusses some of the initial implementations and highlights some first results.

2   In-Situ Visualization

The idea of in-situ visualization dates back to the golden era of coprocessing in the 1990s [3]. As a buzzword in HPC, the term *in-situ* is currently almost as popular as *data avalanche* or *I/O bottleneck*, and reverberated through scientific conferences and papers for years [3,4]. However, the majority of users still tried to avoid it united in the hope that faster hardware could remedy the problems before the need to resort to an in-situ visualization approach would become immanent. So far, also the data analysis and visualization at DKRZ was entirely based on the classic post visualization workflow, but this is – driven by projects such as ESiWACE2 – about to change. Only one simulated day with 30 min

---

[2] ESiWACE2 – Centre of **E**xcellence in **S**imulation of **W**eather **A**nd **C**limate in **E**urope.

output, 75 levels and eight 3D plus twenty 2D variables – there are of course many more variables in the model that would be worth looking at – would accumulate to ≈43 TB (single precision), which is quite a bit, given the fact that such weather simulations often run for several days, weeks, even months.

Several software packages, such as Visit [5] and ParaView [6,7], already provide in-situ visualization capabilities. Other exascale visualization initiatives, such as ALPINE/Ascent [8] or SENSEI [9], directly build upon these tools and extend their functionality. Due to the great familiarity and happiness with ParaView, we at DKRZ have experimented so far only with Catalyst, a VTK-based and ParaView bound in-situ visualization framework [4,10]. ParaView is thereby employed to generate a Python script, that later drives the in-situ processing to create standard visualizations, to threshold and write out reduced data sets, and to create a CINEMA database. The connection to the ICON model is implemented using a so called Catalyst adaptor, compare also with Fig. 2, that handles the data transfer from ICON (FORTRAN) to ParaView/Catalyst (C++). As use cases, we see the following applications/data flows:

- Data reduction
- Verifying the simulation during run time
- Generation of data quicklooks and previews
- Feature detection, extraction and tracking

Once the data is on the C++ side of the adaptor, the data can flow in multiple directions, as are outlined in Fig. 2. Catalyst already supports a number of those applications and comes with a variety of examples. Initially we planned to base our in-situ developments onto the in-situ implementation developed by the MPAS[3] group [11]. However, as the code was quite complex and would have required a lot of work to be customized for ICON, we decided to start the development of a new Catalyst adaptor that is directly tailored to the ICON model from scratch. This proved to be the right decision, as only a few hundred lines of FORTRAN and C++ code, along with some minor modifications within the ICON code itself, already allowed us to run first in-situ visualization experiments. In-situ visualization can be performed either loosely or tightly coupled, that is on dedicated visualizations nodes, or on the same compute nodes on which the simulation is run. We have not yet experimented with different configurations, and so far have only used the tightly coupled setup with an equal number of visualization/simulation processes per node. The data, grid information as well as actual data variables, are transferred from FORTRAN to C++ as zero copy arrays.

The maximum number of nodes that we used so far for parallel simulation/in-situ processing is 540 nodes with 4320 MPI processes, i.e. 1/6 of our HPC cluster. ICON atmosphere was used in a global setup with 2.5 km horizontal resolution and 75 height levels, thereby thresholding two 3D variables *liquid cloud water* and *cloud ice*, which were written out to disk. A threshold of 1.0×10^{-7} kg kg^{-1} (in kilogram water/ice per kilogram air) was applied to discard the *empty* cells,

---

[3] MPAS – **M**odel for **P**rediction **A**cross **S**cales.

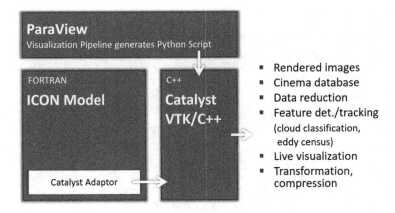

Fig. 2. In-Situ visualization/processing pipeline using ParaView/Catalyst.

and save only those that are above this threshold. This resulted in a mesh reduction from 6.5 billion cells down to ≈150 million cells per 3D variable, which can now be handled easily in a classic post analysis/visualization workflow. Figure 3 shows a visualization of both variables along with an annotation of the Earth's orography. Additionally, a standard visualization (single snapshot per time step) was created, along with a CINEMA database to create quicklooks and previews of the data.

The additional time required to initialize and actually do the in-situ visualization is almost neglectable in respect to the time required to perform the simulation itself. The initialization of the model, as described in the run above, takes 71 s, from which Catalyst needs 6.1 s (≈11%). The first workload, i.e. the transfer of the grid data and Catalyst initialization takes an additional 1.6 s. The model needs an average of about 408 s (total: 408.027 s) to advance the model one time step, from which Catalyst uses on average 0.1 s (max 0.8 s) (total: 12.000 s (≈3%)) to create a standard visualization (single image) and to write out the two thresholded 3D variables.

CINEMA is a useful extension for ParaView developed by the Los Alamos National Laboratory and allows an image-based analysis and visualization of large data sets by creating multiple views of the data per timestep and storing these images together with a data description. Several applications exist to efficiently access this CINEMA database, including a web based viewer [12]. But the evaluation of CINEMA is unfortunately still incomplete, as several issues exist that are also documented on Kitware's Github website[4]. Although the new SPEC-D CINEMA database format is formally implemented, currently only SPEC-A databases are written out and have at the time of writing still to be manually converted into a SPEC-D database to be consistent with the current CINEMA display tools[5]. Nevertheless, once working, CINEMA will be a great

---

[4] https://gitlab.kitware.com/paraview/paraview/issues/.
[5] https://cinemascience.github.io/downloads.html.

Fig. 3. Catalyst extracted 3D cloud ice (turquoise) and 3D cloud water (white) from a 2.5 km global ICON atmosphere simulation.

addition, as it allows scientists to quickly browse through large piles of data (images) in the search for the proper data file to be analyzed in more detail. Other researchers have also utilized the CINEMA database to perform a feature tracking of mesoscale ocean eddies using contours and moments directly on the image data [13].

Another direct advantage of using ParaView/Catalyst as in-situ framework is the possibility to visualize the simulated data live while the simulation still runs on the supercomputer. This allows to precisely track and supervise the progress of the simulation, and to abort in cases of errors. However, in practice, this feature will probably only be used in specific setups and for long simulations, as a batch scheduler maintains the processing of the simulations.

2.1   Feature Detection and Tracking

In-situ processing does not necessarily need to be limited to the generation of images and the storage of reduced data sets alone, but can easily be extended to a detection, extraction and tracking of certain interesting features or structures. A popular object of study in the atmospheric sciences are clouds. Meteorologists are especially interested in their formation, as well as development and evolution over time, i.e. the transition from one type of cloud into another. Clouds and the various cloud types are listed and described in the cloud atlas[6] and can be characterized using boundary conditions defined through specific levels of cloud water/ice, pressure, temperature, humidity, rain and upward wind velocity, as are identified by the International Satellite Cloud Climatology Project ISCCP [14]. Figure 4 shows a visualization of an in-situ cloud classification based on a regional (Germany centered) simulation at cloud resolving scales at 156 m

---

[6] http://www.wolken-online.de/wolkenatlas.htm.

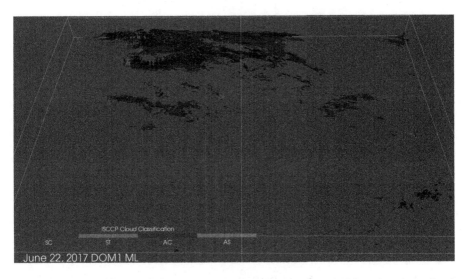

Fig. 4. ISCCP in-situ cloud classification using HD(CP)^2 data [2] with stratus (ST), stratocumulus (SC), sltostratus (AS) and sltocumulus (AC) clouds.

from within the HD(CP)^2 project [2]. It shows four different cloud types over northern Germany: Stratus (ST), Stratocumulus (SC), Altostratus (AS) and Altocumulus (AC). This cloud classification is thresholded, i.e. the empty cells (no clouds) are discarded, and efficiently stored as VTI (VTK Integer Array) file series on disk, to be later loaded and displayed in ParaView.

Another example that we have not yet implemented, but which has been shown by others to be beneficial [11], is an in-situ eddy census from a high resolution ocean simulation, ideally accompanied with the extraction and display of additional quantitative information, such as the size, duration, speed and movement direction of eddies, as well as how much energy and mass they transport.

3   Progressive Data Visualization

One of the drawbacks of an in-situ visualization/processing approach is the indispensable need of a priori knowledge to extract and visualize the right features in the simulated data. Without the domain knowledge where to find interesting features, and which isolevels and/or thresholds to choose, an in-situ visualization is likely to fail. An iterative approach is of course possible, but both time and labour intensive. The finer spatial and temporal resolutions of large scale simulations, also exhibit new – possibly previously unresolved – processes and correlations within the data. The thresholds and isolevels used in simulations at lower resolution can provide guidance, but are probably not a perfect fit at higher resolutions. To correctly find and visualize those new features and structures, one needs to work on the actual data in its original resolution, but the data needs to be transformed and reordered to make the data accessible. To achieve

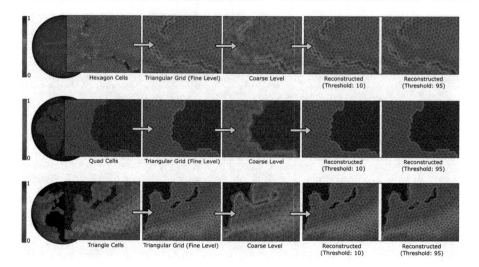

Fig. 5. Exemplary application of DHWT on a low resolution ICON ocean data set. Centroids of hexagons (top), edge midpoints in one direction (middle), centroids of triangles (bottom). Each row (left to right) shows original data, conversion to a triangular grid via icosahedral maps, applying DHWT on the converted grid to obtain coarse data, and reconstructed data using two different thresholds: 10% discarded/90% preserved and 95% discarded/5% preserved.

this, a progressive data visualization approach based on a level-of-detail (LoD) rendering is required. In here, the data is decomposed into different resolutions (LoD) and possibly also compressed before it is written out to disk in a way that facilitates a later interactive access. After the data has been written to disk, a special visualization application that supports progressive LoD rendering is used for a classic user-driven post visualization of the data [15]. Such an application accesses data in an out-of-core fashion, and only the data that is relevant to the current level of detail and which is also contained in the current view frustum is fetched, visualized and displayed.

3.1   Wavelet Decomposition and Compression

A classic tool for a level of detail decomposition of large data sets are wavelets. There are numerous examples on how to use wavelets to perform an efficient LoD based visualization of large data sets, yet those primarily focus on regular rectilinear grids [15,16]. For irregular grids, such as ICON, this becomes a bit more difficult, but it is, nevertheless, still possible. Here, so called icosahedral maps can be employed that are designed to fit the geometry of different cell configurations within the ICON model, as we have discussed in our prior publication [17]. As this research is still work in progress, this section summarizes our previous accomplishments, and outlines our current efforts in this direction.

Icosahedral maps contain the connectivity information in ICON in a highly structured two-dimensional hexagonal representation and facilitate the execution of a multi-resolution analysis on ICON data by applying a hexagonal version of the discrete wavelet transform. A global ICON grid is thereby broken down into ten diamonds, in which the data can be accessed and processed more easily [17], see also Fig. 6:

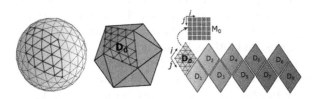

Fig. 6. Global ICON grid unfolded into a net consisting of ten diamonds. The vertex information of each diamond is stored in a 2D rectangular grid that corresponds to the hexagonal lattice associated with that diamond.

Figure 5 shows the principle of this wavelet decomposition for all three ICON grids using a low resolution global ocean simulation. The left column shows the original data, followed by a mapping onto a triangular grid (icosahedral maps), a coarsened grid (lower level of detail) and two reconstructions. In order to observe how the data responds to compression, a quantile thresholding was applied, keeping only those detail coefficients whose magnitudes falls within a specified percentile range. The last two columns in Fig. 5 shows that the wavelet responds very well to compression, i.e. the discarding of certain details. The reconstruction for two different thresholds – 10% and 95% – is shown, and displays that even a very aggressive compression of 95% – i.e. only 5% of the details are retained – is feasible. While this is still only work in progress, it clearly shows that a wavelet based decomposition and lossy compression of ICON data is possible and desirable. The here described wavelet based decomposition of the data would be performed in-situ, and will be implemented on the C++ side of the Catalyst adaptor in the form of an additional data flow branch, as is already outlined in Fig. 2. Researchers at NCAR in Boulder, Colorado, have looked into possible gains and losses by using various lossy compression algorithms, and shown that compression ratios of 1:5 are feasible, without even impairing the statistical signal of the data [18,19].

VAPOR, an interactive 3D visualization platform that is also developed at NCAR can be used to load and display such wavelet decomposed data sets. In fact, VAPOR features the so called VAPOR Data Collection (VDC) data model that allows users to progressively load and visualize their data, thus allowing an interactive visualization of terascale data sets on commodity hardware [15,20]. Initially designed to handle regular rectilinear grids only, it was more recently extended to additionally support the UGRID netCDF-CF[7] standard, i.e. allowing one to also load and display model data on irregular grids, such as MPAS and ICON simulation output.

4   Summary and Conclusion

We have discussed the current status of in-situ visualization/processing at DKRZ, along with a few other ideas to handle some of the extremely large data sets that are produced by current climate simulations. The work presented is still work in progress, and although currently none of the work discussed is used in production mode, it is expected that the in-situ visualization and processing techniques will transition within a few weeks once workflows that are easy to setup and deploy by climate scientists have been devised. After that, other in-situ feature detection and tracking, such as the discussed ocean eddy census, will be added. Steering, as is developed as part of the exascale visualization initiative SENSEI, is also interesting, but probably a topic that lies – at least for us – a bit further into the future [9]. The wavelet decomposition and compression that was outlined in the previous Sect. 3 is implemented as standalone prototype, and needs to be relocated and further optimized into the Catalyst adaptor.

Other interesting aspects include the in-situ generation of high-quality visualizations using raytracing. As our current cluster is based on Intel CPUs, with relatively outdated GPUs, our current choice is OSPRay. Nevertheless, both OSPRay and OptiX are able to create superior quality renderings and are already used at DKRZ within the conventional post visualization workflow [21,22]. A transition of raytracing to in-situ will probably also take some more time.

Furthermore, just a visual display and analysis of large simulations may not be very useful in the near future, as the data is so massive that a single user will have problems finding and detecting the interesting features in the visual output. Here the currently popular machine learning might prove useful to automatically check the plausibility of a simulation, and also to identify outliers and extreme weather/climate events and direct the attention of the researcher directly onto those regions/time steps.

References

1. Zängl, G., Reinert, D., Ripodas, P., Baldauf, M.: The ICON (ICOsahedral non-hydrostatic) modelling framework of DWD and MPI-M: description of the non-hydrostatic dynamical core. Q. J. Roy. Meteorol. Soc. **141**(687), 563–579 (2015)
2. Heinze, R., et al.: Large-eddy simulations over Germany using ICON: a comprehensive evaluation. Q. J. Roy. Meteorol. Soc. **143**, 69–100 (2016)
3. Wes Bethel, E., Childs, H., Hansen, C., et al.: High Performance Visualization: Enabling Extreme-Scale Scientific Insight. Chapman and Hall/CRC Press, London (2016). ISBN 9781138199613

---

[7] http://ugrid-conventions.github.io/ugrid-conventions/.

4. Bauer, A., et al.: In situ methods, infrastructures, and applications on HPC platforms -a state-of-the-art (STAR) report. In: Computer Graphics Forum, vol. 35, no. 3 (2016)
5. Childs, H., et al.: VisIt: an end-user tool for visualizing and analyzing very large data. In: High Performance Visualization-Enabling Extreme-Scale Scientific Insight, pp. 357–372 (2012)
6. Ahrens, J., Geveci, B., Law, C.: ParaView: An End-User Tool for Large Data Visualization. Visualization Handbook. Elsevier (2005). ISBN 13: 978-0123875822
7. Ayachit, U.: The ParaView Guide: A Parallel Visualization Application. Kitware (2015). ISBN 978-1930934306
8. Larsen, M., et al.: The ALPINE in situ infrastructure: ascending from the ashes of Strawman. In: Proceedings of the in Situ Infrastructures on Enabling Extreme-Scale Analysis and Visualization (ISAV 2017), pp. 42–46. ACM, New York (2017). https://doi.org/10.1145/3144769.3144778
9. Ayachit, U., et al.: The SENSEI generic in situ interface. In: Second Workshop on In Situ Infrastructures for Enabling Extreme-Scale Analysis and Visualization (ISAV), pp. 40–44 (2016)
10. Ayachit, U., et al.: ParaView catalyst: enabling in situ data analysis and visualization. In: Proceedings of the First Workshop on In Situ Infrastructures for Enabling Extreme-Scale Analysis and Visualization (ISAV 2015), pp. 25–29. ACM (2015)
11. Woodring, J., Petersen, M., Schmeiss, A., Patchett, J., Ahrens, J., Hagen, H.: In situ eddy analysis in a high-resolution ocean climate model. IEEE Trans. Vis. Comput. Graph. $22(1)$, 857–866 (2016)
12. Ahrens, J., Jourdain, S., O'Leary, P., Patchett, J., Rogers, D.H., Petersen, M.: An image-based approach to extreme scale in situ visualization and analysis. In: Proceedings of the International Conference for High Performance Computing, Networking, Storage and Analysis, pp. 424–434. IEEE Press (2014)
13. Banesh, D., Schoonover, J.A., Ahrens, J.P., Hamann, B.: Extracting, visualizing and tracking mesoscale ocean eddies in two-dimensional image sequences using contours and moments. In: Workshop on Visualisation in Environmental Sciences (EnvirVis) (2017)
14. Schiffer, R.A., Rossow, W.B.: The international satellite cloud climatology project (ISCCP): the first project of the world climate research programme. Bull. Amer. Meteorol. Soc. 64, 779–784 (1983)
15. Clyne, J., Rast, M.: A prototype discovery environment for analyzing and visualizing terascale turbulent fluid flow simulations. In: Proceedings of Visualization and Data Analysis, pp. 284–294 (2005)
16. Balsa Rodriguez, M., et al.: State-of-the-art in compressed GPU-based direct volume rendering. Comput. Graph. Forum 33, 77–100 (2014)
17. Jubair, M.I., Alim, U., Röber, N., Clyne, J., Mahdavi-Amiri, A.: Icosahedral maps for a multiresolution representation of earth data. VMV: Vision Modeling and Visualization, Bayreuth, Germany (2016)
18. Baker, A.H., Xu, H., Hammerling, D.M., Li, S., Clyne, J.P.: Toward a multi-method approach: lossy data compression for climate simulation data. In: Kunkel, J.M., Yokota, R., Taufer, M., Shalf, J. (eds.) ISC High Performance 2017. LNCS, vol. 10524, pp. 30–42. Springer, Cham (2017). https://doi.org/10.1007/978-3-319-67630-2_3
19. Baker, A.H., Hammerling, D.M., Mickelson, S.A., et al.: Evaluating lossy data compression on climate simulation data within a large ensemble. Geoscientific Model Dev. 9, 4381–4403 (2016)

20. Clyne, J., Mininni, P., Norton, A., Rast, M.: Interactive desktop analysis of high resolution simulations: application to turbulent plume dynamics and current sheet formation. New J. Phys. **9**, 301 (2007)
21. Wald, I., et al.: OSPRay - a CPU ray tracing framework for scientific visualization. IEEE Trans. Vis. Comput. Graph. **23**(1), 931–940 (2017)
22. Parker, S.G., et al.: OptiX: a general purpose ray tracing engine. ACM Trans. Graph. **29**, 66 (2010)

Distributed Out-of-Core Approach for In-Situ Volume Rendering of Massive Dataset

Jonathan Sarton, Yannick Remion, and Laurent Lucas$^{(\boxtimes)}$

Université de Reims Champagne-Ardenne, CReSTIC, Reims, France
{jonathan.sarton,yannick.remion,laurent.lucas}@univ-reims.fr

Abstract. This paper proposes a method that allows a fluid remote interactive visualization of a terabytes volume on a conventional workstation co-located with the acquisition devices, leveraging remote high performance computing resources. We provide a study of the behavior of an out-of-core volume renderer, using a virtual addressing system with interactive data streaming, in a distributed environment. The method implements a sort-last volume renderer with a multi-resolution ray-guided approach to visualize very large volumes of data thanks to an hybrid multi-GPUs, multi-CPUs single node rendering server.

Keywords: Interactive visualization · Large volume data · Out-of-core · Multi GPUs · Biomedical imaging

1 Introduction

Several scientific fields rely on the visualization of data represented in the form of 3D regular voxel grids. The characteristics of this representation are particularly well suited to the architecture of modern GPUs. These have become essential to benefit from an interactive visualization of this type of data, with a good rendering accuracy. However, the increase in the size of volume data in science, and particularly in biomedical imaging, is very rapid. The latter is faster than the increase in the physical capacity of the on-board memory on GPUs. One solution to address this problem is to design an out-of-core approach that allows on-demand data streaming of small chunks (bricks) of a large volume to the GPU during interactive visualization. Although these methods are now effective, data transfers to the GPU are still a bottleneck and can be restrictive to allow a fully pleasant interactive visualization. High-performance computing environments can help to reduce this bottleneck. In addition to offering an increase in computing power, useful for interactivity and visualization quality, they increase storage capacities on several GPUs and allow to distribute the load of transfers. The presented method propose a distributed out-of-core management that offer interactive data streaming on heterogeneous node, to allow scientists to visualize large volume data directly after their acquisition from their usual workstation.

© Springer Nature Switzerland AG 2019
M. Weiland et al. (Eds.): ISC 2019 Workshops, LNCS 11887, pp. 623–633, 2019.
https://doi.org/10.1007/978-3-030-34356-9_47

Contributions: The use of an out-of-core approach with a virtual addressing system based on a page table for multi-resolution volume is particularly well suited for the visualization of very massive volume data [7]. However, to our knowledge, any work has been carried out on the possibilities of using this structure in high-performance computing environments for all stages of the pipeline allowing in-situ visualization. In this paper, we present a distribution method to use such out-of-core data structure in distributed environments, on single multi-CPUs, multi-GPUs compute nodes. We address the distribution of virtual addressing space in very large volumes, in line with a distributed sort-last rendering approach for volume ray-casting. Our system is composed of a:

- GPU-based multi-resolution volume ray-casting with a ray-guided approach to render large volume data;
- complete out-of-core pipeline from disk to GPU with a multi-level, multi-resolution page table hierarchy, completely managed on GPU;
- multi-GPUs sort-last volume renderer and a distributed strategy of the out-of-core solution on a multi-CPUs, multi-GPUs single node server;
- remote solution to display, on a thin client, a high frame rate coming from a high-performance rendering server.

2 Related Work

Volume ray-casting, introduced and improved by Levoy [9,10], is nowadays the most intuitive and efficient approach to apprehend direct volume rendering and solve the volume rendering equation [12]. Its implementation on GPUs was first proposed in 2003 [8,17] and then improved in 2005 [19,20], taking advantage of hardware advances and introducing optimization techniques.

Afterward, some work has focused on out-of-core approaches for rendering of large volumes that exceed the amount of memory available on the GPU and even on the CPU. Gobbetti *et al.* [6] were among the first to propose an out-of-core approach for volume ray-casting on GPU, based on a multi-resolution octree. Crassin *et al.* [3] also use an octree and provide a very efficient ray-guided pipeline for rendering large voxelized scenes. While many works in this context have focused on a tree structure to address an entire multi-resolution volume with out-of-core storage, Hadwiger *et al.* [7] introduced a hierarchical page table for efficient virtual addressing. They show that their structure is more suitable than an octree for very large volumes of data. Fogal *et al.* [4] provide a detailed analysis of ray-guided out-of-core approaches on GPU. For more details, we can also refer to a complete state of the art [1]. Parallel volume rendering has also been studied to distribute the computational workload over different units and thus operate on multi-GPUs architectures for efficient rendering [21]. Molnar *et al.* [13] proposed a classification of parallel rendering methods. Although some work in multi-GPUs volume rendering is focused on a sort-first approach [14], most methods are oriented towards a sort-last approach [11,15]. In addition to providing a computational scaling, the latter also provides a memory management scaling. This aspect is the main bottleneck in

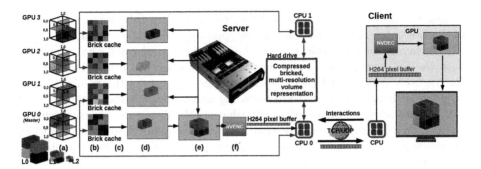

Fig. 1. Pipeline overview. Example of our remote out-of-core rendering pipeline on a 4-GPUs and 2-CPUs server. This pipeline includes the following steps: (a) Virtual multi-resolution volume distribution (b) Out-of-core virtual addressing structure and brick cache (c) Ray-guided volume renderer (d) Local rendering pixel buffer (e) GPUs communications for sort-last compositing (f) H.264 GPU compression.

an on-demand streaming context for interactive rendering of very large volumes of data. Finally, there are very few methods that combine multi-GPUs rendering with an out-of-core approach. Fogal *et al.* [5] propose an out-of-core volume renderer with an MPI-based compositing to render large datasets on multi-node clusters up to 256 GPUs. Beyer *et al.* [2] present a distributed version on 4 GPUs of an octree-based virtual addressing system to visualize a very large volume.

Compared with these works, we propose to introduce a distribution method of an out-of-core approach based on an efficient GPU virtual addressing and caching system [18] on multi-GPUs, multi-CPUs single node server. Combined with a ray-guided volume renderer with sort-last compositing for interactive visualization on datasets exceeding terabytes.

3 Our Method

3.1 Out-of-Core Approach

Figure 1 summarizes the proposed pipeline. It includes an out-of-core data management in order to handle very large volumes that can exceed the amount of GPU and CPU memory. It is based on a virtual addressing system using a multi-level multi-resolution page table hierarchy and a brick cache on GPU. The underlying structure, implemented in GPU texture memory, is fully maintained on the GPU to optimize the communication load with the CPU [18]. This system is able to interactively address a whole multi-resolution volume decomposed into small voxel bricks entirely stored on disk with compression. The bricks required for interactive visualization are streamed to the GPU cache when requested by the application. On the GPU, the navigation in the multi-resolution volume is performed in a normalized virtual volume. The full parallel GPU implementation of our virtual addressing structure management includes a brick request manager. This one takes care of sending to the CPU a list containing the IDs of the bricks required by the interactive application during its whole execution. The streaming of these bricks to the GPU cache is performed asynchronously with the GPU visualization step in order to maintain a constant interactivity for the user. A dedicated CPU thread manages the lists of the required bricks to provide them to the GPU after reading and decompressing. Unlike [7] and [18], we are interested here in the distribution of this out-of-core management solution on a heterogeneous node that includes several GPUs and CPUs with an approach including remote rendering allowing a complete in-situ visualization pipeline.

3.2   Sort-Last Distributed Ray-Casting

The bottleneck of a distributed renderer combined with an out-of-core system lies in the heavy loads of the voxel bricks, streamed to the different rendering units, and in the updates of their associated GPU caches. In this context, a sort-last approach is more appropriate than a sort-first approach to minimize these issues. By pre-determining a sub-domain of the volume on each GPU, this allows limited CPU/GPU and GPU/GPU data transfers and avoids cache flushes.

In association with our sort-last approach, we propose to use a multi-resolution ray-guided volume renderer that efficiently and naturally integrates our out-of-core loading method. This approach ensures to load only the useful bricks on the different GPUs, according to the sampling along the rays in the volume. Our renderer is also suitable for the multi-resolution volume representation by choosing an adapted level of detail for each sample based on its distance to the camera. This allows us to adapt the sampling step, and thus reduce the number of texture memory lookup for areas containing less detail.

In our system, the compositing step, involved by the sort-last rendering, is implemented on GPU with a basic approach applying the OVER operator [16] in front-to-back. At each rendering pass, the local pixel buffer of each GPU is communicated to the pre-defined master GPU, in charge of the compositing. We propose to initiate these transfers from the master GPU, with peer-to-peer communications using CUDA Unified Virtual Addressing system if possible, i.e. if the GPUs are in the same addressing space as the master GPU. Otherwise, our strategy switches to explicit transfers via the CPUs.

3.3   Multi-GPUs Virtual Addressing

The volume partitioning is done on a normalized virtual volume, used on each GPU to navigate through all the multi-resolution volume and to virtually access to any voxels (Fig. 1(a)). This distribution only consists of restricting the addressing range in the normalized virtual volume. This method makes it possible to implicitly distribute the entire multi-resolution representation of the volume. The virtual addressing structure, used to ensure access to all voxels of a very large volume, is distributed as follows. Each GPU has its own instance of this structure with its own brick cache, completely independent of other GPUs.

However, a single virtualization configuration is used for all the GPUs. Thus, the size of the bricks, blocks in the page table and the number of virtualization levels in the structure do not differ from one unit to the other. We also implement a single common CPU brick cache. We use a multi-threaded strategy with OpenMP on the different CPU(s) of the server to communicate with all the GPUs. For each of them, the corresponding CUDA context is linked to one and only one OpenMP thread. The affinity of each thread is essential and is achieved with respect to the CPUs locations according to the server topology. Thus, a thread in charge of communicating with a GPU is necessarily placed on a physical core of the CPU that has a direct physical link with that GPU. At the initialization step, each GPU is responsible for creating all the necessary resources, especially allocating its brick cache and its page table. Then, each OpenMP thread first communicates to its associated GPU the addressing sub-space of the volume on which it must perform its part of the rendering. Each thread can then independently manage the requests and the streaming of the bricks to its associated GPU during the whole duration of the execution of the interactive application.

3.4   Remote Rendering

In order to exploit resources offered by high-performance computing environments from lightweight devices, we propose to integrate a remote visualization system in our method. Thus, after each rendering and compositing pass, the resulted pixel buffer is directly compressed into an H.264 stream on a designated master GPU of the rendering server node. Then, the compressed buffer is copied to the CPU before being sent over the network. A thin client that receives the content of this H.264 stream, decompress it and simply display the result in an interactive display environment. This configuration allows us to provide a single pipeline that can be seen as an in-situ solution in the sense that the visualization can be done on a standard PC in place of the data acquisition. However, this requires sending all the acquired data to the remote rendering server where they are then handled for a pre-processing step. This step only includes the creation of the bricked multi-resolution representation of the 3D volume. The creation of page table entries is done on the fly as needed during the visualization. The initialization of our virtual addressing structure on the different GPUs only consists of allocating the necessary texture memory space for the different cache levels.

4   Results

The results presented here, were obtained on a NVidia Quadro VCA rendering server. It consists of a single computing node containing eight Quadro P6000 GPUs with 24 GB of VRAM, two CPUs Intel Xeon E5-2698 2.2 GHz and 256 GB of RAM. The display is performed on a full HD viewport 1920 × 1080. To illustrate the results, we used two datasets:

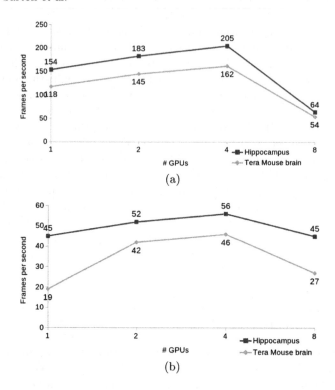

Fig. 2. Out-of-core multi-GPUs volume ray-casting FPS. Average FPS according to two different zoom level for both data sets. (a) For a medium zoom at an intermediate level of detail (see Fig. 3(a, c)). (b) For a high zoom level with a highly detailed full-screen volume (see Fig. 3(b, d)). The averages are calculated on measurements taken over the entire duration of a scenario of several camera rotations around the volume.

- *Hippocampus:* a 2160 × 2560 × 1072 volume with grayscale 16-bits voxels (11.8 GB) of a primate hypocampus from a light sheet microscope.
- *Tera Mouse Brain:* a 64000 × 50000 × 114 volume with RGBA 32-bits voxels (1.45 TB) of a histological slices stack of a mouse brain.

The evaluation is based on these two datasets with 64^3 voxels bricks. In addition, the bricks of the *Tera Mouse brain* volume are stored on disk, cached on CPU and transferred to the GPU with 256^3 voxels, which includes 4^3 bricks of 64^3 voxels.

4.1   Display Frequency

Figure 2 shows the average FPS, based on the number of GPUs used, for two different zoom level. These results were obtained by measuring the number of frames per second over the entire duration of an interactive scenario involving several rotations of an orbital camera around the volume. The results are, among

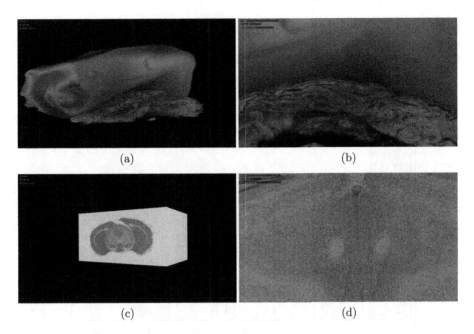

Fig. 3. Rendering illustrations. Rendering of the *Hippocampus* dataset (a, b) and the *Tera Mouse brain* dataset (c, d) at two different level of detail.

other things, dependent on the defined transfer function. Here, the transfer functions are chosen to provide an interesting visualization independently for both datasets.

First, we can note that the behavior of our system is the same for both datasets and, the number of FPS are almost the same. This allows us to show that the performance of our approach does not depend on the input size of the volume to be visualized. The difference between the FPS for the two datasets is actually due to the different transfer function used. With a single GPU, we already achieve interactive visualization time. We also see the gain brought by the multi-GPUs system for the global rendering time. However, there is a significant drop in performance beyond four GPUs. It is due to the topology of the server node where four GPUs are connected to one CPU while the other four are connected to another CPU. According to this topology, four GPUs are not in the same address space as the master one. In this scenario, it is not possible to take advantage of direct GPU to GPU communications with CUDA peer-to-peer and UVA, for these GPUs. The communications with the master GPU are therefore made by explicit transfers, passing through the CPU and crossing a QPI port between the two processors. In order to validate this analysis, Fig. 4, provides details of the different steps required for rendering. We can see the impact of these transfers on the overall rendering time. This behavior could be fixed by using compute nodes that provide direct communication between all GPUs, with the NVLink technology of NVidia for instance.

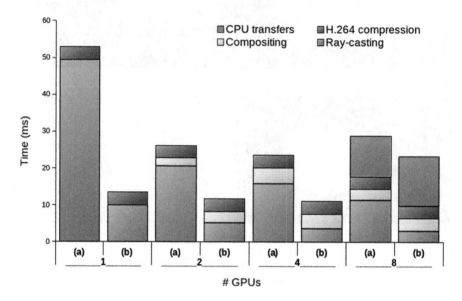

Fig. 4. Analysis of the different step of the rendering. These measurements represent the time required for the different rendering steps according to the number of GPUs for the *Tera Mouse brain* dataset. (a) For a high zoom with full-screen volume display at a high level of detail (see Fig. 3(d)). (b) For a medium zoom with an intermediate level of detail (see Fig. 3(c))

4.2   Data Loading

Figure 5 shows the results obtained by evaluating the data loading time in our multi-GPUs out-of-core management context. This evaluation is done on the loading of all the needed bricks of a complete HD view, in a worst-case scenario, from empty GPU and CPU caches. All the data are therefore only present on the server disk and stored with compression. The trend of these curves shows that the data loading time is greatly reduced by the number of GPUs used for rendering, from few seconds for a single GPU to one second or less with eight GPUs. Indeed, our sort-last rendering solution allows distributing the bricks loading on the different GPUs. Moreover, these values are once again mostly the same for both datasets although their dimensions are very different.

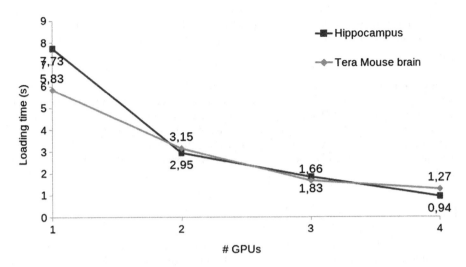

Fig. 5. Loading time of a complete HD viewport in a worst-case scenario. These measurements represent the loading times of all the bricks required to generate the complete HD viewport presented in Fig. 3(b) and (d), based on the number of GPUs used, for the two datasets. They are obtained in a worst-case scenario, with empty GPU and CPU caches.

5   Conclusion and Future Work

In this paper, we have presented a method that proposes a solution to allow in-situ visualization of high dimension volume data. We use an out-of-core approach, based on an efficient virtual addressing system and a GPU caching mechanism, to handle very large volumes of data, in a context of remote parallel volume rendering. The distribution of our out-of-core model is combined with a sort-last ray-guided volume renderer in a multi-GPUs single node environment. This method reduces the main bottleneck of on-demand data streaming, from mass storage to GPU, used by out-of-core approaches to handle data exceeding GPU and CPU memory. The overall data block loading response is accelerated by distributing the charge across all GPUs. In addition, the balancing of the rendering workload allows a smooth interactive visualization. These results are observed on data exceeding terabyte on a server with 8 GPUs. The use of a multi-resolution page table, introduced by Hadwiger for out-of-core addressing of large volumes of data on GPUs, is particularly well suited for very large volumes of data. Moreover, we can conclude with this paper that this structure is also efficient and particularly well suited for the use in a distributed environment on a multi-GPU multi-CPU single node and that its behavior allows to visualize volumes exceeding the terabyte remotely on standard PC. The proposed out-of-core structure opens up a broad application framework allowing complete support of the all pipeline from data acquisition through processing to interactive visualization. We could then consider performing all these steps with our virtual addressing structure to propose an efficace in-situ solution allowing to remotely visualize the data during their acquisition and not only after their acquisition.

Acknowledgments. This work is supported by the French national funds (PIA2'program "Intensive Computing and Numerical Simulation" call) under contract No. P112331-3422142 (*3D Neuro Secure* project). We would like to thank all the partners of the consortium led by Neoxia, the three French clusters (Cap Digital, Systematic and Medicen), Thierry Delzescaux and the Mircen team (CEA, France) for the two datasets as well as the Centre Image of the University of Reims for the VCA server used.

References

1. Beyer, J., Hadwiger, M., Pfister, H.: State-of-the-art in GPU-based large-scale volume visualization. Comput. Graph. Forum **34**(8), 13–37 (2015). https://doi.org/10.1111/cgf.12605
2. Beyer, J., Hadwiger, M., Schneider, J., Jeong, W.K., Pfister, H.: Distributed terascale volume visualization using distributed shared virtual memory. In: 2011 IEEE Symposium on Large Data Analysis and Visualization (LDAV), pp. 127–128, October 2011. https://doi.org/10.1109/LDAV.2011.6092332
3. Crassin, C., Neyret, F., Lefebvre, S., Eisemann, E.: GigaVoxels: ray-guided streaming for efficient and detailed voxel rendering. In: Proceedings of the 2009 Symposium on Interactive 3D Graphics and Games, pp. 15–22. ACM (2009). http://dl.acm.org/citation.cfm?id=1507152
4. Fogal, T., Schiewe, A., Kruger, J.: An analysis of scalable GPU-based ray-guided volume rendering. In: 2013 IEEE Symposium on Large-Scale Data Analysis and Visualization (LDAV), pp. 43–51, October 2013. https://doi.org/10.1109/LDAV.2013.6675157
5. Fogal, T., Childs, H., Shankar, S., Krüger, J., Bergeron, R.D., Hatcher, P.: Large data visualization on distributed memory multi-GPU clusters. In: Proceedings of the Conference on High Performance Graphics, HPG 2010, Eurographics Association, Aire-la-Ville, Switzerland, pp. 57–66 (2010). http://dl.acm.org/citation.cfm?id=1921479.1921489
6. Gobbetti, E., Marton, F., Guitián, J.A.I.: A single-pass GPU ray casting framework for interactive out-of-core rendering of massive volumetric datasets. Vis. Comput. **24**(7–9), 797–806 (2008). https://doi.org/10.1007/s00371-008-0261-9
7. Hadwiger, M., Beyer, J., Jeong, W.K., Pfister, H.: Interactive volume exploration of petascale microscopy data streams using a visualization-driven virtual memory approach. IEEE Trans. Vis. Comput. Graph. **18**(12), 2285–2294 (2012). https://doi.org/10.1109/TVCG.2012.240
8. Kruger, J., Westermann, R.: Acceleration techniques for GPU-based volume rendering. In: Proceedings of the 14th IEEE Visualization 2003 (VIS 2003), p. 38. IEEE Computer Society, Washington (2003). https://doi.org/10.1109/VIS.2003.10001
9. Levoy, M.: Display of surfaces from volume data. IEEE Comput. Graph. Appl. **8**(3), 29–37 (1988). https://doi.org/10.1109/38.511
10. Levoy, M.: Efficient ray tracing of volume data. ACM Trans. Graph. **9**(3), 245–261 (1990). https://doi.org/10.1145/78964.78965

11. Marchesin, S., Mongenet, C., Dischler, J.M.: Multi-GPU Sort-last volume visualization. In: Proceedings of the 8th Eurographics Conference on Parallel Graphics and Visualization, EGPGV 2008, pp. 1–8. Eurographics Association, Aire-la-Ville (2008). https://doi.org/10.2312/EGPGV/EGPGV08/001-008

12. Max, N.: Optical models for direct volume rendering. IEEE Trans. Visual. Comput. Graph. 1(2), 99–108 (1995). https://doi.org/10.1109/2945.468400

13. Molnar, S., Cox, M., Ellsworth, D., Fuchs, H.: A sorting classification of parallel rendering. IEEE Comput. Graph. Appl. 14, 23–32 (1994)

14. Moloney, B., Ament, M., Weiskopf, D., Moller, T.: Sort-first parallel volume rendering. IEEE Trans. Visualization Comput. Graph. 17(8), 1164–1177 (2011). https://doi.org/10.1109/TVCG.2010.116

15. Müller, C., Strengert, M., Ertl, T.: Optimized volume raycasting for graphics-hardware-based cluster systems. The Eurographics Association (2006). https://doi.org/10.2312/EGPGV/EGPGV06/059-066

16. Porter, T., Duff, T.: Compositing digital images. In: Proceedings of the 11th Annual Conference on Computer Graphics and Interactive Techniques, SIGGRAPH 1984, pp. 253–259. ACM, New York (1984). https://doi.org/10.1145/800031.808606

17. Roettger, S., Guthe, S., Weiskopf, D., Ertl, T., Strasser, W.: Smart Hardware-Accelerated Volume Rendering, p. 9 (2003)

18. Sarton, J., Courilleau, N., Remion, Y., Lucas, L.: Interactive visualization and on-demand processing of large volume data: a fully GPU-based out-of-core approach. IEEE Trans. Visual. Comput. Graph. 1 (2019). https://doi.org/10.1109/TVCG.2019.2912752

19. Scharsach, H.: Advanced GPU Raycasting, pp. 69–76 (2005)

20. Stegmaier, S., Strengert, M., Klein, T., Ertl, T.: A simple and flexible volume rendering framework for graphics-hardware-based raycasting, pp. 187–241, June 2005. https://doi.org/10.1109/VG.2005.194114

21. Zhang, J., Sun, J., Jin, Z., Zhang, Y., Zhai, Q.: Survey of parallel and distributed volume rendering: revisited. In: Gervasi, O., et al. (eds.) ICCSA 2005. LNCS, vol. 3482, pp. 435–444. Springer, Heidelberg (2005). https://doi.org/10.1007/11424857_46

Leveraging NVIDIA Omniverse for In Situ Visualization

Mathias Hummel[(✉)] and Kees van Kooten

NVIDIA, Santa Clara, USA
{mathiash,kvankooten}@nvidia.com

Abstract. Typical in situ visualization approaches involve rendering images of the simulation data in step with the simulation itself, using in situ visualization tools such as ParaView Catalyst, VisIt libsim, or SEN-SEI. For these approaches, one has to determine visualization parameters such as camera perspective, color maps, or scene properties in advance. The resulting frames can later be combined to produce animations, but leave little room for improving the presentation.

Alternatively, simulation data can be distilled in situ to a geometric representation, which is then transferred to a workstation and used for live exploration and visualization.

Producing high-quality animations, for example for outreach purposes, typically requires a somewhat tedious process of exporting the geometry to different formats and postprocessing using dedicated modelling, rendering, or compositing software.

We propose a method that allows interactive, high-quality visualization of distilled simulation geometry. Omniverse is NVIDIA's collaboration platform for 3D production pipelines. It is integrated with a number of freely and commercially available 3D software packages and game engines and enables content creators to work on different aspects of models or entire scenes simultaneously.

By integrating ParaView and Catalyst with the Omniverse, the visualization geometry becomes immediately accessible to a number of 3D content authoring and rendering tools without the requirement of invasive software changes in situ or tedious postprocessing and conversion workflows.

Since Omniverse can directly communicate with game engines, the visualization can be augmented using advanced features such as game physics simulation to improve insight and enhance intuition. We demonstrate this by placing architectural building models on a surface that is deformed by an earthquake-like wave. This makes it possible to immediately assess the impact of the earthquake on buildings in a live, interactive way, while leveraging the advanced rendering capabilities of the game engine.

Keywords: In situ visualization · NVIDIA Omniverse · ParaView · Catalyst

© Springer Nature Switzerland AG 2019
M. Weiland et al. (Eds.): ISC 2019 Workshops, LNCS 11887, pp. 634–642, 2019.
https://doi.org/10.1007/978-3-030-34356-9_48

1   Introduction

In the past years, the available computing capability has been outpacing the capacity for I/O. This leaves scientists no choice but to severely limit the amount of data stored as the simulation runs. In situ visualization is a broad term for approaches that do not rely on writing simulation data to persistent storage and then transferring them elsewhere (e.g. a dedicated visualization cluster or even a workstation), but instead perform visualization tasks *in situ*, alongside the simulation.

One approach to in situ visualization is to render images as simulation data are produced, alongside with the simulation. Once an image (or a set of images) is available, the original data can be discarded. The produced images can then be collected and combined into animated videos. With such an approach, fundamental parameters such as camera positions and angles, color coding of physical quantities, and the visualization pipeline itself, have to be set in advance of the simulation. Since the full data are no longer available, there is little opportunity for improving the visualization after the fact.

A different approach consists of setting up a visualization pipeline, and then storing the output of this pipeline. The result is a time series of geometries, which are typically considerably smaller in size than the original simulation output, and can, therefore, be produced at a higher temporal frequency. These geometries are then available to be used with established visualization tools.

Offline visualization purposes including outreach, presentation, and collaborative exploration in virtual reality, are typically facilitated by 3D authoring tools and rendering engines, which are not themselves geared towards scientific visualization. Therefore, they typically require a sequence of file transfers and format conversions before the data can be rendered. Especially in the presence of time-varying data, this process can be tedious and time-consuming.

In the area of media and entertainment, the NVIDIA Omniverse collaboration platform aims to solve similar issues by integrating with a number of established tools, game engines, and renderers [13]. We have implemented the Omniverse bridge for in situ visualization, an adapter that integrates ParaView Catalyst with the Omniverse.

Section 2 describes the in situ visualization challenges that we are addressing in this paper, and lists some relevant previous efforts at NVIDIA. In Sect. 3, we provide a short overview of the NVIDIA Omniverse collaboration platform. The main contribution of this paper, the Omniverse bridge, is introduced in Sect. 4. We present two examples of applying the Omniverse bridge to visualization data in Sect. 5, before concluding our results in Sect. 6.

2   In Situ Frameworks and Workflows

A number of in situ frameworks are available to researchers that make it possible to attach widely used visualization tools to simulation codes with minimal manual effort [5]. Typically, a small piece of adapter code has to be written that runs in step with the simulation and, for each time step (or with a predefined frequency), converts output of the simulation to a format that can be ingested by the visualization software and fed into a visualization pipeline. Examples for such tools include *libSim* [10], which interfaces with *VisIt* [7], *Catalyst* [4] for *ParaView* [3], and *SENSEI* [2], which provides a more general approach that can be used in conjunction with a number of existing in situ frameworks. For each time step ingested by the in situ framework, a visualization pipeline is executed that applies a range of filters, and produces distilled geometry for the purpose of visualization. One option is to render this geometry from a number of predefined view angles, and for a variety of visualization parameters such as color maps. The resulting images can be assembled into image databases for interactive exploration, for example using *ParaView Cinema* [1]. Alternatively, the distilled geometry can be streamed directly to a workstation for live viewing. Also, it is often saved to persistent storage for later retrieval and processing.

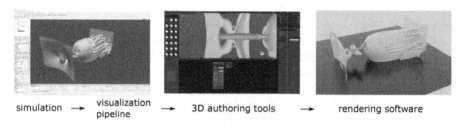

simulation → visualization pipeline → 3D authoring tools → rendering software

Fig. 1. For outreach and presentation, the output of the visualization pipeline (left) is often converted and imported into 3D authoring applications (center), where a scene with context geometry is put together. Finally, this scene is then rendered using cinematic rendering software. This example uses *Blender* [6] for scene setup and rendering.

For outreach and presentation purposes, where high visual quality is desired, the distilled geometry is often converted to formats ingestible by established 3D authoring tools from the media and entertainment world. These authoring tools are then used to set up scenes and animations, together with background and context geometry. From this, high-quality images and videos are produced using cinematic rendering software. Such an approach requires a number of data transfer and format conversion steps, which can consume considerable amounts of time and effort. These steps have to be repeated whenever changes are made to the underlying data or visualization pipeline.

For interactive and collaborative exploration in virtual reality (VR), game engines are often used to ensure sufficient performance and appealing visual quality. These applications are fundamentally subject to the same challenges as outreach and presentation, in that visualization geometry has to be transferred and converted before being added to a VR scene. Achieving the desired interactivity often requires even more work on the conversion side, by having to break up a geometry into logical pieces and attaching certain physics properties.

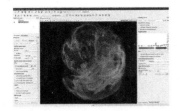 

Fig. 2. Left: NVIDIA IndeX can be used inside ParaView for scalable, high-quality, GPU-accelerated volume rendering. Right: VisRTX provides GPU-accelerated path tracing inside ParaView, enabling advanced rendering with reflections, global illumination, and physically-based MDL materials.

At NVIDIA, several efforts have been made previously that make high-quality visualizations more accessible to researchers. Several technologies have been integrated with ParaView, and can already aid in situ visualization. The NVIDIA IndeX volume rendering framework [12] for scalable, GPU-accelerated volume rendering can be directly used in conjunction with ParaView through the NVIDIA IndeX Plugin (Fig. 2, left). VisRTX [15], an open source library for scientific visualization rendering, leverages the NVIDIA OptiX hardware-accelerated ray tracing engine [14] to produce high-quality, path-traced images. The ParaView integration of VisRTX (Fig. 2, left) is scheduled to be publically available as part of an upcoming release of ParaView. In addition, the Unreal game engine was coupled with ParaView to support virtual reality applications with visualization data without the need for separate transfer and format conversion [9].

3   NVIDIA Omniverse

In the field of media and entertainment, artists often work independently on different parts of a scene withing a movie or video game. They use a variety of industry-standard tools to create and modify assets. Before such changes can be collectively visualized, they have to be reconciled through a tedious process consisting of data transfer, format conversions, imports, and compositing. NVIDIA Omniverse, which was announced in March 2019, is a collaboration platform for 3D production pipelines that makes it possible for artists to work independently on different parts of a scene, using a wide range of tools, while supporting live updates and changes across those tools[1]. Assets such as geometry and materials are accessed centrally through the Omniverse server, which can be run locally or hosted externally. Content authoring and manipulation applications are directly integrated with the Omniverse, so that changes are immediately reflected on all other connected clients. In addition to content authoring tools, the Omniverse is also integrated with game engines and cinematic rendering software, which virtually eliminates the need for tedious data transfer and format conversion.

---

[1] Further information about NVIDIA Omniverse is available at https://developer. nvidia.com/nvidia-omniverse.

```
#usda 1.0
(
    upAxis = "Y"
    defaultPrim = "mesh"
)

def Mesh "mesh"
{
    uniform bool doubleSided = 1
    int[] faceVertexCounts = [3, 3]
    int[] faceVertexIndices = [0, 1, 2, 0, 2, 3]
    normal3f[] normals = [(0, 0, 1), (0, 0, 1), (0, 0, 1), (0, 0, 1)]
    point3f[] points = [(-1, 1, 0), (-1, -1, 0), (1, -1, 0), (1, 1, 0)]
}
```

Fig. 3. A minimal example of a USD mesh in the human-readable, text-based usda format.

To achieve this, assets and scenes are represented using an extended version of Pixar's Universal Scene Description (USD) [17]. Figure 3 shows a minimal example of the human-readable usda format; typically, assets are stored and transferred in binary or compressed form. Changes are pushed to the Omniverse through incremental updates. In addition, the Omniverse supports material descriptions written in the Material Definition Language (MDL) [16] for physically based materials. The Omniverse comes with a reference viewing and editing application, *Omniverse Kit*, which utilizes the newest features of current GPUs to produce high-quality visuals at maximum performance.

4   The Omniverse Bridge

Some of the challenges addressed by the Omniverse in media and entertainment also apply to scientific visualization, especially when data transfer and format conversions are required. We propose to utilize the Omniverse as a 'Rosetta Stone' for in situ visualization geometry, to allow the direct combination of

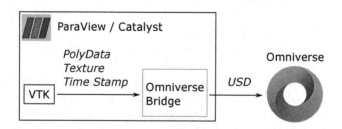

Fig. 4. The Omniverse bridge converts distilled visualization geometry from the in situ visualization framework to USD, and pushes the results into the Omniverse.

scientific visualization data with creative tools, assets, and engines. To this end, we have implemented the Omniverse bridge, an adapter that connects in situ visualization tools with the Omniverse. Distilled geometry, textures, and color maps are converted on-the-fly to USD and pushed to the Omniverse as they become available (Fig. 4). If the visualization geometry is annotated with time step information, time steps are represented as time samples in USD.

Currently, the implementation is integrated with ParaView, where the Omniverse bridge acts as a specialized render view. Any geometry that is flagged to be 'rendered' using the Omniverse bridge render view is automatically converted to USD and transferred into the Omniverse. In a Catalyst script, this view can be registered with the coprocessor in the same way as a regular render view would be used to render and save images.

Even though the current implementation supports ParaView and Catalyst, the concept of the Omniverse bridge itself is sufficiently generic to make integration with other in situ visualization frameworks straight-forward.

5 Examples

To provide a first impression of how the Omniverse can be used to address the mentioned challenges of in situ visualization, we have applied the Omniverse bridge to two example scenarios.

Airliner Flow Simulation: The Airliner example consists of an OpenFOAM [8, 18] simulation of flow around an A320 jet aircraft. ParaView Catalyst was used to compute an isosurface of the pressure field in situ, which was then pushed into the Omniverse using the Omniverse bridge together with the aircraft boundary mesh. The visualization geometries from the Omniverse were combined with some planes serving as contextual background in Omniverse Kit. A polished aluminum material, described in MDL, was applied to the aircraft mesh. When the visualization geometry that is fed into the Omniverse bridge is modified, for example by choosing a different isovalue, the changes are automatically reflected in Omniverse Kit. Advanced rendering methods such as ray traced reflections, ray traced ambient occlusion, and ray traced shadows provide high-quality visuals at real-time frame rates.

"Earthquake:" The "Earthquake" sample is not based on an actual simulation, but instead employs a programmable filter inside ParaView to apply a time-varying, wave-shaped distortion to a planar surface, which is then pushed into the Omniverse (Fig. 5, bottom row). As the filter produces time samples of the surface, the USD representation is updated by the Omniverse bridge, and differential updates are transferred to the Omniverse server. A client, such as Omniverse Kit, can play back all currently available time samples of the surface. As additional time samples arrive, these are incorporated into the animation.

In Omniverse Kit, a number of buildings are placed on the ground surface. Both the building models and the ground surface are registered with the particle-based NVIDIA FleX engine for real time physics simulation [11]. Playing back

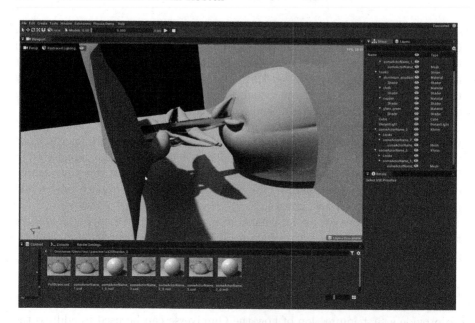

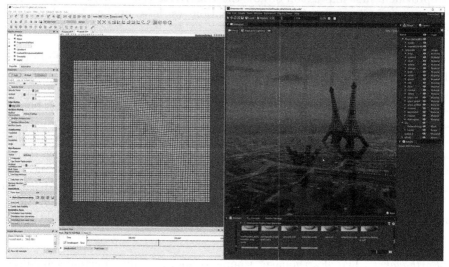

Fig. 5. Two examples making use of the Omniverse bridge. Top: An isosurface of the pressure volume and the airliner boundary mesh, both pushed into the Omniverse by the Omniverse bridge, are visualized using the Omniverse Kit application. Materials and background geometry were added in the Omniverse Kit; the underlying visualization geometry is updated when it changes in ParaView/Catalyst. Bottom row: A programmable filter is used in ParaView to generate a time-varying, wave-shaped distortion on a planar surface (left). The resulting, time-varying mesh is pushed into the Omniverse using the Omniverse bridge. The mesh is used as an animated ground model in Omniverse Kit (right), where a number of physics-enabled building models are attached to it (Map Data: Google, GeoBasis-DE/BKG). As the animation is played back, the wave passes underneath the buildings and causes them to sway.

the surface animation results in the base of the buildings being deformed as the ground wave passes underneath them. The physics simulation model then causes the buildings to sway and wobble, providing an immediate, visual impression of how the ground wave's impact.

6   Conclusion and Future Work

We have discussed some of the challenges associated with in situ visualization, specifically when it comes to data transfer and format conversion for live visualization, outreach, and presentation. We have shown how the NVIDIA Omniverse collaboration platform can help address these challenges by acting as a 'rosetta stone' that removes the need for tedious transfers and conversions. As a proof of concept, we have introduced the Omniverse bridge, which interfaces with in situ visualization frameworks such as ParaView Catalyst. We have provided two examples to show that, using the Omniverse bridge, visualization geometry can be pushed into the Omniverse with minimal additional effort. We have shown that this geometry can be immediately accessed, combined with additional context geometry and materials, and rendered in another Omniverse client. In addition, we have shown how time-varying geometry produced in situ and pushed into the Omniverse can serve as input for real time game physics simulation.

In the future, we plan to apply the Omniverse bridge to more elaborate settings, for example involving live collaboration, large geometries, and virtual reality. Further, we would like to discover applications of game physics engines, involving features such as rigid bodies and fluid simulation, in real-world applications.

Acknowledgments. The authors would like to thank CFD SUPPORT LTD. for providing the Airliner OpenFOAM case: https://www.cfdsupport.com/download-cases-a320.html.

References

1. Ahrens, J., Jourdain, S., OLeary, P., Patchett, J., Rogers, D.H., Petersen, M.: An image-based approach to extreme scale in situ visualization and analysis. In: Proceedings of the International Conference for High Performance Computing, Networking, Storage and Analysis, SC 2014, pp. 424–434, November 2014. https://doi.org/10.1109/SC.2014.40
2. Ayachit, U., Whitlock, B., Wolf, M., Loring, B., Geveci, B., Lonie, D., Bethel, E.W.: The SENSEI generic in situ interface. In: 2016 Second Workshop on In Situ Infrastructures for Enabling Extreme-Scale Analysis and Visualization (ISAV), pp. 40–44, November 2016. https://doi.org/10.1109/ISAV.2016.013
3. Ayachit, U.: The ParaView Guide: A Parallel Visualization Application. Kitware Inc., New York (2015)
4. Ayachit, U., et al.: ParaView catalyst: enabling in situ data analysis and visualization. In: Proceedings of the First Workshop on In Situ Infrastructures for Enabling Extreme-Scale Analysis and Visualization, ISAV 2015, pp. 25–29. ACM, New York (2015). http://doi.acm.org/10.1145/2828612.2828624

5. Bauer, A.C., et al.: In situ methods, infrastructures, and applications on high performance computing platforms. Comput. Graph. Forum **35**(3), 577–597 (2016). https://doi.org/10.1111/cgf.12930

6. Blender Online Community: Blender - a 3D modelling and rendering package. Blender Foundation (2019). http://www.blender.org

7. Childs, H., et al.: VisIt: an end-user tool for visualizing and analyzing very large data. In: High Performance Visualization-Enabling Extreme-Scale Scientific Insight, pp. 357–372, October 2012

8. Jasak, H., Jemcov, A., Tukovic, Z., et al.: OpenFOAM: a C++ library for complex physics simulations. In: International Workshop on Coupled Methods in Numerical Dynamics, vol. 1000, pp. 1–20. IUC Dubrovnik Croatia (2007)

9. van Kooten, K.: Bridging scientific visualization and unreal VR. In: Sherman, W.R. (ed.) VR Developer Gems, chap. 9. AK Peters/CRC Press (2019)

10. Kuhlen, T., Pajarola, R., Zhou, K.: Parallel in situ coupling of simulation with a fully featured visualization system. In: Proceedings of the 11th Eurographics Conference on Parallel Graphics and Visualization (EGPGV) (2011)

11. NVIDIA: FleX. https://developer.nvidia.com/flex. Accessed 19 July 2019

12. NVIDIA: IndeX. https://developer.nvidia.com/index. Accessed 19 July 2019

13. NVIDIA: Omniverse. https://developer.nvidia.com/nvidia-omniverse. Accessed 19 July 2019

14. NVIDIA: OptiX. https://developer.nvidia.com/optix. Accessed 19 July 2019

15. NVIDIA: VisRTX. https://github.com/NVIDIA/VisRTX. Accessed 19 July 2019

16. NVIDIA: NVIDIA material definition language 1.3 (2016)

17. Pixar: Pixar animation studios open sources Universal Scene Description (2016). https://graphics.pixar.com/usd/docs/Open-Source-Release.html. Accessed 19 July 2019

18. Weller, H.G., Tabor, G., Jasak, H., Fureby, C.: A tensorial approach to computational continuum mechanics using object-oriented techniques. Comput. Phys. **12**(6), 620–631 (1998)

Hands-On Research and Training in High Performance Data Sciences, Data Analytics, and Machine Learning for Emerging Environments

Kwai Wong[1], Stanimire Tomov[1(✉)], and Jack Dongarra[1,2]

[1] University of Tennessee, Knoxville, TN 37996, USA
kwong@utk.edu, {tomov,dongarra}@icl.utk.edu
[2] Oak Ridge National Laboratory, Oak Ridge, TN 37831, USA

Abstract. This paper describes a hands-on Research Experiences for Computational Science, Engineering, and Mathematics (RECSEM) program in high-performance data sciences, data analytics, and machine learning on emerging computer architectures. RECSEM is a Research Experiences for Undergraduates (REU) site program supported by the USA National Science Foundation. This site program at the University of Tennessee (UTK) directs a group of ten undergraduate students to explore, as well as contribute to the emergent interdisciplinary computational science models and state-of-the-art HPC techniques via a number of cohesive compute and data intensive applications in which numerical linear algebra is the fundamental building block.

Keywords: Computational science · Educational outreach · Research Experiences for Undergraduates · Data analytics · Machine learning (ML) · Hands-on experiences and education · HPC

1 Introduction

Computational science is an emerging field of study that is truly interdisciplinary, involving researchers from mathematics, computer/information science, and many domain science areas. Computational modeling and simulation have become indispensable tools in nearly every field of science and engineering. The RECSEM predecessor, called CRUSE (2013–2016), and the current RECSEM (2017–2019) programs give students a synergetic set of knowledge and skills that are useful for them to perform scientific research in HPC. These programs aim to deliver a synergetic hands-on research experience to the students by combining the expertise at the Joint Institute for Computational Sciences (JICS) [11] and the Innovative Computing Laboratory (ICL) [4] at the University of Tennessee, focusing at HPC simulation in engineering applications, emergent schemes of numerical mathematics, and state-of-the-art numerical linear algebra software,

© Springer Nature Switzerland AG 2019
M. Weiland et al. (Eds.): ISC 2019 Workshops, LNCS 11887, pp. 643–655, 2019.
https://doi.org/10.1007/978-3-030-34356-9_49

and data intensive computing. ICL is leader in enabling technologies and software for scientific computing, developing and disseminating high-quality numerical libraries like LAPACK, ScaLAPACK, PLASMA, and MAGMA [13].

The RECSEM program focuses on scientific domains in engineering applications, images processing, machine learning, and parallel numerical solvers on HPC and emergent platforms. Figure 1 shows the principle idea of the REU program. In general, the program starts with a two-week training session, introducing the students to the supercomputing environment and the common computational methods and tools to be used later. Each student is assigned a project complemented to his/her academics background and computing skill level and solves a computational modeling problem under the supervision of a team of mentors and advisors.

From 2013 to 2018, these programs have admitted a total of 92 students. Forty of them are international students from our four collaborating institutes from Hong Kong and three local students are supported under a separate REU grant from other colleges at UTK. The CRUSE and RECSEM programs have attracted students from 28 different colleges across the nation. Out of the 52 domestic students, 15 are women and 11 are African Americans (3 females). The students worked on a total of 55 different research projects with a total of 23 different lead advisors and 18 mentoring research staff and student associates at JICS and ICL. The program also enjoys tight collaborations with researchers at the Oak Ridge National Laboratory (ORNL).

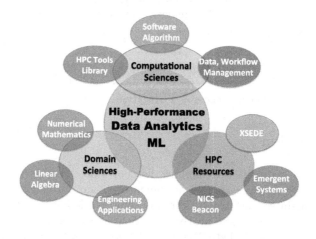

Fig. 1. Design of the RECSEM computational science program.

2 Program Design and Plan

The CSURE program started in 2013 and lasted for four years. The revised RECSEM program streamlines the operation and begins in 2107. These programs draw from the computational sciences experiences of JICS staff and the expertise of numerical linear algebra building on the HPC platform from ICL.

The principle goal was to promote the ability of undergraduate students to succeed in a research-oriented program in computational sciences. *Hence the REU programs seek to mimic the pace and intensity of graduate-level or industrial-level projects with well-defined deliverable deadlines.* The intention is to provide the participants a good knowledge of how a graduate project is organized and executed. In addition, its intellectual focus is not only to push for publishable research outcomes, but also to expose the students to research experiences through appropriate levels of motivations and accomplishments. These are major reasons we choose to do a ten-week long research program, giving students enough time to master the skills in accomplishing their research goals.

While the primary goal of these programs is to develop students' interest in pursuing research careers in computational sciences, we also provide strong professional development, post-program development opportunities, and social networking for the REU participants among themselves. Students are encouraged to continue their research activities at their home institutions afterward. There are several major tasks that the students are asked to follow. These tasks start with an informal in-class presentation, a midterm lecture presentation, an open poster presentation, and conclude with a final presentations and a final report in the last week. These tasks aim to gradually assist the students towards finishing their research goals in time. A detailed listing of the program is available at the program's webpage, www.jics.utk.edu/recsem-reu.

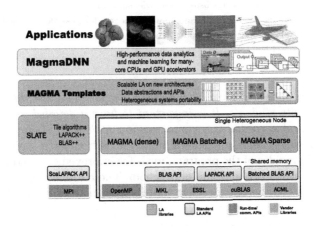

Fig. 2. Software stack for high-performance data sciences in RECSEM using linear algebra, data analytics and ML

2.1 Schedule of the REU Program

To deliver such a diverse program, a well-planned step-by-step schedule for the entire summer is desirable to be in place by early December. Event items for the preparation period include logistical arrangements, program announcement and recruitment, selection of students, payroll registration, social activities, preparation of training materials, evaluation instrumentation, mentor selection and training, and most importantly identification of research projects and mentoring teams. Following that will be the ten-week summer program starting the first week of June and ending the first week of August. A typical daily schedule for the last three years can be found on the RECSEM webpage [9]. A typical timeline of the program is listed in Table 1.

Table 1. Timeline of the REU program

Jan.–March	Student recruitment and research project identification
March	Student selection and research project selection
April-May	Prepare training materials, setup research plan, post detailed schedule
May	Mentor training, prepare reference materials, coordinate travel & logistics
First day	Goal statement, projects assignment, schedule, survey, social issues, Q&A
1st week	Training and hands-on workshop, meeting mentor, define and formulate research goals and plan of projects
2nd week	Students finalize research plan with mentors, 1st social gathering
$2–4^{th}$ week	Preliminary study, in-class presentation
5th week	Mid-term presentation, 2nd social
$6–8^{th}$ week	Research and HPC implementation, final poster
9th week	Prepare for final presentation, extending work
10th week	Final presentation, project report, concluding
Last day	Survey, Q& A, retrospective movie, summary
August	Summarize results, follow up with students for possible extended work
September	Survey report, final report, project continuation
October	Final NSF yearly report submission

The last week of the program is reserved for reporting, presentations, surveys, and meetings with students. It is important to have a detailed check-out list for each student and a cordial discussion session with each student. The discussion session involves soliciting general impressions from each student, including upsides and downsides of the program, ideas for improvement, and future opportunities for project work and graduate school. These discussion sessions provide valuable insights to the advancement and improvement of the program.

2.2 Recruitment and Student Selection

The NSF Computer and Information Science Engineering (CISE) directorate has a joint recruitment program for REU students [10] but the program opts to do additional recruitment because of the diverse, interdisciplinary nature of the program. We rely on recruitment through emails and contacts with collaborative institutes of JICS and ORNL, particularly with an established outreach partner, Morehouse College in Atlanta. Many of the applicants are highly recommended students through the contacts of our collaborators.

Candidates considered for the program fill out an application form and write a short essay describing their background, interests in science, and their goal statements. This information is used to select students and then to assign them to work on the proposed core science domains, to ensure that the specific proposed projects are beneficial to the students and matched to their interests, background knowledge, and skills.

Student selection is not always a straightforward process because of the diverse, multidisciplinary nature of this program and the challenge in finding participants that match for the various research topics. A group of mentors meets to iterate over the applicants, ranking the students for their suitability to the program and the research topics. The deadline for applications is in the late February but generally moved back depending on the need for more applicants interested in specific research topics.

Participants are selected based on three major factors: the nature of their home colleges, their interests and background, and their letters of intent and references. Students from smaller schools with fewer research opportunities are preferred in order to expand the national research community. Rising senior students are preferred. GPA is a deciding factor only if two candidates have comparable qualifications. Over the course of CSURE, we have not seen that GPA is necessarily predictive of success with the program.

Two students are usually assigned to work on one research subject. Each pair starts off together but often splits up to work towards separate research aspects of the same topic at the midpoint of the program.

Acceptance letters will be sent out as soon as the first deadline is passed. Getting a written commitment from each accepted student is important. A second set of acceptances is always needed as there are always students declining to attend. Declination letters also need to be sent out in a timely manner; however, it's wise to keep in contact with a few applicants in case of unexpected availability. There are cases that students withdraw late in April for sundry reasons.

2.3   Computing Resources

The JICS facility represents an investment by the state of Tennessee and features a state-of-the art auditorium, conference rooms, and suites for students and visiting staff. It also provides the access to different parallel computing platforms available at NICS and XSEDE [14]. The ICL has expertise in the fundamental building block of numerical libraries on HPC systems, with emphasis on GPUs. In particular, RECSEM uses the MAGMA libraries to build new data analytics and ML capabilities, e.g., MagmaDNN [1–3,5–8,12], as well as computational support for applications in various fields, as illustrated on Fig. 2.

In the RECSEM program, we turn to XSEDE to support the computing need for the research projects. An educational allocation is obtained to access resources in PSC, SDSC, and TACC. Such arrangement has huge impact to the multi-discipline nature of the program that we organize, not just the variety of hardware platforms ranging from traditional core-based component to various types of accelerators, but also the availability of software and the interactive access for development and testing purposes. Matlab is openly available on XSEDE's bridges system, which helps tremendously. The GPU platform available on XSEDE's comet and bridges platforms provide excellent computing platforms fro data science projects. In addition, we have also arranged individual multicore workstations fitted with a low end P100 compatible GPU card used for code development. These workstations provide a good alternative to accessing supercomputing remotely.

3   Research Work and Mentorship

This REU program addresses the growing importance of computational sciences in many advanced degree programs. The agenda of the program is organized around a synergistic set of ideas and practices that are common to many scientific domains. The focus of the projects leverages the multidisciplinary expertise of the staff in JICS, UTK, and ORNL.

In order to provide students with the most valuable and realistic experience in computational sciences we have identified several different areas of significant interest and expertise within out organization. A participant will select a scientific area in which he/she would like to be involved. Students are paired to work as a team together with their assigned scientific mentors and advisors.

One of the major theme in the RECSEM program is to deliver the fundamental concepts of numerical linear library which is the major building block of computational intensive and data driven sciences. We will provide exemplary data science projects using the home grown numerical libraries, LAPACK and Magma.

3.1   Stages of the Research Plan and Mentor Experiences

The schedule of the research program is organized into six progressing stages shown in Table 2.

Table 2. Timeline of the program

Stage	Week	Project targets
Training	1.5	Lectures, exercises, research skills
Science study	1.5	Overview and set research plan
Formulation	1.0	Objectives and algorithm, short talk
Prototyping	2.0	Description, midterm presentation
Implementation	2.0	Results, poster presentation
Concluding	1.0	Final presentation and report

The program begins with a kick-off meeting to highlight the agenda of the program and introduce the team of researchers and staff working in the project.

A set of tutorials containing a series of lecture materials and a clear calendar of schedule of work and activities is listed on the program website [9] and is available to the participants at start.

The first day is reserved for payroll paperwork, initial survey, introduction, exchanging email addresses, Q&A, introducing a local student team leader, and a campus walk. *A list of safety reminders, health concerns, complaints, and emergency contact information is discussed in detail.* During the program sessions, occasional health issues arise and absence and sick policy will be given.

The first stage of the program includes an in-depth introduction to the use of supercomputers, including programming languages and compiling procedures, batch queuing systems, and I/O tools. Training activities include classroom instruction, hands-on exercises, research and modeling design, and computational studies. Tutorials come with hands-on exercises that put them to work as teams. Recognizing there is an uneven level of expertise in computing, we always pair the team up to compensate for their knowledge in computer and domain sciences. The introductory sessions intersperse lectures with discussion questions, emphasis on group effort on problem solving, and hands-on exercises.

Research topics are assigned to students ahead of time; however, should they change their mind, they may do so in the first week. An important task of the first week is to give specific assignments to students to help them begin making progress on their research topic.

The second week of work includes an introduction to the domain science areas and the specific project content assigned to each team of students. This involves hour-long talks by the subject mentors. We avoid asking students to spend time on learning materials that they will not use. The rest of the week moves to scientific study with literature review, reading and discussing relevant articles, and hands-on practice with relevant computational methods and tools.

In later stages, students start to draw their research plan under the direction of their mentors. Every student will conclude the research plan and project goal in three weeks. Student progress toward their planned goals is evaluated frequently during the program. Mathematical formulation and algorithmic prototyping and testing are then followed. The last week will be reserved for concluding the project, presenting the final results, and finishing the final report.

3.2 Progress Oversight and Deliverables

The Program has Five Deliverables. These are designed to steer the students to finish their projects on time. The timeline of these deliverables is listed clearly on the webpage and emphasized in the first week of the program. *The first deliverable is a short in-class summary talk* of the research topic and the approach. *The second deliverable is an open presentation* of their research work and initial results. It is aimed to orient the students to focus on their works, help crystallize the approach, and make students aware of the project timeline.

The third deliverable is a public poster presentation, organized with other groups of REU students. The posters help students to organize their results.

Students also have the opportunity to review other projects and potentially seek ideas to improve theirs.

The last two weeks of the program have the students working toward *concluding their projects with a final presentation.* Each presentation lasts for 40 min and usually receiving a number of questions from their peers and attendants. Final presentations are great experiences for the participants and represent a concluding milestone for their research endeavors.

The Last Piece of Work is a Report. This is, in fact, a continuous process from the beginning, with students organizing their weekly summaries and articulating their results in detailed reports. Each student is encouraged to keep a weekly summary report. The final report will be a combined work that documents the student's progress and findings. *Yet in fact, this turns out to be the most demanding part of the 10-week program. Hence, it is very important to keep reminding students throughout the program to work on documenting their efforts and results.*

3.3   Research Projects and Mentorship

The research topics available for the participants span a wide range of scientific and engineering domains. Each of the areas corresponds to significant capabilities at NICS or ORNL with active researchers and projects. All projects include hands-on experience and use of parallel computing in the various scientific and engineering domains of the program.

Research projects are selected based on the expertize of the core team of mentors and the backgrounds of applicants. Descriptions of previous research projects, from traditional domain sciences to cross-disciplinary data computation are listed in the following sections.

Data Analytics and Machine Learning: A common theme for all projects is the use of high-performance numerical libraries, data analytics, and machine learning. Several projects are specifically targeting the development of such capabilities. Examples are the development of MagmaDNN [1–3,5–8,12], a high-performance data analytics and deep neural networks (DNN) framework for manycore GPUs and CPUs. Students learn state-of-the-art algorithms and performance optimizations techniques for data analytics and machine learning, implement them in open source library, and also help other students use these capabilities for data-driven science projects. Projects have included the development of the MagmaDNN DNN framework [6], extensions with convolution algorithms [2], including Winograd [5], mixed-precision FFTs using the new FP16 Tensor Cores units on Nvidia GPUs [3,12], parallelization and addition of new features [8], hyper-parameter optimization framework [1], and scalability improvements [7].

Computational Engineering Applications: Engineers have been using supercomputers to analyze and resolve many challenging problems for many years. Nowadays, computer simulation has become a mandatory step in the process of design and development for many industrial applications. Projects completed by the participants include climate and pollution transport simulations, biomechanics modeling, traffic flow computation, and power system evaluation.

Numerical Mathematics and Data Science Projects: Numerical mathematics is the building block of computer simulation of every scientific application. A science problem can usually be modeled by a set of mathematical equations and then numerically solved on computers. The effectiveness of these solvers is often determined by the combination of the specific choice of numerical schemes and implementations, which is particularly true on HPC platform. A theme of the research projects is to develop efficient numerical schemes for equation-based and data-based applications, generally needed in a lot large-scale engineering simulations. Projects completed by the participants include continuous and discontinuous finite element formulations, machine learning algorithms for microscopy and brain signal problems, topological analysis of high-dimensional data, variational inequity problems, and stochastic programming modeling.

Linear Algebra Software Implementations: Linear algebra is the backbone of HPC. Many numerical simulations depend of efficient linear algebra libraries to scale on HPC platforms. Projects completed by the participants include parallel dense solve implementation on GPU and multi/many-core CPU processors, fMRI data analysis using Intel DAAL library, randomized SVD calculations, and building workflow and graphical user interface for specific applications.

Natural Sciences Applications: Computational chemistry, physics, and geography have big footprints on large scale supercomputers. Participants have completed a number of projects in quantum mechanics, molecular dynamics, neutron image reconstruction, and GIS modeling.

The lead mentors are designated persons committed to the program. Mentors are selected based on their availability and commitment. They are leading researchers in their domain science working at UTK and/or ORNL. The team of mentors defines the major element of success of the program. They are chosen early and are involved in the selection of students. The student research projects vary every year but fall in the scope of the major program subject areas. In general mentors meet with their students at least twice a week and are available for questions. Graduate students of the mentoring team are in general also available to provide constant guidance and direction to the students. Given the reality that travel for conferences, reviews, or other purposes makes it likely that mentors will be occasionally absent, having additional advisors is important to ensure steady progress. General oversight of the research progress by the program director is also recommended. Regular discussions between the program director and the mentoring team are also helpful.

4 Accomplishments, Challenges, and Lessons Learned

4.1 Survey

Evaluation of the program is centered on the toolkit distributed by the NSF CISE REU program as published by the University of North Carolina, Charlotte [10]. The evaluation provides the mentoring team with regular feedback for ongoing assessment of the program via in-person meetings along with formal mid-program and annual reports. Reports include evidence-based recommendations for program improvements in the form of clear actions items that program directors can apply directly to further program improvement. A final summary report examines and determines to what extent the program succeeded in meeting its stated goals.

Surveys for the students are performed at the start of the program and at the end of the program. We use the standalone A La Carte student survey from the CISE REU toolkit [10]. In order to evaluate the project's impact on participants, students are given pre- and post-evaluation surveys that assess their attitudes toward and interests in computational science, as well as their knowledge of computational science and its use in the domain focus area. The results of these surveys each year guide modifications to the project for future years. Surveys and summative evaluations are independently instrumented either professionally by a contract agency or a person that is familiar with the process. The REU program engaged Dr. Christian Halloy, a retired computational science leader to conduct the summative program evaluations. Dr. Halloy conducted pre- and post-participant surveys, a personal discussion with each participant, and provided a detailed final report. He also attended and critiqued the progress of the students' final lecture and poster presentations.

In summary, U.S. students' scores for survey constructs of self-efficacy, graduate school intentions, computing attitudes, help-seeking and coping, scientific leadership, and scientific identity were favorable at the start and end of the program (means above 4.00 on a 1 to 5-point scale for pre- and post-surveys). The largest improvement gain for REU participants after the 10-week period was found for the research skills and knowledge scale with a mean increase from 3.93 (SD = 0.48) to 4.38 (SD = 0.41). Overall, participants were satisfied with the program (M = 4.25, SD = 0.43) and their mentor (M = 4.12, SD = 0.63).

Participants rated their mentors quite highly for all the indicators, the highest average score being for "approachable" (M = 4.89, StdDev = 0.31), while the lowest average score is seen for "accessible" (M = 4.56, StdDev = 0.50) which is nevertheless quite high per se.

In general, the following recommendations were provided as examples of practices the REU may consider to include or maintain to ensure continued and future success of the program.

1. Expand the evaluation to include feedback from additional stakeholder groups (i.e., faculty advisors/mentors and program administrators) in order to gain an additional understanding of the REU program.
2. If possible, create a system to follow the student participants over time to assess additional project impacts on a long-term basis. (e.g., graduate school attendance, career choice, presentation and publications, awards and honors, etc.).

3. Continue to integrate strategies that will enhance the experience across diverse backgrounds, considering that students in the program possess differing academic backgrounds and research preparation.
4. Carefully recruit faculty and graduate students who will be available throughout the duration of the program. Consider a back-up strategy to support students if a volunteering mentor is unavailable during parts of the program.
5. Continue to include and potentially increase hands-on instruction at the beginning of the program to engage and motivate participants.
6. Continue to provide opportunities for students and mentors to network at the start of the summer and throughout the research experience.

4.2   Accomplishments, Challenges, and Lessons

The success of the program counts on dedications and efforts of our mentors. We have instituted a total of 55 different projects with only a few of them sharing some levels of similarities. Selection and availability of mentors are constant subjects of concern even we enjoy having a large pool of volunteer scientists. As this REU program continues, we learn to streamline the dimension of projects and maintain the core subject areas the team of resident mentors and PIs are familiar with. Often the program director has to be prepare to spend over half of his time a day answering questions for the entire group.

Parallel computing to many participants has a steep learning curve, pairing students in their comfort knowledge backgrounds is essential to get a project done in time. In addition, to avoid duplication effort within a team, we often design a team project with multiple themes allowing every student has his/her research own contribution.

Human dynamics, emotion, frustration, and conflicts among students, however rare, are unavoidable issues. Listening, patience, caring, and professionalism are appropriate answers to most. After all, we put research experiences as the primary theme of the program. Having international students gives a good mix of cultural interaction, in fact, improves overall group dynamics.

4.3   Program Outcomes and Impacts

Over the last five years, we have instituted a multidisciplinary computational sciences REU program that encompasses 55 different projects, including a total of 92 students from 28 colleges. This program has established a continued relationship with undergraduate institutions such as Morehouse College in Atlanta, Maryville College near Knoxville, Centre College in Kentucky, and Slippery Rock University in PA. This is important in sustaining long-term viability of the REU program, which can continue to evolve and improve from listening the feedback and suggestions from our partner colleges. The outcomes of the students' research work included six sponsored conference presentations, three conference papers and a number of conference and journal papers. A list of their reports is posted in the RECSEM website [11]. Close to 70% of the students have gone to or are applying for graduate schools. The program director has maintained yearly contacts with the participants. This is important to our sponsor. It helps to track the progress of the students and overall impact to the REU program.

5   Conclusions

This REU program intends to provide participants with an experience with a similar level of effort as in graduate school. The program provides students an exposure to research with high performance computing applied to a variety of scientific applications. In three summers, we have resolved many problems and met even more challenges. In particular, the following items summarize the highlights of the program:

1. A well-defined step-by-step timeline leading to the end of the program is in place in early December.
2. The participants are selected based on three major factors: the nature of their home college, their interests and background, and their letters of intent and references.
3. The project assignments are sent to students ahead of time.
4. Getting a written commitment from each enrollee is important.
5. A midterm preliminary presentation of the research topic and the approaches of the research, is very important.
6. Housing for students must be prepared in the early stage of the program. The entire group stays together in the arranged housing to get them to blend together socially.
7. A program director is important, with regular availability to the participants.
8. Co-locating all students and helpers in a multi-purpose lecturing room enhances the cohesiveness of the program.
9. A list of safety reminders, health concerns, and emergency contact information is discussed in detail in the first day.
10. An effective team of mentors represents a major element of success of the program. They are chosen early and are also involved in the selection of their students.
11. We have arranged a local student to serve as the site lead to the group, particularly for social activities.
12. The most demanding part of the 10-week experience is the final report. The program director should keep reminding participants and constantly check for progress.
13. A detailed checkout list for each student and a meeting with each student before the program ends are needed.
14. Surveys for the students are performed at the start of the program and at the end of the program.

Acknowledgments. This work was conducted at the Joint Institute for Computational Sciences (JICS), sponsored by the National Science Foundation (NSF), through

NSF REU Award #1262937 and #1659502, with additional Support from the University of Tennessee, Knoxville (UTK), and the National Institute for Computational Sciences (NICS). This work used the Extreme Science and Engineering Discovery Environment (XSEDE), which is supported by National Science Foundation grant number ACI-1548562. Computational Resources are available through a XSEDE education allocation award TG-ASC170031.

References

1. Betancourt, F., Wong, K., Asemota, E., Marshall, Q., Nichols, D., Tomov, S.: OpenDIEL: a parallel workflow engine and data analytics framework. In: Practice and Experience in Advanced Research Computing (PEARC 2019), July 2019. ACM, Chicago (2019)
2. Chen, S., Gessinger, A., Tomov, S.: Design and acceleration of convolutional neural networks on modern architectures. Technical report, Joint Institute for Computational Sciences (JICS), UTK, 2018 Summer Research Experiences for Undergraduate (REU), Knoxville, TN, p. 2018 (2018)
3. Cheng, X., Sorna, A., D'Azevedo, E., Wong, K., Tomov, S.: Accelerating 2D FFT: Exploit GPU Tensor Cores through Mixed-Precision, November 2018 (2018)
4. Innovative Computing Laboratory (ICL). http://icl.cs.utk.edu
5. Ng, L., et al.: MagmaDNN 0.2: high-performance data analytics for manycore GPUs and CPUs. In: MagmaDNN, 2018 Summer Research Experiences for Undergraduate (REU), January 2019
6. Ng, L., Wong, K., Haidar, A., Tomov, S., Dongarra, J.: MagmaDNN - high-performance data analytics for manycore GPUs and CPUs. In: MagmaDNN, 2017 Summer Research Experiences for Undergraduate (REU) (2017)
7. Nichols, D., Tomov, N.S., Betancourt, F., Tomov, S., Wong, K., Dongarra, J.: MagmaDNN: towards high-performance data analytics and machine learning for data-driven scientific computing. In: ISC High Performance, June 2019. Springer, Frankfurt (2019)
8. Nichols, D., Wong, K., Tomov, S., Ng, L., Chen, S., Gessinger, A.: MagmaDNN: accelerated deep learning using MAGMA. In: Practice and Experience in Advanced Research Computing (PEARC 2019), July 2019. ACM, Chicago (2019)
9. RECSEM REU Program at UTK. http://www.jics.utk.edu/recsem-reu
10. Research Experience for Undergraduates (REU): Socially Relevant Computing. https://reu.uncc.edu/cise-reu-toolkit/results-cise-reu-toolkit
11. Computational Science for Undergraduate Research Experience, 2013–17 internal reports. http://www.jics.utk.edu/csure-reu/csure13/projects, http://www.jics.utk.edu/cure-reu/csure-14/projects, http://www.jics.utk.edu/csure-reu/csure15/projects, http://www.jics.utk.edu/csure-reu/csure16/projects, http://www.jics.utk.edu/recsem-reu/recsem17/projects
12. Sorna, A., Cheng, X., D'Azevedo, E., Wong, K., Tomov, S.: Optimizing the fast Fourier transform using mixed precision on tensor core hardware. In: 2018 IEEE 25th International Conference on High Performance Computing Workshops (HiPCW), pp. 3–7, December 2018. https://doi.org/10.1109/HiPCW.2018.8634417
13. Tomov, S., Dongarra, J., Baboulin, M.: Towards dense linear algebra for hybrid GPU accelerated manycore systems. Parellel Comput. Syst. Appl. **36**(5–6), 232–240 (2010). https://doi.org/10.1016/j.parco.2009.12.005
14. Towns, J. et al.: XSEDE: accelerating scientific discovery. Comput. Sci. Eng. **16**(5), 62–74 (2014). https://doi.org/10.1109/MCSE.2014.80

Correction to: High Performance Computing

Michèle Weiland⬛, Guido Juckeland⬛, Sadaf Alam⬛,
and Heike Jagode⬛

Correction to:
M. Weiland et al. (Eds.) in: *High Performance Computing,*
LNCS 11887, https://doi.org/10.1007/978-3-030-34356-9

In the original version of this LNCS volume, four papers were erroneously released as open access papers. This has been corrected to only two papers – papers 5 and 7.

The updated version of these chapters can be found at
https://doi.org/10.1007/978-3-030-34356-9_5
https://doi.org/10.1007/978-3-030-34356-9_7
https://doi.org/10.1007/978-3-030-34356-9_23
https://doi.org/10.1007/978-3-030-34356-9_41
https://doi.org/10.1007/978-3-030-34356-9

M. Weiland et al. (Eds.): ISC 2019 Workshops, LNCS 11887, p. C1, 2019.
https://doi.org/10.1007/978-3-030-34356-9_50

Author Index

Abeni, Luca 1
Aghakhani, Hossein 101
Akhavan-Safaei, Ali 101
Almgren, Ann S. 113
Aloisio, Giovanni 240
Ambert, Kyle 463
Antonio, Fabrizio 240
Ara, Gabriele 1
Arenaz, Manuel 352
Asiminakis, Marios 88
Azab, Abdulrahman 61

Baker, Joshua 36
Baker, Matthew B. 514
Benedicic, Lucas 46
Berrill, Mark 330
Betancourt, Frank 490
Betke, Eugen 169, 214
Bjørgeengen, Jarle 69
Bode, Mathis 541
Boehm, Swen 155, 330
Boku, Taisuke 561
Bombace, Nico 441
Brim, Michael J. 330
Brown, Nick 528, 567
Budiardja, Reuben D. 330
Burnett, Nicholas 80

Campos, Isabel 478
Carminati, Federico 432
Carpenter, Paul 13
Castellane, Alexandre 317
Chalker, Alan 504
Cheema, Ravi 183
Chiusole, Alberto 300
Choi, Sun 463
Chrysos, Nikos 88
Chu, Ching-Hsiang 361
Clementi, Cecilia 397
Cozzini, Stefano 300
Cruz, Felipe A. 46
Cucinotta, Tommaso 1

D'Anca, Alessandro 240
Datta, Kushal 463
David, Mario 478
Der Chien, Wei 528
Dimou, Nikolaos 88
Dongarra, Jack 490, 643
du Toit, Jacques 124

Elia, Donatello 240
Elwasif, Wael 330
Engels, Jan Frederik 612
Entezari, Alireza 601
Ezell, Matt 330

Farooqi, Muhammad Nufail 113
Fiameni, Giuseppe 61
Fiore, Sandro 240
Foster, Ian 240
Franz, Eric 504
Fuson, Chris 330

Gallo, Steve 504
Garrido, Luis A. 13
Gauding, Michael 541
Gerhardt, Lisa 183
Gianoudis, Michalis 88
Gibb, Gordon 528
Giuliani, Graziano 300
Godinez, William J. 463
Gomes, Jorge 478
Grupp, Adrian 478

Halem, Milton 379
Hanley, Jesse 330
Hater, Thorsten 418
Hazen, Damian 183
Hernandez, Oscar 330
Herten, Andreas 418
Hesam, Ahmad 432
Homölle, Bernhard 258
Hossain, Imtiaz 463

Hudak, David   504
Hummel, Mathias   634

Jackson, Adrian   258
Jiang, Chao   587
Johnson, Doug   504
Jones, Matthew D.   101
Jones-Ivey, Renette L.   101
Joubert, Wayne   330
Jumah, Nabeeh   142

Kallimanis, Nikolaos D.   88
Kalokairinos, Giorgos   88
Katevenis, Manolis   88
Khattak, Gulrukh   432
Khorassani, Kawthar Shafie   361
Kleinheinz, Konstantin   541
Klijn, Wouter   418
Kontak, Max   528
Kordenbrock, Todd   275
Kozlov, Valentin   478
Kufeldt, Philip   198
Kumar, Nalini   561
Kunkel, Julian   142, 169, 214
Kurth, Thorsten   587

Lam, Herman   587
Lamanna, Massimo   300
Lawson, Margaret   227
Leibovici, Thomas   288
Leverman, Dustin   330
Levy, Scott   275
Liu, Jianshen   198
Lockwood, Glenn K.   183
Lofstead, Jay   36, 227
López García, Álvaro   478
Lozinskiy, Kirill   183
Lucas, Laurent   623

Madonna, Alberto   46
Maltzahn, Carlos   198
Mariotti, Kean   46
Martin, David E.   561
Martorell, Xavier   352
Mascagni, Michael   452
Maxwell, Don   330
Mesnet, Bruno   317
Michel, Martial   80
Monjalet, Florent   288

Moore, Branden   124
Moore, Edgar   504
Moro, Marco   25
Mudalige, Gihan R.   124
Muscianisi, Giuseppa   61

Nash, Rupert   528
Nguyen, Tan   113
Nichols, Daniel   490
Nishtala, Rajiv   13
Noé, Frank   397

Ojika, Dave   587
Olshevsky, Vyacheslav   528
Oral, Sarp   330
Ossyra, John   397
Ossyra, John R.   514

Palazzo, Cosimo   240
Panda, Dhabaleswar K.   361
Papaefstathiou, Vassilis   88
Parsons, Mark   258
Patel, Bhavesh   587
Patra, Abani K.   101
Pelfrey, Daniel   330
Peristerakis, Panagiotis   88
Piras, Marco Enrico   25
Pireddu, Luca   25
Pitsch, Heinz   541
Pleiter, Dirk   418
Ploumidis, Manolis   88
Pophale, Swaroop   155
Prabhat   587
Prathapan, Smriti   379
Prodan, Bianca   528
Psistakis, Antonis   88

Reguly, Istvan Z.   124
Remion, Yannick   623
Röber, Niklas   612
Ryan, Ashleigh   227

Saletore, Vikram   463
Sarton, Jonathan   623
Schmielau, Tim   124
Sedova, Ada   397, 514
Settlage, Robert   504
Shalf, John   113
Simakov, Nikolay A.   101

Smith, Jeremy C.   397, 514
Steinke, Thomas   561
Suarez, Estela   561
Subramoni, Hari   361

Templet, Gary   275
Tharrington, Arnold   330, 397
Tomov, Nathalie-Sofia   490
Tomov, Stanimire   490, 643
Tzanakis, Leandros   88

Ulmer, Craig   275
Unat, Didem   113

Vallecorsa, Sofia   432, 587
van der Ster, Daniel   300
van Kooten, Kees   634
Velusamy, Kaushik   379

Vergara Larrea, Verónica G.   155, 330
Vitucci, Carlo   1

Weiland, Michèle   258, 441
Widener, Patrick   275
Wong, Kwai   490, 643
Wright, Nicholas J.   183

Xirouchakis, Pantelis   88

Younge, Andrew   36

Zanetti, Gianluigi   25
Zhang, Kai   601
Zhang, Weiqun   113
Zhang, Xian   463
Zimmer, Christopher   330

Printed in the United States
By Bookmasters